TRAPPED

A CAPE BRETON FISHERMAN'S ABDUCTION TO NIGERIA

LEIF MORRISON

This book is based on real events. Some names have been changed but the actual events are real and based on real characters.

Edited by Cynthia McMurray and Kathleen Healy
Cover illustration includes a photo of the Zurich taken by Leif Morrison.
Cover design by Harve Grant
Printed and bound in Canada at Friesens

Library and Archives Canada Cataloguing in Publication

Morrison, Leif, 1964-
    Trapped: a Cape Breton fisherman's abduction to Nigeria / Leif Morrison.

ISBN 978-0-9813819-8-5

    1. Morrison, Leif, 1964- --Travel--Nigeria.   2. Lobster fishers--Nova Scotia--Cape Breton Island--Biography. 3. Sailing--Atlantic Ocean. 4. Atlantic Ocean--Description and travel. 5. Nigeria--Description and travel. 6. Morrison, Leif, 1964- --Kidnapping, 1995. 7. Kidnapping--Nigeria.
8. Betrayal. I. Title.

HV6604.N54M67 2010   364.15'4092   C2010-906921-8

First printing 2010
Published in 2010 by Bryler Publications Inc.
Suite 1035,
Chester, NS
B0J 1J0
Visit our website at www.brylerpublications.com

10   9   8   7   6   5   4   3   2

For my loving family
Marlene, Justin Donald and Aleisha Janel

Acknowledgements

I have been blessed with some great friends and family who have been nothing but supportive during this time in my life.

I will always be grateful to Hugh Kennedy and author Rob Kennedy for their significant contributions in the creation of this book. Their support and direction were critical to the process.

Thanks to the readers who previewed my work in progress and gave their feedback with overwhelming support.

Many thanks to my publisher, Cynthia McMurray, of Bryler Publications, for her consideration of my work, technical support and promotion and for bringing my story to you.

All said and done, I think what really made it worthwhile were the people around me and in the end, they are what really matters.

Preface

The following is a true story. I have attempted to recount my experience for you as accurately as possible. The near tragic circumstances I put my family and myself through were purely my own doing. I felt a need for adventure and, unfortunately, the excitement of the opportunity and the challenge of sailing a boat across the Atlantic Ocean to Africa, nearly destroyed my idyllic life.

I owe much to my family and the Foreign Affairs staff at the Canadian Embassy in Lagos, Nigeria, for my safe return.

I hold no grudge against the people of Nigeria and the intention of this book is not to cast aspersion on them but rather to highlight the activities of the few men who had such an impact on my life.

Prologue

A s we go through life, we often forget what is most important. For the most part, it is often our health, family, and freedom. When we lose sight of these things in our pursuit for more of the things we desire rather than those things we actually need, we lose focus on what is truly important. I often use the phrase 'today is worth two tomorrows', which I coined from the adage 'a bird in the hand is worth two in the bush'.

As a young man, my heart was not in the academic side of life. Instead, I gave up those treasured high-school years to quell a never-ending restlessness that seemed to haunt me daily. At the age of seventeen, I was employed as an unskilled labourer in a nickel mine three thousand miles from home. But like a four-thousand-square-mile magnet, Cape Breton and all it had to offer, drew me back home like so many before me.

My grandfather once told me, in an effort to keep me in school, that Cape Breton was a wonderful place but you can't eat it. This was becoming apparent as I languished from job-to-job for the next several years, pursuing everything from slinging Coca-Cola to all types of construction.

One day, an older gentleman extended me an invitation to join him in his commercial fishing business. That person happened to be my father-in-law and for the next nine years, he would teach me the necessary skills to become a successful commercial fisherman. It was as if I had found my calling. Here was the way of life I had been searching for. It offered me everything Cape Breton had to offer. Not only was it a good source of income but it gave me the freedom and independence to wallow in the beauty of my island and bask in Her sunshine.

To be a fisherman, successful or not, depends greatly on an individual's skills and expectations. Success in the fishery business is not always measured in the weight of the catch and its value but instead, in the appreciation for a way of life and all it has to offer. Still a young man with a family to raise, I was quick to apply the many skills I had acquired, bouncing from one job to the next. I had become a jack-of-all-trades and with my love and appreciation of the outdoors, I was tailor-made for the industry.

As a fisherman, you must also be versatile and able to turn your hand to just about anything, from maintaining an engine—new or old, gas or diesel—to the ability to twist more than just a wrench because there are no service stations out at sea. It's also not likely you'll have an onboard plumber or electrician. Since the mainstay of our fishing industry is lobster and the season begins in mid-May, shortly after the ice clampers have floated south, the water remains very cold.

With a crew of two, often consisting of family and friends, we are frequently challenged by fog and stormy seas. The threat of someone falling overboard into the icy water places great responsibility on the skipper, which leads to another aspect of the industry.

My boat was a forty-foot-long Cape Islander. A wooden boat of that length and age needs a lot of tender loving care. The one-inch pine planking in her hull must be monitored closely for signs of rot and wear. Her seams must be re-caulked yearly, which means countless hours of pounding cotton cord into the many cracks with a hammer and chisel.

The twelve hours a day, six days a week vigil of hauling and maintaining two-hundred and seventy-five lobster traps continues for nine weeks straight. The crew tends the traps, removes the tasty crustaceans, and carefully stores them for sale, then each trap is re-baited, usually with mackerel. Throughout the day, there is plenty of time for laughter and idle conversation as we steam from location to location. Cruising along a silhouette of majestic coastline and a blue horizon, it's easy to feel like the luckiest man alive.

At season's end when money is earned, a soul is left free to repair and prepare his boat and gear at his own pace, while he enjoys friends, family, and all that Cape Breton has to offer.

An Offer for Adventure

T he sun rose warm and bright on a mid-September morning. As I lingered in bed, I enjoyed basking in its soothing rays in anticipation of what the day would bring. I was a seasonal lobster fisherman and with harvest completed, I now had the freedom to live the day as I saw fit.

From the sun drenched bedroom of our modest two-story home, I could hear the clatter of dishes as Marlene, my wife of fifteen years, prepared breakfast while she hummed a soft melody as she had always done. She was a kind and loving, soft-spoken girl with the face of an angel. As routine would have it, every morning about this time, her voice would flutter like a silk scarf from the kitchen to the bedrooms above.

"Justin, Aleisha, come down, your breakfast is ready," she would call.

Justin, the eldest of our two children, had turned nine that spring. He was a smart, outgoing and fun-loving lad with blonde hair and a dimpled chin who always brought laughter and fun to any situation. Justin had a never-ending thirst for what he had yet to learn and although I did not have all the answers to his questions, I took pleasure in helping him find them. We had a wonderful time living in a world of make believe, where we imagined that dinosaurs still roamed the earth and pirates could conquer the world in a single day. As a proud father, I took great comfort in knowing my son.

As for my daughter, Aleisha, she held a special place in my heart that only a dad can comprehend. At six, she beamed with life and held many of the characteristics of her mother. She was blonde haired and blue eyed with the skin of a porcelain doll. Her beautiful little face always held a smile that could melt my heart. Surrounded by dolls and stuffed animals, Aleisha danced her way through life like a butterfly and filled my days with constant joy.

After a little prodding from their mother, they sleepily made their way to the kitchen table. So was the school morning routine.

I was not far behind and before long, we were all seated in our familiar positions. What started out as just another day at the Morrison's would eventually produce a sequence of events that to this day, seem like a faded nightmare.

The sharp ring of the telephone broke our customary morning chatter. I slowly raised my head from the bowl of Corn Flakes I was eagerly devouring, thinking it was likely for the kids. I lifted the receiver from the nearby wall and simply said, "Yeah, who are you looking for?"

"Leif," the voice replied. I knew right away it was 'Big Mike' as everyone referred to him. "What are you doing?" he asked.

"Not much right now, just having breakfast."

"Take a run over," he said. "I want to see you about something." Mike was a one-of-a-kind type of guy. He was a heavyset man with a rough exterior and usually sported baggy trousers that somehow matched his attitude of never giving a damn about much of anything. He was employed as maintenance manager at the Glace Bay Fishery processing plant. Since he was in charge of maintenance, he didn't do any of the hands-on work himself but often employed my services as a carpenter to repair or build almost anything. I got along well with Mike in our business dealings. Our relationship basically consisted of, 'here is the job' and I did it. Naturally, I assumed I was being called in for a few days work. I ended the call by saying I'd see him in a little while.

Later that morning, I found myself making my way through the fish processing plant, which by this time of year, was in full production. The chatter of machinery and the pungent odour of processed fish engulfed me as I walked past the many smiling faces, replying in kind to the greetings of the workers with whom I had become acquainted over the years. I made my way to the heart of the plant where Mike's office was located.

"Hey big guy, what is so important?" I got right to the point knowing he would do the same. He swivelled toward me in his rickety metal chair, its ancient hinges creaking as though the whole thing might collapse at any moment.

Peering over the top of his round-rimmed glasses without expression, he boldly asked, "Would you be interested in helping to take a boat to Africa?"

After a slight pause, I asked him to tell me more. Throughout our professional relationship, Mike and I had had many conversations, including one in which I had expressed an interest in seeing the world.

He drew a heavy sigh as he leaned back and began to explain, "As you probably know, my business partner and I run an operation in which we repair fishing boats of all sizes. I got one now and she's a big sucker. She's tied up at North Sydney Harbour."

"How big is big?" I asked, my curiosity now getting the better of me.

"One hundred and sixty feet long," he grinned.

"Yeah, that's a pretty big boat Mike but what does it have to do with me?"

"Well it's like this, a fellow was hired to sail the vessel from Halifax and deliver her to Africa. Not long out to sea he experienced mechanical failure and was towed to North Sydney and I got the job of fixing her."

"Is she running now?" I asked.

"No, not yet, we are waiting for some parts."

"How long before she's ready?"

"Oh, it'll be three or four days at least," he replied. He shifted his gaze back down to the cluttered desk.

Getting detailed answers out of Mike was like pulling teeth.

As I thought about it, I made myself comfortable on a neighbouring chair. Although not quite as old as the one Mike teetered on, I braced myself as I folded my hands across my chest and stretched my feet forward. Familiar pangs of restlessness had begun to surface and I could feel my endless need for adventure inch its way through my body. Out of curiosity, I continued to pry more information from him.

"You know, Africa is a big place... where exactly in Africa?"

In typical Mike fashion, he replied with a casual gesture and general lack of concern, as if it were simply a vacation destination. "Nigeria."

I could almost hear the wheels turning in my head. I was intrigued. I knew nothing about Nigeria and quite honestly, deep down that really didn't seem to matter. All I could think about was what a challenge this would be—possibly, even an adventure of a lifetime. From the time I was a young lad, daydreaming in school, I longed for the opportunity to do something exactly like this. Perhaps, my Norwegian genes on my mother's side or even the fact that my name was Leif, like that of Leif, the adventurous son of the Viking Eric the Red, were the root of my insatiable need for adventure. Who knows, but to me, it seemed the natural thing to do.

Looking back, I now realize I was foolhardy and I merely enjoyed taking unnecessary risks; especially those that served my interests, which at that time, included a need for adventure. This was certainly an unbecoming characteristic of a man with a wife and two small children—a man who had everything in the world to live for.

"When can I see this boat?" My words finally broke the silence.

"You can see her today at the government wharf," Mike replied, once again peering at me over his large round glasses. He continued to tell me the captain would be on board and would be glad to show me around. He even phoned ahead to inform and prepare captain Etlar Clausen that he had an employee who may be interested in helping take the vessel to Africa. After a brief conversation about nothing in particular, we shook hands and parted company.

As I made my exit through the plant, my excitement rose. The familiar faces and sounds of the twenty-thousand square foot plant merely a blur as I thought about how fortunate I was to have been given this opportunity and during a time in which I had the flexibility to come and go as I pleased. Once again, I was only thinking of myself.

The smell of the warm ocean air welcomed me as I exited the door to the parking lot. I climbed into my half-ton pick-up truck deep in thought and drove straight to North Sydney. My mind reeled with excitement as I anticipated the adventure and challenge that would unfold in the up-and coming-weeks.

Captain Clausen

Stretched out between one-hundred-foot cliffs bordering Sydney Mines and Cape Petrie, lies a body of water that has played host to mariners since the days of John Cabot. This once thriving harbour, some three miles wide, was a lifeline between Europe and the New World.

North Sydney Harbour lies wide open to the eastern Atlantic Ocean. Being the most easterly harbour able to cater to large ocean going vessels, she was not long in claiming her fame as one of the first building blocks in the foundation on which Canada was built. In the 18th and 19th centuries, ships travelled from all around to take advantage of her protective coves five miles inland. Schooners to steamers, large and small, sailed for hundreds of years into the morning sun, laden down with fish and lumber destined for the beloved northern land of Europe. On their return, they brought with them immigrants with their few worldly possessions and dreams of helping to build this New World. Now, like a retired old servant, lying quiet and peaceful as if taking a deserving rest, she caters to the service vessels supplying the Island of Newfoundland, a few lobster fishing boats, and little more.

Being familiar with North Sydney Harbour and its surroundings, it didn't take me long to find the boat. In fact, it stood out. She was the only vessel moored at this deserted pier. There was no sign of anyone else, just this old beaten up compact-type car, parked in front of the gang plank, which should have borne a sign warning visitors to enter at their own risk. The boat's railings were long since gone and gaping holes scattered its planked floor. I stood back far enough to view her entirety. Despite her obvious disrepair, I thought to myself, "Not bad". In my opinion, she was beautiful, with her hull painted a bright red and her upper deck white, its patches of rust only accentuating her beauty.

At first glance, I thought her to be quite sea worthy. She was one hundred-and-sixty-feet long and her narrow width gave her the look and style of a military cruiser—fast and sleek—which would help her make good time wherever she went. With mixed emotions, I felt the adrenaline as it rushed through my veins. My heart began to pump, each beat echoing in my ears. I turned toward the gang plank, oblivious to its failing condition.

The S.S. Zurich

I drew a deep breath of the sweet sea air, releasing a large sigh as I put aside any rational thinking and common sense God had given me. I anxiously made my way over the gangplank and onto the dilapidated deck. As I followed my way through the maze of doors and stairs, I moved slowly, taking in my new surroundings. It didn't take me long to realize she was no luxury liner. To the contrary, she was an outdated fish trawler, with rusted winches, cables, and an array of accessories from days gone by. Eventually, the unmistakable screech of metal striking metal brought me to the top of a stairway that led into the dark and dirty underbelly of the S.S. Zurich. A nauseating mixture of putrid oil and sweat hit me and I instinctively gasped as I carefully made my way down the steps where I came face-to-face with the new captain, who for whatever reason, was now racing upstairs.

"Get out of my way," he grumbled as he pushed me aside.

"Right on, big fellow," I replied, as I proceeded to the bottom of the stairs where I met William, a small and frail looking man. I had no idea at this point that William and I would form a bond through a harrowing experience that would take us to hell and back.

Remaining crouched on one knee William slowly raised his oil-stained face. I immediately noticed how tired the man looked. His dark eyes looked like craters, only accentuating his sunken cheeks. A half-smoked cigarette dangled between his lips, its red tip glowing in the dim light of the ship's engine room.

"Who are you?" a soft, gentle voice asked.

"My name is Leif Morrison and I am going to help you take this boat to Africa," I replied. With that said, William slowly made his way to his feet, wiped his grease filled hands on his trousers and extended a friendly handshake. With his outstretched hand he introduced himself as William Wells, a mechanical engineer.

William, his small frame revealing every one of his close to seventy years, spoke openly in a down-to-earth manner that quickly put me at ease.

"I'm a buddy of Big Mike." I just assumed he knew Mike since he was in charge of getting the crew together for the voyage. "Have you known him long?" I asked.

"No, not very long," William replied. "Just long enough to get myself into this mess."

He went on to say that Mike called him the night before after a contact had referred him. When they spoke, William told Mike he had spent the last thirty years working on the 'goddamn boats' as a mechanic and since he was out of work, he was interested.

"I haven't worked in over a year and really could use the employment," he added, looking to the floor.

Suddenly, like a hurricane sweeping across the Atlantic, the same figure I had encountered only minutes earlier, came bounding down the stairs. This was my first real encounter with the captain. As I looked into his deep blue eyes, shadowed by a single light in a poorly lit engine room, I was immediately intimidated by his massive six-foot five, two-hundred-and-eighty-pound frame. His greasy blonde hair framed his badly disfigured face, a result of a barroom brawl and a broken beer bottle. The man towered over me, as if he owned the world, giving me the impression he was no saint. In fact, as I was to learn as time went on, the captain had lived a colourful past. His broad shoulders and overly long arms reminded me of a primate. With long, dirty fingernails, he pulled his scraggy mop of hair back from his eyes and turned his attention toward me.

"Who are you?" he demanded, his tone flat.

I paused for a moment not knowing what to make of this individual who was in stark contrast to the meek and mild William still standing in front of the engine he had been working on.

"Leif, Leif Morrison," I replied.

With that said, the captain's demeanour suddenly softened. He seized my hand and at the same time, cradled my elbow with his left. He began to shake my hand as if we were long-lost brothers.

"Mr. Life," he exclaimed, "I am so pleased to meet you." As I attempted to regain my composure—I was still reeling from our initial overwhelming introduction—he introduced himself as Etlar Clausen, emphasizing his name as though I should be impressed. "Mike has told me so many good things about you and I look forward to getting to know you and becoming very good friends in the future," he stated.

"Have you met Mr. Wells?" Etlar asked, stretching his enormous arm toward William who was standing quietly behind him. The captain swung around and pulled William closer to the stair railing. In a stern voice, he introduced me to William, whose face now seemed so gaunt and tired he might actually collapse before me.

William obediently looked me in the eyes, took my hand and shook it. "I'm William Wells," he blurted, obviously trying to maintain his dignity. It was evident William did not like Etlar's quick manner but to his credit, he maintained his composure, a quality I immediately admired in him.

After several minutes of awkward silence, Etlar invited me to see the wheelhouse. I followed Etlar to the top of the boat, keeping a few steps behind him. Along the way, he boasted about his magnificent boat, flirting with information about her specifications, as if describing a beautiful woman. He showed me everything from the compasses to the steering system, which looked quite new and well maintained.

Etlar went on to show his charts and where he had meticulously outlined the course we would sail in pencil. It was a concave course from Cape Breton, Nova Scotia to Warri, Nigeria by way of the Canary Islands. Hoping not to sound inexperienced, I asked him why we would sail in a wide arch and not a straight line. He informed me it was to avoid the fall hurricane season, which in my opinion, made perfect sense. Etlar spoke confidently about his ability to take the huge piece of scrap iron halfway around the world. He went on to explain that by taking this particular course we would be following the sea currents and make better time.

In spite of the gentle cordial nature in which he presented himself, there lingered a nervous uneasiness about him. At the time, I dismissed it for several reasons. Somehow, I was trying to convince myself to see this through because the challenge and adventure excited me. Etlar's uneasiness seemed natural, at least that was what I thought, especially considering the task that lay before him.

In a clumsy fashion, Etlar moved about the wheelhouse room, skirting from window to window as he told me about himself. He began by saying he was from Nigeria and had a Nigerian wife and two young daughters, although with his blue eyes, blonde hair, and fair complexion he certainly did not appear to be Nigerian. When I inquired about his origin he stickhandled around the issue quite smoothly, a talent I would become well acquainted with.

Etlar did go on to say, however, that a Nigerian man educated in the US and who had made large sums of money in the oil industry, purchased the boat from Fisheries Product International for the sum of $60,000. The new owner, Madu Okoro, president of the Sannu Corporation, was planning to convert her into a longliner. In order to do this she would be equipped with large spools of cable and hooks spaced several feet apart for the purpose of catching swordfish and blue fin tuna along the Ivory Coast.

"I can make much money, the waters are full of fish on the Ivory Coast and I'm just the man for the job." Etlar became excited as he went on to tell me how he had fished in Denmark in his earlier years. He explained that he could have the entire Ivory Coast, which was rich in swordfish and tuna, all to himself and stood to make big profits working for Madu Okoro. As Etlar continued, I looked out over the stern of the boat, where three old cars, referred to as 'one hundred dollar specials', sat neatly arranged on the deck, each well shackled against any foul weather they might encounter.

A longliner is just that. On a smaller commercial scale, boats are loaded with barrel-type containers known as tubs. Each tub consists of a half-mile of rope with a hook and line every six feet, which are joined together to form one long line that is then weighted to the bottom of the sea to catch bottom-feeding fish such as cod and haddock. The larger of the longliners, such as the ill-fated Andrea Gail, used a spool of cable and baited hooks every twenty four feet. This very long cable is tethered out over the stern and lies close to the surface in search of larger prey such as tuna and swordfish.

Converting a boat to a longliner wasn't anything out of the ordinary, but in the case of the Zurich, things would be on an even grander scale. The Zurich was more than twice the size of even the largest longliner. A large portion of her side, at water level, was to be removed. This would be the area where huge spools of steel cables fitted with baited hooks would be connected to a yet lighter cable spaced one hundred feet or so apart. For fifty miles or more, this line would be allowed to soak in the waters of the Ivory Coast in search of blue fin tuna or swordfish. A second line may or may not be used to increase productivity. After several hours of soak time, the cable is then hydraulically winched over the side where the large, sometimes four hundred-pound, fish are gaffed and hauled aboard by able-bodied, but poorly paid seamen.

By now, Etlar had finished his spiel and added that he was fluent in five languages; English, French, German, Dutch and a Nigerian dialect. Looking at him, I was surprised he could write his own name.

"Let me show you more, Mr. Life," said Etlar. I didn't know it at the time, but this was to be my new name.

Etlar led the way as I followed him down an iron stairway past thirty years of rust, grit and grime that lead to the galley. As we neared the room, a foul smell permeated the air, clinging to everything in its path.

"What in the name of God stinks so bad?" I asked. I was sure a cat or some other small animal had died and decayed somewhere in the vicinity. But where?

Without expression, Etlar made a small sniffing gesture and dismissed it as if it were unnoticeable. He spread his long arms wide and asked, "Well, what do you think. You like?"

Standing in the doorway, holding my breath, I looked to my left and stared at a sink overfilled with dirty dishes covered in mould so thick that even Frederick Banting would have been alarmed. Could this be the source of the foul smell?

Next, there was a stove large enough to feed a crew of sixteen men in its heyday that was billowing far too much heat for this warm fall day. There was a small cupboard well stocked with spices, dishes and utensils. "This must be the pantry," I said, as I pulled the handle on a large wooden door. I closed it as quickly as I opened it after realizing it contained another stench, although different from the first. To my great pleasure, I noticed one small porthole, which I immediately opened in spite of its stiff, partly seized hinges.

Leaving the galley, we filed past a large table at which many a hungry fisherman would have chased their supper on cold and stormy nights out on the unforgiving North Atlantic Sea. Two new portable fans, which looked totally out of place, were positioned over the table. The fans would prove invaluable in the weeks to come.

"We have food, lots of food," Etlar blurted, as he directed me toward a large deepfreeze. Inside there was a good assortment of steaks, hams, chops and vegetables.

"Great," I thought, since it was the first real positive thing I'd seen in the galley.

As we continued our tour, a faint voice echoed from down in the engine room. William was in need of Etlar's attention, which gave me the opportunity to do a little exploring on my own. A door situated to the right of me is where I found the first mate's quarters. "Not bad," I thought, eyeing its clean linen sheets on the bed and pillows. There was a chest of drawers and another one of those new fans. I thought it could be my room. "Yes, this will do quite nicely," I thought, providing William hadn't already claimed it.

From there, by way of a narrow corridor, I found the inner workings of what was once a vibrant and profitable fishing operation, which now lay as an outdated, inoperable pile of scrap metal. Looking out over the stern of the boat where the huge nets were once brought on board, sat the old cars, neatly placed and securely fastened to the deck. I found out later that Etlar bought them in Halifax with the intention of selling them for a profit in Nigeria.

My wandering eventually led me through another narrow corridor and down a flight of stairs, which brought me to the sleeping quarters of the former crew. Small iron, cell-like rooms contained upper and lower bunks and not much more. Etlar used one of these rooms to store his personal belongings, some of which he had purchased in Halifax. My attention was drawn to two small pink bicycles with matching pink flowered baskets, streamers and little bells on the handlebars. I naturally assumed they were for his two small children and, since I had a six-year-old daughter whom I loved dearly, they gave me the impression he, too, must be a kind and loving father. Looking back, however, I may have just been trying to convince myself of that fact.

"Life, are you down there, Life?" he called. I quickly closed the door and climbed up the stairs.

"Well, what do you think?" Etlar asked. "Is she not a beautiful boat?"

Beauty obviously being in the eye of the beholder, I reluctantly agreed.

Etlar was not one to beat around the bush and got right to the point. "Are you coming with us?" he asked.

"What's in it for me?" I asked. One of my personal character flaws was that I never was one for asking a lot of questions so I decided now would be a good time to start. "How much will I be paid for making the voyage?"

"One hundred American dollars a day from the time we leave port until your return home," he explained, adding that my return flight arrangements would be taken care of and paid for by the Sannu Corporation.

"Okay then," I replied. "How long do you figure the crossing will take?"

"Come, I will show you my charts," replied Etlar, and back to the wheelhouse we went.

Standing over a neatly organized table, he laid out his plotted route. Etlar explained in detail that we would sail over the Grand Banks of Newfoundland, make a southeast arch toward the Canary Islands and the Azures. Once there, we would hold over for fuel and supplies, although he did not specify what kind of supplies or the details of how long we would be there. From the Azures, he said we would follow the currents along the African coast to Nigeria, which would enable us to make good time. He figured it would take about sixteen days; all the while he spoke in a friendly manner and was quick to put his arm around my shoulder, as if we were old pals. But at the same time, I sensed he was nervous and somewhat anxious. This became apparent when I asked him, "When are you leaving?"

"The day after tomorrow, if she is ready," he said, as he nervously chewed on his fingernails, something he did quite often.

"The day after tomorrow…that's a little too soon for me," I replied. "As of this morning, I had never heard of you, this boat or Nigeria. I have a lot of things to get in order," I stated. I knew my wife, Marlene, was certainly not going to take kindly to this.

Etlar became frustrated. He told me it was getting late and hurricane season was fast approaching and we must leave as soon as possible.

"Well, I'll run it past the wife and see what she says," I answered. I didn't realize it at the time but this was the only card he had to play.

Even though I was being hired I still was not sure of my duties, so I finally asked, "What is it that you want me to do?"

Etlar was eager to refer to me as his first mate. "As long as you and William keep the engine running, I will do the rest," he answered. As it turned out, that's the way it really was for eighteen days of hell.

With a day-and-a-half to get ready I had no time to waste. As crazy as it seems now, I was pumped for the challenge of a lifetime; three total strangers taking a thirty-year-old piece of junk across the Atlantic Ocean to an African country of which I knew nothing. I must have been crazy.

"All right, I'm out of here," I exclaimed. "I'll be in touch but before I go, I'm going to bring those dirty dishes home to be sterilized

," I stated. I knew one thing for sure, we would have to eat well and stay healthy to make this trip.

I left that day with dishes in tow like a peddler holding his sack. I went over the gangplank and jumped into my modest half-ton truck.

On the way home, I think I was in some sort of a trance, again putting aside all rational thinking. My mind was made up—I was going to Africa.

Convincing Marlene

"Honey I'm home," I called out. Oh, if Marlene only knew what she was in for?

"What in the name of goodness have you got there?" she asked.

"Ahh, ahh," I stammered. Okay, so it wasn't my finest hour. I hadn't yet figured out a way to convince Marlene that my newest form of off-season employment was a sane idea. Suddenly, I felt like the cornered rat and weasel I had become.

"Remember when Mike called me this morning? Well, he just got me a job…to help deliver a boat to Africa. Isn't that great?" I asked. I still remember the look of total disbelief on her face. She definitely didn't think it was great.

"A boat to where?" she exclaimed.

"Yeah, Africa," I stated. "A wealthy Nigerian bought the boat from the Canadian government and a Dutch guy was hired to deliver it."

"Don't be ridiculous," she said. "You don't know anything about these people."

"The Dutch captain gave me a phone number for the Rhode Island-based company. Let's call it and check it out."

"No, you are not taking any boat to Africa, you're foolish."

I was already expecting this type of response since Marlene was the cautious type and liked to think things through. Deep down I was naïve enough to truly believe this job really was okay, so I turned on all my powers of persuasion until Marlene finally agreed to make the call to the contact in Rhode Island.

A soft spoken lady, representing the Sannu Corporation, assured us both that they indeed had purchased the Zurich and that it was scheduled to arrive in Nigeria by the end of the month. We asked her about the wages and the prepaid flight arrangements for return to Nova Scotia. She gave further assurances that everything would be taken care of just as Mr. Clausen had previously described. She advised us that I would need a passport and then, after exchanging a few pleasantries, we ended our brief conversation.

Marlene looked at me and said, "You don't have a passport." I knew that even with a passport I still had more convincing to do.

"We still don't know anything about this Etlar person, why don't you bring him here for supper," she suggested.

This was going very well I thought and replied, "That's a wonderful idea."

With this new information I was anxious to return to the boat but I hung back until three o'clock when Justin and Aleisha's school bus usually dropped them off. Every day Marlene or I would be there to receive them and in return, I would be rewarded with big hugs and lots of laughter that was as precious as life itself. We were very happy. We sometimes called ourselves the four bears living in our cedar house in the forest. We would often sing our own four bears song, a ritual that consisted of holding hands, hugging snugly and hopping in a circle while singing and laughing. We had a good thing going and we knew it. Today, we all shared in some of that joy at the end of the driveway and as I looked back, I realized it was the best time of our lives.

By now, it was four o'clock and I was heading back to the boat to extend an invitation to Etlar for supper. Etlar was only too glad to accept, or seize the moment. In his eagerness to come, he asked if he could take a bath at our house and change his clothes since there were no such working facilities on board.

It was a one-hour drive back to the house and along the way Etlar often made comments about the scenery of the third most beautiful Island in North America, Cape Breton Island.

Perhaps, it's due to the fact that Cape Breton is an almost four-thousand-square mile island consisting of soft rolling mountains that seem to cradle its countless blue lakes and streams or maybe that she is isolated, being the one of the most easterly points in North America. It could even be her people, a mix of Scottish, Irish and European descent, all committed to hard work and family. Whatever the case, Cape Breton is and will always be entrenched in my heart and soul, as is true for everyone who lives here. A sense of belonging always filled the hearts of all Cape Bretoners, as they lived out as their lives working as coal miners, steel workers and fishermen.

As we continued to the house, Etlar seemed different, somewhat shy and soft spoken, as a gentleman should be—not at all like the authoritative character I met earlier that day.

Before long, we pulled into my driveway and it was obvious by the look on his face that he did not expect my home and property would be so nice. He had a renewed interest and did not hesitate to ask to see my boat and gear or anything else I had for that matter. After the grand tour of my boat, workshop and property, I introduced Etlar to Marlene.

Marlene, being a soft gentle girl, was quite taken aback by this large, longhaired, poorly clothed stranger, an intimidating figure to say the least. I was amazed by his transformation to this gentle ladies man who was quick to apologize about everything from the length of his hair to the state of his hygiene. Marlene was always the perfect hostess and when she had company, she would go all out and make them feel special and Etlar was no exception. In fact, Etlar was invited to take a bath, something he had himself hinted upon earlier on the boat. This made it easier for me to extend the invitation. We made light when he later apologized for the state of the bathroom and the thick grey ring, which now circled the bathtub.

The dining room was set with her fine bone china and a pork roast was cooking in the oven. With all the trimmings, Marlene made Etlar feel most welcome. The evening proceeded as planned and we all enjoyed a three-course meal and shared casual conversation. Much of the attention focused on Etlar, as we were very interested in his family and background. Justin and Aleisha peered over their suppers at this longhaired stranger while swinging their legs under the table trying not to be noticed. After dessert, Etlar and the children were encouraged to get acquainted in the living room while Marlene and I took care of the supper dishes.

Etlar seemed relaxed with the children. We could hear them laugh and giggle in the next room, as I washed and she dried the dishes. We were silent until I gave her a gentle splash of suds and Marlene said in an uncertain tone, "He seems to be a good person but I just don't know."

I made light of the fact that we were only taking a boat across the Atlantic Ocean. "It will only be for a few weeks, people travel by ocean all the time." I was trying to assure her not to worry. I made a point to tell her there was a computer with Internet service on board and that I would surely keep in touch with her all the way. There was silence for the most part as we finished our kitchen duties.

Etlar, was the perfect houseguest. He was very inquisitive that evening, asking a barrage of questions, almost as if he were taking notes. He was quick to point out that he had a wife and two daughters who were five and six years old.

By the end of the evening, Marlene was a little more settled with the idea of me traipsing off to Africa, having now met and spoken with Etlar. She actually surprised me when she told Etlar straight out, "You make sure you get him back here safe and sound."

Etlar, in a warm and gentle manner, wrapped his arms around both our shoulders, telling us we were very lucky to have such a wonderful family and that the voyage would be a safe and expedient one. He boasted that he had years of experience with this sort of thing. It is only now, ten years later, that I am able to come to terms with the fact that it was me, who let this stranger into our lives and me, who would leave lasting scars on our perfect world for years to come.

By now, it was getting late and time to return Etlar to the boat. On the drive we shared conversation about our fishing experiences, as if we were long-time friends. At one point, a reference was made to the necessity of a passport and I told him I would get right on it since I needed it so quickly. And the next day, I did travel to our province's capital, Halifax, to acquire the passport. Now, with passport in hand and Marlene's blessing, I would be free to go.

A Foreboding Sign of Things to Come

I arrived at the boat to find Etlar nervous and agitated as he tried to put his best side forward. I was relieved when I learned the necessary part to repair the engine had not arrived and our departure would be delayed another day. This extra day gave me the time I needed to finish preparing for the trip and most of all, spend more time with my family.

Big Mike, who had referred me for this job, called that night to get an update on what was taking place. He told me he had a going-away present for me, a top of the line survival suit, which was valued at about one thousand dollars. It was the kind of suit worn by the coast guard. He had acquired the suite during his marine dealings and wanted me to have it, jokingly stating, "I hope you won't need it." Mike went on to tell me he would be going to the boat the following day and would drop it off. I always believed Mike to be a straight shooter and I appreciated him taking the time to wish me a safe return, asking if there was anything else I needed to make the trip. Taking into account I was not one to ask a lot of questions, and that Mike had pretty much done his part, I thanked him for his efforts and bid him a good night.

The next day, I had a long list of things to do and people to see. It was late evening by the time I arrived at the boat with a box of sanitized dishes and a carton of cigarettes, something I did like to indulge in at the time but only when Marlene was not present.

"How did you make out?" I asked, wondering if Etlar got the needed part. He was in a fine mood as he was quick to point out that William had done an excellent job on the repairs and had gone home for the evening.

"We leave tomorrow," Etlar exclaimed, wide eyed and smiling. In some way, I didn't share in his excitement. I felt anxious, a feeling I naturally understood to be quite normal considering the challenge that lay before me. But before I could say much of anything, he was quick to interrupt me saying, "You wait, Mr. Life, you can't imagine how magnificent Africa is, trust me, you will be amazed."

With that, I stored the heavy box I had brought and was anxious to return home to have one last night with Marlene and the children. Before leaving I asked if our good friend Mike happened to stop by.

"Oh yes, Mike was here and left not more than an hour ago."

"Where's the survival suit he dropped off for me?" I asked.

"A what? A survival suit? No Life, Mike left no such thing here," Etlar replied without blinking an eye.

"That old devil," I mumbled to myself, as I made my way down the wretched gangplank.

"See you tomorrow, Mr. Life. We leave at noon." With that I assured him I would be there in the morning.

The Adventure Begins

I t was Saturday morning and, as the children had no school, I was not awakened by the usual hustle and bustle of the weekday routine. It was a delight to arouse the young lad and lass myself. Growing up as the son of a coal miner with five siblings, I recognized the importance of a stable and secure family life, something my mother had always been able to assure. My father, a hard worker and provider, made sure the basics were always there, however, he was a cold, heartless individual who brought more fear than laughter to all of us.

Now, with a family of my own, it was my goal to not only be a good provider, but a kind and loving husband and dad as well. As in most situations where commitment and hard work are applied, goodness and happiness follows, as was the case for the four bears.

Aleisha, with her arms outstretched, wrapped them around my neck and said, "Daddy, please doesn't go away."

I had a hard time holding back my tears as I tried to assure her Daddy would not be gone for long and if I could, I would bring her home something special from Africa. Justin was a little pumped about this whole African adventure, as if he were going. He had done some reading about this vast land and he told me to watch out for the lions and tigers and not to take any chances. When I asked him what he wanted me to bring him home for a souvenir, he asked for a coconut.

Once again, with watery eyes, I hugged him and promised I would
bring him home a coconut.

Marlene, however, was not so chipper and made little or no conversation as she prepared breakfast for the four of us. Of course, they
would see me off and the children were excited to see the boat for the
first time. There were a few last minute things to do, which included
picking up Marlene's parents who were like surrogate parents to me
since mine had passed away. They had a strong influence in our lives
and placed much value and emphasis on family. Today would be no
exception. Their presence would be most welcomed and I was happy
to get their best wishes for a safe trip, but even more grateful they
were there to comfort Marlene. Their support gave me consolation,
knowing my family would be looked after and it certainly made my
leaving much easier. Marlene could easily multitask between work
and family obligations and took pride in being independent, so I knew
she would never ask for help.

Anxious to get going, I packed the family van, secured Justin and
Aleisha in their seat belts and we drove off to pick up Jerry and Florence. We had our own path worn in that four kilometres of pavement
from our frequent visits. They were ready, awaiting our arrival. We
couldn't help but smile at one another as we saw Jerry, an avid gar-
dener, carry a fifty-pound bag of his home-grown potatoes on his
shoulder and then place them into the back of our modest passenger
van, as if they were a bag of feathers. Jerry, in his late seventies,
jumped in with face all aglow and proceeded to tell me that now we
would be able to make a "proper meal". For a man who was raised by
a coal miner during the hard economic times of the great depression,
he certainly knew the value of a good potato. By journey's end, the
crew as well, would come to uphold this single vegetable as our staple
of life.

Before long, the four bears were on their way, with grandma and grandpa bear as much needed support. Things were quiet and the mood a bit tense as we started our drive to North Sydney.

"You don't know much about this fellow, Leif, I hope you know what you are doing," said Jerry, in his best fatherly voice.

"Yes, you have to be careful who you trust these days," added Marlene's mother, Florence, the matriarch of Marlene's very large family.

Not wishing to encourage further conversation on the matter, I merely replied, "I'll be back before you know it."

It was a sombre one-hour trip and I knew the grandparents did not wish to cause Marlene and the children any more stress than they were already feeling.

Jerry and Florence are what we would call "a match made in heaven". They exemplified a gentle loving relationship. Each had lost a parent at a very young age and shared the experiences of that hardship growing up in the thirties. They were a traditional couple in their individual responsibilities but together, they equally shared the nurturing of their eight children. They were hardworking people and passed on this quality to the children as they matured.

Two of the oldest siblings had started businesses of their own and were doing quite well as a fisherman and restaurant owner. When I met Marlene she was working part-time while attending college and she always spoke of wanting to start her own business within three years. She was working on her master hairdressing license at the time, which would allow her to open a salon.

Within those years, I fell in love with her and we married in 1981. We cleared a large lot of land and built a Cape Cod home in which she opened the first unisex hair salon in our area. She worked up to sixty hours a week and loved her customers as though they were an extension of the family.

"Well what do you think of her, guys?" I asked, as we drove onto the pier, hoping their first impression would be the same as mine.

"My son, you'll have no problem crossing the ocean in her, provided she's got lots of fuel and everything is working well!" said Jerry. A commercial fisherman for about forty years, Jerry knew this type of fishing trawler was designed for the open sea.

By now, Etlar appeared in all his glory, exuding an aura of confidence, as if he were the Lord and Master of the sea. He stood on the bridge like the captain of a great luxury liner and wasted no time getting to the lower deck. He turned on his charm like a maitre d' of a fine restaurant and welcomed his guests over the ramshackle gangway while offering words of caution. Pleasantries were exchanged and Etlar greeted everyone with warm and friendly handshakes, much of the attention given to the grandparents. He was eager to show everyone around the boat, which he repeatedly referred to as his own.

The engine was running, and I felt nervous and anxious as our departure grew closer. Although I craved the excitement I knew this journey would offer, part of me longed to walk back to the van, wife and family secure in my grasp. But Etlar was keen to set sail and everyone could sense this.

"Where is William?" I asked, since I hadn't seen his little white battered-up car.

"William is in the engine room making final adjustments and whatever else is needed to be done," said Etlar. That was where William was most comfortable and in reality, that was where he had spent most of his adult life. Poor William had a self-inflicted, hard life and didn't have much to show for a lifetime of toil. I made it a point to make sure he was introduced to my family. With his greasy hands and blackened face, William greeted them in a gentleman's manner. We all posed for a variety of pictures, which now, years later, bring back so many mixed emotions.

The Final Goodbyes

I t was a mild, sunny day with a soft southerly wind blowing across the Atlantic. The sea air was soothing, reminding me how much I loved the ocean. Being anxious to set out on his journey across the Atlantic to West Africa, Etlar announced that we must be leaving. With hugs, kisses, and tears from Marlene and the children, I said my goodbyes. The words "I love you so much" would haunt me day and night in the weeks to come. The last farewells were spent and William returned to his duties below. This was the moment of truth, adrenaline was flowing and my heart was pounding.

Carefully, Mom, Dad, and the children and I, managed to safely make our way over the gangplank to the wharf. From there, we watched Leif and a dockside worker retrieve the gangplank and slide it aboard the Zurich.

I had butterflies in my stomach while I nervously held Justin's and Aleisha's hands. They were scared, too, but I managed to overcome my fear to make sure the children were comfortable. I suggested they blow Daddy some kisses and tried to assure them he would be getting off that old boat in Africa real soon.

"Before you know it, we will be at the Sydney airport waiting for his return."

Mom and Dad knew I was putting on a good front and tried to ad-lib. Dad said, "Justin, you will have to be the man of the house now and help your mother to watch over your little sister."

Justin looked up at me with his big brown eyes and little smile then put his arms around my waist while Aleisha followed his lead. I kissed the tops of their heads and together we all watched the Zurich leave the harbour until it was a mere speck on the horizon. In my head, I could hear Leif say, "Move on," and so I did.

Walking to the van, I spoke up and said. "Let's all go to the 'Tasty Treat' for ice cream."

This local store made the best ice cream treats of every kind. The children loved visiting there and I, too, had special memories as a child when Mom and Dad would take all seven of my siblings there for treats. It was the usual stopover on our weekly Sunday outing and family picnic at Mira Park. Right now, that ice cream was probably more of a comfort to me than to my children.

Leif, Marlene, Aleisha and Justin as they say their goodbyes aboard the Zurich.

The Voyage Begins

At dockside, a worker unwrapped the heavy shorelines while I feverishly pulled to bring them aboard. Slowly, she made her way from her mooring and into the open harbour. I was the only deck hand on this one-hundred and sixty-foot vessel. I scrambled with all my worth to secure the large, heavy shore lines and while doing so, I heard a voice above shouting "Faster, faster!" I looked around at first to see who and where the voice was coming from, only to see Etlar flinging his arms and hands about, making rude hand gestures. It was plain to see that Captain Etlar's personality had made a complete turnaround in the short time since leaving the dock. For the first time, I was seeing the true Etlar.

In spite of his demanding behaviour, I stopped what I was doing. With both hands firmly gripping the side rail, I looked back toward the pier where we had just left. In a state of disbelief, I watched everyone I ever loved waving goodbye and growing smaller and smaller as we picked up speed. For a moment, I thought about jumping over the side but the distance between us was now too far for me to swim. "My God what have I done?" I thought.

At the age of eighteen, I sold my only possession, a 1965 Buick, for the purpose of raising enough money to eventually secure passage to Australia. Still short on cash, I followed a tip, which promised a good paying job in Northern Ontario. The job never panned out and the prospects for world travel were dashed, but not the desire. My yearning for travel started during my school years. I would often daydream about all the amazing places I would see. Now, at the age of forty, and afraid of yet another lost opportunity as I was not getting any younger, I seized the moment and quietly slipped away with the evening sun.

Like so many years ago, when the scolding voice of a displeased teacher would yank me back to reality, my expectations of adventure were quickly squashed by the captain's increasing demands. His gruff shouts echoed across the ship's deck as he bellowed needless orders of his now captive crew. With every order that flew from his scowling mouth, my regret and anger grew. I knew I had made a mistake but there was nothing I could do at this point, so I just stared him down as I pointed my finger, as if to say, "You bastard".

I was not a small man at six-foot two and two-hundred pounds. And if I had known then what awaited me, a fight would have probably ensued and this story would never have come to pass. But I didn't, and so here we are. I once heard it said that everyone has a story, so this is mine.

Eventually, the captain relinquished his tyrannical reign, at least for the time being, and all remained quiet on the Zurich as she made her way out to sea. I finished securing the deck and couldn't help but marvel at the splendid beauty of the island of Cape Breton. It is very easy to understand why it has lured so many visitors for thousands of years. An amazing place where the sand and sea have joined forces with the enhancement of our history and culture to create what is known as 'Nova Scotia's Masterpiece'. A major publication, *Travel and Leisure* magazine, named Cape Breton the best island to visit in the continental United States and Canada in *2008 World's Best* readers' survey. Yes, Cape Breton was indeed a place where life was good and a place I would always call my home.

As I watched it disappear into the horizon, I pushed aside my regret and retreated to the galley where, for the first time since starting the voyage, I met up with William. He was slumped in a corner chair smoking a cigarette. He was quick to welcome me to join him for a coffee. This man's soft, gentle manner always made me feel comfortable. I looked into his tired blue eyes and I wondered whether or not William was fit enough to make the long voyage. Life had obviously taken its toll on this frail, old man.

I sat beside him and we focussed on the task at hand, both of us eager to define our duties: he was the engineer and would keep the great twelve-cylinder engine running, while I would cater to his mechanical needs and prepare him healthy meals, bringing him lots of drinks in his confined quarters. We worked four hours on, four hours off, a schedule which we were regularly able to maintain. The rest of the day usually passed unchallenged without contact from Etlar, which neither one of us minded.

A Gale off the Grand Banks

A s the day slipped into night, I made myself comfortable within my new quarters. I lay awake as I thought about the decisions I had made just seventy-two hours earlier and the familiar pangs of doubt and anxiety filled my body. I was raised a Christian by a kind and loving mother and I now put my trust in God and said my prayers as I fell asleep to the steady droning of the engine below.

I was suddenly awakened by the sound of a heavy thud on my door as Etlar slammed his fist, repeatedly shouting, "Life, Life, come now, come quick, we are sinking!"

Like a fireman during an emergency response, I wasted no time racing toward the frantic shouts coming from the engine room. Making my way down the dimly lit iron stairs, I was amazed to see both William and Etlar covered from head-to-toe with thick, dirty oil. The water level had risen past the flywheel, a part of the engine that connected to the driveshaft and sat approximately thirty inches above the bilge or floor, thus spraying decades of accumulated oil and grime everywhere. Etlar was yelling like a madman while a confused and frightened William tried to find the source of water. Etlar turned to me and began screaming orders to get the pumps.

"I don't know where the damn pumps are," I shouted back.

"You should know!" he shrieked over the clamour of the Zurich's mighty engine. He threw me a roll of hose similar to a fire hose and instructed me to go up on deck and drop it down through a manway leading to the engine room. Without hesitation, I did my best to follow the orders of a man who now reminded me more of a lunatic than a confident captain of a one-hundred and sixty-foot ship.

As I made my way up to the deck, the large hose slung over my shoulder, I fought to keep my balance as the ship pitched and rolled. Upon reaching the outer deck, I became aware we were also battling gale force winds off the Grand Banks of Newfoundland. With waves towering ten to twelve metres high, crashing over her bow, I crawled on hands and knees on the poorly lit deck, searching for the hatchway that lead to the engine room. Fearing I would be washed overboard, I abandoned the cumbersome hose. With scraped hands and bloodied knuckles, I was finally able to find and open the elusive hatch. I retrieved the large hose and lowered its length to the engine room below. In a turtle-like fashion, I retraced my route over the deck to get back inside. The waves continued to crash against the bow, drenching me with cold Atlantic water. The salt blinded me, eating its way into every cut on my hands. Dressed in only blue jeans and a T-shirt, I began shaking uncontrollably. The massive waves slammed into my rigid body, each more painful than the first.

Wet and cold, I took a moment to catch my breath before returning to the hellhole below where at least it was warm and dry. Etlar continued his rage as he realized the large bilge pumps were not working. As the owner-operator of my own forty-foot boat, I would never leave the harbour without the assurance that such critical water pumps be on board and in good working order. This incident certainly made me doubt Etlar's competence.

Saying nothing and looking like a Texan who had just struck black gold, William continued to work diligently, checking valves and tracing pipes until he finally shouted over the noise of the engine, "I found it!"

He turned a large valve, which stopped the flow of water to a broken water line. Now, with rough seas to contend with, Etlar abandoned his worthless bilge pumps and returned to the wheelhouse in silence. It was a traumatic sixteen hours into our voyage.

A New Friend

S till shaken, William and I returned to the warmth of the galley for coffee and cigarettes. It was always my belief that everything in life happens for a reason and on this night, both of us had our eyes opened to the character of our captain and to the potential risks involved in our voyage. Who knew the strangers aboard would bond so quickly and become dependent on one another in what was to be the first of several life and death experiences. After tonight, I knew William was much more than the frail man I thought him to be. Instead, he proved to be a cool, calculating, intelligent man, with the heart of a lion well within his prime. William was also pleased I could rise to the occasion and would not falter in a crisis.

We had been exposed to Etlar's multi-faceted personality. His actions showed his inability to act responsibly in a dangerous situation and his general lack of concern for the crew's safety. I'll never forget the look on William's face as he looked up from his coffee and said, "That man is a lunatic." Making an effort to smile, we tried to make the best of a bad situation and agreed to look out for each other. The bonds of a good friendship were formed.

The voyage, for the most part, went relatively smooth for the next six days as we made our way toward the Canary Islands. It was during these uneventful times that we began to feel better about the trip, settling nicely into our daily routine. Etlar would come down from the wheelhouse from time-to-time, never saying much but always letting us know, in his pretentious way, that he was still in charge. Neither of us paid much attention to his moods.

During these times, Etlar would indulge in small amounts of food, mostly bread and cheese and he never took part in the large evening meals I made a point of preparing everyday for all of us. He never wore a shirt, so his large, round potbelly, a stark contrast to the rest of his build, hung over his dirty trousers, looking like he had swallowed a huge watermelon. During the entire time we were aboard the Zurich, we never saw Etlar bathe. He simply showed up once in a while and then left. That's the way it was, Etlar lived upstairs and we lived downstairs.

As the old twelve cylinders noisily pounded her steady rhythm, we were able to maintain the consistent twelve knots originally projected. To maintain this speed however, William and I were committed to keeping the four-on, four-off schedule. William knew my lack of experience around engine rooms and always simplified my duties, which merely meant keeping a close eye on the gauges and maintaining her oil levels. Since she had seen better days, the importance of keeping oil in her daily was becoming a more vigilant duty.

Diminished Respect for Captain Etlar

N ow, in our sixth day at sea, I asked Etlar about sending an email to my wife and kids. Once again, he blew me off; telling me the Internet wasn't working. This was one of the assurances he had given me before we left North Sydney, promising I would be able to communicate with my family while out at sea. Despite his actions, I still believed him and told myself I would be able to send a message the following day. But as the days went by, I became angrier with myself for putting myself in position of absolute helplessness. My life and well-being were now in the hands of a man I did not like, nor could I trust.

Since leaving, we had travelled south at an average of two-hundred forty miles a day. The once cool air off the shores of Cape Breton now felt like mid-summer and I enjoyed lying out on deck, basking in the sun while the long, narrow boat sliced through the calm glistening waters. The Canary Islands were not far off and William and I took pleasure in the idea that we would soon enjoy the fruits of our labour. For me, to visit the Canary Islands would be exciting, but for William, it meant he could replenish his cigarette supply, which was quickly dwindling. Cigarettes were the ultimate necessity in William's life and he asked for no more or no less.

All was going well so Etlar decided we should celebrate. That afternoon, he and I shared a large bottle of rum and got shitfaced drunk. We laughed and carried on as if we were old pals while William, a non-drinker, looked on in wonderment. Late that afternoon, the heat became so intense out on deck, we sought shelter inside. Although that day came and went without incident, it was followed by a well-deserved morning of headache and nausea.

The next day, Etlar announced we were not going to stop at the Canary Islands but continue on to Nigeria. For the first time, William displayed anger toward Etlar, telling him he must call to port.

"Everything is going fine and we don't have to stop," said Etlar. He shoved his large belly into William and looked down at him. He sneered, "You don't tell me what to do, this is my ship and I say what happens." Bewildered and outranked William discretely turned away. It was not his nature to be aggressive.

Later, William told me he thought the "son-of-a-bitch" never had any intentions of going to the Islands in the first place. I agreed whole-heartedly.

Life on Board—Did Someone Say Flies?

Although I was not able to contact my family, I did finally learn that the supposedly broken computer was always able to work for Captain Etlar. My anger grew, but William and I kept our focus, which helped to keep our sanity in order to keep the one–hundred sixty-foot piece of scrap metal running for another nine days while we reached our destination. The further we sailed, the warmer it got, and the temperature made the conditions very uncomfortable. Like true sailors however, we continued working.

As the temperature rose, so did the number of houseflies. They were everywhere and before long, it was as if the good Lord had sent a plague upon us. I can only surmise there was a connection with what was causing the foul smell I had detected the first day I boarded the Zurich. It must have become a breeding ground for maggots, which now sent forth a thick harvest of flies into the galley, our only place of refuge from the steady noise, dirt, and drudgery of the engine room. The situation made it impossible to carry on any type of normal behaviour in the following days. Determined to reach our objective, which was to arrive safely in Africa, we were not deterred by a few thousand flies. This was just going to be one of those inconvenient conditions we had not anticipated along the way.

Measures were taken to protect our food by wrapping and storing what wasn't frozen. But the situation forced us to retreat to the outer deck with our meals in hand. The heavy, thick doors on our bunkhouse rooms were kept shut. William entertained himself by swatting flies with a roll of newspaper any time he wasn't in the engine room, until everything, from the walls to table, was covered in fly carnage. Finally, the battle was won and the flies were no more. Fortunately, the galley heat worked in our favour for once. The intense heat dehydrated the disgusting massacre of thousands of flies, which were brushed away as tiny dust particles. I am sure traces of the battle remain to this day. On a positive note, the terrible, foul smell slowly evaporated without ever revealing its source.

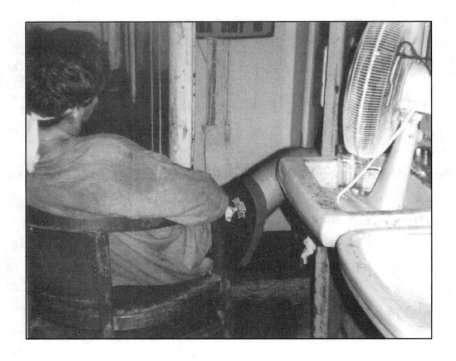

Leif, battling the unbearable heat in the galley aboard the Zurich.

By now, Leif had been gone about two weeks. Before they left, Etlar promised they would keep in touch by computer or radio and contact us to let us know their location and estimated time of arrival. Etlar also gave us an address and fax numbers to use in case of an emergency. Since I had not heard from them, I decided to send a fax to the head office for the Sannu Corporation in Rhode Island. Surely, they would have heard where the Zurich was at sea. I made a second attempt to use the computer address Etlar gave me, but it was not recognized as a valid address. I had no luck at all.

The children went with me to my sister Catherine's office in Glace Bay, the nearest town from home. At this time, we did not have a computer at home so she offered to send my messages. The children wrote letters and photocopied their hands on the copier, thinking this was so cool. They wrote messages on their pictures and hoped to surprise their Dad. When all seven attempts failed and the faxes would not go through, I felt we had been duped. I never told Justin and Aleisha their letters had not been sent to their Dad.

In the following days, Catherine tried several other numbers we found but none were successful. I tried not to let on but I was getting worried and it bothered me not knowing where they were. The sea can be very unforgiving, especially in an old boat, badly in need of repairs, that was meant to sail in the cold waters of the Atlantic.

A Tyrant Dictates our Routine

We began to tire as the twenty-four hour routine became more vigilant. I continued to ensure William's well being. Without him, we didn't stand a chance of completing the voyage. He worked hard and through his diligence, kept everything running below. Just as he would solve one problem another would arise.

By now, the Zurich had crossed the Atlantic Ocean and was steadily making her way down the African coast. We were getting closer to the equator. Etlar now estimated another seven days until we reach our destination. We found out this week would be the most gruelling seven days of our lives.

The heat was excruciating. The Zurich, a fine ship in her day, had been engineered to function in the cold North Atlantic waters off the coast of Newfoundland. And she had done just that for many years. She would now face her greatest challenge—the hot tropical waters off the coast of Africa. Designed to cool her engines with seawater, she struggled daily, like a marathon runner gasping for her next breath in order to reach the finish line. She was spewing oil into the bilge and her stress became mine. Five days to go and William was showing severe signs of exhaustion as we shared this constant vigil.

In the last two days, a concerned William made several comments to me that the engine was in serious trouble and we could no
longer take the stress of doing ten knots. William, covered in grease
and sweat, stormed up to the wheelhouse to confront Etlar. "Slow
this damn thing down," he demanded.

Etlar remained in his captain's chair, unfazed by William's
abrupt entrance. From his position he was enjoying the ride to Nigeria and looked down at the toil and sweat of his two bilge rats
below. Overruling William, who had thirty years of experience, he
replied, "Don't worry about it."

By now, I had developed a serious hatred for the man. He neither respected our hard work nor our ability to take total control
over any given situation. His irresponsible manner put our lives in
danger many times and on a personal level, he still refused to allow
me to contact my family. Etlar could care less about any of us and
he made no effort to keep his end of our deal.

With each passing day, the heat grew more intense, making our
working environment almost intolerable. The ocean was like glass,
not a breath of wind to cool the discomfort of our relentless vigil.
We slowly made our way, edging closer to what we thought would
be the end of a great challenge. The entire boat was like a pressure
cooker. There was no place to take refuge from her large engines
and generators and it was only compounded by the heat from the
galley stove. The temperature both inside and outside was unbearable. Our drinking water was hot but we rectified the problem by
always keeping three one-gallon jugs in the deep freeze–a practice
we would pay a heavy price for later.

William and Etlar were becoming more and more agitated with
each other. Etlar insisted on maintaining the speed and this in turn,
placed much stress on William to keep the engine from overheating

and breaking down. I was twenty-five years younger than William and much more physically fit, yet I, too, found this situation, and the constant stress, took its toll on me. It was my job to regularly monitor the heat gauges and keep her oil levels up.

Poor William, I sympathized with him and feared he was going to have a heart attack but in the long run, he proved to be much stronger than I thought. By now, he had run out of cigarettes, his only true pleasure and addiction. He was beginning to say the hell with it, which scared me because without William, there would be no crossing the finish line.

Silence is Not Golden

The sun crept over the horizon, its crimson glow introducing the dawn of a new day. William and I sat quietly at the galley table as he stared aimlessly into his coffee; exhausted from the monotony of yet another long, hard night. He said nothing. We both dreaded the thought of one more day in the sweltering heat.

Without warning, William jolted upright. His eyes widened as he listened. Staring right through me he said, "Oh my God!"

The steady drone of the engine had been interrupted with a strange thud. Scrambling to his feet, he wasted no time racing to the engine room. I chased after him, catching a glimpse of Etlar as he reared up behind us.

Etlar shoved me aside and began screaming at William over the clamour of the engine. "What is wrong, what is the matter?" He continued to screech as William worked diligently checking gauges and turning valves.

"I told you, I told you…but you wouldn't listen."

Shutting down this huge twelve-cylinder engine was not as simple as turning a key, but all too quickly, the steady drone we had listened to for fourteen days now, fell silent as the Zurich lay motionless, forty miles off the coast of Liberia. William was enraged and wasted no time venting his anger toward Etlar. The captain knew we were in serious trouble. We all knew. Out on the warm South Atlantic Ocean, there was no coast guard to patrol the sea— just pirates.

Etlar informed us that Liberia was in turmoil, being torn apart by three warlords. The fear was that if one of them were to notice a floundering vessel such as ours, they would waste no time in seizing it. Having no use for the crew, one could only surmise what actions they would take. Etlar knew this from his past experiences and it actually brought the big guy to tears as he looked up and said, "Oh God, if you get me out of this mess, I'll become a Christian."

Eventually, William collected himself and went back to work for the greater purpose of saving our lives. One of the cylinders had scored, causing a control arm on the piston to break. His years of experience as a mechanical engineer proved to be invaluable. It was more than a calculated guess that lead him to the conclusion that it was a broken control arm—or maybe two.

Running on adrenaline, William worked steadily doing the necessary repairs and within twelve hours, we were on our way. The large engine was fixed on either side with huge steel plates, twenty-four in all. They were fastened tightly with hundreds of steel bolts, which were often seized tight. Not knowing which ones to remove, William quickly put me to work with the wrench. For twelve consecutive hours in temperatures well over one-hundred degrees Fahrenheit, we did battle with the seized engine, using our best efforts to remove the bolts. We removed one end of the broken control arm from the crankshaft. The process of replacing the steel plates in their rightful position proved to be even more difficult. Being the mechanic he was though, William was able to fine-tune the valves and gauges to fix the engine using what was available. But the continuous labour in the hot, greasy pit left us both exhausted. There was one consolation—the captain upstairs had not set foot in the engine room, which William and I were thankful for.

Every voyage, or so it seems, is not without incident. The only asset we had going for us was quickly coming to an end. The cold drinking water we used to quench our overwhelming thirst was now gone. Our deep freeze unit had burnt out. Overworked by cooling the steady input of hot water jugs coupled with the extreme heat outside, the old appliance had finally given up. In only a short time, the remainder of our food thawed and turned sour as well. It would be another two-and-a-half days to our estimated time of arrival, with only hot water to drink and no edible food.

We spoke very little to each other and had to reach deep within ourselves to remain focused on one thing—LAND or at the very least, convince ourselves we were going to make it.

Relentlessly, as if we had nothing else to lose, we sliced our way at nine knots without incident. It was as if the good Lord had sent me a sign. While on break, I sought refuge from the hot rays of the sun by sitting in a doorway on the upper deck. From there, I peered out over the horizon. The good Lord had indeed sent us a sign—out of nowhere.

Looking up, I recognized the large, black rain cloud and I raced down three flights of stairs shouting, "William, William, stop whatever you are doing and come quick."

By the time William had followed me to the upper deck, I had already stripped naked. William wasted no time in doing the same and we danced around like two happy schoolboys as a torrent of cool, fresh tropical rain water fell heavily upon us for ten minutes or more. It was truly a piece of heaven.

To reach our destination, we only needed to travel one more day, a real boost to our morale. Even Etlar was smiling and happy now, as he made efforts to befriend us both. We welcomed the change in character and kept in mind that we still needed his help to catch a flight to the perfect world we so foolishly left behind many days ago.

At last, the sight of land made me feel as though I had just planted a flag on top of Mount Everest. We really made it! The challenge had been met and now it was time to go home.

Little did we know, we were about to encounter the first of many obstacles in our quest for a safe and quick return home.

A Foreboding Place

Etlar received a radio message informing him we could not enter the river we were supposed to travel through. The sixty-mile passage up the Escravos River to a place called Warri, our final destination, was not to be as easily conquered as we expected. The word Escravos, meaning slave in Portuguese, makes reference to a river with a dark past. Little did we know, we were about to experience its foreboding reputation for ourselves.

While waiting permission to enter the river, the Zurich paddled slowly up and down the coast until we finally received word we could proceed to the mouth of the river, going no further than the marker buoys. It was over two days since we had eaten. The combined mental and physical stress and the fatigue of the voyage, without any contact from home, left us nearing our wits' end.

At the mouth of the large river, Etlar was able to nudge the Zurich's bow, with the utmost skill, only inches away from one of many large marker buoys while battling the strong currents of the dangerous river. Beneath her bow were two young men in a dugout canoe who paddled intensely to maintain their position in the river's current as Etlar fought to do the same. I lowered the bowline with a large shackle to the lads below. With great expertise on the part of both the captain and the canoers, we were now tethered to a buoy at the mouth of the Escravos River.

Three thousand miles from home and after eighteen days of misery, the first order of business for William and me was to find some food and cigarettes. I told him it was a good time to quit, but he would have nothing to do with the idea.

It wasn't long before there were several groups of curious paddlers curious lined up to see this odd spectacle. We made verbal contact with two of the women by shouting over the side of the boat. They soon returned with cigarettes and green bananas. After retrieving the precious goods by rope, we settled our debt by tossing an empty forty-five gallon barrel over the side and everyone was happy. The Nigerians used barrels for water storage and for cooking, so for them, this was a good trade.

Later that evening, we received an official visit from a military gunboat. By request, a rope ladder was dropped over the side, which was met by a young man ominously toting an AK-47. In contrast, he seemed harmless enough and even uncertain of his duties. Protect us or guard us—it was never made clear.

Etlar was as anxious as I was to set foot on dry land so when he somehow made arrangements for a canoe and two paddlers to take us to shore, I jumped at the chance. William, however, opted to stay on board and get acquainted with his new friend.

Food at Last

A fter being cooped up in the decrepit boat for almost three weeks, I was very excited to finally climb down the rope ladder we had thrown over the side of the ship. As I stepped into a large dugout canoe, I was never happier to see the shoreline. The canoe, which looked primitive to me, was paddled by two quiet, well-built young men who only took ten minutes to reach the shore in spite of the river's swift current. It was exhilarating to step foot on land again. I dared to think this meant I had made it. Whatever happened in that moment, it sure felt good.

The closer we got to the shore, it became apparent the people in the village were expecting our arrival. I assumed the village must have been quite large considering the fifty or more villagers that now lined the water's edge. Many crowded aboard two small fishing boats, coming out to meet us with our escort. I was actually quite nervous when a hush came over the crowd as we walked across the narrow, poorly constructed platform where our transport had been tethered. Our two paddlers continued to escort Etlar and me past the other onlookers standing onshore.

Being from Cape Breton, I had seen my share of star-filled nights, but this night was brilliantly lit by millions of stars like nothing I had ever seen before. I also have to say, the silence of the fresh night air was a pleasant change from the pungent odours and continuous racket of the past eighteen days aboard the Zurich.

The closer we moved to the centre of the crowd, the louder the whispers grew and many of the villagers were becoming more vocal, offering what I assumed were polite greetings. I was momentarily startled when a loud voice called out, "Adweebo, adweebo", followed by a distinct hissing sound that echoed across the crowd. Later, I would learn that a/dwee/bo meant "white man" in their dialect.

My first experience setting foot in Africa was, to say the least, a bit unnerving, but it was far overshadowed by the fact that it felt much safer to have the earth beneath my feet. Despite our mishaps and my growing anger at the captain for his misrepresentations, I couldn't help but feel that same sense of accomplishment experienced by all voyagers and explorers, now that we were actually in Africa.

As we made our way up to the village, a small kerosene lantern was handed to our lead paddler, which he used to navigate our way through a maze of pathways that crisscrossed the village, which consisted of numerous mud and stone huts with large thatched roofs.

Etlar was clearly on a mission and the stoic beauty of the riverside village was lost on him. He wanted a drink and nothing was going to get in his way, so I trailed behind him trying to keep my footing in the dark. We trudged past many huts until we were led to a modest metal-covered shack with a dirt floor—the local tavern I gathered. Once inside, Etlar was quick to order a strong drink in his typical less than polite manner, showing no respect for the bartender. When the bartender looked at me and asked what I would like, I mustered the last of my strength and asked, "Do you have any food?"

With a toothy smile, he proudly showed me his pantry, which consisted of an assortment of canned goods placed neatly on two thin shelves. By the light of the old kerosene lantern, I made my selection and devoured a can of corned beef and beans, eagerly washing it down with warm beer. As I threw my head back to drain the last sip from the bottle, I noticed a unique ceiling fixture that looked like a spoked wheel. Affixed to it were five blackened kerosene lanterns, which did little to illuminate the dark, grimy dwelling. Six small, very heavy, and poorly constructed tables were neatly placed within the dank room. Each table was accompanied by two high-back chairs, which seemed somewhat out of place in comparison to the rest of the décor–if you could call it that.

Etlar and I made our way to a table in the back where an eager host was lighting the single candle that adorned each table. I plopped myself down on the rickety chair and glanced around the room. In the far corner, I noticed an old man with a short beard. He sat motionless, almost blending, like a chameleon, into the dimly lit background. Every so often he would take a long draw on his cigarette, causing a bright red glow around his large nose. It was obvious he was comfortable and in no hurry. He nursed his drink while surveying the room. After a while, it became apparent he was interested in us, which was understandable since we weren't your typical patrons in this establishment

. Etlar seemed oblivious to the others in the bar. He leaned back, riding precariously on the back two legs of the tall chair then stretched his legs and feet forward to brace himself. The gracious bartender asked if we would like another drink. Etlar immediately commanded he bring him a good size bottle of whisky. It was certainly no Jack Daniels that arrived, but rather a bottle of home-brewed moonshine. Etlar eagerly poured us a drink and ordered me to drink up. It didn't take me more than one swallow to know the stuff was lethal. My face twisted and contorted as the bitter liquid burned its way down my throat then continued its way down to my toes. Barely catching my breath, I graciously decline another.

Etlar stumbled out of his chair, nearly taking the table and me with him, and then declared it was time to go back to the boat.

When we arrived on ship, William greeted me with a huge smile. I had lugged enough corned beef and beans back for all of us and I was now struggling to heave it over the side of the boat.

"Yes, William, there are two packs of smokes in the bag as well," I said, noticing his concern as he scanned the bag of canned goods.

In the days to come, some of my most fond memories would be of William and the time we had spent preparing our meals or just talking in the galley, which turned out to be our only refuge during the relentless voyage across the Atlantic. It was entertaining just to watch William slice the canned corned beef with the precision of an old English gentleman carving a prime rib for the Sunday dinner. He would purse his lips tightly around a cigarette as smoke wafted from his nostrils and encircled his head like a tough old dragon.

It had been days since we ran out of the fresh potatoes and frozen vegetables. But we now had enough corned beef to fill the void so William was content. He was the sort of man that always lived his life in the moment, and in this moment, he wasn't going to be hungry–for William, all was well with the world. Meanwhile, my only thoughts were directed toward the hard green bananas that hung on the far wall.

Still No Contact Home

William and I smiled. Our bellies were full, we weren't facing any gale force winds at the moment, and Etlar was nowhere in sight. Everything was good and we would soon be on our way home. The only thing that worried me was that it had been eighteen days since I had any contact with Marlene and the kids. The last week-and-a-half had been so hard it overshadowed the issue, but now that we were supposedly safe and we weren't facing a major crisis, it was really hitting me hard—I missed my family.

Two-and-a-half weeks ago, I set sail on a pile of scrap metal with a person I knew nothing about and took off to a foreign country on the other side of the world, a place my family and I knew nothing about. Nothing else mattered now except making that phone call.

The following day, I approached Etlar as soon as I got up. "Look pal, I busted my ass getting you here, now get a message to my family."

"You're in Nigeria, in the jungle, there are no phones here." He laughed at me, his eyes mocking me as though I were an idiot.

"Well, use the fucking radio and ask someone to make a call."

"Life, you just don't understand, do you? You'll make your call in Warri." With that, the conversation was over.

My animosity for Etlar grew daily, but what could I do? I was stuck with him. I could not tell him to fuck off and go my own way even though, in all honesty, nothing would have given me more pleasure. Thousands of miles of water, hundreds of miles of dense jungle, and evil forces I had yet to encounter, lay between me and my freedom. Totally ignorant of the country, I would soon be exposed to the ways of some pretty sinister people in Warri.

The anger brewing inside me was not just the result of Etlar's betrayal but also the disappointment I had in myself for getting into this situation in the first place. I had blindly placed my trust and well being in the hands of a man I knew nothing about.

There was no doubt in my mind that something was wrong. I could drive myself crazy trying to figure out why Leif neither called nor had a message forwarded, so I chose to keep busy and maintain a regular schedule for myself and the children. During the weeks of the voyage, my Dad and brothers, seamen themselves, kept a close watch on the marine forecasts. We were happy to know there had not been any storms or bad weather. They would remind me that "No news is good news." (A well used fisherman's quote—until you know it's bad news, then getting no news is good!) Dad, a well-seasoned fisherman, always believed, "You had to keep the Faith," and keep the Faith was what I did.

The First of Many Strange Visitors

That afternoon, two military police boats arrived, carrying two uniformed officers accompanied by two heavy-set, cheerful-looking chaps, dressed in boubous, the long flowing, wide-sleeved robes worn by Muslim men in much of West Africa. They seemed quite taken with me and paid me a lot of attention. After telling me they were from the desert and had never seen a boat before, they posed for pictures wearing one of the only life jackets we had on board. After a private conversation with Etlar, they left as quickly as they came.

Etlar was all smiles because they had given him the go ahead and we could now proceed to Warri. All I could think about was my phone call and then the trip back to Canada and my family. I was getting excited. Etlar, however, was mortified by the fact that he was told he could not proceed up the river without a pilot. In past conversations, he had told me he had fished a large trawler out of Warri and that he knew the river like the back of his hand. At this point, I didn't know what to believe about the man, but in this situation, the pilot may have been necessary since we were instructed to travel only by night.

Before leaving, Etlar extended an invitation to accompany him to back to the village. Although I didn't want to share his company, I accepted the opportunity to get acquainted with the local people and experience their culture since this was one of the reasons I came to Africa in the first place.

Standing on the bow of the boat, Etlar was able to wave his long arms and draw the attention of two young women in a dugout canoe. They understood his gestures and were able to send his message on to the same two paddlers we had the night before. By now, William had become well acquainted with his new friend and opted to once again stay aboard the boat.

Etlar and I made our way down the rope ladder to the water's edge and met the paddlers as they arrived. I climbed in the large dugout canoe and was perched high on a narrow stick that ran from one side of the canoe to the other. Like a foreign dignitary, I was placed higher than the others while these strong and healthy young men paddled the canoe in a steady rhythm across the water. I was impressed by their ability to manoeuvre the large cumbersome canoe skilfully through the swift currents at the mouth of the harbour.

Since we had left home, it was the first time I felt good about the whole ordeal.

I looked back at the Zurich to view her from this position. I thought she was a beautiful boat from the outside and since she had delivered us safely, she was worthy of the respect and gratitude that William and I had for her. Those who earn their living on the sea know all too well the relationship that forms between fisherman and Mother Nature.

Now, as I looked back at the boat, the only thing that could override her beauty was the rich blue sky and the lush green forest that magnificently lay before me. The rainy season had just passed and the jungle was awakened and alive with sounds and colours. The royal blue sky and the deep green of the thick foliage were in stark contrast to the brown, silted waters of the Escravos River. It was an amazing sight.

The paddlers expertly guided the canoe ashore. With utmost respect, the two young men stood in the shallow water to steady the canoe and reminded us to watch our step as we vacated. Being the first to step ashore, Etlar was quick to get moving. He never looked back at the two men, or me for that matter, and he certainly didn't thank them.

They were curious about our purpose here and lingered as if they wanted to make friends and engage in conversation. I was glad I had taken some small American bills and without hesitation, I handed the closest lad a ten dollar bill. I tried to make them understand that I wanted them to share the meagre note. They were overwhelmed by my generosity. Etlar would later boast to me that when he was captain of a fishing boat at the Warri Harbour, he would get three days work from one of them for that same ten dollars and for a month's wages, he paid a man one hundred dollars. In my opinion, I thought he should hang his head in shame.

I looked up the path but Etlar had not waited for me, which didn't bother me. I felt quite comfortable with my two new friends and I was in no hurry to trail behind him.

Up ahead, I could see the remnants of stone foundations that lined the shoreline. I asked the men about their origin and the eldest of the two was quick to answer. In a storytelling fashion, using many hand gestures, he tried his best to outline a detailed history of a Portuguese slave station. From what I was able to understand, it was said that the river itself flowed from the tears of the slaves' cries. From what was translated to me, I learned that the river had shifted, as they often do, partially covering some of the grizzly reminders of this time, although it was not able to erase everything.

The lads offered to continue from there and show me the remains of a slave ship that was somewhat submerged in the mud of the jungle floor. As interested as I was, I need to find Etlar, so I thanked them for their guidance and left to catch up with the captain before it was too late to find him.

As I followed the trail, I recounted the story the men had told me. I was fascinated. This was the reason I had worked so hard to get here. I wanted to learn of the people, their history, and their culture. This was no resort; it was the real thing, the real Africa. The sights and sounds in this seemingly thriving village were amazing.

As I looked out over the village, it occurred to me that although crossing the Atlantic had been tough, it was over now and this adventure would be worth it. I put aside all of my anger and my fears and decided to enjoy the country. On either side of the narrow dirt road sat rectangular homes, about twelve feet by twenty feet in size. They were built with mud and stone and finished with a pink stucco coating. The roofs were adorned with a thatched covering and despite their simplicity, all of them displayed a true sense of pride. Many homes had livestock such as chickens and goats and the properties were kept neat and tidy.

As I continued to walk through the village, a dozen or more children followed along out of curiosity. Some were dancing and skipping in front of us as if we were in a parade. Some older children were a little more cautious and trailed behind. There was a mixed reaction from the elders of the village. Some made friendly gestures while most lingered and stared, which gave me an uneasy feeling. Young girls would make a hissing sound and call out "Adweebo".

At this point, I was almost glad to have caught up with Etlar. The children, who were familiar with him, were eager to gain his attention but he slapped them away with the back of his hand. He shouted "Life, come!" He placed his arm around my shoulder and told me he found another watering hole.

The wooden remains of a small, green, ramshackle house was our next stop. This was located on the other side of the village. When inside, Etlar did all the talking. It was difficult for me to understand what he was saying. After several years of living and working with the Nigerians, he had managed to master their language. Etlar could speak four other languages as well. With a mix of bad English, slang and this new tongue, he had a key into the lives of a people he had no care or respect for.

Trying to remain focused and keep my wits about me, I chose not to participate in an afternoon of drinking. While I waited for Etlar to get his fill, I entertained myself by peering out through a broken window, watching the local people going about their daily business. Etlar's constant prodding to drink with him was beginning to annoy me so I left the tattered building to escape his harassment.

Nearby, an old lady tended a flock of chickens. Thinking of William back on the boat, I decided to approach her and try to buy one for our supper. She was nervous about my presence but when I showed her a twenty dollar American bill, her fear became excitement. I bargained for two birds but at the sight of the money, she wanted to sell me the entire flock of about twelve or so. We finally agreed to the purchase of just two and I was glad to see her so happy about the exchange, as she handed the chickens over with a big toothless smile. It made me feel good to see her benefit by the trade and besides, I would be going home in a few days and still had about two hundred dollars left.

I was reluctant to stray too far from the watering hole, as Etlar called it, so I hung out by the door and sipped on a warm beer—I thought it wise not to drink the local water. While I waited, I was given some fruit and nuts that Etlar had ordered for me and I made sure William was not left out. By the time we were ready to leave, Etlar was feeling no pain.

I went to collect the two chickens. The old lady had bound their legs and tied the pair of discontented fowl to the end of a stick, which she had prepared for me to carry over my shoulder during the walk back to the boat.

On the way, Etlar questioned me about the purchase and how much I had paid for the birds. When I told him I gave her twenty dollars for the two chickens, he nearly lost it and called me a darn fool. As he continued laughing at me, he told me the word of the big fool would be spread for twenty miles up the river by now. Once again, he reminded me that wages for a month's labour aboard his boat were only about one hundred dollars.

Heading to Warri and a Phone

T he river pilot was brought on board and at dusk, I eagerly heaved the large bowline aboard. The last time I had done so, I had watched all I held dear, fade in the distance.

It was an exciting time for all of us! William and I stood on the deck as we made our way up the river, which became quite narrow in places. I marvelled at the sight of flare stacks not far from the riverbank. They lit up the night sky with a brilliant orange glow that danced across the horizon. An hour or so later, as our boat pushed forward, they faded from sight and all that remained was an eerie blanket of ebony air. I was amazed at how the river pilot navigated the sometimes narrow river with only the moonlight to aid him.

Feeling tired but too excited to sleep, I peered into the darkness, remembering the past three weeks. The engine started to reduce speed as we began to veer to port. The silence was broken when Etlar gave me instructions to ready the bowline.

"What the hell is this all about?" I asked. "We are not going to Warri tonight?"

"We must stay here until daybreak," he replied.

The river pilot nudged the Zurich's long, narrow nose slowly toward an old abandoned tanker at the water's edge. A large man was standing on the tanker's deck, waving his arms and shouting profanities at Etlar.

"Back off, you can't tie your boat here!" he yelled. He was quite adamant about it and when I looked into his face, I could tell he was a force to be reckoned with.

Etlar was quick to turn on his charms, "Please sir, I beg of you. I will pay you money." After a heated debate, a deal was struck and the Zurich lay motionless once more.

There was a small village not more than a stone's throw away and it wasn't long before we were receiving company. Half dozen good-looking local girls, who were dressed surprisingly well, were climbing over the tanker and onto the Zurich. Etlar, preoccupied with other affairs, was unaware that William and I had invited them into the galley area. One had received a severe gash to her foot and William, being the kind and gentle soul he was, was quick to administer first aid while the remaining five made me out to be like some sort of a rock star. Caressing my face and elsewhere, and running their hands through my hair, they were quite fascinated with my moustache, which they referred to as a "toto brush".

Suddenly, from out of nowhere, there was Etlar clutching the fire axe. He looked like a madman from a horror movie. "Get those whores out of here!" he yelled. As he raised the axe over his head I truly feared for their lives, but they were quick to scurry up to deck level. The girl with the injury was last to leave, trailing a bloody dressing from her half-bandaged foot. They tried to reason so they had to be forcibly removed. The door was pulled shut but one tiny hand remained caught. Etlar, still in a rage, lowered the mighty axe toward her hand. I shoved him to one side like a linebacker defending his quarterback, causing a stream of sparks to spray down the wall where the axe hit, narrowly missing the young girl's hand. The girls got the message and never returned.

After the adrenaline stopped pumping, both Etlar and I calmed ourselves. He collected his thoughts and went on to explain to William and me the seriousness of the situation.

"They would have planted drugs on the boat so the police would know where to find them and we would be done for." With that said he spun around and stormed off to his cabin, slamming the heavy steel door behind him.

"What kind of a place is this?" William asked.

At that moment, I realized we were no longer in Kansas. Fatigue had taken its toll. We turned in for the night—tired, confused, and somehow, less innocent. The following day we slept long into the morning.

An Ominous Visit

While enjoying coffee together in the galley, William and I tried to make sense of everything we had witnessed the night before, only to conclude that Etlar was crazier, more untrustworthy, and possibly even more dangerous than we had ever thought. The sound of motorboats caught our attention and out of curiosity, we went topside to see what was going on.

Three river patrol boats were just pulling up alongside us and the sight of these three heavily armed boats gave me a feeling of genuine foreboding. Two of the motor boats were mounted with large calibre machine guns. Though the other, a large zodiac, had no mounted weapons, all three craft were manned with uniformed officers, each carrying an AK-47. Etlar saw me from the wheelhouse and said, "Life, throw over the ladder." Being in no position to argue, I wasted no time in doing so.

Four men climbed aboard followed by a young woman. Two of the men had AK-47s strapped over their shoulders; another chap, a heavy set man, was well dressed, wearing a suit coat and trousers. The fourth was a tall, slender man who wore a leather trench coat that nearly dragged on the ground as he walked toward us. He was carrying two bags containing a lot of money. His expressionless face unnerved me. I had no desire to even make eye contact with him. The woman, wearing a black toque, a white T-shirt and shorts, bounced across the deck, nearly colliding with me as she headed straight for the wheelhouse. Although I didn't know it at the time, this was Etlar's Nigerian wife.

No sooner had the four men stepped aboard, another speedboat arrived carrying two more well-dressed older men, who climbed aboard using the ship's rope ladder. They all greeted each other and shook hands as if old friends. Despite their rather imposing look, they were quite respectful and pleasant when they asked me if they could see the captain of the vessel.

"Follow me," I replied. Though I was feeling uneasy about their presence, they wasted no time getting down to business. When the two bags of money were dumped on the table, I felt it was time for me to leave. Something did not seem right. When they spoke, they each glanced in my direction. This is when I believe I was bought and paid for by the powers that be.

The Captain Disappears

Returning to the galley, William and I decided to have our coffee as far away as we could get from the gathering aloft. After a half hour or so, curiosity got the better of me however, and I felt the need to go topside and take a peek.

All was quiet as I reached the upper deck. Looking out over the bow, I could see the wake of the three boats as they sped away into the distance. Despite my initial uneasiness with the visit, I still did not think it was a big deal.

The captain's quarters were located directly across from the wheelhouse entrance. As I made my way to the bridge, I noticed that Etlar's door, which was always kept shut, was wide open—but not as wide open as my eyes became when I discovered that every single possession that man owned had vanished, along with Etlar himself.

My jaw dropped, as did my heart, when I entered the room in utter disbelief. I stood motionless, gasping, shocked at what I was witnessing. Something caught my eye as I peered into the almost empty closet. There, on the floor, was my survival suit, the one my old pal Mike had dropped off for me.

"That lousy bastard," I mumbled aloud. My suspicions were confirmed. Etlar had deceived me and now, as I stood, thousand miles from my family and all that I loved, I had no idea what lay ahead for me.

My heart was pounding so loud, I didn't hear William come in. He was standing behind me with the same look of shock on his face.

"Look, the son-of-a-bitch had my survival suit all the time," I said.

William was speechless. Our looks of surprise and anger now turned to fear.

"Come with me." I said abruptly, then raced down the stairs to the crew's quarters below, where Etlar had stored his personal belongings. Everything was gone.

Words cannot explain how I felt at that moment. It felt like a tidal wave of emotions had washed over me and swept me off my feet. In that moment, I could only image what it felt like walking out of a doctor's office after being diagnosed with terminal cancer. All I could think was, "My God, what have I done? This can't be happening, someone pinch me please and wake me up."

The faces of Marlene and our two children flashed before me. Here, thousands of miles from home and miles up a river without a paddle and no one, absolutely no one, knows where I am. My only conclusion was that we were shanghaied and now left to fend for ourselves.

After the initial shock wore off, William and I drank coffee and smoked cigarettes the rest of the day, hardly speaking a word. We tortured ourselves trying to make sense of it all while devising a plan to get us out of this mess.

That evening, I made it a point to befriend the muscle bound keeper of the old tanker to which we were tethered. He turned out to be a gentle giant who went by the name Young. Young had no family and claimed the old tanker as his home. He occupied his time lifting his homemade weights. He told me that at one time, he was a merchant marine. He had seen a lot of the world, including Canada, but he was now forced to live out the rest of his life here, on the river, because he had no money and no passport. And without either, he was a prisoner in this foreign country.

The air was warm that night. The moist heat stuck to our skin as Young and I sat under the open sky filled with a million stars. His open, simple manner put me somewhat at ease. I told him about everything that had happened over the past weeks in hopes he could somehow advise me on what to do, since it was evident I had not so much as one ace to play at this point. He seemed to become nervous as I appealed to him and could only offer me this advice, gently saying with his large hand on my forearm, "Be careful, my friend. This is not a good place."

Help Arrives from Local Immigration?

"**G**reat. Just what I wanted to hear," I thought, rising to my feet and bidding Young goodnight.

If I wasn't worried before, Young's friendly advice had put me on alert. I paced the deck until finally I got the idea to get the phone number for the Canadian embassy in Lagos from my passport papers. Folding it neatly, I shoved it, and a one hundred dollar American bill, down inside my knife pouch, which always hung from my belt. Now tired, both physically and mentally, I returned to my quarters for the evening. In light of the past twenty-four hours, I slept very little.

After a long, sleepless night, it was back to the galley for a breakfast of bananas and coffee. Neither William nor I had any idea of what to make of the past night's events. We said little to each other. Our nominal breakfast was interrupted by an unknown voice coming from the upper deck.

"Hello. Is anyone there?" a man's voice called out.

My first thought was that someone had come to take us to Warri. Jumping to my feet, I raced up the stairs, relieved that I may finally be heading home. A small, thin man dressed in a light grey uniform was there to greet me.

He reminded me of a vagrant looking for a handout, with his uniform torn and tattered and shoes so worn his toes protruded from one side. He wore an officer's cap, as tattered as the rest of his uniform, pulled tightly over a pair of dark sunglasses. I noticed a series of neatly placed markings on his face—not tattoos, but decorative markings—etched and scarred into his skin by what must have been a sharp object. Standing behind him, just off to one side, was a young man at least six foot six and two-hundred-and-eighty pounds, barefoot and clothed with only a wrap around his middle. As he stared at me, I tied to ignore his presence. Instead, I gave my full attention to the ragged little man with the big attitude.

"I am with the immigration department and I wish to see your passport," the uniformed man said in a flat, expressionless voice.

Taken aback by this strange encounter, I hesitated, speechless for a moment.

"Is there a problem?" he asked, as he flipped open what appeared to be his credentials.

Frightened, tired and bewildered, I replied, "Yeah sure," and slowly turned away to retrieve the passport from my quarters.

William was more reluctant to do so. He told me he wasn't going to give him his. I felt we had no choice in the matter and assured William the guy only wanted to see them.

Moments later, the passports were handed to the little man in the tattered uniform and he accepted them with great enthusiasm. Softly stroking the covers, he commented on their fine quality as he flipped through their pages. Now, with both passports, he promptly informed me he would keep them and proceeded to place them in the breast pocket of his ragged shirt. Shocked, yet again, I instinctively made a grab for them.

"You can't just take our passports," I told him.

He reacted quickly and pulled them from my grasp.

"You don't tell me what to do. You are in my country now," he snapped. I was about to speak when he added, "You will disappear for twenty years and never be found."

I felt a cold chill run down my spine as I looked into his unnerving, dark eyes, and I knew he meant it.

I turned my gaze toward the big lad. My street smarts told me to back off as I watched him change his stance and realign himself in order to pounce on me.

"On Allah, you will get your passports back. My God is your God," the little man pronounced, as though I should be impressed.

"And my God is your God," I replied, as he slowly stepped back, turned and walked away.

They got into their dugout canoe, never to be seen again.

The Captain Returns

"I knew it!" exclaimed William.

Not knowing whether or not I had done the right thing, I tried to pacify him by saying we had no choice and that I felt confident they would bring them back. Although William wasn't buying it, he said no more about the subject. With our situation now gone from bad to worse, I tried to think of a way out the mess I had gotten myself into. But as I looked out over the side of the Zurich, there was nothing—nothing but jungle and water and I thought that, at best, we would be taking up residence as Young's new neighbours. Unable to settle, I paced the deck of the boat for an hour while William continued to smoke his cigarettes and drink coffee in the galley.

I could see people moving about in the nearby village and thought, "Maybe I can make some friends and get some insight into the little man's whereabouts." It has always been my belief that the one common denominator mankind has with one another is that everyone loves their children, and by showing kindness to people's children, you can connect with their better side. With that in mind, I armed myself with a pocket of assorted hair bows. Marlene, knowing Etlar had two small girls, had gathered all of Aleisha's old hair ornaments and instructed me to give them to his children.

As I made my way across the old tanker, down the makeshift ramp and along the riverbank, I could see a small group already starting to form. Two small children were the first to come and greet me and I was quick to let them pick from the more than one hundred bows. It wasn't long before I was swarmed by happy little faces all seeking to share in the spoils of the odd-looking stranger.

In the background, a number of village residents made kind gestures of approval as they enjoyed the happy faces on their children. It was a nice moment. About a half hour or so later, as I sat with the village members, they wanted to know all about me, and I them.

An older man was in the process of telling me about an official office some two hours walk from there when suddenly, I heard a familiar voice behind me.

"Life, Life!"

There he was. The person I had learned to hate so much was standing on the Zurich's bow, waving his hand in a gesture to come. And come I did, just like an obedient little puppy, clambering through water, over rocks and across boats, in three minutes flat no less.

Etlar was happy—happier than I would ever see him again. "We are good to go, everything is fine. Quickly untie the lines."

And once again, that was exactly what I did. Bearing bread, cheese and wine, he wanted me to celebrate with him as we travelled the last ten miles to Warri.

On to Warri and a Telephone—I hoped

As I enjoyed the last few moments of our long-awaited arrival to Warri, I climbed to the very top of the wheelhouse. It had begun to rain. Large drops of warm water pounded the deck as the sky let loose a torrential downpour. I looked up to the sky as the rain washed away the tears of joy and I thanked God. The day I tasted the rain down in Africa was one of the happiest days of my life.

The rainfall did not last long and by the time we had docked the boat, the sun was beginning to shine again.

"So this was Warri," I thought. If someone had landed here thirty years ago, I am sure they would have been quite impressed. Its huge cranes, two of them to be exact, were mounted on railroad tracks which now lay rusted and obsolete. The facing on the dock itself was clad in timber and still in relatively good shape. The dock work area was paved and was still intact except for patches of weeds growing up through it here and there.

A group of Chinese sailors, maybe fifteen or so, were taking part in their daily exercises. As the Zurich approached however, they took a break to get a better look at the boat and its crew. I found out later they were living on the ship docked directly ahead of us. William, who befriended them in the days that followed, learned the company they had worked for had gone bankrupt and had abandoned the ship. For three-and-a-half years, they had been living on the vessel, supported by meagre rations of rice and fish, which they traded for by slowly stripping the boat of anything of value.

A very large warehouse, the size of a football field, dominated the landscape with a flat roof and boarded-up windows. Guards bearing arms were posted around its perimeter. I never knew what was in the large building. I never asked nor did I want to know. There was also a mill and a large silo to hold grain. This, I was told, was the breadbasket for the region—producing enough bread to feed several million people. A large Greek freighter was having its cargo offloaded as a huge vacuum pumped the precious staple into the silo. The entire compound was encompassed by a ten-foot high chain-link fence topped with a roll of razor wire. A large pile of mahogany logs, once destined for India, now lay abandoned in the tropical sun, and all of this meant nothing to me since there was not a single phone in sight.

It was starting to get late in the day and I was not going to let another day go by without making that so desired phone call. The happiness I felt moments earlier now gave way to anxiety as I marched into the wheelhouse and demanded of Etlar that he take me somewhere to make my phone call.

"Yes Life. Yes, there are people coming tonight to take us to town. Be patient, these things take time."

Sure enough, just after dark, a small, beat-up car picked us up. William again opted to stay aboard the boat. We were driven to a small two-room shack not far from the compound's guarded gates. Escorted in by a man dressed in what looked to be a military uniform, Etlar was introduced to two more uniformed men who continued to glance my way as they whispered softly to one another.

This made me very uneasy and in light of the day's events, it was not without just cause.

All four men then stepped into a poorly lit adjacent room and with the door partially closed, I could hear my name being mentioned. Tired and fed up with all the bullshit, I walked into their meeting, demanding to make a phone call.

"Either someone here takes me to make a phone call right now or I will go and find a phone myself."

"No, Mr. Life. You can't go into the streets yourself for you may be molested."

"Molested," I thought. "Isn't that what sick minded people do to innocent children?"

"I don't care, take me to make a phone call now," I demanded.

By the tone of my voice and the look on my face, they must have seen I was dead serious. After a few more whispers, two of the three men agreed to accommodate my demands. Etlar stayed behind, but was quick to point out the fact that he was true to his word and I was indeed going to make my phone call just as he had promised.

The Long Awaited Call

B y now, it was twenty days since those regrettable farewells and finally, the long awaited moment was at hand. It was tearing me up inside thinking of the anguish my family must have been feeling not knowing whether I was dead or alive or anything else they must have been thinking.

"Take him to Nitel, you know what to do," the third man instructed the others.

Five minutes later, after a short ride through town, I found myself standing before a ten-foot high solid steel gate. A stone wall, topped with razor wire, ran the full perimeter of this place. I felt very uneasy, to say the least, as one of my escorts pounded on the huge gate. It looked more like a prison than a telephone office but at this point, I didn't care as long as there was a phone inside. With some more pounding on the door, it was finally unlatched from the inside and cracked opened enough for us to enter.

Within the confines of the wall was a two-story block and stucco structure. Poorly lit and in desperate need of repairs, it was still a pleasant sight as long as a phone awaited me. On the inside, I took note of three telephone booths set side-by-side on a slightly elevated platform. Directly across, was a wicket booth similar to what you might see at an old train station. One of my escorts went straight to the booth and handed the operator the piece of paper that held the phone number I had given him earlier in the car. A green light appeared over one of the booths and I was told to go ahead and have my conversation. Not once did anyone there look me in the eye or smile for that matter.

"Hello, hello Leif?"

"Is that you Marlene?"

"Yes, it's me."

"Thank God, are you alright?"

"Yes, I'm okay." I tried to make conversation but every time I said anything other than I was okay, it was blocked out with a click, click, clicking sound.

Marlene, frustrated, would repeat, "Are you sure you are okay?" The only response she would receive from me was confirmation that I was indeed okay while everything else was blocked out. The conversation was then abruptly cut off. After twenty days, all I got was a thirty-second phone call, but at least she knew I was okay — or so we thought.

I Meet the Man

I mmediately after my short conversation with Marlene, my two poker-faced escorts delivered me back to the Zurich where my only trusted friend awaited my return.

"Well, how did it go?" William knew how much this call meant to me and was there to lend his support.

"I really don't know. I don't know what to make of the entire evening. Something is not right about this place to say the least." And with that, I turned in for the night.

William and I were exhausted from our long ordeal and, once again, slept late into the morning. We woke to find ourselves among a multitude of strangers who had made themselves at home on the deck of our home away from home. Many were young men seeking employment on this new fishing boat that had, by now, raised quite a stir in the local township. William shared coffee and cigarettes with them and they all seemed to be a fine bunch of lads just looking to earn a day's wages.

Our social gathering was not to be long. Etlar, escorted by a young man of twenty or so, arrived back to the boat from his house–a place he and his wife, Isa, were renting. From out of the old, beat-up scrapheap of a car, Etlar strutted back toward us, waving his arms and shouting, "Get off my boat, you lazy dogs!"

Obediently, without saying a word, the dozen or so men quickly exited by way of the gangplank and stood or sat on the pile of mahogany logs on the shoreline.

Etlar was angry and very troubled about something, which I have to admit, I took great pleasure in.

"Do you believe it, do you believe it?" he grumbled. "Those sons of bitches just put a one-hundred-thousand-dollar import tax on my three old cars. What am I to do?"

I wanted to laugh but from the way he was carrying on, I knew it was no laughing matter.

Not long after, only twenty minutes or so, a shiny white Mercedes Benz showed up. A chauffeur quickly walked around and opened Mr. Madu Okoro's door. Out stepped the finest dressed man I had ever seen, standing five-foot eight, one hundred-and-sixty pounds, he appeared larger than life. Bulky, dark sunglasses that covered most of his face were accented by a long, gold chain as thick as my pinkie finger and a pink silk shirt tucked neatly into linen slacks with a sharp crease. What impressed me the most, however, were his snakeskin shoes.

Etlar was suddenly transformed from his typical chest-beating ape-man personality into that of a grade-school girl vying for the attention of the captain of the football team.

Madu did not care to challenge the rickety gang plank, so instead sent word for me to meet him beside his car. My mother once told me first impressions are last impressions. Despite the long list of lies I had been told from the moment I heard about this voyage to Africa, I believed Madu when he thanked me in his smooth and charismatic manner, for helping to take his boat to Warri. He softened me up with words of praise for being so strong and brave and saying that he could never do such a thing as that. With a gentle handshake he looked me in the eye as he apologized for the passport incident and promised that he would take all measures necessary to assure my safe return home. That was the first and last time I saw Mr. Okoro. It was also the first and last time during this whole ordeal that someone would look me in the eye with an honest face.

Looking back now, it seems strange that he didn't speak to William, but focused all of his attention on me. Etlar it seems, had fallen from grace—Madu, the only person in the country to which the captain had any connection—a connection he needed in order to sustain a life for him and his family—had washed his hands clean of him. Madu's boat, with its damaged engine, was now in the hands of the customs department to whom Madu owed one hundred thousand dollars due to the importation of the three old cars on her deck, a fact that Etlar disclosed to me when he told me not to bother him with my problems as he had enough of his own.

The Rat Ladies

L ater that morning, another vehicle pulled in. This one displayed an emblem on either side indicating it was from the health department. Two well-dressed women wearing navy blue dresses boarded. They asked no permission to board nor did they speak to the captain, but went straight to work spreading a white powder throughout the galley and living quarters.

"Rats," one said. "This vessel is infested with rats."

By now Etlar was aware of their presence and merely looked on in disgust and disbelief. The spreading of the powder was only an excuse to quarantine the ship and quarantine it they did. Straight to the top of the wheelhouse by way of ladder went one of the young ladies with a quarantine flag in hand. This meant no one could leave or enter the vessel until the rat issue was resolved. Except there were no rats and all concerned knew there were no rats. Later that day, the flag was removed.

Etlar was sitting on the deck in the midday sun, tired and bewildered. He rubbed his hands through his long greasy hair and said, "The pied piper has come by way of Madu's chequebook."

By now, I was overwhelmed with emotions, still trying to make sense of all the events over the past seventy-two hours. With my passport literally taken from me and a captain who was a liar, a thief, an absolute lunatic and who had obviously lost all control of his boat and the situation, my problems were my own. The Captain would be of no further help.

The Tribal Brother

The small group of men looking for employment had grown to around fifty. They would approach us with letters or pleas for an opportunity to work aboard the Zurich. Etlar seemed to take joy in their desperation and merely scoffed at them. At one point, he even threw a handful of Canadian Tire money at them over the side of the boat and laughed while they frantically clambered for the worthless currency. He had no respect for these men and they knew it. Etlar was a fool with no friends among the local people and he certainly had no job opportunities for them. The only thing he had going for him was the knowledge of how to play ball with the greater powers that be.

We spent the rest of that afternoon simply waiting for something to happen. We had no idea what to expect when another white Mercedes pulled up. Etlar, however, jumped to his feet upon its arrival, as if he knew it was coming.

The driver, a short, heavyset man, came straight toward me upon boarding the boat. He shook my hand firmly and introduced himself as Tobi Okoro, brother to Madu Okoro. Not a blood brother, but a tribal brother. He informed me that he and his companion, a long, slender man dressed in a suit and tie, were representatives of the Sannu Corporation and that they would ensure my well-being. Tobi's companion was introduced as Adisa. He presented himself with a warm smile and handshake and he wasted no time trying to befriend me with a bottle of peanuts and a dozen eggs—which turned out to be rotten—and one hundred dollars US. This guy was to be my new best friend and I had no reason to doubt him when he told me he would watch out for me and see that I got my passport back.

As a young man, I left my parent's home at the tender age of eighteen. Alone in the world, I developed a sixth sense, which enabled me to read signs of danger. I had always gone when and where I wanted so being able to take care of myself was imperative. Like that fateful day I met Etlar, my senses were now failing me. Even though Tobi and Etlar were having what looked to be an argument just out of earshot, casting glances my way, I took Adisa at his word. After all, he was working for Mr. Madu Okoro—he told me he was one of Madu's bankers. With this in mind, I started to relax, thinking I now had an ally among the all the foes and uncertainties I had encountered up to this point. I couldn't help but wonder, however, why all the attention was focused on me and not William.

Even with my renewed hope, there was still one thing that overshadowed everything else—I needed to make a proper phone call home. This was all I wanted at the moment from this stranger and he assured me he would look into things as soon as he returned from an important meeting. I suddenly felt as if a great weight had been lifted from my shoulders. It was now three weeks since I had left Cape Breton and my family. Adisa and Tobi promised to return mid morning the following day.

By the next day, the number of young men looking for employment on the Zurich had swollen to one hundred. As they watched me pace up and down the dock, they must have thought I was crazy. The truth is, I was becoming more confused, angry, and concerned with each passing moment. As the evening drew to a close, there was still no sign of Adisa.

William and I sat on the lighted deck of the Zurich trying to make sense of yet another day. The night was still and the air warm, embracing us with a false sense of security. It would have been easy to feel comforted, lulled by the fresh air and the hypnotic, steady drone of the Zurich's large generator. But the more I tried to make sense of it all, the more agitated I became. My heart began to pound, the warm air now feeling thick as I tried to catch my breath. I paced the deck again, willing myself to ignore the dark paranoia that was rising within my cluttered thoughts. But deep down, I knew something sinister was taking place—I just had no idea how sinister.

An Endless Pursuit for a Phone Call

"I can't stand this William." I jumped to my feet. "I'm going for a walk. Do you want to come?"

"No, the hell with it. I think I'll stay right here."

I already knew William wouldn't want to go but I could see he was becoming more and more depressed as the hours and days went on. He felt safe on board the Zurich. It had become his haven in an unknown and frightening country. After I left, I watched as he pulled in the gang plank.

I walked toward the grain freighter where I could hear music and laughter. The Greeks were having a party and many of local girls had obviously been invited. In my mind, I assumed the Greeks would be neutral and unaware of the situation as I had always considered them to be an orderly and sophisticated society. I also thought their modern, ocean-going freighter would have all the latest communication devices. So, with the memories of the past days' events still raging through my mind, approaching them to make a phone call seemed like the logical and obvious thing to do. Unfortunately, I was the only one to think so.

A guard at the bottom of the gangplank denied me access when I attempted to board the ship. I figured if I explained the situation to the captain, he would certainly allow me to make my much needed and desired call. I couldn't get past the guard however. He was quite adamant about not allowing me on board, and was becoming quite agitated with me, as though he had already been specifically instructed not to let me on.

Quick to realize I shouldn't aggravate the situation any further, I retreated to the shadows at a safe distance. I waited for over an hour only to realize the guard wasn't going anywhere and would remain at his post for the remainder of the night.

Had it not been for the guard's reluctance, I would have gladly paid handsomely for the privilege of making one call home. Tired and frustrated, I slunk back to the Zurich where I decided I had better get a good night's sleep since I was beginning to believe this was going to be a much longer and harder adventure than I had originally anticipated.

The following morning, William and I took our usually places in the galley with our coffee and smokes in hand. We spoke very little about our situation, probably more so because we didn't want to worry one another anymore than we already were, but I did tell him of the previous night's events.

"Hello." A deep voice echoed through the top porthole. I sped upstairs to investigate and was pleased to see that Young had travelled ten miles up the river just to see how I was getting along.

"Nothing yet." I said.

Young seemed to be to be a genuine person but I really didn't know him, so I held my cards close to my chest. I was grateful for his sincerity, however, as he thanked me for the filthy, grease-stained blue jeans I had given him. They looked clean and new now and Young wore them with great pride.

While sitting with him out on the deck like two wealthy men on their yacht, I was entertaining the idea of asking Young to call the embassy for me, giving him the number that was shoved deep in my knife pouch and paying him with the hundred dollars I had stashed in my shoe. As I looked at Young, I thought, "You are about to become a hundred dollars richer." In the end, my doubts and my very realistic revelations about people in general over the past few days, won out. I later regretted not taking that chance but I also realized that by doing so, I would have put Young at great risk. Instead, we talked, enjoying the evening air.

As the evening rolled on, I saw a car approaching in the distance. As it grew nearer, I could see it was an old beat-up Datsun. The car stopped on the wharf and dropped Adisa off. Still wearing his suit and tie he wasted no time apologizing for his absence the evening before. With my tongue clenched between my teeth, I said only, "We go now."

"Go where?" he asked, dismissing my request as if was nothing.

When I pressed him further on the issue, he conveniently told me the nearest phone was too far away to walk to. I then asked him about the status of our passports to which he nonchalantly replied, "These things take a bit of time," reassuring me things move more slowly in Nigeria.

"Just be patient, everything will work out," he added.

As a young lad, I witnessed my father and uncle slaughter a pig. My father spoke kindly to the pig as he scratched her behind the ear. The pig enjoyed this as she purred like a kitten. While this act of affection was taking place, my uncle positioned a small calibre gun to her head in order to penetrate her walnut-size brain with a single shot. What I learned from this experience was that if someone you don't know or trust is going out of their way to be nice to you, you should always ask yourself, are they 'scratching the pig behind the ear'? At this moment, I was asking myself if Adisa was scratching my ear.

The Passport Shuffle

That day, several cars drove up, their passengers stopping for a quick look at the docked ship. At one point, two men in official looking uniforms requested that William and I go with them to the local immigration office. Excited that we may finally get our passports back and not wishing to offend the officers in any way, we agreed.

The car sped away and we found ourselves being driven to the outskirts of town and then down a long, dirt road in the middle of nowhere. We eventually stopped at a small, tin-clad building with a large, expensive looking black car parked outside. I immediately felt uneasy. It didn't feel right but I told William to cooperate in every way, as it was always my belief to never let your adversaries know what you are thinking, and this was definitely one of those times. We needed to act like there was no problem. At least that was what I wanted everyone to think because by now, everything was resting on one thing: would Madu Okoro pay to get my passport back?

As we walked down a dirt-covered path toward the dilapidated building, I got a quick whiff of gasoline. I looked up to see a man wearing military boots, a pair of old jeans and a dirty white T-shirt, cleaning his gun using the fuel, presumably to remove any dirt and residue.

We entered the building and the two officers told us to wait outside in a small waiting room while they joined several other men in an adjoining room. The building was divided into two halves, the first was a much smaller room where we now sat and waited—me on a three-legged chair supported by a small wooden box, William on an old, but sturdier chair.

After several minutes, we were ordered to bring our chairs into the room with the officers. I tucked the small wooden box under my one arm and carried the gimped chair with the other. As soon as I entered the room, I was met by the biggest black man I had ever seen. His huge body flowed over a tiny chair that was jammed in behind a modest desk. He looked right through us, his face expressionless, as a young officer placed a sheet of paper and pen before us. The big uniformed man instructed us to write down who we were and where we had come from. Since I had nothing to hide, I did as I was instructed. He said nothing as he gathered up the two papers and placed them into an old and tattered briefcase and then simply exited out the back door. That was it. We were escorted back to the boat and nothing more was said. Once again, we were left trying to make sense of everything.

Evening was now fast approaching. The warm, orange glow from the setting sun was slipping into darkness. William, Adisa, Young and I sat out on deck, soaking in moist jungle air.

"Look, there's a bat," I said, startled. The bat was actually the size of a large crow and it seemed to lumber across the evening sky. I watched transfixed, as more began to follow and before long, there were huge bats as far as the eye could see. If you were to hold a saucer at arm's length, you would only block twenty or so out of view. As I marvelled at the estimated one million bats, I thought that all was not lost.

Today, I had fulfilled a promise to a little man so very far away in a not forgotten land. A nice young man, who had come to the boat with resume in hand, eagerly retrieved a few coconuts for me. It is amazing how something as simple as a coconut gave me the strength and courage I would need in the days to follow. I had a delivery to make, and by God, I was going to make it.

It was dark now, and Young had left to visit a friend. The night was still when the same car that had dropped Adisa off earlier, crept up to the dock with its lights turned out. Two men exited. One of them was uniformed and he identified himself as Ngozi, a junior immigration officer. Ngozi informed William and me that he had good news, the entire time only making eye contact with Adisa. He explained he was going to take us to see our passports. William and I looked at each other, but Adisa seemed to know what the young officer was talking about, which led me to believe he had known all day. I was concerned this meeting was taking place after business hours and even more so, after dark but the thought of getting our passports back seemed more important.

"Yes, I would like to see the passports..." I said, thinking we would have to go into town to do this. "But I want to phone my family first."

"First, we must go see the passports and then you can make your call since we don't have time," the young immigration officer replied. With reassurance from Adisa that the call would be made, we were on our way to see the passports.

Once again, we found ourselves well past the town limits and driving deep into the dark countryside. I was becoming very nervous and I instructed William to open his four-inch pocket-knife, mine was already opened and clutched firmly in my hand. But our uneasiness was unfounded.

After about a half hour, we stopped in front of a large set of decorative gates. The young officer identified himself and we were granted entry. After driving through a maze of narrow, unlit streets, we parked in front of a small bungalow. Two men, one armed, the other wearing a suit, stood in military form at the back door. We were told to wait so we decided to take a short moonlit stroll down the street. I was amazed at the magnificent foliage growing among the row upon row of bungalows. Adisa told me this place was known as Steel Town and that the Germans had once run a steel mill here, but that had all changed with time. The place was completely deserted now, giving it an almost eerie feel. Not wishing to offend our host, we returned shortly.

A plain clothed man escorted William and I into a room, which consisted of a small table, a lit candle and three chairs, two on one side and on the other. We were instructed to sit in the two side-by-side chairs. As we sat waiting for whoever would eventually fill the remaining chair, I stared aimlessly into the candle's hypnotic glow, my brain numb, not knowing how much more suspense I could take. Suddenly, from out of the shadows, a man wearing the traditional boubou, yanked the chair out and sat before us. He didn't say a word as he reached his hand inside his baggy sleeve and smoothly flashed a passport open in front of William. Holding it close to the candlelight, he asked, "Is this not your passport?"

"Yes," replied William, as it was quickly tucked away. He then turned to me and repeated the simple process, which ended in the same result.

As suddenly as we were escorted in, we were escorted out. We knew by the nature of the meeting that idle talk or any questions were not going to be part of the curriculum so we said nothing. We obediently got into the car and headed back to Warri.

We rode back in silence, the two lads in front feeling a little out of sorts for one reason or another I believe. William and I were also speechless. We had no idea what had just happened and once again, we were left trying to make sense of yet another experience. Why the security? Why didn't we get our passports back? Could this mean we were in more trouble than I suspected? My head was spinning with questions. How, what, when, why, where? It was all too much to deal with at the time so I dismissed it once again as paranoia. This dismissal was to be short-lived, however. Just inside the town limits, something would happen that would affirm the seriousness of this whole ordeal.

Reality Hits Home

T wo men dressed as local police officers stepped out into the street in front of us, one fired two warning shots into the air and then, with feet planted firmly, they quickly lowered their AK-47s, pointing them directly into the windshield of our car. One officer moved toward us as the other remained in position. The officer then threw open Adisa's door and began beating him. He tried desperately to fend off the steady barrage of blows with his feet, but at least one of the man's fists found its mark and Adisa's head was now bleeding quite badly. The police officer then moved to the other side of the car and dragged the junior immigration officer from the car. With the AK-47 still aimed squarely at us, the second police officer began kicking his young victim who eventually found the strength to scurry back inside the car, where he wasted no time speeding away.

We were stunned. Neither Adisa nor the young officer spoke a word about the beatings as we sped back to the boat. Once we pulled up to the Zurich, we were quickly dropped off and left alone to fend for ourselves.

By this time, the stress, along with the lack of proper nutrition and many sleepless nights, had started to take its toll on William and me. But after tonight, we knew this could not be allowed to happen—we had to be courageous, there would be plenty of time to sleep once we were safely back home.

That evening, I came to terms with the fact that something was seriously wrong with this picture. I realized I could not let emotions get in the way of the two phone calls I knew I had to make: one to Marlene and the other to the embassy. I decided that knowing the facts at this point, was irrelevant.

Not wanting anyone to know what I was thinking, I remained calm and respectful to everyone involved. I thought by acting ignorant and asking no questions, I wouldn't raise any alarms, which might cause my movements to become more restricted or worse, be completely isolated. It was a sleepless night to say the least. These past events were taking a toll on me. I paced non-stop, whether on deck or dock, the reality of this nightmare sinking in. I truly felt like I was caught in a bad dream and my stomach was in knots. My appetite was all but gone.

That morning, I began to think that possibly I might never see Marlene and the kids again. My heart raced, my pulse quickened and I was having a hard time catching my breath. I decided then and there to put my feelings aside and focus on the task at hand.

As I paced back and forth between the boat and the security gate, half a mile or more each way, I racked my brain about how best to position myself in order to get myself out of this mess. I no longer thought staying aboard the Zurich was an option. Here, at the Warri port, I was completely isolated and had no chance of contacting anyone. I thought of the ship's radio but who would I call? I had to let someone know where I was. I had no doubt now that someone, or many people for that matter, were making sure this would not happen. Since it was now twenty-two days and there was still no contact with home, except for that one brief moment, I knew I had to get help.

The Paranoia Deepens

E tlar and Adisa arrived around noon the next day.

"What a sneaky pair," I thought; my suspicions about Adisa were growing stronger. I no longer believed he was my trusted friend but I certainly had no intentions of letting him know this.

"Good morning, guys," I said, with as perky and positive a voice as I could muster under the circumstances.

Adisa handed me a bag containing bread and fruit, saying very little. He quickly turned away without making eye contact. As for Etlar, I never cared to speak to him at the best of times, but today, he focused all of his attention on getting some much needed parts for the Zurich—he obviously still had hopes of fishing her one day. No one even mentioned the incident the previous night but I could tell by the look on Adisa's face, he was very concerned about something. My gut was telling me, he was feeling guilty about something as well. Possibly, he was a pawn caught up in something he did not want to be a part of. I didn't know. All I knew was that I needed to look out for myself because I could no longer trust anyone.

It was another hot day and we lingered about the boat as if waiting for something to happen. I think the stress was finally getting to

William, who spent the day mumbling to himself. He would re-peatedly run his fingers through his hair as he stared into his coffee, cigarette after cigarette hanging from his lips.

Not knowing what to expect after last night's events, I held off on the phone call issue but now the time seemed right to make an-other request. To my surprise, Adisa agreed whole-heartedly and soon we were on our way to town in his old clunker. I watched the road pass beneath my feet as the rotted out frame sped along the old dirt road. Adisa said very little but stared straight ahead until we reached the main streets of Warri. I, on the other hand, felt like a young child with his dad, going to the circus or some other exciting prospect. The moment I had long awaited had finally arrived and I would soon be getting out of this place. I had it all planned out. I would call Marlene, she would call the embassy in Lagos and I would be home free.

My excitement and anticipation were soon to be dashed as we spent the next hour bouncing from one business to the next in search of a working phone. My suspicions rose when I realized that every location Adisa picked resulted in the same "Sorry the phones are not working" excuse. I felt like crying. At one point, I felt the stress and fatigue begin to wash over me again but I forced myself to be calm and I put my trust in God. Marlene had placed a small cross around my neck before leaving and she forbade me from re-moving it. Rubbing it between my fingers now, I asked God to give me the strength to see this thing through.

On the way back to the boat, I noticed a Shell Oil administration building. "Stop, stop, let's go in there!" I insisted.

Since Adisa had chosen the other locations he was reluctant to grant my request, but he soon realized I was adamant about the idea. Now, standing in the lobby far removed from the inner work-ings of the business, I pleaded with the security guard that it was

urgent that I make a phone call. The man was only too glad to accommodate my request—that was until Adisa pulled him aside and
whispered something in his ear.

Form the corner of my eye, I noticed Adisa passing him a folded
paper. The guard then left for a moment and returned shortly only
to inform me they were experiencing technical difficulties and they
were not able to accommodate me today. I wanted nothing more
than to scream at the top of my lungs but I knew I had to keep my
cool if I was going to get what I wanted. So, I somehow found the
strength to say, "Oh well, maybe tomorrow," even though I knew
this was a deliberate act to prevent me from calling home.

The Coconut

O n the way back to the boat, Adisa began to relax. He even started to make short, simple conversation. This was what I wanted. Adisa was the one person I needed to convince that everything was cool, since I was beginning to realize he was assigned to me not for my well-being, but to keep an eye on me.

William was anxiously waiting for us to return and he greeted me with many questions; "How did you get along?", "Did you make your call?", "What did they say?" but he was quick to realize by the look in my eyes that I had nothing to tell him. Meanwhile, 'el Capitan' as I now nicknamed Etlar, staggered slightly on the deck, brandishing a bottle of cheap whisky.

"Life, Mr. Life, come have a drink with me." He caught me at the right moment, feeling tired, disgusted, angry, scared, betrayed, confused, and lonesome. I thought "what the hell". Not wanting Etlar to know my true feelings, we now found ourselves once again like old pals sharing a drink and telling stories.

All was fine until he returned carrying a coconut. Sitting on the deck with his back to the wall and the coconut cupped in his hand, he be began slamming it against the steel deck. Suddenly, realizing that he was destroying the single greatest symbol of strength I had left, I lost it, releasing a dam of pent up frustration and anger. This simple, seemingly meaningless object meant more to me than anyone could have imagined. I had a delivery to make and this fellow was destroying it. With the bottle held firmly by the neck and raised over my head, I yelled, "You son of a bitch! What gives you the right to destroy my property?"

This was the first time I had stood up to Etlar since meeting him over three weeks ago. He knew I was serious and immediately handed over the simple but precious object.

"Life, take it easy Life." He threw his arms up then laid back and went to sleep.

Off the Boat with my Ungracious Host

Another day passed and no phone call. "I can't stay here any longer," I thought, so far removed from everything. Etlar didn't know it yet but he was about to receive an uninvited house guest.

That evening, I made it known to Adisa that there was no way I was staying aboard the Zurich any longer. As I watched the crew of abandoned Chinese sailors perform their evening exercises, I vowed that was not to be my fate three years from now. Not a chance, I was going to get out of this place or die trying.

I began putting pressure on Adisa to take care of the passport issue, still treating him as a trusted friend. I believed he was starting to feel some compassion for my situation. I never believed him to be a bad person but someone who was caught between a rock and a hard place.

"I've be on this damn boat for almost a month and it's time for me to get off," I said, with great conviction.

"Go, go where, Life? You must be patient. I told you these matters take time. If you leave here you may fall into harm's way and we must not let this happen."

Not realizing the brutality and dangers, which were a way of life in the streets of Warri, it was easy to convince Adisa that I was not going to stay. I threatened to make my way to Lagos with or without his help.

"Why not," I thought. I had nothing to fear, right? Adisa became very uneasy with this idea and was quick to reassure me he would take care of everything.

By now, time was beginning to have little meaning and I began to eat or sleep whenever it was convenient. Adisa convinced Etlar I was to stay with him for safety reasons. Although I am sure Etlar was not happy about having a new house guest, I believe he had no choice.

As we left the boat and William behind, I realized I was beginning a new leg of my journey through West Africa. We drove through the streets of Warri where I stared aimlessly at the sights of poverty and despair. I wondered if anyone really cared about me when considering the state of the country. The reality of it all set in once again and that overwhelming feeling of fear and despair began to take hold. All I could do was buck up and take control of my mind and emotions and steer the course, stick to my game plan, and wait for the right opportunity to do what it was I had to do—even though I did not know exactly what that was yet.

Arriving at Etlar's rented house, I was surprised to find it was relatively upscale compared to what I had seen of the city so far. It was surrounded by a ten-foot wall filled with gaping holes due to a lack of maintenance. Around the top of the wall, I could see the remains of razor wire. Two solid, rusted steel gates sealed the entrance to the yard.

Etlar pounded on the gate with his closed fist, shouting for his wife, Isa, to open up. The 'Master' was definitely home. A bright smiling young girl eagerly let us in. This was Isa, a new entry in the list of personalities I had encountered in Africa. I had only seen her briefly on the Zurich that day but I would soon learn she was a character that was unique in every way, a person whose charm and sincerity would become a bright light in a dark world.

Isa knew me by name and excitedly invited me into her home as if she were anticipating my arrival. Isa's rented home was a block and stucco structure that was dyed light pink. The entrance was well kept and its old and cracked marble tile continued throughout the floor area. There were plenty of plants and shrubs and a lime tree, all of which were doing well after the rainy season. All of this played host to a healthy population of lizards. Inside, I was disappointed to find there was not so much as a chair let alone a bed or a table. There wasn't even a pillow to sit on. The large empty room, however, was brightened by Isa's two young daughters who were busy enjoying the open spaces on their new bicycles.

Adisa was never far away and would spend most of his time sitting poised in his suit and tie, which looked out of sorts with the rest of the surroundings. Isa was very eager to learn about my part of the world and she and I spent the rest of the day in the yard making small talk—she answering my many questions about her garden while I was careful not to mention my situation. A young girl was busy preparing a meal of goat meat and potatoes in a small kitchen, which was off to one side.

When supper was ready, Isa instructed the six of us that it was time to eat. I was positioned, although I didn't realize it, sitting on a granite floor with my back to the wall while Adisa was busy taking pictures of me eating this large meal, which had been set before me. It didn't register as anything significant at the time, but when it happened the second day, I began to have an uneasy suspicion. Here was proof that Mr. Life was well fed and well treated. It just seemed strange that the only two real meals that I had eaten during my time there were photographed. There was another occasion, a day or two later when Etlar and Adisa and I went to what seemed to be a deserted outdoor play area with a tennis court, swimming pool, tables with umbrellas, and a barbecue with a cook. Adisa told me that it had all been arranged on my behalf, a way for the Sannu Corporation to send its apologies for my inconvenience. Adisa must have taken thirty pictures that day and was always ready to snap a shot whenever I took a bite of food or put a smile on my face.

Out of Service

I continued to play their game but I was becoming more and more concerned as time went by. I knew something very wrong was unfolding and it was obviously more serious than I could have suspected or even imagined. In my heart, I knew I was not being paranoid by the extended measures Adisa was taking to pacify me. The lavish outing only took place after two days of me insisting on knowing the whereabouts of the passports and when I would get to make my illusive phone call.

For two days, Adisa continued to assure me the passports were on their way and that Tobi Okoro was delivering them personally. For two days, I paced the grounds with doubt and anticipation, my patience all but worn out and Adisa knew this. Adisa finally submitted to my insistence that he take me to make a phone call when I said, "Screw you, I'll go myself."

I stormed out of the house and made it only a short distance from Isa's before I was picked up by Adisa and escorted to several different locations in and around Warri, only to experience the same disappointing results as the last time. I think Adisa had as much at stake in this as I did and the obvious look of concern on his face was all the proof I needed.

It was Saturday morning and the streets of Warri were alive as the locals went about their daily routine of buying, selling, begging, or rummaging through garbage, all in a quest for survival. It was not uncommon to see very expensive cars parked here and there in stark contrast to their surroundings. Banks and churches were everywhere, while the rest of the town consisted of old and neglected buildings, roads and sidewalks. Today was just another day in which Warri remained out of touch with the rest of the world — or so you would think since, once again, there wasn't a single working phone in the whole area.

"This is bullshit," I thought, although neither Adisa nor I ever said a word to each other about it.

As we headed back to Etlar's house, there were no words to describe my feelings for this place and the people who were making my life so miserable. I felt like choking the life out of Adisa, but instead I slumped down in my seat and peered aimlessly out the car window, seeing only the faces of my wife and children.

Isa offered kind words of sympathy after she had learned of my disappointment. I said very little and went off to find a quiet, out-of-the-way place in the yard. Sitting on a wooden box with my head hung low, I spent the rest of the day trying to take control of the many emotions that were raging inside me.

That evening — I can't say after supper because there wasn't any, not that I felt like eating anyway — I found Etlar drinking a beer on the front step. I had seen very little of him the past few days. He appeared to be as tired and stressed as I was, brought on perhaps by his falling out with Madu. Without Madu in his corner, Etlar was nothing. Life, as I was seeing it, could be very hard here and he knew this. I somehow felt bad for him. I now realize Etlar had only one thing working for him and that was being able to play ball with the immigration big boys so they could achieve their goal, which I believe was to acquire what they could in my name.

"Life, come have a drink with me," he said, as he beckoned to Isa to fetch me a beer. "Life, I would really like you to come with me to Mar's Bar." It turned out that the owner's name was Mar.

I accepted his offer for various reasons, but I wasn't going to drink. I wanted to experience the culture and even more importantly, take advantage of an opportunity to perhaps access a phone or at least, a true and honest face.

Mar's Bar was like nothing I had ever seen. It was basically two shipping containers fused together in an 'L' shape and it was apparently Etlar's favourite watering hole. Everyone there knew him and viewed him as a novelty as he boasted about his great adventure. I was feeling out of place but I felt better when Adisa walked in, noting this immediately brought Etlar to attention. Adisa, always in suit and tie and a smile from ear to ear, informed me that we were invited to a party and that Isa would meet us there. Etlar made it clear that he would not attend. Adisa said nothing and made his way to the door with me in tow. Etlar was quickly becoming drunk and I felt more at ease with Adisa in spite of everything.

The Party

The party turned out to be in a hotel room somewhere. We walked up two flights of stairs and to the third room on the right where I was shown a comfortable chair by the window. The room was large and poorly lit but the décor was rather nice.

"This is how the Nigerian people party," I thought.

Two men dressed in suits and a third wearing a boubou, sat on the far side of the room. These men made quiet conversation and acknowledged me with only a slight nod.

"Strange party," I thought.

Adisa sat, as if taking his place, while a girl in her late twenties served me a drink. I had had only two beers for the entire evening and saw no harm in having one drink of alcohol; after all we were having a party. After having several sips of my drink, the young woman sat on the side of the bed and offered to show me something in a magazine, inviting me to sit beside her. Feeling woozy and numb, almost as though I were floating, I obeyed her wishes, and to this day, it is still hard for me to make sense of what happened next. Before long, we were tickling each other and having a great laugh. She pushed me over on my back so we were both lying down. I began telling her my version of the Adam and Eve story, why I don't know, because up until then, I had never had one. I went on to tell her that Adam was banished from the Garden of Eden because he had committed adultery, as the other woman is the forbidden fruit. So, if a man today samples the forbidden fruit, then he, too, will be banished from his Garden of Eden and lose all he holds dear.

They all must of thought I was nuts because in no time, the party was declared over. As I look back on the situation now, I can see it was suspicious. There was only one girl there. There were no cameras that I was aware of but it is my belief they were testing my resolve and my commitment to my wife and home ties. I drank very little of the drink they gave me. That, perhaps, was why I felt no after affects the following day, although I do believe I was drugged.

Isa never did show up and no mention of it was ever made. As usual, Adisa and I never said a word to each other about it. I now saw him as nothing more than a chauffeur and possibly a protector, guarding the merchandise.

Etlar had told me early on not to wander off on my own. He warned me that the street police known as the State Security Services (SSS), would be everywhere applying their trade. The SSS was supposedly formed to protect and defend the Federal Republic of Nigeria against domestic threats, while upholding and enforcing the criminal laws of the country but I had seen their work first hand and these guys scared me, so I thought it wise to take his advice.

The following day, I hung out with Isa and the kids while Etlar was off trying to solve his own problems. Isa told me she sang in a local band and was singing at Mar's Bar that night. She said she wanted me to come. I believed that Isa was truly a kind and honest person and she was being kept in the dark about what was going on. Out of the blue, she took my hand in hers and looked up at me. "Life, be careful," she told me.

A cold chill ran through me as I struggled to keep myself from thinking the worst. Up until now, thoughts of me ending up dead and my family living in a cardboard box seemed outrageous. But another day had gone by and still no passport or phone call. By now, I was coming to terms with the fact that I was trapped.

Just Shoot Me

Adisa, Etlar and I were once again sitting at Mar's Bar, this time watching Isa and her band perform for the locals. Adisa did not drink, claiming it was against his religion. Etlar was already on his way to being drunk and I was nursing a single beer as I needed to keep my senses sharp.

I suddenly began to feel nauseous, so much so that I thought I might vomit. I headed outside for a little fresh air and immediately lost what little potato I had eaten for supper. My gut churned, the muscles aching as though I had been sucker punched. I wiped my mouth with the back of my hand and returned inside to tell Adisa I was going to lie down in the car. It was not long after that the front door opened and Adisa told me he was taking me home.

Whether the motion of the car or whatever bug had infiltrated my weary body, the nausea intensified and Adisa was forced to pull over as I wretched my guts beside the road. For the first time, I was actually glad to be going to my room, which was essentially a small rectangle with stucco walls and a granite floor and only a pillow and a thin blanket to lie on.

This was to become the worst two-and-a-half days of my life. I remember seeing a bucket in the kitchen, which I quickly claimed as my vomit bucket. That night, and all the next day, I spent curled up in a fetal position as I continuously wrenched every ounce of fluid from my stomach. As it continued into the next day, I began dry heaving. My stomach muscles burned, as did my throat when acidic green bile filled my mouth. I was so weak and exhausted that I was unable to wipe the burning drool from my lips and chin. To make matters worse, I also developed diarrhea, which only added to my severe dehydration. Isa tried to help, but I could not even hold down the water she had boil for me.

I spent most of the day in a delirious state, only moving to throw up or run to the washroom. That night, however, I remember hearing gunshots outside my window—apparently the police had caught and killed a robber. As I watched the reflection of the flashing blue lights bounce off the ceiling in my prison-like room, I briefly thought how lucky he was. His suffering had ended and as far as I knew, mine was only beginning. This was truly the lowest time in my life.

Somewhere in the back of my confused and fevered mind, I could hear a little voice saying, "I cannot die, not here like this. I have a delivery to make."

I prayed to God that night to see me through this setback and by morning, the wrenching and diarrhea had eased somewhat. Adisa was there early with bottled water and medications to help rehydrate my withered body while Isa boiled the peelings from limes, which she had picked from her tree in the front yard. Still too sick and weak to care about anything, now compounded by a growing depression, I spent the next twenty-four hours curled up on the floor, sipping water and clutching my lone pillow.

The following morning, I forced myself to begin a fresh new day. Isa, who looked in on me from time-to-time, was cooking something in a large pot.

"It's goat stew," she replied, when I inquired into what it was.

The smell was not the least bit enticing, but I hadn't eaten in three days and I knew it was important to eat something in order to retain my strength. Still dazed and extremely weak, I retrieved a large piece of goat from the pot and after chewing for longer than I cared to, I swallowed with near grave consequences. It immediately became lodged in my throat and hard as I tried, it would not go down. I was choking, I could not speak nor could I breathe. My legs began to wobble and I fell to the floor. Sitting on all fours now, I desperately tried to dislodge the obstruction. I could feel myself starting to black out and I knew it was now or never so with one excruciating final hurl, I was able to force it up. Tears streamed my face, which was no longer blue, but returning to the ghostly white it had been before the incident. I collapsed to the floor in pure physical and emotional exhaustion.

"Enough," I remember thinking. I pounded my fist on the floor and begged. "Please God, get me out of this forsaken hellhole."

That's It...I'm Leaving

I had had enough, my mind was made up—I was leaving for Lagos one way or another. By now, I had come to terms with the fact there would be no phone call home and as for the passport and airplane tickets, I had also come to realize they were not going to arrive. It was time to stop dismissing my better judgment as paranoia and face the fact that I was being held under house arrest while the powers that be were assessing my assets back home. Anger and fear were now my driving forces.

The day was spent pacing the grounds as I tried to come up with a realistic plan. Adisa arrived early evening with some fruit and his familiar phoney smile.

"I've had it with this bullshit, I'm walking out of this fucking place with or without your help."

Adisa was stunned by my announcement. "Go, go where?"

"I don't care if someone shoots me in the fucking back but I'll walk to Lagos and buy my own fucking ticket out of here."

Adisa, taken aback by my anger, was quick to point out the fact that even if I had an airline ticket, I could not leave without a passport.

"I told you Life, that these things take time and that you have to be patient."

Not wanting him to know what I was really thinking, I told him I was frustrated and tired of the living conditions.

"Life, don't do anything foolish like wander the streets alone. I don't want you to be molested. Stay calm, I will try and take care of it."

Within an hour, Adisa returned happy and smiling. "I have good news for you, I was talking to Tobi Okoro and you are leaving in the morning."

This was good news. I sighed heavily, like a huge weight had been lifted from my chest.

"Tobi said for you to have your things ready and that he will be here to pick you up first thing in the morning." It was music to my ears.

That morning, I was awake at daybreak with my few meagre possessions already stuffed into a small canvas bag. Although filled with anticipation, a part of me was already expecting to be let down again as I stood outside waiting for my ride. At one point, Isa joined me and we sat for two hours with no sign of Tobi. Finally, an old blue car drove though the iron gates. I found it strange that Tobi Okoro, who normally drove a white Mercedes, was picking me up in a beat-up, piece of junk, driven by a ragged old man but once again, the thought of possibly going home was more important.

With a friendly beckoning from Tobi, the back door of the decrepit car was held open by the old man who eagerly took my bag.

It had now been about twenty-six days since I watched my perfect world fade off into the distance.

Another Visit from Immigration

Before leaving, Isa gave me a warm hug. She patted my back and whispered in my ear, "Be careful." That was the last time I would ever see Isa or Etlar.

We drove about five minutes through a narrow maze of roads and alleyways. We stopped in front of a large, well-kept home furnished with the usual razor wire and iron gates.

"This is it," said Tobi. "This is where you'll be staying now."

"What the hell?" I thought, as we exited the blue junk heap.

This was obviously just one more measure to pacify me. Tobi simply looked at me and nonchalantly said goodbye then walked down a small dirt road. I quickly followed after him and watched as he got into his white Mercedes and drove away. This was not the first time I was stunned, and as I watched the dust trail from behind Tobi's luxury car, I thought it would probably not be the last.

I turned toward the house to see a one-legged man in his mid fifties waiting for me in the doorway. He seemed to be a nice enough fellow and from what I could tell, he seemed happy to share his home with me. Gerald, whose leg had been shot off by a robber's shotgun blast only a year before, was from Boston and an employee with the Sannu Corporation. This was a company guesthouse. From what I had seen since arriving in Nigeria, this place was a palace.

Gerald showed me to my bedroom. I was pleasantly pleased to see a queen-size bed perched in the middle of the large an air-conditioned room, complete with all the trappings of any modern home. My pleasure quickly turned to anger however, when I realized I had just spent a week lying on a hard granite floor, most of which was spent puking my guts out, and all of this was only five minutes away. I hated every last one of them at that moment.

The house was amazing. I had all the comforts I could ask for; large couches and chairs, remote television, a bar and even a cook, an amazing old man who claimed to be over ninety years old.

That afternoon Adisa and three uniformed immigration officers showed up. By this time, I was tired of playing their games, so I basically ignored them and continued to watch a television program as they hovered over me, asking questions and feigning concern for my well-being. I was keenly aware I was the centre of attraction and they were probably just trying to get a good look at the poor fool in front of them.

Adisa and Gerald were out of earshot, having their own discussion about me, no doubt. The third officer, a woman, took the opportunity to pass me a letter she said was to her brother now living in New York. She was very nervous as she explained its contents. She said it contained a plea for her brother to get her out of the country. She squeezed my hand as she leaned over and whispered in my ear, "This is a very bad place and I believe you are in danger. Be careful my friend." She smiled and then returned to her co-workers who all left with Adisa, whom I never saw again.

Time to Make My Own Call

Walking through the valley of the shadow of death I did fear evil. I not only had no idea who I could trust, but I had no way of defending myself against these people. I felt extremely vulnerable and alone. I felt threatened. One thing I knew, however, was that when someone feels threatened, whether those feelings are founded or not, they still have a mental advantage over their enemies. And I, too, had that advantage. I had the ability to act without warning, whether it was a quick exit or a frontal assault. In any situation, it is important to never let your adversaries know what you are thinking.

After the immigration officers left, I sat staring at the TV. I had no idea what they were up to but I had an idea it was not good.

The next day and a half was spent enjoying my new comforts and getting to know Gerald, who seemed to be a pretty nice fellow. Everything was quiet. Except for Gerald and myself, there wasn't a soul around when I decided to take a stroll down a narrow dirt road that ran past the house. I raced down the path feeling strong and rested and encouraged that nobody knew my whereabouts. I thought this might finally be the moment I had been waiting for. In the back of my mind however, I was certain someone was trying to buy a little more time, but for what, I wasn't sure. I believed they were planning on extorting me or my family, at least that was my theory. I had no proof. But whatever was happening to me, it was big enough to involve a lot of people.

I knew it was now or never and I needed to find a working phone. I removed my small knife from its leather holster and made a tiny cut in the bottom of the pouch. I then pushed out the phone number for the Canadian embassy. With my lifeline in hand, I found myself adjusting my pace so as not to draw attention to myself. My heart raced. I could hear it pounding in my chest as I realized this might be my only shot at contacting someone.

I continued down the dirt path. I could now hear the sounds of traffic, which grew louder with every stride. The road had brought me right to downtown Warri! With no plan of action in mind, I didn't hesitate to flag down a young man riding a scooter. I also didn't wait for an invitation, as I quickly saddled his bike.

"Nitel!" I shouted in the lad's ear and we were on our way. At least I hoped he knew the way to the biggest phone company in Nigeria.

After a long and unnerving ride over potholes and debris, we were there. The place where I would at last make that cherished call to the Eden I had so foolishly left behind.

"Wait here, okay," I told him, making sure we were on the same page.

"No problem," he replied.

With a nod and gentle slap on his shoulder, I replied with a "Thanks."

Adisa had given me some Nigerian money earlier that I had been saving and right now, I was truly grateful I had it.

As I passed through the gates, a young man in uniform holding an AK-47 was obviously making mental notes of my presence. I had only seen one other white man in weeks and I was the visible minority. People stared at me wherever I went, so I took little stock in his glaring look. I was so scared—not about the thought of bodily harm, but that maybe someone had been told not to let someone fitting my description use the phone. I suspected this had been the case in the past and I wouldn't be surprised if this was the case today.

Walking up to the wicket as if I were the most important person in Warri, I tossed the crumpled piece of paper with the embassy's number on it to a middle-aged woman.

"I would like to place that call, please." She paused for a moment as I stared at a block wall, glancing to the floor occasionally.

"That will be thirty nira." Those were the sweetest words I think I've ever heard.

A green light was displayed on one of the three telephone booths. I couldn't believe this was happening.

"Hello."

Without any pleasantries, I got right to the point, "My name is Leif Morrison and I am in Warri with no passport. I feel I am in danger and I need someone to come and get me right away."

"Oh my God," replied the lady on the phone. "Leif Morrison, I just got off the phone with your wife, Marlene, and they are very worried about you."

I was in no mood for idle conversation as I was fearful our conversation would be cut off at any time, so I immediately told her I was calling from Nitel in Warri and that William and the boat were at the Warri port. The woman instantly advised me to stay put and her driver would find me. She explained that it would take them about ten hours to reach me.

"No, that is not acceptable," I replied.

"Look mister, if I leave right now I might make it in ten hours." I apologized and explained I didn't realize it was so far.

"You just sit tight. We are on the way."

This was the third time I had experienced an incredible feeling of relief. I hoped it was the last because I honestly didn't think I could handle another disappointment.

A Ten-Hour Wait for my Angel

My driver was waiting patiently and was very happy to see me return with payment in hand. He didn't know what to charge me, so I gave him forty nira. He smiled as he waved goodbye.

The ten-hour wait was made easy with the help of an old woman affectionately known as Jemima. She was the proud owner and operator of a small fruit stand tucked away in a shaded corner where she also sold beer and peanuts. The elderly lady was a true representative of who the average Warri citizen was. Poor and uneducated, she took a real interest in this strange man who was able to give her a glimpse into a distant world of which she became fascinated. Her demeanour did not hide her thirst for knowledge and she appeared to be quite intelligent for her lot in life. I used the opportunity to sit with her inside the small booth. I gathered two large stones and a flat piece of wood nearby. She found it strange that I rejected her offer to sit on a wooden crate. She was not aware that my makeshift bench didn't allow me to be seen over the countertop. The uncomfortable seat was well worth the sacrifice to be out of sight—and hopefully, out of mind.

From my perch, I was able to watch the people of Warri come and go as they went about their daily lives. The shack was off the main street, away from mainstream traffic so I felt safe.

I had plenty of time to take in my surroundings. This quiet corner of town bore the scars of years of neglect. An attempt was made to build a church out of block and mortar. It was half completed and abandoned where it lay. It was accented with wooden rafters and a cross still adorned its peak. Amid all the bad I had encountered, it gave me a sense of security to think there were good people here, too. Churches like this one were quite common throughout Warri.

For every church, there was always a bank. Banks were everywhere, in all shapes and sizes and they were the well-kept buildings by comparison to all the other structures. There were no really large buildings, no grocery stores, retail, or fast food outlets. Instead, there were many rundown, shabby shacks, each one and two storeys that dotted the roadside as far as I could see. They had no running water or electricity, but they were homes to the many local residents.

I could see heaps of steaming garbage and someone actually digging through the refuse with a stick. I couldn't imagine why someone would want to dig through the garbage of these poor people; there was obviously nothing of any worth.

A few old cars, long stripped of any value lay here and there. It was obvious to see where the spare parts had gone. Small, imported cars, dented and beaten, seemed to rattle about the street as their owners tried to navigate the broken, potholed roads. There were few people out and about, which was much to my liking. However, by dusk, the streets were alive. People rushed home to get off the roads before it got dark. People of all walks of life, some in rags, some in suits and ties, busied the streets. The women wore mostly rags but some wore bright, colourful dresses with matching head wraps.

The day passed slowly as I anxiously awaited my rescue. It was the first time I allowed myself to be entertained by my surroundings. I watched the people carry on their routines in this seemingly lost world. Nervously, I cracked peanuts and smoked more cigarettes than usual. I watched an older couple who appeared to be in their seventies, married I presumed, work all day to build a block and mortar wall. The old man carried and placed the blocks while the old woman gathered water from nearby mud puddles then emptied the small bowls into a larger basin. She balanced the larger basin on her head and carried this to a trough where she would mix the mortar. By the end of the day, they had built a wall, seventy-feet long by four-feet high. Jemima told me they had started the wall at daybreak and did not stop to take a single break.

I could see the coming and going of people and vehicles around the entire area. I sat back feeling like a freed man as I drank three warm beers, cracked nuts and smoked cigarettes as Jemima and I talked. Once darkness fell, two men came and helped her take her cart away for the night.

Now, I was alone, standing in the shadows with only my thoughts to torture me. What if she doesn't come? What if there is someone in uniform looking for me? Here I am a lone, white male, easy prey for foul play.

It was another long three hours, staring into the darkness. Then a car approached. I knew at once, this was no ordinary vehicle. Its headlights were high and wide and very bright. It wasn't until it was closer that I was able to see the red embassy plates on its front.

As I stepped out of the darkness, the vehicle stopped at once. The lady from my earlier phone call got out of the late-model suburban and introduced herself as Joyce Loosli from the Canadian Consulate Services. As she reached to shake my hand, I put my arm around her neck and hugged her gently. I told her she was my angel of mercy.

"That's my job my boy, that's my job." I was nothing she hadn't seen before in her past twenty years of service. "Get in the car, boy," she instructed. "I'm tired and I'm not hanging around here."

It had only been twelve hours since I left the guest house. Acting on an impulse, I found myself in the streets of Warri where I impulsively flagged down an unknown person, who was kind enough to help me. I found my way to the phone company where I was finally able to make a call to the woman who had just got off the phone with Marlene, who, herself, had just made a plea for help. Fate had definitely been on my side. Now, after countless sleepless nights and endless days of living in fear, not knowing whether I would ever see my family again, it was finally over. I could go home—or so I thought.

Rescuing William

T ired from her ten-hour drive, Joyce got right to the point. "All right, where is this other fellow?" she asked. I was always careful when I was with Adisa to make mental routes of where he had taken me so I had a pretty good idea of how to get to the Warri Port.

We spoke very little, apart from giving my directions to the driver, it was a silent ride. Joyce napped part of the way and I reflected on the events of the past weeks.

Once we arrived at the gates to the port entrance, an older man in uniform told our driver he could not enter. Joyce wasn't long straightening him out. She flashed her credentials and said matter-of-factly, "If you don't like that, check the license plate."

I was quickly learning that as long as I was in that vehicle with the big red license plate, I was entitled to as much protection as if I were at the embassy itself. Without hesitation, the barricade was quickly lifted. I couldn't wait to see the look on William's face, especially since I hadn't seen him in over a week.

When we arrived at the vessel, we had to honk the horn and shout his name as the gangplank had been pulled on board. This was William's way of locking the door. I knew he rarely left the Zurich apart from the few times he would walk over to speak with the Chinese, who were living aboard their abandoned ship.

I would have to say William was more confused than happy when he saw me. There was no time for explanations however, so all he received were instructions to gather whatever belongings he had and come immediately. Now that I had poor old William worked up and scurrying about his room, Joyce walked in with her cigarette in hand, as cool as can be.

"So, you must be William Wells. Your sister is quite worried about you."

After five weeks had passed and I still hadn't heard from Leif or received any information that the Zurich had arrived in Africa, I decided to call the Glace Bay fish plant and question Mike, the gentleman who got Leif the job. He was very surprised I hadn't heard from him and asked if I had called William's family. I told him I didn't know anything about them but if he could get me their phone number, I would be obliged. Strangely enough, while I was waiting to get the phone number from Mike, William's sister called me. I was glad to talk to her and she didn't have any more information than I did. She said it was very unusual for William to have been gone for so long without calling home. She felt as uneasy as I did. We promised each other we would keep in touch and share any new information.

I had to figure out where to go from here and after a few calls to various local government agencies, I decided to call the Canadian Embassy in Nigeria. I had to follow my instincts, so what if I was wrong; I felt I could not take that chance.

To this day, I will never forget the conversation with a gentleman named Peter Marshal. He was very receptive and in a lengthy conversation, I did my best to state my concerns in an effort to find my husband. I hoped and prayed my plea was not falling on deaf ears. I was somewhat relieved by his close attention and by the end of the conversation, he gave his word he and his staff would look into this matter and give it their full attention. I felt much better for having called and for asking for help.

Within an hour, I received a return call from a lady named Joyce Loosli. She said she and Peter knew where Leif was because he had just called the embassy and asked for help. They told him they had just spoken to me. What a coincidence...or was it?

I was so relieved that by the time the conversation ended with Joyce, I could feel the hot tears roll down my cheeks. I could hardly breathe from the anxiety that filled my chest and throat as I made every effort to remain on the line.

"Leif is safe," she said, and at this time, I understood it as being safe from his journey across the sea to Africa, not knowing she meant safe from the local criminals who pillaged and plundered the workers and visitors who came to their land.

Graciously, I thanked Joyce for her help and thanked God for answering my prayers. Little did I know the task of getting him home was far from over.

Now, composed and relieved, I called my parents to let them know Leif was well and should be home soon. I couldn't wait for Justin and Aleisha to come home from school to tell them the good news. They had asked so many times, "When is Daddy coming home?" Finally, I had the answer they wanted to hear. Then I called Heather Wells to let her know Leif and William were safe and I explained the contacts we had made at the Canadian Embassy. Joyce Loosli would pick William and Leif up in Warri and take them with her to Lagos where they would stay until she could make arrangements for them to fly home. Heather was as excited as I was at the good news and neither of us took the time to question their lack of communication because we were so grateful our men were okay. We felt we could always ask those details when they got home.

Are you Nuts? Stay in Warri...

W e wasted no time getting off the boat and away from the dock. Joyce was tired and I was a pile of nerves. All I wanted to do was to get as far and as quickly away as possible.

Upon entering the town limits, Joyce thought it appropriate to inform the local police of our departure. "Are you nuts?" I blurted out. "That's the last thing we want to do!" I had had my own experience with the local police and that was enough for me.

"Trust me babes, I know what I am doing," was her quick retort.

After some brief directions from one of the locals, our driver navigated the narrow streets until we came to what looked like Jed Clampett's old shack—only larger. There were half a dozen men with large weapons placed here and there with another three or four young girls hanging about.

"Who is in charge?" shouted Joyce.

A short, fat man wearing only trousers, which sat well below his protruding belly, swaggered slowly toward us asking, "Yes, what is the problem?"

When Joyce briefly explained, he merely shrugged his shoulders and walked away without saying a word.

"Cripes, that was a waste of time," Joyce muttered in a low voice. "Okay, the next thing we have to do is find a place to eat and a place to sleep."

Joyce insisted we pick up my belongings first. I had no desire to collect the meagre possessions and was more than willing to leave them behind but Joyce was the boss and that's the way it would be.

I had no problem finding the guesthouse as I had taken note that the narrow dirt road was directly across from a half-built block and mortar church. When Joyce saw the guesthouse for the first time she instantly said, "This place looks decent. We will stay here the night."

"No, no, you don't understand, we must go now!" But before I could say another word, Joyce was out of the vehicle with her overnight bag in hand. She had so much confidence, or was it ignorance? Either way, we were staying the night.

Gerald was there to greet us. I explained who Joyce was and that William, who never spoke a word the entire night, was my partner from the boat. Joyce and Gerald exchanged pleasantries and he instructed her to take my room. I never trusted Gerald and told him little about myself but when all was said and done, he smiled, nodded his head, and gave me a quick wink.

Escape From Warri

I slept little that night. All I wanted to do was distance myself from Warri. At the crack of dawn, a quick breakfast was had by all and we were back on the road again for our ten-hour drive to Lagos. William and I sat in the back like two happily freed prisoners. There is an old saying about not being able to see the forest for the trees and now that we were distancing ourselves from Warri, a much clearer picture of the last five week's events were coming into focus.

There was little conversation except for the repeated thank yous William and I gave to Joyce and the driver. When not dozing, I gazed out the window at the countryside and the small towns along the way. I couldn't help but notice how time seemed to stand still. The road was wide, with proper on and off ramps, but time had taken its toll and it was now only a mere shadow of days gone by. Large road signs dotted the road, but most were so black and worn, you couldn't read them. Unfinished and windowless block and mortar apartment buildings dominated the heavily populated towns. As we approached the town limits of Lagos, there were an unusually large number of people with missing limbs begging for handouts wherever the traffic slowed.

Joyce, being a kind and generous person, informed William and me that even though the Embassy had full accommodations for wayward travellers such as ourselves, we were to be her guests in her home for the next few days, thinking the passport issue would be sorted out by then.

William and I had made several attempts to enlighten Joyce on the details of our ordeal but instead, she would pass it off as just another day at the office—and rightly so. After twenty years in the business, here was a lady whom I'd never met before, she had just driven more than twenty hours over roads that sometimes seemed to disappear and now, she had invited us to share her home and family. This was no ordinary person. She is a person who lives in my heart to this day. She is the most courageous person I have ever known.

Our day's journey ended when we pulled up to a big decorative gate. Joyce's large home was one of three within the confines of a huge rectangular compound. The three homes sat one behind the other, each separated by its own large stone wall, which gave everyone both privacy and security and a nice backyard, yet all were gated to the adjacent one. The entire compound was encircled by the usual ten-foot-high wall topped with razor wire. At the entrance was a gatehouse with two armed guards.

"Ah, home at last," Joyce said with great relief.

Her three children, Tanya, Nicholas, and the youngest, Christopher, were there to greet her. After Joyce had introduced everyone, I got the feeling her children did not welcome our presence although, over the next two days, a real friendship would grow between us. The kids were especially taken with William as he always took the time to play games and talk with them. I, on the other hand, continued to fester over that damn passport. All I wanted to do was to go home.

The Long Awaited Call Home

My first order of business was to phone home. Finally, after five weeks, I was able to make that call. I was feeling guilty, so very guilty, because I knew I had nobody else to blame for bringing so much heartache and worry to the people who loved and cared for me the most. My guilt was no match for the love I had for my wife and two children and soon we would once again be the four bears.

Joyce, being the wonderful person she was, and a kind and caring mom as well, had no problem putting my call ahead of everything and everyone. While placing the call, she told me to use the phone at the top of the stairs because it would be more private.

The moment of truth and all I could say was that I was sorry. Marlene couldn't understand why I was apologizing and she sobbed tears of joy to have the world's greatest fool back in her life. Due to the time difference, the children had not returned from school yet, but that was a reunion that would take place later that day. I was happy for the first time in what seemed to be an eternity—at this moment all was well with the world. I made it in spite of everything. I felt like I had accomplished something and for the next few days, I would hang out here until the embassy issued William and me new passports—I was pretty certain I would never see the old one again.

Finally, after all the worry, Leif arrived safely in Lagos. William and Leif would be able to breathe easy and know the comforts of a real home. Joyce was wonderful to them and went out of her way to be a gracious host. From here, Leif called to have the first normal conversation in over five weeks. What started out as a routine morning soon became a day to remember. As I answered the phone, expecting to hear a customer requesting a hair appointment, I was overjoyed to hear Leif's voice cry, "Is that you Marlene?" Before I could say too much, he kept saying, "I'm sorry, I'm so sorry."

I told him everything was fine and I was so happy just to hear his voice and know for myself that he was okay. I told him how much I missed him and how worried I was that I was never going to see him again. I was disappointed the children were not home to hear from their Dad but I insisted he call back in a few hours when they were back from school. We were so happy to know he had made it that we didn't dwell on other issues. There would be plenty of time for that. For now, all I knew was that he had to be there a little longer to get another passport but knowing he was well was all I needed for now.

After our conversation, I called my parents and both of our family members to let them know he was coming home soon. Everyone was thrilled. I put my coat on, went out to sit on the step and waited for the bus. I knew two little bears who were going to have their best day this week!

A Gracious Host

Our host was the best that she could be and she made us feel welcomed in her beautifully decorated home, making it easy for these two wayward travellers to settle in.

After freshening up, we all sat in for supper like one big happy family around a large oak table. Booboo, a young man and the hired cook and housekeeper, made us a wonderful meal. It was easy to get comfortable considering the living conditions we had endured over the past five weeks.

The evening passed quickly and on several occasions, I tried to enlighten Joyce and the kids about the past events but they didn't seem interested. I figured because of the nature of her work, she had seen and heard it all. Besides, the kids had school in the morning and we were tired from our long drive. Everyone was looking forward to a good night's sleep.

I will never forget that first evening as Joyce prepared her home for another night in Lagos. She affixed three large padlocks to a wrought iron gate at the front door. A half-inch thick steel door was secured with two more key entry systems. At the bottom of the stairs, was a third wrought iron gate to which she affixed yet another heavy padlock. Finally, she set the alarm system. With two armed guards at the compound entrance along with a stone wall and razor wire, her comfortable oasis was not only her home but a fortress.

By the time William and I had awakened the next morning, the house was quiet. Joyce had gone to work at the embassy and her children were off to school, all chauffeured in a large bullet-proof car. William and I spent the day lounging about and feeling good about life, something we hadn't done in a long time.

As I peered through the barred living room window, I couldn't fathom the world that lay beyond as I hadn't researched the country in which I was now imprisoned. Little did I know, this would be my window to the world for another two weeks.

The time passed quickly and before we knew it, Joyce and the kids were back home after finishing another routine day. She was more herself, perky and quick with her dry wit. At first opportunity I asked about getting out of this place, careful not to sound like an ungrateful guest.

"We're working on it, sweetie," she said with a smile. I left it at that knowing she was in my corner.

Sitting around the dinner table, eating another meal prepared by Booboo within the confines of our little fortress, I felt an enormous appreciation for Joyce and her family, which gave me a real sense of normality.

The next couple of days came and went without incident. By now, Joyce's family had become comfortable with our presence. As for me, I was admittedly not the perfect houseguest. My days were spent staring out the window through two sets of iron bars and gates, trying to make sense of everything that had happened.

On several occasions, I noticed the same man lingering beside the road directly across from the gates. I also got to know Joyce's neighbour who lived directly off her backdoor. Reece was a tall good-looking woman who enjoyed a solitary life, never coming to visit.

That evening, Joyce suggested she send the driver to pick William and me up at noon the following day, thinking an afternoon at the embassy's recreation center would do us good. The large limo-like car arrived at noon sharp as promised. I didn't like going out but I felt secure behind the one-inch glass and large red license plate. As we were leaving, I once again noticed the same man lingering outside the gate, watching us with great interest. Careful not to make eye contact with him, out of the corner of my eye, I watched him leave as we slowly drove away.

"Am I being watched?" I asked myself. This was not an unreasonable question in light of the past several weeks' events.

Soon, William and I were busy smacking pool balls on the green rag and eating BBQ hamburgers. The recreation centre was nice and its Nigerian staff friendly. After a few hours however, I was telling myself that this was bullshit. I had no intention of, nor any desire to become complacent with the fact that I wanted to go home to Cape Breton—and I wanted to go now. I was miserable and I was beginning to take it out on everyone around me, even though I still refused to let my true thoughts be known.

Now, in my fifth day at the embassy and thinking everything would have been resolved by now, I was becoming somewhat angry at the establishment for taking so long to process a new passport. With my fear and uncertainty now replaced by anger and discontentment, I found myself never too far from a glass of scotch.

That evening, Booboo had made his version a pizza for supper. It was a sombre evening as I sat in the chair I had claimed as my own, sipping Scotch whisky and thinking of my family. Reece popped in for a minute to ask Joyce to feed her two large German Shepherds while she was away the next twenty-four hours dealing with some business in the neighbouring country. Appearing to be very serious and professional, she merely made her point and left with a causal smile and wave to me. She was gone as quickly as she had come.

The Dirty Word—Canadian

A day-and-a-half later, Reece returned with the story of her experience at the airport. Thinking it humorous, Reece went on to tell us of the commotion a young woman checking travel documents made when she had seen the word Canadian. As Reece described it, the airport employee shouted loudly to nearby armed guards.

"Canadian... Canadian."

Airport officials were quick to realize however, this was not the Canadian they were looking for. I don't think Reece or Joyce made the connection that the Canadian they were looking for was in fact me, otherwise they would never have entertained the ill-fated attempt to get me out of the county.

I did not press Joyce on the passport issue, as I trusted she was doing everything possible to rectify the situation. Personally, I couldn't understand what the big deal was. I thought that once I was at the embassy, I was home free—make me a new passport and be done with it. This wasn't the case for some reason and I wasn't going anywhere without it. I told Peter Marshall, who was in charge of all leading matters, that he would never retrieve it. It wasn't that it was simply misplaced or on a slow moving caravan from Warri, but instead, I tried to give him some insight into what was going on.

Now, going on the ninth day at Joyce's and still made to feel as welcome as ever, someone came up with the idea to smuggle William and me into the Ivory Cost by crossing the border in the trunk of the big car. This was truly their plan! I told Peter what I thought of the idea and that it bothered me this was their best plan of action. Once again, I found myself slipping back into a state of despair. All I could do was to continue to wait.

As I continued my daily vigil by the window, the same unknown man lingered across the road. A man I believed was assigned to keep tabs on my whereabouts.

Meanwhile, top members of the embassy were receiving pressure from Joyce, at my request, to take some hard-line action, and take it now. Enough was enough, no more bullshit. It was time to go.

The idea of smuggling us out in the trunk of the car was scrapped but instead, we were going to be issued what Peter referred to as emergency documents. It was logical to believe this was a good idea and the embassy officials knew what they were doing, after all, these were the experts with years of experience. On several occasions, I attempted to enlighten them on what I thought was taking place. With nothing to prove my theory, I outlined that immigration was in the process of assessing my worth in Canada in order to ransom me for a sum of money they knew would be obtainable. In return, they would release me—or not. It was of my belief that dead men tell no tales and I would be no exception, but again, that was my assumption. But the members of the embassy had not yet taken hold of this theory and therefore, they did not grasp the seriousness of the situation.

Amsterdam, Here we Come

I did nothing but think about the situation I was in for nine days straight. In a safe and comfortable environment, I had thought only of the series of bizarre events, which had gotten me to this point. Safely tucked away, I could now afford a realistic analysis of it all without experiencing another panic attack.

When we reached the embassy, our driver led us up two sets of granite stairs that led to a series of offices, which looked for the most part, empty. Peter, a small and gentle man, was waiting for us. He had two rather unofficial looking papers on his desk that were to be our emergency documents.

"You leave tonight," was Peter's instruction. He then went on to say that there was only one airline that flew to and from Nigeria. The carrier would be KLM International, which made two flights weekly to Amsterdam.

"What time will you be picking us up?" I asked. To my surprise and disappointment, Peter informed us that he would not be taking us but instead, our driver would be taking us.

"You can't be serious!" I exclaimed. "That won't work, you don't realize the situation."

Peter was taken aback by my outburst. His reaction was, "You don't tell me what to do; you're in my office now."

Once again, I was at the mercy of someone else who was making decisions with my life. Peter assured me the driver, a Nigerian who now worked for the embassy but once worked at the airport, was a trusted and competent person who would take good care of us.

"But Mr. Marshall, you don't understand, I believe we need official representation."

"Don't worry, we know what we are doing and everything will be fine."

With what appeared to be little more than a piece of scrap paper in hand, William and I returned to Joyce's house. Booboo was busy preparing a last meal for us while Joyce encouraged us to get ready, as our driver was picking us up at six o'clock sharp.

"Joyce, this is crazy, you can't expect this to work. Your people just don't understand the seriousness of the situation." As far as they were concerned we were just two travellers who lost their passports.

"You'll be fine, Peter has years of experience at this and I'm sure he knows what he is doing."

At six o'clock sharp, our driver was waiting and with his own personal car, a modest piece of junk. With the usual hugs and kisses of good friends departing, we began the uneasy half-hour ride to the airport. As we passed through the gates and onto the main road, I made it a point to see if the mystery man was still lurking about. Sure enough, there he was. I wouldn't find out what he did next until later on.

Off to the Airport and Home

I wasn't listening to the voice in my head, which was telling me not to go. Once we were on the main highway, a car passed in front of us and exited down an off ramp. I got a quick look at the mystery man behind the wheel and he was accompanied by two other men. It was very unnerving and it was beginning to feel like Warri all over again.

It was getting dark as I tried to make a mental route back to the embassy if ever I needed it. The driver, who I called Joe since I could never pronounce his name, decided he had to make an un-scheduled stop at his house. Off the main highway and on a dirt back road, we were left sitting in total darkness. Joe was very apologetic, however, as he explained it was important that he visit his wife who was not well.

Joe disappeared as he headed down an earthen path toward a single faint light, which appeared to be a kerosene lantern. As we sat alone in the darkness in the middle of nowhere, the idea of leaving this place once again seemed like a dim reality. I didn't think arguing with Joe about going straight to the airport would have made any difference. If Joe could not be trusted, it was out of my hands and whatever was going to take place would.

After a tense five minutes, Joe returned out of breath, again apologizing for the inconvenience.

Arriving at the airport, I was not at all surprised to see that it, too, was only a mere shadow of its former self. Poorly light, dirty, and rundown from a lack of maintenance, it looked more like a prison than an airport. There was no shortage of armed guards and there were a few male travellers dressed in suits and ties while the women were dressed in brightly coloured dresses and head wraps. Everyone appeared to be unhappy, certainly not your typical cheery travellers.

William and I stuck out like two pink fluorescent light bulbs. Joe, in his best efforts, played diplomat as he spoke to two gentlemen who appeared to be his old friends. After presenting his presumed old colleagues with the embassy documents, William and I were instructed to take a seat on a bench against the wall. A small group of men, some in uniform, began to gather outside an office door. It was obvious that William and I were the focus of attention as they talked in hushed voices. Some cast glances while others stared. It felt as though they had been awaiting our arrival and everyone wanted to have a good look at the two mysterious Canadians.

William and I were now instructed to take a seat in the nearby office where two chairs were neatly placed before a rustic old desk. For several minutes, I sat there drained of any emotion. I felt this was the moment of truth. I had come so far and I was so close to freedom. I couldn't help but feel that once again, not listening to my own instincts and instead letting others decide what was best for me, would be my undoing. I didn't even bother to raise my head as what was just another uniformed person acting like someone of great importance, placed a sheet of paper and pen before William and me.

With no sign of respect to either of us, we were simply instructed to write down who we were and our reason for being there. I recall performing this task some four weeks earlier as I scribbled across the page. The papers were collected and we were told to leave.

Our Courteous Staff is ready to Serve You

J oe was waiting outside with a small group of men who continued to gawk at our departure. Joe was a small quiet man who spoke very little, even less than William.

"Follow me," he said, as he led us to what was to be our boarding gate.

On the way there, I witnessed a well-dressed young man who was sobbing uncontrollably while making pleas for mercy as he was being escorted from the building. His small frame was supported by an armed guard on either side so his toes barely touched the floor as he was dragged across the room. Arriving at what was to be our boarding gate, I couldn't help but notice that we were the only ones there. William was excited at the idea that he was finally going home.

"Don't whistle Dixie yet, William, at least not until we see the fasten your seatbelt sign come on."

No sooner did I get the words out of my mouth, when I heard the sound of hard-soled shoes clapping in perfect unison racing up behind us. We turned to see two very serious looking officers, eyes fixed on Joe, standing directly in front of us. We were informed that, "The Canadians cannot leave for there is a problem in Warri."

My first thought in response to this was that someone had laid bogus drug charges on us and under international law, our embassy would not be able to help us. A familiar wave of anxiety washed over me as I witnessed the look of horror on Joe's face. He knew this was bad and he had to act quickly and decisively.

Joe did indeed rise to the occasion, armed with only his two-way radio and sense enough to step into a nearby restroom, he was able to get in touch with Peter Marshall. Joe informed us to act relaxed and take a seat close to the main entrance so as not to raise suspicions of our pending escape.

I have to applaud Mr. Marshall's response time because before we knew it, he was instructing us to stay close to him and not look back. As we exited the building at a casual pace, it turned into a full out run as I heard Peter shout into his radio, "Now, now, now!"

The embassy's bullet-proof car sped toward us. Close on our heels, two armed guards shouted for us to stop. As I opened the rear door of the car, one of the guards fired two shots into the air. With that, I gripped William by the belt and threw his one-hundred-and-twenty-pound body across the seat. With everyone now on board, we began our hasty retreat back to the embassy.

The retreat turned out to be much faster than expected however, since we were now being chased by three cars, which were occupied by what I refer to as thugs. Instead of going to the embassy, Peter instructed our driver, who by now was a nervous wreck, to take us to Joyce's residence. Since her fortified home had the same rights and status of the main embassy, it was indeed the best place for William and me.

In spite of all that had happened that night I had to laugh at the sight of Joyce and her children as we made a quick hard right turn through the gates of the compound—they looked like the Three Wise Men plus one. Joyce was holding a bottle of scotch, Nick a bottle of soda, Tanya two glasses and Christopher a bowl of ice.

"I told you, I told you that was a lame plan."

With that, Joyce gave me the scotch and a warm hug. Feeling some-what embarrassed she told me, "We will get it right the next time." Gently rubbing my shoulder, she escorted me inside.

The first order of business was to calm my nerves with the large glass of scotch Joyce had instructed Tanya to give me. William, however, being a non-drinker, quietly sat in his corner, visibly rat-tled by the ordeal. He chose to smoke his cigarettes, one after the other.

From my chair by the window, I could plainly see Peter and an officer of sorts exchanging words, using many expressive hand ges-tures. Finally, the officer retreated to his car and the three vehicles left as quickly as they arrived.

Peter returned to the house but never proceeded beyond the front door. Upset and shaking, I could hear him tell Joyce, "Can you believe those guys, they were out there trying to convince me they had called the airplane back and they would be kind enough to es-cort the two Canadians back to the airport."

With that, he left without addressing William or me.

How About Plan B?

As I spent the rest of that evening in safety and comfort with my feet perched high, determined to polish off the remaining scotch, I was taking great pleasure in the fact that their cash cow had eluded them once more. I sincerely hoped that heads would roll as a result.

I slept late the following day and awoke to find the house quiet. It was business as usual for the Loosli family. With Joyce at work, and the children at school, William and I were once again left to try and make sense of it all.

Joyce and the kids returned later in the day and Joyce was excited but remained professional as she told us we were to be at the immigration office in Lagos first thing in the morning. Before I could say a word, she grinned, affirming that both she and Peter would be going with us.

The following morning, Peter and his driver collected the three of us, as promised. We were dropped off outside an old rustic shack, which was covered in rusted corrugated steel siding. A young girl on her way to the market happened by carrying a large disk-like pan on her head, piled high with ripe oranges. With a sweet and tender smile, she was only too glad to sell me half a dozen, as I marvelled at her skill in lowering the heavy, cumbersome load to the ground. With the shared oranges now eaten, I found myself at peace somehow. As I put aside all my worries and woes and took the time to smell the fresh tropical air, I took in the sights and sounds around me. Without warning, Joyce gave me a gentle poke in the belly and said, "Come on mister, we're up."

The long, rectangular shack was divided into two halves; one consisting of office space with desks, chairs and office paraphernalia reminiscent of the sixties. We were immediately escorted into the second chamber that looked like a small courtroom. At one end, there was a beautiful curved mahogany desk that had to be at least fifteen feet long. Behind it, sat a large man in full uniform. His hard-billed military cap was pulled tightly to his forehead, and on each shoulder, he wore the large yellow brushes, while a long collection of medals streamed down from his breast pocket. He sat motionless, his hands folded on the desk before him. He was by far, the most intimidating figure I had ever seen.

Standing behind him in semi-circle formation, were seven large officers in full uniform. These men stood at attention for the duration of our meeting, adding to the overwhelming presence of the large man before me.

William was not so easily intimidated and began to mutter, "Money, that's all they want, is money."

With that, Peter quickly got in William's face and whispered softly but firmly, "Shut up and sit down." Without hesitation he did just that.

A bailiff of sorts instructed me to sit in what could only be described as a witness box. From where I was sitting, I could hear Mr. Marshall telling the large man behind the desk that the Canadian government was working hard to foster good relations with Nigeria and that if any harm were to come to these gentlemen, it would not be in the best interest of those relations. This was a very sombre moment as Peter then bowed slightly before quietly returning to his seat.

The officer turned his attention toward me, lifting his sullen face with its high cheekbones and sharp, chisel-like chin, all of which played host to eyes that seemed lifeless and cold, almost shark-like. A chill ran down my back and my hands began to sweat. With no emotion or gestures of any sort he looked through me, asking, "Why are you here?"

I suddenly found myself reaching deep inside for the courage I now so desperately needed. As a young boy, I had a newspaper route. While delivering my daily papers, I was harassed by a dog, who would stare me down and growl, threatening to pounce. A man once told that if I were brave and didn't show the dog fear, the dog wouldn't bite me.

Right now, my eyes were fixated on the big man before me, certainly not to stare him down but instead, I found myself drawn to him like a moth to a candle. You could have heard a pin drop as he and everyone awaited my answer.

As I swallowed to clear the lump in my throat I thought, "This guy is nothing more than a big dog to whom I must show no fear but instead, respect".

So, with a clear and determined voice I softly but deliberately spoke.

"I am only a poor working man in my country. I helped sail an old fishing vessel to your country to earn wages to help feed my family. I wanted a challenge, to make some friends, to see your countryside and then go home."

Not knowing where these words came from, I sat frozen in my chair as we continued to stare at each other. The top corner of his lip rose slightly, possibly revealing the start of a smile. Reaching for a pen, the formidable figure scribbled something across a paper that lay before him. After receiving a slight glance from the officer, the bailiff quickly ushered the four of us out of the building. As we returned to the car, Peter put his hand on my shoulder and told me I had done well and it was now a matter of wait and see.

William and I were given the option of going to the embassy or returning to Joyce's house so we chose Joyce as we felt more comfortable there.

Expecting we would receive word on the status of our situation, I was not able to settle. I paced non-stop for an hour. To my surprise, Joyce stepped through the door with a smile from ear-to-ear waving the illusive passports. She was as happy as we were when I hugged and kissed her, thanking her for everything she had done for us. I wasted no time asking, "When is the next flight out?"

Joyce responded, tears flowing down her angelic face, "The day after tomorrow and your tickets are being processed as we speak."

Up until this point, I don't think Joyce had ever gotten the full gist of the ordeal but she was every bit as happy as we were.

On to Amsterdam...Again

I n spite of being on the receiving end of a few warning shots fired over our heads and the little issue of a high-speed chase in a bullet proof car, we were feeling a little cocky under the protection of the Canadian embassy. It was the first time we were not scared and we relished in the security of the compound. We were like two school children who thumbed their noses at the school-yard bullies in the safety of our own back yard.

That night, Reece had come for her first real visit after hearing the good news. Her visit made that evening just that much more delightful. Reece thought it would be nice if we came with her to an outdoor market the following day.

"What sort of market?" asked William, who was now rested and refreshed as a result of Joyce's wonderful hospitality and care.

"A type of flea market with all sorts of handmade African Folk Art," she replied. Both Joyce and Reece thought it was a good idea if we went with them.

The idea of finding a few trinkets to take back home was appealing, so we gladly accepted her offer. Bright and early as promised, our chauffeur-driven car picked us up. Sitting in the back seat, I was enjoying the ride for the first time. I was finally able to take interest in everything I saw. As we stopped at an intersection, a group of young lads around ten or twelve years old gently tapped on my window, begging for a handout. Loving children as I do, I ordered our driver to wait a moment so I could share the money I had for the market with them. I hastily cranked down the half-inch thick window. Excited that this huge, black shiny car had acknowledged their pleas for kindness, the ragged, hungry children began to draw closer. It was then that I noticed the single most burning image I had witnessed yet. There, standing behind the small crowd was a young boy about the same age as my own son, barefoot with only a rag wrapped around his middle. He stood speechless as he clutched a small blue bowl. The fact that he had no hands was bad enough but what was more gut wrenching was the obvious reason why. It was plain to see that someone had hacked his hands off, one higher than the other and then cauterized them with an open flame. My eyes filled with tears as I instructed the others to move aside. With my arm stretched out the window I beckoned the lad to come closer. With the look of a frightened puppy, he inched his way toward me. After placing every cent I had for the market in his bowl, oncoming traffic forced the driver to pull away. I hung my head, trying to hide my tears. I could only say, "Get me out of this fucking hole."

Before arriving at the market, I warned William to stay close to me and not to wander in the crowd. He needed no such warning and the two of us stuck like glue to Joyce. We were like two little schoolboys with their mother. We stayed in talking distance to both Joyce and Reece. In a short while, the crowd grew and the market was brimming with noise. The two women, our protectors, suddenly seemed insignificant as the crowd continued to expand, jostling us about. The face of the man who watched us from across the street was beginning to look all too familiar in the horde of people, which were still gathering. Pulling William close to me, we agreed it was best to just snatch up a few trinkets and get the hell out of there.

Despite our uneasiness, our trip to the market actually went without incident and William and I were able to find some authentic local handcrafts.

Tomorrow was the big day and I could think of nothing else. The faces of Marlene and the kids were sharp in my mind and for the first time in seven weeks, I wasn't haunted by the idea that I may never see them again.

The following day seemed to drag on forever. Our flight wasn't leaving until seven o'clock that evening and much of my time was spent on the phone reassuring the family that I indeed would be home in two days. They were oblivious to the events of the past weeks and never really did get a full account until now.

Homeward Bound At Last

E very once in a while, I would remove my passport from my
pocket and study its every detail. For right now, it was the
most precious thing on earth.

Finally, it was time to leave but not before having a proper supper, something Joyce made sure of. Our few meagre possessions
were gathered by the door. For the past ten hours, William and I had
been more than ready to meet Mr. Marshall when he arrived in his
big car. Joyce had promised me that this time, they would get it right
and that was a promise she intended to keep.

Now, escorted by two embassy officials and my passport in hand,
it was as if this whole ordeal had never really happened, a mere bad
dream. I felt dazed. I said nothing during the short half hour drive to
the airport. Not wanting to spoil this occasion, I tried not to focus on
the darker side of this nightmare so I reflected on the many kind and
sincere Nigerian people I had met over the past five weeks.

Upon entering the airport, the four of us drew a lot of attention
but unlike celebrities, nobody was looking for autographs or to shake
our hands. Instead, we were the center of whispers and stares as even
the armed guards cast sideways glances so as not to be caught. I felt
like a prisoner being set free, and it felt good.

Peter took charge and steered us through the necessary details to
get us to the boarding gate. I told William to stay close to me and in

turn, I stayed close to Mr. Marshall, not leaving his sight for a moment. As I had told William many days earlier, I will not truly relax until I see the 'fasten your seatbelt' sign.

I felt at least somewhat of a slap in the face when my passport was handed back to me and as I glanced at the still wet stamp, I thought I saw 'deported' brandished across its first page. Nevertheless, all was going well and we were now finally ready to board. Keeping in mind that this was not your everyday, run-of-the-mill airport, but instead, a dark, rundown building that resembled a prison, I was just happy to be leaving, deported, departed or otherwise.

The tunnel connecting the building to the awaiting aircraft was nothing more than a poorly lit plywood box. It seemed longer than most others I've been in. Being the last one to board, I could see only a lovely young Dutch girl awaiting my arrival. A soft light from the fuselage cast the look of a heavenly aura around her. With eyes fixated on her, I passed the halfway mark. For what reason I do not know, I turned and looked back. There, in the dark distance, the only thing I could see was a single exit sign. With a small canvass bag slung over my shoulder, I stood motionless, peering into that exit sign. With a turn of my head, I focused my attention back on the young angel waiting for me, taking one last glace at the exit sign, I moved forward.

This, I thought, was indeed a bad dream, a dream in which I was no longer trapped.

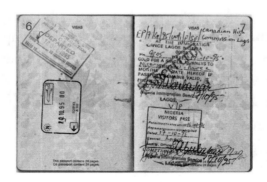

Epilogue

S ince I left Nigeria I have boarded several flights destined for both work and pleasure. But none has ever had such an impact as that fated flight home. Being the last to board, we were not met with the usual congestion in the aisle, instead we found ourselves nervous and very much out of place as we tried not to stare back at the rows of well dressed but sombre looking Nigerians.

Now, on each of my departures, when the seat belt sign flashes, I think of my old buddy William. The guy I had met aboard the Zurich in what seems to be a lifetime ago. With his oil blackened face and sunken cheeks, he was a man to whom I owed so much. At such times, I reminisce about how relieved we both were and laugh when I think about when he looked me in the eyes and jokingly asked, "Can I whistle Dixie now?"

We were both proud independent men and through this whole ordeal we mostly kept our feelings to ourselves. We did however agree that had we known then what we know now, we would have thrown Etlar overboard in one of his drunken stupors and abandoned the Zurich at the Canary Islands, sincerely expressing our grief over his unfortunate accident. Although we would have never done such a thing in reality, it felt good to laugh about it in that moment. From that point on, however, we spoke very little on the subject of Etlar or our seven-week ordeal, instead we were grateful for its outcome, although I may occasionally still take a poke at one of the many characters we met along the way, mainly Etlar.

Etlar, in my opinion, was a very intelligent person. He seemed possessed with a never ending struggle to succeed in life but he was always running away from something. A dark past? Possibly...who knows. I think so but the truth is, Etlar's attitude eventually became his own demise. He cared nothing about the hardship he brought to others, so long as his actions and deeds served his own interests. When I saw him last at the gates of his home, I saw a broken and defeated man. He had all but destroyed the engine of the Zurich and with that compounded by a one hundred thousand dollar import tax on his old cars, he had fallen from grace with Madu. This was his only link to survival. From all I witnessed, Etlar was alone. I noticed on different occasions, members of the street police and other young able-bodied males staring him down while making threatening gestures. Etlar was on the verge of losing his rented home and life on the street for him would have grave consequences, which he knew all too well. Who knows, maybe he rose above it, but somehow I doubt it.

As we taxied down the runway, I couldn't help but to reflect back on the numerous times I had pictured this moment in my head. With my middle finger stretched firm and held tightly to the window, I would shout, "Screw you, you bastards!" but somehow, it didn't fit the moment now. Who was I angry with? Certainly not the people of Nigeria, but instead, a few bad men.

We were off to Amsterdam like two old war buddies, our minds and souls exhausted. During the flight neither William nor I spoke about our ordeal. It was as if we were already trying to forget the entire nightmare. Later, when I tried to recount the experience to family and friends, words could not do it justice, and the story was often met with doubt.

As any routine flight from point A to point B, we landed in Amsterdam as scheduled. We would have to stay overnight and catch a flight to Sydney later the next day. Neither of us wished to linger about the airport until then, so we took a cab into the city. As tourists, it would have been a real treat to wander the old historical streets. William seemed to drag his feet, showing little interest in these new and unique surroundings. I felt much the same and we were content to just sit on a park bench and watch the world go by.

In the city square we saw a small carnival with an assortment of rides and games. Its centre piece consisted of the largest Ferris wheel I have ever seen. This, I thought, would be the perfect vantage point to use up the few remaining photos I had left on my camera as I was reluctant to take photos in Nigeria. Now, with historic Amsterdam stored in my pocket and William in tow, it was nearing dinner time.

We made our way along the cobblestone streets lined with beautiful shops in search of a suitable place to eat. I was eager to take advantage of one of the many phone booths. Something so simple as placing a phone call made me realize how little we appreciate the simplest things in life.

With the four-hour time difference between Amsterdam and home, I knew Marlene would just be getting the kids ready for school. After a warm and cherished phone call, she handed the cordless phone to that little man whose coconut I had tucked safely inside my backpack. Still half asleep, he was excited to tell me that he had just awakened from a dream. In his dream, he and I were at a circus riding a Ferris wheel.

William smiled when I told him of my conversation over dinner. As strange or coincidental as that conversation may have been, we both agreed it fit in perfectly with the seemingly bizarre events of the past seven weeks.

Of course, not wanting to spend the night in the airport, we set out in search of a room. Three hundred dollars was the going rate and between us both, we barely had one hundred. We did however, find a room for less than one hundred dollars in the red light district—a simple, single bed in a room the size of a large closet. I need not go into details of its history or the state of this place, but suffice it to say, we spent the night stretched across several seats back at the airport.

The following day, was met with the usual aches and pains experienced by most people who are subjected to over-nighting in the airport terminal. It did however, make the overseas flight back to Sydney all that more relaxing. Along with a now stress-free mind and the anticipation of the long awaited reunion, it was all good from here on out.

William, like myself, had had numerous life experiences up to this point and along the way, he encountered an array of characters and personalities. Although he and I had gone through so much together, there would come the sad reality that we would eventually go our separate ways.

It was a small consolation for the endeavour of a lifetime, but payment for the seven-week ordeal, less the two weeks at the embassy, was paid to both of us in full.

Home at last: Leif and family at J.A. Douglas McCurdy Airport in Sydney.

Marlene's Search for Answers

From the beginning, I really didn't want Leif to take this job. Sailing the old Zurich in the familiar waters of the Atlantic was risky enough, let alone taking the dilapidated old girl across the open sea to another continent. Logically, there were just too many uncertainties. She was outdated, relinquished from service and tied to the wharf in Halifax waiting to be refitted.

After purchasing the boat for the Sannu Corporation, Etlar made his first attempt to leave for Africa. He was two hours out to sea when the Zurich's engine failed. She had to be towed in to North Sydney for repairs. Her full crew abandoned the Zurich and the idea of going any further. Etlar was on the hunt.

In meeting Mike who supplied materials, parts and tradesmen to service boats in for repair, Etlar made his request known for an engineer and a seaman. So the story unfolds as Leif and William were introduced to Etlar. The mystery, coupled with the adventure of seeing a new world, intrigued Leif. He saw this as an opportunity to fulfill a boyhood-dream and welcomed the challenge as an experienced fisherman.

I felt there were too many risks and I was not on board with the idea. Leif tried to convince me at every opportunity to see otherwise. We called the Sannu Corporation in Rhode Island to find out if the boat's purchase and employment were legitimate and they were. They confirmed Etlar's word and assured Leif and William they should have no worries about the purpose of the boat or receiving their wages. They also said they would pay for their return fares upon arrival in Africa. Making reference to Etlar, they confirmed he was an experienced seaman and navigator and he had been an employee for several years.

Next, a meeting was planned with William, Etlar, Leif, and Mike. I went with Leif a few days later to tour the boat. I didn't understand the extent of the mechanical failures but was assured by William and Etlar, they were being resolved and the engine would be fit and run smoothly. The facilities on the boat were deplorable. It was filthy and its former owner had even left used dishes, pots and pans in the sinks, which smelled. One consolation, the food Etlar had bought was stored in a large freezer unit, which ran efficiently. Etlar advised that it would be cleaned up and the trip would take approximately two weeks, so they could manage their surroundings for that amount of time. With certainty, he advised Leif would have full use of the computer and radio in order to reach home. When out of range, he would get his contacts to relay their position and well being to us at home. Upon arrival, Leif could then tele-phone us from the Port of Warri.

Not one word of this promise was ever kept and looking back, Etlar knew he was lying in order to convince the crew he so desperately needed to get the Zurich to Africa for the benefit of his own employment.

Before their departure, Etlar gave me fax numbers, email addresses, and phone numbers, none of which worked.

Two weeks had passed and I started to feel uneasy. I tried to reach Leif us-ing Etlar's fax and phone numbers for the contacts in Nigeria. As well, I called the Sannu Corporation in Rhode Island to find out if they had received any information. I was told they didn't have a current location but said they expected them to arrive in Africa in another week. They told me, "Not to worry."

Another week passed before I decided to contact Mike. He led me to Wil-liam's sister, Heather. She had not heard from William either and thought it very unusual. I informed her that no one else had heard anything.

Now, I was really convinced something was wrong and by the fifth week, I decided to contact the Canadian Embassy in Nigeria. If my instincts were wrong the consulate would just think I was a foolish woman. No matter what, I had to follow my intuition, which proved to be right.

As it turned out, Leif and William were victims of some unlawful characters who were taking advantage of their positions for their own personal gain. Even though their passports had been confiscated illegally, William and Leif were able to place their trust in our representatives of the Canadian Embassy and after many weeks of uncertainty, they were safely returned home to their families and loved ones. For that, we are forever grateful.

Justin, Aleisha, Marlene and Leif today—The Four Bears again.

ABOUT THE AUTHOR

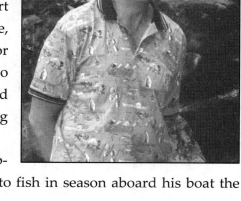

Leif Morrison, a native of Cape Breton Island, lives happily in the coastal community of Port Caledonia. He and his wife, Marlene, have been married for twenty-nine years and have two grown children: Justin (24) and Aleisha (21), both attending University.

Leif is a self-employed lobster fisherman who continues to fish in season aboard his boat the *Aleisha Janel*.

In recent years, he has become an entrepreneur, providing rental homes to senior citizens, many of whom have become close friends.

By trade, Leif is an experienced carpenter and scaffolder, which has through the years, earned him employment across Canada, Bermuda and Germany. Despite his experience in Nigeria, he continues to fulfill his desire for adventure and travels as a tourist whenever he can. His last trip led him on a hiking tour across New Zealand

Ethics in Canadian Nursing Practice
Navigating the Journey

Kathleen Oberle
University of Calgary

Shelley Raffin Bouchal
University of Calgary

PEARSON
Prentice
Hall

Toronto

Library and Archives Canada Cataloguing in Publication

Oberle, Kathleen, 1946-
    Ethics in Canadian Nursing Practice : Navigating the Journey / Kathleen Oberle,
    Shelley Raffin.

    Includes index.

    ISBN 978-0-13-124889-2

1. Nursing ethics—Canada. 2. Nursing—Standards—Canada. I. Raffin, Shelley, 1959-

RT85.O24 2009   174.2'9073   C2008-905179-3

ISBN-13: 978-0-13-124889-2
ISBN-10: 0-13-124889-8

Vice President, Editorial Director: Gary Bennett
Acquisitions Editor: Michelle Sartor
Marketing Manager: Colleen Gauthier
Senior Developmental Editor: Madhu Ranadive
Production Editor: Lila Campbell
Copy Editor: Tom Gamblin
Proofreader: Deborah Cooper-Bullock
Production Coordinator: Sarah Lukaweski
Composition: Laserwords
Art Director: Julia Hall
Cover Design: Michelle Bellemare
Cover Image: Veer

    4 5   12

Printed and bound in Canada

Table of Contents

Preface

It is with excitement that we offer this new undergraduate ethics textbook for Canadian nursing students. The two of us have been teaching ethics to nursing students for some time and have been aware that, despite courses in ethics, many (if not most) students seem to have little understanding about how ethics theory and the Canadian Nurses Association (CNA) Code of Ethics for Registered Nurses can help to guide their practice. Our first question as we started to plan was, of course, how this book might be different from those currently on the market. That led us to the idea that we might construct a book around the Canadian Code of Ethics, and so began a lengthy journey of thinking and writing. The result is *Ethics in Canadian Nursing Practice: Navigating the Journey*. We hope you find it both interesting and useful.

Writing this book was truly an adventure: sometimes exciting, sometimes frustrating. It has taken four long years to come to fruition, because professors, like everyone else, experience life events that get in the way of getting the job done. Both of us lost our fathers during this process, leaving huge holes in our lives and hearts. Another of the many challenges we experienced was writing a book around a constantly shifting foundation. Our work coincided with the CNA's revision of its Code of Ethics. The final revised Code was the result of a process that involved many iterations based on consultations with Canadian nurses. The final version of the new Code of Ethics for Registered Nurses was released in June 2008 at the CNA annual meeting. After the revised Code was released we made our final changes, and are happy to have prepared what we think will be a good addition to the Canadian market.

We feel that there are two unique features of this book. First, it is shaped around a model for nursing ethics that we developed. The model integrates a variety of normative ethics theories, environmental influences, and other factors into a Framework for Ethical Decision Making. This model and the resultant framework have relational ethics at the core, which we believe reflects current beliefs about the nature of nursing practice. The second feature is that the book is based on values in the Canadian Code of Ethics for Registered Nurses. It is our hope that in framing the book this way we have provided students with a clear and logical way to link their practice to the Code of Ethics. We also believe that the book could have utility for nurses who are currently in practice and want a way better to understand how the Code of Ethics might guide them in providing ethical care.

The first three chapters of the book provide a foundation for the model and framework, and should ground the reader in current thinking about health care ethics and its relationship to nursing practice. Chapters four through ten are dedicated to exploring each of the Values in the Code from theoretical and practical perspectives. Each chapter includes scenarios that are reflective of current ethical issues in nursing practice, and concludes with an in-depth analysis of one or two scenarios, using the Framework for Ethical Decision Making. Key words are highlighted throughout the text and compiled in a glossary. For educators who might be using the book in undergraduate classes we have included a series of exercises and activities at the end of each chapter. These are designed to focus students' thinking and help them apply the content in their own growing understanding of ethical nursing practice. They could be used as in-class discussion topics or take-home assignments. Practicing nurses might want to use the questions to stimulate their own reflection on the various topics addressed.

To assist instructors, an Instructor's Manual is available that provides supplementary exercises and suggested answers to some of the exercises in the text. The Instructor's Manual also contains a sample course outline for a Nursing Ethics course and a link to the 2008 CNA Code of Ethics for Registered Nurses. The Instructor's Manual can be downloaded by instructors from the Pearson Education Canada website (**www.pearsoncanada.ca**).

This text is also available as a CourseSmart eTextbook. CourseSmart is a new way for instructors and students to access textbooks online anytime from anywhere. With thousands of titles across hundreds of courses, CourseSmart helps instructors choose the best textbook for their class and give their students a new option for buying the assigned textbook as a lower cost eTextbook. For more information visit **www.coursesmart.com.**

ACKNOWLEDGMENTS

We would like to thank the many people who have helped to make this book possible. First are our families, whose unfailing confidence in our ability to complete this task, made it possible for us to continue despite the challenges. We truly could not have done it without you. Second are the undergraduate students whose ideas, questions, and commitment to becoming excellent nurses made us want to produce something that would contribute to their learning. Third are our graduate students, whose ongoing feedback, questions, and enthusiasm gave us hope that we were on the right track. Fourth are our colleagues, particularly Dr. Janet Storch, who took the lead in the Code revisions. Her ongoing encouragement and willingness to share her work made it possible to complete the book in a timely fashion, and to have confidence that the product was good. We also want to thank the many people at Pearson Education who gave their time and attention to this project and maintained their "cool" when we told them, once again, that there were yet more changes to be made. They were wonderful to work with and provided us direction when needed, but also gave us space to "do our own thing." Thanks to all of you – and we hope you share our belief that this book will make a positive impact in shaping ethical nursing practice in Canada.

The publisher and authors to would like to thank the following people who provided feedback and reviewed the manuscript at various stages of the development of this text. Their comments are very much appreciated.

Connie J. Canam   University of British Columbia

Kathleen Carlin   Ryerson University

Shelley Frizzell   Conestoga College

Lyle G. Grant   Douglas College

Lorena Harvey   Fanshawe College

Amandah Hoogbruin   Kwantlen University College

Jean Hughes   Dalhousie University

Sandy Leadbeater   Humber College

Manon Lemonde   University of Ontario Institute of Technology (UOIT)

Patricia Marck   University of Alberta

Heather McAlpine   University of British Columbia

Karen Motherwell   Lambton College

Carole Orchard   University of Western Ontario

Linda Patrick   University of Windsor

Bernie Pauly   University of Victoria

Elizabeth Peter   University of Toronto

Wanda Pierson   Langara College

Thelma Riddell   University of Western Ontario

Sandra Romano   Red River College of Applied Arts and Technology

Yvonne Savard   Douglas College

Carla Shapiro   University of Manitoba

Kathleen Stephany   Douglas College

Janet L. Storch   University of Victoria

Colleen Varcoe   Langara College

Chapter 1
What Is Ethics?

Chapter Outline

Ethics Theory Described

Deontological Theories

Consequentialist Theories

Virtue Ethics

Bioethics and Biomedical Ethics

Feminist Ethics

The Evolution of Nursing Ethics

Chapter Summary

Learning Objectives

After reading this chapter, you should be able to:

- construct beginning definitions of morality, morals, and ethics
- describe the key elements of deontologist and consequentialist ethics
- describe the main principles of Kant's and Mill's ethical theories
- describe the key elements of virtue ethics
- describe the key elements of bioethics theory
- describe the key elements of feminist ethics
- discuss the evolution of nursing ethics from an historical perspective

It's safe to say that everyone has some idea of ethics and moral behaviour. Each day we make decisions based on what we think is right or wrong, or on what we think we ought (or ought not) to do. If the sales clerk returns too much change, ought we to return the extra? If we are asked for money by a panhandler on the street, ought we to walk by and ignore her, or would it be right to give her what she asks for? When we see someone apparently stranded by the side of the road, with his car hood up, ought we to stop or keep on driving? On what basis do we make these decisions? Generally speaking, we are guided by what we were taught as children and what we value.

Sometimes the response is very clear to us; other times it is not. I know without doubt I should return the money to the clerk, because I was taught that honesty is a virtue, but I'm not so sure about the panhandler. On the one hand, I think I should be charitable and help others in trouble; on the other hand, if I give her money and she spends it on something I would disapprove of, have I made her situation worse in some sense, rather than better? The stranded motorist might benefit by my help, but he might also do me considerable harm. Can I trust him? Do I owe my fellow traveller any obligation? If I leave him unaided, will I be distressed and worried about it all day?

These kinds of questions and the reasoning associated with them are the "stuff" of everyday ethics. We are constantly barraged with possibilities and choices, and must make decisions based on our understandings and our **values**, the core beliefs we hold about what is important to us. On one hand, for example, I might choose to stop at a stop sign because it is the law, and if I am caught not obeying the law I will be punished. On the other hand, I might choose to stop at the stop sign not because I fear getting caught, but because I believe that it is my duty to obey the laws of my country. I believe that laws were designed to maintain the overall good, and if citizens don't obey laws, the civil order and safety I know and cherish will disintegrate. In the first instance, my decision to obey the law is based on my fear of retribution; in the second instance, my decision is based on my understanding of my duty as a citizen. In both cases I come to the same conclusion, that I should stop at the stop sign, but the reasoning underlying my decision is very different.

Clearly, people can have varying ideas about what should be done in any of the above circumstances. Susan might be of the mind that if the clerk makes a mistake, it was meant to be, for Susan needs the money far more than the store does. Ivan might make a personal rule never to help a panhandler because he thinks that everyone should make his or her own way. Rashida might conclude that she should not stop to help a stranded motorist because if anything happens to her, she may be unable to look after her children. Each of these sets of reasoning reflects certain values and beliefs.

How, then, do people arrive at these values? Where does our understanding of "the good" come from? Are there common patterns to peoples' reasoning? Whose decision is right? The branch of philosophy that tries to make sense of all this is called **ethics**. The term **morality** is often confused with ethics. Some maintain that morality is about very personal, closely held values, while ethics is about the formalized study of morality. Others suggest that the distinction lies in the relative importance of the issues being addressed: morality is about relatively trivial, personal views, while ethics is about important issues that can be generalized. Still others would argue the opposite viewpoint: morality is about important issues, while ethics is more personal. Given the lack of agreement, we have chosen to use the terms more or less interchangeably in this book. Thus morality and ethics will both be taken as relating to how individuals (and groups) make choices about how they ought to behave or act in situations. That is, we maintain that ethics and morality are both about "right and wrong" or "ought and ought not" in human behaviour. (Generally speaking, by convention the word "ethics" is taken to be singular. We say "nursing ethics is" (rather than "nursing ethics are") when we mean the overall body of knowledge. However, we might also say "what is the nursing ethic?" when we mean a general way of thinking about things. When we use the term ethics on a more personal level we usually treat it as plural, saying "what are your ethics?").

In a profession, ideas of right and wrong might be structured in a very particular way. Our perception of our duty as professionals might change how we think about our responses to certain questions. These understandings are shaped in large part by the mandate of the profession: what the public requires from practitioners. In the health care environment, there are certain expectations of nurses, which help us recognize or define "right" behaviour. Thus nursing ethics is distinct in that it is an expression of the values and beliefs that guide nursing practice. These values and beliefs are not necessarily unique to nursing, but they are configured in a unique way because of nursing's particular mandate. Nursing is an applied discipline, so nursing ethics cannot be merely theoretical; ethics must guide action in real situations. In fact, ethics is the foundation of nursing practice, as "doing it right" is what practice is all about. Ethics is a fundamental part of every nursing action.

The purpose of this book is to help nurses think about the ethical dimensions of their practice. Every nurse will face dilemmas, where values and obligations seem to conflict. Every nurse will encounter situations in which there is no clear path to "doing good." Every nurse will discover that people view things differently, and will be challenged to defend a position which she or he thinks is "right" regarding patient care. In order to resolve those questions, make decisions with confidence and a degree of comfort, and be able to take a stance when action is called for, the nurse requires a way of reasoning and reconciling differences. We have deliberately chosen to focus on ethics rather than law in this text, as we believe that putting the two together often makes it harder to differentiate between ethical and legal issues. We recognize the importance of law, and will make reference to relevant legislation when appropriate, but we want to maintain a distinction between ethical and legal considerations in this book.

As part of developing an understanding of nursing ethics and ethical decision making, nurses should equip themselves with a working understanding of some of the ways philosophers across the ages have talked about ethics in general and how ethics is understood today. In this first chapter, we introduce you to some basic terms in ethics and to some traditional and modern ethics theory. We use practical examples to help you understand how each of these theories might affect ethical decision making. Then we turn to nursing ethics, and discuss how nursing ethics is evolving from an historical perspective, to prepare you for discussions of modern thinking about nursing ethics.

ETHICS THEORY DESCRIBED

Philosophers strive to find answers to perplexing questions that help us understand the world. They attempt to structure this understanding in the form of philosophical theories, such that their ideas can be shared, examined, and criticized. A **theory** is an idea or belief about something that is arrived at through speculation and/or research. Some theories can be tested through research, and some, such as philosophical theories, are not really testable. Instead, they simply provide us with an idea about how different things might work, the meanings of abstract concepts, or how things ought to be done. Thus theory can be descriptive, explanatory, or prescriptive. A **descriptive theory** describes phenomena as observed, and is therefore generally an outcome of research. Such theory is generally developed by social scientists and nurses, rather than moral philosophers. An **explanatory theory** explains how things might work, what meanings people give to certain events, or how people think about abstract concepts. Theories of this type are based primarily on reflection and conjecture. **Prescriptive theory** gives us direction. It tells us how we should think about things, or how things ought to be done, and is usually generated as a result of research and reflection.

Philosophy is divided into branches depending on the kinds of questions philosophers are attempting to answer. The field of ethics, also called moral philosophy, addresses questions of right and wrong, or ought and ought not. Moral philosophers who tell us what people do or think about moral issues generate descriptive moral theory. Such theory describes the rules, principles, and values that people apply when making moral decisions or judgments, and how those rules, principles, and values apply differently in different situations. For example, a descriptive theory might emerge from studies of how nurses make moral decisions in practice. However, philosophers are seldom satisfied with mere description. Ethics is about what ought to be, not just about what is. Therefore, when looking at a descriptive moral theory philosophers ask, "Do we believe this is the right way to make moral decisions just because many people do it this way?" Answering that question requires an understanding of what "the right way" would be. The area of philosophy that generates descriptive theory about where our understanding of right or good comes from is called **metaethics**. A person studying metaethics might ask if "good" is a social invention, an expression of emotion, or the will of a higher power. When we say something is good, are we really just saying "I approve of this and you should as well," or does our understanding of what is right and good come from a higher authority such as God? Is good "out there" to be discovered, or is it really socially constructed? In other words, is there a true "right," or do we in society just make it up as we go along, and on what basis can moral judgments be assessed as true or false?

Another branch of moral philosophy is normative ethics. A **normative ethics theory** is prescriptive, in that it tells us how we ought to think about moral questions. Normative ethics theories present us with rules, values, and principles that allow us to judge the quality of moral decisions. In other words, they give us a set of rules that are meant to direct the way in which we make and evaluate decisions. Normative ethics theories are theories of obligation, that is to say, they deal with what we are morally required to do.

Applied ethics (or practical ethics) deals with more specific questions about how decisions should be made in particular situations. Using concepts from metaethics and normative ethics, applied ethics seeks to provide answers to controversial issues, and to suggest what moral beliefs and values should apply in specific contexts. Applied ethics theory is both descriptive and prescriptive. Theories that address issues of right or ought in different professions are included in the domain of applied ethics. Thus there are branches of applied philosophy that deal with ethics in journalism, law, medicine, and business, among others. Of particular concern to us in this book is the branch of applied ethics that helps us understand "right" behaviour within the practice of nursing.

In order to understand the development of nursing ethics, we need some understanding of normative theories that have shaped our thinking. We will begin our discussion by outlining three kinds of moral theories that have had a huge impact on thinking about ethics in nursing: deontological theory, particularly that of Immanuel Kant; consequentialist theory as espoused by John Stuart Mill; and virtue theory. We will then describe feminist ethics and bioethics before turning to nursing ethics.

Deontological Theories

Deontology, from the Greek word *deon*, which means duty, and *logos*, which in Greek can mean a theory, a rule or law, or even the ability to reason, is based on the belief that humans have the capacity to think through problems and determine right action based on **duty**, the obligation to act according to particular rules or principles. According to deontologists, doing one's duty is right, and failing to do one's duty is wrong. Thus, if we are to make correct moral choices, we need to know the rules and follow them. There are numerous deontological **theories of obligation** that tell us what the rules are or where they come from. For example, **theories of Divine Command** tell us that we must follow rules determined by a deity or god. **Rights theories** say that our duty is in ensuring that human rights are protected. **Contractarian theories** suggest that our duty lies in following rules that all rational people engaged in social interaction, that is to say, in a social contract, would agree were right. There are many versions of each of these approaches, but they go beyond the scope of this book. Here we will address in more detail the most famous deontological theory, that of Immanuel Kant.

Kantian Ethics Immanuel Kant (1724–1804) is considered the father of modern deontology. He published *Foundations of the Metaphysics of Morals* in 1785, and it is still debated and challenged by moral philosophers to this day. Although Kant's thinking is very complex, the essentials can be summarized fairly easily. The following interpretation reflects content from a number of Kant-related web sites, listed in the reference section of this chapter.

Kant's central concepts were reason and freedom, the duality of the human condition, good will, and duty. First, Kant started with the assumption that people are free to make choices. If human behaviour was predetermined, perhaps by fate, then thinking about choice would make no sense. Kant's view was that we *are* able to make choices, and that these choices, at least the ones related to morals, must never be based on emotions, but on reason alone. He believed that we cannot know the ultimate nature of things, but we can work out rules of conduct through observation and reason. The duality of the human condition refers to Kant's belief that humans do not act only according to reason, nor wholly according to natural impulse, namely emotions, senses, or feelings. Instead, we are capable of acting on either. Therefore, we need ways to determine what is the right way to act, as our reason might be affected by our emotions, senses, or feelings.

According to Kant, the only thing that has true moral worth is good will. Good will must be the underlying motivation for action, and it is realized only when we act according to our duty, not out of emotion or consideration of consequences. Our duty is determined from **maxims**, logical principles that are based on reason. One way we can determine what the maxims should be is by considering what Kant called the **Categorical Imperative**, a rule that has no exceptions. Kant gave several versions of the Categorical Imperative. One is stated as: *Act only on that maxim whereby you can at the same time will that it should become a universal law.* In other words, only act according to those rules that you believe should be applicable to all persons in all cases. To illustrate how this would work, Kant used an example, asking us to imagine that we needed to borrow money, but knew that we would not be able to repay it. We could, he suggested, lie and say that we would pay it back. However, if we thought about our actions and tried to put them into a universal law, we would quickly see that the law would be unworkable. If all persons who wanted to borrow money were permitted to lie about repaying it, no one would ever trust borrowers, and lending would cease. More broadly, if everyone were permitted to make promises they had no intention of keeping, the whole idea of promises would be ridiculed, as no one would ever expect a promise to be kept.

Thus Kant's basic premise was that we are only acting morally if we act according to duty as understood through universal laws or maxims. Doing something because we want to do it, even if it has good consequences, cannot be moral. If we do something we do not want to do because it is our duty, it would be moral even if it has bad consequences for someone else. Doing something just because we want to or because we think it will make someone feel better is not moral, even if it has good consequences. For example, consider the statement "one must never lie," which Kant suggested was a good example of a maxim. Assume for the moment that you have accepted this maxim. Now consider the following case:

Martin is a private in the Canadian army, doing a tour of duty in Afghanistan. When his troop was on routine patrol, a terrorist bomb exploded, killing Martin's best friend Andy and wounding several others. Andy's death was an agonizing one, as a large piece of metal had penetrated his chest. According to Martin, who held Andy and tried to comfort him as he died, he drowned in his own blood. As he and Andy had been very close, Martin phoned Andy's parents. They asked him, "Did Andy suffer?" and Martin replied, "He didn't know what hit him—it was all over so fast."

Was Martin's action morally acceptable? If one accepted the maxim never to lie, Martin's actions would be unacceptable. On deciding whether or not to tell the truth, a

Kantian would reason along the following lines. "For me to say it is acceptable to lie in this situation, I must be able to form a universal rule that lying is acceptable. If I am permitted to lie because I think I am helping someone, then others must be permitted to lie to me. If lying is acceptable, then people will expect others to lie, and there will be no trust. I cannot accept that. Therefore, I cannot form a universal rule that says lying is acceptable." Once a Kantian had established that one could not form a universal rule that permitted lying, her or his duty would be clear: she or he would be obligated to tell the truth. This kind of reasoning led to Kant's idea of the **golden rule**—*do unto others only that which you are prepared to have them do unto you.*

Kant offered another formulation of the Categorical Imperative, stated as: *Act so that you treat humanity, whether in your own person or in that of another, always as an end and never as a means only.* In other words, one must never use others as a means to an end, but must always consider them as an end unto themselves. The basis of this maxim was that people are inherently deserving of respect, and using others as a means to an end is disrespectful. If a person is treated only as a means to an end, it implies that the person has worth only insofar as he or she enables an end to be reached. This is contrary to Kant's belief that people have intrinsic worth.

As part of his treatise on moral thought, Kant also spoke about the importance of treating people as autonomous agents, that is to say, as being able to make decisions for themselves. This kind of thinking is the basis of much of today's dialogue about autonomy and informed consent, important concepts in the ethics of health care. If we were to act according to Kant's view of ethics, we would never make decisions for others if they are able to make decisions for themselves, even if we believed we were acting in the person's best interests. To do so is morally unacceptable.

If we were to use Kant's deontological theory of obligation to guide our actions, then our duty would be to act always according to universalizable rules, as outlined above. We would always have to ask ourselves if the action we proposed to take were based on a principle that could be applied in all cases. We would question ourselves as to whether our actions degraded others by using them as a means to an end or by taking away their autonomy.

The strengths of Kantian ethics include its appeal to reason as a measure of the rightness of our actions. It allows us to be impartial and to act consistently. The major criticism of Kant's moral theory is that it does not allow us to make exceptions. In the example above, most people would want a moral theory that would permit us to save Andy's parents additional grief. In other words, most of us would want to be able to say that the consequences and the intent of our actions ought to count. Following Kant's view, we would act according to duty or reason, but never according to kindness (a natural impulse). For most people that would seem unsatisfactory. However, elements of Kantian thinking can be found in most debates about health care ethics. Certainly the idea of duty is a part of any nursing dialogue. In later chapters we will examine this influence more thoroughly, as we consider specific clinical situations in which the nurse must examine her or his duty and relevant rules of conduct guiding practice.

1.1 Using a Deontological Perspective

Ardith works on a pediatric plastic surgery unit in a large urban hospital. One of the surgeons specializes in facial reconstruction for children who have been disfigured by accidents, surgery, or congenital diseases. Lupe is eight years old. She was born with a number of congenital anomalies, including cleft lip and palate, a deformed nose, an almost absent chin, and very prominent orbital bones. As a result, she has suffered merciless teasing from her classmates, and her schooling has suffered. She was admitted to the unit for a radical rebuilding of her face. The bandages have just come off, and Ardith looks at the child's face with horror. It looks like the surgeon failed in his mission to make Lupe more normal looking. In fact, she looks worse, if possible. Ardith has a lot of experience on the plastics unit and has never seen anything as troubling as this. From her experience, it seems unlikely that Lupe will ever have a good

result. As soon as the bandages are off, Lupe asks excitedly, "How do I look?" Her parents look shocked, but they are not familiar with post-operative appearance, and ask Ardith what she thinks.

Ardith is truly perplexed about how to respond to this question. Should she tell the truth? She has always thought of herself as a good nurse who does her duty, but what is her duty in this case? She thinks about Kant's Categorical Imperative and thinks about his position on lying. From a Kantian perspective, reasoning would suggest that lying for any reason is wrong, but how can she answer Lupe and her parents? What should she say?

1. As a person using a Kantian deontological perspective, how would you answer Lupe and her parents?

2. Does using a version of Categorical Imperative feel comfortable to you in this situation? Why or why not?

Consequentialist Theories

Consequentialism suggests that we think about right and wrong in terms of the consequences or outcomes of actions and of one's obligation to act to make sure certain outcomes are achieved. They start with the premise that happiness or pleasure is a moral good, and that we can bring about such happiness as a consequence of our actions. Obligation is then defined in terms of maximizing good consequences and minimizing bad. Unlike deontological ethics, consequentialism says there are no absolute rules or duties that guide action. Instead, each act is evaluated based on its anticipated outcome. There are many versions of consequentialism. We will explore one consequentialist theory in more detail.

Utilitarianism Perhaps the most famous consequentialist theory is that of **utilitarianism**, which defines "good" in terms of utility or usefulness in promoting happiness. There are a number of utilitarian theories dating back to the time of the Romans, but John Stuart Mill (1806–1873) proposed the most famous utilitarian theory, building on ideas put forward by earlier philosophers such as David Hume (1711–1776) and Jeremy Bentham (1748–1832). Mill maintained that our main obligation is to maximize happiness overall. Mill's key idea was the **principle of utility**, which called for *the greatest good for the greatest number*. According to Mill, our obligation is to act to ensure the maximum amount of happiness for the greatest number of people. Mill described happiness as a form of pleasure that was not restricted only to the physical, but included intellectual pleasure as well.

Consider euthanasia, or mercy killing, as an example of how a person might approach a problem from a utilitarian perspective. An individual in extreme agony requests release in the form of euthanasia. A utilitarian might justify complying with this request on the grounds that it would produce the greatest happiness for the individual involved, as well as those who must watch that person suffer. Moreover, it would save resources that could then be used to help others. "Greatest good" arguments are often brought into play when considering issues of **distributive justice**, or, in other words, how scarce dollars can be best distributed, or how we can get maximum benefit from our resources. Utilitarianism would also allow us to override an individual's objections to immunization, arguing that the greatest good would be served if that individual were prevented from contracting and then spreading a contagious disease.

Of course utilitarianism has its critics. Reasoning on the basis that the *end justifies the means* could allow one to justify some rather questionable acts if they led to a greater good. For example, they could lead one to say that torture of terrorists is acceptable if it means that it might help prevent further terrorist atrocities. Not everyone would agree with the conclusion that the greater good justifies such action. Utilitarian reasoning supports capital punishment as well, and clearly that is a matter of hot debate.

Some moral philosophers have concluded that the underlying concepts of utilitarianism are reasonable, but the problem lies in interpretation. That is, they suggest that the idea of maximizing good is a sound basis for moral thought, but what is needed is a clearer understanding of how we can achieve maximum good. They believe that the classical approach described above, which they call **act utilitarianism**, is limited because it requires us to anticipate the outcomes of every act, and judge it on the principle of utility. This, they say, is unwieldy and fails to take into account long-term consequences of acts. For example, act utilitarianism could lead one to the conclusion that harvesting organs from a healthy person and distributing them to a number of unhealthy people is reasonable, because it leads to a greater good. This could lead to some unpleasant long-term consequences for healthy individuals and is contrary to what most people would think is right. As an alternative, philosophers have suggested that a better approach would be what they call **rule utilitarianism**, which is still consequentialist, but would require us to adopt general rules likely to promote the greatest good for the greatest number. In other words, one should ask, "What general rules would maximize happiness?" In the above example, rule utilitarianism would call for a rule that protects healthy people but still makes healthy organs available to transplant candidates, as our current organ donation system works. Thus it requires us to use rules to bring about certain consequences.

Even with this rule-based reformulation of the classic theory, critics still argue that utilitarianism does not properly take into account ideas of justice, rights, or respect for persons. Judging an act simply for its consequences seems to go against our moral intuition that some things could be morally right in and of themselves. Still, it is difficult to reject utilitarianism outright. It seems logical to suggest that the consequences of one's actions are important, and that actions that promote happiness and lessen misery are, to some extent, right. Many philosophers continue to maintain that utilitarianism is the soundest basis for modern moral thought that we have to date.

Utilitarianism is very much a factor in many discussions of health care ethics, and in subsequent chapters we will discuss clinical cases in which utilitarian ethics offers us important insights. It is important to recognize that even though people are using utilitarian (or deontological, or feminist) theory, they may not be aware of the basis of their beliefs or the congruence between their beliefs and ethics theory. In fact, many, if not most, people do not reflect upon or know the basis of their decision making. They may even fail to see that their decision making involves ethics at all. We will attempt to demonstrate how thinking about clinical situations can be influenced by ethics theory in any of its many forms.

Trying It On

1.2 Applying a Utilitarian Perspective

Howard is a public health nurse working in an inner-city community. He is somewhat troubled about one of the practices in his health unit. The administration wants at least 95% of the children in the community to be immunized. Nurses seek consent for immunization from the children's parents. Howard has noticed that many of the parents do not speak much English, and he worries that they are not really giving informed consent. Instead, he believes they are just signing the form without any understanding of it because they want to do what is expected. There are few interpreters in the area, so for efficiency, most of the nurses choose to ignore this ethical concern. They also want to get their immunization numbers up.

Howard understands that it is important that children be immunized, because immunization has dramatically reduced the incidence of communicable diseases and their associated symptoms and side effects. He realizes that some common childhood diseases, such as measles, can have long-term consequences. He is also aware that if immunization numbers decrease and more people contract these preventable diseases, it will put a huge strain on the already overburdened health care system. Still, he wonders whether it is right to ignore the fact that some parents are not giving fully informed consent.

1. How would a person using a utilitarian perspective think about these issues?

2. Do the utilitarian arguments you have constructed seem comfortable to you?

3. What do you think Howard should do?

Virtue Ethics

The two theoretical approaches we have discussed thus far focus exclusively on actions, requiring us to consider how we ought to *act* in a given situation. These approaches pay little attention to how we ought to *be*. Asking how we ought to be enables us to focus on the characteristics of a moral person. The importance of putting the person's characteristics at the centre of moral thought was first articulated by Aristotle (384–322 BCE). He believed that a person who demonstrated certain **virtues** or moral elements of character would make correct moral choices. Virtues can to some extent be learned or acquired. Aristotle articulated a number of virtues, the highest of which was self-respect. **Virtue ethics**, which is the school of thought that says good people will make good decisions, was considered less than useful by most moral philosophers, particularly after Kant's ideas were published. This was partly because the virtues Aristotle described (including temperance, civility, and friendliness) seem somewhat outmoded or out of place in more modern moral theory, and partly because there was debate about which virtues were important. Recently, however, there has been a resurgence of interest in virtues, particularly among those who focus on health care ethics. Virtue ethics appeals to our intuitive sense that one who cares for vulnerable people ought to demonstrate particular personal characteristics.

Aristotle defined human good loosely in terms of well-being, a similar concept to happiness. However, unlike the utilitarians, he did not suggest that people should evaluate their actions according to whether they would maximize well-being. Rather, he believed that people who possessed certain dispositions or characteristics, which he called virtues, would naturally choose well, such that well-being for themselves (and others) would result. He discussed what he called "practical wisdom," which he said is about making right choices. According to Aristotle, making right choices requires having the requisite virtues, then learning to use them appropriately through practice. He held that one has to practice "virtuous actions" to become virtuous and that to be able to choose virtuous actions one must possess virtues. This seems like rather circular thinking, but it means that one must have the motivation and basic character elements to *want* to choose well, and that with effort one can learn to make more virtuous decisions. The emphasis on choice makes it clear that, as moral agents, we are responsible for our actions.

When Aristotle talked about choice, he indicated that a virtue enables one to choose the middle ground between excess and deficiency. He called this the **golden mean**. Thus a virtuous person would be brave but not reckless, controlled but not unduly limited, industrious but not obsessed with work. In other words, the virtuous person would make balanced choices that would lead to well-being.

As was mentioned above, Aristotle's theory of ethics had for some time fallen out of favour. One criticism of virtue ethics is that it does not provide us with definitive answers to moral questions. It is more about personal characteristics, not moral decisions as such. It assumes that if we are good people we will make good decisions, but it does not give us any way to determine what a good decision is. Another criticism has been the difficulty

1.3 Thinking about Virtue

"All I have to do is pass" was Nadine's motto in nursing school. She decided right from the beginning that she would do the bare minimum required to get through. She didn't like the nursing program much and wasn't really sure that she wanted to be a nurse, but she knew the money would be good when she graduated, so she kept going. Every weekend she partied until late into the night, and was often hungover in her Monday classes. Most of her weekday evenings were spent on her two part-time jobs. It wasn't that she really needed the money, as her parents were supporting her, but she liked nice clothes and needed the extra cash to keep up her sense of style. She wasn't worried much about whether she was learning enough to enable her to provide safe care in the future. By her reasoning, passing with a low grade was no big deal—it was only important that she pass at all. She often made mistakes when she was in clinical, but the instructor was divided between two units and was seldom there to catch the errors. Really, the errors hadn't been all that serious, and patients didn't know the difference, so what did it matter? She reasoned that it was up to someone else to tell her she should leave nursing. As long as they didn't fail her, she was satisfied with doing as little as possible.

1. What are the links to virtue theory in this scenario?
2. What characteristics should a nurse possess? Does Nadine demonstrate these characteristics?

in defining which characteristics are virtues. Nonetheless, Aristotle's ideas require us, when faced with difficult decisions, to ask fundamental questions such as: "What kind of person do I wish to be in this situation? What will this require of me, and do I wish to be the kind of person who can fulfill this requirement?" Without such questions it is difficult to imagine one reflecting on moral decisions or growing in ability to make right choices. Increasingly, those who think about health care ethics are suggesting that characteristics such as honesty, trustworthiness, and compassion are needed in the provision of excellent care. Thus virtue ethics is becoming more a part of ethical thinking as our understanding of health care ethics grows and evolves.

Bioethics and Biomedical Ethics

To this point we have been discussing important normative ethics theories (and their critiques) that are very general in scope. Theories of this type are intended to help us understand and structure moral thinking in the broadest perspective. The problem is that, because they are so general, these theories often fail to provide guidance in specific situations. Of particular concern to us is the limited direct application of such theories in professional settings such as health care; none of the theories cited above gives a satisfactory account of what to do when conflicts arise. Certainly, anyone who has worked in health care recognizes that conflicts do arise and difficult decisions have to be made. How, then, are we to resolve these conflicts or, at the least, make the best possible decision? How can ethics theory help us in specific situations?

These were questions facing a group of young scholars at Georgetown University in the United States in the early 1970s. They had concluded that the current theories were not sufficiently practical in that they did not give sufficient guidance for the important moral questions arising in medicine. They decided to try to rectify that deficiency by proposing theories that would specifically serve medicine. The most famous of these theories was put forward by Thomas Beauchamp (pronounced "beecham") and James Childress in their landmark book *Principles of Biomedical Ethics* (1979). As mentioned, **biomedical ethics** as a theory was intended to guide medical practitioners in ethical decision making; however, the basic ideas were quickly adopted by other health professionals, including nurses, and new terminology came into play. Biomedical ethics came to denote ethical reasoning for physicians, while **bioethics** became the more general term for principled reasoning across health care professions. Bioethics is often used interchangeably with health care ethics, but there are some important differences. **Health care ethics** is generally understood to refer to ethics in the broader sphere. That is, it includes ethical decision making at the policy and systems level, whereas bioethics generally refers to the provider-patient relationship.

Biomedical ethics as first described by Beauchamp and Childress was in some sense an amalgamation of elements of the theories described above, but it was unique in its approach. Certainly it was a theory of obligation, but it was obligation of a very particular kind, that of physician to patient. It was clearly outcome-oriented, as the physician is seen as obligated to achieve the best possible health care outcome, and it was based on reason. However, it also required the physician to take into account the consequences of his or her actions. In essence, the theory suggested that doctors should examine each situation; consider their response to the situation in terms of a set of four principles, autonomy, beneficence, non-maleficence, and justice; determine which of the principles has priority; and use that principle to guide action. Criticisms levelled at this approach (often by feminists), such as its neglect of issues related to the physician-patient relationship, have resulted in numerous revisions, and the book is now in its fifth edition. Each revision has attempted to address challenges to the theory, bringing in new thinking. The result is that the book has stayed current and remains probably the most widely cited and taught medical ethics textbook ever written for North American audiences. Certainly it has had considerable impact on nursing ethics, and as such deserves detailed attention here.

Despite the many revisions, basic elements of the theory are essentially the same as first proposed. The original four principles—autonomy, beneficence, non-maleficence, and justice—remain central to decision making. These principles were not invented by Beauchamp and Childress; rather, the principles had first been described in an earlier document (The Belmont Report) designed to address issues in the ethics of scientific research. Beauchamp and Childress's contribution was in bringing them directly into the domain of medical ethics, and showing how they could guide decision making by doctors in ethically problematic situations.

In describing the autonomy principle, Beauchamp and Childress (2001) explain that it involves one's ability to make choices for oneself, and that these choices should be based on full understanding, free of controlling influences. **Autonomy** is about having both the right and the ability to make meaningful choices about oneself (and one's care). The principle of autonomy dictates that physicians should respect a person's autonomy whenever possible. When health care decisions are made, the person's right to choose must be given primary emphasis, and the physician must consider whether the individual is free to make a choice and has the capacity to do so. For example, when deciding whether or not to write Do Not Resuscitate (DNR) orders, physicians must determine whether patients have the capacity to decide for themselves how they want care to proceed. In the absence of such capacity, the physician is obligated to get as much information as possible to determine what the patient would probably choose if capacity were present, and then make a decision, with support of the family if present. Autonomy is the key concept driving our current insistence on informed consent for health care interventions and research. As discussed above, the notion of autonomy comes directly from Kant's ethics and his idea of respect for persons.

The second principle is the principle of **beneficence**, which is the obligation to do what is best for the patient. Thus it speaks directly to duty or obligation, as do deontological theories. Before bioethics emerged as a key force in health care, beneficence was the main focus in care delivery. It was generally expected that the physician would know what was best for patients and make decisions accordingly. For example, a physician might make a decision to do a high amputation of the patient's leg and both arms, knowing that the presence of gangrene necessitated that action for the patient's survival. Today we take a somewhat different view of who should make decisions, believing that paternalism is undesirable. Paternalism is a term that originated from the idea of a father having the right to make decisions for his child in the child's best interests, without the child's consent or involvement. In the health care context **paternalism** is defined as doctors (or other health care providers) making decisions for patients in the patients' best interests, again without their consent. Making a decision without seeking the patient's consent clearly conflicts with the principle of autonomy. In the example above, had the patient been asked, he might well have refused treatment, believing it was better to die than live without limbs. If we maintain the principle of autonomy, however, decisions made on the principle of beneficence will not be paternalistic. The physician has an obligation always to act in what she or he believes to be in the patient's best interests, to the best of her or his ability, and with as complete knowledge as possible. Such knowledge includes patients' wishes. Conflicts arise, though, when the patient's best interests conflict with what the patient wants. Consider the patient who is suicidal and has declared his intent. Is the physician obligated to prevent this act or not? If we consider capacity, we might argue that the patient does not have the ability to make good choices, and the decision should be made on the basis of best interests. But we might argue equally strongly that the patient does have the capacity—that the fact that he is making a decision different from what we would think reasonable does not automatically mean he lacks capacity—and autonomy should be honoured. The conflict between autonomy and beneficence leads to some of the most powerful and thought-provoking reflections and debates in health care.

The principle of **non-maleficence** is in some ways the "flip side" of the principle of beneficence. It means *do no harm* and is generally recognized as the primary duty of the physician. Consequently, non-maleficence becomes a key principle in debates about such things as termination of treatment. Clearly, the question arises as to how "harm" should be defined and who should define it. If the physician feels that a suffering patient's treatment should be stopped because it is futile and merely extending the patient's pain, but the family, hoping for a miracle, wants care to continue, whose viewpoint should be given priority? Which would do more harm to the patient, continuing treatment or stopping it? Such debates happen with great frequency in the acute care environment.

The last principle is the principle of **justice**. The common understanding of justice is "fairness"; however, a more philosophical definition would be to "treat equals equally and unequals unequally." For example, if one person has less than another, justice dictates that considerations or compensations are put in place to make it fairer to the disadvantaged person. In other words, we "level the playing field" to equalize advantage and disadvantage. Justice usually becomes an issue when scarce resources must be distributed. That is, when there is competition for a scarce resource, justice demands that decisions be fair and, to the extent possible, unbiased. In decisions about who gets the heart for transplant, for example, it is understood that the heart will be allocated as fairly as possible. Understandings of fairness will depend on community values. Thus, in Canadian society, community standards dictate that it should not be sufficient to say that one patient will pay more or is of more value to society. The decision should not turn on who has the higher intellect or larger salary; instead, we demand that the decision be made on need alone. Of course, the definition of need can be debated, and when two people are of equal need there is nothing in the theory that helps us decide between them.

Other scholars of bioethics, including Canadians Michael Yeo and Anne Moorhouse who have written about nursing ethics (1996), have incorporated a number of other principles such as fidelity (honouring promises, faithfulness), veracity (truth-telling), and confidentiality. However, Beauchamp and Childress maintain that these are not principles of the same moral weight as the original four. Instead, they suggest that all these are not separate principles, but rather a part of the patient-physician relationship. As such they are still important but are not given the same kind of emphasis as the principles themselves (Beauchamp & Childress, 2001).

The principled approach to moral reasoning does not offer foolproof answers to moral questions. It may be difficult to define capacity, harm, and justice in particular situations. There may also be overlap among the principles, or competition between them. It may not be possible to respect a patient's autonomy and at the same time serve the principle of justice if, for example, the patient chooses something that must be given to someone

1.4 Using Bioethical Principles

Mei, a nurse on a medical unit, was very distressed. Her 94-year-old stroke patient, Mr. Jonas, had just been told that the stroke had permanently damaged his ability to swallow. The physician recommended a PEG tube, a permanent feeding tube inserted through the abdominal wall into the stomach, as Mr. Jonas would be unable to take nourishment any other way. He was already on tube feedings and had severe diarrhea. With the partial paralysis from his stroke, he was unable to get to the bathroom in time and had been incontinent of liquid, foul-smelling stool on numerous occasions. He realized that the problem would not disappear with a permanent PEG, and he also knew he would not be permitted to eat or drink anything. With tears rolling down his cheeks, he refused the procedure and any further active treatment, including intravenous fluids. He could not live with the indignity of this diarrhea and couldn't bear the thought of never being able to enjoy a cup of coffee or a piece of chocolate for the rest of his life. He said he would rather die than face that kind of life. In refusing feeding he hoped he would die quickly. That fact did not frighten him; his fear and sorrow were for his family, who would have to watch him die. Mei and the doctor left the room, both of them very shaken up, and the doctor questioned Mr. Jonas' capacity to make the decision to stop feeding and treatment. Mei believed him to be entirely competent and wondered what she should do. Should she stand up for his right to choose?

1. How do the principles of autonomy, beneficence, and non-maleficence come into play here?

2. How do they conflict? Which principle has priority?

3. What would you do if you were the nurse? Why? What is the basis for your decision? What kinds of issues would you consider?

else. However, the principles certainly provide a structured way of thinking about problems, provide a basis on which to approach problem resolution, and open possibilities for discussion and exploration. The theory has its critics, but overall, the bioethical principles outlined by Beauchamp and Childress have been hugely influential in shaping thinking about medical ethics. The principles have also been used widely in nursing ethics, as will be discussed below.

Feminist Ethics

As mentioned earlier, all the above theories have their critics. One of the most important recent challenges to traditional ethics and bioethics theory has come from feminist scholars. In general, feminist ethicists have denounced traditional ethics theory for being based essentially on a male point of view. For example, the virtues Aristotle described (such as courage) tend to be those of men in the public domain, whereas more feminine virtues (such as nurturing) are ignored entirely. Feminists charge that traditional theories do not serve women well because they do not take into account the kinds of issues that are of importance to women. In other words, feminists believe that traditional ethics theory is gender biased and based on customs that subjugate women and make them subservient to men. Surely, they maintain, an ethics theory should question these traditions and speak against gender-related issues of powerlessness, inequality, and injustice. From the feminist perspective an ethics theory that does not address such issues is incomplete. There is no single feminist alternative to traditional ethics theory. Rather, there are many feminist approaches, all of which are similar in that they challenge existing theory, raise key questions, and attempt to expose issues of gender bias, power, and oppression. The underlying values, according to a group of noted feminist nursing scholars, are social justice, relationships, and community (Peter, Lunardi, & Macfarlane, 2004).

Hilde Lindemann Nelson, a noted American feminist scholar, has provided an interesting history (2000) of the development of feminist ethics and bioethics. She notes that the feminist attention to gender and gender issues gave rise to an important perspective called **care theory**, a type of virtue ethic that gives moral weight to caring for others. This was an important development in thinking about ethics because it moved attention away from the traditional masculine virtues toward those that had traditionally been considered more feminine. In fact, some have called care theory a feminine, rather than a feminist, ethic. Many, if not most, feminist scholars maintain that feminist ethics is about more than just care theory. It is also about thinking about ethics in a totally different way that is neither utilitarian, Kantian, virtue, or biomedical theory. These scholars "reject the role of the ideal ethical reasoner as a solitary and powerful—read masculine—judge who applies lawlike principles derived from one or several of these theories to the case at hand" (Nelson, p. 494). Instead they see "ethical deliberation as an expressive-collaborative process" (p. 494) in which people work together to find common meanings and understandings about "who is responsible for what to whom" (p. 494). Narrative ethics is a form of feminist ethics that enables such understandings to be developed through story or narrative. That is, narrative ethics requires that we listen to details about social context, personal history, and factors that have shaped the "who" of the story. As Nelson points out, "understanding how we got 'here' is crucial to the determination of where we might be able to go from here, and this is where narrative is indispensable" (p. 501). In other words, if we are to make ethical decisions, we must hear the voices and stories of those involved and consider their social context.

One of the great contributions of feminist scholars is that they have placed culturally embedded elements that were not formerly thought of as moral issues, for example, the dominance of men's values and ideas, into the domain of ethics. Feminists have made it evident that there are other perspectives and voices that need to be acknowledged and heard, and have challenged us to take these into account. More specifically, in health care ethics feminists have caused us to think about our relationships with patients as part of any consideration of ethics and ethics problems. They suggest that the people with power in a health care situation are the professional care providers, not the patients. A kind of vulnerability is built into being a patient; patients require something from care providers that could be withheld, which gives care providers power. The voice of the patient (or family) has seldom been heard in deliberations about care decisions, and the most vulnerable, such as the elderly or the mentally challenged, have been silenced the most.

Feminist theory asks that we look at relationships and power differentials, and make sure that the voice of the vulnerable is heard and that power differentials are reduced or eliminated. They also call for us to consider whether there is gender bias in the way resources for care and for health research are allocated. They raise awareness about the gendered nature of research and the kinds of thinking that are given privilege in the allocation of research dollars. In showing how the concerns of the rich and powerful may be studied more readily than the needs of the poor and vulnerable, feminists point to the need for research that is free of gender and power imbalances. They argue for science that is more inclusive and more open to the subjective experience of the person or persons being studied.

It seems reasonable to think that issues of power, oppression, and social context would be of concern in health care ethics, as medicine is one of the strongest, most dominant forces in our culture. However, according to Nelson, early feminist influences on bioethics were largely limited to considerations of women's reproductive issues. As recently as the year 2000, she charged that there was much work to be done in moving feminist critique to broader health care issues, such as organizational ethics, which addresses the hierarchical structures that shape experiences of patients and caregivers alike (Nelson, 2000). Since that time there has been a lot more interest in developing feminist bioethics or health care ethics. Interestingly, some of the most important recent advances have come from feminist nurse scholars, who have had enormous influence in shaping nursing ethics. Examples include Varcoe and colleagues, a group of nurses from the Universities of Victoria and British Columbia (Varcoe, C, et al., 2004; Varcoe, Rodney, & McCormick, 2003) and Elizabeth Peter (Peter, Macfarlane, & O'Brien-Pallas, 2004; Peter, Lunardi, & Macfarlane, 2004) from University of Toronto.

These scholars have begun to expose some of the forces of dominance and oppression that influence nursing work and life. Their questions and concerns have led to a revolution in how nursing ethics is being thought and written about. As a result of feminist thinking, ethics of care and relationship are being placed at the centre in nursing ethics. We will discuss this shift in thinking again as we examine how nursing ethics is evolving, and you will find evidence of feminist thinking woven throughout our entire discussion of nursing ethics in the remainder of this book.

THE EVOLUTION OF NURSING ETHICS

Having considered the most common theories influencing ethics in nursing, we now turn to the idea of nursing ethics theory as a separate entity. To understand current thinking, nurses need an understanding of how nursing ethics has changed over time. We will therefore outline a brief history of nursing ethics, particularly as it has evolved in the North

Shaheen is a research nurse working for a group of physicians in a neurosurgical research program. The group has several clinical trials under way to study new procedures and medications. Part of Shaheen's responsibility is to recruit patients to the various studies. She has an ongoing concern about recruitment, because she feels that patients are sometimes pressured into taking part in the studies. The researchers are also caregivers, and Shaheen feels that sometimes patients agree to be in the studies just because they want to please the doctor or because they are afraid they will not get the same care from the doctor if they don't take part. She worries that some patients might be highly inconvenienced or even put at risk as a result of being part of a study, and she is not always sure that they fully understand the risks or consider them in their decision making. She thinks their decisions are based more on trying to please the doctor than on a true understanding of the risks and benefits of the study. She wonders if this is a problem she should bring up at the group meetings.

1. How might a person using a feminist approach identify the problem?

2. Do you see links between Shaheen's concerns and feminist ideas?

3. What do you think Shaheen should do? What might be the implications of different actions for Shaheen as an employee? As a nurse?

American context. Much of this abbreviated version of events is based on the writing of Dr. Marianne Lamb, a prominent Canadian nurse historian and ethicist (Lamb, 2004).

The history of nursing ethics is embedded in the history of nursing as such, because nursing ethics is about how nurses ought and ought not to act. It cannot, therefore, be understood outside the social and political context in which nurses practice. It is clear that the values of the nursing profession in Canada were highly influenced by the French Roman Catholic nuns who provided care for the sick very early in Canadian history. Not a great deal is documented about ethics at that time, but certainly Christian values were paramount. At the time of Florence Nightingale, when formalized nursing and nursing education became a reality, nurses worked primarily in the home setting, providing care for patients in their own environments. Nursing writings from this era emphasized characteristics of the nurse related primarily to etiquette and general comportment. A "good" nurse was one who was courteous, quiet, loyal, obedient, and respectful, which were qualities expected of any "well bred" woman of the time. Nurses were also expected to be unselfish and kind in their care of patients. These kinds of traits were emphasized in nursing education for several decades, although nurses at the beginning of the twentieth century were beginning to write about nursing ethics as such and were calling for a code of ethics to guide practice. By the mid-1920s, there was discussion that the ideal of unquestioning respect for authority might be inappropriate for a professional body.

In the period from about 1930 to the late 1960s, there was a shift in location of nursing work, with a move from home to hospital. This brought the idea of professional nursing obligations into focus, as nursing became more visible and at the same time more theory-based. Nursing was no longer considered to be under the absolute control of medicine, which made it even more important that it have its own professional ethical standards. The idea of "ethics as etiquette" was beginning to lose ground, as it became clear that nurses had responsibility for decision making about their own practice. The concept of human rights was beginning to gain acceptance. For example, in a book titled *Nurse and Patient*, a British nurse named Evelyn Pearce (1969) outlined the importance of human relations in nursing and focused on patient dignity and rights.

By the 1970s, nursing scholars were beginning to take up the idea of nursing ethics in earnest, as evidenced by a growing number of articles on the subject. Terry Pence, an American philosopher, noted in an annotated bibliography of nursing ethics (Pence, 1983) that on average five articles on nursing ethics were published per year in the 1960s; whereas, by the early 1980s, nearly 160 books and articles on issues in nursing ethics were published annually.

M. Josephine Flaherty was one of the earliest Canadian nurses to write extensively on the topic of nursing ethics. Her landmark book, co-authored by a prominent American nurse, Leah Curtin (Curtin & Flaherty, 1982), was based primarily on human rights and the ideas of nursing commitment and the nurse-patient relationship. Many of the concepts were presented in case-study format, in an attempt to provide nurses with practical examples of issues they might face and ways of dealing with them. Flaherty's thinking was influential in Canada, and her ideas became even better known when she later became a consultant on nursing issues to the Canadian government.

As nursing ethics became more visible, scholars began to seek a more theoretical foundation for their work. There had been little mention of traditional ethics theories in typical nursing ethics books such as Curtin and Flaherty's. However, bioethics had been introduced at the end of the 1970s, and nursing scholars in Canada and elsewhere began to use that work as a foundation for nursing ethics. Frameworks for decision making began to emerge. Dr. Janet Storch, another Canadian nurse scholar and ethicist, based her early work on human rights (Storch, 1982), then later developed a framework based on bioethical principles that was much cited and used in Canadian nursing education (Storch, 1988; 1992). Storch's work has been and continues to be hugely influential in shaping Canadian nursing ethics. Michael Yeo, a Canadian philosopher working with Anne Moorhouse, a Canadian nurse, first published *Concepts and Cases in Nursing Ethics* in 1991. This book was clearly based on bioethical principles, addressing issues in Canadian nursing ethics from a strong theoretical perspective. In 1995, a pair of Canadian authors, Margaret Keatings and O'Neil Smith, put forward (Keatings & Smith, 1995) their ideas about ethics and law in Canadian nursing practice, drawing clear distinctions between the two, but showing how they are inextricably linked. Again, their approach was largely based on bioethical principles. To understand just how "young" the idea of nursing ethics is as a distinct area for inquiry, consider the fact that many, if not most, of these pioneers in Canadian nursing ethics continue to publish today.

Advances in nursing ethics on the Canadian scene paralleled changes across other parts of the world. Some of the most prominent ethics scholars include Verena Tschudin (Tschudin, 1992; 1994), a British nurse and current editor of the journal *Nursing Ethics*; Anne Davis and Mila Aroskar, American nurses whose collaborative work began in the late 1970s, and who are still highly influential today (Davis & Aroskar, 1978; 1983); and Megan-Jane Johnstone, an Australian nurse who continues to publish books and articles on nursing ethics (Johnstone, 1989; 1999; 2004).

As we have discussed, bioethics as outlined by Beauchamp and Childress had a huge impact on thinking about medical ethics, and it was also adopted with enthusiasm by other health care disciplines, including nursing. It is probably safe to say that essentially every nursing student in the United States and Canada since 1980 has at least been exposed to the bioethical principles, generally in preference to other ethical theories.

Questions soon arose, however, as to whether bioethics and nursing ethics theory were the same thing. Was nursing ethics merely a subset of medical ethics? Sara Fry, an American philosopher, was one of the first to suggest that nursing ethics should be thought of as separate and distinct from medical ethics (Fry, 1989), although in her collaborative work with medical ethics philosopher Robert Veatch, Fry used bioethical principles as the foundation for nursing ethics (Fry & Veatch, 2000; Veatch & Fry, 1987).

Andrew Jameton, another prominent American philosopher and ethicist, also wrote about nursing ethics as a separate area of inquiry. In his book, *Nursing Practice: The Ethical Issues* (1984), he introduced a number of interesting concepts that are widely used today in explorations of nursing ethics. He explained that nurses seldom experience what are termed true ethical dilemmas. An **ethical dilemma** is a situation that requires a choice between two mutually exclusive courses of action. For example, if I decide to stop treatment, I cannot at the same time continue treatment. The reason nurses may not experience true dilemmas as often as doctors is that the kinds of decisions that are required in such situations are not often nursing decisions. Jameton described other concerns that are part of the moral domain and more likely to be part of a nurse's experience. **Moral distress** happens when one believes that something should be done but is constrained by institutional pressures from acting on that belief. When a nurse feels she should tell an inquiring patient about his diagnosis, but is prevented from doing so because the physician has ordered that the patient not be told, the nurse may experience moral distress. Similarly, a nurse being asked to continue treatment on a patient whom the nurse believes would prefer to be allowed to die with dignity suffers moral distress. **Moral uncertainty** occurs when one has an idea that something is morally amiss and/or that something should be done but is not certain what that something should be. Part of the difference between the ethical concerns of doctors and nurses in the clinical setting is a result of the hierarchical nature of the health care structure. Physicians write orders for nurses to carry out; the reverse is not true. Consequently nurses often complain that their **moral agency**, namely their ability to act on their moral beliefs, may be compromised by the system. This fact is at the root of much of the feminist critique of bioethics for nursing. Feminists suggest that it is not reasonable to ask doctors and nurses to use the same approaches to moral decision making when there is an imbalance of power in the health care system itself. More recently another important term was added to the list of moral issues of particular importance to nursing. **Moral residue** was defined by Canadian philosophers George Webster and Françoise Baylis (2000) as the long standing feelings of guilt, remorse, or inadequacy an individual experiences because of unresolved ethical conflicts or morally distressing situations. Nurses who are unable to exercise their moral agency often suffer moral residue.

Jameton also emphasized the importance of nursing competence and professionalism, and described important issues of nursing autonomy. Unlike most authors writing about nursing ethics at that time, Jameton did not frame his work around bioethical principles. In contrast, most other works published in the 1980s and early 1990s were mainly based on bioethics, as nurses were encouraged to consider how the principles could help them reason toward a resolution to nursing issues. Another exception to the bioethics orientation came from philosopher Sally Gadow, who argued for something she called "existential advocacy," based on the nurse-patient relationship, as a foundation for nursing ethics (Gadow, 1980). Her ideas did not get as much attention as they might have, because of the popularity of bioethics. More recently, the generally unquestioned idea that bioethics is a suitable approach for nursing has been strongly challenged. Criticisms, particularly from feminist nursing scholars, suggest that bioethics is not sufficient in and of itself to inform nurses' ethical decision making. It has been argued that nursing ethics is not the same as medical ethics, in that nursing's mandate and relationship with patients is different, as are nursing's decision-making responsibilities. Consider, for example, that it is the physician, not the nurse, who writes the DNR order, decides what treatment to deliver, and determines who gets the heart (or even the bed), while it is the nurse who carries out the orders and looks after the patient. Thus many of the moral quandaries experienced by doctors are not a problem for nurses, and conversely, many moral problems experienced by nurses are not a problem for doctors. We will discuss more recent developments in nursing ethics in greater detail in the next chapter.

In summary, close scrutiny of the nursing ethics literature reveals many interesting changes over time. As we have seen, early writings emphasized personal characteristics of the nurse and proper nursing comportment. Then, as nursing became more recognized as a profession, nursing ethics began to focus on the nature of the nurse-patient relationship and human rights. A shift toward a more theoretical approach was evident. In the 1980s the focus turned to the kind of principle-based reasoning mandated by bioethics. More recently there have been criticisms of the medically oriented approach suggested by bioethics. Nurse scholars have begun to look at how nursing ethics is unique as they struggle to untangle differences between nursing and medical ethics. In the next chapter, we will explore some of the more recent ideas in greater detail and consider the role and influence of codes of ethics. We will then introduce a model that integrates traditional ethics theory and current nursing thinking to demonstrate the many influences on the development of nursing ethics. In Chapter 3 we will offer a framework for use in the practical setting of Canadian nursing.

CHAPTER SUMMARY

In this chapter the terms morality and ethics are used more or less interchangeably. Both terms are about considerations of right and wrong, of ought and ought not in how we behave in interactions with others. Different kinds of theories have been developed to help us think about what our obligations are, and how we ought to behave. Descriptive ethics theories tell us about how people think about right and wrong. Metaethics is a branch of ethics scholarship that asks questions about where our ideas of right and wrong come from. Normative ethics theories are prescriptive, in that they tell us what we should do and how we should think, that is to say, what we are morally required to do. Applied or practical ethics theories can be descriptive or prescriptive, and deal with moral thinking in specific situations such as health care.

Two categories of normative theories that have shaped our thinking about ethics include deontology and consequentialism. Deontological theories, the most famous of which is that of Immanuel Kant, are based on understanding of duty. Kant said that we must use reasoning to work out what our duty is in any given situation and that we must never base our decisions on consideration of consequences or emotions. He suggested that we use maxims or universal rules to guide our behaviour. Whenever we are making decisions, we must ask if our reasoning can be applied in all cases. If we believe it can, then we have a maxim suitable for guiding action. Kant also talks about treating persons as ends in themselves, never as just means to an end. Kant's ideas are still evident in health care ethics today. His notions of respect for persons are the basis of much of our thinking about autonomy and informed consent. Kant's theory has been criticized, however, because it does not take consequences into account.

Consequentialist theories, by contrast, are based entirely on consequences. John Stuart Mill's utilitarianism is the most famous consequentialist theory. It suggests that moral choices are guided by a principle of utility that says "the good" is achieved when we maximize happiness and minimize suffering. This generally translates into "the greatest good for the greatest number." Some criticisms of utilitarianism are that in considering only consequences, it does not take into consideration issues such as individual rights. Nonetheless, utilitarian thinking is still much in evidence in health care ethics, particularly when discussing how scarce resources might be allocated.

Another approach to thinking about ethics is virtue theory, of which Aristotle's is the best known. In contrast to other theories just described, virtue theory is less about what we do and more about who we are. That is, virtue theories start from the premise that if people have the right personality characteristics they will make right choices in difficult situations. Virtue theory is becoming more popular among theorists working in health care ethics, because it seems intuitively correct that the kind of people we are should influence the kind of care we give. However, virtue theory does not tell us what to do in specific situations.

In response to the need for a very specific way of thinking about health care ethics, or, in other words, for an applied ethics theory, a new field of ethics inquiry called bioethics sprang up in the late 1970s. Bioethical principles of autonomy, beneficence, non-malefi-cence, and justice, as described by Beauchamp and Childress, have had a huge influence on medical ethics. Autonomy is about being able to make choices for oneself. Beneficence is about our obligation to do good, and non-maleficence is about our obligation to do no harm. Justice is about fairness and equal distribution of resources. These principles have formed the foundation for medical ethics for the past 35 years, and have strongly influenced thinking about nursing ethics.

Feminists criticize traditional ethics theories for reflecting men's interests and for not paying attention to the moral issues important to women. Feminism has been the basis of the ethic of care and narrative ethics. Feminist ethics in health care has strongly influenced nursing ethics and has drawn attention to issues of power and dominance, politics, and social context. Feminist ethics puts much greater emphasis on values of community and relationship.

A brief history of nursing ethics reveals that it has changed substantially over time. Whereas early nursing ethics was largely about etiquette and the personal characteristics of the nurse, more recent work has been based on ethics theory in general and bioethics theory in particular. Nursing scholars are working to uncover the real nature of nursing ethics, as distinct from medical ethics, and to develop ethics theory for nursing practice.

Questions for Reflection

1. Having read this chapter, how would you explain ethics to someone who has not been exposed to this analysis and these theorists?

2. Based on your understanding of this chapter, how do you think professional ethics might be different from everyday ethics?

3. Keeping in mind the different ethics theories, what role do you think personal values play in professional ethics?

Exercises

1. Consider the scenarios presented in the boxes. For each one, try to adopt another ethics perspective and see if you would come to a different conclusion. For example, in Box 1-2, how would a deontologist's perspective change how you would approach the problem? Would you come to a different conclusion using that form of reasoning? Which theoretical perspective are you more comfortable with?

2. In a small group, consider the following questions: Where do you think "the good" comes from? That is, what is the source of moral authority? See how many possibilities you can generate. Find out if members of the group have strong opinions about the source of "good" or right and wrong, and examine whether their ideas differ from yours.

Research Activities

1. Talk to nurses in practice, and discuss their views about nursing ethics. How do they come to an understanding of right decisions in the practice setting? Document your findings, and compare them with one another. Consider which of these ideas is closest to your own understanding of practice.

2. Find one web site for each of the major ethics theories discussed above. Identify a key point about each theory that is not mentioned in this chapter. Share your findings with your classmates.

Key Terms

act utilitarianism	maxim
applied ethics	metaethics
autonomy	moral agency
beneficence	moral distress
bioethics	moral residue
biomedical ethics	moral uncertainty
care theory	morality
Categorical Imperative	non-maleficence
consequentialism	normative ethics theory
contractarian theories	paternalism
principle of utility	prescriptive theory
deontology	principle of utility
descriptive theory	rights theories
distributive justice	rule utilitarianism
duty	theories of Divine Command
ethical dilemma	theories of obligation
ethics	theory
explanatory theory	utilitarianism
golden mean	values
golden rule	virtue ethics
health care ethics	virtues
justice	

References

Beauchamp, T., & Childress, J. (1979). *Principles of biomedical ethics*. New York: Oxford University Press.

Beauchamp, T., & Childress, J. (2001). *Principles of biomedical ethics* (5th ed.). New York: Oxford University Press.

Curtin, L., & Flaherty, M. J. (1982). *Nursing ethics: Theories and pragmatics*. Bowie, MD: Robert J. Brady.

Davis, A. J., & Aroskar, M. A. (1978). *Ethical dilemmas and nursing practice*. Norwalk, CT: Appleton-Century-Crofts.

Davis, A. J., & Aroskar, M. A. (1983). *Ethical dilemmas and nursing practice* (2nd ed.). Norwalk, CT: Appleton-Century-Crofts.

Fry, S. (1989). Toward a theory of nursing ethics. *Advances in Nursing Science, 11*(4), 9–22.

Fry, S. T., & Veatch, R. M. (2000). *Case studies in nursing ethics* (2nd ed.). Sudbury, MA: Jones & Bartlett.

Gadow, S. A. (1980). Existential advocacy: Philosophical foundations of nursing. In S. F. Spicker & S. A. Gadow (Eds.), *Nursing: Images and ideals* (pp. 79–101). New York: Springer.

Jameton, A. (1984). *Nursing practice: The ethical issues*. Englewood Cliffs, NJ: Prentice-Hall.

Johnstone, M. J. (1989). *Bioethics: A nursing perspective*. Sydney, Australia: Harcourt Sanders.

Johnstone, M. J. (1999). *Bioethics: A nursing perspective* (3rd ed.). Sydney, Australia: Harcourt Sanders.

Johnstone, M. J. (2004). *Bioethics: A nursing perspective* (4th ed.). Sydney, Australia: Elsevier.

Keatings, M., & Smith, O. (1995). *Ethical and legal issues in Canadian nursing*. Toronto: W. B. Saunders.

Kemerling, G. Immanuel Kant. *Britannica* philosophy pages. Retrieved June 8, 2008, from www.philosophypages.com/ph/kant.htm.

Lamb, M. (2004). An historical perspective on nursing and nursing ethics. In J. L. Storch, P. Rodney, & R. Starzomskil (Eds.), *Toward a moral horizon: Nursing ethics for leadership and practice* (pp. 20–41). Toronto: Pearson.

McCormick, M. Immanuel Kant's metaphysics. *The Internet encyclopedia of philosophy*. Retrieved June 8, 2008, from www.iep.utm.edu/k/kantmeta.htm.

Nelson, H. L. (2000). Feminist bioethics: Where we've been, where we're going. *Metaphilosophy, 31*, 492–508.

Pearce, E. C. (1969). *Nurse and patient: Human relations in nursing* (3rd ed.). London: Faber & Faber.

Pence, T. (1983). Ethics in nursing: An annotated bibliography. National League for Nursing, document #20-1936.

Peter, E., Lunardi, V. L., & Macfarlane, A. (2004). Nursing resistance as ethical action: Literature review. *Journal of Advanced Nursing, 46*, 403–416.

Peter, E. H., Macfarlane, A. V., & O'Brien-Pallas, L. L. (2004). Analysis of the moral habitability of the nursing work environment. *Journal of Advanced Nursing, 47*, 356–367.

Ross, K. M. Immanuel Kant. Retrieved June 8, 2008, from www.friesian.com/kant.htm.

Storch, J. L. (1982). *Patient's rights: Ethical and legal issues in health care and nursing*. Toronto: McGraw-Hill Ryerson.

Storch, J. L. (1988). Ethics in nursing practice. In A. J. Baumgart & J. Larsen (Eds.), *Canadian nursing faces the future: Development and change* (pp. 211–221). St. Louis, MO: C. V. Mosby.

Storch, J. L. (1992). Ethical issues. In A. J. Baumgart & J. Larsen (Eds.), *Canadian nursing faces the future: Development and change* (2nd ed., pp. 259–270). St. Louis, MO: Mosby.

Tschudin, V. (1992). *Ethics in nursing: The caring relationship* (2nd ed.). Oxford, UK: Butterworth-Heinemann.

Tschudin, V. (1994). *Deciding ethically: A practical approach to nursing challenges*. London, UK: Balliere Tindall.

Varcoe, C., Doane, G., Pauly, B., Rodney, P., Storch, J. L., Mahoney, K., McPherson, G., Brown, H., & Starzomski, R. (2004). Ethical practice in nursing: Working the in-betweens. *Journal of Advanced Nursing, 45*, 316–325.

Varcoe, C., Rodney, P., & McCormick, J. (2003). Health care relationships in context. An analysis of three ethnographies. *Qualitative Health Research, 7*, 957–973.

Veatch, R. M., & Fry, S. T. (1987). *Case studies in nursing ethics*. Sudbury, MA: Jones & Bartlett.

Webster, G., & Baylis, F. (2000). Moral residue. In S. Rubin & L. Zoloth (Eds.), *Margin of error: The ethics of mistakes in the practice of medicine* (pp. 217–230). Hagerston, MD: University Publishing Group.

Yeo, M., & Moorhouse, A. (1991). *Concepts and cases in nursing ethics*. Peterborough, ON: Broadview Press.

Yeo, M., & Moorhouse, A. (1996). *Concepts and cases in nursing ethics* (2nd ed.). Peterborough, ON: Broadview Press.

Suggested Reading

The interested individual can find a wealth of resources regarding ethics and ethical theory on-line. Simply type your topic of interest, for example, "Kant," into the search line in your search engine, and you will find any number of web sites devoted to the topic. Take caution to ensure that the web site has a reputable host, for example, the University of Stanford or the Routledge Encyclopedia of Philosophy.

Some resources that we have found particularly helpful, in that they describe the basics of ethics theory in a language and format that is easy to understand, are listed below.

Honderich, T. (Ed.) (2005). *The Oxford companion to philosophy* (2nd ed.). New York: Oxford University Press.

Keatings, M., & Smith, O. (2000). *Ethical and legal issues in Canadian nursing* (2nd ed.). Toronto: W. B. Saunders.

Larrabee, M. J. (Ed.) (1993). *An ethic of care: Feminist and interdisciplinary perspectives*. New York: Routledge.

Martin, R. M. (2002). *The philosopher's dictionary* (3rd ed.). Peterborough, ON: Broadview Press.

Rachels, J. (1986). *The elements of moral philosophy*. Philadelphia: Temple University Press.

Sherwin, S. (1992). *No longer patient: Feminist ethics and health care*. Philadelphia: Temple University Press.

Taylor, R. (1991). *Virtue ethics: An introduction*. Interlaken, NY: Linden Books.

Waluchow, W. J. (2003). *The dimensions of ethics: An introduction to ethical theory*. Peterborough, ON: Broadview Press.

Chapter 2
Developing Nursing Ethics

Chapter Outline

Professional Codes of Ethics

Traditions of Professional Practice and Codes of Ethics

Strengths and Limitations of Professional Codes of Ethics

Values and Ethics in Nursing

Ethics Theory in Nursing

Developments in Nursing Ethics Theory

Relational Ethics in Nursing

Practice as the Moral Foundation for Nursing Ethics

A Model for Ethics in Nursing

Virtues and Nursing Ethics

Relational Ethics as Central

Decision Making in Clinical Practice

Chapter Summary

Learning Objectives

After reading this chapter, you should be able to:

■ summarize the nature of professions and the purpose of codes of ethics

■ discuss the importance of values in nursing and perform values clarification exercises

■ discuss the evolution of nursing ethics and the focus of current thinking

■ describe the nature of ethical nursing relationships, using the six main elements of ethical relationships

- define practical wisdom and list the three main components of excellent nursing
- illustrate a model of nursing ethics

Suppose for a moment that you are working in a long-term care institution. The patients on your unit are almost all elderly, and all have some form of dementia. You provide physical care for them, and for the most part believe it is adequate, but you know that many times their emotional and spiritual needs are ignored. You have too little time to sit with them and their families, as only one nurse and three care aides are on duty at any given time, and there are 40 patients on the unit. You are quite sure that the patients are all kept safe, and their basic needs for nutrition and hygiene are met, but you have a sense of unease about the care they receive. You feel sad each time you see them sitting and staring into space and suspect that they are bored, even if they are suffering from dementia. There is really nothing to keep them occupied, and you feel their quality of life is far from optimal. You wonder if you are meeting your obligations as a nurse and experience something that you have come to call moral distress each time you go to work.

This kind of ethical problem is one of many that could occur in nursing practice, and it should prompt you to ask, "As a nurse, what are my ethical obligations? What should guide my decisions in practice?" These questions, as we have seen in Chapter 1, could be answered in many ways. We could rely on ethics theories, referring to our understanding of duty and universal laws, as proposed by Kant. This would, of course, require that nurses agree on a set of universal laws, or else each nurse would have to generate his or her own. It would be difficult to engage in practice discussions if each person was working from a different set of laws. Besides, it would be difficult to think of universal laws that would apply in the above situation. We could appeal to notions of greatest good, as per utilitarianism, but we would have difficulty ensuring that individual rights were protected. Or we could adopt bioethical principles that are derived from both deontology and utilitarianism, but what are the principles that are important in this scenario? As we consider the situation it becomes clear that many of the problems encountered by nurses are rooted in relationships and issues that none of the above theories seem to take into account. Nor do they focus on the important aspect of personal characteristics of the nurse and the way she or he relates to others. Virtue theory suggests that this is important, but where does it fit in our understanding of nursing ethics? It seems that nursing ethical issues might require a somewhat different approach from any of those described in Chapter 1.

In this chapter we will continue our discussion of nursing ethics theory and its development. This will lay the groundwork for a model of nursing ethics that brings together traditional normative ethics theory, virtue theory, bioethics, and feminist ideas, and addresses nursing ethical issues in a unique way. First, we will discuss the nature of professions and the role of codes of ethics in establishing a baseline for ethical practice, which will show us the kinds of values Canadian nurses need to be concerned about. You will be invited to consider how your own values and approaches toward patients/clients might affect the care you give. Next, we will talk about how nursing ethics theory has grown and evolved over time in its attempt to provide direction to nurses. This will give you an opportunity to think about how nursing ethics might be different from medical ethics and what that might mean for nursing practice. The relational aspect of nursing ethics, namely the ethical foundations of how we act toward others in our care, will be described. We will introduce the topics of clinical competence and practical wisdom to help you understand how your skills as a nurse have ethical dimensions, and finally we will describe a model for considering how nursing ethics might be depicted. Throughout the discussion we will use the term "patient" to indicate the recipient of care, understanding that this could mean an individual, family, or community. We prefer the term patient to client because it reminds us that there is often a power imbalance: the nurse has services that the patient requires, and hence the patient is in a vulnerable position. While we realize that this idea is often controversial in nursing, we believe it is important not to mask the potential vulnerability of those receiving care.

PROFESSIONAL CODES OF ETHICS

Professions are bodies of persons recognized in law as having the capacity to be self-governing, to be responsible for their own definitions of professionalism, and to set their own standards of training and practice. The practice of a profession requires a specialized body of knowledge and skills for which professionals are responsible and accountable to the public. Not only do professionals have to be competent in certain skills, but they also have to conform to a particular ethical code. In other words, those who enter a profession are obliged to take on the duties and ethics of that profession. Self-regulation allows professional bodies to set standards by which they can evaluate individual members' conduct and enact disciplinary procedures if necessary.

Traditions of Professional Practice and Codes of Ethics

Professional practice is **teleological**, which means goal-oriented. Professionals are educated in a particular way to meet a particular need in society. The public must have confidence in the professional and should have a reasonable expectation that the profession's mandate will be met. Therefore, the scope and limitations of practice are outlined in legislation, and professional conduct is carefully monitored both by the government and by professional associations.

One set of standards that a profession uses to evaluate and shape practice is called a **code of ethics**. Codes of ethics reflect the set of values agreed upon by members of the profession. A value is a core belief we hold about what is important to us, that is to say, we care about it a great deal. Anyone reading a code of ethics should be able to understand what values a given professional can be expected to uphold. A lot of emotion is attached to values, and given that nurses work with some of the things people value most highly, such as life and health, values can easily become a source of controversy and conflict. Codes of ethics are therefore necessary to help nurses understand their unique obligations and responsibilities with respect to certain values. In Canada, the Code of Ethics for Registered Nurses (CNA, 2008) has been the responsibility of the Canadian Nurses Association and acts as a national standard. The Code has been developed by expert practitioners through extensive consultation and debate with those working in the field and with the public to be served. It is framed around seven primary values:

- providing safe, compassionate, competent, and ethical care;
- promoting health and well-being;
- promoting and respecting informed decision making;
- preserving dignity;
- maintaining privacy and confidentiality;
- promoting justice; and
- being accountable.

The preamble to the CNA Code of Ethics for Registered Nurses states that the Code is "a statement of the ethical values of nurses and of nurses' commitments to persons with health care needs and persons receiving care . . . It is developed by nurses for nurses and can assist nurses in practising ethically and working through ethical challenges that arise in their practice with individuals, families, communities, and public health systems" (CNA, 2008, p. 1). In essence the Code is a document devised for the purpose of guiding professional conduct.

To be effective, professional codes of ethics must be dynamic documents that change over time in response to changing needs and values in society. The CNA Code is no exception. The first code of ethics followed by Canadian nurses was developed by the International Council of Nurses (ICN) and adopted by the Canadian Nurses Association in 1954. This early ICN Code was based on a general understanding of human rights that emerged after the atrocities of World War II. It emphasized that nursing's responsibilities included providing care for all, regardless of race, colour, or creed. By 1965, when the next revision of the ICN Code came out, there was greater emphasis on obligations to the community as a whole and the nurse's obligations as a citizen. In the 1970s, as medical treatment and technology advanced, nurses began to assume more responsibility and become more accountable for their practice. The nature of nursing practice was changing, and the CNA decided it was important to develop its own Code of Ethics, which first appeared in 1980 (CNA, 1980). Recognizing that many changes were still ahead, the CNA made a commitment to revise the Code every five to six years, and several versions of the CNA Code have been released. Nurses who have considerable practice experience as well as knowledge of ethics and ethics theory have made the revisions. Revision committees are selected from among the many nurses who volunteer. When the most recent (2008) Code was drafted, it was sent out to all Canadian nurses, who were invited to give their input.

The final version therefore included the collective wisdom of practising nurses across the country.

Since the CNA's first Code of Ethics for Registered Nurses was published, the basic values underlying nursing practice have remained fairly constant, but the specific responsibilities have changed somewhat, with more emphasis being placed on certain factors. To get an idea of how the Code has changed, refer to Table 2-1 for a comparison of the values statements in the 1991 and 2008 Codes. Just looking at the difference will give you some sense of how nursing is changing with time. The 2008 entries reflect a number of recent changes in health care and nursing. Some examples are listed in Appendix B of the Code under the following headings: challenges and opportunities impacting the public; challenges and opportunities impacting nurses and other health care providers; and challenges within the socio-political context of the health care system. Other factors that have had an influence on the revisions include changes in the Canadian health care system. Recently there has been a shift toward a more business-oriented approach to health care reform, and this is having a large impact on nursing practice, so the Code makes reference to nursing responsibilities within the system as a whole and places greater emphasis on policy and politics. It also takes into account the fact that nursing practice takes place in a global community, and helps nurses understand their obligations to others in developing countries. It reflects a growing awareness of the ethical obligations arising from the nurse-patient relationship and speaks to the evolving importance of relational ethics in nursing. Values in the CNA Code are very general, as they are meant to guide a wide range of practice activities.

Strengths and Limitations of Professional Codes of Ethics

Professional codes of ethics play an important role in guiding what professionals ought or ought not to do when faced with ethically problematic situations, such as ethical dilemmas or ethical violations. Codes of ethics are used to improve decision making in matters of ethical concern. They enhance ethical awareness, encourage right behaviour, and increase the probability of self-evaluation and self-reflection regarding practice. Nursing codes of ethics also provide a common language to help nurses talk about matters of ethical concern.

It is also important to understand that codes of ethics have only general moral authority and can be overridden by other, stronger moral considerations. They do not offer direction as to which values should take priority or how to interpret the values in a given circumstance. Moreover, codes are shaped by the particular context in which the practice occurs and are not stand-alone documents in professional decision making. They must be considered in relation to laws, professional standards, and normative ethics theory.

Table 2.1 Comparison of CNA Codes of Ethics

1991 Code of Ethics for Nursing	2008 Code of Ethics for Registered Nurses
Value 1: Respect for Needs and Values of Clients: A nurse treats clients with respect for their individual needs and values.	Value 1: Providing Safe, Compassionate, Competent, and Ethical Care: Nurses provide safe, compassionate, competent, and ethical care.
Value 2: Respect for Client Choice: Based upon respect for clients and regard for their right to control their own care, nursing care reflects respect for the right of choice held by clients.	Value 2: Promoting Health And Well-Being: Nurses work with people to enable them to attain their highest possible level of health and well-being.
Value 3: Confidentiality: The nurse holds confidential all information about a client learned in the health care setting.	Value 3: Promoting And Respecting Informed Decision Making: Nurses recognize, respect, and promote a person's right to be informed and make decisions.
Value 4: Dignity of Clients: The nurse is guided by consideration for the dignity of clients.	Value 4: Preserving Dignity: Nurses recognize and respect the intrinsic worth of each person.
Value 5: Competent Nursing Care: The nurse provides competent care to clients.	Value 5: Maintaining Privacy and Confidentiality: Nurses recognize the importance of privacy and confidentiality and safeguard personal, family, and community information obtained in the context of a professional relationship.
Value 6: Nursing Practice, Education, Research, and Administration: The nurse maintains trust in nurses and nursing.	
Value 7: Cooperation in Health Care: The nurse recognizes the contribution and expertise of colleagues from nursing and other disciplines as essential to excellent health care.	Value 6: Promoting Justice: Nurses uphold principles of justice by safeguarding human rights, equity, and fairness and by promoting the public good.
Value 8: Protecting Clients from Incompetence: The nurse takes steps to ensure that the client receives competent and ethical care.	Value 7: Being Accountable: Nurses are accountable for their actions and answerable for their practice.
Value 9: Conditions of Employment: Conditions of employment should contribute in a positive way to client care and the professional satisfaction of nurses.	
Value 10: Job Action: Job action by nurses is directed toward securing conditions of employment that enable safe and appropriate care for clients and contribute to the professional satisfaction of nurses.	

Despite the general limitations of codes of ethics, nursing codes of ethics contribute to professional nursing ethics in two important ways. First, they make the values that nurses are expected to uphold clear to them. Second, they inform the public about what to expect from professional nurses and outline those things for which nurses can be held accountable. In addition, a code of ethics outlines ethical values and standards for those thinking of entering nursing. Although codes of ethics do not address all issues in nursing practice or offer complete guidance for complex situations, they are key in setting a standard for ethical professional behaviour. It should be noted that a code of ethics reflects local values and beliefs. Thus the code of ethics for Canadian nurses will reflect somewhat different values from the codes for other countries (see Appendix, p. 308, for the full version of the 2008 CNA Code of Ethics for Registered Nurses as an example).

In subsequent chapters of this book we will engage in a detailed exploration of the CNA Code of Ethics for Registered Nurses (CNA, 2008) and what it means for practice. We will examine each of the values that are set out in the Code and consider how they might be played out in nursing practice. This is not as straightforward as it might first appear, however, as there may be many sets of values present in any given situation. For example, the nurse might hold both personal and professional values, which may or may not be in conflict with each other and with the values of the patient, other caregivers, and the institution.

VALUES AND ETHICS IN NURSING

As we discussed above, key professional nursing values are outlined in the CNA Code of Ethics for Registered Nurses. But there are always at least two persons in nursing relationships, and their values and beliefs might be different. **Values conflicts** arise when two or more individuals hold different values calling for actions that cannot both be fulfilled. The challenge for nursing is in trying to come to a position where the values of all involved are respected. Nursing ethics is concerned with values as lived in everyday practice and in values conflicts arising out of practice and research. Values govern how we treat one another and the systems we create for delivering care to one another.

Values and beliefs in nursing practice are both shared and individual. While a value is something we hold dear, a **belief** is a cherished notion, something we think is true. Beliefs and values are closely related; a belief might be the basis of a value, and a value might lead to a belief about how we should act in a certain situation. As discussed above, professional values are those put forward by the nursing profession and expressed in the Code. Individual values and beliefs are learned in the context of family, community, and culture. Therefore, each nurse will bring to the health care setting a unique set of values and beliefs that guide behaviour. The expectation is that a nurse's values will be congruent with professional values, but sometimes they are not. For example, a nurse might hold the professional value that it is important to respect a patient's choice, but at the same time might be reluctant to act on a patient's request for a Do Not Resuscitate (DNR) order because of a conflicting, deeply held personal value about the sanctity of life. This value might lead the nurse to believe that a DNR order is wrong. Individual value differences might arise between nurse and patient, colleague, or system as a whole. Therefore, it is essential that nurses examine and reflect on their values and discuss them with one another in the course of practice. Values are the foundation of ethical action, but there can be a discrepancy between what we value and what we do when these values are called into action. In other words, we do not always act on our values or beliefs for a variety of reasons, sometimes because our values are not the most important in the situation. For example, a patient's values will often take precedence over what a nurse values. However, failure to act on one's beliefs often leads to moral distress among nurses. Learning how to recognize one's values and when it is appropriate to act on those values is one of the key reasons for studying nursing ethics.

Sometimes values are not immediately evident, and values clarification exercises can be helpful. **Values clarification** is a process used to increase one's awareness about what one values most. The nurse, particularly a new graduate, needs to be aware of what he or she values in the professional context. Personal and professional values may be challenged as the nurse is socialized to the demanding, sometimes competitive workplace. Nurses who gain an awareness of their own values are more likely to feel comfortable engaging in dialogue that leads to problem solving and decision making in relationships that acknowledge the values of others.

There are many ways to enhance awareness of your own values. **Journalling** involves writing about practice situations and reflecting on what one has written. You may already engage in journalling for personal reasons, or you might have been required to journal as part of your nursing courses. It may not have been evident to you that journalling is one way to engage in values clarification or increase awareness of values. We suggest that journalling helps one learn to recognize what is important in the situation and can therefore help you come to a better understanding of ethical practice. Another approach to clarifying your own values about particular issues is to engage in deliberate reflection; the questions in Table 2.2 are a guide for initiating this process. Dialogue with colleagues is also an effective way to develop understanding of the values that inform nursing practice. It is especially useful for a student or novice nurse to ask more experienced colleagues about what they consider notable in care situations. It is important to be aware, however, that such dialogue must be undertaken in a spirit of openness to be effective. All parties to the conversation must feel safe in expressing their views and having them examined and perhaps challenged.

If nurses are to make effective use of their code of ethics, they must have a solid understanding of what it means. Canadian nurses need to be familiar with the values put forward in the CNA Code of Ethics for Registered Nurses and should give thought to practice situations in which these values are supported or challenged. This kind of reflection makes it likely that, when faced with a patient situation that has challenging ethical dimensions, the nurse will have a clearer idea of how to act.

Table 2.2 Values Clarification Questions

- Describe a situation in your personal or professional experience in which you felt uncomfortable or felt that your beliefs and values were being challenged, or in which you felt your values were different from others.

- As you record the situation, include how you felt physically and emotionally at the time you experienced the situation.

- Write down your feelings as you remember the situation. Are your reactions now any different from when you were actually in the situation?

- What personal values do you identify in the situation? Try to remember where and from whom you learned these values. Do you completely agree with the values or is there something you question or wonder about their validity?

- What values do you think were being expressed by others involved? Are they similar to or different from your own values?

- What do you think you reacted to in the situation?

- Can you remember having similar reactions in other situations? If yes, how were the situations similar or different?

- How do you feel about your response to the situation? Is there something you would change if you could repeat the scene? Rewrite the scene with the same changes. What might be the consequences of these same changes?

- How do you feel about the new scenario?

- What do you need to do to reinforce behaviors, ideals, beliefs and qualities that you have identified as personal values in this situation? When and how can you do this?

From *Ethics and Issues in Contemporary Nursing*, Second edition, by Burkhardt/Nathaniel. 2002. Reprinted with permission of Delmav Learning, a division of Thomson Learning: www.thomsonrights.com Fax 800 730–2215.

ETHICS THEORY AND NURSING

The CNA Code of Ethics for Registered Nurses summarizes the values that Canadian nurses are expected to uphold. To understand how those values might be realized, however, nurses need to have knowledge of ethics concepts in general and nursing ethics concepts in particular. When faced with values conflicts, nurses need to have a way of approaching such conflicts and working toward a resolution.

Developments in Nursing Ethics Theory

Ethics theories such as those described in Chapter 1 can help nurses understand their obligations in particular situations. They provide a useful starting point for thinking about various aspects of situations; however, as was pointed out, each of the theories has its critics, and no theory alone serves as an adequate guide for nursing practice. Consequently, the ethical foundations of nursing are becoming a popular field of study for nursing scholars and ethicists. In Chapter 1 we showed how bioethics became central to nursing ethics in the 1980s. Not everyone saw this form of principled reasoning as the answer for nursing, however. An important critique of bioethics came from feminist philosophers, and some nursing scholars picked up these criticisms and began to look at their application to practice. As a result, feminist thought has had a very strong influence on the evolution of nursing ethics. We will describe in more detail some of the current thinking, but first we need to describe how the concerns arose.

One of the key points made by feminist critics of bioethics theory such as philosopher Annette Baier (1987a; 1987b) is that the kind of reasoning required by the principled approach is not necessarily the kind of reasoning employed by women, and therefore it misses an enormous aspect of moral thought. Since the vast majority of nurses are women, and since nursing upholds values of nurturing and caring that are traditionally feminine values, this could be a serious concern. In support of their arguments, feminists cite important work in moral reasoning by two developmental psychologists, Lawrence Kohlberg and Carol Gilligan. We will discuss this work below, showing how it has formed the basis for considerable controversy in discussions on moral development.

Contributions of Developmental Psychologists and Feminists Kohlberg's aim was to understand how people came to think about moral problems. He conducted extensive research with children, adolescents, and young adults, and developed a theory of how moral reasoning develops. According to Kohlberg (1981), moral reasoning progresses in stages: preconventional, conventional, and postconventional. At the preconventional level, a person follows society's rules out of respect for authority or fear of being punished for bad behaviour. At the conventional level, people conform to certain standards to try to preserve social order because they believe it is right to follow the rules. They also begin to take others' feelings and needs into account. At the postconventional level, thinking moves beyond feelings and needs and is characterized by a search for abstract principles of justice. Kohlberg considered this the highest or most sophisticated level of moral reasoning.

Kohlberg's theory of staged reasoning was quickly accepted by many scholars, who used it to develop measures of moral reasoning. Researchers using these measures generally came to the same conclusion: girls are more likely to stay at the conventional level, while boys are more likely to move to the postconventional level. In other words, after a certain point (adolescence), boys, on average, demonstrate more sophisticated moral reasoning than girls of the same age. Gilligan, who had worked with Kohlberg in his early research, challenged this conclusion (Gilligan, 1982, 1988). She noted that Kohlberg had studied only boys as his research subjects, but had assumed in forming his theory that the findings could be applied to girls, which she said was inappropriate. Based on her research, Gilligan claimed that girls' reasoning is often different from, but not less sophisticated than, boys' reasoning. She explained this difference by suggesting that as boys grow they are encouraged to become more objective and detached from others, while young girls are more often encouraged to develop a growing sense of connectedness with and care for others. The result is the unfolding of a feminine ethic of "care," which Gilligan contrasted with the more typically masculine orientation described by Kohlberg. She suggested that boys' reasoning is more oriented to rules, principles, and ideas of justice and rights, while girls' reasoning is more likely to be focused on caring and relationships. Therefore, girls and boys (and women and men) might come to very different conclusions about the right thing to do in a given situation.

Around the same time that Gilligan and followers were doing their research into the development of moral reasoning, the philosopher Nel Noddings wrote a book titled *Caring: A Feminine Approach to Ethics and Moral Education* (1984). Noddings offered the idea that women's natural instinct to care for others should be recognized as a legitimate source of moral knowledge, something that was notably absent in traditional ethics theories. She called this innate caring "feminine" because it occurs more naturally in women and suggested that it become the basis for exploring a whole new approach to ethics theory. An ethics based on relationships, she maintained, might look very different from an ethics based on abstract rules of right and wrong, which was the foundation of most normative theories.

Feminists picked up this argument as they looked at ethics in health care in general. They agreed with the general criticism that standard ethics theories privileged male points of view and essentially dismissed women's concerns and those issues important to women in particular. They began to criticize bioethics for its implicit acceptance of the kinds of power relationships inherent in the health care system. They suggested that the appeal to rules and laws (which are developed and supported by those in power) silences those who are most vulnerable and gives privilege to those with the most power. A number of feminist ethics scholars suggested that the feminine or caring ethic might offer a partial solution to the problem by offering a different approach to understanding ethics. A feminine ethic, they said, could help give voice to those who are silenced because it depends on relationships, and to build a relationship with another, one must listen to his or her story. However, many feminist scholars also raised the concern that a feminine ethic such as that proposed by Noddings was not, in itself, sufficient to address the kinds of power imbalances present in health care. Issues of context, politics, and hierarchy are not well addressed by a feminine ethic, but are nonetheless of vital importance in generating rich moral understanding. They suggested that ethics must take these issues into account in a meaningful way.

Evolving Nursing Ethics Theory It is interesting to note that several studies of nurses' moral reasoning done in the mid- to late 1980s, using instruments based on Kohlberg's work, cast doubt on the ability of nurses to reason beyond the conventional level (see, for example, the work of Patricia Munhall [1982], a nurse researcher who explored moral reasoning). This created considerable controversy, as it suggested that nurses' moral reasoning was somewhat unsophisticated. Taking up the idea of a feminine approach, nursing scholars began to explore reasons for these findings. They used both Noddings's and Gilligan's work as a basis for examining the idea of an ethic of care in nursing and suggested that nurses' reasoning in ethical situations might look different from, for example, physicians' reasoning, but was not necessarily less sophisticated. The problem was that the scale used to measure moral reasoning was based on the more male-oriented appeal to rules and laws, and neglected the relational aspects of situations.

Nursing scholars then began to question specifically whether bioethics, which in many ways reflects a male, or androcentric, point of view, was the most appropriate theory for nursing ethics. Bioethics, based as it is on principled reasoning, effectively promotes the position that an impartial judge can select from among rules or principles and make the "correct" decision. Feminist ethics scholars disputed that position, saying that ethical decision making is much more complex than that, and more complex than even a feminine ethic of care suggests. They argued that ethics requires a detailed understanding of the context in which the problem occurs, that is to say, the "how we got here and where we might want to go" approach described in Chapter 1. The bioethical impartialist approach to ethics neglects moral understandings that are rooted in relationship and influenced by social context, hierarchy, power, and politics. Feminist nursing scholars argued that a theory of nursing ethics should be developed to take those issues into account. Such a theory would need to pay particular attention to relationship and to the hierarchical structures and power imbalances that limit nurses' ability to act morally and that foster oppression of the vulnerable in the health care system.

With the idea of a separate nursing ethics in mind, nursing scholars have conducted considerable research over the last two decades and have written extensively about what nursing ethics is and how it can be described. A detailed analysis of developments across the world is beyond the scope of this book; however, it is fairly clear from research and conferences that the issues of nursing ethics are very similar in most developed countries. Of particular interest is the work of Patricia Benner, a prominent nurse researcher from the United States. Her research began with an exploration of how nursing expertise developed (Benner, 1984). As her work progressed it became increasingly evident that she saw relationship as being the foundation of nursing. She began to express her ideas in the language of ethics, pointing out that ethical practice *is* relational practice (Benner, 1989, 1996, 1999). She was one of the first to speak of nursing ethics in this way and as such was a leader in the evolution of nursing ethics theory. Benner continues to write articles about ethics and ethical nursing practice and remains an active researcher and popular speaker at conferences.

Another important advancement in nursing ethics was the contribution of American nurse Anne Bishop and philosopher John Scudder (1996), who introduced a novel approach to nursing ethics. A second edition of their book (2001) expanded on their original ideas. They initially described nursing ethics in terms of therapeutic presence and later spoke in terms of "holistic caring practice." Thus it was evident that they, like Benner, saw nursing practice as an inherently ethical endeavour based on relationships.

It is interesting that some of the most influential and important work in nursing ethics has been done by Canadians. For example, a group of academic nurses in British Columbia has recently been focusing on the nature of nursing ethics as described by practising nurses, and group members have published a number of papers based on their research. Their findings demonstrate that nursing ethics is, indeed, rooted in relationships and that principled reasoning is inadequate for the kinds of issues nurses face (Rodney et al., 2002; Rodney & Varcoe, 2001). Drs. Patricia Rodney, Janet Storch, and Rosalie Starzomski, part of this group, have recently published a book in which many of the theoretical aspects of nursing ethics are discussed by a number of Canadian authors (2004). Two other nurses, Dr. Elizabeth Peter from the University of Toronto and Dr. Joan Liaschenko from the University of Minnesota, have written convincingly about the need for a nursing ethics that is rooted in practice and that considers issues of oppression and power as they affect health care (Liaschenko & Peter, 2004; Peter & Liaschenko, 2003, 2004). Recently, nursing scholars have begun to explore the impact of power and politics on nursing and nurses' ability to act morally and have begun to expose some of the ethical implications of the hierarchical structures in which nurses work (Peter, Macfarlane, & O'Brien-Pallas, 2004; Varcoe et al., 2004; Varcoe, Rodney, & McCormick, 2003). In all this work the feminist influence is strongly evident, and a nursing ethics based on relationship and on considerations of power and politics is emerging. To this point, however, no single commonly accepted theory of nursing ethics exists, and much more research and philosophical reflection is needed. Franko Carnevale, a Canadian pediatric nurse from Toronto, argues that the only way we can hope to develop useful theories of nursing ethics is to conduct research by using methods that allow for rich descriptions of practice (Carnevale, 2005). As these descriptors mark feminist approaches, it is evident that nursing ethics is moving toward a feminist base.

Clearly nursing ethics is evolving in Canada (and elsewhere). Based on this recent work, we are convinced that nursing ethics goes beyond the application of bioethical principles. The practice of nursing seeks the well-being of others, and as a professional the nurse has a moral obligation to try to meet that goal. The nurse-patient relationship has characteristics that call for a particular kind of moral response. Nurses do not simply care for patients' physical bodies. Rather, nurses pay attention to the patient's whole experience: mind, spirit, and social connections. Consequently a common theme in any discussion of nursing ethics must be the nature of the nurse-patient relationship, which is seen as the foundation of "good" nursing. This development in nursing ethics has been paralleled by developments ethics theory in general. The idea of relational ethics as a separate ethics theory is gaining strength. In the following paragraphs we shall further explore the application of relational ethics in nursing.

Relational Ethics in Nursing

It is becoming increasingly apparent that relationship is at the heart of ethics in nursing. **Relational ethics** says that our ethical understandings are formed in, and emerge from, our relationships with others. Relational ethics refers to individual relationships, but also helps us consider how we relate within an institutional structure. It is important that nurses understand the concept of relational ethics, as we believe it is the foundation of our moral understanding in nursing. Nurse educators, philosophers, and ethicists have suggested that "being in relation" with others is the core of nursing practice. If that is true then nursing ethics as such must be relational. In other words, to these scholars the basis of nursing ethics is relationship with others: patient, family, community, colleague, or environment. Vangie Bergum and John Dossetor, two Canadian ethics scholars, have explored relational ethics through extensive research focused on ethics in health care. They suggest that ethical relationships require certain elements: embodiment, mutuality, engagement, non-coercion, freedom, and choice (Bergum & Dossetor, 2005).

In relational ethics, **embodiment** means recognizing that the mind/body split is an artificial one and that healing for both patient and family cannot occur unless "scientific knowledge and human compassion are given equal weight [and it is recognized that] emotion and feeling are as important to human life as physical signs and symptoms" (Bergum, 2004, p. 492). This approach requires us to connect with others in a particular way such that nurses become truly aware of what others might be experiencing. This demands attention and focus on other people's experiences to such an extent that they become a part of the nurse's own experience. It is a kind of reaching out to others by going beyond oneself. As a dimension of the nurse-patient relationship, it becomes a moral imperative that requires that the nurse value others and treat them with respect. It goes far beyond just being "nice" to people. Instead, it requires a commitment to care about others and their experiences. **Mutuality**, loosely defined as a relationship that benefits both and harms neither, requires a willingness on the part of the nurse and the patient to participate in a relationship. While some might argue that nurses provide a professional service and should expect no benefit to themselves, we believe that mutuality *requires* that the interaction go both ways. It is a human-to-human exchange in which the nurse takes a genuine interest in the other, and therefore is rewarded by a feeling of "knowing" the person. **Engagement** means connecting with others in an open, trusting, and responsive manner. That takes skill and practice, as it requires a commitment to keeping the relationship caring and respectful. Engagement requires that the nurse connect with the patient, but at the same time set boundaries such that the relationship remains on a professional level. Knowing how much to engage with another is one of the greatest challenges in nursing. It will be discussed at length in subsequent chapters.

Coercion is pressuring or forcing someone to do something she or he does not wish to do, thereby limiting choice and freedom. **Choice** means making one's own decisions, or being self-determining, and is closely tied to **freedom**, which involves creating an environment in which choices are available. **Non-coercion** is the opposite of coercion; it means *not* forcing others to make a particular choice. In the context of a relational ethic, this means regarding the other as someone who can be self-determining and make moral decisions. Coercion is to be avoided, except in very particular situations such as preventing children from harming themselves, because it means taking away an individual's freedom to choose. A relational ethic therefore requires that nurses enter into dialogue with persons (or groups) receiving care to determine their wishes and goals. As part of open dialogue, nurses must always remember that interpretations other than their own may be correct. An ongoing commitment to the patient requires that nurses set certainty and authority aside and are open to others' points of view.

Another theme identified as part of a relational ethic is that of environment (Bergum & Dossetor, 2005). Bergum (2004) describes this in detail, saying that environment "is each of us—a living system—that changes through daily action. We are the health care system; we are environment" (p. 489). Every action that is taken as part of care delivery, whether by nurse, patient, family, or other health care providers, affects the system in some way. Bergum encourages us to consider the entire health care arena as a network or matrix, in which each part connects either directly or indirectly to the other. Having an awareness of this connectedness encourages us to look beyond the immediate, to try to envision a larger picture. It also makes us very aware of the ways in which the power structures and politics of the overall system can affect care and relationship. For example, if a nurse feels silenced or oppressed by hierarchical structures, his or her relationship with the patient and family could be jeopardized, and at the same time the nurse's relationship to the system itself could be damaged. Understanding ourselves as part of a web or network helps us to think about our responsibilities, not just to the individual patient, but also to the family, our health care colleagues within and outside nursing, the administration, and the political system.

Relational ethics theory suggests that the elements described above—embodiment, mutuality, engagement, non-coercion, freedom, and choice, plus environment—are key to an ethical relationship (Bergum & Dossetor, 2005). However, they are not unique to nursing. What makes a nursing relationship distinct is partly the knowledge the nurse brings to the relationship and partly its goal, which is to enhance well-being. Within the relationship the nurse uses nursing knowledge and acts with intent to work toward that goal. Another aspect emphasized in nursing is the awareness of our interconnectedness and our responsibility toward sustaining an intact network or web of relationships such that all involved feel supported. It has often been said that nurses are the "glue" that holds the health care system together. Relational ethics and an awareness of the environment help us understand why that is part of nursing's function.

From the above it should be clear that being in relation is at the core of nursing's philosophy. At the individual level, this means that each person is respected as being unique and having particular needs, wants, and beliefs. This is the key focus of nursing interactions. In each interaction the nurse responds to the other, including the system as a whole, in a way that is essentially moral. Thus it seems reasonable to think that nursing relationships are central to nursing ethics.

What the public wants and expects from nurses and what they are educated and able to do determine the context in which the nursing relationship exists. Questions such as "What kind of relationship is important in the clinical situation? What makes for right and good health care relations? What are our ethical commitments to one another in a professional relationship? What must the professional be and do? What guides us and fosters a healthy moral climate in our relationships with others?" become the foundation of relational nursing ethics. We can find the answers to some of these questions in the work of nursing ethics scholars and by exploring broader ethics theory such as that described in Chapter 1. However, for many questions arising in nursing practice there will be no clear answers. Theory provides only a general guide. To be confident in ethical decision making the nurse must actively examine and reflect on clinical situations, seeking guidance from theory and more experienced practitioners.

If the relational elements of embodiment, mutuality, engagement, non-coercion, freedom, and choice are to be present, the nurse needs different approaches and ways of connecting with each person or group receiving nursing care. Skills required for forming relationships with patients, families, and communities are learned in basic nursing education, and are outside the scope of this book. What is important here is that the nurse think about the ability to form such relationships not only as a skill, but also as a moral obligation. Seeing environment from a relational perspective is vital to this process. The nurse who understands that being in relation goes beyond the individual, and that "the system" is not "out there" but part of us, will be acutely aware of how each part affects the whole and will understand obligation in a much different way. Simply put, such an understanding helps the nurse comprehend more fully the relationship between care and context.

We realize that relational ethics might look, at first glance, very similar to narrative ethics and the ethic of care described in Chapter 1. We want to point out, however, that there are key differences. Whereas narrative ethics depends on hearing the other's story, relational ethics requires that we enter into a relationship with that person in such a way as to better understand the meaning of that story. The ethic of care is essentially a virtue ethic that gives moral weight to caring for others. In other words, it says that caring is a virtue in and of itself. Relational ethics is broader in scope. It is about action and about how our shared experience informs that action. It means understanding that every encounter we have is part of, and changes, the network in which care takes place, and as such every nursing action is essentially moral in character.

Certainly there have been critiques of this relational approach to ethics. Philosophers Beauchamp and Childress (2001) suggest that it is underdeveloped, too contextual, and hostile to principles. Nonetheless, they conclude that a more relational approach has benefits in that it may correct "undue obsession with impartiality requirements in traditional ethics theories" and "promises to have positive consequences because many aspects of character, forms of sensitivity, and modes of practical judgment excel appeals to impartial principles" (p. 92).

PRACTICE AS THE MORAL FOUNDATION FOR NURSING ETHICS

Whenever we think about making a "right" decision in nursing, or anywhere else, we are assuming that there is a way to understand right and wrong. The idea that any and all ideas have equal moral weight is called **moral relativism**. Moral relativism implies that no single solution to a problem can be considered more right than another; however, we know that in nursing this is not the case, so the question is, "what is the moral authority in nursing?" In other words, the question that a nurse should ask is, "where does our idea of 'right' come from in nursing?" We maintain that the nurse is guided to an understanding of right behaviour by a number of professional standards. Earlier we talked about the CNA Code of Ethics for Registered Nurses as the guide for what nursing values should be upheld. We showed that the Code was developed by nurses who had expertise in ethics theory and who were highly experienced in nursing practice, and that the latest version (2008) was offered to all Canadian nurses for input before it was finalized. Philosophers (and astute students or practitioners) would challenge this process, saying that a code of ethics developed in such a way represents only what nurses themselves think is morally important in nursing practice: it talks about what "is," but not necessarily what "ought to be." However, we argue that in the absence of a clearly defined, universally accepted version of where "good" comes from, the understanding of good in nursing must come from practice. The values expressed in the Code grew out of the practical wisdom of expert practitioners through reflection on practice, and in consideration of ethical theories. Therefore we consider it an acceptable standard and authority on ethical behaviour. In other words, in the absence of one clear set of rules or standards that apply to everyone in all situations, we accept the reflective wisdom of practitioners as the standard of ethical practice. We also recognize that standards change over time, as demonstrated in the Code's history. Therefore, to be meaningful and constructive, such change requires active reflection on the part of all practitioners.

Patricia Benner shows how understanding of the good in nursing and nursing's moral identity are grounded in practice. Because the caring practices of the nurse have the good of the patient built into them, they have an inherent moral dimension. The meaning of what is "good" is embedded in the nurse's commitment to care (Benner, 1991; see also 1989, 1994, 1996, 1999). Everyday health care encounters with patients, and the relationships formed with them, are the foundation of moral practice. Thus a morally good nurse is actively concerned with fostering well-being through a caring relationship in the context of attentive, efficient, and effective nursing practice.

Nurses seek through ethical reflection to understand values and varying perspectives on issues. Ethical nursing practice involves working through the particulars of a situation, and this requires engagement in a relationship as well as skill and practical judgment. This kind of engagement means trying to understand what the experience means to the patient, because if the nurse does not know what matters to the patient, it is difficult to make decisions that are in the patient's best interests. Through questioning and understanding, ethical actions ought to become clearer and possibilities for actions should translate into reality. The nurse's respectful, insightful, and creative use of knowledge is essential in determining a correct course of action and fulfilling excellent nursing practice. It is also a requisite part of changing the system through leadership and policy development. Ethical thinking can be informed by many factors, as we shall discuss below.

A MODEL FOR ETHICS IN NURSING

Health care and nursing practice are constantly growing and changing. Technological advances, institutional practices, social influences, and fiscal constraints give rise to new ethical challenges almost on a daily basis. Practice has led to common understandings about what ought to be done in many situations. This common understanding is passed from one nurse to another through education, dialogue, and mentorship. With the complexity of practice and the rapid changes occurring within it, however, nurses may be faced with moral questions that have not previously been examined and for which no common wisdom exists. Each individual (patient and nurse) has a unique understanding of a situation as it arises in a particular context, so it will not be possible to cite "standard practice" as an answer to all moral questions. Nurses must be able to examine issues and bring ethical knowledge to bear in each situation. To do that, nurses must have **moral sensitivity**: they must be able to recognize the moral dimensions of situations and to call on a sound knowledge base for guidance in making right decisions. That knowledge base includes, but is not limited to, practical and theoretical knowledge, professional values, and the particularities of each situation.

Clearly, nurses need to have a way of thinking about ethical issues that will help them know how best to act in a given situation. We have shown that there are many theories that can help structure thinking, but none of them alone seems to be sufficient for the kinds of problems nurses face, so what will be of greatest use to nurses in their practice? Is there a theory of nursing ethics that nurses can turn to? Susan Sherwin, a noted Canadian philosopher and ethicist, has offered an idea that is useful for our purposes. She suggests that it is not productive to try to establish a single ethics theory that can answer all questions, because that is unrealistic. Instead, she suggests that we consider ethics theories as perspectives or *lenses* that we can look through. Each lens will give us a somewhat different picture, and we can select the lens that gives us the clearest view in a given situation (Sherwin, 1999). Similarly, Peter and Liaschenko (2003), building on the work of noted feminist philosopher Margaret Urban Walker, have suggested that we consider nursing ethics to be a "negotiated morality." In other words, they say that answers to moral problems must be negotiated in the context in which they arise. People bring different perspectives to the situation, depending on the lens they look through, and all these different viewpoints must be taken into consideration in coming to a resolution of the problem. This way of thinking of ethics in context seems to be more in keeping with what actually happens in health care situations and seems like a useful way of thinking about how to use different types of information. It also helps us to consider the broader moral environment in which we work and how we act in professional encounters within nursing and with other colleagues.

In nursing we use models to understand how concepts are related and how we can apply various theories to our practice of nursing. A **model** is an abstract representation of reality that can be depicted through either pictures or words, or a combination of the two. We have constructed a model, which we call the Ethics Composite Model, to represent how different factors and perspectives can affect thinking in nursing ethics (Figure 2.1). In the model we show how various ethical theories described in Chapter 1 and earlier in this chapter can work together in nursing. Specifically, we show how virtue ethics, normative ethics theories such as deontology and utilitarianism, bioethics, and relational ethics can influence thinking. But we also realize that other considerations such as law, societal demands, and the professional code of ethics play an important role. Finally, we show that **clinical competence**, or the skills of professional nursing practice, are an inseparable part of ethical action in nursing.

As you will see from Figure 2.1, the first element in the model is *virtue*, which provides the nurse with the motivation to act in the patient's best interests. The patient's best interests are represented as *beneficence*. Although you learned about beneficence as the bioethical principle that states our obligation to good, in this model we see it as the goal of care. Nurses' work is aimed at doing "good" for the patient, which also translates into promoting their well-being and not doing harm (*non-maleficence*). In order to know what the patient believes is good, the nurse needs to establish a relationship with the patient, described earlier in this chapter as *relational ethics*. Knowing what is important to the patient is not sufficient, however, as one must also take into account *bioethical principles*, which are a useful way of focusing on different aspects of the situation. The nurse also needs some understanding of *normative ethics* theories, particularly Kantianism and utilitarianism, as they help in interpretations of duty. For instance, a nurse needs to have some concept of "greater good" versus "individual good," and how that might influence decision making. Nursing ethics issues always arise in a particular context, which includes the values and concerns of other health care professionals (*institutional values*), societal expectations of nursing and health care (the *social context*), and relevant law (the *legal context*). The nurse's professional mandate, as expressed in the CNA *Code of Ethics for Registered Nurses*, will necessarily guide action. Professional or *clinical competence* is what brings all

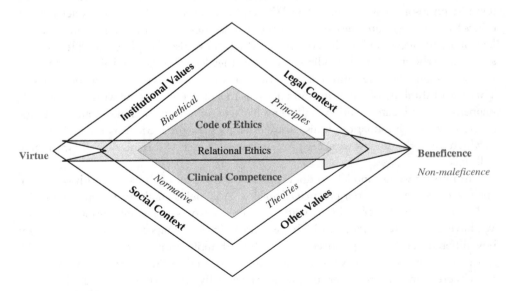

Figure 2.1 Ethics Composite Model

these elements together and enables the nurse to take appropriate action. We will describe each of these elements in more detail below.

Virtues and Nursing Ethics

Virtue is the starting point for ethical practice. In our earlier discussion we explained that the virtuous person, as described by Aristotle, was one who aspired to be the best person possible. In part because of the difficulty of defining "best person," this idea of an "ethics of aspiration" had fallen out of favour with moral philosophers, to be replaced by an "ethics of duty" or obligation. However, virtue theory is now attracting greater interest, as it seems only logical to think that the kind of person one is has something to do with ethics. It makes sense that "ways of being" would play an important role in nursing ethics, considering the importance of relational ethics and the centrality of the nurse-patient relationship.

Ethics in a practice profession requires understanding of virtue as well as obligation. In other words, the practitioner must consider not only "what must I do?" but also "what kind of person should I be?" According to the ancient Greeks, virtue meant personal excellence and aspiration toward it. With this in mind, it is fair to think that the virtuous nurse is one who aspires toward excellence as a professional. As Aristotle suggested, being virtuous includes the desire to choose well; accordingly, we believe that virtue provides the moral motivation that makes the nurse wish to act to bring about a particular goal, in this case the goal of increasing human well-being (beneficence).

Virtue in nursing, then, has to do with aspiring to be the best possible nurse one can be. Part of being a "good" nurse means having the moral motivation to work toward a professional goal of acting in the patient's best interests. Besides motivation, the good nurse needs personal characteristics such as compassion, caring, trustworthiness, fidelity, and integrity. **Compassion** in nursing means having a feeling for the pain and suffering experienced by others; **caring** implies acting for the benefit of others; **trustworthiness** means being dependable, someone who can be counted on; **fidelity** is loyalty to one's vows and promises; and **integrity** implies honesty, sincerity, and uprightness. Such characteristics may be inherent in persons attracted to nursing, but they are further developed in a professional nursing program. In particular, the student nurse learns ways to express compassion and learns to recognize situations that require particular kinds of trustworthiness and integrity. Students also learn that nursing involves a commitment to caring for others and that loyalty to that commitment is vital.

As we explained in Chapter 1, Aristotle argued that virtues grow through practice and the development of practical wisdom. In nursing, **practical wisdom** is knowing the how, when, and why of appropriate interventions, or in other words being able to make good practice decisions. The practical wisdom needed by the professional nurse can be enhanced through what nurse scholars Peggy Chinn and Marlene Kramer (2004) have called **praxis**, or "reflection in action." Thinking about practice and working to improve it are key characteristics of professionals. Put another way, nurses must begin with the moral motivation to "do good," and it is then through reflection on practice that they can develop the skills to interpret situations and make the best moral choices. If we think of virtue in this way, it is possible to see how it can be taught by training and practice. Much of what we do in nursing programs is aimed toward developing this kind of virtue.

Thus the virtue of the nurse is the starting point for a model of nursing ethics. A virtue-based approach considers the characteristics nurses require in their practice to be ethical, focusing on intentions, dispositions, and motives. In other words, it encourages us to consider the kind of person the nurse ought to be in her or his practice. Exploring one's virtue through self-reflection is an active part of the nurse's commitment to ethical care, because thinking about virtues helps the nurse to see how her or his unique characteristics as a person have an impact on relationships with others. The way in which a nurse responds to the patient or client is as important as, or perhaps more important than, the concrete action performed.

Another element of virtue in nursing is what we call **moral courage**, meaning the strength and commitment to act on one's beliefs. It is important to have the intent to act in the patient's best interests, and to have the skills and knowledge to do so, but it is not always easy to do the right thing. Having the moral courage to do what is necessary is part of ethical practice. In acting on her or his beliefs, the nurse becomes a moral agent, moral agency being the actual carrying out of a moral act. Virtue in nursing, then, means having the intent to act well, having the necessary characteristics that enable one to choose well, having the skills and abilities to carry out the chosen actions, and having the moral courage to act. This results in moral agency in nursing, which is necessary for ethical care.

Relational Ethics as Central

We believe that being in relation is at the heart of practical wisdom and ethical understanding. To accept this, one must first acknowledge that the goal of nursing is to act in the best interests of the patient. Without a connection to the patient as person, the nurse can have little idea of what would matter to that person, and therefore cannot begin to understand how to act in that person's best interests. In other words, relationship plays a vital role in informing practice, for it enables us to understand what would be the best choice of action in a given situation. It also helps us understand our part in the broader ethical environment. Our Ethics Composite Model (Figure 2.1) suggests that the goal of nursing is to act in the best interests of the person, family, or group through direct care and/or through leadership and policy development. Virtue is the motivation that drives the nurse to achieve this best-interests goal, and relational ethics is key to achieving it. To reflect our thinking, we have placed *relational ethics* in the centre of the model.

Bioethical Principles and Nursing Ethics Relational ethics is central to our conception of nursing ethics, but the bioethical principles are also important because they help focus thinking in particular ways. There is a rich history in nursing and medical ethics of using bioethics principles as the framework for analysis, and bioethics continues to have much to say to practising nurses. Recall that the bioethical principles are beneficence, non-maleficence, autonomy, and justice. We have already indicated that the principle of beneficence is what we see as the goal of nursing. Non-maleficence is essentially the reverse of beneficence, and says that we have an obligation to do no harm. It is important to consider non-maleficence as a principle because it requires us to think about possible harms in our actions, so in our model we have situated it close to beneficence.

Autonomy and the right to make decisions for oneself have had a huge influence on how we think about practice. The concept of autonomy has been the basis of the whole idea of informed consent. It might surprise you to learn that informed consent for medical or other procedures was not required until a few decades ago. Before that it was just assumed that the health care provider would know what was important and right for the patient. Today, we would not consider acting without seeking the patient's consent.

Similarly, issues of justice must be considered in practice. If a nurse manager is called upon to decide whether or not to allow another patient to be admitted to intensive care when there is a shortage of nurses, relational ethics alone will not be sufficient. The nurse manager might favour the patient with whom she had the relationship over the new patient, even if the new patient had a greater need for the bed. Hence, nurses should not rely on relationships alone when making care decisions. In this instance the nurse manager must look at the broader picture and consider what would be fair and just. Consequently, as we review cases in the remainder of this book, we will call upon the four main bioethical principles to help us sort through obligations and determine right action.

Normative Theories and Nursing Ethics While relational elements are central to ethical nursing practice, "being in relationship" with someone does not necessarily prevent values conflicts. Certainly it is essential for the nurse to know what matters to the person, family, or group receiving care; however, values and beliefs among all those involved in care situations may conflict, leading to questions about right action. As well, the nurse may experience competing obligations, for example when a duty to a particular individual conflicts with a duty to a larger group or to the institution. To help resolve these issues, the nurse might try looking through the lens of a utilitarian or a deontologist, and imagining what kind of solution this might evoke. Using normative theories in this way gives the nurse an opportunity to view the situation from different perspectives, and helps him or her see alternative solutions.

Context: Social, Legal, Institutional, and Professional Much has been written about the reality that nursing ethics issues always arise in a particular context. Nurses are employees and as such are influenced by many factors that can affect decision making. For example, nurses' work is generally governed to a large extent by institutional values and the values of other professionals, notably physicians. For example, a nurse might believe that a patient should not be discharged because of insufficient support at home, but the physician might feel the patient is able to cope, while the institution supports the shortest length of stay. In this case, the nurse must consider whether she or he has an obligation to "fight" for the patient's right to stay in hospital a little longer. Nurses are not always at liberty to exercise their moral agency, or in other words to do what they believe is best, because their work is regulated in numerous ways. Expectations of nursing care are also controlled in part by what society believes nurses and other health care professionals are supposed to do. If the family wants everything done for a critically ill relative, but the nurse believes there is no hope for this person's recovery and continued care promotes further suffering, the nurse is still obligated to provide care until the physician and family agree to stop treatment. Here the nurse will probably experience moral distress and might consider refusing to care for the patient but will have to consider whether the institution (and possibly the law) would support such a refusal of care. In addition to all the above considerations, there is another important factor that is essentially a part of the social context: the economic factor. As a society, we decide how much money is available for health care, and as we shall see in subsequent chapters, the amount of money can also be a limiting factor. As much as most of us would like to say that dollars should not have an impact on care decisions, the reality is that there is a limited amount of money to be spent, and care priorities will be affected. For example, a choice about whether to make more beds available in neonatal intensive care or to put the beds in long-term care will certainly limit what the health care system is able to offer in one way or another.

Code of Ethics and Clinical Competence At the core of the model are the Code of Ethics and clinical competence. We placed these near the centre because they are the key factors that influence the nurse's professional values and ability to act on those values. We have said that nursing ethics begins with the virtues of desiring to do good and be a good nurse, which require personal characteristics such as compassion, caring, and integrity. This does not imply, however, that *intending* to be a good nurse and having these characteristics is sufficient. Goodness or virtue in nursing also implies excellence in action, which requires the demonstration of particular skills or competencies. By **competency** we mean a practised ability to perform required nursing actions at a high level of proficiency. Nursing excellence has many components: **technical competence** (psychomotor skills, pattern recognition, knowledge of procedures, knowledge of the health care system); **relational competence** (ability to engage with others respectfully and authentically); and **theoretical competence** (knowledge of the why and how of possible interventions). To put it another way, nursing excellence requires "know what" (pattern recognition), "know how" (practical knowledge), "know who" (relational knowledge), and "know why" (theoretical knowledge). The nurse must be able to understand physical, psychological, social, and spiritual aspects of situations, and know when and how to act to help the recipient of care come as close to well-being as possible. This is what constitutes practical wisdom in nursing and the basis of nursing practice. Linking this to virtue, we believe that the desire to gain the necessary competencies to be a good nurse is a virtue, and that practical wisdom, meaning the competencies themselves, become virtues as they are learned. In this way, achieving competence in nursing becomes an ethical obligation.

As discussed earlier, the CNA Code of Ethics for Registered Nurses tells us what values are to be upheld by Canadian nurses. Its positioning near the centre of the Ethics Composite Model indicates that it is a central factor in ethical nursing practice. As moral agents, nurses act on what they believe, and the values of the Code are an articulation of what Canadian nurses believe to be important. These beliefs are upheld through enactment of clinical skills. Thus competence and the Code are what make ethical nursing practice "happen." However, as we have pointed out, nurses are not always free to act on their beliefs, which is the cause of moral distress and moral uncertainty.

DECISION MAKING IN CLINICAL PRACTICE

This is just a brief introduction to our model of nursing ethics. In subsequent chapters of this book we will use the Ethics Composite Model as a basis for analysis of case situations, and each of the different elements will be expanded upon. It may not be immediately obvious to you how the different parts of the model could translate into clinical practice, so we have developed a framework that you can use as a practical guide. Before we describe this framework in Chapter 3, we will discuss a case to illustrate how the different elements of the model could be brought into play and how difficult practice decisions can be (see Trying It On 2.1).

If we use the model, we can examine the case more systematically. Clearly, the nurse (Nancy) has the motivation to choose well on behalf of the patient. She appears to have the clinical competence to recognize an urgent situation and to act appropriately in starting oxygen and calling the physician. If we look to the centre of the model, we see that Nancy had established a relationship with Mrs. Jones. However, we are not certain that Nancy was doing all she could, as we do not have evidence that she asked Mrs. Jones to explain what she would consider a heroic measure. When we look at the CNA Code of Ethics for Registered Nurses, we find that one of the key values is choice. Nancy should be expected to honour the patient's choice, but without a clear understanding of what Mrs. Jones had in mind, we are not able to establish whether Nancy in fact did that. From a bioethical principles standpoint, we can see that the principle of autonomy, or freedom to choose, is probably the most important here. Again, if Nancy is to act in Mrs. Jones' best interests, she needs to understand what Mrs. Jones would choose in this situation. From a normative ethics standpoint, we understand that Nancy has an obligation to act in Mrs. Jones' best interests, but what is that action in this case? Without more information, it is difficult for us to answer this question.

Other factors at work in this situation include the hierarchical structure of a hospital, where nurses are generally expected to follow doctors' orders unless there is a very good reason to do otherwise. We do not know if the institution would support Nancy if she failed to do what the doctor asked. Nurses also need to know their legal position: Is there anything in law that requires the nurse to assist the doctor in this procedure? Finally, we need to know the social context and what exactly the family understood when they agreed with Mrs. Jones' desire for "no heroic measures."

On the surface of it, if we understand Mrs. Jones' wishes for no heroic measures to include such things as intubation, Nancy was not acting ethically when she assisted the physician in the intubation. However, if we look at the situation more closely, we can see that it comes right back to communication and relational ethics. We can't really judge

2.1 Conflicting Obligations

Mrs. Jones was an 83-year-old woman hospitalized for ulcer surgery. She had severe arthritis and had been bedridden at home for over a year. Post-operatively she developed respiratory complications, which resulted in an extended stay in hospital. During this time she frequently talked to the nurses and the surgical resident about her prognosis. She indicated on numerous occasions that if her condition should worsen, and particularly if she had a respiratory arrest (stopped breathing), she did not want "heroic" measures to be taken. She did not wish to continue a life of pain and dependency. Her family understood her position and agreed with her.

On May 6, Mrs. Jones was alert and oriented, and her general condition appeared to be improving. During her morning care, she and her nurse, Nancy Martin, had been discussing Mrs. Jones' wishes not to have aggressive treatment. Suddenly, Nancy noticed that Mrs. Jones was having increasing difficulty breathing. Nancy turned the oxygen on and hurried out to the desk to call the surgical resident. The resident was in surgery and unavailable, so the nurse, recognizing the seriousness of Mrs. Jones' condition, called the attending physician. The physician did not know Mrs. Jones well, but he came immediately, and after assessing her rapidly worsening condition, called ICU for advice. The resident in ICU stated that the patient required artificial ventilation and should be transferred to ICU. The attending physician called Nancy to assist him in intubating Mrs. Jones (putting a tube in her throat to enable mechanical ventilation).

Nancy told him about what Mrs. Jones had said, but he insisted that they follow the suggestion from the ICU physicians and intubate. Nancy complied and assisted the physician. Mrs. Jones was intubated and transferred to ICU, where she died four days later.

1. Do you see an ethical problem for Nancy?
2. What do you think Nancy should do in this situation?

This scenario was developed as part of a study one of the authors (Oberle) conducted on ethical issues experienced by practising nurses. This version is a compilation of similar stories told repeatedly by study participants and reflects their actual observations. Embedded in the scenario are many of the elements we discussed above. The question is whether Nancy should or should not assist with the intubation. Interestingly, when this scenario was presented as part of the research to a number of practising nurses, there was little agreement as to how it should be handled. Some felt that Nancy had done the wrong thing in going against the patient's wishes; others thought that Nancy had little choice but to comply with the doctor's request. Still others thought that there was no problem at all, because putting a breathing tube in a patient's throat is not what they would call a heroic measure, but rather a comfort measure. This scenario vividly illustrates that there can be many points of view and shows why nurses need a more organized ethical approach.

whether Nancy did the right thing if we don't know what Mrs. Jones wanted. The Code and bioethics principles point to the right of the patient to choose. Kantian ethics would also support that, as Kant was very concerned about paternalism and making choices for others. He, too, believed in a person's right to choose. Utilitarian ethics doesn't add a lot in this particular instance; it is more useful when questions of justice are being considered.

What makes this scenario interesting and relevant is whether Nancy would be able to act to support the patient's autonomy if Mrs. Jones wanted no intubation. Even if she thought that it was the wrong thing to do, Nancy might feel compelled to assist the doctor. It would be important for Nancy to know if the institution would support her if she chose to refuse the doctor's request. She might need a lot of moral courage to stand up to the doctor and ensure that the patient's wishes were followed. Of course, we could also consider whether a Do Not Resuscitate (DNR) order had been written and whether the patient had a written advance directive. We will explore similar issues later in this book, but in the meantime, this scenario acts as an introduction to some of the complexities of clinical decision making and shows how a model can help us consider various aspects.

CHAPTER SUMMARY

A profession is a self-regulating body that has its own set of practice standards. Canadian nursing is a profession with a specialized body of knowledge and skills. Its members are guided by the CNA Code of Ethics for Registered Nurses, which outlines the values and beliefs of the profession and the standards of ethical practice. The CNA Code was first published in 1980 and has since been revised approximately every five years to reflect changes in societal values, the health care system, and the changing role of nurses as professionals. The Code is an invaluable guide for practice. However, it provides only general guidelines and does not give clear direction for specific nursing ethics problems. Therefore, the practising nurse needs critical thinking skills informed by nursing ethics theory.

Ethics is about values, and it is essential that nurses have a clear understanding of the values that guide their care. All people involved in a care situation bring their own sets of values to it, and sometimes these values can be in conflict. Peoples' beliefs, which are influenced by their values, help determine what is important to them in a care situation. Nurses need to engage in conscious reflection and values clarification exercises to help them recognize their own values, and they need skill in finding out what values others hold. Awareness of values differences helps nurses develop moral sensitivity, the ability to recognize the ethical dimensions of care situations. Nurses also need some understanding of ethics theory to help them understand issues as ethics problems.

Nursing ethics has only recently emerged as a separate topic for scholarly analysis. It is becoming increasingly clear that normative ethics theory and bioethics are insufficient to guide nurses in the kinds of ethical situations they encounter. Nursing ethics is rooted in relationship, and relational ethics are the foundation of ethical care. Ethical relationships in nursing require six key components: embodiment, mutuality, engagement, non-coercion, freedom, and choice. Relational ethics requires nurses to pay attention to the patient's story and the meaning he or she attaches to the care situation.

A model of nursing ethics can help nurses understand the interrelationships among virtue theory, normative theory, and bioethics, and how they relate to nursing practice. The first component of the Ethics Composite Model presented in this chapter is virtue ethics. Virtue ethics in nursing asks the question, "Who must I be to be an ethical nurse?" It is about being the best possible nurse one can be. This includes having the intent to act in the patient's best interests, as well as having certain characteristics such as compassion, competence, caring, trustworthiness, fidelity, integrity, and moral courage.

In the model, the goal of nursing is beneficence. In order to know what is important for the patient, and what she or he would see as beneficence, nurses need to have a relationship to the patient. Therefore, relational ethics is the core of this model of nursing ethics.

Another element of the model is bioethical principles, which include autonomy, beneficence/non-maleficence, and justice. Originally expounded as the basis of medical ethics, they also have great utility in nursing ethics. They help nurses understand important aspects of situations and decide which elements have priority. These concepts can be useful tools for nurses in trying to determine what is most important in care situations. Normative ethics such as Kantianism and utilitarianism can also provide the nurse with some ways of structuring thinking around ethical issues.

Ethical issues in nursing always arise in a particular context. Institutional values, the values of others including other professionals, relevant laws, and societal beliefs can all have an impact on how a nurse thinks about ethical issues. These contextual features may make it hard for a nurse to act on his or her values and beliefs in a given situation. They may also make it necessary for nurses to develop moral courage.

Nursing ethics resides in nursing practice, so clinical competence is also a key component of nursing ethics. Practical wisdom, which is the ability to make good decisions, develops with experience. It includes components of practical, theoretical, and relational knowledge, as well as pattern recognition. Being competent is a moral obligation because care cannot be beneficent if the nurse is unable to carry out requisite tasks.

Questions for Reflection

1. What values do you think influenced you to select nursing as a career?
2. What values do you hold that you think might cause conflict for you in your nursing career?
3. What values do you hold that you think are easiest to realize in practice?
4. In your experience to date, to what extent do you think that your relationships with patients have been respectful?
5. What virtues do you think you have that are important in nursing?

Exercises

1. With a small group of student colleagues, engage in a discussion of how you think nursing ethics might be different from, or similar to, medical ethics. Provide the class with five points of similarity or difference.
2. In small groups, discuss the components of relational ethics (embodiment, mutuality, engagement, non-coercion, freedom, and choice). Each student should give an example of those elements in a patient-nurse relationship in which they have been involved.
3. Pick one care situation you have experienced, and journal the ethical concerns it posed as a values clarification exercise.
4. Using the same or a different care situation, engage in deliberate ethical reflection, using the values clarification questions in Table 2-2.
5. Imagine that you are the nurse described in Trying It On 2-1. Select the method of values clarification you prefer, and engage in reflection on this situation.

Research Activities

1. In your clinical setting, ask three staff nurses about what they consider to be the main elements of nursing ethics. Prepare a brief report for the class describing the top three to five main elements.

2. In your clinical setting, talk to three staff nurses about ethical concerns that they have experienced in practice. Write a report explaining how these concerns relate to the CNA Code of Ethics for Registered Nurses and how they could be approached using the Ethics Composite Model.

3. In your clinical setting, show three staff nurses the scenario Trying It On 2-1. Ask them what they think Nancy should do in this situation. Relate their answers to the model presented in this chapter.

Key Terms

belief	moral courage
caring	moral relativism
choice	moral sensitivity
clinical competence	mutuality
code of ethics	non-coercion
coercion	practical wisdom
compassion	praxis
competency	relational competence
embodiment	relational ethics
engagement	technical competence
fidelity	teleological
freedom	theoretical competence
integrity	trustworthiness
journalling	values clarification
model	values conflicts

References

Baier, A. (1987a). The need for more than justice. In M. Hanen & K. Nielsen (Eds.), Science, morality, and feminist theory. *Canadian Journal of Philosophy*, 13 (Supplement), 41–56.

Baier, A. (1987b). Hume, the women's moral theorist? In E. F. Kittay & D. T. Meyers (Eds.), *Women and moral theory* (pp. 37–55). Totowa, NJ: Rowman & Littlefield.

Beauchamp, T., & Childress, J. (2001). *Principles of biomedical ethics* (5th ed.). New York: Oxford University Press.

Benner, P. E. (1984). *From novice to expert: Excellence and power in clinical nursing practice*. Menlo Park, CA: Addison-Wesley.

Benner, P. E. (1989). *The primacy of caring: Stress and coping in health and illness*. Menlo Park, CA: Addison-Wesley.

Benner, P. (1991). The role of experience, narrative, and community in skilled ethical comportment. *Advances in Nursing Science*, 14, 1–21.

Benner, P. (1994). The role of articulation in understanding practice and experience as sources of knowledge in clinical nursing. In J. Tully (Ed.), *Philosophy in an age of pluralism: The philosophy of Charles Taylor in question* (pp. 136–155). Cambridge, MA: University Press.

Benner, P. E. (1996). *Expertise in nursing practice: Caring, clinical judgment, and ethics*. New York: Springer.

Benner, P. E. (1999). *Clinical wisdom and interventions in critical care: A thinking-in-action approach.* Philadelphia: Saunders.

Bergum, V. (2004). Relational ethics in nursing. In J. L. Storch, P. Rodney, & R. Starzomski (Eds.), *Toward a moral horizon: Nursing ethics for leadership and practice* (pp. 485–503). Toronto: Pearson Education Canada.

Bergum, V., & Dossetor, J. (2005). *Relational ethics: The full meaning of respect.* Hagerstown, MD: University Publishing Group.

Bishop, A., & Scudder, J. (1996). *Nursing ethics: Therapeutic caring presence.* Boston, MA: Jones & Bartlett.

Bishop, A., & Scudder, J. (2001). *Nursing ethics: Holistic caring practice* (2nd ed.). Sudbury, MA: Jones & Bartlett.

Canadian Nurses Association (1980). *CNA Code of ethics: An ethical basis for nursing in Canada.* Ottawa: Author.

Canadian Nurses Association (1991). *Code of ethics for nursing.* Ottawa: Author.

Canadian Nurses Association (2002). *Code of ethics for Registered Nurses.* Ottawa: Author.

Canadian Nurses Association (2008). *Code of ethics for Registered Nurses* (Centennial Ed.). Ottawa: Author.

Carnevale, F. (2005). Ethical care of the critically ill child: A conception of a "thick" bioethics. *Nursing Ethics,* 12, 239–252.

Chinn, P., & Kramer, M. (2004). *Integrated knowledge development in nursing* (6th ed.). Toronto: Mosby.

Gilligan, C. (1982). *In a different voice: Psychological theory and women's development.* Cambridge, MA: Harvard University Press.

Gilligan, C. (1988). Moral orientation and moral development. In E. F. Kittay & D. T. Meyers (Eds.), *Women and moral theory* (pp. 19–33). Totowa, NJ: Rowman & Littlefield.

Kohlberg, L. (1981). *The meaning and measurement of moral development. The Hinz Werner lecture series, Vol. XIII.* Worcester, MA: Clark University Press.

Liaschenko, J., & Peter, E. (2004). Nursing ethics and conceptualizations of nursing: profession, practice and work. *Journal of Advanced Nursing,* 46(5), 488–495.

Munhall, P. (1982). Methodologic fallacies: A critical self-appraisal. *Advances in Nursing Science,* 4(7), 43–47.

Noddings, N. (1984). *Caring: A feminine approach to ethics and moral education.* Berkeley, CA: University of California Press.

Oberle, K. (1993). Evaluating nurses' moral reasoning. Calgary, AB: Unpublished doctoral dissertation, University of Alberta.

Peter, E., & Liaschenko, J. (2003). Whose morality is it anyway? Thoughts on the work of Margaret Urban Walker. *Nursing Philosophy,* 4, 259–262.

Peter, E., & Liaschenko, J. (2004). Perils of proximity: A spatiotemporal analysis of moral distress and moral ambiguity. *Nursing Inquiry,* 11, 218–225.

Peter, E. H., Macfarlane, A.V., & O'Brien-Pallas, L.L. (2004). Analysis of the moral habitability of the nursing work environment. *Journal of Advanced Nursing,* 47, 356–367.

Rodney, P. & Varcoe, C. (2001). Towards ethical inquiry in the economic evaluation of nursing practice. *Canadian Journal of Nursing Research,* 33(1), 35–57.

Rodney, P., Varcoe, C., Storch, J. L., McPherson, G., Mahoney, K., Brown, H., Pauly, B., Hartrick G., & Starzomski, R. (2002). Navigating towards a moral horizon: A multisite qualitative study of ethical practice in nursing. *Canadian Journal of Nursing Research,* 34(3), 75–102.

Sherwin, S. (1999). Foundations, frameworks, lenses: The role of theories in bioethics. *Bioethics*, 13(3/4), 198–205.

Storch, J. L., Rodney, P., & Starzomski, R. (Eds.) (2004). *Toward a moral horizon: Nursing ethics for leadership and practice*. Toronto: Pearson Education Canada.

Varcoe, C., Doane, G., Pauly, B., Rodney, P., Storch, J.L., Mahoney, K., McPherson, G., Brown, H., & Starzomski, R. (2004). Ethical practice in nursing: Working the in-betweens. *Journal of Advanced Nursing*, 45, 316–325.

Varcoe, C., Rodney, P., & McCormick, J. (2003). Health care relationships in context: An analysis of three ethnographies. *Qualitative Health Research*, 13, 957–973.

Suggested Reading

Baylis, J., Downie, B., Baylis, F., Downie, J., & Dewhirst, K. (1999). *Codes of ethics*. Toronto: Hospital for Sick Children.

Bergum, V. (1992). Beyond rights: The ethical challenge. *Phenomenology & Pedagogy*, 10, 75–84.

Bergum, V. (2002). Ethical challenges of the 21st century: Attending to relations. *Canadian Journal of Nursing Research*, 34(2), 9–15.

Bergum, V. (2004). Relational ethics in nursing. In J. L. Storch, P. Rodney, and R. Starzomski (Eds.). *Toward a moral horizon: Nursing ethics for leadership and practice* (pp. 485–503). Toronto: Pearson Education Canada.

Bishop, A., & Scudder, J. (1999). A philosophical interpretation of nursing. *Scholarly Inquiry for Nursing Practice: An International Journal*, 13(1), 17–27.

Brown, H., Rodney, P., Pauly, B., Varcoe, C., & Smye, V. (2004). Working within the landscape: Nursing ethics. In J. L. Storch, P. Rodney, and R. Starzomski (Eds.), *Toward a moral horizon: Nursing ethics for leadership and practice*. Toronto: Pearson.

Cameron, B. (2004). Ethical moments in practice: The nursing "How are you?" revisited. *Nursing Ethics*, 11(1), 53–62.

Gastmans, C. (1999). Care as a moral attitude in nursing. *Nursing Ethics*, 6(3), 214–223.

Hartrick Doane, G. (2002). Am I still ethical? The socially-mediated process of nurses' moral identity. *Nursing Ethics*, 9(6), 623–635.

Johnson, J. (2004). Philosophical contributions to nursing ethics. In J. L. Storch, P. Rodney, &R. Starzomski (Eds.), *Toward a moral horizon: Nursing ethics for leadership and practice*. Toronto: Pearson.

Lightenberg, J. (1996). What are the codes of ethics for? In M. Cody and S Bloch (Eds.), *Codes of ethics and the professions* (pp. 13–27). Melbourne, Australia: Melbourne University Press.

Nisker, J. (2004). Narrative ethics in health care. In J. L. Storch, P. Rodney, and R. Starzomski (Eds.), *Toward a Moral Horizon: Nursing Ethics for Leadership and Practice*. Toronto: Pearson Education Canada.

Pellegrino, E. (1985). The caring ethic. In A. Bishop & J. Scudder (Eds.), *Caring, curing, coping: Nurse-physician relationships* (pp. 8–30). University, AL: University of Alabama Press.

Raffin, D. S. (2002). *Accompanying the dying: Nurses create a moral space for suffering*. Unpublished doctoral dissertation. Edmonton, AB: University of Alberta.

Storch, J., Rodney, P., & Starzomski, R. (2002). Ethics in health care in Canada. In B. Singh Bolaria & H. Dickinson (Eds.), *Health, illness, and health care in Canada* (3rd ed., pp. 409–444). Scarborough, ON: Nelson Thomson Learning.

Chapter 3

A Framework for Ethical Decision Making in Nursing

Chapter Outline

Engaging in Ethical Action: Issue 2

Reflecting on and Reviewing the Ethical Action: Issue 2

Chapter Summary

Learning Objectives

After reading this chapter, you should be able to:

- articulate what constitutes an ethical problem in nursing

- describe the Framework for Ethical Decision Making in nursing

- discuss how the Framework links to the Ethics Composite Model

- use the Framework to analyze a clinical case

You have probably already experienced some situations that made you feel uncomfortable in your nursing practice. You might have wondered whether they were ethical problems as such. In Chapter 1 you learned that ethics is about "ought and ought not." That is, ethics is about how we think about right and wrong behaviour. In nursing, every encounter with a patient has ethical elements, because as a nurse you have to make choices about what to do and how to act toward patients and the environment in any given situation. You will need to be aware of the quality of your relationships and whether you have the clinical competence to work effectively with particular patients. You will also need an awareness of what is expected by your employer, the patient and family, other health care professionals, and the law, and an awareness of what values nurses are expected to uphold. Every time nurses work with patients, they make ethical decisions. Whether or not these decisions become problematic depends in part on how the nurse feels about them. Any time you have been in a situation where you were not sure of the right thing to do, or which made you feel morally distressed, you were experiencing an ethical problem. This is part of what we meant by "embodiment" in Chapter 2. If you have felt something in your "gut" or have had some other bodily response, then it was probably an embodied ethical response.

If you have experienced ethical problems in your practice, you will be aware that they can be highly complex and difficult. Our purpose is to help you think about how you might deal with such problems. To begin this part of your learning about ethical decision making, we ask you to picture yourself on an acute care nursing unit. The patient is comatose, and the family has requested a certain treatment that the physician does not feel is appropriate. It has many horrific side effects, and there is no research to support its use in this kind of illness. In fact, the physician believes that further treatment would be of no use, as the patient's condition is beyond hope. She feels that what the family is asking for would just prolong the patient's suffering. The patient's wife and son have been at the bedside for most of the discussions, and they are very angry. They are convinced that the treatment will help the patient, and believe that it is being denied for cost-saving reasons only. After the doctor has left the room, they turn to you and ask your opinion. They plead with you to intervene with the doctor and convince her that the treatment is warranted. You realize that the wife and son are distraught and feel abandoned by the system. What should you do? Clearly the decision as to whether to start the treatment is not a nursing decision. What, if any, are your ethical obligations in this case?

In Chapter 2 we presented the Ethics Composite Model to show what a nurse needs to consider when faced with an ethical problem. As important as all these aspects are, however, they may not help the nurse in a situation such as the one described above if the nurse is unclear as to what his or her ethical obligations are. The situation is likely to produce moral uncertainty in the nurse, and, if he or she has a belief about what should be done, may also produce moral distress. A systematic approach to the problem is required for the nurse to determine where responsibilities lie. It is only then that the nurse can begin to think about the "right" thing to do.

To make the Ethics Composite Model more applicable to practice situations, we have created the Framework for Ethical Decision Making, which shows how a nurse might approach each situation. The Framework is the basis of what we call "Questions for Ethical Reflection" that will guide the nurse in decision making. While we recognize that asking these questions does not guarantee good answers, we can assure you that practice in approaching problems systematically will sharpen your skills. Reflection on actions taken will then help you decide whether they were morally sound. We will use the above scenario to illustrate parts of the Framework and will then present another clinical case to demonstrate how you might use the Framework.

A FRAMEWORK FOR ETHICAL DECISION MAKING

A **framework** is a structure of related concepts that is somewhat more concrete than a model, and consequently gives more direction for practice. Our Framework for Ethical Decision Making, shown in Figure 3.1, reflects the process a nurse should follow in thinking about ethics in care situations. It is meant to be a companion to the Ethics Composite Model and to reflect the elements that are present in it. In other words, each step in the Framework is influenced by elements of the model: virtue, relational ethics, bioethical principles, and normative theory, all directed toward the goal of acting in the patient's best interests. As we have seen, contextual factors that influence ideas about ethical action include law, institutional and societal values, and other values (including professional and family) at work in the situation. Therefore, the Framework takes these into account.

We would like to emphasize here that the Framework is a way of examining ethical problems in a systematic way. As such it will be of use in helping the nurse select "right" action in moral dilemmas, but it will also be useful as a guide for reflection on what we call **everyday ethics**, the day-to-day ethical encounters that a nurse has with patients, families, colleagues, and the broader environment. Everyday ethics is largely about the choices a nurse makes in relationships with others. In other words, it is about how nurses

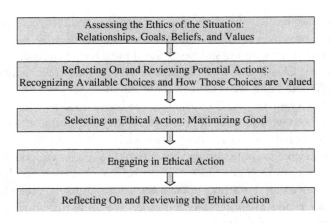

| Assessing the Ethics of the Situation: Relationships, Goals, Beliefs, and Values |
| Reflecting On and Reviewing Potential Actions: Recognizing Available Choices and How Those Choices are Valued |
| Selecting an Ethical Action: Maximizing Good |
| Engaging in Ethical Action |
| Reflecting On and Reviewing the Ethical Action |

Figure 3.1 Framework for Ethical Decision Making

ought to "be" with others, and as such is not necessarily about conflicts or problems, but merely about being in relation. Everyday ethics also includes the nurse's ability to provide care, that is to say, her or his competence. Thus everyday ethics is about relational ethics and competency in daily encounters with patients. Relational ethics is part of everyday ethics but is also an essential aspect of the complex and difficult ethical problems that nurses experience, as described in Chapter 1, such as moral distress, uncertainty, and dilemmas.

Framework Overview

The Framework is presented as a series of steps:

Assessing the Ethics of the Situation: Relationships, goals, beliefs, and values. What is happening here?

Reflecting on and reviewing potential actions: Recognizing available choices and how those choices are valued. What could I do?

Selecting an ethical action: Maximizing good. What should I do?

Engaging in ethical action. What will I do?

Reflecting on and reviewing the ethical action. What did I do?

The first step is *Assessing the Ethics of the Situation*. This requires what we referred to in Chapter 2 as moral sensitivity. When faced with a situation in which there appears to be an ethical issue, the nurse must try to come to an understanding of the issue through relationship, dialogue, and information gathering. Next, *reflecting on and reviewing potential actions* asks the nurse to take into account the possible options for care and to consider factors that might impact on available choices. In *selecting an ethical action* the nurse must decide what he or she believes would do the most good, and whether he or she can act on that belief. The ability to act will be determined in part by what others, including the patient and other care providers, believe should be done. The nurse must then examine whether he or she possesses the necessary skills and knowledge to act appropriately and must assess the relative risks and benefits of different choices of action. The next step is *engaging in ethical action*, which implies that the nurse must consider ethical, legal, and social aspects of the situation. The nurse must be mindful of the possibility of making an error and be able to justify and validate the decision. Finally, *reflecting on and reviewing the ethical action* allows the nurse to consider the action taken and learn from the experience, with the objective of strengthening her or his ability to provide ethical care. Details for each step are presented below.

Assessing the Ethics of the Situation: Relationships, Goals, Beliefs, and Values

Every care encounter a nurse has with a patient has ethical dimensions. A **care encounter** is any situation in which a nurse is working in a professional relationship with a patient, with intent to improve the patient's well-being (*beneficence*). The nurse must first possess the necessary *virtue* of wanting to choose well in making decisions that will fulfill that goal. Then he or she must assess each situation to determine what ethical elements are present.

The first step in assessing the situation involves relational ethics. As was mentioned in Chapter 2, a key theme in relational ethics is embodiment, which requires an awareness of the links among mind, body, and healing. Supportive, nurturing relationships that attend not just to the body but also to the caring and connections that contribute to "who" the patient is, are central to embodiment. With this in mind the nurse must first consider whether her or his relationships with the patient and family are supportive, nurturing, and caring. Through relationship the nurse seeks to determine the beliefs and values of those involved in the situation and what goals they hope will be achieved through the care encounter. If the nurse is unaware of what the patient and/or family want(s) and expect(s) from care, then it is difficult to establish what actions they would consider to be in the patient's (or their) best interests. The question to be asked is "What would the patient and family consider a good outcome?" This does not imply that caregivers always act on the patient's or family's beliefs, as their expectations might not be realistic or achievable in the circumstances. Part of the nurse's role is to help patients and family clarify their expectations. This kind of discussion can be quite difficult, because patients and family may have limited understanding of what might be possible for themselves or their loved one, and they may feel that caregivers are simply refusing care when they say that certain things cannot be done. In the scenario at the beginning of the chapter, we saw that the patient and family had a belief that the new treatment would be effective. The nurse should try to determine the source of that belief. Do they have information that the care providers do not? Have they had prior experiences that make them believe that this treatment might work? Is it a question of simply finding something that can give them hope? Do they have religious beliefs that guide their thinking in a meaningful way?

The nurse should explore how patient and family understand the patient's illness and whether they have all the information they need for their decision making.

The next step is to ask what other relationships, such as those the patient has with family and friends, are particularly important and to question the quality of those relationships. They may have a strong influence on how the situation is understood by all concerned. It would be worthwhile to examine the kinds of relationships that exist within the family and establish whether everyone has the same views of the situation. Disagreements among family members might become important to decision making. For example, in the above scenario we heard about the wife's and the son's views. There might be others whose opinion the patient would value, such as an absent child or another close relative. The nurse should inquire as to whether all those who are likely to have a part in decision making are present.

Part of the nurse's assessment should include relationships of patient and family with the health care providers, as well as relationships among those involved with the patient's care. Are there power imbalances? Does everyone feel supported and respected, or do some feel vulnerable or powerless? In care situations it is essential to show consideration for others' values. When relationships are not respectful, some may have difficulty expressing their views or feel their values are not understood. This can lead to moral distress for patients and caregivers alike. The patient and family might feel silenced or disrespected, but so might the nurse and other caregivers. For example, in our scenario the patient and family want more done than the care providers believe is reasonable, and the family's anger suggests that they do not feel that they have been heard. It seems that the care providers are placing emphasis on the patient's prolonged suffering, believing that further treatment is futile. They seem to be of the opinion that the best outcome would be for the patient to be allowed a peaceful death, and the patient and family appear to be interpreting this as abandonment. It is also possible that the care providers feel frustrated or disrespected because their views are not being honoured. It is important to remember, too, that care providers don't always agree. In this instance we do not know if the nurse agrees with the doctor's position or not. Nurses will be guided by their professional Code of Ethics and personal beliefs, while other care providers will be guided by their own professional codes and beliefs. Sometimes the different codes suggest different actions. In situations where there are disagreements about treatment options, it is essential that all have an opportunity to express their views. Without open dialogue some might feel their values have not been taken into consideration. The nurse should establish exactly where differences exist so attempts can be made to resolve them. This underscores the importance of relational ethics and strong communication skills in nursing.

From this discussion it should be clear why relational ethics is central to ethical practice. You should also be able to see that, as we discussed in Chapter 2, feminist ethics has an important influence on the kinds of questions a nurse might ask. Feminist ethics has made nurses sensitive to the hierarchical structures in health care and the effect of power and politics (context and environment) on relationships. In fact, relational ethics and the need to attend to issues of connectedness essentially arose from feminist thought.

Reflecting on and Reviewing Potential Actions: Recognizing Available Choices and How Those Choices Are Valued

Once goals, beliefs, and values have been established, the nurse should then consider the possible actions that could be taken. The way in which one interprets the situation and thinks about what options are possible will be influenced by bioethics theory and normative theories. For example, a nurse might ask, "Is the patient's autonomy an issue here? Ought I to act to protect that autonomy [bioethics]? Is there concern about individual rights versus the greater good [utilitarianism]?" The patient and family are largely responsible for decision making, but it is important that they have sufficient information. Much of the explanation of reasonable options is the physician's responsibility, but nurses have an important role in interpreting what has been said and in ensuring that the patient's voice has been heard in the discussion. This is part of what has been called the advocacy role in nursing. **Advocacy** in nursing means taking the part of another, speaking for persons who cannot speak for themselves, or intervening to ensure that their views are heard. The idea of advocacy is strongly influenced by feminist ethics in which a core concept is helping the voice of the vulnerable or silenced to be heard. Advocacy requires that we have a strong awareness of the context in which situations arise and an understanding of the influence of power and politics on how we make decisions. The nurse who experiences **constrained moral agency**—who feels powerless to act for what she or he thinks is right, or who believes his or her actions will not effect change—will have difficulty being an effective advocate.

Part of the nurse's responsibility in considering action involves thinking about his or her own values and beliefs about care. These values and beliefs may or may not be the same as those of the patients and family or of other caregivers, as discussed above. Some situations call for nurses to make decisions about care, while others require the nurse to act on someone else's (usually the physician's) orders about care. Nurses always have the option about how to treat patients in relationship, but do not always have the option about what treatments are offered to patients. This can create conflict, as when a nurse believes one action should be taken, but the physician believes something else ought to be done. If nurses are not able to express their values, they will find it difficult to engage in meaningful dialogue with others.

In situations that involve nursing decision making, nurses need to look at a variety of perspectives and determine what actions they think will do the most good. This also means taking into account how others in the situation will be affected. For example, a choice to discharge a patient might mean that others in the family will have to take time off work to provide care, which might not be possible for them. The key questions to ask are about the potential consequences of the actions: Who will be affected? How will they be affected? Are those effects acceptable? In the opening scenario, for example, it is important to understand that there are essentially only two options: to treat or not to treat. That is not a nursing decision, but nurses can help ensure that all the information is "on the table." They can also take part in discussions with the physician and family, ensuring that the family's views are understood. For instance, the nurse could point out that a decision not to treat could be devastating for this family at this time; perhaps the wisest course would be to wait until they are more ready to accept that further treatment will not be beneficial.

Sometimes the choice of treatment or options offered to a patient or family can cause the nurse moral distress. Considerations that seem to be in conflict with the patient's best interests might come into play. The nurse needs to recognize factors that impact on how decisions are actually made. For example, in the above scenario the nurse might feel strongly that the patient ought to be treated, just in case the family is right. However, medical judgment also needs to be respected, and it may be difficult to justify providing treatment that has no proven worth, particularly if it is very expensive. Again, awareness of power structures in the situation will help the nurse understand just what might be possible, and what might be out of the question. In another example, a nurse might feel that the patient should not yet be discharged, but there might be a serious shortage of beds, and one patient must be discharged to permit another, sicker patient to be admitted. In other cases, a treatment might not be available because there are no nurses available or because the cost of the treatment is seen to be excessive. These are economic realities of today's health care in Canada. Not all things can be offered to all patients at the time they need or want it. Political factors might also be evident. Fortunately, political considerations are not usually a concern, but when they are they are usually linked to economics. For example, a decision might be made to limit home support to the elderly or to a rural Aboriginal group in preference to giving more home support to new mothers and babies in the city. This might seem to nurses to be based more on a desire to serve a highly visible or politically favoured group. These kinds of considerations call for action at higher levels, removed from the individual care situation. We will be discussing questions of political action later in the book. For now, it is important for you to realize that economics and politics might limit possibilities.

In Chapter 2 we discussed some of the contextual elements that can limit the action a nurse might take. These must be taken into consideration when deciding on possible options for ethical action, so we will expand a little on them here. Nurses' decision making may be constrained by institutional policies and rules. Every institution will have policies designed to regulate nurses' behaviour. For example, there might be a policy directing nurses to initiate resuscitation proceedings if there is no medical Do Not Resuscitate (DNR) order. The nurse might have knowledge about a patient's wish not to be resuscitated, but must start the process because there is no DNR order. This might feel unethical to the nurse, because he or she knows it is against the patient's expressed desires, but it is not really a matter of choice for the nurse as an employee. In selecting an ethical action, the nurse needs to take into account the likelihood that the institution will back up the decision. In other words, will the nurse have the necessary support from his or her employers? In our opening scenario, the nurse will not make the decision as to whether or not treatment will continue, so it is not a dilemma for the nurse. However, the nurse might have to decide whether she or he can continue to provide treatment that prolongs suffering. It would then be very important to know what options are available and whether the institution will be supportive of the nurse's decision.

The law is another potentially constraining factor on nurses' moral agency. Legislation guides some nursing actions by stating specific responsibilities. For example, in some provinces there are acts detailing how vulnerable persons in care must be protected. There are also acts around end-of-life decision making and the legality of the patient's written directives about care (such directives are often called "living wills"). Tort laws concerning issues of consent and duty of care must be taken into account, as they will be the reference point for standards of practice. Employment law also binds nurses: in accepting a position they are, in effect, agreeing to follow institutional policies and procedures, and failure to do so can put them in breach of contract. Failure to follow the law can have serious consequences ranging from discipline by the professional association (which can include loss of licence to practice) to loss of employment and even charges of misconduct or negligence. It is important to note that law and ethics are not always congruent, and following legal requirements may or may not result in action the nurse considers most ethical.

Nurses faced with decisions about what to do need to know relevant legal requirements. For example, can a nurse refuse to carry out a doctor's order for an unconscious patient on the basis that the nurse believes the patient would not want the treatment? Is a nurse obliged to report drug abuse in the patient's home, even if it means destroying that patient's trust? Nurses are responsible for being aware of legislation that impacts their area of practice. Another reality is that society as a whole has certain expectations of care, which then shape individual beliefs. For example, there seems to be a general view in society today that death can be defeated if we just spend the money or use the right resources. When caregivers believe that care should be withdrawn but the family believes it should continue, caregivers might fear the threat of a lawsuit if they act on their understanding that further care is futile and a waste of scarce health care resources. This could be the case in the scenario that we have been discussing. If options are not made available to the patient or family, caregivers might feel at risk of legal action. This may lead them to feel they have to extend care for a longer period. Nurses might believe this is unethical, but the threat of repercussions can sometimes be a real factor in decision making. This kind of situation demands sensitivity to relationships as well as goals and expectations. As mentioned earlier, nurses will often play a central role in helping families understand what is reasonable and appropriate.

Selecting an Ethical Action: Maximizing Good

As we discussed above, in everyday ethics the nurse always has an obligation to treat patients with dignity and respect. This is not really part of decision making but is simply understood. However, some decisions about action may cause values conflict. When this happens, nurses must ask themselves about their own actions: what they can and are willing to do in the situation. They must ask themselves if they can support the patient's choice or the choice of other care providers. They must also be aware of their own options: do they have any choice in how they act? Are they at liberty to refuse to provide care or act on their own values? Health care institutions are generally hierarchical: there are lines of authority that might put the nurse's values at risk. For example, if the nurse radically disagrees with the views of the physician, does the nurse have the right to withdraw from the care situation? In other words, does the nurse have the right to act on his or her beliefs, and thus act as a moral agent?

The nurse's first objective is to act in the patient's best interests, but this is not always possible. Sometimes, the fact that the nurse works with patient, family, and community might complicate a decision; what is good for the individual might not be best for the community. For instance, a sexually promiscuous patient with HIV/AIDS might request that you not reveal his status to his sexual contacts or his wife. Here you would have to decide whether the patient's right to privacy supersedes the rights of others who might have contracted the disease from him. In this instance, legal parameters about reportable diseases would give you some guidance but would not necessarily answer your moral questions. Selecting the right action—the action that maximizes good—is not always easy. The nurse might not be sure what the best thing to do is or might be prevented from making the decision he or she believes is best. Ethical decisions in nursing are often very difficult. The purpose of this book is to help you think through those decisions and be confident that you have taken the important factors into account.

Another consideration for the nurse in selecting an action is whether she or he has the necessary knowledge and skills (clinical competencies) to carry out the action. For example, if the preferred ethical action involves ongoing support of a palliative patient at home, does the nurse have the necessary knowledge to help the family when the patient dies? Does the nurse know what needs to be done when a patient dies at home? The nurse must also assess whether he or she has the necessary virtues in the form of moral sensitivity and moral courage to do what needs to be done. If those are lacking, then no amount of right decision making will ensure that the right thing is done.

Engaging in Ethical Action

As part of engaging in ethical action, the nurse enters into negotiations with others in the situation, seeking their input and cooperation and working to foster their autonomy and dignity. Again, the nurse's ability to act as a moral agent will depend in part on his or her understanding of the situation based on relational ethics, bioethics, and normative theory. Factors influencing the nurse's action will include knowledge and skills, others' beliefs and values, codes of ethics, social context, and legislation. A constraining factor may again be the hierarchical structure of the organization in which the nurse works. Others, such as physicians, may be in charge of the care situation and may have certain expectations of the nurse's behaviour. Such constraint may be a source of moral distress for nurses as they strive to act on their beliefs. Sometimes nurses know what should be done but lack the moral courage to take appropriate action.

Questions a nurse must ask include whether or not he or she is acting with care and compassion and according to the CNA Code of Ethics for Registered Nurses. Another important question is whether the action is what a reasonable and prudent nurse would do in a similar situation. The court holds nurses to this standard if a care situation is ever challenged in court. The nurse cannot be held negligent if it is determined that she or he acted in a way that one would expect of a reasonable nurse with equivalent experience.

Reflecting on and Reviewing the Ethical Action

The final step in the model is evaluation. In reflecting on and reviewing the action, the nurse looks at both process and outcomes, asking whether the situation was handled in the best possible way. It is not sufficient to examine only the final result, as the process itself may have caused harm. Consequently, it is important to ask questions about *how* things were done, as well as *what* was done. The nurse must examine how everyone involved in the situation was affected and whether harm was minimized and good maximized. It is important to consider what might have been done differently and what was done well. Especially vital is examination of relationships: Were all individuals treated with dignity and respect? Were all voices heard? Were differing values taken into account? As part of the evaluation, the nurse should seek input from others involved and, if possible, consult experts. If a situation has been particularly troubling, the nurse might turn to other nurses, other caregivers, ethics experts (most institutions have an ethics committee or ethics expert who can be approached), and perhaps articles written by others about similar care situations. Improvement in practice depends on this kind of detailed assessment and analysis.

QUESTIONS FOR ETHICAL REFLECTION: USING THE FRAMEWORK IN NURSING PRACTICE

Ethical problems in nursing can be very complex, as you can see. Nursing obligations are often unclear, and a nurse's freedom to act in the most ethical manner is not always guaranteed. In fact, a good deal of nurses' moral distress comes from feeling constrained as a moral agent. Whatever the situation, the nurse needs to have a way of approaching it. The Framework for Ethical Decision Making provides that approach, but to clarify the kinds of questions you would need to ask, we have also developed the Questions for Ethical Reflection (see Table 3.1). You won't necessarily ask every question in every situation, and you might think of many more questions that are important; these questions are just a starting point, based on what we have discussed so far.

Table 3.1 Questions for Ethical Reflection

1. **Assessing the Ethics of the Situation: Relationships, Goals, Beliefs, and Values**
   - What relationships are inherent in this situation?
   - Who is significant in this care situation, and how should they be involved?
   - Are my relationships with others in this care situation supportive and nurturing?
   - What are the goals of care in this situation?
   - Are these goals shared by the patient, nurse, and others?
   - What beliefs and values are most important for the patient/family/community receiving care?
   - What are my beliefs and values?
   - What values in the CNA Code of Ethics for Registered Nurses are inherent in this situation?
   - What values are important for others in the situation, including other health care providers?
   - Do the individuals involved in this situation have different values? Do the differences create conflict?

2. **Reflecting on and Reviewing Potential Actions: Recognizing Available Choices and How Those Choices Are Valued**
   - What expectations do the patient/family/community have for care? What action(s) do the patient/family/community think will do the most good? Have I helped this patient/family/community become clear about what they value and the actions they think should be taken?
   - What action(s) do I think will do the most good? What do other care providers think?
   - What action(s) will cause the least amount of values conflict and/or moral distress? What are potential consequences of the actions? How will key persons be affected?
   - What values does society view as important in this situation? What are societal expectations of care?
   - What economic and political factors play a role in the patient's care? What actions are possible given the existing resources and constraints?
   - What legislation applies to this situation in terms of my obligations, the institution's obligations, and the obligations of other health care professionals? Are there legal implications of different actions?

3. **Selecting an Ethical Action: Maximizing Good**
   - What do I believe is the best action?
   - Can I support the patient's/family's/community's choice? The choice of other care providers? If not, what action do I need to take?
   - Are there constraints that might prevent me from taking ethical action?
   - Do I have the kind of virtues required to take ethical action? Do I have the necessary knowledge and skill?
   - Do I have the moral courage to carry out the action I believe is best? Will I be supported in my decision?

4. Engaging in Ethical Action

- Am I acting according to the CNA Code of Ethics for Registered Nurses?
- Am I practising as a reasonably prudent nurse would in this situation?
- Am I acting with care and compassion in my relationships with others in this situation?
- Am I meeting professional and institutional expectations in this action?

5. Reflecting on and Reviewing the Ethical Action

- Were the outcomes of this action acceptable?
- Was the process of decision making and action acceptable? Did all involved feel respected and valued?
- How were the patient/family/community affected? How were care providers affected?
- Were harms minimized and good maximized?
- What did I do well?
- What might I have done differently?

To give you more practice using the questions, we will now turn to another scenario, Trying It On 3.1.

Trying It On
3.1 Conflicting Obligations

Issue 1

Marnie is having a bad day. As a public health nurse working in the city downtown, she spends part of her time making home visits and part of her time in a middle school (Grades 5 to 9). Marnie's unit manager has just told her that the school wants her to teach the sex education classes. This has created a real moral dilemma for Marnie. She has very strong religious beliefs, and one of the things her church teaches is that birth control and premarital sex is wrong. She knows that if she teaches these classes, she will have to talk about birth control and safe sex. How can she get up in front of a class and discuss things she believes are morally wrong, even if they are "right"

from a health point of view? To complicate the problem, her two daughters, who are in Grades 7 and 8, go to the school. At home their teachings have been about not having sex before marriage. Marnie doesn't know what to do about this because on one hand she believes that teaching about sex is important, and she wants students to have accurate information, but on the other hand she is concerned that the school will want her to teach aspects that go against her beliefs. She really likes her work in the school, where she believes she has made a number of positive changes. She is worried that she won't be allowed to continue if she takes a stand and refuses to teach the classes.

(Continued)

3.1 Conflicting Obligations

Issue 2

Later in the day Marnie visits Jasmine, a young single mom with two children under two years of age. The younger child has a high fever and an earache, and needs to see a doctor. Marnie knows that Jasmine has no family physician, so she will have to take the baby to the nearest medical clinic, which is some distance away. Since Jasmine has very limited means, a taxi is out of the question, which means that she will have to take the children on the bus. The temperature outside is −20°C, and the bus requires a transfer. Marnie will be making another home visit about two blocks from the clinic and could easily drop Jasmine off, and perhaps even pick her up after the doctor has seen the baby. In fact, this is just what Jasmine has requested; however, there is a regulation that nurses are not to transport patients in their cars for insurance reasons. She tells Jasmine about the rule, and Jasmine says, "But surely they could make an exception. It's right on your way, and I just can't take the kids on the bus. It's too cold. It will make the baby worse." Marnie wants to be a good employee and follow the rules, but she feels a duty of care to Jasmine and her children. Her obligations to the institution and to the patient are in conflict, and she really isn't certain what she should do.

1. What do you see as the ethical issues in this scenario?
2. If you were Marnie, how would you approach the two problems?

In approaching these problems, Marnie would select the questions that seem to have the most relevance for her situation and modify them as necessary. We will address each problem in turn, showing how the questions might help to clarify the issue.

Assessing the Ethics of the Situation: Issue 1

■   What relationships are inherent in the situation?

In the first of Marnie's concerns, the important relationships are between Marnie and her unit manager, the school, and her children.

■   What beliefs and values are most important? Are the values shared?

Marnie's values, based on her religious beliefs, are incongruent with the job she has been assigned. There is no direct caregiving in this scenario, but Marnie does value giving students accurate information about sex. She also values being consistent in her teachings with her daughters and being true to her church and her beliefs. The school values providing the students with the most up-to-date and valid information, which is why they thought Marnie, as a health professional, would be the best person to teach this health topic. The institution (her unit manager) also values providing the students with the best possible health teaching. Clearly values conflicts are present.

Reflecting on and Reviewing Potential Actions: Issue 1

- What action(s) will do the most good and cause the least amount of values conflict and/or moral distress? What are the potential consequences of the actions? How will key persons be affected?
- What values does society view as important in this situation?
- What economic and political factors play a role in the patient's care? What actions are possible given the existing resources and constraints?

In this situation, Marnie has two main options for action. She can refuse to teach the classes, but then she has to consider the potential ramifications in terms of both the students' knowledge and her position as an employee. Or, she can agree to teach the classes, which will undoubtedly cause her moral distress. If she looks at ethics theory, she might see that utilitarian theory would direct her to teach the class, as this would lead to the greatest good. Bioethics does not give her much help in this situation, as it is not clear what principles would be given precedence. Bioethics does not say much about how to address issues that are primarily centred on a caregiver's personal values, such as in this scenario. The CNA Code of Ethics for Registered Nurses suggests that nurses are not obligated to provide care or services that are morally repugnant to them, unless there are no other options. In Marnie's situation it is not clear whether the institution she works for would support her if she refused the assignment.

If Marnie agrees to teach the classes, she might lessen her personal sense of conflict by explaining her position to her daughters and seeking their support and understanding. She might also try to negotiate with another colleague to trade this particular task for another task. For instance, she might offer to take another nurse's immunization clinic in exchange for teaching the classes. The economics of the situation are probably that no one else can be hired to give the classes, so the task will have to be arranged within the current staff roster. Not offering the classes does not appear to be an option, as the unit manager appears to believe it is important to have the public health nurse do the teaching. Marnie could approach the unit manager with her concerns, however, and attempt to negotiate an alternative. If there is no satisfactory resolution to the problem, Marnie will have to decide if she wants to compromise her personal values or lose her role in the school or even her job.

Selecting an Ethical Action: Issue 1

- What do I believe is the best action?
- Are there constraints that might prevent me from taking ethical action?
- Do I have the kind of virtues required to take ethical action? Do I have the moral courage to carry out the action I believe is best? Will I be supported in my decision?

As Marnie works through the scenario, she will have to decide what she values most. Once she has collected all the information, she will have a better idea of what her options might be. This might present as a true dilemma for Marnie, depending on whether or not she can make arrangements not to teach the classes. If she feels that she must teach the class or lose her position, she will have to consider the ramifications and whether she has the moral courage to leave the job. She will also have to consider whether losing her job would have a negative impact on her family. Here we see that the nurse exists in a web of relationships that can strongly influence her decision making.

Engaging in Ethical Action: Issue 1

■   Am I acting according to the CNA Code of Ethics for Registered Nurses?

■   Am I practising as a reasonably prudent nurse would in this situation?

■   Am I acting with care and compassion in my relationships with others in this situation?

■   Am I meeting professional and institutional expectations in this action?

Whatever decision Marnie makes, she will have to consider the above questions. Of course, if she quits her job there are no such issues, as she will not be providing care. If she continues in the job she will have to consider whether or not she is providing full information to the students. She will also have to consider whether she is comfortable that her daughters are not confused by the apparent inconsistencies in her teaching. It is important to acknowledge that Marnie has an obligation not to do harm to her family. This is the kind of "care ethic" that Nel Noddings, whom we discussed in Chapter 2, would say is legitimate as a moral concern, but it does not find a place in traditional normative ethics theory.

Reflecting on and Reviewing the Ethical Action: Issue 1

■   Were the outcomes of this action acceptable?

■   Was the process of decision making and action acceptable? Did all involved feel respected and valued?

■   How were the patient/family/community affected? Were harms minimized and good maximized?

■   What might I have done differently?

Once the decision is made, Marnie has to assess whether this was the best action she could have taken. She will have to consider all the outcomes and whether she used her negotiation skills to best advantage. It is not possible for another to assess the outcome in this case, as Marnie's personal values are at the centre of this scenario. Only she can decide whether she has been morally compromised.

Assessing the Ethics of the Situation: Issue 2

- Are my relationships with others in this care situation supportive and nurturing?
- What are the goals of care in this situation?
- What beliefs and values are most important for the patient/family/community receiving care?
- What are my beliefs and values?
- What values in the CNA Code of Ethics for Registered Nurses are inherent in this situation?
- What values are important for others in the situation, including other health care providers?
- Do the individuals involved in this situation have different values? Do the differences create conflict?

In this second situation, Marnie's conflict is a difference between what she believes ought to be done for the patient and what the employer will allow. Marnie appears to have a caring, supportive relationship with the patient. The problem is that the health unit has regulations that prohibit Marnie from doing what she thinks is right for this patient. Marnie needs to clarify her position by asking herself which values she thinks are most important to her. She values being a good employee, but she also values providing transportation for Jasmine. She believes that Jasmine's need is great. Jasmine clearly values getting support for her daughter and is apparently not concerned about the regulations.

Reflecting on and Reviewing Potential Actions: Issue 2

- What expectations does the patient have for care?
- What action(s) will cause the least amount of values conflict and/or moral distress? What are the potential consequences of the actions? How will key persons be affected?
- What economic and political factors play a role in the patient's care? What actions are possible given the existing resources and constraints?
- What legislation applies to this situation in terms of my obligation? Are there legal implications of different actions?

In examining possible actions, Marnie realizes that Jasmine expects her full support. She also knows that the institution expects her compliance with regulations. Marnie has several potential actions. She could take Jasmine and the children, against regulations. She could refuse Jasmine's request. Or she could consult with her supervisor to see if she could get permission to transport Jasmine and the children. In the latter instance, if she is refused permission, she will have to decide whether to follow her employer's direction or act on her belief that she should help Jasmine. What should she do?

In this instance, bioethics and normative theories are not especially helpful, as they do not facilitate sorting out priorities of this type. If one were to look at what is best for the patient, the goal is clear, but if one were to consider the principle of justice or a utilitarian ethic, it is less so. What is in the best interest of the patient may not serve justice or the greatest good, because if something happens that the employer's insurance does not cover, this choice might be very costly, which might mean reducing services for other people. There is no clear rule that says what is right in this situation. The CNA Code of Ethics for Registered Nurses says that patients deserve support, but at what cost to Marnie and the institution? Marnie could probably get away with taking Jasmine in her car, unless something went wrong, but would that be the right thing to do? If Marnie followed Kant's beliefs, she would probably not take Jasmine, because that would require being dishonest with and disloyal to her employer. If she were to say such dishonesty or disloyalty was acceptable on this occasion, she would logically have to say it is acceptable whenever "the end justifies the means," which Kant would say is wrong. Marnie feels a duty of care, however, which is supported by feminist ethics. There is probably no relevant legislation that can give her guidance. Finally, it seems evident that this is a situation where one's duty of care conflicts with economic realities, a relatively common experience in today's health care system.

Selecting an Ethical Action: Issue 2

■ What do I believe is the best action?

■ Are there constraints that might prevent me from taking ethical action?

■ Do I have the kind of virtues required to take ethical action? Do I have the necessary knowledge and skill?

■ Do I have the moral courage to carry out the action I believe is best? Will I be supported in my decision?

Again, as an employee Marnie has to decide whether the repercussions would be worth it if she helped Jasmine against the rules. If Marnie were told that she should not take Jasmine, it is likely that Marnie would comply, as she does have certain responsibilities as an employee. It is not entirely clear, however, whether this is the right thing to do in this instance, particularly as we have little information about why the rule was initiated in the first place. If there is little basis for the rule, a care ethic would suggest that Marnie break the rule and take Jasmine. However, this might have serious consequences for Marnie. Also, if Marnie were to say it was acceptable to break the rule this time, would she feel it was acceptable to break the rule every time the patient had problems with transportation? If so, then she could become a glorified taxi service. If not, she would have to figure out some rules to guide her in deciding whom she could transport and whom she could not. Otherwise, she would simply have to decide on some other parameter, such as whether she liked the patient or not. This would not appear to be an acceptable alternative.

Engaging in Ethical Action: Issue 2

- Am I acting according to the CNA Code of Ethics for Registered Nurses?
- Am I practising as a reasonably prudent nurse would in this situation?
- Am I acting with care and compassion in my relationships with others in this situation?
- Am I meeting professional and institutional expectations in this action?

In this difficult situation, if Marnie acts with care and compassion, then according to the Code she will be in conflict with her employer through not acting according to the employer's expectations. The Code would not require her to do that. Again, Marnie would have to make a decision based on what her own values are, how she understands Jasmine's needs, and how she understands the possible consequences. This is a true dilemma, in that the two ethical actions (honouring Jasmine's request or refusing it) are in conflict. The best Marnie could hope for would be a compromise with her manager that would allow her to take Jasmine and have the rule reexamined. If no compromise is possible, Marnie will have to consider all the issues at stake and make a choice. Again, she has to consider her own needs and the needs of her daughters as well: If she does not have a job, will her family suffer? She also has to take into account the concerns raised above. If she were to take Jasmine in her car, would this set a precedent for her with regard to transporting patients? In the final analysis, Marnie should probably abide by the rule but take action to have the rule reexamined and its basis made more clear.

Reflecting on and Reviewing the Ethical Action: Issue 2

- Were outcomes of this action acceptable?
- Was the process of decision making and action acceptable? Did all involved feel respected and valued?
- How were the patient/family/community affected? How were care providers affected?
- Were harms minimized and good maximized?
- What did I do well?
- What might I have done differently?

As in the first issue, Marnie needs to look at her action and decide if she acted in the most ethical way possible. She might want to discuss this with her colleagues and her supervisor or unit manager to see what others might have done in the same situation. Ideally, problems such as this that create conflicts for staff should be openly discussed without penalty to staff. It is only through dialogue and reflection that problematic rules and procedures can be exposed and their basis uncovered. It might be much easier for Marnie to refuse Jasmine if she understood the reason for the rule and could see, for example, that it was important for the long-run protection of the institution.

CHAPTER SUMMARY

Ethical decision making in nursing practice is a complex set of skills that nurses need to develop. In this chapter we provided the Framework for Ethical Decision Making, which can guide a nurse in identifying ethical issues, considering important actions, selecting the best action and carrying it out, and reflecting on the outcomes as a way of improving decision making for the future. The framework is based on the Ethics Composite Model described in Chapter 2. We then presented a series of Questions for Ethical Reflection that a nurse should ask whenever an ethical problem is encountered and a choice about ethical action has to be made. These questions are based on the Framework, but are only a starting point for the kinds of key questions nurses might ask themselves. We then showed how a nurse might select relevant questions from the list in analyzing two nursing-practice problems.

Nurses must learn to incorporate reflection and questioning into all their daily activities if the model and framework are to have utility in nursing practice. In the remainder of this book, we will provide more examples of how this might be done, using case studies that reflect typical moral issues in nursing. Since the CNA Code of Ethics for Registered Nurses is the primary moral guide for professional practice in Canada, we will organize our thinking around the eight primary values in the Code. For each value we will provide some theoretical background, then present case studies in which the value under study is challenged. We will use the framework and reflective questions to analyze the case study and consider what nursing actions would have been morally defensible in the situation. While we realize that our analysis is not the final word on any case, we hope to stimulate the reader to begin a journey of ethical reflection that will form the basis for ongoing ethical practice.

Questions for Reflection

1. Have you ever encountered a situation in which you were not sure what your obligations were? Why do you think it was unclear?

2. What is the basis for moral sensitivity? Do you think that it is possible to learn to be more sensitive to ethical issues?

3. What is the role of the nurse as patient advocate? How often have you seen nurses act as advocates for patients? Did you think of this as a moral obligation of the nurse?

Exercises

1. Consider the Framework for Ethical Decision Making, and think about how it compares with other processes you might have learned, such as the nursing process or patient assessment. What similarities and differences do you see? Do you see overlap among the steps of the Framework? Discuss this in small groups with your classmates.

2. Think about the Questions for Ethical Reflection. Can you think of other questions that might be important? Discuss this with your classmates, and see if you can add to the Framework.

3. Think about a care situation in which you felt some moral uncertainty. Think about whether the Framework might have helped you work through the situation.

4. In small groups, role-play with your classmates the scenario described at the beginning of the chapter. Members of the group should take the parts of nurse, doctor, patient, wife, and son. Try to imagine what kinds of things the family might say. After the role-play, discuss what the nurse's response might be, and, as a group, try to determine what the nurse should have done based on how members of the group played their parts.

5. In small groups, discuss what you think Marnie should do in the care situations described in Trying It On 3-1. Try to determine the basis for differences: What points of view do others present, and what are their perspectives?

Research Activities

1. Go to the literature, and find an article about ethical problems in nursing practice. You may choose from the selected readings if you wish. Consider what kinds of questions you might need to ask in a given situation. What would you need to know to assess the situation?

2. Talk to your nursing preceptor or other staff nurse about the Framework, and ask him or her to think about whether the questions could be useful. Ask the nurse to consider what barriers there might be to acting ethically in the clinical situation.

3. Discuss Marnie's two problems with three staff nurses. Make a brief report of similarities and differences in their views about what Marnie *should* do, and what they *would do* if they were Marnie. Discuss the various perspectives in class, and compare them with your fellow students' viewpoints.

Key Terms

advocacy

care encounter

constrained moral agency

everyday ethics

framework

Suggested Reading

Altun, I., & Ersoy, N. (2003). Undertaking the role of patient advocate: A longitudinal study of nursing students. *Nursing Ethics*, 10, 462–471.

Blasszauer, B., & Palfi, I. (2005). Moral dilemmas of nursing in end-of-life care in Hungary: A personal perspective. *Nursing Ethics*, 12, 92–105.

Blondeau, D., Lavoie, M., Valois, P., Keyserlingk, E. W., Hebert, M., & Martineau, I. (2000). The attitude of Canadian nurses towards advance directives. *Nursing Ethics*, 7, 399–411.

Bosek, M. S. D. (2001). Ethical decision making by emergency nurses: A descriptive model. *Journal of Nursing Law*, 7, 31–41.

Chaowalit, A., Hatthakit, U., Nasae, T., Suttharangsee, W., & Parker, M. (2002). Exploring ethical dilemmas and resolutions in nursing practice: A qualitative study in Southern Thailand. *Thai Journal of Nursing Research*, 6, 216–230.

Dawe, U.,Verhoef, M. J., & Page, S. A. (2002). Treatment refusal: The beliefs and experiences of Alberta nurses. *International Journal of Nursing Studies, 39,* 71–77.

Doutrich, D., Wros, P., & Izumi, S. (2001). Relief of suffering and regard for personhood: Nurses' ethical concerns in Japan and the USA. *Nursing Ethics, 8,* 448–458.

Jezuit, D. L. (2000). Advanced practice: Suffering of critical care nurses with end-of-life decisions. *MEDSURG Nursing, 9*(3), 145–152.

Koller, K., & Hantikainen, V. (2002). Privacy of patients in the forensic department of a psychiatric clinic: A phenomenological study. *Nursing Ethics, 9,* 347–360.

Oberle, K., & Hughes, D. (2001). Doctors' and nurses' perceptions of ethical problems in end-of-life decisions. *Journal of Advanced Nursing, 33,* 707–715.

Schwarz, J. K. (2003). Understanding and responding to patients' requests for assistance in dying. *Journal of Nursing Scholarship, 35,* 377–384.

Schwarz, J. K. (2004). Responding to persistent requests for assistance in dying: A phenomenological inquiry. *International Journal of Palliative Nursing, 10,* 225–235.

Smith, K. V., & Godfrey, N. S. (2002). Being a good nurse and doing the right thing: A qualitative study. *Nursing Ethics, 9,* 301–312.

Solum, L. L., &, Schaffer, M. A. (2003). Ethical problems experienced by school nurses. *Journal of School Nursing, 19,* 330–337.

Sorlie V., Jansson L., & Norberg, A. (2003). The meaning of being in ethically difficult care situations in paediatric care as narrated by female registered nurses. *Scandinavian Journal of Caring Sciences, 17,* 285–292.

van Rooyen, D., Elfick, M., & Strumpher, J. (2005). Registered nurses' experiences of the withdrawal of treatment from the critically ill patient in an intensive care unit. *Curationis: South African Journal of Nursing, 28,* 42–51.

Chapter 4

Value 1: Providing Safe, Compassionate, Competent, and Ethical Care

Chapter Outline

Learning Objectives

After reading this chapter, you should be able to:

- articulate what constitutes an ethical problem in nursing

- describe the first primary value in the CNA Code of Ethics for Registered Nurses: *providing safe, compassionate, competent, and ethical care*

- discuss the concept of professional self-regulation

- summarize the historical development of self-regulation in Canadian nursing

- discuss the concept of competence in nursing

- outline mechanisms for ensuring continuing competence in Canadian nurses

- articulate the relationship between law and professional competence

- define compassion in nursing

- describe issues of safety and moral obligation in nursing

- describe how Canadian nurses demonstrate *safe, compassionate, competent, and ethical care* as a lived value

- apply the Framework for Ethical Decision Making to a clinical problem in which the first primary value is challenged

What does it mean to be a nurse in Canada? How does the CNA Code of Ethics for Registered Nurses help nurses in their practice? How can nurses use the Ethics Composite Model and the Framework for Ethical Decision Making to help them make ethical decisions about the care they give? These are some of the questions that the remaining chapters of this book will address. The first three chapters provided you with a foundation for thinking about ethical issues; now we will begin to look more specifically at practice decisions. We will organize our discussion around the values in the Code, as that represents the values Canadian nurses have said are most important to practice. In this chapter we will discuss the first value and how it is related to practice. We will consider the notions of competence and nursing practice standards. Competence must be continually demonstrated, so we will discuss how a nurse maintains competence and assesses her or his fitness to practise. We will define compassion briefly and consider some of the issues related to ensuring safety. Finally, we will describe two clinical scenarios that reflect this value and use the Framework to analyze them.

THE FIRST PRIMARY VALUE: PROVIDING SAFE, COMPASSIONATE, COMPETENT, AND ETHICAL CARE

The first value in the CNA Code of Ethics for Registered Nurses is stated as "Nurses provide safe, compassionate, competent, and ethical care" (CNA, 2008, p. 8). We have already discussed several aspects of this value in Chapters 2 and 3, where we talked about nurses' obligations to strive for the highest quality of care possible, to be clinically competent, to recognize their own levels of competence, and to understand their own values. We also discussed the need to minimize harm. All these obligations are detailed in the Code in responsibility statements associated with this first value.

Safe, compassionate, competent, and ethical care is the first value because it is the foundation of nursing practice and the ultimate goal of nursing. Nurses have a responsibility to safeguard the quality of care that patients receive. Society holds nurses to high standards. Consequently, nurses must keep up to date with changes in practice, follow current guidelines, and integrate research findings into their practice. It is part of nursing's mandate to take preventative or corrective action to protect patients from unsafe, incompetent, or unethical care from nurses or other health care providers. The safety of workplace conditions in which they practice is also a concern for nurses, whether it be their or their patients' safety. Upholding the value of *safe, compassionate, competent, and ethical care* is an enormous responsibility that nurses do not take lightly. One way this value is realized is through self-regulation and practice standards.

NURSING COMPETENCE

Nursing competence refers to integration of knowledge, skills, abilities, and judgment in enacting care delivery. If nurses do not have the necessary knowledge and skills to provide care to patients, mistakes will happen and patients may suffer harm. The Canadian Nurses Association proposes that providing for patient safety involves a wide range of actions at the level of the individual nurse, the profession, the multidisciplinary team, the health care organization, and the health care system (CNA, 2003). Nursing competence is in part about psychomotor skills and working with technology, but it also involves other things. Abilities to assess, plan, organize, and delegate are critical. Communication skills such as listening to the patient and family, and providing information in a language that they can understand, are essential to safe nursing practice and to making health care experiences as positive as possible. Open, clear, and honest communication with members of the health care team, including other nurses, physicians, other health care providers, and administrators, is crucial for optimal care and risk management. It is part of a nurse's responsibility to ensure that communication is clearly received and understood. Documentation of care is another important element of practice, as it allows communication among members of the health care team and provides evidence of the kind of care that was given.

Practice Standards

In Canada Registered Nurses (RNs) have the privilege of being members of a **self-governing or self-regulating** profession. That means that nursing has been given the responsibility under law to ensure accountability for practice. It follows that nursing associations must monitor the practice of their members and discipline them for poor performance. In Canada the Canadian Nurses Association, to which all provincial and territorial associations belong except Quebec, articulates overall practice standards. **Practice standards** are written statements detailing those things for which nurses must be accountable, and as such are closely tied to the CNA Code of Ethics for Registered Nurses. Practice standards are designed to ensure nursing competence, which is the minimum standard for ethical practice. Provincial or territorial professional nursing associations have been granted responsibility for regulation and are required to enforce the national standards. In addition, every province or territory has its own specific standards and legislation that guide nursing practice. Nurses are obligated to maintain those standards and laws through the ongoing acquisition and critical application of relevant knowledge, attitudes, skills, and judgment (CNA, 1987).

Self-regulation is recognized as a professional privilege because it enables a profession to define and monitor its own practice. Laws allowing nursing to be self-regulating are relatively new. Historically, nursing education was based on an apprentice system of hospital training. Students learned on the job, through observation and sharing of knowledge by experienced nurses. Formalized nursing education began in Canada in 1874 after worldwide recognition of the work of Florence Nightingale. Nursing practice was defined and guided by a list of delegated medical responsibilities, which served to outline the boundaries between nursing and medicine. Gradually it became evident that nursing had a specific body of knowledge and that those who understood what nurses were educated to do and what could reasonably be expected of them should monitor nursing competency. Therefore, Canadian nurses began to lobby to become self-regulating. Nursing Practice Acts were passed at various times across the country. For example, nursing has been self-regulating in Manitoba since 1913, whereas self-regulation in Ontario has been in effect since 1963, and in Alberta, the Nursing Profession Act was passed in 1980. The relevant legislation in each province not only gives nursing the power of self-regulation but also defines its scope of practice, which is protected by the title Registered Nurse. That is, the **scope of practice** legislates the activities that only those with the title of Registered Nurse are permitted to undertake.

Definitions of nursing practice and professional responsibilities are always changing. For example, the Alberta Nursing Profession Act was revoked in 1999 and a Health Professions Act proclaimed (in part) in 2004. This new legislation allows other professions, such as Licensed Practical Nurses, to perform some of the activities that were formerly restricted to RNs. Other provinces and territories are experiencing similar transitions. It is important that nurses be up to date on what they are permitted and/or expected to do under law in the course of their daily work. Nursing professional organizations in Canada are also required to change with the times, modifying professional practice standards as required. At present, all professional standards in Canada require nurses to promote good practice, prevent poor practice, and intervene with unacceptable practice. If nurses are to know what "good practice" looks like, nursing practice standards must include a list of **competency statements**. These are detailed lists of the skills nurses must have and the tasks they must be able to perform in all areas of practice. Such competency statements form the basis of nursing curricula and the accreditation of nursing programs in education and clinical practice. **Accreditation** is a formalized approval process whereby a nursing education program, or indeed an entire health care institution, is evaluated by external reviewers to see if it meets minimum standards. Competency statements are also used to define specialist practice. Finally, they give guidance to nurses, providing a clear set of expectations as to what nursing practice should entail.

Each provincial or territorial association has the responsibility of developing practice standards and for ensuring that they are maintained. The exception is Ontario, where regulatory and professional development responsibilities are divided; the Ontario College of Nursing is the regulatory body. The development of standards has been recognized as an important milestone in nursing's evolution toward professionalization. To become an RN, one must first become registered with the appropriate body, and registration must be renewed each year. **Registration** involves a formal assessment of credentials and granting of a licence to practise. If a nurse has the required educational background, having graduated from a recognized nursing program, she or he is eligible to become registered, and will be granted a licence upon applying and paying a fee. Under legislation, no one is permitted to work within the nursing scope of practice unless she or he is registered. This process is the key to self-regulation, because the professional must meet certain standards in order to retain a licence.

The professional nursing associations are responsible for **discipline**, namely imposing sanctions on nurses who do not meet nursing standards. Each province or territory has a procedure for receiving and investigating complaints against practising nurses. If an investigation proves that the nurse violated professional standards, disciplinary actions may be instituted. These could include requiring the nurse to take a short course, temporarily suspending the nurse's licence to practise, or even permanently revoking the nurse's licence. Instances of professional misconduct for which disciplinary proceedings might be initiated include continued demonstrations of incompetence, breaches of professional conduct such as altered performance due to misuse of alcohol or drugs, or abuse of patients.

Professional associations have put into place many supports for nurses to assist them to meet professional standards. For example, most associations have one or more nursing practice consultants who are available to answer questions, direct nurses to appropriate resources, and provide on-the-job assistance. These consultants also serve as a resource for the institution in offering advice about what an employer should be able to expect of an RN. For example, as one way of helping nurses to understand and work with provincial practice or professional standards, the College of Registered Nurses of British Columbia (CRNBC; formerly the Registered Nurses Association of British Columbia or RNABC) established a network of workplace representatives who act as an important support for other nurses, health care facilities, and agencies (RNABC, 1999). The goal across the country is to ensure that the public has a reasonable expectation of consistently safe, competent, and ethical care. Please refer to the provincial and territorial web sites listed at the end of this chapter for more information.

Student nurses learn the basic elements of nursing competence in undergraduate education programs and are expected to perform at a beginning level of competence on completion of their programs. According to Patricia Benner (1996), a noted nursing scholar who has done considerable research in the area of nursing competencies, it takes a novice nurse about two years of working in a particular area before he or she is able to master the skills and knowledge necessary for competent practice. Different areas of practice require different skills and knowledge, and when a nurse moves to a new role in nursing, she or he can expect to feel less than competent at first. Nurses are expected to keep up to date with changing standards and new knowledge that emerges from research. Clearly, competence in nursing is very complex. When a nurse's practice is evaluated for regulatory purposes, it is compared against the minimum standards and what one could reasonably expect from a nurse with similar education and experience.

Provincial/territorial associations attempt to define the basic elements of practice through practice standards and competency statements, as discussed above. In order to be applicable to the many areas of nursing practice, these statements must be very broad. For example, the CRNBC has outlined six areas of nursing responsibility in its practice standards:

Standard 1   Responsibility and Accountability

Standard 2   Specialized Body of Knowledge

Standard 3   Competent Application of Knowledge

Standard 4   Code of Ethics

Standard 5   Provision of Service in the Public Interest

Standard 6   Self-Regulation

Competency statements or indicators are outlined for clinical practice, education, administration, and research. For example, indicators for clinical practice for Standard 3 include:

1. Collects information on client status from a variety of sources using assessment skills including observation, communication, and physical assessment.
2. Identifies, analyzes, and uses relevant and valid information when making decisions about client status and reporting client outcomes.
3. Communicates client status, using verifiable information, in terminology used in the practice setting.
4. Develops plans of care that include data about assessments, decisions about client status, planned interventions, and evaluation criteria for client outcomes.
5. Sets priorities when planning and giving care.
6. Carries out interventions in accordance with policies, guidelines, and care standards.
7. Evaluates client's response to interventions and revises the plan as necessary.
8. Documents timely and appropriate reports of assessments, decisions about client status, plans, interventions, and client outcomes.
9. Initiates, maintains, and terminates professional relationships in an appropriate manner. (RNABC, 2003).

Continuing Competence

We have indicated that competencies for which nurses are accountable are defined by each provincial or territorial association. To be sure that patient care meets the same standards of competence, safety, and ethics across the country, it is important that expectations of nurses be relatively uniform. To address that issue, provincial and territorial nursing associations participated in the National Nursing Competencies Project (NNCP) from 1995 to 1997. This project was aimed at achieving national consensus on entry-level competencies for Licensed Practical Nurses (LPNs), RNs, and Registered Psychiatric Nurses. The purpose was primarily to ensure a degree of national consistency in education. Once there was agreement on the basic competencies, each provincial and territorial association went back to its membership, namely practising nurses, and asked for feedback on whether the competencies were valid and relevant for local nursing-practice settings. Revisions were made as appropriate. The final list of competencies is used in designing undergraduate programs that will prepare nurses with the skills they need to practise safely and ethically. It is also the basis of provincial and territorial practice standards. Of course, as mentioned earlier in this chapter, at entry to the profession a novice nurse has only beginning skills. The question then arises as to how to ensure that nurses maintain their basic competency and continue to grow and develop throughout their professional careers.

Historically, once nurses became registered in a Canadian province or territory, they were permitted to re-register annually provided they had completed a minimum number of practice hours over a certain period. They were not required to demonstrate that they were competent. Today, the Canadian Nurses Association believes that the public interest is best served when regulatory bodies adopt a **continuing-competence** policy. That is, as part of the annual registration process nurses must indicate what they have done to maintain their competence or learn new skills and knowledge. The purpose is to provide some measure of assurance that nurses remain current throughout their nursing careers (CNA, 2001).

Across Canada all provincial and territorial associations are developing or have developed a mandatory continuing competence program of some type. Competency assessments require that individual nurses undertake a process of self-review. This usually involves development of a personal portfolio demonstrating what the nurse has done to maintain competence. No standardized measures of competence are used across the country. Instead, the process for reporting self-assessments and the standards used to determine adequacy of the methods used to maintain competence are (or will be, depending on the state of development of the program in each province) clearly outlined in nursing association documents. This process of holding nurses accountable for their own competence is relatively new. For the most part it is gaining acceptance as a necessary way of ensuring public safety; however, some nurses perceive it as very threatening. They question why they should have to show that they are competent to do a job they are already doing. Despite this opposition, nursing associations are proceeding with their continuing competence programs. The issue is one of quality and public trust in the profession: it is essential that the public be able to maintain confidence in nurses' preparedness to practise. To reduce the perception of threat, some provincial associations have gone to great lengths to involve nurses in developing the process for annual review. For example, in Alberta the Continuing Competence Program was developed after extensive consultation with RNs across the province and with representatives from the United Nurses of Alberta, the government of Alberta, and nurse educators.

Continuing competence is a lifelong learning venture. Formal continuing-competence programs provide nurses with tools to demonstrate how they have maintained their skills and enhanced their practice. Self-assessment requires **reflection**, a conscious effort to evaluate one's own practice and determine what one needs to improve. Reflection on practice is not new to nursing. Nurses have always engaged in various activities to examine their own practice. What is new is the documentation or continuous development of a portfolio, so that nurses have a critical appraisal of how they might build on existing skills and develop new ones, or, in other words, enhance their own learning. In consideration of the value of safe, competent, and ethical care, developing a portfolio to assess practice becomes an ethical imperative for every nurse.

Peer review, certification of specific skills, and chart audits are other approaches used to measure continuing competence in the practice setting. Some institutions have put in place regular checks on nursing performance. **Peer review** involves having another nurse observe and evaluate one's functioning. **Certification** is a formalized approval process to permit a nurse to carry out a particular task. It usually requires a written test and demonstration of the skill, and may be required by institutional policy. Certification is generally required for very complex tasks such as starting an intravenous infusion. Many certifiable skills were formerly done only by physicians and have only recently been delegated to nursing. If certification is required, a nurse may not perform the skill unless he or she has completed the certification program. Sometimes nurses are not permitted to practise in the institution unless they have completed the certification program. For example, many hospitals require certification for cardiopulmonary resuscitation as a condition of employment. For most skills the certification only lasts for a limited time, and the nurse has to recertify, or take the tests again, to be allowed to continue performing the skill. A **chart audit** is a formalized quality control mechanism whereby someone, usually from nursing administration, reviews charts looking for particular indicators of good practice, such as recording the effectiveness of pain control mechanisms. Audits are generally done at regular intervals, and an institutional "report card" is produced. They seldom point to individual behaviours, but instead give a measure of the quality of care overall.

The Law and Professional Competence

We have explained that scope of nursing practice is legislated in provinces and territories across Canada and that practice standards guide everyday nursing practice. A nurse's licence to practise is based on conformity with these standards, and disciplinary proceedings can be initiated against a nurse who fails to meet minimum requirements. Discipline is a professional matter, but not necessarily a legal one. A nurse may be in breach of practice standards, but if there is no immediate harm to an individual or group the nurse may not be in contravention of the law. When harm occurs, the nurse may be charged in civil or criminal court, depending on the nature of the injury. When a charge is laid, the court measures the performance and behaviours of the nurse in question against professional and ethical standards. In receiving care, a patient relies on the nurse's knowledge and expertise, and nurses have a legal duty to provide what the court considers a reasonable level of care. According to the Canadian Nurses Protective Society (CNPS, 1994, p. 1), a non-profit liability protection organization for RNs in Canada, a nurse's behaviour will be evaluated in court according to what would "reasonably be expected of a competent prudent nurse of the same experience and standing in similar circumstances." A nurse who works in a specialized area such as obstetrics or intensive care will be held to the standard of care on that unit, and the court will examine her or his practice against peer assessments of what is reasonable and prudent. Thus a nurse can be held accountable under law to perform to a certain standard but cannot be held accountable for skills that would not normally be required in a similar situation. Nursing practice standards act as a guide for the court regarding what should be expected of a nurse.

COMPASSION

In Chapter 2 we defined compassion as having a feeling for the pain and suffering experienced by others. If we are to give compassionate care, then our actions as nurses must be based on a recognition of that suffering and a desire to do something about it. Giving compassionate care does not necessarily mean that all nursing is about suffering. For example, in health promotion activities such as counselling about lifestyle changes, we are not acting to relieve suffering (although we might be acting to prevent it). However, we must always be aware that we have the ability to cause or worsen suffering, and giving compassionate care implies acting with that awareness. If we are disrespectful of patients and their families, or if we act in such a way as to cause a person to feel a loss of dignity, we can be responsible for some of their suffering. Compassionate care demands relational ethics, because we must "be in relation" with patients and families in such a way that we act in their best interests. In the Ethics Composite Model (Chapter 2) we described virtue as the moral motivation for practice and said that one of the virtues for nurses is compassion. Being a compassionate nurse requires an awareness of others' needs and clinical competence such that you can act to reduce suffering and provide comfort. Part of competence is having the skills to recognize suffering and to relieve it. In other words, compassion and competence are tightly linked to one another, and a nurse who acts without compassion will not be practising competently or ethically.

SAFETY AS A MORAL OBLIGATION

Nurses have a responsibility to ensure that patients are given safe care. That is, care must be such that harm is minimized. It is not always possible to ensure that patients are not harmed, as sometimes the care we give causes harm in itself. For example, a surgical incision is a harm of a kind. Debriding a burn (removing the necrotic tissue so the wound can heal) is painful and causes immediate suffering. Tying a demented elderly woman to a bed to prevent her from falling can cause the patient considerable suffering if it is frightening for her and takes away the woman's autonomy. It can also create moral uncertainty and distress in the nurse, who may be unsure about whether or not it is an ethical thing to do. Sometimes caregivers make choices that cause temporary suffering with the understanding that the long-term outcome will be positive. It is not always easy to keep the long-term view in mind when one is causing a patient discomfort. Even something as simple as requiring a patient to get out of bed immediately after surgery can be perceived by nurse and patient alike as a form of cruelty. This can be especially difficult for the novice nurse who sees the immediate effects more easily than the long-term effects. The ability to resolve this kind of conflict comes with experience, active reflection on practice, and discussion with colleagues.

Sometimes nurses find it hard to care for a patient when other health care providers, usually physicians, make choices that nurses think are causing more harm than good. For example, a patient in intensive care who is comatose but seems to experience great pain when turned can create a very upsetting situation for the nurses. They may experience moral distress if they feel that they are, in effect, torturing the patient each time they turn him. Keeping patients safe from harm can be difficult, and sometimes it requires great ethical sensitivity to be aware of harms being caused. Some harms may be less obvious than others. For example, it is easy for a nurse or other care provider to do things that damage a patient's sense of dignity and self-worth. We will discuss this problem in detail in later chapters, but at this point it is important to remember that relational ethics is central to this issue. Relational ethics helps us know what the patient considers harm, and it is crucial to engaging in discussions with colleagues. Approaching another colleague, especially one who appears to be in a position of power, such as a physician, can sometimes be difficult. It is particularly important to open dialogue in a non-confrontational way. As we discussed earlier, the nurse needs to develop relational skills that enable him or her to advocate for the patient in a way that does not challenge the integrity of the other caregiver. It stands to reason that if you as the nurse are feeling that action is unethical, and you raise the issue with your colleague, she might assume that you are challenging her ethics and become defensive. Effectively engaging another in this kind of discussion is a learned skill. Finding a colleague who does it well, and watching and learning from that colleague, is an important step in gaining that skill.

Other kinds of harm can come to patients because of inadequate or inappropriate caregiving. Sometimes these harms are a result of mistakes that can be explained; sometimes they are a result of carelessness or incompetence. For example, a nurse who makes a medication error might be excused if the context was such that errors were almost inevitable. For instance, on one hand, when a nurse has a lot of very ill patients to care for and there are many demands on her time, medication errors may occur because she is distracted and rushed. These kinds of errors are unfortunate but are not breaches of ethics as such. On the other hand, if a nurse made a medication error because she had been out partying all night before her shift and was not fit to practise that day, it would be considered unethical. Either way, nurses need to monitor their own competence to practise and admit to their mistakes. Regardless of the cause, if a nurse makes a mistake and does not admit it, this is considered unethical.

In a multi-disciplinary environment, everyone must take responsibility for the care that is provided. Nurses need to be aware of what others are doing for and with their patients. If **adverse events**—"unexpected, undesirable incidents resulting in injury or death that are directly associated with the process of providing health care or services to a person receiving care" (Hebert, Hoffman, & Davies, 2003, as cited in CNA, 2008, p. 22)—occur, then they must be reported, regardless of who is responsible. The person who is most directly involved when the adverse event occurs should be the one to report it, but sometimes that does not occur. In that situation, a nurse who observes the event must report it. It is the nurse's obligation to ensure patient safety, but this is not easy when it can mean exposing a colleague. Imagine, for example, that you observe another nurse drop a frail elderly patient during transfer. The patient doesn't seem hurt, and the nurse doesn't seem to plan to report the incident. Should you report it yourself? Your obligation is to speak to the nurse and ensure that the incident is reported. If the nurse doesn't do it, you must, as this is a clear issue of patient safety, and your obligations are clear. **Whistleblowing**, or reporting a colleague's errors, incompetence, unsafe/negligent practice, or patient abuse, is one of the most difficult things a nurse must do in ensuring that this first value is met. We will discuss some other issues related to whistleblowing in more detail in Chapter 10.

Sometimes the environment is so difficult for nursing safely that it becomes dangerous for patients. This is particularly the case when there are staffing shortages. When such a situation arises, the CNA Code of Ethics for Registered Nurses explains that it is a nurse's responsibility to do the best that she or he can, but to let patients, families, and employers know of the situation and the possible problems that could arise. Nurse leaders have a particular obligation to work toward a practice environment in which safe care is supported. The idea of a safe environment for care includes relationships among health care providers, because a dysfunctional team is more likely to make errors or perform ineffectively. All nurses are obligated to work collaboratively with other care providers and to try to create a harmonious milieu in which everyone feels supported and respected.

Up to this point we have been talking about the safety of the patient, but there is another aspect of safety that must be considered: the nurse's own safety. Sometimes the nurse is put in a situation in which he or she may be in physical danger. There are increasing reports in the literature and the popular media about physical violence against nurses. Overcrowded emergency rooms and long wait times, for instance, can raise frustration levels, and patients sometimes take their frustrations out on a nurse. There are many reports of nurses being struck by patients, either intentionally or when the patient is in a confused or delirious state. The CNA Code of Ethics for Registered Nurses makes a strong statement about violence, stating that "nurses work to prevent and minimize all forms of violence by anticipating and assessing the risk of violent situations and by collaborating with others to establish preventative measures. When violence cannot be anticipated or prevented, nurses take action to minimize risk to protect others and themselves" (CNA, 2008, p. 9). This includes violence done to patients in the context of care. It goes without saying that it is unacceptable to use violence against a patient. A possible exception is when a patient is at risk of harming herself or himself or others, and has to be restrained in such a way that she or he is injured. Nurses and other care providers must do everything in their power to ensure that no injury occurs, but if the choice is between restraining the patient and allowing him or her to hurt someone else, and there are no other options, it is possible that harm might come to the patient in the process of restraint. It is the nurse's ethical responsibility to ensure that this risk is minimized as much as possible. It is important to mention that this prohibition against violence also relates to violence against nurses. Nurses need to understand that they are under no obligation to allow themselves to be injured by patients, whatever the reason. Self-protective action could include leaving the scene and calling for assistance from security to restrain the patient or using sedative medications as ordered. Nurses should make it clear to patients that violent or abusive behaviour of any kind will not be tolerated. Sometimes the patient may be cognitively impaired and unaware of having injured the nurse. In such instances it is necessary to ensure that adequate sedation is ordered so staff (and other patients) are protected in future. However, mental illness is not an excuse for violence against nurses, and patients must be informed of that fact; all nurses need to adhere to a policy of zero tolerance. Most acute care institutions have special procedures for dealing with violent and abusive patients, and nurses should be aware of those procedures and implement them as necessary.

Not all care occurs in hospitals, however. Home care and public health nurses who visit patients in their homes can be at risk. If they sense danger they are under no obligation to remain in the home, even if care is required. They should leave, contact their supervisors, and ask for backup assistance before they re-enter the home. For example, one of the authors (Oberle, 2000) interviewed nurses for a study on ethical problems in public health nursing. A participant spoke of making a home visit to a new mother and being frightened of the mother's partner, who appeared to be making a drug deal in an adjacent room. She left as quickly as possible and decided never to return unless in the company of another nurse.

Violence in health care is one of the kinds of concerns exposed by feminist ethics scholars. Until recently little was said in the public domain about violence against nurses. It was more or less accepted as an occupational hazard. However, this is no longer the case. Protection for nurses has even been written into negotiated contracts in the form of requirements for more than one nurse to be on duty at any given time, including nights. As more people become aware of the real threats to nurses, many of whom are exposed to potential violence on a daily basis, we can expect that more effective strategies for dealing with violence will be developed.

Finally, we need to say a word about another possible risk to nurses: the risk to health through exposure to communicable diseases. The 2003 outbreak of Severe Acute Respiratory Syndrome (SARS) is a good example of how nurses can be endangered; dozens of nurses in Toronto contracted the disease after caring for infected patients. New and emerging diseases pose similar threats, and there is a real concern about a pandemic influenza sweeping the globe. The CNA Code of Ethics for Registered Nurses has addressed nurses' obligation during this and other kinds of disasters. It states, "During a natural or human-made disaster, including a communicable disease outbreak, nurses have a *duty to provide care* [emphasis in original] using appropriate safety precautions" (CNA, 2008, p. 9). This raises ethical concerns for nurses who might be worried about the adequacy of safety precautions, as well as their duty to protect themselves and their families. Following the crisis created by SARS, the University of Toronto Joint Centre for Bioethics developed a position paper outlining moral responsibilities during a communicable disease outbreak. The interested reader can find the full report on-line (www.yorku.ca/igreene/sars.html). Some of the points in this report include the kinds of decisions health care workers had to make about safety issues. One key concern was the need for organizational support of nurses and other health care providers. Nurses cannot be expected to provide direct care to patients if there are insufficient protections, such as adequate masks and gowns, available. Although it is commonly accepted that health care providers do have an obligation to provide care, the Code suggests that such an obligation holds only if adequate safety measures and protections are in place.

ATTENDING TO NURSES' ETHICAL FITNESS

Earlier in this chapter we discussed mechanisms to help nurses maintain their competence to practise. One aspect of such competence deserves further mention here, and that is ethical competence and ethical fitness to practise. Nurses cannot expect to provide safe, compassionate, competent, and *ethical* care unless they have well-developed ethical sensitivity and moral agency. Our moral identity and integrity as nurses is closely tied to how we practice. In order to maintain integrity in stressful environments and to be able to navigate their way through the ambiguous and shifting grounds of ethical nursing practice, nurses need to be critically aware and attuned to their emotions and bodily experiences through a self-discovery process. As with ethical practice, the vital balance of the person's subjectivity and the objectivity of reason is essential to the creative process of attending to ethical fitness.

Nurses regularly face physically and emotionally charged situations. They encounter intense interpersonal, interprofessional, and intraprofessional conflict in the workplace and try to make appropriate and safe decisions. Chronically stressful work environments can lead to absenteeism, low morale, and poor work performance. For example, consider Nancy's story. Nancy works on a busy surgical floor. Palliative patients are often admitted to the surgical unit because of a shortage of beds throughout the hospital. Caring for these patients has caused Nancy to rethink whether nursing is really for her because it is difficult for her to see them experience so much pain, mental anguish, and fear. She feels these problems are seldom acknowledged or alleviated as there are too few nurses available on the unit to deal appropriately with the patients' suffering. Nancy encounters this moral problem much too often. She normally has care of seven patients, of whom six are surgical patients who cry for pain medication, vomit, or come and go to the operating room. Most can have their concerns dealt with immediately through medications or skilled tasks. By contrast, the dying patients need nurses to be present, to listen, and to give holistic care. This takes more time than Nancy has to give. On this unit nurses are encouraged to get the tasks accomplished as quickly and efficiently as possible, which means a minimum stay at each patient's bedside. Time after time Nancy feels overwhelmed and frustrated, and she is angry that she cannot be the nurse she wants to be for the palliative patients. This is not a dilemma, because she knows what the right course of action is. Instead, it is a situation of moral distress. To deal with it she does her best not to get emotionally attached and avoids meaningful conversation with her patients. She makes sure that the patients' physical pain is taken care of and tries to satisfy herself that pain control is sufficient. In reaching this point, Nancy has come to use such invisible barriers as a form of relief. She is no longer aware of the painful and distressing feelings she is blocking in order to protect herself.

Developing Ethical Fitness

Canadian nurse ethicist Janet Storch says that to be "ethically fit" is to be mentally engaged in the human activity of ethical reflection and justification. Such fitness requires a degree of knowledge and skill in ethical problem solving. It involves being or becoming a person of good character, engaging in ethical conduct, and building a moral community (Storch, 1999). This kind of fitness requires nurses to nurture and sustain themselves in order to maintain their physical, mental, emotional, and spiritual well-being.

It is common for nurses to cope with emotional and physical exhaustion and pain by developing ultimately self-destructive habits and shields such as Nancy has. Addressing these issues can cause nurses shame, embarrassment, and guilt, but recognition of the problem is a beginning step toward healing. Physical health is a factor in mental health and moral fitness. Eating healthy foods, getting adequate (which likely means more) sleep, and engaging in aerobic and fun physical activity are successful beginning strategies to developing ethical fitness.

Emotional self-care also requires setting boundaries, a process that involves identifying which caring (work) demands should be accepted and which should be rejected as well as judging the conditions under which help might be sought from others. Personal boundaries give us a sense of safety and a means of regulating our interactions with others. More importantly, they begin to give us some insight into ourselves as ethical persons.

Listening to one's own voice is a process of knowing personal limits and strengths, trusting judgments, and reflecting on values and philosophy of care. In doing so, we pay attention to how the physical, relational, and emotional processes of caring are affecting our abilities to use knowledge and strategize for self-protection and self-healing. More specifically, knowing personal limits and strengths involves acknowledging physical, financial, emotional, and intellectual limits and strengths that emerge as nurses respond to caring demands of work, and using that knowledge as a basis of care. Nurses should look for indicators of stress such as fatigue, low tolerance for frustration, and feeling that work is meaningless. Recognizing ethical distress and personal limitations may contribute to a decision either not to provide care or to limit the scope of the caring response, or to indicate that more assistance is needed. This process of self-care also directs nurses' attention toward types of practice that they may or may not want to engage in in the future.

Trusting judgments involves appreciating that the ethical decisions one makes can be reliable and valuable. It is based on knowledge of one's strengths and limitations, and to some extent on intuition. Trusting judgment develops over time and with experience. Ethical reflection on situations, personal responses, and outcomes help nurses to learn from both successes and mistakes. Nurses will more likely be able to honour the public's trust when the values they consider important in their professional lives are aligned with those of the people with whom they work. Therefore, in building a moral community of care, nurses negotiate and repattern care in ways that make sense in their relationships with patients, families, and interdisciplinary colleagues.

Another aspect of listening to one's own voice is to reflect on one's philosophy of care. As nurses, we should reflect honestly on our beliefs and values about nursing. Rediscovering thoughts and feelings that brought us to nursing and that inspired our desire to care may help us reflect on what is truly important. Recognizing that there are many givens in the workplace that we cannot control and searching for other nursing practices that we can and will control makes the moral community more ethical.

Referring to the CNA Code of Ethics for Registered Nurses can help nurses clarify ethical relationships, responsibilities, behaviours, and decision making that give rise to ethical distress. The Code provides a basis for self-evaluation and self-reflection. When nurses can name the type of ethical concern they are experiencing, they are better able to discuss it with colleagues and supervisors, take steps to address the concern, and receive support and guidance in dealing with it. Role modelling, mentoring others regarding ethical decision making, and creating an ethical environment are leadership skills that can be assumed by experienced nurses. In a mentoring capacity, nurse leaders can help colleagues in raising ethical concerns, thus fostering an environment where diverse views are expressed and moved toward resolution. Informal learning opportunities with interdisciplinary team members, such as ethics rounds and case reviews, are ways to engage colleagues in moral dialogue. The ethical climate also needs to encourage patients and caregivers to express diverse views and raise questions about the ethical elements of clinical care.

Developing an Educational Foundation for Ethical Fitness

The process of becoming ethically fit for practice needs to begin with the education of student nurses. Students need to be supported to become moral agents. Gwen Hartrick Doane, a prominent Canadian nurse ethicist, challenges nurse educators to develop a pedagogy that teaches students to consider ethics as a way of being, not simply as something they follow, and to develop the knowledge and ability to live in and navigate through complex health care environments (Hartrick Doane, 2002). She suggests that a creative pedagogy should "inspire students to tap into and use their creative, imaginative power to revise, adapt, expand, and alter themselves and their knowledgeable practice as moral agents" (p. 523). This would require helping students learn strategies and language that prepare them for entering into ethical dialogue with other professionals and for the realities of day-to-day practice. Directly in clinical practice, and in the classroom, students need to enter into dialogue that uncovers sources of conflict among core beliefs, professional traditions, and institutional expectations. Nursing students need a more realistic understanding of the system within which they work and the social ethic of the many health care professionals they will encounter to become sensitized to the political and cultural workplace.

Preventative Ethics

Thus far we have addressed healing strategies stemming from stressful environments. In becoming ethically fit and creating an ethical climate, it is also crucial to consider preventative ethics. An ethical environment fosters early identification of issues and anticipation of possible dilemmas. The ability to predict conflict and develop plans in a proactive rather that reactive manner will avert some potentially difficult dilemmas. Rather than having to choose one value over another as in a dilemma, preventative ethics emphasizes that all values should be reviewed and examined prior to a conflict arising so that situations where values may differ can be anticipated. The goals of the health care team must always be in the open. Preventative ethics is akin to the philosophy of palliative care, in which the goals of care are always discussed honestly and openly, both initially and as the patient transitions from cure to comfort care. In palliative care, patient, family, and caregivers anticipate and acknowledge changes in the patient's condition and are aware and indeed expect that changes in treatment goals will occur. Modelling this preventative approach in ethical deliberations encourages early identification of values and beliefs that may influence treatment decisions and allows time for reflecting on and resolving issues before they surface.

SAFE, COMPASSIONATE, COMPETENT, AND ETHICAL CARE AS A LIVED VALUE

The explanatory statements listed in the CNA Code of Ethics for Registered Nurses under *providing safe, compassionate, competent, and ethical care* demonstrate two kinds of ethical responsibilities. The first is the obligation of ensuring that care is of the highest quality, which includes maintaining one's own ability to provide that care. This is what we referred to in Chapter 3 as everyday ethics. In other words, since nursing is an inherently moral activity, one must be alert to the issues of competence and relationship at all times. Every care action must be understood as a moral act. Nurses must be aware that performing safely, compassionately, and competently is, in fact, the essence of their ethic as a nurse.

There is, however, another kind of ethical responsibility that arises when there are values conflicts or when the nurse experiences moral uncertainty as to what should be done. These situations, which cause nurses moral distress, arise frequently in the practice setting. Part of *safe, compassionate, competent, and ethical care* involves dealing with these conflicts or uncertainties in a way that maintains the dignity and self-worth of all involved. Everyday ethics requires an awareness of and reflection on how one acts toward those receiving care, including performing technical and relational skills. Ethical dilemmas require an even deeper reflection about what, in a situation where choices and decisions must be made, would be the *right* thing to do. Sometimes these choices reflect values conflicts, and at other times they are inherent in the systems designed to deliver care. In any of these situations, the nurse has to maintain a personal sense of moral integrity but must also respect the values of others. This is where it is important to have a framework to help structure your thinking. The Framework for Ethical Decision Making that we presented in Chapter 3 is designed to help you consider all the elements of the Ethics Composite Model, each of which can add to your thinking in important ways.

The following case study involves a classical ethical dilemma around minimizing harm. It reflects the value of *safe, compassionate, competent, and ethical care*. We will use the Framework to analyze the case, showing how the primary value discussed in this chapter might be threatened and how the nurse might respond to uphold the value. This is the first analysis we have presented using this Framework; in subsequent chapters there will be more cases that will provide opportunities for you to consider the Framework and its application in practice situations.

Trying It On

4.1 Maintaining Safety

Miriam is Charge Nurse on a general psychiatry unit. Her shift has started badly and is steadily getting worse. To begin with, staffing was already minimal when Cindy called in sick. Miriam has been frantically trying to find replacements, but none of the nurses on the casual roster are home or answering their phones. It looks as though the staff are just going to have to make do until someone can be found to cover, despite the fact that the unit has only one empty bed and several very sick patients who need a great deal of care. Already on this shift one patient has slashed her arm, requiring that the surgical resident be called to suture the wound. Another patient with bipolar disorder is extremely agitated and has been pacing and talking incessantly, making patients and staff even more tense. A third, alcoholic patient has been experiencing hallucinations. A fourth patient has just been brought down from intensive care after an unsuccessful suicide attempt, and a fifth, certified patient has left the unit without permission, which means that one nurse is tied up on the phone with the police and security. And these are just a few of the problems. The unit is as busy as it had ever been and is already short-staffed. Not only

(Continued)

4.1 Maintaining Safety

that, but all the nurses are very tired because they have been working a lot of mandatory overtime.

Just as things appear to be settling down, the phone rings. Admitting wants to send Miriam a woman who is five days post-partum after a Caesarian section. She is showing signs of post-partum psychosis and extreme agitation. The woman's husband brought her to emergency because her abdominal wound had split open (dehisced) and her intestines are visible. She is in shock and possibly septic. Her husband says that since they brought their baby daughter home, his wife has been hearing voices telling her to kill the baby.

Miriam doesn't know what to do. She knows that she lacks the staff to provide adequate care for this patient. Although all the nurses on the unit have plenty of experience in psychiatry, she is sure that none would feel confident in caring for a woman with a dehisced abdomen and gynecological needs. If the patient is truly psychotic, they will have to watch her very closely. They clearly do not have the staff to take another patient on close supervision requiring that level of care. And if the patient is in fact septic, will the psychiatric nurses even know how to assess or when to intervene? Miriam simply doesn't feel it is right to take

this patient, but she is equally sure that the gynecology unit will not want her, as they are not prepared for dealing with her mental problems. Clearly the patient has to come to psychiatry, and they do have an empty bed, but how can they care for her?

Miriam is also worried that if they admit the patient to psychiatry and anything related to her physical needs goes wrong, her nurses may be blamed for not providing adequate care. Another potential problem is the infant's care. There is a possibility that other care providers might help, but will they be able to provide safe care? The patient is apparently breast-feeding, so does the ward have to admit the infant as well? If so, will they be able to watch carefully enough to ensure that the infant is not harmed? Miriam is quite sure that administration will not be sympathetic to her concerns, as there is an obvious need to admit the patient somewhere, but she is equally sure that they won't support the nurses if there is a problem. She feels torn about taking this patient, as it would simply be asking too much of her already over-worked and highly stressed nursing staff and would be putting both the staff and the patient in jeopardy. However, she doesn't think she would be permitted to refuse the patient. What can she do?

Applying the Framework

Maintaining Safety

Unfortunately, the scenario described above is not unusual in the acute care setting. Nursing is becoming increasingly

specialized, and patients often have needs that cross specialties. In this case, the issue is whether the psychiatric nurses have the skills and knowledge necessary to provide safe, competent, and ethical care to this particular patient. There is also the problem of having too few nurses to provide the necessary support for the patient (and perhaps the infant).

Assessing the Ethics of the Situation: Relationships, Goals, Beliefs, and Values

Miriam's situation is truly perplexing. The main value of importance here is safe, competent, and ethical care. The goal is to help the patient and family deal effectively with this psychosis and the surgical complications. Miriam does not want to put the patient in jeopardy, and as a result is experiencing moral uncertainty. She truly does not know what would be the best thing for this patient. She reasons that the surgical problems are acute and serious, but so is the mental problem. She is concerned about nursing competence in caring for this patient. If the patient is admitted to psychiatry her surgical problems will probably not be dealt with adequately, as psychiatric nurses often lack skills and knowledge related to surgical issues. However, Miriam does not want to leave the psychiatric problem to the surgical nurses, who are likewise ill-prepared to handle it: surgical nurses seldom have the kind of specialist knowledge needed to care for a psychiatric patient, especially one with an acute psychiatric problem such as this patient's. Her psychosis could be life-threatening if she is suicidal. There is also the infant to consider. Miriam has been told that the mother is breast-feeding, and, therefore, they will likely have to admit the infant as well, which further complicates the situation.

At this point Miriam does not have a relationship with the patient. She does, however, have a relationship with and an obligation to her staff and the patients currently on the unit. She is reluctant to put her nurses in a situation where their ability to deliver excellent care is compromised. They are already tired and short-staffed, and admitting a patient with complex physical problems is inviting accidents to happen. If nurses are asked to work beyond their competencies, patient safety is threatened. Another problem is that if this patient is admitted it will take attention away from other patients on the unit. Given the shortage of nurses, these patients are already receiving less nursing attention than they normally would, which translates into a lower standard of care. Admitting another seriously ill patient could further compromise the care being given to other patients on the unit. Thus, the ethical dimensions of this situation are related primarily to resource allocation. The resource, skilled nursing care, is in short supply, and Miriam has to decide how to best meet the needs of patient and staff.

Again, if we look at the issue from a bioethical perspective, we will see that Miriam's desire is to "do good" for the patient, but she is uncertain what "good" will look like. This is a situation in which she is experiencing moral uncertainty. There is also an issue of justice, as Miriam is reluctant to admit a patient who will take time and attention away from other very ill patients. She would have to ask herself whose rights are most important. In this sense, she could also consider utilitarian views, which would suggest to her that the greater good of the group should not be sacrificed to the good of one individual. At this point we don't necessarily see these principles in conflict; we merely point out that each of the two principles casts a different light on the problem.

(Continued)

Maintaining Safety

Reflecting on and Reviewing Potential Actions: Recognizing Available Choices and How Those Choices Are Valued

Miriam is asking herself if she or her nurses have the knowledge needed to provide safe, competent, and ethical care, and whether there are enough nurses to attend to the needs of this patient (and possibly her infant) without putting other patients at risk. She must make a decision about whether to resist the admission of the new patient and her baby on the grounds that the unit is insufficiently staffed. She is very concerned with preventing harm to the patient and infant; however, she also has concerns about the nurses on her unit, and whether it is ethical to give them a patient who they are clearly not equipped with resources or time to care for.

In this situation, Miriam is dealing with the system rather than with individuals. She recognizes that certain economic and political factors must be considered. First, the hospital is chronically underfunded and consequently rarely replaces nurses who are off sick or on vacation. Therefore, a number of part-time casual nurses have resigned because they were unable to get sufficient hours. Tonight there are no nurses available on the casual roster to make up the staffing shortfall. Secondly, hospital administration does not appear to recognize the importance of specialized knowledge in nursing. They want to admit a surgical patient to a psychiatric unit, but Miriam has doubts about the wisdom of that action. She is being pressured to admit the patient, even though she is aware that her psychiatric nurses do not

have surgical nursing skills. It appears that hospital administration holds the belief that "a nurse is a nurse" and that a patient should be able to expect equally skilled care regardless of where in the institution she or he is admitted. Miriam realizes that this is not the case. She knows there is clear evidence that nurses develop specialty knowledge and cannot provide expert care outside their areas of expertise. She also knows that her nurses do not have sufficient recent experience with septic surgical patients to be able to make highly skilled assessments and interventions. Yet she fears that administration will not take this into consideration when sending the patient to her unit. If we refer to the Composite Model, we can see that Miriam's decision making in this case is constrained by institutional beliefs and values.

Moreover, Miriam is concerned that if she assigns a nurse to care for the new patient, the other patients will not receive the care they need. She feels torn because she knows the patient needs psychiatric care, but her unit is so short-staffed that the nurses might not even be able to provide that care competently. That might put the patient and infant at risk. The mother has a history of wanting to harm the baby, and if she is not carefully supervised the nursing staff might not be able to prevent her from doing so. At the same time, Miriam knows that if she refuses the patient, she will have to answer to hospital administration and defend her position. She is not confident that her choice will be supported. She also wonders what the legal implications might be. If she permits the patient to be admitted, other patients might be placed at risk. If she does not, is she abandoning the patient?

Selecting an Ethical Action: Maximizing Good

As she works through the situation in her mind, Miriam reasons that the best thing to do would be to admit the patient to psychiatry and request that a nurse from one of the surgical units come in to consult on the surgical care. She also decides that she will put in a call to the lactation consultant to advise on breast-feeding and the effects of antipsychotic medications on the infant. By involving nurses with different areas of expertise, she will give the patient a better chance of having her complex needs met. However, the problem of the shortage of nurses to care for the remaining patients is still unresolved. Miriam reasons that, for the most part, the problems of the remaining patients are not as acute as those of the new patient and her baby. The unit could manage if they had a security guard to watch the patient who is suicidal. She puts in a request for security and calls the resident to request sedation for the patient with bipolar disorder, which isn't her first choice of treatment, but might be the best they can do under the circumstances.

Engaging in Ethical Action

In making these decisions, it is essential that Miriam record all her concerns and her efforts to secure the very best care for the patient. If there is a serious problem and a patient is injured in some way, it is possible that a nurse could face legal charges of negligence or worse. The legal standard is what a "reasonably prudent nurse" would do. It is imperative, therefore, that Miriam make it clear that the nurses were given responsibilities beyond what they could reasonably be expected to manage. She will have to document that they were acting prudently and attempting to provide the best care within their limits of expertise and availability. She will also have to evaluate the outcomes of her decision by monitoring the care received by the new patient, her infant, and the other patients on the unit. She will need to be especially vigilant to be sure that no new problems emerge. If the situation becomes worse, she will have to report to hospital administration, and perhaps even to the provincial nursing association. It is important that Miriam protect her nurses if they are put in an untenable situation. It is even more important that the patients get the best possible care.

Reflecting on and Reviewing the Ethical Action

In reflecting on her decision, Miriam will probably realize that she had arrived at the best possible solution. She will be aware of the issue of scarce resources and how nurses and nursing care are recognized and valued. These are some of the realities of today's health care system. The escalating costs of health care and other social forces have led to cost constraints that may be reflected in shortages of all kinds, including shortages of RNs. It is possible that nurses may find themselves in situations where it is not possible to give "safe, competent, and ethical" care at all times. The "right" thing to do in such situations is to make every effort to secure adequate care, to ensure that those efforts are recorded, and then to perform to the best of one's ability.

CHAPTER SUMMARY

The first value in the CNA Code of Ethics for Registered Nurses is *safe, compassionate, competent, and ethical care*. In Canada, a number of processes are in place to ensure that this value is upheld. Self-regulation is one such process. A self-regulating profession is one that has responsibility for the practice of its members and has processes in place to evaluate practice, investigate charges of substandard performance, and invoke disciplinary procedures if practice is found to be below minimum standards. All Canadian provinces and territories have developed practice standards that outline the basic responsibilities of nurses.

Self-regulation of the nursing profession in Canada is defined in legislation outlining the scope of nursing practice and the aspects of care for which nursing is responsible. The nurse must be aware of the most recent legislation governing practice, since legislation is changed periodically, and the nursing scope of practice is constantly being redefined. Competency statements indicating those things that all nurses must be able to do are outlined in nursing practice standards and are constantly being revised. Accreditation of educational programs and institutions is one way of ensuring adherence to competency statements. Accreditation involves review by external reviewers to determine whether standards are being maintained.

Self-regulation means that a profession must have procedures in place for investigating charges of inadequate or substandard performance. In Canadian nursing, this is the responsibility of the professional associations. Nurses in Canada must be registered with their professional association and must be given a licence to practise in that province or territory. This means that they must demonstrate the ability to perform to minimum standards. Normally registration is based on educational credentials, and it is assumed a nurse is practising to standard unless there is reason to believe otherwise. Each association receives and investigates complaints about nursing practice. If care is found to be below minimum standards, the association can discipline its members. Discipline will vary depending on the seriousness of the charge and can include temporary or permanent suspension of the licence. The professional association also has consultant support for nurses who require advice on acceptable practice.

Nursing competence is essential to safe and ethical care. Competence is difficult to define but is now understood to include psychomotor skills, relational and communication skills, assessment, planning, organizational and delegation skills, and the ability to document appropriately. Competencies are described somewhat differently across the provinces and territories, but all are based on national competency standards first developed in 1997 and periodically revised. This allows patients to have confidence that nursing competence will be defined consistently across the country. The national standards are also the basis of nursing curricula in all provinces, so all nursing education programs contain the same essential content.

Nurses must be registered to practise in Canada and must renew their registration every year. Recently, provincial and territorial professional associations have agreed that there must be measures in place to ensure continuing competence to practise before registration can be renewed. They have begun to institute programs that require nurses to submit evidence that they have kept up to date with changing standards and new procedures. These programs are in varying stages of development across the country. One of the main challenges in instituting such programs is convincing nurses to accept the need for, and to comply with, the requirements. Some nurses find the idea of being required to demonstrate their competence insulting or threatening. Nonetheless, most nurses see it as an important step to ensuring that safe, competent, ethical care is a reality in Canada. Other processes such as peer review, certification, and chart audits are also important ways to ensure continuing competence.

Legal standards are also important for regulating the quality of nursing care in Canada. A nurse can be charged in court if a patient is harmed. In judging a case, the court will use nursing standards to judge whether a nurse acted reasonably and prudently compared with other nurses with the same background and experience.

Compassion is an element of nursing ethics. Nurses must understand that relationship is the foundation of care and that ethical practice includes attending to the social, spiritual, and psychological concerns of patients and families. Another consideration for ethical practice is the safety of both patients and nurses. Issues of competency, including monitoring of others' practice and whistleblowing, are inherent in this value. Also of concern are all forms of violence, including violence against nurses. Ethical practice requires action taken to minimize risk and harm associated with any form of violence. Finally, safety includes the obligations of nurses during communicable disease outbreaks, and their duty to provide care while taking reasonable precautions to protect themselves.

Maintenance of ethical fitness is key to safe, compassionate, competent, and ethical care. Nurses can use many strategies to help them gain the necessary strength of character and virtue. Nurses can learn to become strong ethical practitioners through basic education and ongoing reflection on their practice.

Cases reflecting the value of *safe, competent, and ethical care* show that many concerns must be taken into account. The nurse has responsibility to endeavour to provide the best possible care for the patient, taking all relevant factors into consideration. This process can be aided by use of the Framework for Ethical Decision Making (Chapter 3), which encourages the nurse to consider all the elements in the Ethics Composite Model (Chapter 2).

Questions for Reflection

1. Consider your own readiness to practise. What are the limits of what you can do safely? What are the key elements of ethical practice for you at this point?
2. What are you doing to maintain your readiness to practise?
3. What do you think about the concept of "nursing as a lifestyle"?
4. What is your reaction to the idea of continuing competence in nursing?

Exercises

1. Working in small groups, discuss the following statement: "Failure to maintain a healthy lifestyle is unethical for a nurse." Do you agree with this statement? Why or why not?

2. Write a half-page description of a situation from your clinical practice in which you felt that the value of safe, competent, and ethical care might have been in jeopardy. Examine your own role (if any) in that situation. What were the main contributing factors? What might have been done differently? Taking care to protect confidentiality, share the key elements of the circumstance with your classmates, and see if they can offer alternative possibilities for what might have been done.

Research Activities

1. Go to the web sites of at least three provincial or territorial associations and find the statement of practice standards. Compare the main points, and prepare a brief list of the key similarities and differences.

2. From the provincial and territorial web sites, determine which associations have a mandatory continuing-competence program. Provide a brief summary of the different approaches.

3. Look in your library or on-line for three copies of a provincial association newsletter (e.g., Alberta RN, RNABC Newsline) that has a column about professional misconduct. Identify reasons for professional discipline and the nature of the discipline. Prepare a one-paragraph summary to share with the class.

Key Terms

accreditation

adverse events

certification

chart audit

competency statements

continuing competence

discipline

listening to one's own voice

nursing competence

peer review

practice standards

reflection

registration

scope of practice

self-governing or self-regulating

trusting judgments

whistleblowing

References

Benner, P. (1996). Expertise in nursing practice: Caring, clinical judgment, and ethics. New York: Springer.

Canadian Nurses Association (1987). A definition of nursing practice. Standards for nursing practice. Ottawa: Author.

Canadian Nurses Association (2001). Position statement: Quality professional practice environments for Registered Nurses. Ottawa: Author.

Canadian Nurses Association (2003). *Position statement: Patient safety*. Ottawa: Author.

Canadian Nurses Association (2008). *Code of ethics for Registered Nurses* (Centennial Ed.). Ottawa: Author.

Canadian Nurses Protective Society (1994). Negligence. *InfoLaw, 3*(1), 1–2.

Hartrick Doane, G. (2002). In the spirit of creativity: The learning and teaching of ethics in nursing. *Journal of Advanced Nursing, 39*(6), 521–528.

Hebert, P., Hoffman, C., & Davies, J. (2003). *The Canadian safety dictionary*. Edmonton, AB: Canadian Patient Safety Institute.

Oberle, K., & Tenove, S. (2000) Public health nurses' perceptions of ethical problems. *Nursing Ethics, 7*, 425–437.

Registered Nurses Association of British Columbia (1999). *Nursing self-regulation: Nurses governing nursing in the public interest*. Vancouver: Author.

Registered Nurses Association of British Columbia (2003). *Standards for registered nursing practice in British Columbia*. Vancouver: Author.

Storch, J. (1999). Ethical dimensions of leadership. In J. Hibberd and D. Smith (Eds.), *Nursing Management in Canada* (2nd ed., pp. 351–367). Toronto: W. B. Saunders.

University of Toronto Joint Centre for Bioethics. *Ethics and SARS: Learning Lessons from the Toronto Experience*. Retrieved July 11, 2007, from www.yorku.ca/igreene/sars.html.

Suggested Reading

Jeffrey, Y. (2000). Using competencies to promote a learning environment in intensive care. *Nursing in Critical Care, 5*(4), 194–198.

Purkis, M. E., & Nelson, S. (2003). Nursing competence: Constructing persons and a form of life. In M. McIntyre & B. Thomlinson (Eds.), *Realities of Canadian nursing: Professional, practice, and power issues*. Philadelphia: Lippincott Williams & Wilkins.

Web Sites

Below is a list of web sites for Canadian nursing associations. We have made a few suggestions as to how you might use each web site to obtain more information about the nursing practice standards and ethics documents prepared by the web site's association.

Canadian Nurses Association

www.cna-aiic.ca

This site has links to all the ethics documents prepared by the Canadian Nurses Association. Clicking on the tab labelled "Nursing Practice" and then on "Nursing Ethics" will take you to the CNA Code of Ethics for Registered Nurses and a number of other resources.

Provincial Web Sites

British Columbia

www.rnabc.bc.ca

On the CRNBC web site, go to the tab for Registered Nurses for such things as practice standards and the process for addressing complaints.

Alberta

www.nurses.ab.ca

On the CARNA web site are practice standards, continuing competencies, and relevant legislation. Look in particular under the "Nursing Practice" tab.

Saskatchewan

www.srna.org

See in particular the "Professional Conduct" and "Nursing Resources" tabs.

Manitoba

www.crnm.mb.ca/

The College of Registered Nurses of Manitoba is the professional regulating body. See particularly the "Nursing Practice Expectations" tab.

Ontario

www.cno.org

The College of Nurses of Ontario is the regulating body that sets and enforces standards. See the "Practice Standards" and "Quality Assurance" tabs in particular. See also:

Registered Nurses Association of Ontario

www.rnao.org

The RNAO is the professional body that offers education and development. Membership in the CNO is required for practice; membership in the RNAO is optional.

Quebec

www.oiiq.org/

The OIIQ (Ordre des Infirmières et Infirmiers du Québec) is the only association that does not belong to the CNA. Therefore it has its own Code of Ethics. (This is the only web site listed here that is exclusively in French.)

New Brunswick

www.nanb.nb.ca

This web site is in both English and French. See in particular the "Public Protection" and "Professional Practice" tabs.

Nova Scotia

www.crnns.ca

Recent legislation changed the name of the RN association to the College of Registered Nurses of Nova Scotia. See in particular the "Member Services" and "Resources" tabs.

Prince Edward Island

www.anpei.ca

There is little info on this PEI web site with respect to practice standards. See the "Nursing Practice" and "Conduct Review" tabs. There are good links to other relevant web sites.

Newfoundland and Labrador

www.arnnl.nf.ca

An excellent web site with direct tabs for "Standards," "Legislation," and so on.

Yukon

www.yrna.ca/

The Yukon Association has clearly stated practice standards (see the "Nursing Practice" tab). Disciplinary procedures appear under the "Your Association" tab.

Northwest Territories and Nunavut

www.rnantnu.ca/

Nursing practice standards are the same as those of the College of Registered Nurses of Manitoba and are obtainable through a link under the "Standards" tab.

Chapter 5
Value 2: Promoting Health and Well-Being

Chapter Outline

Learning Objectives

After reading this chapter, you should be able to:

■ describe the second primary value in the CNA Code of Ethics for Registered Nurses: *promoting health and well-being*

- discuss the concepts of health, wellness, and health promotion

- discuss how Canadian perspectives on health and wellness have evolved over the past few decades

- describe factors that can influence health and health behaviours

- describe some nursing responsibilities for and ethical implications of health promotion

- discuss some of the critiques of health promotion

- discuss how research can help nurses find better ways to promote health

- demonstrate an understanding of health promotion within illness

- discuss ways in which the current structure of the health care system can challenge nurses' abilities to promote health

- apply the Framework for Ethical Decision Making to a clinical problem related to health and well-being

Assume for a moment that you are a public health nurse making a home visit. Your patient, Maria, is a 39-year-old woman who is blind and confined to a wheelchair due to a car accident. Until the accident, which occurred 15 years ago, she was employed as a nurse in an intensive care unit. She was engaged to be married and was thinking about graduate school. After the accident she was in a rehabilitation hospital for over a year, during which time her fiancé left her. She tells you that at first she was devastated by all the changes in her life, but then she decided she would make the best of it and try to rebuild her life. She moved into an apartment where personal care was available if she needed it, learned how to read Braille, and got a seeing-eye dog. Soon she was moving about the community in her wheelchair. She enrolled at a university and completed a law degree. On graduation she joined a law firm and began a successful practice, specializing in human rights issues and medical malpractice. Three years ago she became engaged to one of the firm's senior partners, and they were married last fall. She is now pregnant, and you are visiting her to do some prenatal teaching and check on her recurrent bladder infection, for which she was recently hospitalized.

When you think about Maria, do you think about her as being healthy or ill? How would you report her state of wellness? These are important questions because as a nurse you are required to uphold the second primary value of the CNA Code of Ethics for Registered Nurses: *promoting health and well-being*. Nurses need to have a clear understanding about what health means to them and the people in their care if they are to practise ethically.

In this chapter we describe the second primary value and discuss in depth what it means to Canadian nurses and their practice. We begin by exploring some definitions of health and wellness and tracing how family and culture impact our thinking about health. We then move on to descriptions of four models of health and show how ideas about health have been shaped over time, particularly as reflected in some important Canadian documents. Next we turn to the concept of health promotion and what that means in terms of nursing practice, including ways in which nurses can promote health within illness. In the final section of the chapter, we describe some of the moral implications of health promotion in nursing, as presented in two case studies.

THE SECOND PRIMARY VALUE: PROMOTING HEALTH AND WELL-BEING

As discussed in previous chapters, ethics and values are part of every nursing act. Nurses cannot avoid making moral choices or debating matters of moral principle in health care, since health is one of the things valued most by individuals. Health is central in family life, our work, and society. We desire good health and seek to avoid pain, injury, disease, and death. Canada today is a health-conscious nation. Over the past 20 years, there has been a major shift in health care toward an emphasis on health promotion and illness prevention, rather than simply curing disease. This shift is reflected in the second primary value in the CNA Code of Ethics for Registered Nurses, stated as: *"Nurses work with people to enable them to attain their highest possible level of health and well-being"* (CNA, 2008, p. 10). Health is a very complex concept, as we shall demonstrate in this chapter. If nurses are to act on the second primary value they must understand what health means to others. There are many different understandings of what it means to be healthy, and nurses must be open to others' beliefs. They must also be aware of current thinking about factors that contribute to good health and those that make a person susceptible to illness. We will begin our discussion of health as a nursing value by looking at the evolving definition of health.

HEALTH AND HEALTH BEHAVIOURS

Health is a complex concept that is not easy to define. In general, we think of health as having many dimensions: physical status, emotional well-being, social relationships, intellectual functioning, and spirituality. **Wellness** is "a dynamic state of health in which an individual progresses toward a higher level of functioning, achieving an optimum balance between internal and external environments" (Mosby's, 2002, p. 1829). Wellness, too, is highly subjective. There are no lab tests for diagnosing wellness, or objective measures that say how well one is.

Some of the most important work on wellness was conducted by a physician named Halbert Dunn (1959, 1977). He coined the phrase **high-level wellness**, which he defined as "an integrated method of functioning which is orientated toward maximizing the potential of which the individual is capable, within the environment where he [sic] is functioning" (Dunn, 1977, p. 9). More recently, two Canadian nurses have characterized wellness–illness as "the human experience of actual or perceived function–dysfunction" (Jensen & Allen, 1994, p. 349). These definitions are necessarily somewhat vague, because a person's wellness can only be assessed by himself or herself, and there are as many ways to define health as there are individuals. Maria, described above, would probably define herself as well because she is able to do all that she wants and needs to do to most of the time. Afaf Meleis, an influential nursing scholar, suggests that "the quest for a single definition of health is not appropriate, possible, or useful" (Meleis, 1990, p. 109). She argues that we need a diversity of ideas about health and wellness, and that health care professionals should be aware of this diversity and knowledgeable about the different ideas. Meleis also suggests that, while wellness may be difficult to evaluate objectively, there are a number of indicators of it. These include:

1. a person's capacity to perform to the best of his or her ability

2. an ability to adjust and adapt to varying situations

3. a reported feeling of well-being

4. a feeling that everything is together

Health as wellness is a basic concept that underlies the framework for many modern approaches to health care. Simply defined, it is a state of optimal health or functioning. This definition allows for the fact that people rarely attain perfection in all aspects of their health. Most people have some minor physical problems, such as an allergy to certain pollens, or even major health problems, but they can still strive to be the healthiest that they can be. The key is that people define their own health and wellness according to the indicators important to them. It is essential for nurses to understand this because, to practise ethically, they must be aware that people assess their own health needs in different ways, and an individual, family, or community might have ideas that are unlike those of the nurse.

CULTURAL AND FAMILY INFLUENCES ON HEALTH

Individuals acquire an understanding of health as they grow and develop. Many forces, including family and community values, influence our beliefs and values. These values are shaped by, and in turn shape, the culture. By **culture** we mean the beliefs, customs, practices, and social behaviours of a particular group of people. Ethnic origin is often equated with culture, because people belonging to a particular racial group often have similar beliefs and practices; however, there are many other ways to develop common social behaviours. Any community that shares certain experiences will develop a culture. For example, we can speak of the culture of being on the street and addicted to drugs. Such a group will have its own belief system, language, and priorities. We can also speak about the culture of computer hackers or long-distance truckers. When people share beliefs and ideas, they share culture. Culture affects how individuals and communities view health and illness, and, in part, determines how they care for themselves and what expectations they have for treatment when illness occurs. For example, in North America we generally believe that obesity is unhealthy, and we encourage maintenance of a lean body weight. By contrast, in some African communities obesity is considered desirable, especially in women, where it is seen as a sign of fertility. Similarly, in some cultures the elderly are expected to be sedentary and relatively inactive; whereas in North America we value the ability to maintain an active lifestyle for as long as possible. Clearly, if nurses are to promote health, they require knowledge about cultural beliefs that shape the health practices of those for whom they provide care. Imposing one's own cultural norms about health on someone who holds a different set of beliefs is unlikely to be effective and may even be unethical.

EVOLVING PERSPECTIVES ON HEALTH

Over the years our ideas about health and illness have changed considerably. Understandings of health are shaped by the time and place in which we live. At one time health was simply defined as the absence of illness; people were considered healthy as long as they were not ill. In the mid-1960s there was a shift toward a belief that health is more than the absence of disease; it is also about high-level wellness. It came to be understood that individuals have control over their own health, and their behaviour has an impact. For example, we began to consider things such as smoking, lack of exercise, and overeating as a cause of many illnesses. Today we recognize that health is affected not only by physiological and lifestyle factors but also by the social and economic conditions in which people live. As we discussed in Chapters 2 and 3, ethical nursing practice depends in part on peoples' expectations of care and what they believe to be a good outcome. If our goal is beneficence, and nurses value health and well-being, we need to understand what that looks like to our patients and how we believe it can be achieved. To a large extent, the nature of the health care system and nurses' roles in that system will be shaped by how the population understands health and illness. We will review evolving concepts of health as represented by four different models: *biomedical*, *behavioural*, *socioenvironmental*, and *population*.

The Biomedical Model

Tremendous advances have been made in the physical sciences over the past hundred years. "Scientific medicine" has dominated Western thinking for most of the twentieth century. This way of thinking, known as the **biomedical model**, focuses on the physiological determinants of health and disease. Disease is considered to be a breakdown in or malfunctioning of one or several parts of the body. According to this belief system, health is achievable primarily through medical expertise. Diagnosis and interventions such as medication or surgery are necessary for cure of disease. Achieving higher levels of health involves removing the cause of disease, decreasing the symptoms, and/or removing and replacing the diseased body part. Such an approach puts less emphasis on health promotion and disease prevention.

A key challenge to the biomedical model came from the World Health Organization (WHO). In its constitution, written in 1946, it published the statement that "health is a state of complete physical, mental, and social well-being and not merely the absence of disease and infirmity" (WHO, 1946). This recognition that health and disease are personal and social values and not simply medical labels offered a new perspective on health. It moved beyond focusing on the physiological basis of illness and challenged us to consider health in a broader way. It did have its critics, however. Some suggested that the definition was too vague and all-inclusive, and therefore impractical. Another concern was that describing health as a "state" implied that it is fixed and measurable, rather than a unique and ongoing process. Nonetheless, this new vision of health caused considerable rethinking, particularly in the nursing profession, as people began to question whether health and health care could be less attached to medical interventions.

The Behavioural Model

In the early 1970s Marc Lalonde, then the Canadian federal Minister of Health and Welfare, authored a document entitled *A New Perspective on the Health of Canadians* (also called the **Lalonde Report**). The report, introducing what is known as the "health field concept," indicated that "Future improvements [in health] . . . lie mainly in improving the environment, moderating self-imposed risks, and adding to our knowledge of human biology" (Lalonde, 1974, p. 18). The Lalonde Report made significant contributions to the discussion of health by emphasizing the *lifestyle* element. This was a turning point in broadening the understanding of health and health promotion. In suggesting that lifestyle could have an impact on one's health, the report shifted responsibility from the medical profession to the individual.

Following the Lalonde Report, in 1978 the Canadian government established a Health Promotion Directorate under the Department of Health and Welfare. The aim of the Directorate was to decrease behavioural factors that were known to put a person at increased risk of disease, such as smoking, substance abuse, lack of exercise, and unhealthy diet. The nurse's role grew to include teaching and counselling on lifestyle factors. An increased interest in what motivated people to engage in healthy or unhealthy behaviours and lifestyles prompted many research studies by nurses. It was found that individuals with greater access to primary prevention information benefited most. Education and the ability to access resources, as well as stable employment and higher income, were shown to have a positive effect on health.

The focus following the Lalonde Report was on health education and disease prevention, and on promoting physical well-being, feeling well, having energy, and being fit. In this way, it moved thinking away from illness care toward a more positive approach. There was, however, some opposition to the Lalonde Report. There was a concern that its emphasis on lifestyles could result in victim blaming. In other words, the report could be interpreted as suggesting that people become sick simply because they do not have a healthy lifestyle. Strong emphasis on individual or personal responsibility might result in blame for poor health. This could lead us to abandon and/or devalue the sick, which would be a matter for ethical concern. Another criticism of the report was that it focused on the physical environment, while giving little attention to cultural, social, educational, and economic factors associated with risk behaviours.

Critics suggested that health-related behaviours cannot be separated from the social contexts in which they occur.

The narrowness of the lifestyles approach was recognized not only in Canada but also internationally. Setting the stage for the future, leadership again came from the WHO. "Health for all by the year 2000" was adopted at the Alma-Ata International Conference of the WHO in 1978 as a policy objective (WHO, 1978). The WHO recognized the significance of social conditions on health and proposed focusing on issues of equity, accessibility, and social justice. It specified that communities should take a more active role in health promotion and initiate more active health strategies. This came about through attention to the ethical and political implications of good health as something of personal and social value.

Socioenvironmental Models

The Ottawa Charter and the Epp Report were two documents that emerged in the 1980s which reflected a socioenvironmental approach to health. The **socioenvironmental model** emphasizes connectedness to one's family and community, self-efficacy, self-determination, and capacity to do things that are important and meaningful. Health is seen as encompassing the whole person, including relationships between person and environment. It is not static but is a process of growth and a feeling of well-being. Prerequisites for health are expanded from strictly medical and behavioural health determinants, such as disease prevention and lifestyle, to include psychological, social, environmental, and political elements.

The Ottawa Charter for Health Promotion In 1986, Health and Welfare Canada, the Canadian Public Health Association, and the WHO met at the first International Conference on Health Promotion to develop a health promotion plan. The **Ottawa Charter** was the result of that meeting and was an important document impacting health policy (WHO, 1986). The Charter explored the concept of "responsibility for health" and suggested that a balance between medical, behavioural, and socioenvironmental or ecological approaches was needed. A revised definition of health in the Charter emphasized interrelationships between personal health behaviour and the environment. Health was viewed not as an end goal but as a "resource for everyday living." It promoted a social model where health is a dynamic process that is the responsibility of everyone, not just experts. Health was understood as a positive concept emphasizing social and personal resources as well as physical capabilities. The model required coordinated action from all sectors of society, including governmental and non-governmental organizations, to promote the health of populations. This called for a very different way of working with and viewing professionals; they should be seen as facilitators, mediators, advocates, and supporters rather than experts. The most important component of the Ottawa Charter was a shift from treatment and prevention methods of health care to health promotion strategies that featured empowerment and community involvement. The next step was to develop implementation strategies.

The Epp Report Following the WHO initiative and the Ottawa Charter, Jake Epp, the Canadian Minister of Health and Welfare from 1984 to 1989, developed a policy statement entitled *Achieving Health for All: A Framework for Health Promotion*, also known as the **Epp Report** (1986), which recommended:

- fostering public participation in a national effort to achieve health;
- strengthening community health services to include the public in accomplishing community objectives; and
- coordinating public health policy to provide all sectors of society with opportunities to participate in health choices.

Epp's framework clearly identified the notion of health as a resource that belongs to the people. The strategies reinforced community action in health promotion, community identification of priority needs, use of local resources, and community affiliations. Health had become the responsibility of the community.

The Population Health Model

The Lalonde Report, the Ottawa Charter, and the Epp Report were vital to changing Canadian views about health. In 1989 the Canadian Institute for Advanced Research (CIAR) introduced the concept of population health, proposing that **determinants of health**, or those factors that contribute to one's health and well-being, include social, environmental, and economic factors. It is the interaction among determinants that has a significant effect on health. For example, unemployment can lead to social isolation and poverty, which in turn influences one's psychological health and coping skills. Together these factors can lead to poor health. The term **population health** has come to mean that the health of people improves only when society tackles all these determinants. With a population health approach, action is directed at an entire population or sub-population rather than individuals. In 1994, the population health approach was officially endorsed by the federal, provincial, and territorial Ministers of Health in a report entitled *Strategies for Population Health: Investing in the Health of Canadians*. The report proposed a framework to guide the development and implementation of policies and actions to improve the health of the population. At present, federal, provincial, and territorial policies are based on this report and the population health model.

These ideas continue to evolve and be further refined as our health care system changes. Most recently, two important documents have been released as guides to health care reform. By the millennium it was becoming increasingly evident that health care is expensive, and costs continue to rise. There was concern that, with increasing levels of spending, the Canadian public system was not sustainable. Consequently, the Canadian government appointed Roy Romanow, a former Premier of Saskatchewan, to head a federal commission to examine our health care system in detail and make recommendations about health care reform. Romanow traversed the country seeking input from Canadians and conducting exhaustive examinations of how public health policy was affecting the population. After 18 months the **Romanow Report** was released in November 2002 (Romanow, 2002). The report suggested sweeping changes in how we think about and fund our health care system. One of the most important changes was to alter our focus to primary care. In other words, Romanow recommended that we focus on health promotion and illness prevention. He suggested that we place a much greater emphasis on wellness, including programs to decrease smoking and reduce obesity. Romanow clearly saw the key to a healthier population as resting in determinants of health. The Romanow Report has been criticized, particularly by feminist scholars, for focusing too much on individual behaviours and paying too little attention to the environmental context and determinants of health. Nonetheless, the report certainly attempted to further shift the focus from illness care to health care and health promotion.

The focus on determinants of health and population health was also seen in the Premier's Advisory Council on Health, commonly known as the **Mazankowski Report** (Premier's Advisory Council on Health, 2002). Don Mazankowski, a former federal cabinet minister, was commissioned by the Alberta government to lead a council delegated to make recommendations about health care spending in that province. Some of the ethical implications of a focus on population health and wellness are evident in the Mazankowski Report. For example, the report's first suggestion for reform was to make the population healthier by strengthening health education in schools, supporting children living in poverty, altering Canada's food guide, increasing support for tobacco reduction programs, and providing incentives to Canadians for staying healthy. In other words, the report suggested spending more public dollars on health promotion and illness prevention. How it differed from the Romanow Report was in suggesting that fewer public dollars be spent on illness care as such. At present the Canada Health Act permits very limited private health care, as Canadians have demonstrated that they value payment for health care through public funds (taxation dollars). Mazankowski's analysis led to controversial recommendations to permit private hospitals and clinics for illness care, where individuals who can afford it can buy an increased level of care. This would create a two-tiered (public and private) system of health care, in which the wealthy would have greater access to services. The report has generated significant debate, not just in Alberta but also across Canada. It calls into question many of our cherished beliefs about illness care and places more responsibility for health on the individual.

What does the population health approach mean to nurses and nursing? First, it suggests that health care must be about more than just curing illness. It requires nurses to be aware of the influence of community and environment on health. It points out that individuals are shaped in large part by their environments, and poor health choices may, in fact, not be choices at all. This means that nurses must understand the social determinants of health and work to address broader health concerns at the policy level. Placing the emphasis only on individual behaviours may miss the point entirely. For example, individuals who have little access to education, healthy food, clean water, and primary prevention, as happens on many Aboriginal reserves, may not be able to make healthy choices. Population health therefore suggests that nursing as a profession has a moral obligation to work to ensure that health policy and health promotion strategies are accessible to the greatest number and have the greatest effect. With this in mind, the Canadian Nurses Association and provincial and territorial nursing associations all take an active role in interacting with government in an attempt to influence health policy development. It is becoming increasingly important for nurses to speak up when public input is invited into policy decisions. It is also becoming evident that nurses have an increasing role in health promotion. A report commissioned by the CNA to examine current and future nursing roles has suggested that the main focus for nurses by the year 2020 will be health promotion and primary care and prevention (Villeneuve & MacDonald, 2006).

HEALTH PROMOTION

Health promotion as a concept is frequently confused with the related terms health protection and disease prevention. **Health promotion** is motivated by the desire to increase well-being and actualize health potential. **Health protection** is motivated by a desire to prevent illness, detect it early, or maintain functioning within the constraints of illness. It is often used in conjunction with the term **primary care**, which refers to accessible and coordinated health services focused on both prevention and cure. This is usually thought to take place in the family practitioner's office or even the home. Disease prevention is often discussed in terms of primary, secondary, and tertiary prevention. **Primary prevention** is an action or program designed to help people grow up with or maintain healthy behaviours that will help them resist disease. Recommendations in both the Romanow and Mazankowski reports are examples of primary prevention. **Secondary prevention** aims to help people change unhealthy behaviours and strives for early detection of disease. **Tertiary prevention** is treatment that prevents a person from becoming more ill or dying from a disease. Health promotion, then, is not the same as disease control or disease prevention. Disease prevention is problem oriented, with an emphasis on slowing, changing, or eliminating disease processes, whereas health promotion is more a matter of integrating concepts of health as wellness and fostering activities that move people toward wellness. It is action taken to enhance the quality of life, and it takes into consideration the whole person in interaction with the environment.

Health Promotion and Its Relationship to Nursing

Although health promotion seems to be a relatively recent concept, it has actually been a part of nursing dating back to the time of Florence Nightingale. Certainly health teaching has been a prominent aspect of nursing's mandate since earliest times. In her writings, Nightingale talked about the need for clean air and clean water, rest, and exercise. The public health movement in the United States was led by another famous nurse, Lillian Wald, early in the twentieth century. In Canada the Victorian Order of Nurses, concerned about determinants of health as early as the beginning of the twentieth century, provided prenatal education, well baby clinics, and school health services.

Traditionally, nurses have been leaders in health promotion, with an emphasis on primary prevention. However, with growing awareness of the many factors to be considered, it is becoming clear that health promotion is, by nature, interdisciplinary. Each of the health disciplines brings a different knowledge base to the care of individuals and communities. For example, psychologists have in-depth knowledge about mental health and wellness, while kinesiologists have expertise in developing wellness through exercise, and nutritionists are experts in diet. Nursing has been challenged to find its unique contribution to health promotion.

There are many definitions of health promotion and many perspectives on the nature of health promotion activities. Health promotion as a part of professional nursing practice can be understood in terms of the various definitions of health. Nurses who view health as the absence of disease will focus primarily on illness care and symptom management, as well as disease prevention strategies such as immunization. Those who ascribe to a behavioural model will focus on primary prevention and will emphasize lifestyle factors such as exercise, smoking cessation, and nutrition. Nurses who adopt a broader, more socioenvironmental or population view of health may address topics such as nutrition, poverty, and domestic violence. There will certainly be overlap among the different approaches, for they all view health promotion as an activity that increases individuals' control over their health and lives. What varies is the emphasis. Prior to the 1990s, most health-related practice and research focused on behaviours that prevent illness. With the publication of the Ottawa Charter, nursing efforts in health promotion moved from a focus on lifestyle to more emphasis on psychological, social, environmental, and political considerations. This view of health promotion also introduced the idea of empowering or enabling people as a way of promoting health.

Currently the focus is on behaviours that promote wellness. Health is no longer thought of as simply the absence of illness but instead as wholeness or integrity. On that notion, health promotion practice in nursing involves the nurse as partner, engaging clients in dialogue about health determinants, working with clients to generate health promotion strategies, and fostering positive lifestyle behaviours conducive to optimal health status, harm reduction, and disease prevention. This may be, but is not necessarily, done in the context of illness and illness care. In other words, nurses can work to enhance wellness even within illness. Nurses work toward enhancing clients' capacity for self-care, reducing barriers or modifying situational factors that interfere with health.

Another important issue in health promotion is recognition that a focus on individual behaviours may not be sufficient. Nurses must recognize that the most socially just way to reduce inequities in health care is to look to social determinants of health that affect whole communities. There is an urgent need to increase understanding of these influences on health. This can best be accomplished through research, and nurses have a moral obligation to be aware of research findings, critique and apply findings as appropriate, identify research questions, and conduct research according to their levels of educational preparation. Best practices in nursing are founded on research evidence. The CNA Code of Ethics for Registered Nurses says that "Nurses support, use, and engage in research and other activities that promote safe, competent, compassionate, and ethical care, and they use guidelines for ethical research that are in keeping with nursing values" (CNA, 2008, p. 9).

Enhancing Capacity: Identifying and Building Strengths Individuals are more likely to change their health behaviours if they believe that they have the capacity to do so. This is the notion of **self-efficacy**, which is the degree to which a person believes in his or her ability to perform a certain task. Self-efficacy is a strong influencing factor on behaviour. A person with a low level of self-efficacy is less likely to attempt to undertake a change in health behaviour, believing that she or he will probably not succeed. Nurses can enhance individuals' self-efficacy by helping them clarify their values and what they want to do. Through teaching, coaching, and mentoring, nurses can help individuals recognize and enhance their own strengths. This requires great sensitivity and an understanding of how others learn. For example, when teaching a patient how to monitor blood pressure at home, the nurse breaks down the tasks into small manageable objectives and has the patient demonstrate mastery of the task. Immediate feedback encourages further success.

Empowerment is the process of helping another find strength to do whatever he or she has to do, or in other words to gain self-efficacy. It is an interactive process facilitated by relationships. As nurses, we help patients become empowered through attentive listening. This allows nurses to become aware of clients' strengths and abilities, as well as their goals and desires. As the nurse engages in relational communication with the client, the client can be helped to develop awareness of root causes of problems and to determine readiness to take action for change. This means approaching individuals with an attitude of trust in their abilities to know what they need and make the best choices for themselves. In the past, nurses have been reluctant to trust people to act in their own best interests. The prevailing attitude was that health professionals knew what was right and would direct the patient along the appropriate path. By contrast, a health promotion orientation views people as experts of their bodies and experiences. The nurse's role is to understand the patient and family's values and decision-making style, the cultural context, and social, political, and economic influences on choices, and help the patient and family understand and select the best options for them.

The Importance of Attitudes and Beliefs Nurses value health promotion and view it as an important part of their practice, but they must recognize that not everyone in society values the concept of health promotion equally. People may hold negative beliefs about health promotion. Beliefs are powerful shapers of behaviours. Attitudes about health and personal vulnerability, which are often learned in the family, influence what we think about health and health promotion activities, and our willingness to participate in health activities. Consider a man with a prominent family history of heart disease and stroke. He may hold the belief that health promotion practices have not made a difference in his family as several members have died of the disease regardless of their lifestyle habits. Therefore he does not make the choice to eat more nutritiously and stop smoking.

Individual teaching is a major intervention for promoting health, and motivation is a key component of achieving and maintaining health. Nurses can better help individuals engage in healthy behaviour by considering their beliefs and experiences when planning care and teaching. Many factors help individuals feel motivated to change health behaviours, including self-efficacy, a belief that their health status will improve, a perception of positive outcomes from behaviours, and the receipt of confirmation of these changes from others.

Systems Issues The health care system itself can pose a challenge to nurses wishing to focus on health promotion at the individual or environmental level. One issue is **resource allocation**, the way in which dollars, supplies, and staff are assigned to different aspects of health care. Often health promotion is given less attention than illness care. In other words, there is generally less money allocated to health promotion activities than there is to hospitals and home care for those who are ill. Another related issue is the health status of vulnerable populations who do not have resources comparable to society in general. For example, statistics demonstrate that health concerns in Canada are much greater among Aboriginal people than among the remainder of the population. Many Aboriginal people live in remote areas with little access to health care. The question of resource allocation asks: How do we apportion our health care resources among programs and individuals in need of them? Allocation decisions can involve money, goods, and time. When we talk about resource allocation we often refer to three levels of decision making:

1. **Micro level:** decision making about specific individuals or groups; for example, what level of support should this family receive?

2. **Meso level:** decision making at the institutional level; for example, should the budget for home care be increased within a health region?

3. **Macro level:** decision making at the level of broader society; for example, how much money should the province allocate for health care?

While nurses and other health care providers can and do make decisions daily at the micro level, they are rarely involved in decision making at the meso and macro levels. As discussed previously, however, health promotion, harm reduction, and disease prevention are all viewed as part of a nurse's mandate, particularly in public and community health. This leads to the conclusion that nurses should be involved at all levels. One might argue that this is the mandate of the profession as a whole and not individual nurses, as nurses often feel that they have no control over decisions made at higher levels. Unfortunately the reality is that nurses do not escape the issues of cost and resource allocation in their everyday care at the micro level, and it may be necessary that they take action to promote change at higher levels.

Health Promotion and Social Determinants of Health Most of the focus in this discussion has been on the individual and the factors that affect individual choice. There is, however, another important area that must be considered in any conversation about health and health promotion and that is the effect of environment and context on choice. Socioeconomic factors such as income and educational level are, on the one hand, individual concerns, but on the other hand they may also be community concerns. In some communities access to health care, good nutrition, and clean air and water are markedly limited. These factors have far-reaching effects and can influence capacity, empowerment, and attitudes at the community level. Understanding these influences is of vital importance, as any attempts to change individual behaviours are unlikely to be successful unless the underlying problems are addressed. One of the criticisms of the health promotion approach is that it can lead to victim blaming, as was mentioned above. It is easy for nurses, who in many ways are in a privileged position of relative power, to assume that individuals are too lazy, unmotivated, or lacking in knowledge to make change. This is sometimes the case, but again we must emphasize that very often environmental effects disempower individuals to the point where they are *unable* to exercise choice. Sometimes unhealthy behaviours become the norm in a community because of lack of understanding or community disempowerment. Such things as low economic status, poor nutrition, inadequate education, and ongoing lack of access to primary prevention services make it harder for individuals to understand the importance of health behaviours. More research is urgently needed to look at interactions among a variety of factors thought to influence health. This is an area where nursing expertise in identifying questions and designing excellent studies is critical.

Promoting Health and Well-Being within Illness According to the CNA Code of Ethics for Registered Nurses, "Nurses provide care directed first and foremost toward the health and well-being of the person, family, or community in their care" (CNA, 2008, p. 10). Health promotion can be considered even while patients are dying. As we mentioned before, health is more than just the absence of disease. One of the nurse's responsibilities is to help individuals be the "best" that they can be, regardless of their state of illness. This means helping them maintain their dignity and self-respect, preserving their autonomy to the extent possible, and helping them feel empowered to make choices that are important to them. These are some of the values discussed in later chapters of this book. As you read them, consider how these values relate to health and health promotion. Helping patients (and families) maintain their sense of wholeness despite devastating illness and even dying is one of the most important health promotion activities nurses can undertake.

MORALITY AND HEALTH PROMOTION

At this point you might be asking yourself why we have presented such a detailed discussion of health promotion in a nursing textbook on ethics. The answer to that question is that we believe a strong connection exists between health, health promotion, and morality. And indeed, so does the Canadian Nurses Association, as it has indicated that one of the primary values of its Code of Ethics for Registered Nurses is promotion of health and well-being. Clearly we believe that it is part of the profession of nursing's moral obligation to help others attain or maintain wellness. However, ethical dimensions related to this concept involve more than simply saying "it is a nurse's job to try to promote health."

It may be obvious by now that the moral significance of nursing is not just a matter of working toward certain objectives such as health promotion. Part of the ethical dimension of nursing involves *how* these activities are carried out. Nurses strive toward relational practices in all their activities, including health promotion. This means trusting patients as partners in health promotion practices. It also means respecting and supporting individuals' rights to make decisions and identifying and using individuals' strengths and assets to empower them to promote their own health and healing.

Respecting and Supporting Individuals' Rights

In the past, health care professionals were given considerable authority for decision making. Often the person's wishes were not sought. Information was frequently withheld. Student nurses were instructed not to provide health information to patients or clients, even about minor things such as blood pressure. The doctor made the decision as to what the patient should be told and either delivered the information himself (and most doctors were male) or gave the nurse careful instructions as to what was to be discussed. Today, we hold individuals responsible for their own health as much as possible. No longer is the health care provider the key decision maker. Patients expect to be given information so that they can make informed decisions. Health care is to be tailored to an individual's particular needs according to his or her beliefs and desires. Patients expect to be shown respect and to have their wishes honoured in regard to matters of their own health.

In Chapter 1 we discussed the ethical principle of autonomy, which we said refers to the individual's right to choose and the ability to act on and find meaning in that choice. Increasingly, we try to promote autonomy in health care and avoid paternalism. Recall that paternalism is deciding for others in what we believe to be their best interests, without giving them choices. This is the kind of decision making that used to be expected in health care. Today nurses work to ensure that patients have autonomy to make their own decisions, respecting their rights to choose and protecting those who are not able to decide for themselves. Nurses strive to avoid paternalism and instead enter into dialogues with patients. Decisions about treatment or health promotion activities are made through a process of discussion whenever possible.

It is particularly important to consider and respect peoples' decisions about their own health promotion activities. A growing awareness of the influence of risk factors and lifestyle on health might lead a nurse to be critical of individuals who do not make lifestyle choices that the nurse thinks are right. Above we discussed the concept of victim blaming. We described how a strong belief in a behavioural or even population health model could lead nurses to hold individuals responsible for their own illnesses if they fail to make lifestyle choices that reduce their risks of disease. As nurses we need to be aware that people have widely different beliefs about health and illness, and make choices for a lot of different reasons. We no longer believe that people make decisions all on their own. Thanks in large part to the work of feminist writers such as Susan Sherwin, a feminist philosopher and ethicist from Dalhousie University in

Halifax, we have come to understand that people make decisions within a complex web of relationships, responsibilities, and social structures (Sherwin, 1998). Sherwin calls this **relational autonomy**. For example, a mother might be aware that she should eat more healthful food but decides to eat mostly fatty foods and carbohydrates because they are less expensive, and she wants to use her limited funds to buy more fruits and vegetables for her children.

The concept of relational autonomy requires nurses to seek a better understanding of how and why their patients or clients make decisions. Not everyone feels free, or has the ability, to make the decisions we might think are appropriate. Nurses often assume that patients experience the same sense of autonomy that nurses do, and fail to recognize that patients may feel disempowered or vulnerable. They may make decisions for reasons we do not understand. Nurses need to be conscious of their own beliefs and values, and not judge others for their choices. Michael Yeo, another Canadian philosopher and ethicist, points out that power, knowledge, and vulnerability are not always evenly balanced in the client-professional relationship (Yeo, 1996). Individuals who need health care services often feel vulnerable, believing that health care providers will withhold care or treat them disrespectfully if they make "wrong" decisions. To some extent their perception may be accurate. Health care professionals can be insensitive to the way in which the health care system dehumanizes people and takes away their sense of autonomy. Violation of an individual's autonomy might occur if nurses assume that individuals have the same values and goals as the nurses. Or nurses may fail to recognize that individuals' thought processes are different from theirs.

Because we as nurses have a strong belief in health promotion, we assume others have the same belief. This kind of assumption can be dangerous, however. It can make it hard for nurses to understand why others make choices that do not lead to optimal health. It can lead nurses to devalue others who make choices incongruent with health promotion. Often nurses' enthusiasm for health promotion leads them to expect that patients will accept whatever health plans the nurse suggests. When patients do not follow our advice, we often label them as "difficult" or "noncompliant." We may demonstrate contempt for or frustration with their choices. For example, we might feel that an overweight person with high blood pressure who refuses to lose weight and exercise is not deserving of our respect. Such a response to another's decision making is not acceptable in nursing. We emphasize that it is not our position to judge another's choices. What we can do as nurses is explore their reasons for making such choices and provide them with information and support.

HEALTH PROMOTION AS A LIVED VALUE

The two case studies below reflect some of the ethical issues in health promotion that nurses might encounter. One was drawn from recent research on ethical issues experienced by Canadian public health nurses that one of the authors conducted with a colleague, Sandra Tenove (Oberle and Tenove, 2000). In this study, nurses were asked to report frequent ethical concerns that they experienced in nursing practice. The first case study is derived from an actual story nurses told us. The second case study is set in acute care and drawn from the clinical experience of a Masters in Nursing student in a clinical practicum. Both scenarios involve a conflict of values and beliefs in which the nurse is unsure how emphatic to be in encouraging health promotion strategies. Both involve relational ethics rather than classical ethical dilemmas.

Trying It On
5.1 Other Voices, Other Beliefs

Sharla was a public health nurse working in an inner city program for new mothers. She had made a home visit to Estelle, a 22-year-old woman who had a 14-month-old son named Theo. Estelle and her husband lived with Estelle's parents and grandmother. The family appeared to have strong religious and cultural beliefs. This was not Sharla's first visit to the home. In fact, she had seen Estelle and Theo frequently since she had learned of a problem at a follow-up home visit. She was concerned that Theo was not thriving. It had been difficult for Estelle to establish breast-feeding as Theo was not an energetic feeder, and Estelle was shy about the whole process. At first Theo had been colicky and had frequent watery stools. Sometimes his stools had bright blood in them, and he was very small for his age. He was often lethargic and sleepy. The family physician had diagnosed severe food allergies.

Together, Sharla and Estelle had worked out a strategy. They had discovered that when Estelle ate certain foods, Theo had more diarrhea, so these had been eliminated from Estelle's diet. Now Theo was starting to fill out and look much healthier. He was alert, and was beginning to master age-appropriate tasks. Yesterday he had even pulled himself up to standing and walked around the furniture!

On this visit, Sharla and Estelle were discussing how long Estelle should continue to breast-feed Theo. Sharla was of the opinion that Theo should be introduced to solid foods very slowly and that breast milk was the best thing for him at this stage. She was concerned that the diarrhea, which was now under control, would return if new foods were introduced too quickly.

Estelle seemed to think so too. She now seemed to be comfortable with breast-feeding; however, she was not sure that she should continue. She said to Sharla, "I'm really wondering if I can try Theo on formula and more solid foods. My husband thinks it's unnatural and disgusting that I'm still breast-feeding such a big boy. My grandmother thinks so too. She has come up with some foods that I should try him on—things that they always used to feed babies when Mom was little. She says he should be drinking milk out of a cup and eating meat and vegetables. Every time I start to feed Theo she clucks like a wet hen and gets very annoyed with me for not listening to her. Mom sides with Grandma. She thinks these new feeding ideas are ridiculous. They can't understand why I won't listen to Grandma! They say it's disrespectful."

Other Voices, Other Beliefs

The case study reflects a very real concern in nursing practice. The problem here is that what is considered appropriate action can be greatly affected by individual and cultural beliefs. The nurse requires an awareness of this, particularly when attempting to influence health promotion practices and lifestyle choices.

Understanding the Ethics of the Situation: Relationships, Goals, Beliefs, and Values

In this scenario, Sharla is concerned that Estelle's choices will influence her baby's health. She wants to give good advice to Estelle, but a number of conflicting beliefs and values are at work. First, Sharla values the infant's health and well-being, and wants to ensure that he receives the best possible nutrition. That probably means he should have breast milk for as long as possible. However, the family has strong beliefs about the appropriate length of time for a mother to nurse a male infant. They have not said what the underlying concerns are, but clearly they do not agree with breast-feeding a 14-month-old child. They are convinced that other approaches are better and that the elder member of the family (the grandmother) has important knowledge that they consider correct. They also believe that the grandmother's views should be respected, as she has a particular kind of wisdom and possibly simply because she is old.

If Sharla decides to interfere with these beliefs, there is a strong possibility of disrupting family harmony, which in the long run might be bad for the baby and for Estelle. Sharla also worries that, if she is seen to be in opposition to the elder members of the family, she will be refused admittance when she next comes to visit Estelle. She is not certain what would be the right thing to do. Should she continue to promote what she believes to be in Theo's best interests and risk upsetting the family dynamics and jeopardizing her access to the home, or should she try to accept the family's cultural beliefs and values? Which is the more ethical approach in this situation? Which would maximize the good?

If Sharla were to consider normative theories or bioethical principles she would find little guidance for a situation such as this, for it is essentially an issue of relationship, which is not addressed directly by such theories. One might suggest that there is a conflict between beneficence for the child and autonomy for the mother, but that does not capture the nuances of the situation. Even if one decided to give priority to the principle of beneficence, what would that look like? On one hand, if Sharla does not respect the relationships present, she might ultimately cause harm to the child if the family decides not to let her visit any more. On the other hand, without Sharla's support Estelle might be overwhelmed by her family's opposition to continued breast-feeding, and Theo might experience worsening health. Considering the Ethics Composite Model, Sharla would see that the core of this situation rests with virtues and relationships.

Reflecting on and Reviewing Potential Actions: Recognizing Available Choices and How Those Choices Are Valued

In this situation Sharla has several options: she can go along with what the grandmother and others suggest regarding Theo's nutrition; she can concentrate on trying to convince Estelle to follow their original plan of continuing breast-feeding and introducing new foods very slowly; or she can focus on convincing the family of the importance of this course of action. Sharla is basing her beliefs on her knowledge of allergies and the development of antigen-antibody responses. However, she is unfamiliar with the foods that the grandmother is suggesting they try, so is unable to establish whether or not they would be dangerous to Theo. Sharla is also aware of the emphasis Estelle's cultural group places on respect for elders. She has observed that within the family Estelle is expected to obey her elders and her husband. Therefore, to suggest a course of action that is contrary to this cultural code would be wrong on Sharla's part. It is important to protect the infant, and Sharla is quite confident that the health promotion strategy she suggested earlier to Estelle is the right one, but she also knows that the situation is complex and that she has to take into account the beliefs held by the family.

Selecting an Ethical Action: Maximizing Good

After reflecting on the possible approaches she might take, Sharla decides on the following action: she asks if she can come to the house on Friday afternoon and requests that all the family members are present. It is her intent to try to explain her rationale for recommending that Estelle continue to breast-feed. She also knows, however, that it is important that she listen to what the family has to say about their concerns.

Engaging in Ethical Action

The day before her meeting with the family, Sharla is somewhat worried because she does not want to cause conflict. Part of her moral obligation, then, is to become somewhat more familiar with the family's cultural and religious beliefs. She goes to the library and does some reading on the key values expressed by Estelle's cultural group. She realizes that their issues are involved with beliefs about how a male child is to be treated, how his development is understood, and how religious beliefs might affect their understanding. When she meets with the family, she is able to be more informed in her questioning and more effective when working with them. As she explains some of the underlying science to the family, they appear to be more accepting. Estelle's husband expresses a belief that they are in a new country now and should go with the new ways, as he wants his son to grow up to be a strong and healthy Canadian.

Reflecting on and Reviewing the Ethical Action

Sharla is satisfied with the outcome of her intervention, as the family has agreed to the plan she and Estelle had developed. She is also aware, however, that she has not been as careful in the past and has been much more insistent on certain courses of action with other families. She wonders if her past practices have done more harm than good, and she makes a vow to be more attentive to the patient's and family's beliefs in the future.

Trying It On

5.2 Understanding Health Choices

As an experienced cardiac nurse, Rob was actively involved in patient teaching. He prided himself on doing the best job of it: all his patients commented on how thorough he was, although some seemed not to pay much attention to what Rob was teaching. One of his patients, Shane, was ready for discharge. He had been admitted with chest pain five days earlier and then diagnosed with a mild anterior myocardial infarction. He was being discharged on a variety of medications and was scheduled for an angiography in about four weeks. Rob entered Shane's room and began to talk to him about the lifestyle modifications necessary to prevent recurrence of his cardiac problems. Rob had brochures and pictures to show Shane, but when he started to talk about the need to lose weight and restrict his fat intake, Shane got upset and told Rob quite rudely to "get lost." Rob was quite surprised, and asked Shane what was wrong.

Shane replied, "My life is horrible. My wife left a year ago and took the kids. I lost my job about four weeks ago, and I haven't been able to find anything else. I'm living in a hotel. I used to drink and smoke too much, but I got those habits under control. Now my only comfort is a decent meal, but all you high and mighty nurses keep telling me to give that up too. You don't know anything about my life, and I wish you would just leave me alone."

Rob didn't know what to do. He was concerned about Shane's decision but wasn't certain about whether he should try to give more information at this time. He felt it would be wrong not to try, as he felt obligated to give Shane the information he needed to make healthy choices, but he wasn't sure Shane would get much out of it.

Applying the Framework

Understanding Health Choices

This scenario is not unlike the previous one, in that the key element is understanding the other's perspective. Again, it is essentially an issue of relationships, not conflicting principles. Analysis will therefore be somewhat briefer.

Understanding the Ethics of the Situation: Relationships, Goals, Beliefs, and Values

As an experienced cardiology nurse, Rob is certain that his teaching is important and that Shane needs to make better lifestyle choices. Rob believes that, as it stands, Shane is a victim of his own poor health practices and is doing himself harm. Ron has never questioned the importance of risk factor management and has always undertaken patient teaching with enthusiasm. His belief is that patients will make correct choices if they are just given the right information. The current situation has made him stop and think, however. He realizes that he has made a lot of assumptions about Shane and the cause of his problems, but has never actually stopped to ask him about his life and its stresses. Rob sees that he has been pushing his own values on Shane without considering the context in which Shane makes his decisions. Rob now wonders if insisting on the importance of changing Shane's diet is the most effective intervention for him just now. The stress of changing his diet at this point in time might be harmful to Shane, given all he is dealing with. Rob begins to shift his understanding from a focus on lifestyle choices to a focus on minimizing harm. He begins to see that he has a moral obligation to consider the factors influencing Shane's decisions and try to determine if there is anything he can do to support Shane in this difficult period.

Reflecting on and Reviewing Potential Actions: Recognizing Available Choices and How Those Choices Are Valued

In this situation, how can Rob fulfill his obligation to give the patient important information and still respect the patient's request to be left alone? Clearly, the two positions are incompatible. However, Shane has given Rob an opening to explore the issue further, in that he has made several statements about the quality of his life. One choice that Rob might make is to attempt to explore Shane's issues and understand the context in which he has made his choices. This might be more effective than simply giving Shane information that he won't use. Shane's choices are based on what he is currently experiencing, and for Rob to push ahead with his own agenda without taking Shane's issues into account seems wrong from a relational ethics perspective.

Selecting an Ethical Action: Maximizing Good

Like Sharla, Rob realizes that the most ethical approach in this situation is to stop and listen to the patient. Perhaps if he can help Shane find solutions to his other problems, Shane might be in a better position to make more positive health choices. If Rob's focus changes to one of minimizing harm, he might look at the situation differently and understand that he has an obligation to try to work with Shane to deal with his immediate problems. Later they can start to consider his lifestyle choices.

Engaging in Ethical Action

Rob's approach to Shane will need to be very sensitive. Shane has already indicated that he does not want to be bothered further. Rob will need to use excellent communication skills, including engaging authentically with the patient, listening actively, and reflecting on what is said. Rob's moral obligation as a cardiology nurse is in part to respect the patient's choices, but he also has an obligation to help the patient see the importance of more healthful lifestyle decisions. Before he can do that, however, he needs to try to engage Shane in a conversation about the contextual factors that are making it so difficult for him to change. This requires that Rob indicate a sincere desire to help, not just deliver a "formula" risk-management plan. Not only must he listen to Shane's problems, but he must use his relational skills to help Shane find ways to deal with the underlying issues shaping his current lifestyle, and then they can move on to beliefs that are more likely to lead to healthy choices.

(Continued)

Understanding Health Choices

Reflecting on and Reviewing the Ethical Action

Rob's approach of listening and respecting the patient's right to make his own choices is an example of relational ethics in action. Not only does he listen, but he works with the patient to find more healthful ways of dealing with his problems. This requires enormous professional skill that is gained only through experience and practice. The details of how this might be done are beyond the scope of this book. Our purpose here is to raise awareness of its importance as a part of ethical practice.

CHAPTER SUMMARY

In this chapter we explored the second value in the CNA Code of Ethics for Registered Nurses: *promoting health and well-being*. To draw out the ethical elements of that value, we began our discussion by differentiating between health and wellness, and between illness and disease. We talked about the importance of understanding how health and wellness might exist within illness, and various factors that could contribute to how one views health. For example, we described how family beliefs and values could impact how an individual views health behaviours.

Nursing is evolving as societal understandings change. To demonstrate how nursing care might be influenced by different views of health and health care, we talked about four different models of health. The biomedical model was described as being primarily about disease and disease treatment and management. That model is the model most clearly linked to medical care. The behavioural model grew out of a need to curb rising health care costs, as it was becoming evident in the 1970s that, despite advanced technology and the best possible medical care, the health of the population was not improving dramatically. Marc Lalonde's report on Canada's health emphasized the need for prevention and health promotion as a way of limiting health care spending. Rather than treat people when they become ill, it seemed reasonable and less costly to prevent them from becoming ill. Lalonde emphasized the importance of lifestyle choices. In the 1980s new socioenvironmental models were introduced. These models demonstrated the importance of considering not just an individual's own lifestyle choices but also the social and environmental context within which a person makes those choices. The Ottawa Charter and the Epp Report gave direction to Canadians for health promotion based on socioeconomic models. More recently, the population health model has been used to shape health promotion strategies. This model takes into account the determinants of health and includes personal health practices as well as the physical, social, and economic environment, individual capacity, and health services. Recent analyses on health care reform, including the Romanow and Mazinkowski reports, support the concept of health promotion as a key to containing health care costs.

From that detailed discussion of concepts of health, we moved on to discuss health promotion and the nurse's role in it. We discussed the importance of enhancing capacity and building strengths in patients and families, considering attitudes, beliefs, and values, and understanding systems issues at the micro, meso, and macro levels. We then went on to describe the moral elements inherent in health promotion, including the obligation to respect and support others' rights and beliefs. We discussed at length a concept called relational autonomy, in which patients and families are understood to make autonomous choices within a network of relationships.

Finally, we discussed two case studies: a problem with conflicting cultural beliefs around infant feeding, and a situation in which the nurse had limited awareness of the patient's needs and was challenged by the patient regarding the wisdom of particular health teachings. In both, the key factor in resolution of the problem was relational ethics. Both scenarios were chosen because they reflected situations in which the nurse was making assumptions about the right action, without exploring it in detail with the patient and family. Once the relational aspects of the situation were attended to, a resolution to the problem could be found.

Questions for Reflection

1. Consider your own ideas about health. When do you consider yourself healthy? What has to happen to make you feel you are not healthy? Do you think of health as absence of disease? Can you feel healthy if you have a disease?

2. What do you think about people who put their health at risk? Do you think that this belief will influence how you provide care?

3. Consider your own understanding of health and health promotion. Do you know others who have a different view? What do you think about their beliefs?

4. Can you think of any time when you have judged others for their actions regarding health promotion? Was that appropriate?

5. Consider your clinical practice. What kinds of health promotion activities have you observed? Who was doing these activities? In what areas of practice do you see the most health promotion activity? What obligations do you see nursing having regarding health promotion in acute care? Public health?

6. What ethical issues regarding health promotion have you encountered?

Exercises

1. Working in small groups, discuss ideas about health. What different views emerge in your group? Discuss how different views might impact whether and how nurses undertake health promotion activities.

2. Again working in small groups, discuss some approaches that Rob might have taken with Shane. Be specific, drawing on your understanding of communication theory and relationships nursing. Develop four questions that Rob might have used to help Shane with his lifestyle choices.

Research Activities

1. Obtain and examine mission statements of your health region or hospital. What emphasis is there on health promotion? Working from Health Canada statistics, determine what proportion of the annual health care budget is allocated to health promotion and illness prevention. Then consider nursing activities that might promote a more health-oriented care delivery system. Present your conclusions to the class.

2. From the library, locate three articles that discuss health promotion. Try to determine the models they are working from. Consider differences that the models might make in how one approaches the patient.

Key Terms

biomedical model

culture

determinants of health

empowerment

Epp Report

health

health as wellness

health promotion

health protection

high-level wellness

Lalonde Report

macro level

Mazankowski Report

meso level

micro level

Ottawa Charter

population health

primary care

primary prevention

relational autonomy

resource allocation

Romanow Report

secondary prevention

self-efficacy

socioenvironmental model

tertiary prevention

wellness

References

Canadian Nurses Association (2008). *Code of ethics for registered nurses* (Centennial Ed.). Ottawa: Author.

Dunn, H. (1959). What high-level wellness means. *Canadian Journal of Public Health, 50*(11), 447–457.

Dunn, H. (1977). What high-level wellness means. *Health Values, 1,* 9–16

Epp, J. (1986). *Achieving health for all: A framework for health promotion.* Ottawa: Health and Welfare Canada.

Jensen, L., & Allen, M. (1994). A synthesis of qualitative research on wellness-illness. *Qualitative Health Research, 11,* 349–369.

Lalonde, M. (1974). A new perspective on the health of Canadians. Ottawa: Government of Canada.

Meleis, A. (1990). Being and becoming healthy: The core of nursing knowledge. *Nursing Science Quarterly, 3*(3), 107–114.

Mosby's medical, nursing, and allied health dictionary (6th ed.) (2002). St. Louis, MO: Mosby.

Oberle, K., & Tenove, S. (2000). Public health nurses' perceptions of ethical problems. *Nursing Ethics, 7,* 425–437.

Premier's Advisory Council on Health (2002). *A framework for reform.* Edmonton: Government of Alberta. Retrieved August 2008 from www.mapleleafweb.com/features/2002-mazankowski-report-health-care-alberta.

Romanow, R. J. (2002). *Building on values: The future of health care in Canada. Final Report.* Ottawa: Health Canada. Retrieved August 2008 from www.hc-sc.gc.ca/hcs-sss/alt_formats/hpb-dgps/pdf/hhr/romanow-eng.pdf.

Sherwin, S. (1998). A relational approach to autonomy in health care. In S. Sherwin (Ed.), *The politics of women's health: Exploring agency and autonomy* (pp. 19–47). Philadelphia: Temple University Press.

Villeneuve, M., & MacDonald, J. (2006). *Toward 2020: Visions for nursing.* Ottawa: CNA.

World Health Organization (1946). *Constitution of the World Health Organization: Chronicle of the World Health Organization 1*. Geneva, Switzerland: WHO.

World Health Organization (1978). *Declaration of Alma-Ata*. Geneva, Switzerland: WHO.

World Health Organization, Health & Welfare Canada (HWC), & Canadian Public Health Association (1986). *Ottawa Charter for Health Promotion*. Geneva, Switzerland: WHO.

Yeo, M. (1996). *Concepts and cases in nursing ethics*. Peterborough, ON: Broadview Press.

Suggested Reading

Gadow, S. (1990). Existential Advocacy. In T. Pence & J. Cantral (Eds.), *Ethics in Nursing: An Anthology* (pp. 41–51). New York: National League for Nursing.

Green, L., & Kreuter, M. (1993). Are community organization and health promotion one process or two? *American Journal of Health Promotion, 7*(3), 221.

Hood, L., & Leddy, S. (2003). *Conceptual bases of professional nursing* (5th ed.). Philadelphia: Lippincott.

Labonte, R. (1993). Health promotion and empowerment: Practice frameworks. *Issues in health promotion series 3*. Toronto: Centre for Health Promotion, University of Toronto and ParticipACTION.

Pender, N. (1982). *Health promotion in nursing practice*. Norwalk, CT: Appleton Century Crofts.

Pender, N. (1987). *Health promotion in nursing practice*. Norwalk, CT: Appleton Lange.

Pietroni, P. (1987). The meaning of illness-holism dissected: Discussion paper. *Journal of the Royal Society of Medicine, 80*, 357–360.

Raeburn, J., & Rootman, I. (1999). *People-centered health promotion*. New York: John Wiley.

Reilly, S. (2004). Health and wellness. In B. Kozier, G. Erb, A. Burman, K. Burke, S. Raffin Bouchal, & S. Hirst (Eds.), *Fundamentals of nursing: The nature of nursing practice in Canada* (1st ed.). Toronto: Prentice Hall.

Romanow, R. (2002). *Building on values: The future of health care in Canada*. Ottawa: Health Canada. Retrieved from www.hc-sc.gc.ca/english/care/romanow/index1.html.

Smith, J. A. (1981). The idea of health: A philosophical inquiry. *Advances in Nursing Science, 3*(3), 43–50.

Somers, A. (1976). *Promoting health: Consumer education and national policy*. Germantown, MD: Aspen.

Young, I. M. (1994). Punishment, treatment, empowerment: Three approaches to policy for pregnant addicts. *Feminist Studies, 20*, 33–57.

Chapter 6
Value 3: Promoting and Respecting Informed Decision Making

Learning Objectives

After reading this chapter, you should be able to:

- articulate what constitutes an ethical problem in nursing

- describe the third primary value in the CNA Code of Ethics for Registered Nurses: *promoting and respecting informed decision making*

- discuss the concepts of choice, autonomy, and informed consent

- discuss the history and interpretation of choice/autonomy in ethics and bioethics

- describe nursing implications related to choice

- apply the Framework for Ethical Decision Making to a clinical problem related to choice

Mary is a 24-year-old single woman who is nine months pregnant with her first child. She has been admitted to an acute psychiatry unit because she is suffering from a very severe depression that is causing her to feel suicidal. In fact, she had slashed her wrists just prior to her admission but was found by her landlady and rushed to hospital. Mary's physicians have advised her that she is a candidate for electro-convulsive therapy (ECT). This would involve applying electrodes to her head and administering an electric shock to her brain after giving her a muscle relaxant and anaesthetic. This form of treatment has been shown to have some positive effects by "resetting" brain impulses that cause feelings of depression. Mary has no family or significant other to help her with this decision. Sometimes she feels confused and finds it difficult to make decisions, so she is not certain she understands all that she is being told about the treatment. Another problem is that no one seems to be able to tell her how her unborn baby will experience this treatment. It seems reasonable to assume that the baby will feel the shock, but will it be painful or unpleasant? Is there any risk of harm to the baby from the shock or the drugs?

THE THIRD PRIMARY VALUE: PROMOTING AND RESPECTING INFORMED DECISION MAKING

The third primary value of the CNA Code of Ethics for Registered Nurses is *promoting and respecting informed decision making*. The Code states, "Nurses recognize, respect, and promote a person's right to be informed and make decisions" (CNA, 2008, p. 11). Embedded in the concept of decision making is the idea of choice and the right to choose for oneself. Sometimes issues of choice and decision making are fairly straightforward, and present no ethical dilemma. For example, an adult man who is competent to make decisions about his own welfare may be easily able to decide whether or not to have a wart removed from the sole of his foot. Other decisions are much more complex and difficult, as Mary's situation illustrates.

If you were the nurse in Mary's situation, what kinds of questions might arise for you? Would you wonder about Mary's ability to give informed consent? Would you wonder about whether it was right for her to decide on a treatment that might cause discomfort or harm to her unborn baby? How would you proceed in helping Mary come to the best decision for herself and her child? To help you reach some answers to these questions, in this chapter we will provide you with some background information about how choice is understood in ethics and bioethics. We will discuss the concept of autonomy, how others have defined it, and the moral significance of different interpretations of it. We will consider some factors that can influence understandings of autonomy and choice, such as culture, and describe how the notion of rights has changed the way in which we think about decision making in health care. Questions about how decisions can be delegated to others and whether it is ever morally acceptable to limit choice will be considered. Then we will turn to implications of choice for nursing practice. Finally we will present two case studies in which choice is an issue, and analyze these cases using the Framework for Ethical Decision Making.

UNDERSTANDING CHOICE

The word "choice" is simply defined: it means selecting among various options. That definition does not begin to capture the complexities of choice in a health care setting, however. Making a choice implies making a decision about what one wants to do, or wants done, with respect to one's health and health care. As we discussed in Chapter 4, health is a very strong value for almost everyone. Choices related to health and illness care will, therefore, reflect deeply held beliefs and values. In the above paragraphs, we indicated that a number of concepts are embedded in the notion of choice. The first of these is autonomy.

In Chapter 1 we said that autonomy "involves one's ability to make choices for oneself, and ... these choices should be based on full understanding, free of controlling influences. **Autonomy** is about having both the right and the ability to make meaningful choices about oneself (and one's care) (p. 14). Autonomy has become central to much of the literature on bioethics. The right to choose is at the heart of ethical discussions about informed consent, for example. Autonomy has a number of different elements, and it is important that you understand the concept's origins and the many meanings associated with it, some of which are outlined below.

Philosophical Origins of Autonomy

Much of our current understanding of autonomy is based on the writings of Immanuel Kant and John Stuart Mill, which we talked about in Chapter 1. Candace Cummins Gauthier, an American philosopher, provides a clear account of this in her discussion of autonomy. According to Gauthier, Kant's contributions to understanding autonomy stemmed from his belief that people are to be treated differently from animals and things because people have the ability to reason. Kant's Categorical Imperative that one must "*treat humanity, whether in your own person or in that of another, always as an end and never as a means only*" was based on the idea that people, because of their capacities, must be treated with respect. Treating someone with respect means that we are not permitted to do things to them without their permission. It also implies that we must consider their dignity, which we will discuss at length in Chapter 7. In health care, respecting choice means allowing persons to control what happens to them or their families. It means avoiding making paternalistic decisions for people without involving them in the decision making. This is more difficult than it sounds, however, as we shall discover shortly.

Mill's ideas about liberty suggested that persons could and should make decisions about and for themselves, but only insofar as their decisions do not affect the welfare of others. That is, he said that making decisions for oneself is right and proper, but our decisions are limited by the effects they have on others. He also believed that it was important to recognize that we can allow persons to make decisions for themselves only if they have the capacity to do so. That is, they must have well-developed decisional capabilities (Gauthier, 2002). This thinking is very present in the way we think about autonomy today. You will see evidence of it if you consider the kinds of decisions people with limited decision-making capacity, such as children or the demented elderly, are permitted to make in health care. We will discuss this concept further in our discussion of informed consent, later in this chapter.

Components of Autonomy

The thinking of these two philosophers, Kant and Mill, forms the basis of the bioethical principle of autonomy, as described by Beauchamp and Childress (2001). The belief that autonomy must be respected is at the core of biomedical ethics. Philosophers have described autonomy in different ways, but most understand it to have several dimensions. A Swedish philosopher, Lars Sandman, has summarized much of the thinking about autonomy (2004) and says that it has four components: *self-determination, freedom, desire fulfillment,* and *independence*. You might be asking yourself why you need those kinds of philosophical understandings about autonomy. Our answer is that if you know what autonomy is really about, you will have an easier time recognizing an autonomy issue when you encounter it in nursing practice. As a nurse you need to know whether autonomy is a reasonable goal, what its limits are, and when those limits have been reached. The explanation below should clarify what to look for when you are considering issues of choice.

Self-Determination Self-determination means making decisions related to what happens to oneself. This is the central idea in autonomy. A self-determining person makes choices according to his or her own will, doing what he or she wants to do in accordance with his or her values. Implications of this for practice would seem to be quite straightforward: if our obligation as care providers is to support autonomy, then we should support people in doing what they want to do; however, this is not as simple as it seems. People sometimes do not know what they want to do, or have difficulty deciding what actions they should take. Sometimes they lack sufficient information to make a decision. Sometimes the information they have is wrong. They may choose to do something because they mistakenly fear bad consequences if they do not do it. Sometimes what they want to do conflicts with what others want them to do, or what others want to do. Sometimes what people want to do will cause them serious harm or may cause others harm. Clearly, there must be some limits on self-determination. We do not always have the freedom to do what we want.

Freedom One meaning of freedom is "the absence of necessity, coercion, or constraint in choice or action" (Merriam-Webster on-line). In other words, it means being able to make choices based on what we want, not on what we are forced to do or prevented from having or doing. We may be limited in making our choices because someone prevents us from choosing, because we do not have the ability to carry out an action we would choose to undertake, or because available options do not include what we value most highly. Resources might not be available to allow us to do what we want. For example, as Sandman (2004) points out, people in underdeveloped countries cannot choose to have medications and health care that are available to people in developed nations. If I am a prisoner, I cannot choose to walk to the corner store whenever I wish. Sometimes people cannot choose things because they have been taught that certain choices are wrong. A Muslim woman is not free in certain countries to choose to walk on the street with her face uncovered. Certainly, laws designed to make certain that our choices do not harm others can limit our freedoms. Clearly we do not have unlimited freedom, for many reasons. We must consider, too, that even if we are free to make choices, and have the self-determination to know what we want, our desires will not always be fulfilled.

Desire Fulfillment The notion of **desire fulfillment** suggests getting what we most want. However, as mentioned above, simply knowing what we want and having the freedom to make choices does not always ensure that our desires are fulfilled. Sometimes the choices we make do not lead to the desired result. Sometimes we choose to take a certain path and discover that it did not go where we thought it would go. That is, sometimes people just make wrong choices. For example, I might think that if I dye my hair green I will suddenly become more attractive to the object of my affection. I might be very wrong in that thought. Or I might believe that if I have prophylactic mastectomies (breast removal) I will be free of the fear of developing breast cancer. I might think that pretending I am not having symptoms will make them go away and make me healthy again. I might believe that smoking cigarettes makes me cool. Often people know what they desire but do not know what choices they have to make to ensure that their desires are fulfilled.

Independence If we know what we want and have the freedom to make choices, we may also need **independence**, or the ability to do things ourselves, in order for our desires to be fulfilled. If we are unable to act on our own, our choices may be limited by what others are willing or able to do for us. An elderly man in a long-term care institution who cannot care for himself cannot choose to go home to live with his daughter if she is unwilling to provide the necessary care. A two-year-old child cannot choose to go to the shopping mall unless her parent accompanies her. Independence can become an enormous barrier to autonomy if one requires the support of others to carry out one's wishes. The case of Canadian Sue Rodriguez is an excellent example. She suffered from ALS (amyotrophic lateral sclerosis) and fought with the courts to be permitted to have someone assist her in committing suicide. She no longer wished to live in a state of total dependence but was so disabled that she could not end her own life. Her battle with the courts was unsuccessful; under Canadian law a person who assists with a suicide can be punished with up to 14 years in prison. Rodriguez eventually found a physician to assist her, and she died by lethal injection. This was one of the most famous and dramatic instances in medical ethics and law. The interested student can find many articles and broadcasts devoted to the subject. Many are available on the Internet.

Another issue of independence has to do with how our decisions about ourselves affect others. If we think carefully about it, we will realize that our decisions seldom affect only ourselves. As a mother of three children, if I decide to run off with the mailman, my decision clearly affects my family. If I do not wish to suffer the agonies that can go along with cancer chemotherapy, my decision to forego treatment could have a huge impact on those who love me. In Chapter 1 we used an example of a man who refused a gastric feeding tube (Trying It On 1.4). In making his decision, he wanted to know what his family would have to watch if he were to stop all feeding and starve to death. He was concerned that watching his suffering might be unbearable for his family.

The point we are trying to make here is that decisions in health care cannot always be made without reference to others. My ability to make decisions and carry them out will depend, to some extent, on what others are willing to do, or on how my decision will impact them. Thus decisions in health care have many dimensions, all of which must be taken into consideration. To be truly supportive, a nurse needs constant awareness of the complexity of decision making.

AUTONOMY AND INFORMED CONSENT

Promoting choice as a key value of the CNA Code of Ethics for Registered Nurses implies that nurses are obligated to support the autonomy of patients and families. This belief about choice in health care is relatively recent; until a few decades ago it was assumed that the health care provider knew best and would make decisions for the patient in her or his best interests. With the birth of bioethics and the emphasis on autonomy, it became clear that, if we were to protect people's right to choose what was done with and to them, we must not act without their **informed consent**: their permission for something, based on a good understanding of the situation. This notion of informed consent has had both positive and negative consequences. On the positive side, it has helped us reduce paternalistic decisions by care providers. On the negative side, it has become a way for care providers to turn difficult decisions over to patients and families who might not be prepared to make the decisions. Informed consent is widely considered to have three dimensions: *voluntariness*, *capacity*, and *comprehension*. In the discussion that follows, we will discuss these elements and a number of related concepts. This should help you understand the nature of informed consent and its strengths and limitations.

Voluntariness

Voluntariness means that decisions are made without coercion or undue inducement. Coercion, as we have discussed previously, is pressure to do something because we are afraid that something bad will happen or that something we want will be withheld if we do not do it.

For instance, we might coerce a patient into changing a lifestyle practice such as smoking by saying we will not provide care for him if he does not do as we direct. An opposite kind of pressure is inducement. An **inducement** is a promise that something good will happen if we take a certain action. In health care, we induce patients to accept treatments by promising them a good result. A physician might, for instance, induce a woman to have a facelift by promising that she will look younger and more beautiful. Similarly, we might induce a man to accept radical surgery by promising that his cancer will be removed.

If we have too much, or **undue inducement**, then it becomes a form of pressure. A difficulty arises in determining what is an undue inducement. If we make promises about a certain outcome, even though we do not know for sure how things will turn out, is that undue inducement? To use the above example, promising a woman that the lines on her face will be reduced is not a form of undue inducement, as it is a fact. If, however, she is told that she will definitely be more attractive to her partner, and that is something she really wants, it might be considered undue inducement, because we cannot really promise that will happen. To act as an inducement, whatever we promise or offer must be of value to the person to whom the promise is being made. If I promise that your partner will love you more, but you really don't care because you were thinking of leaving him anyway, it will not be an inducement. If, however, I promise that others will find you more attractive, and you are looking for someone, that might well be an inducement. In health care we have to be very careful that we do not promise something we cannot deliver or something that may be deliverable but is excessive. We must also weigh the effect of our promise. If we offer something that induces a person to take risks he or she might otherwise not take, we must be certain that the benefits outweigh the risks.

Capacity

Capacity means having the ability to understand what you are told. This requires a certain level of cognitive development or awareness. As a result, certain groups of people will be considered to lack capacity. Young children, demented or mentally challenged individuals, and those with certain mental illnesses will have limited or absent capacity. Capacity can change over time and under different circumstances; it is not a fixed entity. A nurse needs to be constantly alert to the possibility of such changes. For example, a patient who has breathing problems might be able to make decisions while his oxygen is running at a sufficient level but might become confused and incapacitated when he takes his oxygen off. A person with Alzheimer's disease might be quite lucid one day and totally incoherent the next. A woman whose baby has just been diagnosed with brain cancer might be so distraught that she lacks the capacity to understand what you are telling her. Capacity assessment is made more difficult by the fact that people might have capacity in one area, but not the next. For instance, someone with dementia might be able to decide whether he wants to eat steak or chicken, but might not be able to manage his financial affairs. A patient with schizophrenia might be able to decide not to take her medication but might not understand the consequences. A 12-year-old child with a chronic illness might be able to decide whether or not to accept a particular treatment but might not be able to understand the nature of a research project for which she is a possible candidate.

Capacity assessment is, therefore, an important part of nursing practice. Sometimes capacity is obvious, but sometimes it is not. If you doubt someone's capacity to give informed consent, it is essential that you begin to investigate. Skill in capacity assessment improves with practice and experience. It is also important to realize that nurses need to work with those from other disciplines, such as psychology, who have more education and training in performing such assessments. A nurse should never hesitate to seek another opinion when capacity is in doubt.

There is also a legal component to capacity. Each province has legislation that talks about consent for health care. Children are considered to have developing, but not full, capacity until they reach a certain age, which will be defined in the legislation. Age of consent varies across provinces. For example, in British Columbia a person is permitted to consent for health care at the age of 19 years; in Saskatchewan the age of consent for health care is 16 years. It is important that you know the legal age of consent in the area in which you work. When capacity is found to be lacking and consent for treatment is required, a **proxy**, that is to say a **surrogate** (substitute) decision maker, will be asked to provide consent. This could be a parent in the case of a minor, or an adult child in the case of a demented elder. It is, therefore, important to know what the law says about who is permitted to act as a surrogate decision maker. Each province constructs its legislation and statutes somewhat differently, so it can require a concerted effort to find relevant legislation, but most is available on the Internet.

Comprehension

The third required component of consent is **comprehension**, which is the person's actual understanding of what she or he is being told. This is similar to, but not the same as, capacity. If I lack capacity, I will also lack comprehension. It is possible, however, that I have the capacity to understand but am not able to understand because of some other factor. Often this factor is language. For instance, if I am seeking consent for chemotherapy from a patient who is a physician but speaks only Russian, she undoubtedly has the cognitive capacity to understand but will not comprehend unless I speak in Russian. Another language barrier is the use of medical jargon. Frequently health care providers will explain a procedure using words that are familiar to them but not to the person who is having the procedure done. It is important to use plain, everyday language, or misunderstandings can develop. For instance, in a study that one of the authors was involved with some years ago, patients were asked to indicate what they thought certain sentences meant. One sentence read, "We are going to take you to radiology." The majority of patients thought this meant "cancer treatment," not "X-ray" (Cochrane et al., 1992). From this example, one can see how use of jargon can make comprehension, and hence informed consent, very difficult. Use of high-level language can become unethical if it obscures, rather than clarifies, meaning. Often nurses will be required to translate language on a written consent form into more recognizable words. It is interesting to note that most consent forms, when analyzed, prove to be written at a level that is much too high for the majority of readers. Surveys have shown that many Canadians have low literacy skills; therefore, health care providers cannot expect that patients will understand written consent forms.

Related Concepts in Consent

Three other concepts are very important in voluntary consent. They are *honesty, trust,* and *power*. **Honesty**, or truth telling, is required of the care provider. As a nurse, I am obligated to give accurate information (although that requirement might sometimes be modified, as we shall discuss in the section on practice implications and culture). I must not promise too much, and I must outline the risks and limitations of whatever it is for which I am seeking consent. Sometimes this is difficult, as I might not know all the risks. Or I might really believe in the treatment and add some emphasis or embellishment to make it more attractive to the patient. I can reduce this risk by considering the idea of undue inducement and being careful to guard against it.

Trust, as defined by Merriam-Webster (on-line) means "assured reliance on the character, ability, strength, or truth of someone or something." We have suggested before that trust is part of a nurse-patient relationship. Patients trust us to act in their best interests, which includes protecting their autonomy. That trust means that we are in a position to do both harm and good, because trusting in someone makes you vulnerable to their actions. In other words, if I trust you it is easier for you to harm me because I believe what you tell me. That said, if I trust you it is also easier for you to help me because I am willing to cooperate with your suggestions or interventions. The trust that patients and families feel for nurses means that nurses must be extra careful to give full information about what they want to do or what they believe the patient should do. Trust requires honesty; patients trust nurses to give them true information, and nurses are ethically required to tell the truth and not distort the facts as they understand them.

Power, in this case referring to possession of control, authority, or influence over others, is always present in a health care relationship. Patients and families have a certain kind of power. They have the power of rights, in that patient rights are protected to some extent by law and to a large extent by our understanding of professional obligation. Health care providers have a **fiduciary** relationship with patients, which means that they are in a position of trust and are obligated to act in the patient's best interests. This obligation exerts some power over the actions of care providers. However, more often we think of a power imbalance arising in the opposite direction, with the care provider having power over the patient and family. This occurs because the care provider has control over much of the environment, treatments offered and/or withheld, and comfort measures. When patients are sick, vulnerable, and transferred from their home environment into an institution, they often feel at the mercy of care providers. Nurses generally have control over such things as when or whether food is delivered to patient rooms, whether family and friends are allowed to visit, whether hygiene measures are freely available, and what kinds of information are given or protected. Although most nurses would not abuse that control, they must be aware of the potential for a power differential, because it can influence the actions of patient and family. If a patient is worried that refusal to take part in a procedure will upset the nurse and pain medications will then be withheld, the patient might well consent to the procedure simply to placate the nurse. This is not real informed consent, because it does not have the element of voluntariness described above. Therefore, power has the potential to impact the patient's or family's autonomy. A choice made because of a power imbalance is not autonomous.

Assent

In this discussion we have been talking about consent and have said that full consent requires capacity, comprehension, and voluntariness. We indicated that when a patient is unable to give full consent, we usually seek a surrogate decision maker to give consent. However, the fact that a surrogate has given consent does not release us from seeking assent from the patient. **Assent** means that the person agrees to receive care or accepts what we offer. It does not require the degree of comprehension and capacity that a fully informed consent requires. For a person to assent to treatment, he or she must have had some explanation about the treatment, and it is expected that a patient's assent will be sought before care is given. This can raise an ethical dilemma for a nurse. Suppose, for example, that a mother has given consent for her child to have a particular treatment, but the child **dissents**, that is she or he wishes to refuse the treatment. Whether the nurse can honour the child's dissent depends on how important the treatment is, how old the child is, and how strongly the child dissents. If a six-year-old child wanted to refuse chemotherapy, but the parent had consented to it, the nurse would be justified in giving the treatment despite the child's objections. However, if a 17-year-old refused to take an antiemetic, the nurse would probably not be justified in forcing the patient to take the drug. Generally, nurses seek assent from a child and often try to persuade the child to agree if the parent has consented to treatment. In this way, nurses recognize the developing capacity of the child, but still honour the wishes of the parent. Similarly, nurses will seek assent of elderly patients who have lost capacity. They will be less likely to force treatment, however, even if a surrogate has given consent. It is understood that adults who have lost capacity still have a right to have their wishes respected to a certain extent. The nurse is expected to act in the patient's best interests, but this does not give the nurse permission to force an intervention unless it is to prevent the patient from harming himself or herself or others.

From this you can see that there is a difference in how we deal with those who have never reached the developmental stage where they could provide full consent, such as children and developmentally delayed adults, and those who have lost the ability to consent, such as demented elderly patients. We are more willing to impose an intervention on a child than an adult, even if that adult is cognitively impaired. Somehow we seem to believe that paternalism—acting in what we believe to be in someone's best interests even if that person resists our actions—is more acceptable with a child. This belief is part of our cultural understandings of how children ought to be protected, and we allow parents a great deal of control over children. It is important, nonetheless, to keep the child's developing autonomy in mind. This is where relational ethics becomes really important. Even though a child cannot understand the details of treatment, he or she can still experience feelings of safety and trust. Children are generally accustomed to having adults take control, and it does not necessarily make them unhappy. How troubling this will be to a child depends to a large extent on the degree of trust that has been established. Nurses who impose treatments on a child without first working to establish that trust may be acting unethically. In an emergency situation there is little choice but to act quickly. In other situations, however, it is necessary to take the time to build rapport and give the child a feeling of safety. Explaining procedures at a developmentally appropriate level is of utmost importance, and the nurse should try to gain the child's agreement and co-operation. However, if the treatment is essential to the child's health it may be inappropriate to seek assent if you do not intend to honour dissent. When the nurse asks a child for permission to proceed with treatment, the child refuses, and the nurse carries on regardless, the child's trust in the nurse will be damaged. It is preferable simply to explain the treatment and indicate that it must be done. Pretending to give the child a choice when you have no intention of honouring the choice (unless, of course, the child agrees with what you want to do) is deceptive and dishonest, and inherently unethical. If it is necessary to impose an intervention on a child, it is important to spend time with the child afterward, providing comfort and perhaps rationale, depending on the child's developmental state. Children are familiar with having to do things they do not want to do and will often understand if a nurse explains that that she or he would rather not have had to force this treatment, but that it was done in the child's best interests.

Sometimes the situation can become very complex, because the idea of developmental capacity is rather vague. In many Canadian jurisdictions, the age of majority is the default age at which a child can give full consent. In others the age for consent to treatment is defined separately in law. It is a nurse's responsibility to be aware of the relevant legislation. A recent headline case in Calgary illustrates some of the difficulties that can arise when balancing law with moral understanding. Bethany Hughes, a 16-year-old girl who was a Jehovah's Witness, was hospitalized for leukemia. Doctors had indicated that blood transfusions were essential for her survival. Bethany's father wanted her to have treatment, but her mother did not. The child herself refused treatment. She was made a ward of the court, and care providers were ordered to go ahead with treatment. Nurses working with Bethany were required to restrain her while she received her transfusions. This caused great moral distress for all concerned, as Bethany fought the transfusions. Sadly, she died seven months later. The case brought to light just how complicated assent and consent can be. In this situation, the surrogate decision makers (the parents) had different views as to the best course of action. Bethany's own preferences were ignored. Care providers believed they were acting in Bethany's best interests, but Bethany and her mother disagreed with them. The interested reader can find details on many Internet sites. What this case teaches us is that the entire subject of children's consent is fraught with ethical landmines, and nurses can be excused if they find it unclear and morally troubling.

Another thing that complicates the issue in seeking a child's assent is that children with chronic illnesses are often very sophisticated in their understanding of their bodily functions and their treatments. In fact, they may be more knowledgeable than the nurse. It is important to listen to the child's point of view, keeping in mind that she or he might well be right. Relational ethics helps us understand this and be comfortable with it. A dismissive attitude does nothing to foster trust and could even result in inappropriate treatment. Again, pretending to pay attention to what the child has to say is not sufficient; children often have very good instincts about who is sincere and who is not. Ethical care of children requires careful attention to honest and authentic relationships, a commitment to being open to the child's point of view, and a willingness to take control when necessary.

The situation with cognitively impaired adults is a little different. Many of the same principles apply, but, as mentioned above, we are often more inclined to honour an adult's dissent. Generally, we will seek surrogate consent when an individual is not able to make choices for himself or herself. Even with surrogate consent, unless the intervention is necessary for the patient's survival, nurses should be reluctant to force treatment on a dissenting patient, as an adult's autonomy is closely tied to dignity. We discuss this at length in Chapter 7. It is interesting that nurses experience moral distress less frequently in taking away a child's autonomy (provided they are convinced that they are acting in the child's best interests and have done everything they can to respect the child's developing autonomy), and do not consider it undignified for a child to submit to an adult's authority. The same is not true of an adult. Nurses may experience a great deal of moral distress in having to take away an adult's power of choice. However, this is sometimes necessary for safety and health, and the challenge is in knowing when it is essential. Sometimes dignity is more important than safety, and nurses have to allow patients to take risks. One of the keys to acting ethically in these difficult situations lies in relationship. The nurse who has formed a connection with a patient is more likely to know what is really essential and what the patient really values. Patients are more likely to give their assent to someone they trust and with whom they have an authentic relationship; therefore, taking the time to make that connection is a fundamental part of ethical care.

RELATIONAL AUTONOMY

To this point we have been discussing autonomy as it has traditionally been understood in philosophy and in health care. A newer way of thinking about autonomy has emerged from feminist ethics (see Sherwin, 1998). In Chapter 5 we briefly mentioned the concept of relational autonomy; we will now expand on this idea.

Traditional notions of autonomy in Western philosophy suggest that individuals make independent decisions based on their own needs and values. Relational autonomy encourages us to think about people as interdependent, making decisions in a network of relationships. In the example that opened this chapter, we talked about a woman who had to decide whether or not to undergo electro-convulsive therapy. Certainly she has the right to make this decision for herself, but she is also deciding for her unborn baby. If she had a partner she would probably want to consult that person, because such a decision would have an impact on her or him as well. If a young father with a wife and children is offered chemotherapy treatment, he will most likely take them into account in making his decision. Discussions about treatment will probably include his wife. Much of the ethics literature on autonomy talks about patient rights, but autonomy is about more than rights. It is also about people's way of being in the world, how they think about choices, and whom they consider or involve when making those choices.

Vangie Bergum and John Dossetor, Canadian ethicists who conducted an extensive study on relational ethics, help us understand what that means in health care. They state, "In practice, we see how autonomy is lived in relation to others . . . While the principle of respect for autonomy has been important in the development of human rights [such] as self-determination and personal freedom, the concept of lived autonomy is found in personal connection to others and responsibility" (Bergum & Dossetor, 2005, p. 53). This statement points out that choice involves responsibility and connectedness to others. A patient's choices will be influenced by his or her beliefs, which are shaped through personal relationships. These relationships are at the heart of trust in the health care environment. Relational ethics requires us to consider who else is or might be involved in decisions, who might be affected by choices that are made, and who might want to participate in discussions. It requires us to think about the responsibilities people have toward others, and how their understanding of these responsibilities is developed. It helps us to move away from notions of individual rights to ideas about how people exist in community, and how the choices they make affect and are affected by that community.

BELIEFS, PREFERENCES, AND CHOICE

Thinking about how relationships shape beliefs helps us understand how culture influences choice. It has an impact not only on the kind of choices people make, but also on the way in which they make those choices. In North America, particularly in the United States, the norm is to value independence and self-determination very highly. As a result, we expect people to make choices for themselves, often without the involvement of others. However, individualism is not valued as highly in all cultures, even within North America, and might even be seen by some as selfish or limited. For instance, Aboriginal people generally have a very strong sense of community, and we can expect that they will want to have others present when decisions are made. Our system, however, does not often make provision for joint or community decision making. We frequently present people with consent forms and want them to sign them immediately; we may even become annoyed if they express a desire to involve others in the decision making if that means a delay in getting the form signed. A nurse who is aware of the importance of relational autonomy will be more sympathetic to a patient's wishes regarding obtaining consent.

Culture and beliefs will also influence how much people wish to be involved in making decisions for themselves. This becomes particularly important in end-of-life decisions. In North America the norm is to give patients and families as much information as possible and let them make decisions about their treatment and care. In Canada we usually expect that most people will want to be told about a terminal diagnosis so they can "get their lives in order," and we consider it wrong to withhold information, but not everyone wants to be told. Nurses need to be aware that giving full information might not be appropriate for all cultural groups. For instance, Lucy Candib, an American physician, talks about different cultural preferences for the amount of information desired (Candib, 2002). She points out that for some groups, such as the American Navajo, it is important to speak of only positive things. To name something is to invite it. In other words, for a nurse to say that death is a possibility would be the same as inviting death to happen. Navajo people in general do not wish to be told about possible negative outcomes, and their belief system would not be congruent with giving directions about what to do when they become ill. If we were to ask them whether they wanted a Do Not Resuscitate (DNR) order written, they would find it offensive, because for the Navajo, talking about critical illness increases the likelihood that it will happen. Similarly, in many Asian and some European countries such as Russia, standard practice is not to tell people if they have a terminal diagnosis. Families expect to be told, but the patient is not informed (Quill, 2002).

The emphasis on choice in our health care system has, therefore, led to some interesting biases. We understand that it is a person's right to make an informed choice; however, we seldom respect the person's right not to choose. We need to consider the possibility that not everyone wants to have full information and to make choices. To a large extent, we act as though everyone has approximately the same information needs, and as a result, we may be giving patients and families too much information. Canadian nurse researcher Carolyn Ross, working with Tom Maguire, a statistician, has explored different coping styles and concluded that some individuals cope best with full information, and others are much more comfortable knowing very little and allowing others to make decisions for them (Ross & Maguire, 1995). Lesley Degner, a prominent Canadian nurse scholar, has conducted numerous studies in collaboration with a variety of other scholars. The studies are about preferred roles in decision making and informational needs in cancer care. All lead to essentially the same conclusion as Ross's: people's needs for information and participation in decision making are variable (Davison, Kirk, Degner, & Hassard, 1999; Degner, Davison, Sloan, & Meuller, 1998; Degner, Sloan, & Venkatesh, 1997; Hack, Degner, & Parker, 2005). This raises important ethical questions for nurses about the obligation to disclose information to the patient and family even if they do not want the information. Does a patient have the right *not* to choose? Much of how we think about providing information and choice is governed, not by ethical considerations, but by legal concerns. There is always the possibility that if we fail to give sufficient information, the patient or family can bring legal action against us if something untoward happens. In the case of a lawsuit, the nurse or physician would have to explain to the court why certain information was withheld from the patient or family. Consequently, usual practice is to give patients and families as much information as possible, which, as we have seen, might not be in their best interests. There is a way to deal with this problem. Nurses should consider that the most respectful approach to patients and families would be to offer to provide information, but not to give it without permission. It is important to note that refusal of information must be documented for legal purposes.

LINKING CONCEPTS OF AUTONOMY AND CHOICE

As we have seen, choice in health care is highly complex. Consider what we have discussed to this point. We learned that philosophy tells us that we must honour autonomy because being self-determining or being able to choose what happens to oneself is an essential part of being human. We saw that, based on traditional philosophical theories, autonomy became the core principle of bioethics. Examining the components of autonomy, we saw that it has several parts: self-determination, freedom, desire fulfillment, and independence. As we looked at consent, we learned that fully informed consent must have the characteristics of voluntariness, capacity, and comprehension. We then examined the concept of relational autonomy, and learned that beliefs and preferences shape how people make decisions about their care.

If health care providers are obligated to preserve the principle of autonomy, then they must have an understanding of how the various components are linked. Self-determination is reflected in the notion of capacity and comprehension. People are not able to make choices for themselves if they are not able to consider the cause and effect, or, in other words, if they lack capacity. Nor are they able to decide what is best for themselves if they do not understand the options, that is if they lack comprehension. Voluntariness is linked to freedom, in that a person must not be restricted in her or his choice, and must make the decisions based on what she or he desires. Freedom, however, is always limited to some extent by the needs and wishes of others. People are not always given the freedom to make a choice. For example, I might choose to have the most expensive drug on the market for my child, but in our health care system I might not be allowed to make that choice because it is too costly for the public system. Independence is also linked to voluntariness because it is not possible to make an independent decision if one is being forced or pressured to take a certain option. In this way the characteristics of informed consent are linked to autonomy. What relational ethics helps us understand is that people exist in a network of relationships, so their choices are seldom really free, and their desire fulfillment often includes the desires of others. In other words, people often make choices that they think will be best for others or that will make others happy. In one sense these are voluntary decisions, but in another sense they lack freedom because they are constrained. Few people are totally independent; instead, most are interdependent and make their decisions based on how they see themselves in relationship.

Some practice examples might make the links among the concepts clearer. We considered the issues of capacity and consent. If a person who needs immediate treatment lacks capacity to make an informed choice and give consent, and no surrogate decision maker is present, health care providers will be faced with a decision about what to do. It is assumed that they will decide based on what they understand to be the patient's best interests and seek support for their decisions when the person regains capacity or a surrogate becomes available. This can mean that they sometimes make wrong decisions, because people make their decisions based on their values, and values may diverge. If I treat you the way I want to be treated, I might find out later that you have very different views about treatment.

For instance, consider a patient who is admitted unconscious to emergency after a motor vehicle collision and treated aggressively with medications and a variety of surgical interventions. When he regains consciousness he tells us that he is a Christian Scientist, and many of the treatments we provided were against his beliefs. Without further information in the emergency situation, it is impossible to know what he would want. He lacks capacity, and therefore freedom, to consent, and we do not know what his desires are. We might desire life above all, but a desire to follow his religious beliefs might be most important to him. Therefore, every effort must be made to find someone who can provide some background information about the patient. In emergency situations there may not be sufficient time to find someone before it is necessary to take action. Caregivers must then be guided by their clinical judgments, which may later be found to conflict with the patient's values and beliefs. Relational ethics can become very important in these situations, because they encourage us to explore values with patient and family, and help us remember that our values may not be shared by others. They help us understand that our ideas about what might be in a person's best interests might not be shared by that person.

We mentioned above that parents are considered surrogate decision makers for a child. However, as care providers we do not always allow parents to make decisions. We may not give them that freedom if we believe, for whatever reason, that the decision they make is not best for the child. In such situations law and ethics may conflict. The case of Bethany Hughes discussed earlier is a case in point. Another example is that of K'Aila, a young Canadian boy of First Nations heritage whose situation made national headlines in the early 1990s. K'Aila was only a few months old when he was diagnosed with a rare form of liver failure. His physicians believed that a liver transplant was in his best interests, but his parents disagreed. Their beliefs led them to refuse the treatment, as they felt it would doom him to a life of pain and suffering, with an uncertain future. A transplant also conflicted with their cultural belief that it was wrong to transplant organs from one person to another. The courts intervened and ordered the parents to accept the surgical procedure. They fled to another legal jurisdiction, and the child died before the courts were able to apprehend him. The story, which was presented on film by the Canadian Broadcasting Company, offers uniquely challenging ethical and legal issues to consider. Key ethical questions are whether parents ought to be free to deny their child the right to life-saving treatment, and whether parental cultural beliefs ought to be respected. The key legal question is whether the court is responsible to protect the child even against wishes of the parents. Interested students can find more information about K'Aila and his parents' difficult decision on the Internet. It raises many interesting concerns for nurses about parental autonomy, power, trust, freedom, and desire fulfillment.

An interesting clinical situation that illustrates issues of choice with an adult is the story of Dax Cowart. In the summer of 1973, Dax was terribly burned in an accident involving explosive gas. He was rushed to hospital and treated for massive third-degree burns. Initially he protested that he did not want treatment, but care providers overrode his decision, believing that the pain made him lack capacity. As time went on and Dax miraculously survived, he continued to protest against the pain, both physical and emotional, that he was experiencing. He continually asked caregivers to stop treatment, but they refused on the basis that he wasn't able to appreciate the implications of his request and that it wasn't right to support someone in his wish to die. They continued to treat, arguing that it was in Dax's best interests. His burns healed, but he required many subsequent surgeries, and he was totally blind. He later completed law school, married, and established a successful law practice. One might conclude that this was a success story: Dax was saved from life-threatening injury to live a full and happy life. However, he remained very angry about the fact that his wishes were not heeded. He felt that his survival was not worth the pain and suffering he had experienced, and long afterward he continued to maintain that care providers were wrong in making him endure that suffering. Like K'Aila's case, Dax's story raised important questions about autonomy, freedom, and control. Reflecting on Dax's case is important in helping us understand that despite our best intentions we might make decisions that are not in the patient's best interests, and that autonomy is important (Bergum & Dossetor, 2005; Rosenberg & Karides, 1994).

Today we are more likely to heed a person's wishes because of the emphasis on autonomy. However, we might continue to question a person's capacity in a life-threatening situation. A fairly recent development in health care is the idea of advance directives, also called personal directives, living wills, or health care directives. An **advance directive** (AD) is a signed document that an individual prepares. It is intended to be put into effect when the individual loses the capacity to make decisions. The document can have two main purposes: first, it may name others who are authorized to make health care decisions for the individual, should he or she lose capacity; second, it may be used to outline treatment decisions individuals would prefer, as insurance in case they lose capacity. For example, an AD might indicate that my son is authorized to make decisions about treatment for me. It is expected that my son will make decisions he thinks I would want. To assist him in knowing my wishes, I could outline whether or not I would wish to have treatment withdrawn if I were in a persistent vegetative state or coma. Advance directives may contain considerable detail about treatment wishes. Each province has legislation as to what an AD may contain and under what circumstances it may be used.

An AD can be useful to health care providers because it provides them with a way to help patients exercise their autonomy even when they lose capacity, but it also has limitations. It may be difficult to interpret what the writer of the AD really intended. For instance, if a woman writes that she doesn't want "heroic measures," what does she really mean? Does that include artificial feeding? Artificial ventilation? If she says that she doesn't want artificial ventilation, does that mean she would not want it for six hours until her condition is stabilized or that she does not want it for the long term? Does it mean "absolutely" no artificial ventilation, even if there is an excellent chance that she will recover to normal functioning? People writing ADs might not truly understand the implications of what they are choosing and might not make such distinctions clear. They might also change their minds. What they write when they are feeling well and healthy might be different from what they would write while ill. When I am healthy I might not be able to imagine a life without being able to walk and might write that I would not want to be "saved" if I were in danger of losing mobility. I might feel very differently if I were in a car accident and realized that I would be unable to walk but still able to care for my children and watch them grow. As you can see, ADs may require considerable interpretation. Caregivers often rely on family members or other surrogate decision makers to help them understand what the patient would want. Therefore, an AD might give guidance but is not a simple solution to a complex problem. Several of the key concepts we have considered—capacity, comprehension, self-determination, and desire fulfillment—all play a part in our understanding of the need for, and limitations of, ADs.

ADs are quite new to Canadian health care, and as a result, many people do not have them. When someone requires treatment and does not have cognitive capacity to give consent, a surrogate decision maker will be sought. If there is an AD that names the surrogate, then health care providers can be more confident that the person giving direction for care has sufficient knowledge of the patient's wishes. If there is no AD, the situation is more difficult. Usually the closest relative is sought, but that relative might be estranged from the patient or might have a different belief system. Sometimes family members have diverse ideas about care, and it is difficult for care providers to know who really speaks for the patient. Sometimes the person whom the patient would want to make decisions does not have the legal status that will permit caregivers to consult her or him. Consider a gay man who was shunned by his parents when he announced his sexual orientation. He might want his partner to make decisions about his care, but in some jurisdictions care providers are required to rely on family members who may have had little contact with the patient for many years, and who might have a set of values that is not consistent with the patient's. Questions of autonomy and choice can cause great moral distress for caregivers and family members when the patient lacks cognitive capacity. An AD can lessen moral uncertainty, and despite the limitations described above, is generally of benefit in ensuring that the patient's wishes are followed.

CHOICE AS A LIVED VALUE

Let us now turn to the Ethics Composite Model we presented in Chapter 2 (p. 46) and consider how elements of the model direct us to think about choice in nursing practice. The outer ring of the model includes institutional values, social context, legal context, and other values. Institutional values are influenced by the social context in which health care is delivered. Generally this means that the dominant values of the culture will determine how autonomy and choice are understood. The legal context is also influenced by social understandings, and has resulted in laws that limit our ability to act without patient permission. The values of patient and family are also influenced by the dominant culture, but may be very different from it. Therefore, nurses need to be conscious of how different ways of thinking about autonomy influence practice. Certainly nurses must be aware of legal standards related to autonomy. Nurses' values will be influenced by the social context in which they practise and their own personal values, and they need to think about how their own beliefs affect their approach to patients and their response to patient choice. It is particularly important to understand how the patient and family view choice, autonomy, and decision making. Questions that must be asked include whom they wish to involve in decisions and what kinds of information they want or do not want.

The next ring in the model includes bioethical principles and normative theories. We have seen that bioethics directs us to respect autonomy almost above all other principles. Normative theories such as those of Kant and Mill help us understand why autonomy is so important. In the centre of the model is the code of ethics, which also directs nurses to support autonomy. Relational ethics runs through the core of the model. It helps us understand that part of our obligation is to think about the network of relationships within which patients and families make their decisions. Relational ethics tells us that the nurse-patient relationship is essential in helping us find out what really matters to patients and their families so we can help them make decisions that will achieve their desires.

Two elements of the model that we have not yet discussed in relation to choice are virtue and clinical competence. Our discussion to this point has been aimed at helping you understand that the virtuous nurse supports autonomy. Part of clinical competence involves understanding what patients and families need to make good decisions. If I, as the nurse, believe that all I have to do is give information and let patients and families decide on their own, I might not be acting ethically. My moral obligation is not just to let them exercise choice but to support them in making that choice. That is, I am obligated to offer my support to families, helping them understand the limits of their choice, what is feasible, whether the choices they make will fulfill their desires, and whether and how others might be affected. I cannot force my assistance on them, but I must make it available. This approach is an integral part of relational nursing, and developing skills in this area is a large part of clinical competence. Nurses might find themselves judging patients for their choices, but engaging in meaningful conversation with patients will help both nurse and patient understand all that went into a particular decision.

In Chapter 1 (p. 14) we discussed paternalism and said that it was morally unacceptable to make decisions for others if they were capable of making decisions themselves. Patients used to expect to be told what to do by health care providers and to get little information. Patients did not expect to make decisions about their care: that was to be taken care of by the doctor or the nurse. In Canada, most people no longer have the same expectations. Bioethics have led care providers to believe that patients and families have the right to make decisions about their own care and the care of their loved ones. The consumer and rights movements have also had an effect on beliefs about decision making in health care. Patients and their families now consider themselves more as consumers of care and less as passive recipients. More people are concerned about their rights to make their own decisions. The availability of a great amount of medical data on the Internet has made it easier for patients and families to be informed, and many come to the health care setting with clear expectations about the care they should receive. Paternalism is no longer considered acceptable by most health care providers and patients.

Supporting a patient's or family's decisions may be difficult if the decisions conflict with the nurse's values. Nonetheless, a nurse's responsibility is to ensure that the decision-making process promotes informed choice. Elements of voluntariness, capacity, and comprehension must be present. All necessary (or desired) information must be given.

Once those criteria are met, it is important to remember that the choice remains with the patient and family. It is not necessary that the nurse approve of the choice. When the nurse experiences a values conflict in supporting the patient's choice, the CNA Code of Ethics for Registered Nurses makes it clear that, as long as the patient's request is in keeping with professional practice, "the nurse provides safe, compassionate, competent, and ethical care until alternative care arrangements are in place to meet the person's needs or desires" (CNA, 2008, p. 19). In other words, the nurse cannot abandon the patient because of that patient's choices. However, the nurse is well within his or her rights to request an alternative assignment, as the nurse's values must also be respected.

The idea of respect has come up several times in this book. Again, it is a vital part of the nurse-patient relationship. Nurses who show lack of respect for patients and families in decision making may be abusing their power. That a nurse might be disrespectful is possible because patients and families do not have much power in the health care system, and there might be little they can do about the nurse's behaviour. In other words, nurses might allow themselves to be disrespectful because they can "get away with it." Consider an elderly patient who has no relatives and is somewhat confused. He may feel (and indeed, be) essentially powerless if no one listens to his complaints. Of course, disrespectful behaviour on behalf of the nurse is unethical and, as such, is certainly not acceptable practice. Nurses must always be on the alert for possible disrespect in their way of being with patients and families. We mention the possibility here because respect must play a large role in decision making. Nurses need to respect patients' and families' need for information and for time and privacy in decision making.

A question that can arise for nurses is when it is permissible to limit a patient's or family's freedom of choice. Earlier we said that this is sometimes necessary if a patient is about to harm herself or himself, or if the patient's choice may harm others, including the nurse. Nurses sometimes use coercion to force an intervention if a patient lacks capacity. Making a decision to limit a patient's autonomy can be painful for nurses. Two American nurses, Paula Vuckovich and Barbara Artinian (2005), conducted a study in which they explored mental health nurses' experiences in administering medications to involuntary patients, that is to say patients who had been admitted to psychiatry against their wills. Findings of the study showed that nurses tried to use inducement and persuasion, rather than coercion, to get the patients to take their medications. If this was unsuccessful, coercion was sometimes necessary. When that occurred, nurses justified it as being in the patient's best interests. The justification allowed them "to engage in behaviour generally disapproved of while retaining a self-image of a 'good' nurse" (Vuckovich & Artinian, 2005, p. 370). This shows how deeply we value autonomy and how strongly we link supporting autonomy with good or virtuous nursing.

Sometimes choices are limited by other considerations, such as lack of resources. A patient may not necessarily be able to choose to have a lung transplant tomorrow if no suitable donor can be found. A family may wish to have a particular nurse care for their loved one, but if that nurse is off duty or her services are required elsewhere, that choice might not be available to them. A family might ask to have treatment stopped for an aging, wealthy, and cantankerous relative, but if the patient has a good chance of recovery and stopping treatment is not medically indicated, this will not be an option. Whenever choice is restricted, nurses must work to ensure that patients and families understand the rationale for the decision. Again, relational ethics becomes particularly important, because patients and families will likely see any limit to autonomy as a threat, and great sensitivity is required.

This lengthy discussion of choice should help you understand why it is such an important value for nurses. We will now explore some of the more direct nursing implications of autonomy and choice as we examine two scenarios. The first of these is a complex situation involving divergent beliefs and values; the second is a story of everyday ethics in nursing care.

Trying It On

6.1 Choices for Azizeh

Azizeh Farudeh is a 36-year-old Iranian woman who has recently arrived in Canada. She was admitted through emergency to the gynecology unit after collapsing at home. She states that for several months her menstrual periods have been very long and her flow excessive. In fact, when her flow is heaviest, she soaks a pad in about 15 minutes and is going through a box of pads a day for two or three days at a time. Most months her periods last from 12 to 15 days. She also has had severe abdominal pain and cramping. On admission her hemoglobin is found to be dangerously low and she is very pale and weak. The admitting physician, Dr. Mark Peters, first saw Azizeh in the ER and ordered an ultrasound. Azizeh refused a physical examination.

Marianne is the nurse caring for Azizeh on Thursday afternoon, the day after the ultrasound. She enters Azizeh's room and finds her lying on the bed crying softly. When Marianne asks what is wrong Azizeh just turns her head away and says, "You wouldn't understand." Marianne nods sympathetically and replies, "Why don't you try me? Help me to know what

is bothering you. It makes me unhappy to see you so upset." Azizeh turns to Marianne and said, "Please, could you close the door?" Marianne complies and returns to the bedside, pulling up a chair beside the bed. Azizeh begins her story. She says, "The problem is, I am a devout Muslim. In my culture women are considered very special. It is important for us to be modest and keep ourselves apart from men other than our husbands. Islam dictates that a woman in my culture be a credit to her husband. It is important that I produce sons who can make my husband proud. In the emergency and again today the doctor came to examine me, and I sent him away. I could not have a man examine me in that way, as it would not be proper. Also, I know that the tests have shown that something is wrong, and I am very worried that I will lose my ability to have a child. We do not have any children and my husband and I both long for a son. That is why I am crying. I'm so afraid and so ashamed."

Just as Azizeh finishes speaking, Marianne hears an emergency bell. She hurries toward the door, telling Azizeh

(Continued)

6.1 Choices for Azizeh

that she will return as soon as she can. Unfortunately, Marianne becomes involved in assisting with a cardiac resuscitation of a woman in the next room and is tied up until the end of shift. With all the activity and documentation she does not get back to Azizeh's room until the next morning when the day shift starts. She walks into the room just in time to find Azizeh sitting on the side of the bed looking very ill and very distressed. Dr. Peters is explaining that the ultrasound showed some disturbing signs, and he is recommending that she have an exploratory laparoscopy. He thinks that she probably has fibroids severe enough to warrant removal of the uterus and is recommending that she sign a consent for that surgery also, in case the laparoscopy findings confirm his suspicions. He says that if her blood loss continues at the current rate she will soon not have enough hemoglobin to meet her oxygen carrying needs. He feels it is urgent that they take immediate action.

Azizeh looks at Dr. Peters, her eyes filled with tears. She says, "I can't consent for this surgery. I need my husband here to make the decision. He is away in Iran and won't be back for two or three months. I don't know how to get hold of him as he is out in the country teaching in small villages."

Dr. Peters replies, "I don't think you can wait that long. You need to make a decision in the next couple of days." Azizeh just turns away. Dr. Peters says thoughtfully, "There is another treatment. We could try you on birth control pills that would trick your uterus into thinking it was pregnant. Sometimes that stops the bleeding."

Azizeh shakes her head and looks down. After Dr. Peters leaves, Azizeh turns to Marianne and says, "I can't make this decision. I need my husband to decide. I can't have the surgery unless my husband agrees. I can't have that doctor look after me. I can't take a birth control pill. Islam forbids it. What can I do?"

Marianne feels frustrated with Azizeh's dilemma. She simply cannot understand why Azizeh cannot make up her own mind. She wonders if she should try to talk to her and help her see that she has the right to choose what will happen to her own body. She hates to see Azizeh put at risk because no man is available to make the decision for her. She has some sympathy for Azizeh's refusal to be examined by Dr. Peters, but mostly because Marianne doesn't particularly like Dr. Peters, not because she is averse to the idea of Azizeh being examined by a male doctor. Marianne does not understand why Azizeh is so worried about producing babies. Nor does she understand how a woman can defer such an important decision to her husband. In fact, the idea that a woman would put her life at risk because she is worried about consulting her husband infuriates Marianne.

Dr. Peters is most worried about Azizeh's physical health. He finds it frustrating that she will not allow him to examine her and worries that she is rapidly reaching a danger point. Her refusal to consent to surgery baffles him. It is difficult for him to understand how anyone could put religious beliefs ahead of such an important and potentially life-saving option.

Choices for Azizeh

Assessing the Ethics of the Situation: Relationships, Goals, Beliefs, and Values

In assessing Azizeh's situation, Marianne has to consider her own and the patient's beliefs. Azizeh has made a clear statement of values related to reproduction and gynecological examinations. She desperately wants a baby and sees it as part of her responsibility as a woman. She also has strong beliefs about being examined by a male physician. Most importantly, she does not feel free to make decisions about her care in this regard without her husband's guidance.

Marianne's views, largely influenced by her cultural belief in individual autonomy and the right of a woman (or anyone) to make decisions about her own body, make it difficult for her to accept Azizeh's views. She needs to be aware of this and consider how it is affecting her approach to the patient. Marianne's beliefs are supported by the dominant model of autonomous decision making that is most accepted in Canada. However, in this situation Marianne's personal beliefs are less important than professional standards. The CNA Code of Ethics for Registered Nurses says that nurses should respect a person's method of decision making, recognizing that "capable persons may place a different weight on individualism and may choose to defer to family or community values in decision making" (CNA, 2008, p. 11). Although Marianne might have approached the situation differently if it were her choice, she needs to understand that it is the patient's right to approach it any way she chooses.

Reflecting on and Reviewing Potential Actions: Recognizing Available Choices and How Those Choices Are Valued

Marianne's and Dr. Peters' options for ethical action are somewhat limited in this case. It is not a classic moral dilemma, but rather a case of moral distress. Azizeh is clear that she will not sign a consent form at this point and will not allow Dr. Peters to examine her. Although this may cause them some personal distress, Marianne's and Dr. Peters' obligation is to support Azizeh's freedom of choice. Even if they disagree strongly with Azizeh's views, they must set aside their own beliefs about choice and treatment. Azizeh is an adult with intact cognitive capacity, and no treatment can be imposed on her without consent. Nor should Marianne and Dr. Peters pressure her to make a decision on her own if that is contrary to her beliefs.

Selecting an Ethical Action: Maximizing Good

After reflecting on the situation Marianne must realize that she has to put her own beliefs aside and try to understand what Azizeh thinks would be best for her. Marianne should ask Azizeh to explain more about her belief system because with more knowledge about the situation Marianne might be more effective in working with Azizeh to come to a creative solution to the problem. As they talk, Marianne should emphasize the importance of getting treatment soon. She should also acknowledge Azizeh's religious restrictions about being touched by a man who is not her husband and should ask Azizeh if she would consider a female physician instead of Dr. Peters. It is also important that

(Continued)

Choices for Azizeh

Marianne explore other options with Azizeh, such as whether there might be an Imam (religious leader) available who could make the decision for her. If that is permissible, then Marianne should undertake to contact that person and arrange for him to come to the hospital when the physician is present. Marianne will need to explain to Dr. Peters why another physician has been called in, and Dr. Peters should accept Azizeh's preferences.

Engaging in Ethical Action

The intervention in this case amounts to supporting the choices of a patient whose beliefs differ from the beliefs of the caregivers. There is little latitude in this situation; caregivers must not try to impose their own beliefs on the patient. Once they establish what Azizeh wants done, they are obligated to act, even if they find it puzzling or worrisome. It is difficult for someone from outside the belief system to understand the importance of such religious preferences to the patient. It is likely that Azizeh would experience a great deal of emotional and psychological discomfort if she were to act against her religious beliefs. Even though health care providers might disagree with her choice, they must honour it.

Reflecting on and Reviewing Ethical Action

Marianne needs to ask herself if her approach to Azizeh demonstrated respect. It is not sufficient to go through the motions of respecting choice if one's manner is disrespectful or shows disagreement. Marianne should ask herself if she did all she could to help Azizeh make the choice that was best for her. It would be acceptable for Marianne to indicate that Azizeh's choices were surprising to Marianne, but it would not be acceptable for Marianne to indicate disapproval or lack of support. As a nurse, Marianne must always be alert to ways in which her own beliefs influence her interactions with patients and must accept that others will make choices with which she disagrees. Relational ethics demands that she continue to provide support to the best of her ability.

Trying It On

6.2 To Bathe or Not to Bathe

When Esther Levy entered her assigned room on Monday morning, she realized that there was a problem. One of the patients, Greg Seutter, had been admitted from Emergency during the night, for possible delirium tremens. He was a known alcoholic who had been admitted to the unit for similar withdrawal symptoms on other occasions. Greg lived on the street, and his hygiene was somewhat lacking, to say the least. This morning, the problem that greeted Esther right away was Greg's body odour, which filled the room. The other three patients in the room looked at her in silent entreaty to do something about it. One even called her over to his bedside and pleaded with her to move him to another room, as he felt that he couldn't stay in the same room with Greg. He said that he had been unable to sleep ever since Greg had arrived, as the smell was so strong. Esther had to admit that it was overwhelming.

She walked over to Greg's bedside and greeted him with a pleasant "Good morning, Mr. Seutter. I see you are back with us again." Greg flinched and pulled away from her, saying, "Get back. Get back. They're all over you. I don't want them on me!" He was hallucinating again, and Esther could only guess as to what he was seeing on her. She tried to soothe him with distraction, mentioning the weather outside and asking him how he had arrived on the unit. He appeared to relax somewhat and answered her questions. Seeing an opportunity, Esther said, "Greg, we really need to get you into the bath. It's important that you clean up a bit. What do you say?" Greg looked at her in horror. He shook his fist and said, "I can't do that. It isn't healthy. You people are always trying to make me sicker!" Esther knew that Greg usually came in infested with lice, and his lack of hygiene was a serious problem for staff and the other patients. He was clearly upset and delusional, but he also resisted taking a bath under any circumstances. She wondered just what she should do. She wanted to give him the choice, but knew the choice he would make was unacceptable. She went off in search of her Unit Manager for a bit of advice.

To Bathe or Not to Bathe

This is an interesting problem because one person's choice clearly has an impact on others. In this case, Greg's decision not to bathe could be based on personal preference or could be a result of his delusional state. Either way, it is difficult to determine just what one ought to do for his sake, and for the sake of the other patients and the staff. It is not clear whether his poor hygiene is causing the other patients harm. If they are prevented from sleeping, one might argue that harm is involved, as lack of sleep can be a cause for concern, particularly when one is ill. If Greg is infested with lice, then the issue becomes quite different. That raises a potential harm for staff and patients alike.

Assessing the Ethics of the Situation: Relationships, Goals, Beliefs, and Values

Greg is clearly acting in a way that is outside mainstream cultural beliefs. In North America being clean and sweet-smelling has become almost an obsession. To be otherwise is considered socially unacceptable. One ethical question then becomes whether or not mainstream values can be imposed on another or whether we must honour his choices. In looking at the situation, Esther would need to have a better understanding of why Greg is unwashed and foul-smelling. Is it a matter of being too ill to understand and complete necessary hygiene practices? Or is it a deliberate choice to turn his back on community values? It is

(Continued)

possible that he has very strong and well thought out reasons for his choice. One could assume that he is not cognitively competent because he is delusional; however, he might still be able to discuss his beliefs about hygiene.

From the scenario it is evident that the other patients in Greg's room value cleanliness and find his choice about hygiene unpleasant. The nurse no doubt has the same opinion. In a hospital, cleanliness becomes particularly important because of the potential for spread of disease. The goal of health professionals generally is to maintain a very high standard of cleanliness in a hospital, but what if the patient disagrees? If there is no potential for harm, what rights do others have to demand that someone adhere to their standards?

Reflecting on and Reviewing Potential Actions: Recognizing Available Choices and How Those Choices Are Valued

The first thing that Esther needs to do is try to establish Greg's cognitive capacity and competence so she can discuss the issue with him. It is possible that he is unaware of the effect he has on others and would be willing to comply with a request that he bathe. However, if he is not cognitively competent, potential actions will be determined in part by whether he is putting others at risk.

In the past Greg has been infested with body lice (pediculosis), and there is a good possibility that he has lice again. In most, if not all, jurisdictions, legislation requires that pediculosis be treated to protect others. In Alberta, for example, treatment of louse infestation is outlined in the Public Health Act. Special precautions need to be in place regarding the patient's clothing as well as his body. If Esther has evidence that Greg has pediculosis, she will be obligated to enforce treatment. She is even empowered to examine him against his will, if necessary.

If there is no evidence of lice, there is probably no real harm being done to other patients and staff. Esther may try to talk Greg into bathing, but if he refuses her options are limited. She can try to find a private room for him, but such rooms are in short supply. Patients often pay for extra health care insurance so they can be assured of a private room. However, private rooms are given to patients first on the basis of medical priority. Even extra insurance coverage will not secure a private room if someone with greater health needs requires it. If all the private rooms on the unit are occupied, Esther might have to check to see whether hospital policy will permit her to move a patient out of the room so Greg can be moved in. Such a move would require a great deal of thought, because it would imply that Greg could be given a room for which someone else has paid extra, simply because of Greg's lifestyle preferences.

If Greg has pediculosis, the question of choice is altered somewhat. He must be treated, but if he refuses to cooperate it becomes a much bigger problem. Questions of whether he is cognitively intact will arise again. It may be necessary to sedate or restrain him to permit staff to carry out the necessary procedures. However, that kind of action is highly coercive, and staff members are certain to find it morally distressing. A more likely decision on the part of nurses would be to try to coax Greg into cooperating or deceive him in some way so that he is unaware of what is happening. Either way, it is a moral problem.

Selecting an Ethical Action: Maximizing Good
Esther's first action should be to establish Greg's ability to understand the problem and to try to determine why he is averse to bathing. Possibly, if she is able to establish a therapeutic relationship with him, she might be able to convince him to bathe. If he has lice she will be required to initiate deinfestation proceedings, as legislation requires. It will be a difficult decision to take away Greg's choice, but Esther might have little option.

Engaging in Ethical Action
Whatever choice Esther makes, she will have to be sure that she is protecting Greg's autonomy as much as possible. Often nurses use persuasion or coercion to get patients to conform. If Greg is cognitively competent and has no pediculosis then persuasion is permitted, but coercion is not. If he is cognitively competent and pediculosis is present, coercion might be required. If he is not cognitively competent, persuasion and possibly coercion are acceptable, depending on the seriousness of the problem, the degree of discomfort of the other patients,

and whether or not pediculosis is present. Coercion might also be warranted if Greg's lack of hygiene has become a serious health risk for him, but only if he is unable to make that decision for himself. Otherwise, Esther needs to accept that individuals who are cognitively competent have the right to take risks with their health.

Reflecting on and Reviewing Ethical Action
We have stated repeatedly that protecting autonomy and honouring choice are of great importance in nursing. Any decision that requires the nurses to limit Greg's autonomy will probably be difficult for them. They will justify their behaviours as being in the best interests of the other patients, especially if pediculosis is present. Again, it is essential that Greg be treated with respect, even if staff members are required to use coercive methods. Regardless of whether his choices agree with what is socially desirable, all nurses involved in Greg's care will have to examine their own actions to determine whether they were able to show respect for him. The essence of ethical nursing is being able to act with respect toward others, even when we have difficulty understanding their choices.

CHAPTER SUMMARY

In this chapter we considered the philosophical origins of respect for choice, and showed how it is related to autonomy. We noted that Kant and Mill both believed that autonomy was a necessary part of being human, although their underlying reasons for this belief were somewhat different. We pointed to the central role of autonomy in bioethics and discussed some of its elements: self-determination, freedom, desire fulfillment, and independence. Next we discussed relationships among autonomy, choice, and consent. Elements of informed consent, namely voluntariness, capacity, and comprehension, were described, and the importance of honesty, trust, and power discussed. We distinguished consent from assent, an important difference when people lack capacity to make their own decisions. Next we returned to the concept of relational autonomy, which was discussed briefly in Chapter 5. We showed how decision making is driven by beliefs and values, and hence by culture and religious beliefs. Then, to link the concepts together, we described two famous ethics cases, those of K'Aila and Dax Cowart. In this way we demonstrated that real-life decision making is completely entwined with notions of autonomy. Deciding for others, as with surrogate decision makers, was also discussed. The idea of advance directives was explored and some of the limitations of advance directives put forward. Finally, we discussed choice as a lived value and used two clinical cases to demonstrate some typical nursing concerns related to choice. Analysis of the cases using the Framework for Ethical Decision Making was presented to help you understand how some of the concepts play out in nursing practice.

Questions for Reflection

1. Think about the decisions you have seen people make about their health care. How many of those people made their decisions without consulting others? When you make decisions about your own health, do you do so independently?

2. Consider how consent is sought in health care. From your observations, do you think adequate attention is paid to issues of comprehension, capacity, and culture? What kinds of issues have arisen for you?

3. Consider your own sense of autonomy. What kinds of limits are there on your autonomy?

4. Reflect on your own developing skills in relational ethics. What skills do you think you would need to strengthen to be able to support patients and families in making autonomous choices?

Exercises

1. During your next clinical experience, talk to nursing colleagues and ask them about consent issues that have arisen for them in nursing practice. Identify three different areas of concern. Document these areas, and report back to the class. Once all members of the class have reported, categorize the consent issues under the headings of self-determination, freedom, desire fulfillment, and independence. Relate these categories to voluntariness, capacity, and comprehension.

2. Role-play a situation with your classmates in which one of you is the nurse, and others are family members trying to decide whether to stop treatment on their aged mother who has been in a motor vehicle collision. See if you can anticipate issues that might arise, and consider how you might deal with those issues. Videotape your interaction and work in a group to critique it.

Research Activities

1. Conduct a literature search on a topic related to choice in practice settings. Identify two articles that you believe reflect different aspects of autonomy/choice. Work with classmates to try to get a broad range of articles. Provide a brief summary of the article and the key concepts related to choice. Enter your summary on an electronic bulletin board such as Blackboard. Examine the summaries prepared by all students, and identify four common themes.

2. Working in small groups, do an Internet search to identify relevant Canadian legislation that guides practice related to choice. Each group should work with a different province. Examine similarities and differences.

3. Conduct a library or Internet search to identify a key ethics case related to autonomy. Post a summary of the case on the electronic bulletin board you used in question 1, and look for common themes across cases. Identify how they relate to the theory in this chapter.

Key Terms

advance directive	inducement
assent	informed consent
capacity	power
comprehension	proxy
desire fulfillment	self-determination
dissent	surrogate
fiduciary	trust
honesty	undue inducement
independence	voluntariness

References

Beauchamp, T., & Childress, J. (2001). *Principles of biomedical ethics.* (5th ed.). New York: Oxford University Press.

Bergum, V., & Dossetor, J. (2005). *Relational ethics: The full meaning of respect.* Hagerstown, MD: University Publishing Group.

Canadian Nurses Association (2008). *Code of ethics for registered nurses* (Centennial ed.). Ottawa: Canadian Nurses Association.

Candib, L. M. (2002). Truth telling and advance planning at the end of life: Problems with autonomy in a multicultural world. *Families, Systems and Health, 20,* 213–228.

Cochrane, D. A., Oberle, K., Nielsen S., Sloan-Roseneck J., Anderson, K., Finlay, C., & Roe, C. (1992). Do they really understand us? *American Journal of Nursing, 92*(7), 19–20.

Davison, B. J., Kirk, P., Degner, L. F., & Hassard, T. H. (1999). Information and patient participation in screening for prostate cancer. *Patient Educaton and Counseling, 37*,255–263.

Degner, L. F., Davison, B. J., Sloan J. A., & Mueller, B. (1998). Development of a scale to measure information needs in cancer care. *Journal of Nursing Measurement, 6*,137–53.

Degner, L. F., Sloan, J. A., & Venkatesh, P. (2007). The Control Preferences Scale. *Canadian Journal of Nursing Research, 29,* 21–43.

Gauthier, C. C. (2002). The virtue of moral responsibility in healthcare decisionmaking. *Cambridge Quarterly of Healthcare Ethics, 11,* 273–281.

Hack, T. F., Degner, L. F., & Parker, P. A. (2005). The communication goals and needs of cancer patients: A review. *Psycho-Oncology, 14,*831–845.

Merriam-Webster on-line. Retrieved June 23, 2006, from www.m-w.com/.

Quill, T. E. (2002). Autonomy in a relational context: Balancing family, cultural, and medical interests. *Families, Systems and Health, 20,* 229–232.

Rosenberg, E. A., & Karides, D. A. (1994). An interview with Dax Cowart. *Journal of the American Medical Association, 272,* 744–745.

Ross, C. J. M., & Maguire, T. O. (1995). Informational coping styles: A validity study. *Journal of Nursing Measurement, 3,* 145–158.

Sandman, L. (2004). On the autonomy turf: Assessing the value of autonomy to patients. *Medicine, Health Care and Philosophy, 7,* 261–268.

Sherwin, S. (1998). A relational approach to autonomy in health care. In S. Sherwin (Ed.) *The politics of women's health: Exploring agency and autonomy,* pp. 19–47. Philadelphia: Temple University Press.

Vuchovich, P. K., & Artinian, B. M. (2005). Justifying coercion. *Nursing Ethics, 12,* 370–380.

Suggested Reading

Aveyard, H. (2005). Informed consent prior to nursing care procedures. *Nursing Ethics, 12,* 19–29.

Churchill, L. R., & Schenck, D. (2005). One cheer for bioethics: Engaging the moral experiences of patients and practitioners beyond the big decisions. *Cambridge Quarterly of Healthcare Ethics, 14,* 389–403.

Hallström, I., & Elander, G. (2005). Decision making in paediatric care: An overview with reference to nursing care. *Nursing Ethics, 12,* 223–238.

Hildén, H. M., & Honkasalo, M. L. (2006). Finnish nurses' interpretation of patient autonomy in the context of end-of-life decision making. *Nursing Ethics, 13,* 41–51.

Kim, S. H., & Kjervik, D. (2005). Deferred decision making: Patients' reliance on family and physicians for CPR decisions in critical care. *Nursing Ethics, 12,* 493–506.

Ramfelt, E., & Lützén, K. (2005). Patients with cancer: Their approaches to participation in treatment plan decisions. *Nursing Ethics, 12,* 143–155.

Sargent, C., & Smith-Morris, C. (2006). Questioning our principles: Anthropological contributions to ethical dilemmas in clinical practice. *Cambridge Quarterly of Healthcare Ethics, 15,* 123–134.

Scott, P. A. (1999). Autonomy, power and control in palliative care. *Cambridge Quarterly of Healthcare Ethics, 8,* 139–147.

Chapter 7
Value 4: Preserving Dignity

Learning Objectives

After reading this chapter, you should be able to:

- describe the fourth primary value in the CNA Code of Ethics for Registered Nurses: *preserving dignity*

- discuss the concepts of dignity and respect for persons

- discuss influences on our ideas about dignity

- describe nursing implications related to dignity

- discuss ways in which the current structure of the health care system can challenge nurses' abilities to maintain dignity

- apply the Framework for Ethical Decision Making to a clinical problem related to dignity

The topic of this chapter is the fourth value of the CNA Code of Ethics for Registered Nurses: *preserving dignity*. To introduce you to this topic, we invite you to consider the following scenario.

Assume you are a nurse working on a busy trauma unit in an acute care centre. One of your patients, Joe, is a 78-year-old man, who until very recently was an independent businessman and president of a large company. Four months ago Joe was diagnosed with lung cancer, and he has been receiving aggressive chemotherapy and radiation. Cancer treatment has not been kind to Joe. He has experienced several serious complications, including a prednisone-induced psychosis that is the cause of his current admission. As you read about Joe in the care plan, you learn that he is unaware of his surroundings, highly anxious, and at times uncooperative during aspects of his care. He says and does highly inappropriate things. When you enter the room you meet several members of his family. They are quick to tell you that Joe is really not himself. They mention that it makes them uncomfortable to see him this way, as they know he would be embarrassed if he were aware of some of the things the psychosis is making him do.

When you think about Joe and his state of well-being, do you wonder how his dignity is being affected by his illness and care? Nurses must think about such things because the CNA Code of Ethics for Registered Nurses indicates that dignity is one of nursing's central values. To uphold this value nurses must grapple with difficult questions, such as: What is dignity? How does a person maintain or lose dignity? How does a nurse enhance or diminish a patient's dignity? How does the health care environment or system enhance or diminish a patient's dignity?

We begin our discussion of the fourth value of the Code with a presentation of several interpretations of dignity. We show that the term is used in a number of different ways and contexts, and thus often lacks clarity. After considering dignity in the abstract, we move to nursing practice and attempt to uncover ways in which dignity can be eroded or preserved in the nurse-patient relationship and the health care system as a whole. Finally, we describe some moral implications of dignity in nursing, as presented in two case studies.

THE FOURTH PRIMARY VALUE: PRESERVING DIGNITY

Dignity can have two kinds of meanings. One, **subjective dignity**, refers to a person's subjective experiences and encompasses the person's own idea of what dignity means. The other, **universal dignity**, is the belief that all persons have worth. The term dignity comes from the Latin words *dignitas*, meaning "merit," and *dignus*, meaning "worthy." Webster's Dictionary (1991) defines **dignity** as

> The quality or state of being worthy; intrinsic worth, excellence; the quality or state of being honoured or esteemed . . . ; formal reserve of manner, appearance, behaviour, or language: behaviour that accords with self-respect or with regard for the seriousness of occasion or purpose . . .

Dignity has come to be understood as a fundamental human right. By **human rights** we mean those entitlements, freedoms, or privileges to which all people are entitled. The idea of human dignity has been given support by recent scientific developments. UNESCO's *Universal Declaration on the Human Genome and Human Rights* gives special status to the possession of uniquely individual human genes (UNESCO, 1997). The *Declaration* states that because the genome is what ties us together as humans, everyone with human genetic material has the right to be respected. In other words, everyone with human genes is a bearer of human dignity. In making *preserving dignity* the fourth value in its Code of Ethics for Registered Nurses, the Canadian Nurses Association shows support for the belief that preserving dignity is everyone's right. It also emphasizes that in health care there is great potential for loss of dignity, and it is nurses' moral obligation to work to prevent that loss.

Statements about preserving dignity in the Code highlight the importance of worth, integrity, and vulnerability. By **worth,** in this context, we mean a belief in the value of every human being. The Code states that "Nurses recognize the intrinsic worth of each person," which implies that every person is deserving of care simply because of being human. Care should protect the **integrity** or wholeness of the person. Preserving integrity means that nurses pay attention to more than just the physical aspect of the patient. The person's sense of self must also be safeguarded. **Vulnerability** implies that persons receiving care may be at risk of emotional or physical harm that could rob them of their dignity.

These words and phrases are frequently used both in clinical and philosophical discussions about the effects of illness and health care. Dignity is associated with our **sense of self-worth**, that is how we think about and value ourselves. In health care today many factors can work to diminish patients' dignity by decreasing their sense of self-worth, and perhaps by taking away some of their human rights. Patients in the health care system are inherently vulnerable because they have needs that they cannot meet for themselves. For example, they might no longer be able to cope on their own with their pain, or they might not be able to feed or dress themselves. They depend on care providers to fulfill their most basic needs. Yet in our current system, technology makes it possible for health care providers to look at the machine, not the person. Consequently nurses must be increasingly vigilant in ensuring that dignity is protected. This requires nurses to be well-informed and reflective about how their care can affect peoples' senses of dignity. In other words, protecting dignity creates special responsibilities for nurses.

Dignity has descriptive, normative, and evaluative elements. We can describe something as dignified, which makes us think of it in a certain way. We can understand it normatively by thinking that certain behaviour is expected from people, and when that behaviour does not occur, they lose dignity (as with Joe's inappropriate actions in the example above). It also has evaluative components because it is assumed that if something is dignified, it is also by definition good. For example, we might say that someone is dying with dignity, which means that his or her way of dying is "good."

Since it is difficult to see dignity directly, its meaning is often revealed in the contrast between its absence and presence. In other words, we pay more attention to the concept of dignity when we think it is *not* present. For example, we might recognize that it is undignified to be incontinent, but we don't think of using the toilet as being dignified. It is when we see something as undignified that we really begin to think about what dignity is.

DEVELOPING IDEAS OF DIGNITY

In looking at ways in which dignity has been defined, it becomes apparent that our understanding of it is very individual. This warns us that nurses cannot take the notion of dignity for granted. We must guard against treating the term as if it has a single meaning. What one person might consider dignity, another person might think lacks dignity.

Daryl Pullman, a noted Canadian philosopher, explains (2004) that dignity defines in large part who we are as moral beings and how we live our lives. Therefore, a deep understanding of dignity is of fundamental importance to understanding morality. Our ways of thinking about dignity have come from many sources. The following discussion will provide more background for you in considering how you think about dignity.

Dignity and the Law

The term dignity in its most modern sense is legal or semi-legal. The word has appeared in the constitutions of many countries and is found in the United Nations' *Universal Declaration of Human Rights* (UDHR). Matti Hayry, a prominent British philosopher, identifies that in Article 1 of the UDHR, "All human beings are born free and equal in dignity and rights. They are endowed with reason and conscience and should act toward one another in a spirit of brotherhood" (Hayry, 2004, p. 588). Including it in constitutions and declarations of human rights means that dignity becomes a fundamental element of our legal processes: law protects our right to dignity. The law does not precisely define dignity, however; that is left up to individual interpretation.

Dignity and Theology

All the great religions consider dignity a foundation for humanity, but each has a somewhat different approach to understanding its source and what it looks like. For example, Hayry (2004) summarizes some key points from Roman Catholic doctrine:

- dignity flows from God
- all human beings are equal in dignity regardless of their social and political status, whether or not they can reason or communicate
- the dignity of individuals must be protected
- unborn human fetuses have a right to dignity, but non-human species do not

This is a view accepted by about a sixth of the world's population and is just one example of how religious doctrine helps define dignity. Further explorations of how dignity is interpreted through religion are beyond the scope of this book. We merely want to point out that religious teachings can have a definite impact on how individuals understand who or what has the right to be treated with dignity.

Dignity and Philosophy

Many of the great philosophers addressed dignity directly in their writing. One of these was Immanuel Kant, whom we discussed earlier in this book. Kant's view followed Roman Catholic doctrine in that he believed that people deserved dignity regardless of social or political status. His thinking was not entirely congruent with the Roman Catholic ideas expressed above, however, as he believed that dignity did not come from God, but rather that dignity is a basic characteristic that all humans have simply because they can reason. Reason gives people the capacity for self-direction or autonomous action. Kant said that humans *never lose* their dignity, regardless of their capacity or incapacity to act. Therefore, in Kant's view, even a person in a persistent vegetative state or a morphine-induced stupor would still have inherent dignity. Since this capacity remains whether or not it is exercised, Kantian human dignity cannot be earned and cannot be taken away (Kant, transl. Ellington, 1994).

This is a very different way of thinking about the concept. Definitions we have discussed earlier seem to imply that it is something that we accord or give to others through our valuing of them. To Kant, opinion did not matter so much, because he felt that people have dignity simply because they are people. If we were to follow Kant's view we would have to worry less about loss of dignity, as such a thing could never happen. In current thinking as expressed in the CNA Code of Ethics for Registered Nurses, dignity can be lost, so the Kantian view is somewhat limiting. Indeed, if we were to follow Kantian reasoning, dignity would be automatic and would occur naturally, but the Code under-stands it differently, believing that nurses must be vigilant in their protection of dignity because of the vulnerability of those in our care.

According to Hayry (2004), utilitarian philosophy sees dignity as based on the capac-ity to feel pleasure and pain, which is possessed by all sentient creatures, including non-human animals. By **sentient** we mean responsive or finely tuned to sense impressions (Merriam-Webster on-line), or capable of responding emotionally, not just intellectually. The foundation of human dignity is the observable phenomenon of suffering: humans have dignity because they can experience suffering. On this view health care providers have an obligation to consider the effect of suffering on dignity. It is important to note that by utilitarian thought embryos and fetuses are not sentient in their early stages of development and therefore do not possess all the rights of fully developed human beings. Utilitarian thinking helps us see the connection between feelings, emotions, and dignity, but it could also encourage us to think that those who appear to have lost the ability to experience emotions or feel suffering, for instance, individuals in a persistent vegetative state, do not have dignity.

Aristotle, who described virtue ethics, saw dignity in a different way. He thought it was connected with status, or more generally with the fulfillment of social roles. According to this view, dignity was an extraordinary quality that gave persons rank and importance and was closely linked to the virtues of thought and character. To live a good life one had to be able to develop and execute complex, long-term plans, which then required some degree of independence and control. Without those abilities one would have limited social status, and therefore limited dignity. From this kind of thinking we can infer that when we speak of living with dignity we have in mind a life in which one is able to fulfill social roles and exercise independence. Again, this kind of thinking can have important effects on how we deliver care. As health care professionals, we will sometimes find ourselves caring for individuals who have limited control over their lives and who are totally dependent on others. An Aristotelian point of view could lead us to understand that circumstances can make it more difficult to develop or exercise one's virtues of thought and character, or to fulfill social roles. For instance, if we consider persons with disabilities unable to fulfill social roles, we could consider them lacking in dignity.

Dignity as Relational

Arthur Frank, a Canadian sociologist from the University of Calgary, offers us an approach that is particularly applicable to nursing. He maintains that dignity arises from "an event happening between persons, rather than [being] a fixed quality" (Frank, 2004, p. 207). As such it is *relational*, which is to say that it exists only in the context of a rela-tionship and is created within a relational experience. It is not something that exists on its own. He considers maintaining dignity to be an essential part of caring and reminds us that "caring is not a unidirectional administration of a standardized treatment. Care that takes dignity seriously is a dialogue" (p. 207).

Dialogue always involves a relationship. How we understand dignity comes from what we know of how the other is feeling or what we would expect him or her to feel based on our own understanding. Put another way, dignity is created in how we respond to others and is shaped by our own experiences. As Frank suggests, "We learned how to feel this way from people like us; and others who learned from other people feel differently" (p. 210).

If we accept the relational view of dignity, we will be aware that in caring for others we influence how they feel about themselves. A person's sense of dignity will be a function of how we respond to her or him. It is something like holding up a mirror. If we reflect to a person a belief that she or he has little worth, then that is what the person may see. As nurses, then, we have to be aware that all our caring actions and gestures will shape others' experiences and to some extent how they feel about themselves. Dignity is present and shaped in the intimate sharing of time together and is continuously learned in ongoing dialogues and relationships. Dignity happens in the way we care for others, how we touch them and respond to them. It becomes our responsibility as caregivers to create an experience in which a person feels a sense of self-worth and value. Frank suggests that dignity is best understood and experienced through dialogue and care. He states, "We learn how to react to dignity's maintenance or loss by seeing the faces made—the smiles of approval and frowns of distress—by others whom we take to be like us, and by having them recognize as appropriate the faces we make" (Frank, 2004, p. 209).

This way of thinking about dignity helps us understand how culture can affect interpretations of dignity. Culture is about common meanings and shared beliefs and values. Meanings and values are learned, so cultural understandings of what constitutes dignified or undignified behaviour in illness (or other) situations might be very different. For example, a nurse might consider it undignified for a woman to cry and shout during labour, whereas her family might expect this behaviour and think it perfectly dignified.

DIGNITY AND NURSING PRACTICE

In Chapter 5 we considered health and well-being as key nursing values. Some interesting questions arise when one thinks about the relationship of these values to dignity. For example, we could ask if dignity should be thought of as a necessary component of health. If, as the many definitions of dignity imply, self-worth is an essential aspect of being human, then it should also be considered a central aspect of health and consequently a significant concept for nursing.

Dignity plays a central role in the nurse-patient relationship, in part because of the shared humanity of patient and nurse. Illness threatens the integrity or wholeness of the person and can produce wounds that are much more than physical. When illness affects human dignity it can go to the very core of what it means to be human. In health care relationships, protecting human dignity begins with knowing the "person" in care. To know individuals as persons is to know them as **subjects** (as opposed to objects), individuals who act with their own desires and intentions. That is, it is important that nurses recognize the humanity and self-worth of each patient, because what is considered an important part of dignity varies from person to person.

Each person values different things and thinks about self-worth in a different way. For instance, I might consider that I lose self-worth and dignity when I have to give up my own clothes and wear a hospital gown, but someone else might not worry about that at all. An athlete might feel a loss of dignity in having to be bedridden. Another person might feel a loss of dignity in having to go to bed at a certain time or take medications. To know their patients and what their patients value, nurses must know something about their patients' biographies, or life stories, their contexts, and how they live in the world.

In their practice, nurses learn to express respect and promote dignity through their caring presence. If you reflect on your practice, you will observe that focusing on technical manipulations and treatments, at the expense of the person receiving those treatments, detracts from your patient's dignity. As a nurse, you must be sensitive to the importance of your actions. The way you treat people is a reflection of the respect you feel for them. It is important to remember that "people like us" who are in need of care have a sense of self-worth that must be maintained, just as we would want our own self-worth to be maintained. In nursing care, recognizing the vulnerability of the patient to loss of dignity is a primary ethical obligation.

Understanding the Erosion of Dignity

In striving for dignified care, nurses need to be attentive to the possibility that their patients' dignity is lost or eroded. Whenever a person is placed in a vulnerable position where opportunities to exercise control and choice are limited, there is the potential for loss of dignity. In the same way that a sense of dignity is created in relationship, it should be clear that environment also has the potential to make one feel valued or devalued, worthwhile or worthless. Thus erosion or loss of dignity can occur whenever illness, loss, and suffering are present. **Depersonalization**, the loss of sense of self as a unique individual, can easily be a part of hospital admission and treatment, and frequently goes unrecognized by health care professionals. When we admit patients, we give them a number and often treat them as a diagnosis. We expect them to follow our rules and routines without paying much attention to their own schedules and established self-care practices. Standard routines ignore the individuality of patients and make it easy to neglect their dignity. Although both routine and protocol are important in ensuring consistency and efficiency, nurses must guard against treating the *patient* as routine.

Again, a story from practice will illustrate how nurses can erode a patient's dignity. Mr. Jensen was a patient in his early thirties. He had been in a car accident several years prior and as a result was quadriplegic, with only gross upper body movement. For some time he had been living in an assisted living complex for people with disabilities. He had his own apartment and was able to manage most of his own care with the assistance of an aide who came in twice a day. At present he was hospitalized for a urinary tract infection. The nurses found him demanding and difficult, as he was always ringing his bell and demanding assistance. Sometimes he was rude to the nurses, and they thought he was arrogant.

At report they were chuckling about how the night nurses had "fixed" him. Not wanting to put up with his constant demands they removed his bell and closed the door to his room. He retaliated by banging on his side rails and making as much noise as possible, but the nurses ignored him. Eventually he knocked down his side rail and fell out of bed. When the nurses found him on the floor, apparently unhurt, they told him that it served him right and that he was too heavy for them to pick up and return to bed. They would have to call the "lift" team, which they did. Before they called, though, they left him lying on the floor for an hour or more. They felt he had it coming for being so obnoxious.

Clearly this is a tale of unethical practice. Even the most inexperienced novice should be able to see that such behaviour from nurses is unacceptable. It was designed to diminish the patient and take away his "arrogance." They even used the phrase "cut him down to size." How can we start to understand the behaviour of the patient and nurses? In the hospital environment, patients often feel an acute sense of loss of control. When they try to regain some of that control, staff may label them as "difficult" or "uncooperative," and occasionally punish their behaviour. Nurses are sometimes resentful of patients who disrupt the accepted routine or who require too much attention.

Ethical behaviour on the part of the nurses would require that they explore with the patient why he was behaving in such a troubling way. Irritability, sadness, rudeness, silence, and anger can be direct expressions of loss of dignity. Actual and potential loss of dignity can erode a person's sense of self. Separation from familiar environments and relationships can strip away parts of the patient's identity. Only the person living the experience can really know what these separations mean. An attentive nurse is alert to signs that the patient is feeling damaged in this way. Recognizing that dignity is lost when individuality is ignored can be the first step in ensuring that your patients feel respected.

Because every patient is unique, nurses cannot presume to know what upsets them. The morally perceptive and responsible nurse will inquire what makes the patient feel undignified. Given that human integrity has to do with exercising thought, character, and choice, the nurse must work to construct an environment that preserves choice to the extent possible. Nurses foster indignity by insisting on rigid routines, limiting options, and ignoring the character of their patients.

Concerns with dignity in nursing are particularly evident in care of the elderly. These patients are often at great risk because they may have relatively little power over their circumstances and because we take certain things for granted. Nurses may make assumptions based on stereotypes or accepted societal values. **Ageism**, defined by Merriam-Webster online as "prejudice or discrimination against a particular age-group and especially the elderly," can take many forms, and as a nurse you might not even recognize it as such. North America in general reveres youth and beauty, and the elderly are regarded as having little to offer. This prevailing attitude can influence your thinking without your being conscious of it; such is the nature of prejudice. It then becomes easy even with the best of intentions to act in ways that damage dignity. That is why an awareness of story and "person" are so vital to ethical care. A scenario will help illustrate this point.

Imagine for a moment an elderly woman on an acute nursing unit waiting for place-ment in long-term care. She is frail and obviously experiencing some dementia. The nurs-ing care plan includes a note that the patient was always very concerned about grooming and hygiene. You have a few moments to spare in a busy day, and know that she has vis-itors coming in the afternoon, so you take the time to brush her hair and make sure she has a clean gown. You think that she is very cute, so you decide to put some blue bows in her hair to match her gown. You feel quite good about the fact that you have done some-thing nice for this patient. When her family comes in they are clearly upset at seeing her. You ask them if something is wrong, and the daughter replies, "It infuriates me to see what they do to Mother. They dress her up and put her hair in pigtails like she was five years old. I know they think they are doing something nice, but Mother would be mortified to be treated like an infant. I don't know why everyone persists in thinking of old women as cute little dolls just because they are old. Mother was always so dignified. She wore her hair in an elegant French roll all her adult life. She looks so ridiculous in pigtails, and it just makes me realize all the more how helpless she has become. It tears my heart out!" Clearly your best intentions were misguided in this situation, and you walk away feeling embarrassed and determined to pay more attention to stereotypes that influence your thinking.

Another area in which prejudicial thinking is evident is in care of obese patients. Our culture has what amounts to an obsession with thinness, and those who are markedly overweight are stigmatized. There is a prevalent belief that being obese is a lifestyle choice, and those who do not control their weight are weak and sometimes contemptible. A nurse who starts with that attitude is much more likely to treat obese patients disre-spectfully and view them as a "management" problem. Consider a morbidly obese patient admitted for abdominal surgery. He requires three nurses to turn him, and even changing a dressing becomes more difficult because of the large panniculus (apron of belly fat). Instead of judging the patient, the nurse should consider what it might be like for him to recognize that he presents a problem for the nurses. It could be humiliating to know that it requires several nurses to turn you or change your dressing. A perceptive nurse might wonder whether the patient is more than usually bothered by having his body exposed to unfamiliar eyes or what it would feel like to have nurses sighing and rolling their eyes as they tried to help you onto a bedpan. The nurse might pause to think about what it might feel like to know that others are watching every bite you take, thinking that you should eat less, or maybe not eat at all for a few days. Feeling that you are an object of contempt or ridicule can be a particular form of pain. Nurses who are complicit in diminishing a patient's self-respect in any way are acting unethically.

Respecting and Restoring Dignity

A concept that naturally fits with dignity is respect. In the context of the nurse-patient relationship we make a distinction between respecting persons and respecting the *rights* of persons. Until recently rights were given the greatest emphasis in health care ethics. This led to a focus on moral entitlements such as self-determination or autonomy. By contrast, the moral obligation to treat persons in themselves with respect is tied to enhancing their self-worth and dignity. This goes beyond respecting their autonomy. It means acknowledging persons for who they are and responding to them in a manner that preserves their integrity and sense of self.

In a caring relationship, dignity begins when the nurse recognizes that the patient has worth. The CNA Code of Ethics for Registered Nurses says "Nurses in their professional capacity relate to all persons with respect" (CNA, 2008, p. 13). A major part of maintaining human dignity is encouraging patients to retain control over their care decisions for as long as possible. When patients are fully involved in their treatment plans, making decisions and evaluating outcomes, their integrity is preserved.

There may be some individuals for whom it is difficult for you to feel respect because of your beliefs, values, and possibly prejudices. For example, in Chapter 5 Rob had difficulty respecting his patient because of his inability or unwillingness to lose weight when it was clearly a health problem for him. Sometimes nurses judge patients for the ways in which they live their lives, but it should be clear to you that there is little place for this kind of judgmentalism in nursing. If you are to give ethical care, your starting assumption should be that all persons deserve to be treated with respect, even if they demonstrate personal characteristics that do not match your values.

In Chapter 2 we discussed embodiment in the nurse-patient relationship. Restoration of eroded dignity may be possible through embodied relations between the nurse and patient. Too often nurses become disembodied in their conversations—they become an instrument, like a machine. To become re-embodied means that the nurse needs to be open to other ways of learning about the patient, including listening and touch. Sally Gadow, a prominent philosopher of nursing, says "the violation of dignity and autonomy that seems to accompany technology is in reality not the role of machines in patient care but of the view of the body as a machine" (Gadow, 1999, p. 65). With such traps there is danger of cultivating insensitivity and indignity through detachment and loss of emotion. This makes the patient feel dehumanized and disrespected. The nurse also has a role to play in helping other members of the health team see the patient as a whole person rather than a disease, a bed number, or a diagnosis. Valuing the person's integrity, uniqueness, and wisdom is the nurse's way of showing respect. Through actions and words, the nurse conveys to his or her patients the perception that their life is of value no matter what physical or emotional state they are experiencing.

Dignity and Privacy

One of the ways in which dignity can be lost in the care setting is through loss of **privacy**, which can be defined as freedom from observation or intrusion by others, or from their attention. In Chapter 8 we discuss privacy and confidentiality at length, but for now we consider it as it relates to dignity. To a large extent, culture defines how we think about personal privacy. In some cultures privacy is considered a luxury for the wealthy; in others it is an expectation for all. Our views about bodily privacy and how we protect it in part define who we are. For example, an Orthodox Jewish woman does not appear in public with her head uncovered, and to demand that she remove her head covering in the presence of strangers would reduce her self-respect. Conversely, a teenage girl in mainstream North American culture might feel diminished if she were required to wear more clothing than she would normally choose.

When we are ill it may be difficult for us to protect our privacy. Caregivers often disregard the importance of bodily privacy in the interests of dealing with physical problems. Consider a case example involving a young woman in intensive care (ICU). Typical ICUs are open so that all patients can be seen easily by nursing staff. The patient has what is called a "flail chest" from a traumatic accident. When she inhales, a segment of the ribcage that has broken free moves in instead of out. This is also called "paradoxical respiration." The movement of the rib segment compromises respiration. When the physician and his junior staff visit the patient they want to view the chest wall motion, so they pull back the covers and pull up her gown, leaving her naked to the waist and exposed for all to see. This kind of event is not uncommon and should be a cause of moral distress for nurses. The nurse in this case should make every effort to remind the physician that exposing the patient in this way contributes to loss of dignity.

Not all privacy issues are related to having body parts exposed to others. For some, intimate details of bodily functioning are considered both private and embarrassing. When a nurse asks a female patient about her last menstrual period in a physician's office waiting room or an elderly long-term care resident about his bowel movements in a room full of other residents the nurse is, in effect, making these details public. Feeling required to provide this information publicly is often demeaning to patients, and the perceptive nurse is aware of this fact. In general, the morally sensitive nurse is alert to any kind of public display or revelation that individuals would prefer to keep private, and the nurse makes every attempt to honour that preference.

Dignity and Boundaries

Another important idea for nurses to consider is that whenever we form relationships with a vulnerable other a potential for exploitation and boundary violations exists. A patient who has come to depend on you for a sense of self-worth might well develop feelings for you that go beyond the professional. This is more often the case in long-term relationships than in the acute care environment. For example, patients on a rehabilitation unit have often experienced many losses. Think of a young athlete who has been left quadriplegic by a diving accident. It is conceivable that he would develop feelings of attachment to a nurse who works with him to help him regain optimal functioning and who demonstrates that she cares about him despite his disability. A nurse making frequent visits to a patient in her home might be the only contact that patient has with the outside world. It might seem to the patient that the nurse is a friend, not simply a professional. A patient in long-term care might develop strong affection for the nurse who is particularly kind to her and sees in her the person she used to be. Such situations make patients especially vulnerable.

The CNA Code of Ethics for Registered Nurses makes it very clear that nurses must maintain **boundaries** that limit the extent and nature of the involvement the nurse has with the patient. It states that nurses "recognize the potential vulnerability of persons and do not exploit their trust and dependency in a way that might compromise the therapeutic relationship" (CNA, 2008, p. 13). That is, nurses maintain boundaries to ensure that their professional relationships are always for the benefit of the persons they serve.

Some aspects of establishing professional boundaries are quite straightforward. It should be obvious to you that engaging in sexual intimacy with persons in your care is not acceptable. Sometimes you might develop personal attachments to patients, but as long as you are in a caregiving relationship with them you must not act on your feelings beyond providing professional care. Clearly, if you are working with patients you are not permitted to use your relationship with them for your own monetary gain. Part of helping patients maintain their dignity is keeping a professional distance from them.

As obvious as these ideas are, some elements of boundary setting are not as clear. There are many grey areas that can lead to confusion and uncertainty. For example, gift-giving has raised some debate. The question is whether accepting gifts from patients is morally permissible. Those who argue that it is never acceptable say it can lead to preferential treatment of some patients. Nurses are compensated for their work, and accepting gifts implies something beyond a professional relationship. Those who argue that it should sometimes be allowed say that it is important to preserving patients' dignity. Some patients need to feel that the relationship is reciprocal, and if they do not give a gift they remain somehow beholden to the nurse. Janice Morse, a nurse researcher working at the University of Alberta, conducted a study to examine the issue of gift-giving in the nurse-patient relationship. She concluded that it can sometimes be important for patients' self-worth and that refusing the gift is insulting to them (Morse, 1991). There has been little, if any, published research on the topic since that time. At present there continues to be little consensus on acceptability of small tokens of appreciation, but it is generally agreed that accepting a large gift is morally unacceptable, as it could be seen as exploitation for monetary or other material gain. From our perspective, gift-giving may be morally permissible in some instances. The nurse must attend very carefully to context and should refuse a gift that implies a relationship outside professional boundaries or that is given to foster affection or attention. The nurse must try to establish what the gift means to the patient, and whether accepting the gift (or failing to accept it) will compromise care in any way. The decision depends on what is best for the patient and/or family.

The question of gift-giving is a reflection of some of the ambiguity around boundaries in the nurse-patient relationship. One of the most helpful sources for guidance can be downloaded from the College and Association of Registered Nurses of Alberta (CARNA) web site. Titled "Professional Boundaries: A Discussion Guide and Teaching Tool," this document outlines some of the issues and provides case studies and commentary. Other professional associations also have policies and support documents. The interested nurse can easily find them on-line using the search term "Canadian nurses boundaries."

Dignity, Death, and Dying

The term "dignity" is often used in discussions about death and dying. Perhaps this is because dying patients are so vulnerable. Uncontrolled pain, suffering, and fear can certainly erode dignity by altering behaviour and limiting control and choice. The fact that dignity is mentioned in this context reflects just how important it is in our society. Being able to die with dignity may be the last hope of the terminally ill patient. What this means in nursing practice will be variable, but generally people think of **dying with dignity** as being able to maintain a sense of self-worth by behaving in a way that they feel is honourable or desirable. It also implies dying without unnecessary pain and suffering.

Dying with dignity has become an important topic in health care ethics in general. There are those who advocate allowing persons to undergo **voluntary euthanasia**—to end their own lives—or seek assistance from others in doing so. At present it is illegal in Canada to commit or assist with voluntary euthanasia, but in the United States the state of Oregon passed the Dying with Dignity Act in 1997. The act permits terminally ill individuals to end their lives through self-administration of medications prescribed by a physician for that purpose.

Clearly the idea of dying with dignity is a powerful and important one. Nurses have an enormous role to play in providing appropriate pain control and other comfort measures, being authentically present for the individual and family, and listening to the patient's and family's wishes. Dying with dignity can be possible, even in the face of painful illness, with appropriate nursing support.

Dignity and Systems Issues

To this point we have been discussing the role of the individual nurse in helping maintain the patient's dignity. We have, however, paid little attention to the context in which care occurs. The environment can have an important impact on the quality of care given, but it can also be part of the whole process by which dignity is eroded. Some examples may help to explain this.

First, it is important that nurses have the time and resources to be able to support patients to maintain their dignity. Staffing shortages can make it difficult to spend the necessary time with patients. Being authentically present requires time for connection and listening. We have said throughout this discussion that nurses must be present for patients, know their stories, and listen to their worries and fears. But what if there is no time for that? In interviews one of us conducted with nurses in acute care (Oberle & Davies, 1993), the commonest ethical concern they had was insufficient time to provide the care they thought was necessary. They experienced moral distress when they felt patients were losing dignity because of lack of adequate nursing care. This can be a significant cause of burnout for nurses. Framing the problem as an ethical one may help nurses articulate their concerns in a way that gets the attention of those who manage the system. Too often those who provide the funding for nursing care understand it only as skilled tasks. Helping others understand that preserving dignity is part of nursing's moral foundation can be important in establishing the validity of requests for better staffing.

Nursing staffing issues aside, the system may contribute importantly in other ways to depersonalizing individuals. Sometimes decisions made in the interests of efficiencies and fiscal restraint can be damaging to patients. Consider the "first available bed" policy that applies in many jurisdictions. This policy says that patients awaiting long-term care will be given the first available bed, regardless of whether or not that seems desirable to the patient and family. An elderly woman who cannot drive might find it an impossible burden to have her husband in a long-term care facility on the other side of the city. The patient himself might lose all touch with family and his sense of self in this situation. Another example is the centralization of medical services. In one jurisdiction, women who are being treated for breast cancer have the needles to localize the tumour positioned in one institution, then they must go to another institution to have the treatment. Having to drive across town with a breast sprouting needles may be distressingly undignified. These are only two examples of the kinds of decisions that are sometimes taken at the macro level. Nurses must be prepared to question such decisions as part of fulfilling their obligations to preserve dignity. Nursing input at the policy level is of vital importance if we are to have a health care system that preserves, rather than destroys, the dignity of patients, families, and even health care providers.

DIGNITY AS A LIVED VALUE

As humans we are all vulnerable to loss of dignity. The morally sensitive nurse acknowledges that in health care relationships there is almost unlimited potential to degrade, devalue, and humiliate. The virtuous nurse strives to be the best nurse possible, which as we have shown requires respecting the dignity of patients. This implies acknowledgement of vulnerability, fallibility, and potential for dignity violations; commitment to reflection for improvement of practice; and knowledge about how dignity has been understood through philosophy and research. Situations arise in relation to dignity every day. Nurses need to reflect continuously "in action" on their own potential to affect the dignity of a patient and/or family. Nurses must cultivate an attitude of moral sensitivity to make dignity a fundamental value in each and every care situation.

We again turn to practice examples to demonstrate how the ethical value of dignity appears in the course of practice. We present two case studies and use the Framework for Ethical Decision Making to uncover moral dimensions of the situations. As in earlier chapters, the framework helps us think about the relative weight of the different elements in the Nursing Ethics Composite Model for ethical decision making: bioethical principles, professional practice standards, legal and contextual considerations, and overall goals of care.

7.1 Choices for Mr. Stanley

Mr. Stanley, an 83-year-old with Parkinson's disease, lives in Shady Pines Nursing Home. He appears alert and oriented, with no obvious signs of major cognitive impairment, but sometimes he seems a bit confused. He is recovering from a fractured hip sustained while walking outside with his daughter. He receives physical therapy but is making very slow progress in his ability to walk. One evening, trying to manoeuvre the few steps from his wheelchair to his bed, he falls. He is not hurt but the next day he gets up from his wheelchair and falls again. He persists in his short journeys even though he has been told not to leave his wheelchair or bed without assistance. After a third fall in which he suffers a cut on his forehead, two actions are taken: his wheelchair is taken out of his room so he cannot attempt to get in it himself, and he is restrained when in bed and in the wheelchair. Mr. Stanley reacts vigorously against this change in independence. He constantly pulls at the restraint and pleads with staff and visitors to untie him.

This evening Mr. Stanley appears agitated. Marjorie, a regular nurse at Shady Pines, hears him from several rooms down the hall calling out, "Nurse! Nurse, help me!" As she comes closer to the room she hears him rattling the bed rails, crying, "Please don't keep me trapped in my bed like a caged animal. I'm not an invalid. Please." Marjorie goes to his bedside. She tries to explain that his falling causes concern and that it is policy for all patients who are at risk for injuring themselves to be restrained. She is concerned that he is being robbed of his dignity, but she is very worried that he will hurt himself. The only way to protect him, if he won't follow advice, is to restrain him or sedate him. Marjorie decides that the restraints are preferable to drugs and must remain in place.

The next evening when Marjorie comes on shift Mr. Stanley's grown children are talking to the nurse in charge. She is explaining why their father is tied in the bed. She says that they need to keep him safe, commenting, "If he falls again and really hurts himself, what freedom will he have then? Consider his long-term status. He might be restrained now, but it's only for the sake of his future mobility. We think that he is confused right now and just want to wait until his thinking is clearer." His children aren't sure, as they don't really think their father is confused, but they reluctantly agree to take the nurse's advice and leave the restraints in place. Marjorie, however, isn't convinced that this is the best course of action. She wonders what the most ethical response to Mr. Stanley's request to remove the restraints would be. She understands the need for safety, but is concerned about how the restraints are affecting his sense of self. She wonders whether Mr. Stanley really understands the risks he is taking when trying to get up. She wonders if he is capable of making that decision for himself and whether the nursing staff members are protecting themselves as much as they are protecting Mr. Stanley. They don't want to see him hurt himself and also worry about their liability if he is not kept safe. But Marjorie wonders if they are doing more damage by taking away his independence.

Choices for Mr. Stanley

The ethical issue reflected in the case study is common in nursing practice. In terms of bioethical principles, it is often cast as a choice between autonomy, in this case respecting Mr. Stanley's right to make independent decisions, and beneficence, or acting in Mr. Stanley's best interests by ensuring his safety. However, the CNA Code of Ethics for Registered Nurses helps us understand that this ethical problem is about more than just autonomy and rights. In restraining Mr. Stanley, the nurses are taking away his sense of self—in other words, his dignity. When nurses consider the use of restraints, they generally propose that safety is the underlying value that initiates their moral actions, but they must also consider how it makes the patient feel. The use of restraints is a moral problem involving professional judgment, safety, and the client's sense of self-worth.

Assessing the Ethics of the Situation: Relationships, Goals, Beliefs, and Values

In attempting to determine the most ethical action in this case, Marjorie must begin by examining beliefs of the patient, family, and care providers. In this instance it is clear that conflicting beliefs and values are present. It appears that Mr. Stanley most values autonomy. He wants to be free to make his own decisions, even if those decisions put him at risk of harm. His goal is to be independent. However, whether he can be left to make decisions depends on whether he has the cognitive capacity to understand the risks. Mr. Stanley's daughter has admitted to feeling guilty about his fall and wants him to be safe, but she is also concerned about his integrity. His son

is also worried, as he is not convinced that his father is confused, and he knows that his father values independence above all. The charge nurse believes that protecting Mr. Stanley from harm is the first priority. She does not believe that he is making right decisions, and therefore questions his cognitive status. Marjorie is suffering moral distress and uncertainty because she is not sure what is the right thing to do. She wants what is best for Mr. Stanley but can't accept that his best interests will necessarily be served by restraining him. She thinks that maintenance of dignity is also in his best interests.

Reflecting on and Reviewing Personal Actions: Recognizing Available Choices and How Those Choices Are Valued

There are several options that Marjorie might consider. She could choose to leave the restraints on and the side rails up whenever Mr. Stanley is alone. She could use other safety devices, such as a bed alarm, and leave the side rails up. Both actions are intended to prevent harm and are justified by the moral obligation to act in the patient's best interests. Alternatively, she might also consider Mr. Stanley's autonomy and his right to make his own choices. That would mean removing the restraints against the direction of the nurse in charge, an action that might not be supported and might cause Marjorie to be reprimanded.

Selecting an Ethical Action: Maximizing Good

It seems evident that the other nurses value Mr. Stanley's safety. However, in attempting to protect him they have not demonstrated respect for his decisions, and so they have impinged on his autonomy and his dignity.

(Continued)

Choices for Mr. Stanley

It is not entirely clear whether restraint is morally justified here. Marjorie decides that her first course of action will be to sit down with the family and Mr. Stanley and discuss their values and beliefs. This will help her understand what "good" looks like to them in the situation. She also needs to assess Mr. Stanley's cognitive status. If he is not capable of making rational decisions, then a surrogate will have to make decisions for him. Usually that is a family member. Marjorie needs to understand what risks the family is willing to accept on behalf of their loved one, and be sure that they understand the relative risks and benefits of the different courses of action. This will help her make a decision based on caring and compassion toward Mr. Stanley as a person wanting to live his life with dignity and happiness.

Engaging in Ethical Action

Reflecting on the situation, Marjorie realizes that her moral obligation is to engage with Mr. Stanley and his family in working toward the best possible care. In considering this, Marjorie will need to reflect on her personal and professional beliefs and values. Has she upheld the values in the CNA Code of Ethics for Registered Nurses? Marjorie's priority of *safe and competent care* to prevent injury is certainly important, but in this case overlooks and is contrary to respect for Mr. Stanley's dignity. His calling out that he feels like an "invalid" and a "caged animal" suggests this. If Mr. Stanley is to be restrained, the psychological harm done to him might be considered equally as damaging as the physical injury he might sustain by falling.

Marjorie needs to take care to foster Mr. Stanley's self-determination, but again, if he is unable to assess the risks for himself, then self-determination may not be possible. If he is cognitively aware and prefers to take the risk of injury, there is no justification for continuing to restrain him. There is a legal issue here also. Marjorie should have relevant knowledge of laws regarding restraint use. For example, the province of Ontario in 2001 passed the first institutional restraint Act in Canada, Bill 85. Legal issues that may arise from the use of restraints include concern related to obtaining informed consent of patients, families, and/or legal guardians, as well as the safety of patients and others. By law, the patient or the surrogate decision maker must be fully informed of the reason for the restraint and must give consent. In case of an emergency situation, consent must be obtained from the patient as soon as possible after the emergency has occurred (Statutes of Ontario, 2001).

Even if nurses believe that patients should follow a different course of action, they have no right under law or on ethical principles to take away a patient's autonomy. Marjorie cannot make this decision by herself. She must talk with the family to get a better understanding of how Mr. Stanley usually acts and whether risk-taking was part of his usual way of being before his hospital admission. She must try to learn whether Mr. Stanley's determination to get up without assistance reflects his need to be independent or deteriorating cognitive status. Instead of assuming that he is incompetent, she must consider the possibility that he would simply rather be independent than safe. Clearly he understands the restraints as taking away his dignity. If he is not competent to make decisions, the question still remains as to whether his safety is more important than his dignity.

What would a reasonably prudent nurse know and do? There are documented research studies, practice and legal standards, and institutional policies that Marjorie needs to consider. First, research indicates that restraints are overused and may not always be beneficial; in fact, they can cause physical and psychological harm. According to nurse researchers, harmful effects including increases in serious falls, skin breakdown, immobilization, cognitive decline, agitation, and even death have been associated with the use of physical restraints (Smith, Timms, Parker, Reimels, & Hamilin, 2003; Sullivan-Marx, 2001). Professional practice standards and position papers across the country adopt the principle of "least restraint practice" where a nurse is to exhaust all possible alternative interventions before deciding to use a restraint. Alternatives to restraints can include a variety of approaches such as redirection, setting limits, using timeouts, the use of medication, psychosocial interventions, and safe physical escort techniques (De Prospero Rogers & Bocchino, 1999; Kozub & Skidmore, 2001). Marjorie needs to be aware of the institutional policies where she works, and whether restraint use is generally supported and encouraged, or sometimes discouraged. Such policies address factors such as comprehensive assessment of the client to determine whether restraint is necessary, and propose alternative interventions to restraint as discussed above.

Marjorie will have to be certain that Mr. Stanley's competency assessment is well documented. If the assessment shows that he is competent, then she will have to remove the restraints. If he is not competent, then she will have to be guided by legal standards, institutional policy, and family wishes. Whatever she decides, she will have to document her decision making carefully. If she were to restrain, she would have to monitor Mr. Stanley regularly and document her observations. Accurate and complete documentation of the use of restraints is essential to protect the nurse against liability and to communicate to other staff the decision-making process.

Finally, in her role as Mr. Stanley's advocate, Marjorie may need to suggest that the policy be reviewed and/or that other staff members are educated about the use of restraints and alternative measures.

Reflecting on and Reviewing the Ethical Action

In this instance, Marjorie's assessment supported the conclusion that Mr. Stanley's cognitive capacity was impaired and that he was in serious risk of damaging himself if he fell. She decided to leave the restraints in place when he did not have someone with him and the staff was busy, but to take them off and use a bed alarm and side rails when staff were less busy and could respond to the alarm. Whenever the family was present or the nursing staff could stay with him, she planned to remove the restraints. In considering her professional and personal values, Marjorie felt satisfied with her decision. She became aware that in the past, she had not considered the holistic needs of her patients. She realized that applying restraints, even according to policy, could overlook clients'

(*Continued*)

Choices for Mr. Stanley

beliefs and preferences, thus violating choice and eroding dignity. However, there are times in health care when safety does have to come first. In this situation, Marjorie felt that she had done all she could to preserve Mr. Stanley's dignity by sharing her beliefs and concerns with the family and with Mr. Stanley, and by arranging for him to have as much freedom as possible. Her attentive, caring presence demonstrated to Mr. Stanley and his family that he was regarded with respect, despite his limited capabilities. This is the essence of relational dignity.

Trying It On

7.2 Prolonging Life or Prolonging Death?

As they prepare for their evening shift in ICU, Su Ling complains to her colleague, "I just hate this. I get her every night, and I can't stand it one minute more!" She is protesting her evening assignment. For the third night in a row she is to care for Mrs. Lee, a very frail, elderly Chinese woman who speaks no English. Mrs. Lee's daughter is always at the bedside, and her English is also very limited. Su Ling is the only person who can speak Cantonese, Mrs. Lee's native language, so it seems logical that she is the primary caregiver whenever she is on duty. However, caring for Mrs. Lee is grinding Su Ling down. She really cares about this tiny, fragile person. The problem is that she thinks the team is working far too hard to keep Mrs. Lee alive. This 94-year-old patient was admitted to ICU following a near-fatal car accident. Her daughter had been driving when a half-ton truck broadsided them. Mrs. Lee's injuries include fractures of several facial bones, her neck, and her left femur. She has serious contusions and lacerations, several of which are infected. She suffered a cardiac arrest early in her admission and never recovered consciousness. For the past 21 days she has been comatose, and she is being sustained on tube feedings and intravenous fluid. Her weight is down to about 35 kg, and her skin is breaking down badly. Her oxygen saturation levels drop dramatically whenever she is turned, and it is obvious to all the nurses that she is experiencing severe pain. When she is suctioned she coughs, her oxygenation saturation drops, and she grimaces with the pain.

At rounds that morning the physicians said that further care would be futile, as Mrs. Lee is now showing signs of renal failure. She is unresponsive to the antibiotics that have been used to treat her lung and wound infections, and her electrolytes are all abnormal. To top it off, she is showing signs of having developed a bleed somewhere, as her hemoglobin has been dropping steadily. All nursing staff members on the unit are of the opinion that they should stop treatment and allow Mrs. Lee to die with some dignity. The respiratory technician and the physiotherapist feel the same way. From what the nurses have been able to understand from the daughter, Mrs. Lee had been a very proud and independent woman before the accident, and it seems wrong to continue active treatment under these circumstances. Most of the nurses feel that they would much rather die than be subjected to the indignities that Mrs. Lee is experiencing: incontinence, skin breakdown, pain, and suffering.

The problem is that Mrs. Lee's daughter, May, is adamant that they continue to treat. She seems to believe that there is at least a chance of some kind of recovery. The physicians are reluctant to take away the daughter's hope, but they do not feel that there is any chance that Mrs. Lee will regain consciousness. From their perspective, death is inevitable; it is really just a matter of time.

Su Ling is very unhappy in caring for Mrs. Lee. She feels that continuing active treatment is a form of torture, as they are prolonging death beyond dignity. In Su Ling's mind, the daughter is simply unable to let her mother go and is making decisions based on her own needs, not on Mrs. Lee's needs. Su Ling wants to refuse to care for the patient, but knows that, as long as treatment is to continue, she will have to follow orders. All the nurses are in agreement that treatment should stop, and they have asked the physicians why it is continuing when it is clearly going nowhere. So far it seems that their concerns have not registered. Su Ling is feeling considerable moral distress but feels powerless in the situation. What can she do if no one will listen to the nurses?

Prolonging Life or Prolonging Death?

Nurses often experience moral distress around end-of-life decision making. In two Canadian nursing studies, dying with dignity and the prolongation of suffering were the most frequently identified ethical issues for nurses (Oberle, 1995; Oberle & Hughes, 2001). As we have discussed throughout this chapter, dignity is about self-worth, respect, and choice. The issue that arises for nurses seems to come from their belief that continuing treatment beyond what a person would want diminishes that person's dignity. The suffering and pain that the patient experiences erodes his or her humanness and makes the patient into nothing more than an object on whom health care providers impose treatments. Su Ling's moral distress and sense of powerlessness are typical of the kinds of concerns raised by nurses in their practice. In terms of bioethical principles, this situation represents a problem of beneficence. Everyone wants to do what is best for Mrs. Lee, but there is disagreement about what that would be.

Assessing the Ethics of the Situation: Relationships, Goals, Beliefs, and Values

In this situation several sets of values must be taken into account: those of the patient, family, nurses, and physicians. We do not have any way of knowing what the

(Continued)

Prolonging Life or Prolonging Death?

patient would want, as she is unresponsive and there has been no mention of a personal directive. Usually it is assumed that the family will be best able to represent the patient's wishes, but in this case the staff do not believe that May is making decisions in the patient's best interests. May wants treatment to continue, despite evidence that it will almost certainly be unsuccessful. We can assume that she values keeping her mother alive at all costs, but it is not clear why she feels the way she does. If Su Ling were to talk to her about her beliefs, it might become clearer. It might be that May simply does not understand how seriously ill her mother is. It might be that she feels guilty about the car accident and cannot accept that her mother might die as a result. Another possibility is that she believes it is her duty to ensure that her mother has every possible chance to continue living, regardless of the quality of her mother's life. Or she might just need a little time to come to an acceptance of the situation. At this point we do not know what she believes and values.

The nursing staff, including Su Ling, have clearly stated that they value dignity in dying and that the continued treatment betrays that value. As care providers, they see their roles as helping the patient to recover or, if that is not possible, to become more comfortable. They are doing neither in this case. They feel that treatment has become futile, as there is no hope of recovery, and therefore they are simply prolonging the patient's agony. Most importantly, they feel that they are doing something to the patient that she almost certainly would

not want, and this robs her of the dignity she should have in dying.

The physicians also believe that Mrs. Lee's treatment will be unsuccessful. So far they have opted to continue treatment, but they may also feel conflicted. If Su Ling were to ask the physicians why they have made the decisions they have, she might find out that they are concerned about the effect on May of stopping treatment. Perhaps they are aware of her feelings and believe she needs more time to come to acceptance; perhaps they are concerned that she will charge them with negligence under the law. It is also possible that they have difficulty admitting that they have not been able to save Mrs. Lee. Physicians are ultimately responsible for writing the "stop treatment" orders, and writing those orders can never be easy.

Clearly, there are many values and beliefs at work in this situation. Coming to a resolution will require considerable dialogue among all concerned.

Reflecting on and Reviewing Potential Actions: Recognizing Available Choices and How Those Choices Are Valued

Su Ling could take several actions that might help the situation. First, it seems important that she talk to May and find out what her values and beliefs are. It is part of Su Ling's responsibility as a nurse and moral agent to be sure that everyone's voice is heard. May's voice could easily be silenced in this situation, for a number of reasons. She does not speak much English, so it is difficult for her to make herself understood. She also comes from a different culture than most of the staff, so it is possible that her cultural beliefs will be ignored or misunderstood. Culture might also make it more difficult for her to be open about her feelings. Su Ling will have to use excellent relational communication skills if she is to enter this sensitive conversation. Part of the conversation will also involve finding out what May wants her to share about what is said with the health care team. If, for example, May confesses to feeling guilt about the car accident, she might prefer that her feelings not be shared with anyone else. Su Ling will have to consider May's dignity and sense of self-worth when considering appropriate action.

If May is in agreement, Su Ling should share her findings with the health care team. This could open up the conversation and allow others to share their views. A potential action would be to arrange for as many members of the health care team as possible to discuss this situation. If she is not able to make these arrangements, she could request that her manager call the team together for a discussion. It will be important to have representatives from all the disciplines involved. In particular, it is important to have physicians participate in the discussion, along with other nurses. All members of the team have values and beliefs, and it is important that they have an opportunity to express their views. If some feel silenced, they will experience moral distress and a loss of dignity.

The values and actions of the physicians in this situation must also be taken into account. Su Ling and the other nurses are frustrated that the physicians are continuing to treat. However, they have not asked the physicians why they have made this choice. It seems important to understand their reasons before condemning them for their decision. Part of ethical practice is supporting the functioning of the health care team. When she enters this discussion

with the physicians, Su Ling will have to be careful that she does not approach it in a challenging way. Physicians as people have dignity that also needs to be considered, and when people feel threatened or devalued they often respond with anger or resistance. Again, relational communications will be of paramount importance.

Another potential action would be to ask her unit manager or charge nurse to contact the institution's clinical ethics committee. Most institutions will have a committee of this type, whose role is to help the team reflect on the situation and arrive at the solution that seems most ethically sound. Margaret Urban Walker, a noted feminist philosopher, says (1993) that the ethics committee must "keep moral space open" so that everyone who has an interest is heard. Generally the committee is not considered to have the authority to tell clinicians what to do. Instead, it gives advice as to what it thinks would be best, and clinicians can choose to act on that advice or not. The purpose of the ethics consultation is to be sure that all sides of the issue are considered in light of common understandings of "right action." In many instances, the committee will use current literature on health care ethics to inform its recommendations.

Su Ling might also decide to do nothing more than refuse to care for Mrs. Lee. However, she would need to think very carefully about that decision. She would have to ask herself whether it is morally acceptable to abandon Mrs. Lee at this time. Her own moral distress would not seem to be an acceptable reason to walk away from the situation without having tried to understand the reasons for what was happening.

It is also important that legal dimensions of the situation be taken into account. There is at present no law that

(Continued)

Prolonging Life or Prolonging Death?

requires care providers to continue treatment that is deemed futile. Determining when this point is reached, however, is never easy. It is possible that the daughter might even charge the physicians and staff with negligence if they discontinue care, although it is unlikely that she would be successful if she did. If there is consensus of medical opinion then the court would not consider that there was cause for prosecution.

Selecting an Ethical Action: Maximizing Good
The options Su Ling might take are not mutually exclusive. In this case she should do several things: talk to May about her beliefs and values; discuss with the physicians why they have made their choices; and, together with her colleagues, present their concerns to the health care team and to May. If no resolution is achieved in this way and the situation remains unchanged, she should also talk to her unit manager about asking for an ethics consultation. Given that the physicians have not so far demonstrated a willingness to consider the nurses' concerns, it might prove necessary to take this step.

The key to the success of all these actions is effective communication skills. If Su Ling does not feel that she has the skills to engage in these kinds of conversations, she should seek someone who has greater skills. It would also be helpful if she could make herself aware of the most current philosophical thinking on the subject of discontinuing treatment so that she can call upon this knowledge in presenting her argument.

Engaging in Ethical Action
It is probable that none of the suggestions we have made seem surprising to you. Most nurses would be able to create this same list of possible actions. The difficulty is that many will not take the actions they know they should take. It is well known that there is often a gap between what people know they should do and what they actually do. In situations like this, it is more common for nurses to complain to other nurses about the situation than to address it directly. This is probably because most people dislike conflict, and many do not have the moral courage to put themselves at risk of being criticized by their colleagues. However, it is part of a nurse's professional responsibility to work to ensure that the patient's best interests are served. Certainly the CNA Code of Ethics for Registered Nurses would support the nurses in questioning the assault on Mrs. Lee's dignity. Nurses have not only the right but also the obligation to make themselves heard. Bringing up the topic might result in some tension, but if sensitively handled it is more likely to relieve it.

Reflecting on and Reviewing the Ethical Action
Once the action is taken, it is necessary to evaluate its effectiveness. In this case, it is difficult to predict whether simply engaging in discussion would alter the situation. However, if everyone feels heard, it is likely that some of the tension will diminish. Su Ling should examine her approach to the situation, what worked and what didn't, and think about how she might improve her approach in future. This is the essence of ethical reflection and action.

CHAPTER SUMMARY

In this chapter we explored the fourth value in the CNA Code of Ethics for Registered Nurses: *preserving dignity*. To uncover the ethical elements of that value, we began our discussion with a presentation of definitions and moved on to a variety of influences on our thinking about dignity. We considered the impact of law, theology, and philosophy, and then turned to a discussion of relational ethics. The discussion revealed that dignity has different meanings, depending on one's point of view. Dignity is unique to individual persons. What one person might consider necessary to maintaining dignity, another person might see as unimportant. This has implications for nursing care delivery in particular and health care management in general.

Next we focused on nursing practice and dignity. First prejudice on how we think about patients and considered some of the factors that can change individual behaviour and make people appear undignified. Some of the ways in which nurses can contribute to loss of dignity and how they can help restore dignity were presented. We then turned to some specific dignity-related aspects of health care, including privacy, boundaries, and dignity in death and dying. We pointed out that dignity can and should be explored as both an other-regarding and a self-regarding value. That is, nurses must have respect for the dignity of others and for their own dignity. We turned next to systems issues and described some of the ways in which the system itself can contribute to erosion of a patient's dignity. Finally we presented two case studies in which dignity had a central role and analyzed them using the Framework for Ethical Decision Making.

Questions for Reflection

1. Consider your own ideas about dignity. What needs to happen in a situation for dignity to be present?
2. Is dignity something that is owed to us by virtue of our humanity? What do you think all nurses need to consider about dignity when they are caring for any patient?
3. What ethical issues regarding dignity have you encountered?
4. What is your belief about the claim that people have a *right* to be treated with respect?
5. What does the claim in the CNA Code of Ethics for Registered Nurses to "respect patients" mean to you? Can you think of situations in your clinical practice where respect for patients was not upheld? How did you respond?

Exercises

1. Working in small groups, discuss critically the right to dignity, in particular dying with dignity. What different meanings about death with dignity emerge? Discuss some ethical issues that might arise in the notion of death with dignity.
2. In small groups, consider the value of dignity and respect for persons from a relational perspective. How is this value similar to or different from respect for autonomy?

Research Activities

1. Working in a group of three, find three articles on dignity in the research databases. Each article should be in a different area of practice. Examine the articles for commonalities and differences in how dignity is presented and actions nurses should take to preserve dignity. Present your findings to your classmates.

2. In your clinical area, speak to three practising nurses. Ask them to describe the biggest challenges to preserving patient dignity in that practice area, and what actions they take to ensure that dignity is protected. Compare your findings with those of others in your class.

Key Terms

ageism

boundaries

depersonalization

dignity

dying with dignity

human rights

integrity

privacy

sense of self-worth

sentient

subjective dignity

subjects

universal dignity

voluntary euthanasia

vulnerability

worth

References

Canadian Nurses Association, (2008). *Code of ethics for registered nurses* (Centennial ed.). Ottawa: Author.

College and Association of Registered Nurses of Alberta (2005). *Professional boundaries: A discussion guide and teaching tool.* Edmonton, AB: Author

De Prospero Rogers, P., & Bocchino, N. (1999). Restraint-free care: Is it possible: Can we make physical restraint a last resort in acute care? *American Journal of Nursing*, 99(10), 26–34.

Frank, A. (2004). Dignity, dialogue, and care. *Journal of Palliative Care*, 20(3), 207–211.

Gadow, S. (1999). Relational narrative: The postmodern turn in nursing ethics. *Scholarly Inquiry for Nursing Practice: An International Journal*, 13(1), 57–70.

Hayry, M. (2004). Another look at dignity. *Cambridge Quarterly of Health Care Ethics*, 13, 7–14.

Kant, I. (1994). The metaphysical principles of virtue. In *Ethical philosophy* (Transl. J. W. Ellington, 2nd ed.). Indianapolis, IN: Hackett Inc.

Kozub, M., & Skidmore, R. (2001). Least to most restrictive interventions: A continuum for mental health facilities. *Journal of Psychosocial Nursing*, 39(3), 32–38.

Legislative Assembly of Ontario (2001). Bill 85: An Act to minimize the use of restraints on patients in hospital and on patients of facilities. In *Statutes of Ontario, 2nd session* (Chapter 16). Toronto: Author.

Merriam-Webster on-line. Retrieved July 14, 2007, from www.m-w.com.

Morse, J. M. (1991). The structure and function of gift giving in the patient-nurse relationship. *Western Journal of Nursing Research*, 13, 597–615.

Oberle, K. (1995). Measuring nurses' moral reasoning. *Nursing Ethics*, 4, 303–313.

Oberle, K., & Davies, B. (1993). An exploration of nursing disillusionment. *Canadian Journal of Nursing Research, 25*, 67–73.

Oberle, K., & Hughes, D. (2001). Doctors' and nurses' perceptions of end–of-life decisions. *Journal of Advanced Nursing, 33*, 707–715.

Pullman, D. (2004). Death, dignity, and moral nonsense. *Journal of Palliative Care, 20*(3), 171-178.

Smith, N. H., Timms, J., Parker, V. G., Reimels, E. M., & Hamilin, A. (2003). The impact of education on the use of physical restraints in the acute care setting. *Journal of Continuing Education in Nursing, 34*(1), 26–33.

State of Oregon (1997). *Death with Dignity Act*. Retrieved July 14, 2007, from www.ohd.hr.state.or.us/chs/pas/pas.cfm, July 14, 2007.

Sullivan-Marx, E. M. (2001). Achieving restraint-free care of acutely confused older adults. *Journal of Gerontological Nursing, 27*(4), 56–61.

UNESCO (1997). *Universal declaration on the human genome and human rights*. Retrieved April 18, 2006, from http://portal.unesco.org/en/ev.php-URL_ID=13177&URL_DO=DO_TOPIC&URL_SECTION=201.html.

Walker, M. U. (1993). Keeping moral space open. *Hastings Center Report, 23*(2), 33–40.

Webster. (1991). *The New Lexicon Webster's Dictionary of the English Language*. New York: Lexicon Publications Inc.

Suggested Readings

Anderberg, P., Lepp, M., Berglund, A., & Segesten, K. (2007). Preserving dignity in older adults: A concept analysis. *Journal of Advanced Nursing, 59*(6), 635–643.

Chocinov, H. (2006). Dying dignity and new horizons in palliative end-of-life care. *CA: A Journal for Clinicians, 56*, 84–103.

Gallager, A. (2004). Dignity and respect for dignity-two key health professional values: Implications for nursing practice. *Nursing Ethics, 11*(6), 587–599.

McClement, S., Chochinov, H. M., Hack, T., Hassard, T., Kristjanson, L. J., & Harlos, M. (2007). Dignity therapy: Family member perspectives. *Journal of Palliative Medicine, 10*(5), 1076–1082.

Statman, D. (2000). Humiliation, dignity, and self-respect. *Philosophical Psychology, 13*(4), 523–540.

Zhang, Q. (2000). The idea of human dignity in classical Chinese philosophy: A reconstruction of Confucianism. *Journal of Chinese Philosophy, 27*(3), 299.

Chapter 8
Value 5: Maintaining Privacy and Confidentiality

I . . . will hold in confidence all personal matters committed to my knowledge in the practice of my calling.

Florence Nightingale Pledge

Chapter Outline

Confidentiality as a Lived Value

Chapter Summary

Learning Objectives

After reading this chapter, you should be able to:

- describe the fifth primary value in the CNA Code of Ethics for Registered Nurses: *Maintaining privacy and confidentiality*

- discuss the concepts of confidentiality, confidential information, privacy, and respect for persons.

- discuss the history and interpretation of confidentiality in ethics

- discuss confidentiality and the law, including privacy law

- discuss personal health information and who can access it

- discuss relational nursing ethics and confidentiality

- discuss situations where confidentiality may be breached

- discuss ways in which the current structure of the health care system can challenge nurses' ability to maintain confidentiality, and when it is appropriate to breach confidentiality

- apply the Framework for Ethical Decision Making to a clinical problem related to confidentiality

Jane's caseload consists of a full spectrum of acute, palliative, and chronic care patients. Her practice situations present complex and challenging issues of confidentiality that emerge on a regular basis. As a home care nurse, Jane works autonomously. She must have excellent communication skills as she is exposed to a variety of situations that involve confidentiality and privacy concerns. Jane needs to communicate effectively with co-workers and other stakeholders through face-to-face contact, voice-mail, fax, telephone, and health records that she leaves in the patients' homes.

Imagine that you are following Jane as she makes her rounds. Today she begins her day by answering telephone calls. One is from the niece of Mrs. Parker, who is dying at home. She wants an update on her aunt's condition. Jane apologizes and tells her that she can only give information to Sally, the patient's daughter, as Mrs. Parker has asked that no one else be told. She suggests that the niece contact Mrs. Parker or her daughter directly.

Next, Jane travels to a seniors' home. Riding in the elevator with some of the residents, she is often asked whom she is visiting and why. She has learned just to smile and say, "You know that's top secret!" Jane visits Mr. Baird, a 78-year-old patient with a leg ulcer that she is monitoring. She finds him in the sun room, together with another resident who has several family visitors present. Dr. Johns enters the room and introduces himself to Mr. Baird. Without asking anyone to leave the room, Dr. Johns begins to discuss Mr. Baird's medical history, which includes a blood disorder that may require a brief hospitalization for a blood transfusion. Dr. Johns asks Mr. Baird whether he will accept the transfusion, saying, "I understand you are a Jehovah's Witness." Jane, surprised by this practice, interrupts Dr. Johns to ask if she can speak with him outside the room. There she voices her displeasure about his disclosing private patient information in front of others.

Jane also visits Bill, a 72-year-old client who has just returned home after a month-long hospitalization following cardiac bypass surgery. Bill's recovery from surgery was complicated by compromised pulmonary function caused by a 50-year history of cigarette smoking. When Jane arrives, Bill is smoking. He is obviously embarrassed and apologizes for his habit, but in the same breath he asks Jane not to reveal his smoking to his daughter who will be visiting shortly. Politely, Jane opens the conversation surrounding Bill's decision to continue smoking. She also offers information on smoking cessation resources and leaves it at that. When Bill's daughter arrives, Jane does not mention or address the smoking issue.

Lastly, Jane visits a Japanese woman requiring palliative care, which is given by her husband, mother, and 14-year-old daughter. Jane has known this family for only a few weeks. During the first visit it was established that the patient was not to be informed of her diagnosis, as this would diminish hope and cause further suffering for both the patient and her caregivers. Jane, aware of their cultural beliefs, respects the family's wishes and carries out her assessments and physical care to the best of her abilities. As Jane leaves the home a neighbour, who happens to be an acquaintance of Jane's, approaches her. The neighbour is curious in a concerned way as to why Jane is visiting this couple so frequently. Jane smiles politely and replies, "They need my help, and out of respect for privacy that's all I can really say."

As you can see, Jane's practice is steeped in situations where issues of privacy and confidentiality are prominent, partly because of the close relationships she forms with patients, and partly because of her visibility in the community. Jane enters and adapts to many unique patient-controlled environments. In each visit, she must develop trusting and respectful relationships with individuals to whom she gives care. She avoids discussing patients outside the clinical setting, telling friends or family about them, or discussing them in the elevator with other care providers, as all these actions violate professional nurse-patient confidentiality.

The kinds of issues described above are very common in nursing, and would be familiar to most practising nurses. They illustrate the topic of this chapter, which is the fifth value of the CNA Code of Ethics for Registered Nurses: *Maintaining privacy and confidentiality*. Direct nursing practice is just one of many situations in which nurses face issues related to confidentiality and privacy. Later in this chapter, we will highlight other areas where confidentiality is important, such as public policy, medical, nursing, or other research involving human subjects, and legal concerns. Broader policy issues exist not just for the profession of nursing but also for society as a whole, suggesting the need for greater public education and dialogue. The Canadian Nursing Association has a position paper (2001) on privacy of health information that raises the issues in a direct way. The position paper states that "Individuals have the right to privacy with respect to their personal health information." However, the Canadian Nurses Association recognizes that "health information is necessary to improve population health status and to improve the effectiveness and efficiency of the health care system" (CNA, 2001, p. 1).

Confidentiality has always been of concern to nurses, but in recent years it has been given even more emphasis. Our understandings of confidentiality have been brought to a heightened awareness with the growth of technology and increasing complexity of health care environments and services. Technology has made rapid transfer of information much easier. While this can be an advantage in care, it also raises many concerns about protection of personal information.

In this chapter we explore various aspects of the concept of confidentiality in relation to health care information in many settings. We consider the nature of confidentiality, privacy, informational privacy, and security. We present the history and interpretation of confidentiality in ethics and the law to show the complexity of the concept in today's health care system and the need for evolving legal perspectives to protect our privacy rights as individuals. After considering confidentiality in the abstract, we move to nursing practice and attempt to uncover the value of confidentiality as it exists in the nurse-patient relationship. Finally, we describe some moral implications of confidentiality in nursing, as presented in two case studies.

THE FIFTH PRIMARY VALUE: MAINTAINING PRIVACY AND CONFIDENTIALITY

Confidential information is "intimate or private knowledge" (Merriam-Webster on-line) protected under a duty of **confidentiality**, which can be summarized as the duty of someone (generally a professional) who has received information in trust to protect that information, disclosing it to others only with permission or when rules or laws authorize its disclosure. Confidential information may come directly from the patient, or may be received through written documents, electronic data, or even from a third party. A common rule frequently noted in policy is that all knowledge is considered confidential unless otherwise stated by the patient.

Often the notion of confidential information is discussed within the framework of the legal right to privacy. In simple terms, privacy is about people, while confidentiality is about duty to protect information. We defined privacy in Chapter 7 as a person's right to control the intrusion of others into his or her life. In other words it concerns what information a health care provider can have. A patient's right to privacy means that she or he has the right to disclose details of her or his life, illness, feelings, finances, and family interactions, or *not* to disclose them. Confidentiality is about what a nurse does with the information he or she is given. When patients give their personal information to a nurse, they trust that the nurse will disclose it only to appropriate members of the health care team. Maintaining patient confidentiality is an important element of trust, and, as such, is a moral obligation of nurses. The ultimate value of keeping confidences and building trust is related to the notion of human dignity. To decrease trust is to cause harm. Confidentiality serves as a cornerstone of a solid foundation on which trust must be built. Privacy and confidentiality are often used interchangeably, although they do not have the same meaning. (For example, privacy legislation is really about confidentiality of health information.) In this chapter we will use them interchangeably except when specific differences must be noted.

CONFIDENTIALITY AND ETHICS

Confidentiality is the ethical principle that requires nondisclosure of private or secret information with which one is entrusted. Historically, respect for privacy and confidentiality has figured prominently in the health professions. Evidence of this is found in such sources as the physicians' Hippocratic Oath, nursing's Florence Nightingale Pledge, the ICN (International Council of Nurses) Code of Ethics for Nurses, and the CNA Code of Ethics for Registered Nurses. However, confidentiality is not approached in the same way in all these documents. The Hippocratic Oath, for example, calls for confidentiality only in reference to those things "which ought not to be spoken abroad [i.e., in public]." The Florence Nightingale Pledge (as shown at the beginning of the chapter) seems to require keeping all confidences without exception. The ICN Code of Ethics for Nurses takes a discretionary position and states that while "the nurse holds in confidence personal information," the nurse may also use his or her judgment "in sharing this information" (ICN, 2006, p. 4).

In offering confidentiality as the fifth value in its Code of Ethics for Registered Nurses, the Canadian Nurses Association shows support for maintaining strict confidentiality, with disclosure permitted to other care providers with the patient's permission. The Code also permits breaking confidentiality in order to protect the patient and other innocent parties. The fifth value is stated as, "Nurses recognize the importance of privacy and confidentiality and safeguard personal, family, and community information obtained in the context of a professional relationship" (CNA, 2008, p. 15). The Code acknowledges that the nurse must comply with provincial or federal privacy legislation, which sometimes requires that information be revealed without the patient's consent. It is essential, however, that the nurse work to minimize any harms that might arise from this kind of disclosure. In our discussion we will work through cases that explore the keeping and breaking of confidentiality.

Understanding Confidentiality

For the fifth value, the explanatory or interpretive phrases that help us understand what confidentiality means suggest the importance of individual control, legal rights, informed consent, and advocacy. By **individual control** we mean, in this context, that nurses must respect the person's right to control her or his own body and bodily functions, as well as what personal information is given, and with whom and how it is shared. **Legal rights** are those entitlements, freedoms, or privileges to which the individual is entitled, as described and protected in law (in this case, privacy laws). *Informed consent* has been discussed at length in Chapter 6, and is directly related to permissions patients give for collection and use of information. The concept of *advocacy*, which we defined in Chapter 3 as taking the part of another, speaking for persons who cannot speak for themselves, or intervening to ensure that their views are heard, also has a role in confidentiality. It requires nurses to have knowledge of and respect for policies and safeguards to protect and preserve the patient's confidentiality. It also requires that they contribute to development of policy to safeguard privacy and confidentiality, and that they support patients who wish to have access to and control of their health records. These words and phrases are frequently used in ethical, legal, and philosophical discussions about confidentiality, privacy, and their impact on the health/illness experiences of individuals.

Philosophical Positions on Privacy, Confidentiality, and Autonomy

In ethics there are two main ethical arguments in favour of preserving confidentiality. The first of these is based on the individual's right to control personal information and protect privacy.

The right to privacy and confidentiality flows from autonomy and respect for persons. The ability to maintain privacy in one's life is an expression of autonomy. The capacity to choose what others know about us, particularly intimate personal details, is important because it enables us to maintain dignity and preserve a measure of control over our own lives. Patients have the right to determine the appropriate time and manner in which sensitive information is revealed to family members, friends, and others. To uphold this value, nurses ought to be reluctant to pry into personal details unless there is therapeutic reason for obtaining such information, and should respect personal confidences. When entering into relationships that expose them to sensitive or intimate personal information, nurses must be mindful of the importance of protecting confidentiality, even if the patient has not made a special request to do so.

The second argument is utilitarian and focuses on long-term consequences if confidentiality is breached. If patients suspect that health care providers reveal sensitive and personal information indiscriminately, they may be reluctant to seek care, which could cause them significant harm. On the other hand, having information might be important to protect others from harm. Providing effective care for socially sensitive conditions such as sexually transmitted diseases, HIV/AIDS, mental illness, and end of life situations require heightened caution regarding privacy and confidentiality. Some philosophical arguments have interpreted preserving confidentiality as an **absolute principle**, meaning that it cannot be breached under any circumstances. In other words, confidentiality could be taken as demanding that information taken in a professional-client relationship must always be kept secret, even when its disclosure might serve a greater public good. Utilitarians would refute the notion that the principle of confidentiality is absolute. John Stuart Mill suggested in the nineteenth century that personal freedom may legitimately be constrained when the exercise of freedom puts others at risk. He said,

> The sole end for which mankind are warranted, individually or collectively, in interfering with the liberty of action of any of their number, is self-protection . . . [T]he only purpose for which power can be rightfully exercised over any member of a civilized community, against his will, is to prevent harm to others. (Mill, ed. Robson, 1977, p. 223)

This suggests that, although patients have the right to control when information about them is shared, this right is limited by the obligation not to harm others. When serious harm is threatened, the principle of autonomy (and hence the duty to preserve confidentiality) no longer takes precedence, and disclosure without patients' authorization may be permissible or required. In modern health care ethics we often consider the greater good when thinking about confidentiality. However, it is not always clear from utilitarian arguments what degree of harm makes it permissible to disclose information. For instance, consider Larry, who is terminally ill. His family is not aware of the seriousness of his condition, and he has asked that they not be told. They will be adversely affected by his death, partly because their financial security rests on Larry's skill in handling the family business, so they need to take some proactive steps to ensure that the business remains intact even after his death. A utilitarian might say that there is a need for the family to be informed, as they stand to suffer serious harm if they are not, and Larry is unlikely to be harmed by disclosure. However, our current understandings of privacy contradict this position. The standard in health care today is to accept Larry's right to confidentiality, despite the family's apparent need for the information, because they will not be harmed physically. Economic harm is seldom, if ever, considered as a legitimate reason for breaching confidentiality.

Research Ethics and Confidentiality

The conduct of research with human subjects adds another layer of complexity to maintenance of privacy and confidentiality. The guarantee of confidentiality of data is held sacrosanct in research as a way to ensure respect for persons and to minimize harm. Ethical issues arise for nurses involved in research regardless of whether they are caregivers, research nurses, trial coordinators, or principal investigators.

Nurses observe practices that protect the anonymity of each human subject in research whenever possible. **Anonymity** exists when no one, not even the researcher, can link the subject's identity to his or her data. For example, if questionnaires were mailed out to home care patients and were returned without any identifying information on them, then the responses would be anonymous. When anonymity is not possible, researchers must implement other confidentiality procedures. Confidentiality in this case means that the researcher knows the identity of the research participant, but does not reveal participants' names or any links between the participant and the data. Confidentiality measures should be taken during recruitment, documentation of informed consent, data collection, data coding, and analysis and reporting of results. The Tri-Council Policy Statement or TCPS (Government of Canada, 2006), which is the Canadian document that regulates the conduct of research, outlines the ways in which confidentiality should be protected in research. As well, the Canadian Nurses Association (2001) details nursing considerations in relation to research subjects' confidentiality. Important points include the need to protect research participants' identity, to observe all relevant privacy and confidentiality laws, and to inform participants exactly how their personal information will be used. If the law requires certain information to be revealed, participants must be informed of that before they give consent. For example, the law requires that any instance of child abuse be reported, so a researcher who learns about child abuse while collecting data is legally obligated to report it. Similarly, if participants are to be involved in group interviews it is important to let them know that their confidentiality cannot be guaranteed, because other members of the group might not keep information confidential.

Researchers may breach confidentiality unwittingly. For example, in published research reports, participants' direct quotations might offer subtle cues that would permit others to identify individual study participants. Another sensitive issue is the distinction between what participants are willing to share as "public" (to be reported) and what is considered "private" (not to be reported), as it unfolds during conversations and observations in the course of data collection. Participants may reveal to the researcher intimate details that they would have never imagined would be disclosed. Thus it is easy to see how breaches of confidentiality could be the unintended result of research reports. Any nurse who is conducting research or participating in data collection as a research assistant must observe professional standards of confidentiality, and must take the participants' wishes and understandings into account.

CONFIDENTIALITY AND THE LAW

The confidentiality of patient information is prescribed in law. The rapid growth of technology over the last decade has increased capacity to collect, analyze, disseminate, and use information to enhance the quality of health care and the efficiency of the health care system. Computerization, however, raises major legal concerns related to the confidentiality of health records because of the potential for unauthorized access and/or data sharing and for uncontrolled use of patients' personal information (Canadian Nurses Protective Society [CNPS], 2005). Although using computers is the norm in many hospitals, health care centres, and physicians' offices, this technology means nurses must be even more vigilant in protecting the patient's or client's right to privacy of health information.

What Are Nurses' Professional and Legal Obligations?

We have made the point that nurses have an ethical and legal obligation to protect the confidentiality of patients' personal information. We have already discussed the ethical obligations outlined in the CNA Code of Ethics for Registered Nurses. Privacy is a right underpinning health care in Canada. This right is addressed in legislation and related publications produced by organizations such as the Canadian Health Record Association and the Canadian Council on Health Services Accreditation (CNPS, 2005).

Nurses must understand the personal **privacy rights** of their patients concerning health information. These include legislated rights to provide or withhold consent with respect to the collection, use, disclosure, or accessibility of personal health information; to access one's own information; and to have personal information recorded as accurately as possible (CNA, 2001).

Privacy Legislation

There have been many key documents in the development and evolution of public policy concerning informational privacy. In 1986 the Canadian Standards Association developed the *Model Guide for the Protection of Personal Information*. This document stemmed from principles of "fair information practices" that significantly influenced policy development in Canada and elsewhere. Recently, new privacy legislation has been introduced at both the federal and provincial levels to protect the personal information of Canadians. The *Personal Information and Protection of Electronic Documents Act* (PIPEDA) was ratified in January 2001. This federal Act governs private sector organizations (such as banks, telecommunications, cable television networks, telephone companies, shipping, railways, and air carriers) in the collection, use, and disclosure of personal information (CNPS, 2006). The intent of this legislation is to protect an individual's privacy by setting basic rules on how businesses compile and share both paper and electronic records. It applies in all provinces and territories unless they have introduced substantially similar privacy legislation. For instance, Alberta and British Columbia have both introduced legislation in the form of a *Personal Information Protection* Act (PIPA) (Office of the Privacy Commissioner of Canada, 2006). These provincial Acts have been declared substantially similar to PIPEDA. In addition, some provinces have developed new health information legislation that provides more guidance for dealing with computerized documents and telecommunication systems in the health care sector. Alberta's *Health Information Act* and Manitoba's *The Personal Health Information Act* are two examples. With such laws in place, PIPEDA will have less direct impact. However, it still applies in some cases. At the very least, PIPEDA requires making patients aware of their privacy rights. That includes providing them with an opportunity to know what personal information is being collected for what purpose, and how it will be used, disclosed, and protected (CNPS, 2006). They must be told how they can seek access to and, if necessary, correct their personal health information, and they must also have an opportunity to discuss concerns about how their information is handled. Under each privacy law, a Commissioner oversees the application of the statute and investigates disputes between individuals and organizations.

How Does Privacy Legislation Apply to Nursing?

The Canadian Nurses Association believes that an individual's right to privacy is paramount (CNA, 2001). To meet the requirements of the new legislation, organizations including hospitals are required to establish a privacy policy and rules to achieve privacy protection. Safeguards include:

- limiting the categories of personal information or the types of files that may be accessed by various employees or groups of employees
- creating security systems to restrict access to authorized personnel only
- creating systems to track access and disclosure of personal information
- establishing protocols to approve and record "non-routine" access and external requests for information
- establishing security measures to protect personal information when it is copied or transmitted electronically or by facsimile
- developing standards for maintaining accuracy of information and deleting information when it is no longer required (CNPS, 2006)

The primary legal consideration with respect to any information that a nurse obtains from a patient during the course of her or his professional relationship is that such information is confidential and may not be disclosed to anyone who has no valid purpose for requesting it. There are exceptions to this rule in both common law and law as provided by statute. But in many provinces, if an unauthorized person accesses a patient's health record or if health information is inappropriately released, a breach of patient's privacy rights may result in legal liability for the custodian of the records and the individuals involved in the incident. Because of that risk it is important for all nurses, health care professionals, and employees to be aware of current developments in, and comply with the legislated requirements of Canadian privacy law. To meet the need for informing patients of their rights, health care agencies have developed brochures and pamphlets, posted notices, and web sites. They also encourage open discussion with health care professionals regarding what will and will not be shared.

What is "Personal Information" and What Information is Confidential?

Even if they are not involved in the development of policies within the organization where they work, nurses must be aware of the legislative requirements and their employers' privacy policies so that they can comply with ethical and legal obligations to protect patients' confidentiality. Knowledge of and compliance with these requirements begins by knowing *what* information is confidential. This notion is often confusing to nurses and may be the primary reason that information is innocently or perhaps ignorantly disclosed. The *Personal Information Protection Acts* (PIPA) in British Columbia and Alberta define personal information as "information about an identifiable individual which includes any factual or subjective information, recorded or not, about that individual" (Office of the Privacy Commissioner, 2004, Key definition 1). **Identifiable data** means data that would provide either access to further information or information about the individual's life or health circumstances. This could include the patient's name, opinions about the patient, his or her birth date, income, physical description, medical history, gender, religion, address, political affiliations and beliefs, education, employment, and visual images such as photographs or videotape in which individuals may be identified. Failure to protect this information can lead to serious repercussions.

Who May Access Personal Information?

Basically, every piece of data recorded and observed by a health care professional would fit into the category of "individually identifiable data." It is the nurse's responsibility to consider with whom these data may be ethically and legally shared. Ethically, as we discussed earlier, the nurse begins with informing patients of their privacy rights and obtaining their consent to use and disclose their heath information for care and treatment. PIPEDA uses the term "circle of care" to describe this practice. This expression includes the individuals and activities related to the care and treatment of a patient. Thus, it covers the health care providers who deliver care and services for the primary therapeutic benefit of the patient. It also covers related activities such as laboratory work and professional or case consultation with other health care professionals. The standard for determining whether patient information can be disclosed is commonly referred to as "disclose only on a need-to-know basis."

What are the Exceptions to Confidentiality?

In nursing as well as other health professions there may be exceptions to the duty of confidentiality. These exceptions might include situations where the welfare of the patient is at stake or where the welfare of other parties is seriously jeopardized. Additionally, as mentioned above, the duty to breach confidentiality may be required by law. Yeo and Moorehouse (1996) describe breaches of confidentiality as deliberate or inadvertent and unintentional. **Deliberate** breach is when health care professionals deliberately decide to subordinate confidentiality to some other good or value; for example, when it comes into the duty to protect harm. An **inadvertent** or **unintentional breach** occurs when care providers do not realize that they are engaging in practices that might result in improper disclosure, for example, when a conversation among nurses and physicians is overheard in an elevator.

When considering to whom information should be disclosed, a nurse should ask whether another health care provider can do her or his job safely and knowledgeably without this information. If the answer to that question is yes, then the information should not be disclosed. For example, if a student nurse not normally assigned to an HIV-positive tuberculosis patient was asked to give eye drops and change his eye patch while another nurse was at coffee, the student would not need to know the patient's HIV status, as the student would normally be using standard practice for blood and body fluids. Precautions needed when entering the patient's room might be posted outside the room to protect against transfer of airborne pathogens. The student would thus not need to know the diagnosis of tuberculosis for the tasks she or he was performing.

When we consider who should access personal information, the use of signs also raises questions and can act as a threat to maintaining confidentiality. Although the use of precaution signs can prevent harm either to the patient or others, each sign discloses a clue to the patient's health or personal circumstances. For example, "fall precautions" can imply that the patient is cognitively impaired or that she has motor deficiencies. Similarly, signs proclaiming such things as "needs assistance with toileting" or "feed soft foods only" can give important clues to an individual's abilities for daily living. Some facilities use information on wristbands that is not readily identifiable to the public's eye, or coloured dots above the bed. The latter, however, have substantial potential for error, if not all health care providers are aware of hospital signage protocol. There is a significant need for improvement in communicating and/or protecting patient information.

Another area of concern is disclosure of health care information to other disciplines. For example, a school nurse might wonder about such things as whether the fact that an elementary school student has asthma should be revealed to the student's teacher, or whether a social worker should be told that a woman with young children is HIV-positive. In the first case, the student could be harmed if information was not disclosed; in the second, the social worker might be harmed. In both cases, it might be important for the individual's care to have the information disclosed, but the CNA Code of Ethics for Registered Nurses is quite clear that "Nurses respect the right of people to have control over the collection, use, access, and disclosure of their personal information" (CNA, 2008, p. 15). Essentially, the nurse must use ethical/professional judgment, but if he or she is uncertain about what should be disclosed, then the organization's policies, other colleagues, and/or the privacy officer should be consulted for advice.

RELATIONAL ETHICS AND CONFIDENTIALITY

Thus far we have discussed confidentiality in terms of ethical principles and the law. We will now turn to what confidentiality and privacy mean for nurses in everyday practice. We will discuss how the value of confidentiality is upheld in the relational practices of nurses, and how confidentiality practices have (or have not) changed over the last decade.

The emphasis placed on confidentiality in health care is relatively recent. Formerly, it was assumed that health care providers would use personal information as they wished, and patients expected to have little say in the process. There were few formal documents protecting confidentiality, and it was believed that professional values would prevent care providers from revealing information that might harm an individual. Now, documents abound. There are policies and laws devoted to the subject. It is almost assumed that without such laws, personal information will be revealed without due care and attention. Of course, nurses do not protect confidentiality because they are told to by written documents, but because of their beliefs about human dignity and personal respect. However, these beliefs can be hidden in the legal maze of privacy rights and individual freedoms.

The fundamental nature of a relational ethic lies in commitment to another and a sense of responsibility toward her or him. The health care encounter involves a particular kind of relationship that connects strangers together in meaningful ways (Bergum & Dossetor, 2005). Nurses' relationships with patients are fiduciary in nature, that is to say, they are based on trust. The information that patients share with nurses in this relationship is often deep, meaningful, and intensely private. Nurses must be committed to upholding confidentiality as they delve deeper into intimate aspects of their patients' lives. Information gained in this context must not be disclosed except as absolutely necessary for care and treatment.

In Chapter 2 we described relational ethics as having characteristics of engagement. When a nurse-patient relationship is engaged, the patient comes to it with a willingness to discuss very personal information related to health care needs. By keeping patients' information private, nurses engender trust and pave the way toward more effective care. If patients cannot trust nurses to keep their information confidential, they may be reluctant to share it or decline to participate in certain therapies. Confidential information can be used to help, but it also has the potential to bring harm. In a trusting relationship, confidentiality is grounded in respect for persons. This can become a particular issue for nurses because of the privileged intimacy inherent in the nurse-patient relationship. This privilege leads to a duty of fidelity: loyalty to one's vows and promises, or, in other words, promise keeping.

Fidelity is a key component of all nursing actions surrounding confidentiality, but this prompts one to ask: What ought nurses to promise patients regarding confidentiality? Clearly, the nurse is expected to keep information in health records confidential. Sometimes disclosure is required by law; for example, if a nurse is making a home visit and witnesses child abuse, she is obligated to report it. There are similar legal requirements around elder abuse. When the nurse encounters such situations, the duty to disclose must be shared with the patient. That is, the nurse must inform the patient about what actions will be taken. If a patient's care were to become a subject of court action, the patient's chart and other documents would become part of the legal proceedings, and as such would be subject to disclosure. The nurse testifying in court would be expected to answer truthfully.

In some situations the nurse's duty might not be so obvious. If the home care nurse observes breaches of social policy, it might be difficult to determine what ought to be done. For instance, consider a single mother who is receiving welfare payments. There are strict limitations on how much she is permitted to work for pay, and if she earns more than the limit her welfare payments will be cut off. If a nurse making a home visit suspected that the mother was working and accepting welfare, ought the nurse to report it? The CNA Code of Ethics for Registered Nurses says little about the subject other than to indicate that disclosure is permissible if there is a substantial risk of harm. This seems to suggest that nurses use their judgment in determining if the risk is substantial, but does not make clear whether the harm is to another, or just to the patient. Nonetheless, it seems clear that in the above scenario the nurse not disclose the information, as there does not appear to be a risk of serious harm. Failure to keep the information confidential could jeopardize the nurse-patient relationship and result in the nurse being denied future access to the home. This could lead to harm for the mother and/or her children. Thus it would seem logical that this information must be kept confidential. It is permissible, according to the Code, to share personal information outside the health care team if the individual consents. That is, the nurse would have to ask the patient, and could release the information if consent were granted.

Another issue related to the nurse's fiduciary obligation of confidentiality arises because of the physical environments in which health care is often given. It may be impossible to protect a patient's confidentiality, despite our best efforts. The physical structures of health care institutions are not always conducive to ensuring privacy. Overcrowding moves patients closer together, flimsy curtains separate patient beds, and large common areas where treatment occurs are open to the eyes and ears of all in the vicinity. When environments are relatively open, nurses can easily breach privacy and confidentiality through carelessness, for example, by leaving charts open on desks or computer stations displaying patient information unattended. Another common transgression of confidentiality is careless conversation among nurses that occurs in the proximity of other patients. It is not uncommon for groups of health care professionals to gather at a patient's bedside and discuss private health information that other patients in the room can hear. Conversations in public places such as cafeterias and elevators are another source of confidentiality breaches. Often one can pick up significant information about patients by overhearing nurses' coffee chat.

To this point we have been discussing privacy of information, but there is also an issue of bodily privacy that must be considered. This was discussed briefly in the previous chapter when we were considering indignities related to disclosure about bodily functions and exposure. Individuals are entitled to **bodily privacy**, the right to control how much of their body is exposed to others' sight. The body as the focus for concerns about privacy is certainly encountered in the everyday routines of nursing. In fact, it is often joked that patients must give up any notions of privacy or modesty when they enter hospital. There is a common perception among health care providers and patients alike that privacy is less important than the convenience of care providers and the efficiency of treatment. For instance, gowns that are open in the back are designed to make changes easier, but they do nothing to protect modesty, especially if the patient is ambulatory. Too often patients are exposed in ways that are acutely embarrassing to them. A frequent example is when a nurse walks unannounced into a patient room without regard for what the patient might be doing, such as getting dressed or sitting on the toilet. In long-term care institutions, patients are often stripped and put into a lift to be hoisted into a bathtub, without any consideration of who might be in the room, or whether doors are closed and curtains drawn. Nurses have a strong obligation to protect bodily privacy. They may be required to intervene to ensure that the patient is not subjected to such exposure, and that dignity is maintained. As part of their fiduciary relationship with patients, they must act as advocates to be sure that patients are kept covered to the extent possible. They must not make assumptions about how the patient might feel about having his or her body exposed, and to whom.

Nurses must use professional judgment when providing care that might expose the body. For the most part, they should assume that patients want their privacy to be protected, and provide privacy to the extent possible whenever giving care. They should warn patients before they begin procedures that might expose them, and ask for permission to proceed. If patients are comfortable with having family members present, then there is usually no need to ask them to leave. However, if the patient is unable to express a preference, the nurse must assume a desire for privacy and have others leave the room. All of these considerations are taught to students in nursing fundamentals classes, and are considered part of basic care. It is surprising, then, that they are so often neglected in the institutional setting. It is essential that nurses remember that providing bodily privacy is not just a "nice thing" but a moral obligation, and an expression of the value of confidentiality outlined in the CNA Code of Ethics for Registered Nurses.

Safeguarding confidentiality and privacy is our ethical and legal obligation as nurses. At the same time, the reality of the world in which a nurse practices raises troubling confidentiality concerns. For example, on many occasions during a shift a nurse might be put in the awkward position of being asked for information by a patient's families and friends. It is not always easy to know to whom you are to give information, particularly if you cannot ask the patient. It is good practice to ask the family to name a spokesperson with whom staff can communicate. That way they will know who is permitted to have information and who is not. Staff can also refer anyone with enquiries to the spokesperson.

On a more personal level, consider going to another unit to check how a friend is doing after surgery. On the surface this seems harmless, but in fact it is a potential breach of confidentiality. Staff might be more likely to give you information that is confidential because you are a nurse. Think also about how often you have thrown identifiable personal information into the garbage in a patient's room or at the nursing station. Your care notes with the patient's name and your recordings for the day would be an example. When disposing of such material, you must ask yourself whether you have compromised the patient's confidentiality.

SAFEGUARDING CONFIDENTIALITY IN THE HEALTH CARE TEAM

The CNA Code of Ethics for Registered Nurses states that "Nurses intervene if others inappropriately access or disclose personal or health information of persons receiving care" (CNA, 2008, p. 16). The fact that this is included in the Code implies that the problem happens fairly often. It is sometimes difficult to uphold this value, because it requires the nurse to be something of a "guardian" of confidential information. This can involve simply reminding others that their conversations can be overheard or that they have left confidential information out in public view. Consider two situations. The first is a doctor's office, where patients sitting in a waiting room can often learn far more about other patients than they should. Nurses and receptionists need to be made aware that their telephone conversations and discussions with patients about presenting problems can be overheard. The second is when physicians discuss a difficult case in an intensive care unit and disclose a great deal that is heard by family and friends visiting other patients. They need to be reminded to hold their conversations somewhere more private.

Challenging others on their behaviour takes great moral courage. The first course of action for the nurse observing breaches of confidentiality is to speak directly to the offending colleague. If that person repeatedly makes private information public, even inadvertently, and does not change behaviour when reminded, the colleague's supervisor will have to be notified. This is a difficult thing to do. The person guilty of the ethical breach will almost certainly be angry and upset when criticized. No one likes to think of himself or herself as being unethical, and to have unethical behaviour identified by a peer is particularly upsetting. If the colleague is someone higher in the institutional hierarchy, such as a physician, the situation can become particularly unpleasant. Individuals who are accustomed to being in positions of relative power may react with anger and defensiveness when questioned by a nurse. Nonetheless, it is unacceptable to ignore the problem simply because it is difficult. The challenge for the nurse is to call attention to the problem as sensitively as possible.

ADVANCED TECHNOLOGY AND PRIVACY CONCERNS

Nurses work in an increasingly information-intensive environment. A recent development with important practice implications is the **Electronic Health Record** (EHR). A definition by the Federal/Provincial/Territorial Advisory Committee on Health Information Structure (2001) that best summarizes the intent of EHRs is:

> A longitudinal collection of personal information of a single individual entered or accepted by health care providers, who have been authorized by the individual as a tool in the provision of health care services. The individual has access to the record and can request changes to its content. The transmission and storage of the record is under strict security.

You can sense from this definition the complexity of issues involving EHRs. Ideally electronic health records should enable nurses and other health care professionals to plan more effectively, deliver higher quality care, and better monitor the care provided. EHRs should also supply information to support research to improve knowledge of nursing practice. Because they are relatively new, there has been little research as to their effectiveness in meeting the objectives outlined. Nahm and Poston (2000) report that nurse and patient satisfaction with EHRs is mixed. Nurses identified a number of considerations in adapting to EHRs, such as time required for charting; time for acquiring appropriate skills and knowledge; quality of documentation; change in care, charting, and privacy related to the use of bedside terminals; technological difficulties related to "viruses" and "worms"; and potential impact on quality of patient care.

The benefit of wide and simultaneous availability of EHRs certainly results in a potential threat to privacy of health records. Consumers and health care providers alike are concerned about how to maintain the privacy, security, and confidentiality of the EHR. National, provincial, and territorial policies and standards are currently being formulated, and nurses have the opportunity to participate in the evolution of these standards (CNA, 2001). The challenge is to balance protecting the privacy of the individual with necessary sharing of information among health care providers. The Canadian Nurses Association believes that there are opportunities within our national health care system to develop national standards by using a consensus approach and involving all stakeholders. Nurses have the opportunity to participate at all levels. Questions that nurses might consider include: Who decides which health care providers have access to information about patients? Should the patient have a role in determining which health care providers are entitled to access? Should there be a mechanism to ensure informed consent around access? What mechanisms should be designed for the detection and sanction of access violations, and who should perform such monitoring? Answers to these questions have ethical and legal implications and, as such, should be addressed before the health care system adopts EHRs as a primary means of record keeping (Care et al., 2003).

APPROPRIATE DISCLOSURE OF INFORMATION

We have already identified many of the confusions that surround the duty of confidentiality and the specifics of what is confidential information or who has rightful control over it. There may also be confusion about information sharing and patient authorization.

The moral basis of the duty of confidentiality is not always clear. Let us consider some general reasons that might justify violating the principle of confidentiality. It is possible that the duty of confidentiality may conflict with the patient's safety. For example, if a patient were severely depressed and threatening suicide, there would be just cause for the nurse to involve a third party (the court) in order to commit the patient to care. That is, when the nurse believes that maintaining confidentiality would put the patient at risk of considerable harm, it might be justifiable to disclose information. This is not meant to imply, however, that nurses can reveal information whenever they believe there is a potential harm. In order to avoid paternalism they must use careful clinical judgment in making such assessments. Unfortunately, the degree of risk that warrants disclosure is far from clear. Consider Mr. Hagen, who is illiterate. He has revealed this information to the nurse and asked her to keep it confidential. The care team has been giving him important discharge information in the form of written brochures and instructions. The nurse realizes that his inability to read these written materials might put his health in jeopardy. However, the nurse would not be justified in revealing the fact of Mr. Hagen's illiteracy to other care team members. He is cognitively competent, has assessed the risks, and has concluded that the embarrassment of having his illiteracy revealed would be more harmful than not understanding the discharge instructions. The nurse must respect this choice.

An instance where the disclosure of information might be justified is when confidentiality conflicts with the rights of an innocent third party. For example, the question of whether to disclose a client's HIV infection to her or his spouse is a difficult ethical issue. In this situation, the client's right to confidentiality is in conflict with the ethical principle of non-maleficence, as failure to disclose could cause the spouse considerable harm. It is generally agreed that disclosure should be negotiated with the patient, but that the duty to protect the spouse overrides the patient's right to absolute confidentiality. When there is potential for a serious conflict between confidentiality and the rights or interests of society in general, legislation is usually enacted to ensure public safety. For example, the law requires reporting of certain infectious diseases. A less clear situation might occur when one discovers a serious medical problem in a patient whose occupation makes him or her responsible for the lives of other persons, for example, a bus driver with epilepsy or a surgeon with failing eyesight.

Finally, we have discussed repeatedly the need for patient consent with regard to aspects of confidential information, including its disclosure. Of course this consent could only be given by a patient with sufficient cognitive capacity. In the absence of such capacity, the nurse is expected to act according to professional judgment and an understanding of the patient's best interests, or alternatively to seek a surrogate decision maker for the patient.

A different question arises when the information refers to an entire community. The nurse must be aware that some kinds of information can be damaging, and take care to avoid disclosure that can harm individuals, families, or communities. For example, if a public health surveillance reveals a high prevalence of sexually transmitted disease or substance abuse in a community, the nurse should be careful about revealing this information. Handling sensitive data requires considerable ethical awareness to avoid stigmatizing the community as a whole. A careful risk-benefit assessment will help the nurse decide who ought to receive the information and for what purposes. That is, the nurse needs to examine the situation carefully and determine the validity of the information and whether disclosing it will be of benefit or harm to the community. Benefits might include programs aimed at prevention; harms might include making the community seem less desirable as a place to live, perpetuating its low status. This is especially important when a particular racial group is dominant in the community, as the stigma could be applied primarily to that group. If possible, the nurse should seek permission from the community before disclosing, but it might be very difficult to know from whom to obtain consent. For example, in a mixed-race inner city neighbourhood there might be no individual or group who can speak for the entire community. In this case, the nurse will have to use professional judgment based on moral awareness and an understanding of the potential for harm and benefit. Even though it is difficult to identify a single spokesperson, it might be advisable to consult with individuals in the community to establish what they would view as damaging. Risks and benefits often look very different when viewed from within the community. In other words, without awareness of a community's sensitivities and understandings it is difficult to predict what they might see as problematic.

CONFIDENTIALITY AS A LIVED VALUE

Our discussion in this chapter has raised several key issues related to the need for good communication between nurses, their employers, and patients. Confidentiality is predicated on good communication with patients about what they can expect nurses to do with their personal information. It also requires communication between nurses and employers about policies and safeguards to protect patient confidentiality, and about steps nurses must pursue when confidentiality is threatened.

The detailed discussion we have given should help you to understand the significant role nurses play in upholding privacy and confidentiality. We will now explore two scenarios common to nursing practice. The first is a case involving an adolescent's experience with pregnancy and abortion, and the nurse's decision making around whether or not to break confidentiality; the second is a question related to working in a small town.

Trying It On
8.1 Confidentiality and Ms. Leonard

Cassandra Leonard was a 15-year-old female patient visiting Stacey, a nurse practitioner at a Primary Health Clinic. Cassandra had attended her orthopedics clinic for a six-month follow up after surgical fixation of a fractured ankle, and was referred to the nurse practitioner for investigation of low hemoglobin.

On assessment, Stacey suggested that they invite Cassandra's mother into the room to participate in some nutrition counselling. Prior to her mother coming into the room, Cassandra shared with Stacey that she was six weeks pregnant and scheduled to have an abortion the following week. Cassandra stated that her mother was not aware of the pregnancy. She also stated that she was planning to move in with her boyfriend and that her

mother knew of this decision. The only reason Cassandra's mother was here with her today was because she had insisted on accompanying her.

After inviting Mrs. Leonard into the room, Stacey discussed the preferred diet and follow up with further blood work. When Stacey asked if Cassandra or her mother had further questions, Mrs. Leonard began to express her concerns about Cassandra's fatigue, nausea, and change in appetite. She wondered if these symptoms were due to her daughter's low hemoglobin. Stacey replied that fatigue was a common symptom of low hemoglobin and assured Mrs. Leonard that with proper nutrition, rest, and follow-up care, Stacey's hemoglobin could return to normal.

Reflecting on the situation later, Stacey felt uncertain that she had done the right thing. She had her own beliefs about abortion, and felt that it was not a good decision for Cassandra. She also thought that Cassandra would have benefited from talking with her mother about the abortion. At the very least, if she was to proceed with it, she could use her mother's support. She was also worried about Cassandra's ability, should she change her mind, to care for an infant, given her poor understanding of nutrition and basic self-care.

Stacey wondered if she should call Cassandra's mother and tell her what was happening with her daughter. She reasoned that she would want to know if it were her own daughter. Although Stacey knew that Cassandra did not want her pregnancy disclosed, she also wondered whether Cassandra was mature enough to make the decision to terminate it.

Applying the Framework
Confidentiality and Ms. Leonard

Assessing the Ethics of the Situation: Relationship, Goals, Beliefs, and Values

In assessing this situation, Stacey has to consider her own, Cassandra's, Cassandra's partner's, and her mother's beliefs. Cassandra has made a clear statement of values regarding her pregnancy. She reports that she is in a solid relationship, although Stacey has not met her partner. Cassandra has sought abortion counselling at a reputable clinic and has a firm commitment to live with her boyfriend. Most importantly, although she has always had a good relationship with her mother, she does not feel that she needs to involve her mother in making a decision about whether to have an abortion. Stacey does not know how Cassandra's mother would view her child's decision, nor does she know what Cassandra's boyfriend thinks.

Stacey's views are largely influenced by her duties as a professional and her beliefs about what would be best for Cassandra. She also has to take into account her own moral beliefs about pregnancy and abortion. As a practising Roman Catholic, Stacey is personally opposed to abortion. She knows that this might affect how she views the situation, so she is worried that she is not seeing things as objectively as she might. Stacey is also troubled about the age of her patient. She has always felt that parents should be the ones to make decisions for their children until they are legally adults, and it is difficult for her to accept that Cassandra has a right to make her own decisions. Legislation in her province sets the legal age for decisions about health care at 14, but Stacey thinks that is too young. She believes that Cassandra would be better off in the long run if her mother knew about her pregnancy. Stacey needs to be aware of her own beliefs and whether they are having an impact on what she does. She is aware of the relevant legislation, but needs to question Cassandra's competency and ability to fully understand

(*Continued*)

Confidentiality and Ms. Leonard

the consequences of her decisions. The CNA Code of Ethics for Registered Nurses states that "Nurses recognize the importance of privacy and confidentiality and safeguard personal, family, and community information obtained in the context of a professional relationship" (CNA, 2008, p. 15), but Stacey feels uncomfortable with this because of her personal beliefs.

Reflecting on and Reviewing Potential Actions

Stacey's options for ethical action are related to her feelings of commitment to many individuals. Cassandra is very young, and when Stacey learns of her pregnancy and plans for abortion she is caught in a moral dilemma. Her judgment about what is in her patient's best interest leads her to want to disclose Cassandra's decision to her mother, whereas her commitment to the duty of confidentiality leads her to want to keep Cassandra's trust by remaining silent. Cassandra is clear that she and her partner have sought counselling, and feel the abortion is the best option for both of them at this time. This causes personal distress for Stacey as she has strong beliefs concerning abortion. She knows that her views are not to be imposed on Cassandra, but wonders if she should be trying to help her see an alternative way of dealing with the situation. She also has strong feelings about needing to involve Cassandra's mother. She does not think that Cassandra fully appreciates the implications of what she is planning to do. However, the law permits Cassandra to have an abortion without her mother's permission. Stacey is also worried about what will happen if Cassandra's mother finds out that her daughter had an abortion and that Stacey

knew about it. Cassandra's mother has some ongoing health problems, and Stacey is concerned that their relationship will be damaged to the extent that her care will be compromised.

Selecting an Ethical Action: Maximizing Good

To disclose or not to disclose, that is the ethical question. Is Stacey's judgment that Cassandra needs to involve her mother in this decision sufficient justification for breaking confidentiality? Or should Cassandra's right to confidentiality be respected? After reflecting on the situation, Stacey realizes that she has to put her own beliefs aside, ensure that she is clear about the privacy laws and laws relating to minors in her province, and try to understand more about Cassandra's relationship with her partner and why she has made the decision to have an abortion. Stacey should ask Cassandra to explain more about her belief system. With more knowledge about the situation, Stacey might be more effective in working with Cassandra. In conversation it might become more evident to Stacey why Cassandra thinks it is best not to involve her mother. It is also important that Stacey explore other options with Cassandra, such as adoption if keeping the baby is not possible for her. Stacey should explain her worries about not telling Cassandra's mother, and see if she can get permission to involve her in the discussion. Regardless of what Cassandra decides, it is important for Stacey to gain her trust and keep her confidence.

Engaging in Ethical Action

Stacey has made a promise that she will keep all Cassandra's information confidential. This may be difficult for her because her beliefs about pregnancy, abortion, and parental involvement are different from Cassandra's. Breaking the confidence could be viewed as disrespectful to Cassandra's autonomy and could bring harm to the nurse-patient relationship. Once Stacey establishes how this situation should best be handled, she is obligated to act, even if she finds it worrisome. She must put aside her personal views and honour Cassandra's wishes. Even though Stacey might disagree with Cassandra's choice, she must abide by it.

Reflecting on and Reviewing Ethical Action

Stacey needs to ask herself if her approach to Cassandra demonstrated trust and respect. It is not sufficient to go through the motions of keeping information confidential if one's manner is disrespectful or shows disagreement. Stacey should ask herself if she did all she could to help Cassandra make the choice that was best for her. It would not be appropriate for Stacey to suggest that Cassandra's choices around abortion were morally unacceptable, but it would be reasonable for Stacey to explore with Cassandra the possibility of involving her mother. As a nurse, Stacey must always be alert to ways in which her own beliefs influence her interactions with patients, and must accept that others will make choices with which she disagrees. Relational ethics demands that she engage in a relationship that shows mutual respect and builds trust.

Trying It On

8.2 Small Town Practices

When Irene Foster graduated from nursing school, she married and returned to work in the town where she grew up. Currently she is working in the acute care hospital and attached nursing home. In both institutions, she frequently cares for parents and grandparents of her own friends. Patients and residents know and trust her, and she feels able to provide meaningful care to them and their families.

Irene and her husband are active members of the community, attending many social events. It is not unusual at these events for Irene to be approached by friends and relatives of patients and residents who are seeking news about them and their conditions. While she believes that these people are generally well meaning and genuinely concerned, and also suspects that most patients and residents would have no objection to her passing information along, she nevertheless feels uncomfortable sharing such information.

Another of Irene's concerns is the fact that the central laboratory in the health region faxes lab results to the hospital and nursing home. The fax machine in the receiving institution is in a central office, where messages are received by clerical personnel. More than once she has heard a secretary exclaiming about a lab result on someone she knew.

Finding herself particularly distressed by the constant requests for information and by her worries about private information becoming "everybody's business," Irene decides to discuss her concerns with her colleagues. Most of the nurses do not see answering simple questions or sharing residents' health status as problematic. Many of them have worked at the facility

(Continued)

8.2 Small Town Practices

for a long time and do not recall ever hearing concern from anyone about inappropriate sharing of information. One of her colleagues says that working in a small town encourages more "friendly and informal care." While the other nurses agree that the fax issue is a problem, they do not see any solution, and feel that it is just an unfortunate fact of life that "word gets around." Irene is unsure how to take their comments and continues to be concerned with these practices.

Applying the Framework

Small Town Practices

Assessing the Ethics of the Situation: Relationship, Goals, Beliefs, and Values

This case highlights how the values of the community dictate how private information and confidentiality might be understood. It appears that much of the personal information obtained in the health care setting seems innocuous because there is no obvious reason why the patient would need to keep it from others. In a small community there is very little "private" information. The context in which the information is shared is unique to rural communities. In this situation Irene is uncertain about what is considered to be confidential and private information. For whatever reason, her beliefs about what constitutes private information seem to be different from her colleagues'.

Reflecting on and Reviewing Potential Actions

Irene is experiencing moral distress as she searches for some clarity in what she senses are breaches of confidentiality. The breaches appear inadvertent and unintentional, perhaps because most of the other nurses have worked in this environment for a long time and have become accustomed to a community standard, rather than a professional one.

Irene's colleagues may have lost sight of the fact that personal patient information is confidential even in a rural community. Irene has to choose between simply accepting her colleagues' point of view, or taking action to change community practice.

Selecting an Ethical Action: Maximizing Good

The ethical question foremost in this case seems to be whether community standards can dictate what information is considered confidential. Although community members seem somewhat relaxed about what they reveal and what they do not, a number of questions arise as Irene considers the problem. She must ask whether it is permissible to disclose information only to family or friends of the patient, who presumably have a genuine concern. One problem with this is that nurses may be mistaken in distinguishing those who are genuinely concerned from those who have a different interest. Futhermore, even if the nurse could be certain that the concern was genuine and that no harm would likely come from others knowing, the patient simply might not want them to know.

Irene needs review her professional obligations as outlined in the CNA Code of Ethics. Here she will see that, despite what the community practice has been, she is correct in believing that the breaches of confidentiality are unprofessional. Once she has identified this, she is obligated to take a stand and try to get the practice changed. She should speak to the nurse in charge, and if that fails, speak to the Chair of the hospital board. If her charge nurse and/or Board Chair are in agreement, she should address the issue with other staff, and should engage in a public forum, where it will be made clear to members of the community that standards of confidentiality must change. If she does not succeed in changing the situation, she should report her concerns to her provincial nursing association, who will institute an investigation.

Engaging in Ethical Action

Once Irene has made her decision, she must find the moral courage to act. She needs to be aware that in taking a stand, she will probably become somewhat unpopular with her colleagues and with others in the community. None of them will be happy to be made aware that their practices are inherently unethical.

Reflecting on and Reviewing Ethical Action

In reflecting on her own actions, Irene needs to consider whether she has approached others with respect. It appears that other nurses and members of the community are unaware or do not believe that they are acting unethically in giving and requesting information. Irene needs to examine whether she has helped them understand the ethical principles involved in a way that preserves their sense of dignity. Inadvertent breaches of confidentiality are common, and in setting a higher standard Irene is acting according to legal and professional obligations. However, she needs to do this in a way that is sensitive to the needs and understandings of the community.

CHAPTER SUMMARY

Because health care reaches so far into patients' lives and makes them vulnerable, it is imperative that health care professionals respect patients' privacy and hold in confidence knowledge disclosed in the course of their relationships with patients. It is important to recognize that the potential exists for confidentiality to be misunderstood and violated because of the inherent power of technology and the intensive part it plays in today's health care system. Nurses work in their relationships with patients to build trust, the foundation of confidentiality and privacy. They must assume a leadership role in advocating for patients' privacy through responsible and responsive practices that begin in dialogue and mutual respect for patients as persons. A relational ethic allows us to see confidentiality as a demonstration of mutual respect rather than as a right. Mutual respect occurs in an atmosphere of interdependence, where I acknowledge that what I do affects you, and what you do affects me.

Questions for Reflection

1. Think about a situation in your clinical practice where you believe that confidentiality of personal health information of a patient was disclosed without consent. How did you and/or others react? Was the disclosure justifiable? Was the disclosure deliberate or inadvertent? What should the next steps have been?

2. You have a new patient being admitted to your unit. What steps or processes would you take to begin to provide information related to informed consent of confidential information?

3. Identify confidentiality issues related to the use of technology in your practice.

Exercises

1. Read the section in the CNA Code of Ethics for Registered Nurses on the value of *confidentiality*. Suggest how you might revise or update the responsibility statements.

2. Examine your institution's policy on confidentiality. How is confidentiality defined? What safeguards are in place to protect privacy of information? What are the consequences of breach of confidentiality?

3. On the next shift you work, ask the staff nurse you are working with about the notes that he or she takes about patients during report time. What type of information is included? What does the staff nurse do with these notes after he or she is done on his or her shift? According to privacy laws and institutional policies, what should be done with these notes?

Research Activities

1. Working in small groups, identify relevant Canadian legislation that guides practice related to confidentiality. Include in your search relevant codes of ethics and policy guidelines. Each group should work on a different province. Examine similarities and differences.

2. Conduct a literature search on an issue related to confidentiality and health care ethics. Explore these issues using different ethical theories such as ethical principles and relational ethics to explore how different perspectives takes up the issues.

Key Terms

absolute principle

anonymity

bodily privacy

confidentiality

confidential information

deliberate breach

Electronic Health Record

identifiable data

inadvertent or unintentional breach

individual control

legal rights

privacy rights

References

Bergum, V., & Dossetor, J. (2005). *Relational ethics: The full meaning of respect.* Hagerstown, MD: University Publishing Group.

Canadian Nurses Association. (2008). *Code of ethics for Registered Nurses* (Centennial Ed.). Ottawa: Author.

Canadian Nurses Association. (2001). *Privacy of personal health information.* Ottawa: Author.

Canadian Nurses Protective Society. (2005). Privacy. *InfoLaw,* 14(2), 1.

Canadian Nurses Protective Society. *New developments in privacy law.* Retrieved May 9, 2006 from www.cnps.ca.

Care, D., Gregory, D., Whittaker, C., & Chernomas, W. (2003). Nursing, technology, and informatics: An easy or uneasy alliance. In M. McIntyre & E. Thomlinson (Eds.), *Realities of Canadian Nursing: Professional Practice, and Power Issues.* Philadelphia: Lippincott.

Government of Canada (2006). *Tri-Council policy statement.* Retrieved September 12, 2006 from http://pre.ethics. gc.ca/english/policystatement/context.cfm#C

International Council of Nurses. (2006). *The ICN code of ethics for nurses.* Geneva, Switzerland: Author.

Merriam-Webster on-line. Retrieved June 15, 2006 from www.m-w.com.

Mill, J. S. (1977). On liberty. In *Essays on politics and society: Collected works,* 1(18) (Ed. J. M. Robson, p. 223). Toronto: University of Toronto Press.

Nahm, R., & Poston, I. (2000). Measurement of the effect of an integrated point-of-care computer system on quality of nursing documentation and patient satisfaction. *Computers in Nursing,*18(5), 220-229.

Office of the Privacy Commissioner of Canada. Fact Sheet. *Questions and answers regarding the application of PIPEDA, Alberta and British Columbia's Personal Information Protection Acts (PIPA's).* Retrieved July 5, 2006 from www.privcom.gc.ca/

Yeo, M., & Moorehouse, A. (1996). *Concepts and cases in nursing ethics.* Peterborough, ON: Broadview Press.

Suggested Reading

Beauchamp, T., & Childress, J. (2001). *Principles of biomedical ethics.* (5th ed.). New York: Oxford University Press.

Canadian Nurses Protective Society. (1996). Confidentiality of health information: Your client's right. *InfoLaw,* 1(2), 2.

College of Registered Nurses of British Columbia. (2005). *Privacy Legislation* (Practice Standard-pub. 335, p. 2). Vancouver: Author.

Haigh, C., & Jones, N. (2005). An overview of the ethics of cyber-space research and the implications for nurse educators. *Nurse Education Today,* 25, 3-8.

Kleinman, I., Baylis, F., Rodgers, S., & Singer, P. (1999). Confidentiality. In P. Singer (Ed.), *Bioethics at the bedside: A clinician's guide* (pp. 55-62). Ottawa: Canadian Medical Association.

Salladay, S. A. (2002). Confidentiality: Stop the gossip. *Nursing,* 32(4), 78.

Schopp, A., Leino-Kilpi, H., Valimaki, M., Dassen, T., Gasull, M., Lemonidou, C., et al. (2003). Perceptions of privacy in the care of elderly people in five European countries. *Nursing Ethics,* 10(1), 39-47.

Chapter 9
Value 6: Promoting Justice

Chapter Outline

Learning Objectives

After reading this chapter, you should be able to:

- describe the sixth primary value of the CNA Code of Ethics for Registered Nurses: *promoting justice*

- discuss the different kinds of justice: legal, social, and distributive

- discuss justice as a philosophical idea and a bioethical principle

- discuss the role of justice in research

- describe elements of justice in the workplace

- discuss how justice might be considered from a relational ethics perspective

- discuss how justice is important for nursing

- apply the Framework for Ethical Decision Making to a clinical problem related to justice

Magda Polanski was not a happy nurse. She was on her way to work, having just come from a union meeting in which there was discussion of an impending job action. Nurses were threatening to strike because of their heavy workloads, unsafe working conditions, and inability to deliver safe, competent care. They were considering taking a strike vote in the next couple of days, and Magda was really at a loss as to what to do. On the one hand, she felt that it was important that nurses speak out about the appalling work situation and deteriorating quality of patient care that had been a result of drastic cost cutting. At the same time, she knew they had many extremely sick patients in the hospital, and she was terribly worried that a strike could result in disastrous consequences for these patients. If there were no nurses to look after them, what would these patients do?

When Magda arrived at the ER where she was working as a staff nurse she noticed that the halls were full of patients on stretchers. The place was a zoo! There were patients everywhere, and nurses running from one to another, trying to make sure that everyone was tended to. She asked the nurse at the desk what was happening, and was told that they had been "crazy busy" since early morning. There had been an industrial accident and five badly injured men had arrived at once. An apparent outbreak of flu had filled the waiting room with mothers and their feverish, possibly dehydrated infants. This also seemed to be the day for heart attacks—there had been three since morning. Two separate motor vehicle collisions had resulted in three patients with serious lacerations and one with an apparent head injury. All the ER beds were full and, to make matters worse, there were hardly any empty stretchers in the hallway. As she walked in to take report, Magda heard two nurses complaining bitterly about a patient who had just been admitted. He had come in with mild chest pain, and because he was a prominent politician he had been whisked upstairs into one of the last remaining medical beds. The nurses were disgusted that he was able to jump the queue and get a bed when so many who had been waiting for so long had to endure even more time in the waiting room. One of the nurses sighed and said, "You know how it is. If you're important enough you can get premium service in this place, but if you're regular folk, you're out of luck!" Magda was outraged. "How could this be right?" she said to herself.

The scenario above illustrates different aspects of the sixth primary value of the CNA Code of Ethics for Registered Nurses: *promoting justice.* In Chapter 1 we defined justice as "fairness," but that definition does not begin to capture the complexities of the concept. In fact, justice is probably the most difficult of the values to define precisely. It also has many different kinds of impacts in nursing. In the scenario Magda is dealing with issues of fairness in the workplace and in the clinical setting. She is considering issues of social and distributive justice. In an attempt to make all this clear to you, we will first describe how the Code directs nurses to think about justice. Then we will consider different ways of thinking about it, including legal interpretations, bioethical principles, and social justice. We will discuss how the concept is understood in nursing practice, and how relational ethics can be helpful or unhelpful in dealing with justice concerns. Finally, we will describe two scenarios that reflect justice issues, and use the Framework for Ethical Decision Making to analyze the situations and consider right actions.

THE SIXTH PRIMARY VALUE: PROMOTING JUSTICE

The CNA Code of Ethics for Registered Nurses defines justice as "respecting the rights of others, distributing resources fairly, and preserving and promoting the common good (the good of the community)" (CNA, 2008, p. 26), but a more precise definition is elusive. In discussing the value, the Code indicates that "Nurses uphold principles of justice by safeguarding human rights, equity, and fairness and by promoting the public good" (p. 17), which differs somewhat from the glossary definition. The explanatory statements concerning justice in the Code (p. 17) indicate implications for nursing. Nurses must do the following:

- not discriminate against patients
- avoid judging or labelling individuals and groups
- avoid (and report) treatment that is inhumane or degrading
- try to make fair decisions about resource allocation
- advocate for the interests of patients in their care and for fair allocation of resources
- support a climate of trust and openness such that individuals feel safe in questioning and reporting practices that might be considered unethical

The broad range of responsibilities described in the Code make it clear that justice is enormously important in nursing. To understand your obligations you need a more complete explanation of what each of the different aspects of justice, such as fairness, social justice, and resource allocation, really mean. It is probably fair to say that everyone has a general idea of what justice means, but clearly it can mean different things to different people. We will begin to uncover some understandings by exploring what it means in law.

LEGAL INTERPRETATIONS OF JUSTICE

When people talk about justice, most often they mean it in the legal sense. That means applying or upholding the law. In fact, a judge in our legal (justice) system may also be called a Justice. The Philosopher's Dictionary defines justice as "what the law requires, or what is fair or correct treatment" (Martin, 1991, p. 124). Again, the idea of fairness comes up. It is assumed that laws are written to ensure fair treatment of members of society and to protect them from harm, but there are many interpretations of how this should come about. Those working within the system have a better understanding of how justice can be interpreted within that system. One common understanding of justice is **retributive justice**, which refers to punishment for wrongdoing. When people say "justice was done," they usually mean that someone "got what she or he deserved." Some believe that retribution or punishment is part of justice and is necessary to restore moral order and that the severity of punishment should be determined by the nature of the crime. This belief is captured in the familiar expression, "An eye for an eye, a tooth for a tooth." Kant, to whom we have referred before, developed a version of retributive justice, or retributism, in his writings (Martin, 1991). However, some criticize retributism, suggesting that it is really not about justice, but merely revenge. Debates about how our legal system should deliver justice are frequent. You have no doubt read or heard media discussions about whether a sentence was sufficiently severe, given the nature of the crime. These discussions are usually about retribution and whether the person who committed the crime was sufficiently punished. A notable debate is whether capital punishment should be permitted. Some (retributionists) would say that a person who killed someone else should be killed. Others would say that this is not justice—taking a life is wrong, no matter who does it, and the state (government) should not be involved, as capital punishment is merely revenge, not justice.

The capital punishment debate also stems from the fact that our legal system is not exclusively or necessarily about retributive justice. In part it is about protecting the public by incarcerating those who might commit crime, and in part it is about **deterrence**, which means discouraging others from taking action by making them afraid of consequences. In the legal system it is assumed that knowing you could suffer consequences such as being fined or put in jail for committing a crime may prevent you from doing so. Our system is also supposed to be about **rehabilitation**: teaching criminals how to meet their needs without resorting to crime. However, the degree of rehabilitation that is present in our justice system is questionable. For the most part, the public considers the justice system to be about punishment and considers adequate punishment to be related to the degree of the crime. A longer jail sentence is expected for more serious crimes.

As part of the legal system of justice, one must also consider the concept of rectificatory or restorative justice, which is usually dealt with in civil court. **Restorative justice** requires that there be equal exchange between individuals. Therefore, it requires that those who have had something such as money, reputation, or goods taken from them be compensated for their losses. In other words, justice is restored when wrongdoing is repaired by "paying someone back." The court decides whether significant wrongdoing has occurred and decides what compensation is required.

JUSTICE AS A PHILOSOPHICAL IDEA

Legal interpretations of justice are only a part of how we understand the concept. Philosophers have pondered the notion of justice for centuries. For Aristotle, justice was a kind of virtue. He felt that people learned to be just by doing just acts and that the state was responsible for shaping peoples' behaviours through legislation. He divided justice into two parts: universal and particular. Universal justice was established by law, while particular justice was fairness in dealing with others and was part of an individual's virtue. A just man, in Aristotle's view, was one who was law-abiding and fair, an unjust man unlawful and unfair (Aristotle, transl. D. Ross, 1998). It was Aristotle who introduced the idea of rectificatory justice. Aristotle also talked about distributive justice, which we defined in Chapter 1, and by which he meant the fair distribution of goods or resources. It was Aristotle who referred to justice as being about "treating equals equally and unequals unequally." In other words, according to Aristotle it is necessary to give more to those with less, to even things out.

Kant's views on justice were very complicated and require more in-depth analysis than we can provide here. It is sufficient for our purposes to say that Kant thought that justice mainly had to do with rights and freedoms, and with the right of the state to use coercion to ensure that individual freedoms were respected. That is, the state could impose penalties to ensure that one person did not take away the rights and freedoms of another.

Mill, on the contrary, was not very clear on the notion of justice. His idea of utilitarianism and the "greatest good for the greatest number" could in some sense be seen as incompatible with justice. Generally speaking, Mill believed that justice was about being sure that people got what they deserved, which in the long run would promote the greatest good for the greatest number. Exactly what that should look like is somewhat vague in Mill's writing.

Justice has also been considered by a number of modern philosophers, notably John Rawls. In A Theory of Justice (Rawls, 1971), Rawls considered justice as fairness and talked about ways in which we might make fair decisions, particularly around distributive justice. He paid special attention to the problem of conflict of interest in decision making. **Conflict of interest** occurs when someone makes, or is in a position to make, a decision based on what is in his or her own best interests, not in the best interests of others who might be affected by the decision. For example, if I were sitting on a selection committee to choose a new dean of nursing and one of the applicants was a close friend, I might make my decision based on the belief that my friend would make my life easier and give me special consideration, rather than on what might be best for the faculty. Rawls suggests that to get around conflict of interest, decision makers should function as if they were operating under a "veil of ignorance." Roughly speaking, this would mean that those making the decision would act as if they did not know their own position in society, so they would not know how the decision would affect them. In this way they would be required to make the decision that was most fair, because a fair decision would be the most likely to benefit them as typical members of society. Rawls' work is probably the most famous of contemporary philosophers' works on justice, but its practical implications for health care are not entirely clear, as the idea of a "veil of ignorance" is hard to put into effect. However, it does help us understand that our own interests and beliefs can influence our decision making.

JUSTICE AS A BIOETHICAL PRINCIPLE

In Chapter 1 we mentioned that justice was one of the principles of bioethics. Beauchamp and Childress (1994) discuss this principle at length. They describe justice as fairness and discuss the right to equal access to health care and the way in which scarce resources can most fairly be distributed. They identify six guiding principles that could be used, either individually or together, to guide thinking about how resources should be distributed:

1. To each person an equal share
2. To each person according to need
3. To each person according to effort
4. To each person according to contribution
5. To each person according to merit
6. To each person according to free-market exchanges (Beauchamp & Childress, 1994, p. 330)

In thinking about how each of these principles might come into action, consider an example from public health. Two programs have been developed, one to provide feeding advice and support for new mothers and their babies, and another to provide home visiting for the frail elderly who are living at home. Both have been operating for some months and by all accounts are highly successful. A recent cut to health care funding has just been announced, and it becomes evident that one of the programs has to be discontinued. Which will it be?

If we use the first principle of resource allocation, *equal share*, we would cut both programs by half. However, under that condition neither program could work. Both are just barely supported with full funding; with halved funding they would be almost useless. If we want allocate according to *need*, we will hear arguments that both groups have a need for the program. The new mothers who have taken part so far have had fewer visits to the pediatrician, fewer infant hospital admissions, and healthier babies. Similarly, the frail elderly have had fewer falls, fewer hospital admissions, and report a better quality of life. If *effort* is the criterion, we can see that the new mothers are all making huge efforts to help their infants thrive. The frail elderly are also making enormous effort, desperately trying to retain their independence, and will do whatever the program nurses advise them to do. *Contribution* is another criterion we might use. Logic tells us that, on the one hand, the infants (and their mothers) are likely to make large contributions in the future. On the other hand, the frail elderly are no longer making an important monetary contribution to society. However, one could argue that they contribute in other ways such as wisdom and reflection, and that they have already made a huge contribution to the society and now deserve to be supported. If we use *merit* for our decision, we find similar contradictory arguments. One could argue that infants have greater merit as they are the future of our society, and we must treasure and protect them. However, we might argue that the elderly formed the foundation of our society, and they ought to be treasured and protected as well. Unless we can ascribe particular merit to being either very young or very old, merit is not a particularly helpful criterion. The final criterion is *free-market exchanges*, which does not seem to have direct relevance in this instance. Neither the very young nor the very old are in a position to exchange goods and/or services for the help provided. If one looked at the issue merely from an economics perspective, one could argue equally strongly that infants should be served because they will contribute to the economy in the future (similar to the merit argument) or that the elderly ought to be served because their health care needs constitute an immediate expense to the system and reducing those needs reduces potential costs.

Thus, you can see that having principles of distributive justice does not solve our problem. There are too many ways to interpret each principle. In the example above, no matter what decision is made, someone will have a counter-argument that could be convincing. It might be that the most just decision will be to choose simply on a "first-come, first-served" basis, or, if that criterion does not enable one to distinguish between the two possible recipients, then it might have to be decided by chance, using a draw or something similar. These kinds of difficult decisions require considerable reflection and a wide array of opinions and input. Eventually, however, someone has to have the final say. Usually in these very complex situations a board or panel makes the decision. Those on the panel will need to have a more in-depth understanding of the elements of justice than is possible to present here. There are many books and articles on the subject outlining various perspectives that might be helpful. Some of these are listed at the conclusion of the chapter. The interested individual can also access considerable information about health care justice issues on the Internet.

SOCIAL JUSTICE

According to the CNA, **social justice** means "the fair distribution of society's benefits and responsibilities and their consequences" (CNA, 2006, p. 7). That is, it is about ensuring that all members of society can benefit equally from that society. In other words, it is about human rights and the benefits to which all people are entitled. In health care, social justice refers to issues around access to resources and whether all individuals have the same opportunities for care. It should be apparent that many issues of distributive justice could also be considered issues of social justice. There is a great deal of overlap between the two concepts. The main difference is that social justice focuses on whether individuals or groups are being discriminated against in some way; whereas, distributive justice is not so concerned with social causes, looking instead simply at fair ways of dividing up that which is in scarce supply.

To illustrate, consider the following examples that deal with social justice issues. Those concerned with social justice in Canadian health care could question whether care is as available to Aboriginal people as it is to others in society. They might look to recent evidence of lack of clean water in some Aboriginal reserves and suggest that the government's failure to ensure equal access to clean water is a matter of social injustice. It could be interpreted as treating certain people as second-class citizens merely because of their racial origin or where they live.

Those exploring social justice issues in health care might also question whether there is discrimination on the basis of gender, cognitive status, sexual orientation, or any of a number of other variables. They might also ask how socio-economic status affects health and health promotion. For instance, how do poverty and environment impact the health of Canadians? Do those living in poverty have equal access to resources? Is there system-wide discrimination based on age or ability? For example, one might look at the availability of long-term care beds and query whether the kind of care delivered in long-term care institutions is acceptable. The issue of social justice in that instance would be about whether those who have the least resources and are arguably the most vulnerable in our society, namely the elderly and those with certain disabilities, are treated fairly and equitably.

One important document with which you should be familiar is the Canada Health Act, enacted in 1984. It constitutes our federal health insurance legislation and outlines the responsibilities for health care in Canada. It was intended to address issues of social justice in health by ensuring that "all residents of Canada have reasonable access to medically necessary insured services without direct charges" (Health Canada, 2002, p. 1). In other words, the Act was designed to make sure that even those of limited means could obtain health care when they needed it. The Act is based on five main principles:

- **Public administration:** The health care insurance plans are administered by the provinces and territories.

- **Comprehensiveness:** The provincial or territorial health insurance plans must insure hospital, physician, and surgical-dental services, as well as the services of other health care providers, as agreed upon at the provincial or territorial level.

- **Universality:** Every resident of the province or territory is entitled to insured health services.

- **Portability:** Residents moving from one province or territory to another must continue to be covered for insured services except during a minimum waiting period.

- **Accessibility:** The health insurance plans of each province or territory must provide reasonable access to insured services without extra billing.

The Canada Health Act has been somewhat successful in ensuring that most Canadians have access to health care services. In fact, our health care system is the envy of many nations. The system is not without its problems, however. In remote communities, particularly in the north, services may not be available in a timely fashion, and health promotion and illness prevention may be severely lacking. As a result, residents of many northern communities have a poorer health status overall than, for example, Canadians in urban settings. For instance, infant mortality rates are much higher in remote communities, particularly among Aboriginal people. Many consider this an issue of social justice and a cause for national shame. We will consider social justice issues in more detail later in the chapter when we examine the nursing implications more closely.

RESEARCH AND JUSTICE

The CNA Code of Ethics for Registered Nurses states that "Nurses support, use, and engage in research and other activities that promote safe, competent, compassionate, and ethical care, and they use guidelines for ethical research." (CNA, 2008, p. 9). One aspect of ethical research involves justice, and nurses need an understanding of some of the issues if they are to support and promote ethical research.

Clinical studies are becoming a fact of life in most health care institutions. The push to find new and better ways of delivering health care has caused an astronomical increase in the number of new studies that are initiated each year. For example, the Calgary Health Region alone currently has upward of 2000 research studies going on at any one point in time. With such an increase, it is becoming even more important to ensure that research is carried out according to accepted ethical standards. Research Ethics Boards (REBs) now exist in all major centres of research. Their mandate is to review all research that will involve human subjects or participants to ensure that it meets certain criteria. In Canada, the Tri-Council Policy Statement, or TCPS, (Government of Canada, 2006) is the document that provides guidance for REBs as they review proposals. The TCPS was commissioned by the three major granting agencies in Canada, the Medical Research Council of Canada, the Natural Sciences and Engineering Research Council of Canada, and the Social Science and Humanities Council of Canada; it was released in 1998 after extensive deliberation and national consultation. In the introduction to the TCPS a number of ethical principles are outlined. One of these principles is justice, as described below.

> *Respect for Justice and Inclusiveness:* Justice connotes fairness and equity. Procedural justice requires that the ethics review process have fair methods, standards, and procedures for reviewing research protocols, and that the process be effectively independent. Justice also concerns the distribution of benefits and burdens of research. On the one hand, distributive justice means that no segment of the population should be unfairly burdened with the harms of research ... On the other hand, distributive justice also imposes duties to neither neglect nor discriminate against individuals and groups who may benefit from advances in research. (Government of Canada, 2006, 1.5)

From the above you can see that an important aspect of justice in research revolves around who will be included in and who will be excluded from studies. One reason for including or excluding an individual could be gender. In times past almost all research was done with men as subjects. Some of the reasoning was either that women were too "risky," in that they could become pregnant or their hormones might alter the effects of the treatment and confound the results. It was assumed that research results could be easily transferred from men to women. In other words, a drug that was tested on men could be given to women with the same expected results. However, we now realize that this reasoning is faulty. First, men's and women's physiology is not the same, so results obtained from male subjects will not necessarily hold for female subjects. Therefore, we are becoming more sensitive to the idea that it is unfair or unjust to exclude women from research. Women have a right to share equally in the benefits of research. Second, it is not fair or just to allow men to share all the burden of research; women who might be using the benefits of the research should share equally in the risk. Nonetheless, it must be acknowledged that some very difficult issues can arise when involving women in research. For example, if a new drug is being tested, should pregnant women be permitted to enter the study if the effects on the fetus are unknown? Clearly there is a risk of endangering the fetus, but if pregnant women are never permitted to be in studies, how can we know what can safely be given to them during pregnancy? It is hardly fair either to assume that pregnant women will never need treatment or that they will simply be denied reasonable care because they are pregnant. This is an issue that continues to be debated on many REBs.

The same kinds of issues arise with children as subjects of research. We know that children are not simply adults in miniature; their bodies may respond very differently to treatments such as drug therapies. It is not reasonable to assume that we can do research on adults and extrapolate the results to children. However, being involved in research studies might put children at risk. How can we even out the risks and benefits of research such that children are not put at unnecessary risk but are still able to be participants? One idea is that if they are to be involved in a study that will put them at risk, there must be a possible therapeutic benefit to them. If there is no possibility of benefit, they should not be eligible for the study.

These are just a few examples of the kinds of justice issues that can arise in clinical studies. In fact, the whole idea of clinical research raises issues when not everyone chooses, or gets the chance, to participate. One might question whether it is fair even to allow people to choose to be in a study or not. Suppose, for example, I decide not to enter a study for a new asthma medication because of possible side effects, but later, when the results of the study are released, I am anxious to have the drug prescribed for me. Should those who refuse to take the risk of being in a study be permitted to benefit from the results?

Another aspect to consider is the social justice issues raised by research in developing countries. You would be right to question whether it is fair and just to conduct drug studies in countries where the population is generally too poor to buy the drug if it is found to be effective. Sometimes these studies are carried out in a developing nation because they are considered quite risky, and the researcher would have difficulty getting ethics approval from an REB. Ethics standards may not be quite so high in developing nations. This raises interesting debates. On the one hand, researchers will argue that testing the drug in the developing nation gives participants an opportunity to obtain drugs to which they might otherwise not have access. In other words, taking part in the trial may be of benefit to them. The other side of the argument is that participants assume all the risks, and usually cannot reap long-term benefits because the drug will be economically denied to them once the trial is finished. Consider, too, the possibility that a drug has been tested in Africa and has been found to be effective for a condition from which you, living in Canada, suffer. Would you think it was ethical to take the drug knowing that it was developed in Africa because Canadians were afraid to take the risk of experiencing unknown side effects?

Yet another issue that can arise around research is one of conflict of interest, which we have mentioned previously. Suppose you are a member of an ethics board that has been asked to approve a study of a new and potentially very lucrative drug. You have just purchased quite a few shares in the drug company that is testing the drug. Should you vote on whether the study is approved? You have some reservations about whether the recruitment strategies are entirely just. You know that they are planning to exclude pregnant women because effects on the fetus are unknown, and the company fears a lawsuit if anything should go wrong. You also know that the drug is very unlikely to affect a fetus and that the drug will probably be given to pregnant women once it is on the market. You want the study to go ahead because you believe it will be effective (and therefore probably profitable, although this may not be your primary motivation). Should you vote on the application for ethics approval?

In our examples above, we have talked primarily about drug trials because the issues are quite obvious. Nursing research is not often as risky as drug trials; however, similar concerns can arise. For instance, I might be studying the effects of music on vital signs in post-operative patients who have had coronary artery bypass surgery. Most of the patients are men, as they have a higher incidence of coronary artery disease. If I want to include women in my study I will have to wait a lot longer to get a sufficient number for analysis. This will delay my study and require considerably more funding. Do I need to feel obligated to include women in my study? From a practical perspective, it is very difficult. From a justice perspective, it is probably necessary. Most researchers will likely take the more expedient choice and leave women out, but the ethics of that choice could be questioned unless you have strong rationale as to why women should not be part of your study. For instance, you might be able to justify excluding women if you had good reason to believe that you would get too few women to analyze separately. If combining their results with men's might alter your findings in some important way, thus making it unfair to men, your choice to exclude women would be just.

As you can see, research can be a minefield of justice issues. As a nurse, you are likely to encounter patients who are enrolled in clinical studies. You might even be conducting your own research. If you are to be an effective advocate for your patients, you need to have some understanding of the issues and be prepared to speak up when concerns arise.

This brings us to another aspect of justice and research: the need to study issues of justice in a systematic way. Much of the more interesting research in social justice issues in health care is conducted by nurses, in part because nurses are often most aware of the concerns. As a nurse it is your obligation to identify justice issues and advocate for just health policies and decision-making procedures consistent with current knowledge and practice. Current knowledge may be insufficient, so it is a moral obligation of nurses to identify researchable questions and, if in a position to do so, conduct research that will inform decision making at the policy level.

JUSTICE AS A LIVED VALUE

To this point we have been considering the theoretical aspects of justice, and some situations in which justice issues might arise. Now we turn to more specific aspects related to nursing care. For the most part, the important justice issues of everyday practice are distributive, such as who gets the bed or community program, or whether an MRI is purchased with scarce dollars. Such decisions are not made by staff nurses, but instead are usually administrative or medical decisions. However, the way in which resources are allocated has an important impact on nursing practice. When there is insufficient funding, staffing levels may be low, beds may be scarce, and other elements of care, such as laboratory and radiography services, may be limited. Time and resource management then become an even more central part of nursing care.

Justice in Nursing Care

We have talked about justice throughout this chapter as an ethical principle and have indicated that it is difficult to define. Our discussion to this point has been mostly theoretical, but in nursing care justice decisions have to be made daily. There will always be choices about who gets what, and questions about whether the decisions are fair. For example, a justice decision integral to everyday nursing practice has to do with how you allocate your own time in giving care. Suppose you have two patients, one of whom is lying in a wet and dirty bed, and one of whom is crying and distressed about her prognosis. Whose need is greater? You cannot be in two places at once, so you have to decide which problem gets priority. In fact, if resources are scarce, you might have time to see only one of those patients. Which one would you attend to? How would the situation make you feel? The decision will be based on your own values and the values of the unit. Often a unit as a whole will have certain priorities. Nursing leadership, and in particular that of the unit manager, is important in setting those priorities. You will find that nurses on a unit will demonstrate unit values in the way they set priorities. For instance, in the example above, if the unit manager stresses clean, neat beds and physical comfort over psychological comfort, you will probably be encouraged to tend to the patient in the wet bed first. If the unit manager views psychological support as a priority, you will likely attend to the crying woman. If you work on a unit where the underlying values differ from yours, you could find yourself quite uncomfortable. Eventually you will need to decide whether to change your own priorities, leave the unit, or continue to experience discomfort. If you recognize that these are values-based justice decisions, you have a much better chance of being able to articulate your concerns and address the issue with your colleagues.

Another concrete example of the problem allocating your own time as a scarce resource is again with two patients. One patient is a frail, somewhat confused elderly person sitting on a toilet. He is at great risk of falling, and you are standing nearby until he is finished so you can help him up and back to bed. Just then you notice in the room across the hall a man who appears to be having chest pain. If you rush to help him, you will put the elderly man at risk. If you stay put, the man with the chest pain is at risk. How do you decide which patient has priority? In this instance you would probably instruct the man on the toilet to stay seated until you come back and run to the man with the chest pain, because his need seems more immediately life-threatening. However, leaving the elderly man on the toilet unattended could be life-threatening for him also. Part of your reasoning about how to respond will be determined by your underlying values. If you really think that the elderly man has little worth, you will have no problem making a decision. Conversely, if you believe that the elderly man is at greater risk and that someone else can respond to the man with possible chest pain if you put on the emergency call bell, you are demonstrating a different set of values.

It is often difficult in the practice setting to get agreement on what is just in any given situation. For instance, if ICU beds are limited, is it the right course of action to discharge a very sick patient to the general nursing unit in order to admit someone from emergency whose needs are more acute? What if the person who is in emergency got there because she was driving while intoxicated? Would that, and should that, influence the decision? This may not be a decision that you, as the nurse, have to make, but you may be involved in giving input, and you do have to live with the decision once it is made. It is important, then, that you have some way of sorting out your own beliefs and values around justice and what is important. These examples may seem like simple priority-setting to you, which is something that you learn in basic nursing education. However, it might be helpful for you to understand that they are really ethical questions around distributive justice. If you can explore situations in light of what you believe to be fair and just, it might be helpful to you in articulating your concerns and arriving at reasonable responses.

As we said earlier, justice decisions are often very difficult to make. In the Ethics Composite Model introduced in Chapter 2, we indicated that ethical principles, including justice, are part of nursing ethics. To "apply" the principle of justice one must sort out what is the fairest thing to do, but that is seldom obvious. Beauchamp and Childress (1994) suggest that one way to deal with distributive justice issues is to consider relevant properties in the situation. By **relevant properties** they mean those things that a person must possess to qualify for particular goods or resources. In other words, if you are to be eligible for a treatment or type of care you must have certain characteristics. You must, for instance, have an infection to qualify for antibiotics.

The difficulty in using relevant properties for decision making is that it is often hard to decide what properties are really relevant. Is the cause of a person's need for an ICU bed a relevant property or not? Does the woman who was drunk driving have the same right to a bed as the man who is recovering from cardiac bypass surgery? The driving accident was self-induced, but could one say the same about the heart disease? Both involved lifestyle decisions, at least to some extent. If you were a home care nurse with time for only one visit, would you choose to visit the young mother with a new baby or the elderly man who had borderline dementia? What would be relevant properties in this case? You might consider prognosis; the elderly man might be less able to benefit from your visit in that his condition will deteriorate no matter what you do. Perhaps availability of support should be a criterion; the young woman has other resources at hand, but the elderly man does not. What about dependents? The young woman has an infant whose health could be affected if you do not make your visit to her; no one is dependent on the elderly man. Another possible criterion is safety; the elderly man needs to be assessed, as he might be making choices that endanger himself and others. On the other hand, the young mother might be making bad choices for her infant.

Establishing relevant properties is a complex problem. Here is one area where relational ethics can be helpful; if you are able to connect with your patient in a meaningful way, you will have a better chance of understanding what is important to her or him. It will also give you opportunities to assess characteristics that might become relevant properties in making a justice decision. For example, you might be able to assess cognitive status, degree of independence, knowledge base, or availability of social support. On the other hand, relational ethics can raise a problem of a different sort. If you become very connected to your patient and/or the family, it might become difficult for you to make a decision that would give another patient priority. Some time ago Howard J. Curzer, a Dutch philosopher, wrote an article in which he made the argument that "care" in nursing was a vice, not a virtue. He suggested that nurses who care too much for their patients lose their justice perspective: they allocate their time on the basis of like, not need. This, Curzer maintains, "opens the door to even more unsavoury practices such as racism, sexism, and ageism. These 'isms' have no place in the health care setting" (Curzer, 1993, p. 58). In other words, Curzer is arguing that your liking of a person for whatever reason is not a relevant property for decision making. The only relevant property is need. Most of us would accept that, in general terms. However, if you had to choose between giving care to your dying mother, who was a patient on your unit, and giving care to a patient with similar needs in a different room, whom do you think you would choose? Some philosophers have argued that obligations of a personal nature, such as family relationships, are indeed relevant properties.

As in much of health care ethics, there is no single clear answer that will satisfy everyone. It is important, though, that you are able to sort through the values and beliefs that you hold about different care situations. This will help you articulate what you consider to be relevant properties. In many care situations, particularly when you are working with a multidisciplinary team, this can help clarify the situation. Consider, for example, a patient on a geriatric mental health rehabilitation unit. The psychiatrist suggests that the patient should be discharged in a week because he has a "personality disorder" and is "playing power games" with the staff. Such a patient, she says, should not take up a bed that might be needed for another patient. As a staff nurse, you believe that the label "personality disorder" is unhelpful, and you do not think that the perception that the patient is playing power games is relevant or accurate. Your relational ethics have led you to deep conversations with the patient, and you are convinced that he is on the verge of a breakthrough in understanding his own behaviours and needs. You believe that he should have more time to sort things through, as that will give him a much better chance for long-term improvement. If you are able to offer a different set of relevant properties in presenting your position to the psychiatrist, you might make this resource allocation decision (who gets the bed) easier and more effective.

This example provides the basis for a good counter-argument to Curzer's position that nurses should not care about their patients. In this instance, you might not even particularly like the patient, but you do care enough to find out what is happening in that person's life and what matters to him. Curzer was suggesting that liking patients and caring about them is the same thing. We maintain that this is not the case, as professional caring is about valuing a person and seeing that he or she has worth, which does not necessarily involve a personal involvement with the person. In other words, it is possible to separate professional caring from personal liking. In fact, as a nurse you are required to establish boundaries around your relationships with patients. Too personal an involvement can impede your ability to make fair or just decisions about priorities in care delivery. That is one reason why nursing professional associations include a statement about boundaries and professional relationships in their nursing practice standards. It is also an important reason for suggesting that health care providers should not care directly for their own family members in a professional context.

Guarding against personal relationships in nursing can be difficult, because engaging with a person in a caring, supportive way often leads to increased understanding of that person, which may lead to greater emotional attachment. We discussed this problem in Chapter 7 when we were considering dignity and boundaries. Here we consider it as a justice issue. Part of your obligation as a nurse is to reflect constantly on your relationships with patients and examine the way in which you are making decisions about how you allocate your time and energy. You need to ask yourself what properties or characteristics of the patient you are taking into account. As mentioned earlier in this book, reflective journalling can be an effective way of examining your own values and beliefs. It is also helpful to talk to colleagues. Consider, for example, a patient whom everyone wants to avoid. Some patients are more difficult or less personable than others. Should this be a reason for withholding or limiting care? Do staff members spend more time with the young, charming man who is very appreciative of their efforts than the elderly, irritable woman who needs help but usually appears critical and ungrateful? Is this a just allocation of staff time? Raising issues such as this can be a difficult and sometimes unpopular move, but if you observe care allocation decisions that are suspect, it is your moral obligation to do so. The CNA Code of Ethics for Registered Nurses states, "Nurses make fair decisions about the allocation of resources under their control, based upon the needs of persons, groups, or communities to whom they are providing care" (CNA, 2008, p. 17). An integral part of nursing practice, therefore, must be critical reflection and discussion, and advocacy to ensure that distributive justice is served.

Nursing and Social Justice

Social justice issues arise frequently at the broader systems level, but they are not always recognized as such. The way in which health care dollars are allocated may be determined in part by understandings of social worth. For example, an enormous amount of money is directed to cardiac care, while long-term care suffers from staffing and bed shortages and inadequate supplies. It is fair to question whether this situation is influenced to some extent by the fact that many cardiac patients are relatively young, relatively affluent white men. As mentioned above, Aboriginal people have very poor health overall when compared with their non-Aboriginal counterparts. One could certainly question why the dollars directed toward Aboriginal health are relatively limited, given their poor health status. These are social justice concerns.

As a nurse, you need to be aware of such issues and be prepared to challenge inequities in care. The CNA Code of Ethics for Registered Nurses discusses **vulnerable groups**, indicating that ethical endeavours include "Understanding that some groups in society are systematically disadvantaged, which leads to diminished health and well-being. Nurses work to improve the quality of lives of people who are part of disadvantaged and/or *vulnerable groups* and communities, and they take action to overcome barriers to health care" (emphasis in original; CNA, 2008, p. 21). This might seem like a lot to ask, when what you are perhaps thinking is, "All I want to do is look after sick people." It is not meant to imply that all nurses should spend their time and energy crusading for human rights. The Code does say, however, that nursing's mandate is to promote health and well-being for *all* people and that awareness of issues of social justice is important. You may choose to work at the higher systems level to correct social inequities. However, attention to social justice is not limited to work at that level. If you are giving direct care and observe what you believe to be unjust allocation of resources based on characteristics such as poverty, race, gender, sexual orientation, or age, you are morally obligated to speak up against such injustice. You do have a responsibility to challenge decisions that you believe are based on social inequities. That is part of being a professional nurse.

Social justice includes not harming vulnerable groups. The Code also states, "Nurses do not engage in any form of lying, punishment, or torture, or any form of unusual treatment or action that is inhumane or degrading. They refuse to be complicit in such behaviours. They intervene, and they report such behaviours" (CNA, 2008, p. 17). We dealt with issues of dignity in Chapter 7, so will not go into detail about degrading or punishing behaviours here. However, it is important to note that the Code prohibits nurses from "any form of lying" as part of the value of justice. This could seem like a rather strong prohibition, given that sometimes nurses choose not to tell the truth if it will cause patients embarrassment, humiliation, or hurt. For instance, a nurse might tell a patient that she was not bothered by the smell of his incontinent feces, when it really makes her feel somewhat nauseated. We interpret the Code statement to be saying that lies that result in degrading or harming the patient are not to be tolerated. However, this stance could be considered controversial, as many nurses would not agree with this interpretation. If they were working from a strong Kantian perspective they would take the position that lying in any form is never acceptable.

Part of the statement above indicates that nurses report activities that they see as degrading or inhumane. This is "whistleblowing," which we described briefly in Chapter 4. Whistleblowing is a difficult thing to do, as most of us have been taught that we should not "snitch" or "tattle" on others. Often the nurse who reports another receives negative social sanctions, as others might feel that the problem could have been dealt with in another way. We provide an example in Chapter 10 when we discuss issues related to accountability and nurses' obligations to ensure that others are able to practise competently. However, as an issue of justice, consider the problem raised for Leanne, a nurse working in long-term care. Leanne was on evenings and was the only RN on duty. It was nearing 2100 hours, and she was just starting to give out her medications in the South wing. Usually by this time she had already finished in the South wing and was working in the North wing. However, tonight she was behind as she had stopped to comfort a family in distress. Just as she prepared to enter Mr. Jacques' room she heard Jerry, one of the aides, saying, "You stupid old man. I told you not to mess in your pants again. I've had it with you! You need to be taught a lesson." She hurried in and saw Jerry with his arm raised, about to strike Mr. Jacques, who was cowering in the chair. She gasped and Jerry turned around. When he saw Leanne his face went white and he stammered, "Leanne. I thought you were on the other wing. This wasn't what you think. I was just trying to scare him because he knows he is supposed to ring the bell. He just does this to drive me crazy. Please don't report me. I wasn't going to hurt him. You know me. I was just fooling around."

Clearly Leanne had no choice but to report Jerry's behaviour. Mr. Jacques was vulnerable, and Jerry was in a position of relative power, which he was clearly abusing. This was a matter of justice, as Jerry's treatment of Mr. Jacques was designed to humiliate and degrade him. In this situation Mr. Jacques was likely also protected by legislation. Most provinces have some legal provision for protecting the vulnerable. For example, Alberta has a Protection for Persons in Care Act that makes the reporting of such behaviours mandatory under law. Reporting is not optional for Leanne, however much she may like or respect Jerry as a person.

Other situations might not be as easily sorted out, or might have difficult consequences for the nurse doing the reporting. For example, a nurse involved in clinical research might experience some conflicts between the demands of the research protocol and what he or she considers ethical. There are a number of documented cases of nurses reporting research improprieties that put patients at risk. For example, see the statement of Cherlynn Mathias (retrieved from www.circare.org/230402Ch.pdf, January 2008; or search on "Cherlynn Mathias"). She was a research nurse who was so distressed by what she considered to be unethical conduct involving patients in a drug trial that she reported it to the authorities. She saw it as her responsibility to protect the vulnerable patients in her care. In her statement she alluded to the need to protect whistleblowers, who can be fired or sanctioned when they report problems. Ms. Mathias' story is inspirational because it reflects the kind of reporting that the CNA Code of Ethics for Registered Nurses demands of nurses, despite the personal costs that they might incur. Justice demands that those providing care not abuse or damage those who receive the care.

Justice in the Workplace

Another important aspect of justice to consider concerns the treatment of nurses in the workplace. As you no doubt appreciate, nurses are people too and deserve to be treated fairly. They have a right to fair compensation for their work and reasonable working conditions. It is unacceptable to put either nurses or their patients in jeopardy. Nurses have a responsibility to speak out when they see any kind of injustice being committed in the health care setting. That includes unfair treatment of other health care providers, not just patients. It follows, then, that nurses have an obligation to treat other care providers fairly, and that nurses have a right to be treated with respect by patients and co-workers. Justice in the workplace demands that everyone be treated fairly and equitably.

Sometimes nurses need to take drastic positions in order to ensure that health care dollars are adequate and distributed fairly. This could require a formal job action or strike. A strike is one way of drawing people's attention to inequities in pay or working conditions. The CNA Code of Ethics for Registered Nurses refers to nurses' obligations during job action under the first primary value, which we discuss in Chapter 4. However, the discussion there is limited to the nurse's responsibility to ensure that patients receive necessary care, even during job action. In the appendices of the Code, there is also a discussion titled "Acting Ethically in Situations that Involve Job Action." Clearly there are important considerations for patient care in the event that such action is necessary. The broader question, though, is whether strike action is ethical in itself. Some might question whether nurses are acting ethically in striking at all. The answer to that should be evident if we consider justice in the workplace. Most job action has several demands, including fair payment for services, acceptable working conditions, and reasonable workloads. Strike action is taken as a last resort when nurses feel they are being treated unfairly with respect to any of those conditions. Workload and working conditions can have moral implications if they are such that nurses are unable to uphold their value of delivering safe, compassionate, competent, and ethical care. A recent news story reported the death of a patient who was given a wrong dose of medication by a nurse. It is easy to place the blame on the nurse, but if she or he were working under highly stressful conditions, for instance, with too many patients, it would also be easy to see that mistakes were bound to happen. Instead of blaming the nurse, perhaps the blame should be put on the system that put the nurse in that difficult position. These kinds of issues are often the basis of strike action. When nurses strike to improve their salaries and working conditions, they are acting to ensure that they are treated justly in the workplace and that working conditions enable them to deliver quality care. Thus strike action can in itself be ethical, as long as provisions are made to ensure that patients get safe care as a minimum. Nurses sometimes have difficulty with the idea of "abandoning" their patients during a strike. It might help them to consider that they are working for social and distributive justice.

Similarly, it is sometimes difficult for nurses to put limits on patient behaviour, as many nurses seem to view nursing as being about self-sacrifice. However, if you view nursing as being about human interactions and consider that all humans deserve to be treated justly, it will help you realize that nurses also deserve just treatment. They must not be put at risk in the context of their work environment.

We now turn to the analysis of two practice examples that demonstrate justice issues. The first involves a scarce resource, whereas the second involves both retributive justice and justice in the workplace.

Trying It On

9.1 The Scarcest of Resources: Mr. Boyd's Liver

Today has been a difficult day for Chris. As a staff nurse on the transplant unit he usually feels very good about his work. It makes him feel part of something really important when someone who was facing certain death is given a good chance at life with a transplanted organ. He likes being one of the people who make this process happen. He came to work here shortly after graduating and has found it an amazing learning experience. One of the things he likes best is being part of discussions about who is going to be receiving organs and what their care will involve. He also enjoys all the patient/family teaching that is part of his everyday practice.

Today, however, Chris is feeling more frustrated than satisfied. He has been asked to work with Mr. Boyd, who is on the list for a liver transplant. A compatible liver had been found at long last. As he reviewed with Mr. Boyd what the procedure would be like, and what Mr. Boyd could expect pre- and post-surgery, Chris began to question whether Mr. Boyd was a good candidate for the transplant. His liver has been damaged from too much alcohol, and it appears to Chris that his patient is continuing to drink, even though he knows he has serious health problems. In fact, Chris isn't sure that Mr. Boyd was sober during their teaching session. He suspects that the patient has been having someone bring him alcohol in hospital.

What bothers Chris is that another patient on the wait list, Mrs. Cathcart, has a genetic profile that was similar to Mr. Boyd's. The same liver could work for either of them. Chris is upset because he thinks that Mrs. Cathcart should be the one to get the liver. Mr. Boyd has been waiting longer, true, but Mrs. Cathcart has two young children. Her liver disease was a result of the hepatitis that she got when she was given a blood transfusion after the birth of her second child. She had been working as a missionary in Africa and had gone into premature labour just as she and her husband were getting ready to return to North America. Her care in the African hospital had been excellent, but then she began to hemorrhage. Blood was in short supply, and the Cathcarts suspected that it hadn't been screened properly before she was given her transfusion. Now she is waiting for a new liver.

Chris feels that Mr. Boyd does not deserve to receive the precious liver. It appears that he has not stopped drinking to this point. If he continues to drink, as seems likely, he will ruin the new liver too. The patient denies that he is still drinking and says he is a "reformed man," but Chris thinks he is lying, and feels so unhappy about the decision to give the new liver to Mr. Boyd that he does not even want to care for him. Chris finds himself feeling angry and resentful whenever he talks to Mr. Boyd, especially when he detects the scent of alcohol. He is also feeling angry with the surgeon for making such a choice. Every time the surgeon comes on the unit Chris feels like he should tell him off. He wonders what, if anything, he should do about his feelings.

The Scarcest of Resources: Mr. Boyd's Liver

Assessing the Ethics of the Situation: Relationships, Goals, Beliefs, and Values

This is clearly a distributive justice issue. Like many justice issues in health care, the primary decision is not Chris's to make. However, as mentioned above, Chris has to live with other people's decisions. Chris is experiencing moral distress because he feels that the decision to give the liver to Mr. Boyd is not fair. He knows how scarce donated livers are and is worried that giving this liver to Mr. Boyd will be a waste of a precious resource. He feels that Mr. Boyd's willingness to comply with the required post-operative regimen is suspect and that if he continues to drink the liver will be damaged and cease to function. Chris believes that Mr. Boyd's liver damage was self-induced, whereas Mrs. Cathcart's occurred through no fault of her own. Therefore, Mrs. Cathcart should have the liver: she is more deserving, and is more likely to comply with the post-op requirement. She is also a mother of young children who are dependent on her, whereas to Chris's knowledge Mr. Boyd has no family. Chris's resentment of Mr. Boyd may be affecting his care of the patient.

The surgeons appear to believe that Mr. Boyd is a suitable candidate for the liver. Chris thinks that if they knew about Mr. Boyd's behaviour they would be less willing to give it to him. In this situation we do not know the surgeons' rationale for selecting Mr. Boyd to be the recipient, but we have to assume that they have considered it carefully. We also assume that their wish is to do the "right thing."

Clearly Mr. Boyd desires to have the transplant, as he has been on the wait list for some time. What we do not know at this point is what he is thinking about his own role in maintaining the viability of the liver once it has been transplanted. We do not know what he is thinking about his drinking habits and how they will affect the situation.

Mrs. Cathcart's views on the situation are not really relevant at this point. We can be certain that she would prefer to have the liver herself, as she is undoubtedly worried about her health and the care of her children.

Reflecting on and Reviewing Potential Actions: Recognizing Available Choices and How Those Choices Are Valued

Chris has several options. He can say nothing and let the decision stand. Then he will have to resolve his own feelings about providing care to Mr. Boyd. If Chris is unable to do this, and provides inferior care, he is acting unethically. Therefore, he needs to examine his own values and beliefs. He needs to reflect on what he believes to be relevant properties in making a decision such as this.

If he is to take action on this problem, Chris could start by discussing the situation with the surgeon. Perhaps if he understood the thinking behind the decision he would be able to accept it. For example, it is possible that the surgeon has made an agreement with Mr. Boyd about his drinking. It might be that the surgeon is equally conflicted, but believes that the fairest way to handle the situation is to take the first person on the list. Perhaps he is concerned that allowing someone to "jump the queue" will set a precedent. He might also be worried that it would be unfair to make a decision based on a perception of social worth. What if Mr. Boyd is really a wealthy philanthropist who does many good works, and Mrs. Cathcart abuses her children and is disliked by almost everyone? How can one decide about the social worth of another? If Chris were able to engage in a discussion with the surgeon, he might develop a better understanding. If he were able to articulate his concerns he might also be able to get the decision changed, as it is possible that the surgeon is unaware of some of the relevant points that are troubling Chris. It is also possible that the surgeon was guided in his decision making by others or that the decision might not have been his to make. Often such decisions are made by a panel that weighs the different aspects of the situation before making a ruling. If Chris knew what they had taken into consideration it might help him accept the decision.

Chris could also address the issue with Mr. Boyd. As we have pointed out on several occasions, relational ethics requires that we attempt to discover meanings that patients ascribe to the situation. Chris might learn that Mr. Boyd has thought a lot about his drinking and is planning on changing his behaviour. It might be that Mr. Boyd needs support, and Chris could play a role in helping him find that support to stop drinking. If Chris is to feel comfortable working with Mr. Boyd, he must have as much information as possible. It might also be helpful to Mr. Boyd to understand what is at stake: that the liver could be given to someone else and that he should not be wasting such a precious resource. Chris doesn't really have any information about Mr. Boyd other than that he has abused alcohol; learning something about how the patient experiences the world might be helpful to Chris in resolving his moral distress.

Another possibility is for Chris to ask his unit manager not to assign him to work with Mr. Boyd. This should be a last resort. If Chris is not able to resolve his concerns, and it affects his care, this would be one way to deal with the situation. However, it is the least desirable of all the alternatives, because it does not really address the issue.

Selecting an Ethical Action: Maximizing Good
In this situation there is no ethical dilemma as such. Chris can undertake more than one action. All the options available to Chris require relational communication. He should start by speaking to the surgeon about the choice to give the liver to Mr. Boyd, but first he should identify the relevant properties or characteristics that he believes need to be taken into account in making a decision. This is essentially a values clarification exercise. If Chris begins an active examination of his own discomfort with the situation, he will uncover the values that make him think the decision is unfair. He will have to admit that he believes Mr. Boyd is less worthy than Mrs. Cathcart. It will probably help him to write down his beliefs. For instance, he might record that he thinks alcoholics are not to be respected or that preference should be given to patients with children or those who make "meaningful" contributions. Perhaps he believes that because Mr. Boyd is an alcoholic, he is probably homeless and therefore of lesser worth than Mrs. Cathcart. Whatever his beliefs, they will affect what he thinks are relevant properties in the situation. It will be an enlightening exercise for Chris to put his ideas down on paper. It is important that he is very honest with himself as he does this. Examining his values in this way may cause him to question what he assumes to be true about Mr. Boyd. It will also enable Chris to have a more constructive conversation with the surgeon. He needs to remember to approach the

(*Continued*)

The Scarcest of Resources: Mr. Boyd's Liver

conversation with the surgeon in the spirit of inquiry, rather than in the spirit of confrontation. That is, it is important that Chris make it clear that he wants to understand the decision, rather than challenge it. Once he has more information, he can present his counter-argument if he believes it is necessary.

Next, Chris should open a conversation with Mr. Boyd. In speaking with him, Chris needs to be careful to remain open and respectful. The topic will be very sensitive. Mr. Boyd has an addiction to alcohol, so Chris will need to remember that talking to someone about an addiction is not easy. Experience has taught him that addicts most often become defensive and hostile if they feel their choices are being criticized or if they feel threatened in any way. In this case, Mr. Boyd's alcoholism has threatened his life, yet he apparently continues to drink. Clearly he has a very deep-seated need. Chris also needs to keep in mind that his assumptions about Mr. Boyd are not verified; he does not have any real information except that Mr. Boyd is an alcoholic. He needs to use the principles of relational communication, namely openness and

engagement, in speaking to Mr. Boyd. Given the sensitivity of the issue, Chris might want to seek advice from an experienced addictions counsellor before he approaches the patient.

Engaging in Ethical Action
The actions suggested above are not mutually exclusive. Chris needs to find the moral courage to address the issue with the surgeon and with Mr. Boyd. All the possible actions require communication skills that should be part of daily practice.

Reflecting on and Reviewing the Ethical Action
If the problem is not resolved for Chris through these conversations, he will have to take more dramatic action. It is possible that he will want to consult the hospital's ethics committee for advice. As mentioned above, he might feel it necessary to ask not to be assigned to Mr. Boyd, but if there are no other nurses available he will have to accept the assignment and hide his displeasure at caring for the patient. However, it is most likely that after engaging Mr. Boyd in a meaningful conversation, his aversion to the patient will lessen.

Trying It On

9.2 Does He Deserve Care?

Annalise had been working on the infectious diseases (ID) unit for over four years and found it extremely interesting. She thought it was fascinating how all the pieces from observations, assessments, and the various lab results were put together to

form a diagnosis and treatment plan. She enjoyed the challenges of the work and felt that her assessments were often important in helping the physician make a diagnosis.

Only one thing about working on ID consistently bothered Annalise: the presence of convicted prisoners on the unit. This happened fairly often, as they would frequently cut themselves and do something such as rubbing feces in the wound to make it infected. This was, she supposed, the act of desperate people who would do anything to get away from the prison environment for a while. When they became infected they were admitted to ID for treatment. They were always accompanied by a guard.

Annalise had been troubled for a while by a certain patient named Mike Spenzle. He was a convicted rapist and pedophile who had been incarcerated for several years. This in itself really bothered Annalise, who could not understand how a person could do such horrible things. And this was not his first admission to the unit. This time he had a very serious leg wound that seemed not to respond to antibiotics. The infection was spreading, and he was in danger of losing his leg, if not his life. Still, he seemed to have a lot of energy for harassing the nurses. Annalise was his particular target. She was an attractive woman and an excellent nurse, and he was delighted each time she was assigned to him. When he was first admitted Annalise had put her feelings of repugnance aside, reasoning that everyone deserves a chance. However, the more she got to know him the less tolerance she felt. He seemed to be entirely self-serving and manipulative. No matter how hard she tried to open a therapeutic conversation with him, it always ended up with him closing himself off from her and making smart remarks. Even worse, the effect of her efforts seemed to be that he thought she actually had feelings for him! Whenever she came into the room he would make lewd and suggestive remarks, using very foul language. If she came too near he would try to touch

her in ways she found highly offensive. When she demanded that he stop he just laughed at her discomfort and said, "Come on, Anna. You know you like it." The guards were no help—they all seemed to enjoy watching Annalise become embarrassed and angry. The patient often became angry, too. If the care wasn't exactly what he wanted he would yell at her and sometimes threaten to throw things at her or hit her. She was actually quite frightened of him.

This whole situation bothered Annalise on many counts. First, she resented the time she spent working with Mike. She could not forgive him for his crimes and felt that he didn't deserve all the care and attention he was receiving. To some extent she felt that way about all the prisoners who were admitted to the unit, but this patient was the worst ever. She was bothered by the fact that every minute she spent with this disgusting individual was time she could have been spending with other patients who did deserve her care. She also felt it wrong that she should be required to put up with the sexual harassment and threats of physical abuse. She didn't believe it was fair to her or the other patients to have this man on the unit. Every time she cared for him she found herself spending as little time in the room as possible and doing little things to "punish" him. She would put the food just a bit out of his reach so it was hard for him to reach it. She would leave his dressing unchanged for as long as she could. She would hold off on pain medication when he asked for it, using the excuse that she was busy with other patients. Each time she did such things, she felt a little badly about not treating him like she did her other patients, but it was somewhat satisfying, too. She felt he

(Continued)

deserved it, and it gave her a feeling of regaining power to make his day a little less pleasant. After all, she reasoned, if everyone made it a treat for him to be in hospital, he would just keep repeating his self-inflicted injuries. Still, she knew she was not behaving professionally. She wondered what she should do about the whole situation. Did she have to put up with his abuse? Did they have to admit such patients when their problems were deliberately self-induced? Was it right to take time away from other patients to care for this man? What was the fairest way to handle the situation? She hated to mention it to Murray, her unit manager, because she felt she should be able to deal with it. She was also reluctant to draw attention to the fact that yet another patient was attracted to her, as it wasn't the first time this had occurred with the prisoners. And she certainly wasn't about to tell anyone about her punishing the patient. But she did want something done about the whole situation. She wondered what she should do.

Applying the Framework
Does He Deserve Care?

**Assessing the Ethics of the Situation:
Relationships, Goals, Beliefs, and Values**
Again, this situation raises justice issues. Annalise's concern about the time this patient is taking from other, more deserving (in her view) patients is a question of distributive justice. The situation also has retributive justice elements, as Annalise is punishing her patient for his behaviour.

In many ways the situation is somewhat similar to that in the previous scenario, in that both nurses are unhappy about providing care for patients they feel are not deserving of that care. The difference here is that Annalise has attempted to establish a therapeutic relationship with the patient. She has come to know him quite well and has already made efforts to engage in relational dialogue with him. He has resisted her efforts and misinterpreted them. He is also abusive toward her and is putting her at risk of physical and emotional harm. In addition, she may lose her self-respect because of her unprofessional behaviour.

As mentioned above, Annalise has had a difficult time working with prisoners in general. Her belief in upholding the law and not harming others makes it difficult for her to think that they are deserving of care. On the contrary, she does have a strong belief that everyone has some worth and, as such, has a right to basic care. This has led her to try to do the best she can to put her feelings aside. Now she has changed her mind about the patient. The way he is treating her makes her angry and uncomfortable. The nature of his crimes is especially upsetting to her, and she has become resentful of the time she spends with him. She knows that punishing a patient is not part of professional practice, but she also feels that she needs to regain some control in the situation. She is able to justify her behaviour by suggesting to herself that it is for his own good: if she makes it less pleasant for him to be in hospital, he will be less likely to damage himself. She wants to protect herself because she doesn't feel she deserves to be abused, and she wants to provide good care to the other patients on the unit.

The patient seems to have ideas about his rights and privileges as a patient. He seems to think that nurses are "fair game" if they provide him with amusement. He also seems to be seeing Annalise as a sexual object rather than a professional. His views about women in general probably play into this. It seems that he has little respect for women, or indeed for anyone else who does not do what he wants. His violent past is reflected in his behaviour with Annalise.

The guards who are supposed to be monitoring Mike's behaviour seem to share his beliefs about women and nurses in general, and Annalise in particular. They do not seem to believe that it is their responsibility to challenge Mike's behaviour.

At this point we do not know what Murray, the unit manager, thinks about the situation. However, Murray's beliefs are vital to determining his actions.

Reflecting on and Reviewing Potential Actions: Recognizing Available Choices and How Those Choices Are Valued

As she ponders the situation, Annalise will soon realize that she needs to act quickly to change things. Mike's advances and threats are making her uncomfortable and affecting both her satisfaction with her work life and her care of the patient. If she

becomes sufficiently upset about what is happening with the prisoners, she might have to leave the unit temporarily or permanently. Annalise is an experienced and caring nurse, and her departure would be bad for the unit and for patient care. Her care of Mike is being affected in a way that could damage her professional reputation and her sense of self as a nurse. She must overcome her reluctance and go first to her unit manager. She should also seek support from the penal institution itself. The behaviour of the guards is unacceptable; they should be putting a stop to Mike's behaviour. It is their duty to be sure that Mike does not cause damage, and what he is doing to Annalise is damaging to her.

Annalise does not have further responsibility to try to engage Mike in relational communication at this point, as he has abused this privilege. Until she has some reasonable assurance that his behaviour toward her will improve, she has the right to avoid contact with him. Annalise's rights as a nurse and a person are as important as those of the patient.

If she does not get support from her unit manager and the guards, Annalise should be prepared to go higher up the chain of command. She should speak to someone in higher authority in nursing and also in the jail. She could also report the situation to her provincial association.

Selecting an Ethical Action: Maximizing Good

Annalise does not really have a choice in reporting what is happening. If she does not, she risks affecting care. Therefore, she must talk to her immediate supervisor and the guards. Annalise's next action will depend on the response she receives. Ideally, Murray will sit down and talk with Mike and Annalise together to try to sort

(Continued)

something out. He will have to make it very clear that Mike's behaviour will not be tolerated. Murray might want to talk to the patient's physician as well. All should be in agreement that any disrespect or abuse of Annalise (and any other nurses involved) must stop. If it does not, Murray has the right to refuse further care of the patient. The patient has full cognitive capacity and is responsible for his actions, so his actions cannot be excused. He should be informed that if his behaviour does not improve, he will be discharged from the unit. Murray should also speak to the guards and make sure it is understood that their responsibility is not just to prevent the patient from escaping but also to protect the staff. Their lack of action in this matter should be reported to their supervisor.

It seems clear that Murray should release Annalise from having to care for this particular patient. He should also meet with the physicians, the prison staff, and all staff members who work with Mike and other prisoners. They should discuss their beliefs and feelings about the situation and work out a strategy to prevent future recurrences. Annalise might be reluctant to share with the staff her concerns about Mike's advances toward her. It is not necessary that she do so; it is enough for her to say that his behaviour has been objectionable. The entire staff should work together to set acceptable boundaries and guidelines for care. It is not acceptable to refuse future patients on the basis that they might behave badly; instead, it is necessary to provide them with rules and consequences that will be enforced. Some might question whether it is acceptable, within the sphere of a relational ethic, to exert so much control over patients. Our response is that in order to be fair and just to nurses and other staff, it is necessary to ensure that they are treated with respect and that they can practise safely in the workplace. That is, the principle of justice demands that the rights and privileges of one person (the patient) do not impinge on those of another (the nurse).

Engaging in Ethical Action

Annalise and the unit manager will both need moral courage to address this situation. Once staff members have agreed on the boundaries, they will all have to adhere to the rules and act consistently toward future prisoners. Justice demands that patients and nurses be treated fairly, and the most just action in this case would be a consistent approach toward patients.

Reflecting on and Reviewing the Ethical Action

Once the problem has been addressed, all staff members, including Annalise, will have to examine their behaviours toward prisoners as patients. This includes Mike. Controlling unacceptable behaviour must not translate into discriminatory practices toward any patient. It will be necessary to have future meetings to assess ongoing progress in this area. In examining how they are doing in this regard, staff should involve patients in the discussions. Otherwise there is a danger that the prisoners as patients will be treated unequally or unfairly.

CHAPTER SUMMARY

In this chapter we discussed justice, the sixth primary value in the CNA Code of Ethics for Registered Nurses. We showed different ways that justice can be defined from legal and philosophical perspectives, including the concepts of distributive, retributive, and restorative justice. We then described justice as a bioethical principle. First we developed the idea of distributive justice in health care and demonstrated how the Canada Health Act was essentially a document about distributive justice. Then we drew distinctions between distributive and social justice. We made the point that there is often considerable overlap between distributive and social justice, because the way in which distribution decisions are made is often determined by beliefs about relative value and worth. To conclude our more general statements we described some issues around justice in research.

Next, we turned our attention to different aspects of justice as it is lived out in nursing. We talked about how decisions about resource allocation get made at the macro or administrative level, and described how such decisions might affect nurses and what they might do to influence these decisions. We then discussed a number of practice examples around allocation of a very scarce resource in health care today: the nurse's time. We pointed out that even at the micro or direct care level, the way a nurse distributes a resource such as time is driven by his or her underlying values. We also touched briefly on issues of justice in the workplace, pointing out that nurses have a right to be treated fairly and equitably in their jobs. Finally, we described two practice scenarios: one involved a decision about distribution of a scarce resource, that is, an organ for transplant; the second involved just treatment of a nurse and a patient in conflict.

We hope that this discussion has helped you see even more clearly that all decisions made about resource distribution and fairness are based on underlying values. Therefore, it is essential that you continually reflect on your own values and understandings about relevant properties in given situations.

Questions for Reflection

1. Consider a time in your personal life when you thought an injustice had happened. Reflect on that situation in light of the kinds of justice we have discussed in this chapter. Consider what would have made the situation more just from your perspective. Think about the values that might have been involved, and how your values differed from those of others involved in the situation. Is there anything you might have done that you did not do to make the situation more just?

2. Think about a situation involving injustice in your health care experience, either as a caregiver or as a recipient. Reflect on that situation in light of the kinds of justice we have discussed in this chapter. Consider what would have made the situation more just from your perspective. Think about the values that might have been involved, and how your values differed from those of others involved in the situation. Is there anything you might have done that you did not do to make the situation more just?

3. Think of a time when you were involved in an act of retributive justice. Think about how that made you feel. Consider whether you would have done the same thing now, given what you understand about justice. Have you ever been involved in an act of retributive justice in health care? Again, consider the situation and reflect on how you would handle it now.

Exercises

1. Consider the following scenario: City Council has just announced an exciting new initiative. They are going to build a shelter for homeless people in the city core. They want to centralize the homeless and get them away from the city streets, where they are constantly harassing other citizens. The homeless are becoming an increasing problem because many of them come to the city in search of work, and there is simply no affordable accommodation. It is time to do something about this problem, and a shelter seems like the ideal solution.

   Working in small groups, think about the social justice elements in this situation and how they are related to determinants of health. As a nurse working in the community, what obligations might you have related to this policy decision of City Council and the health of the homeless population? Did City Council make the right decision? Is this a just way of approaching the needs of the homeless?

2. In small groups, consider the elements of justice in the question, "Who should get the heart transplant?"

   a. A 45-year-old CEO of a small but successful manufacturing company and father of two who has been on the wait list for 14 months

   b. A 14-year-old boy with Down syndrome who has been on the wait-list for 17 months

   Consider what you might think of as relevant properties in this situation. Decide on which patient the group agrees should get the transplant, and consider the values your choice represents. Consider what would have to happen, that is, how the relevant properties might change, in order for you to change your decision.

3. In a small group, develop a scenario that has social justice implications. Analyze the scenario using the Framework for Ethical Decision Making, and present your scenario and analysis to the larger group.

Research Activities

1. Find an article in a recent newspaper that reflects a justice issue in health care. Make a brief summary of the issue, including who was involved, what elements of justice were represented, and who made the decisions and on what basis (if known). Present your summary to the class, and engage classmates in a discussion of what might have been done differently and why, and of what the nurses' roles might have been.

2. Find a published article in a nursing journal on justice in health care. Make a summary of the key points in the article. In small groups, present the key points to other members of the group. Discuss, and have someone record, the kinds of issues that are raised. Report your findings to the class. As a class, try to determine what proportion of the

issues reported are social justice issues, distributive justice issues, or issues of fairness in the workplace.

3. When you are in the clinical setting, ask three nurses to describe an issue in which they thought that an injustice occurred. Report back to the class the kinds of issues described (but not the details, to protect confidentiality). Have the class consider what kinds of issues are talked about most often and why.

Key Terms

accessibility

comprehensiveness

conflict of interest

deterrence

portability

public administration

rehabilitation

relevant properties

restorative justice

retributive justice

social justice

universality

vulnerable groups

References

Aristotle (1998). *The Nicomachean ethics* (transl. D. Ross, revised J. L. Ackrill & J. O. Urmson). New York: Oxford University Press.

Beauchamp, T., & Childress, J. (1994). *Principles of biomedical ethics* (4th ed.). New York: Oxford University Press.

Canadian Nurses Association (2006). Social justice . . . a means to an end, an end in itself. Ottawa: Author. Retrieved August 2008 from www.cna-aiic.ca.

Canadian Nurses Association (2008). *Code of ethics for registered nurses* (Centennial Ed.). Ottawa: Author.

Curzer, H. J. (1993). Is care a virtue for health care professionals? *The Journal of Medicine and Philosophy, 18*, 51–69.

Government of Canada (2006). *Tri-Council policy statement*. Retrieved September 12, 2006, from http://pre.ethics.gc.ca/english/policystatement/context.cfm#C.

Health Canada (2002). *Canada Health Act overview*. Retrieved September 2, 2006, from www.hc-sc.gc.ca/ahc-asc/media/nr-cp/2002/2002_care-soinsbk4_e.html.

Martin, R. M. (1991). *The philosopher's dictionary*. Peterborough, ON: Broadview Press.

Rawls, J. (1971). *A theory of justice*. Cambridge, MA: The Belknap Press of Harvard University Press.

Suggested Reading

Bekemeier, B., & Butterfield, P. (2005). Unreconciled inconsistencies: A critical review of the concept of social justice in three national nursing documents. *Advances in Nursing Science, 28*, 152–162.

Falk-Rafael, A. (2006). Globalization and global health: Toward nursing praxis in the global community. *Advances in Nursing Science, 29*, 2–14.

Giddings, L. S. (2005). A theoretical model of social consciousness. *Advances in Nursing Science, 28*, 224–39.

Kohi, T. W., Makoae, L., Chirwa, M., Holzemer, W. L., Phetlhu, D. R., Uys, L., Naidoo, J., Dlamini, P. S., & Greeff, M. (2006). HIV and AIDS stigma violates human rights in five African countries. *Nursing Ethics, 13,* 404–415.

Miller, P., & Kenny, N. P. (2002). Walking the moral tightrope: Respecting and protecting children in health-related research. *Cambridge Quarterly of Healthcare Ethics, 11,* 217–229.

Ornek, N., & Sahinoglu, S. (2006). Violence against women in Turkey and the role of women physicians. *Nursing Ethics, 13,* 197–205.

Phillips, L. J., & Phillips, W. (2006). Better reproductive healthcare for women with disabilities: A role for nursing leadership. *Advances in Nursing Science, 29,*134–151.

Smoyak, S. A. (2004). Gender differences: From discrimination to acceptance. *Journal of Psychosocial Nursing and Mental Health Services, 42*(6), 6–7.

Turner, L. (2005). Bioethics, social class, and the sociological imagination. *Cambridge Quarterly of Healthcare Ethics, 14,* 374–378.

Vehmas, S. (2004). Dimensions of disability. *Cambridge Quarterly of Healthcare Ethics, 13,* 34–40.

Welchman, J., & Griener, G. G. (2005). Patient advocacy and professional associations: Individual and collective responsibilties. *Nursing Ethics, 12,* 296–304.

Williams, L. L. (2006). The fair factor in matters of trust. *Nursing Administration Quarterly, 30,* 30–37.

Chapter 10
Value 7: Being Accountable

Chapter Outline

Learning Objectives

After reading this chapter, you should be able to:

- describe the seventh primary value in the CNA Code of Ethics for Registered Nurses: *Being accountable*

- discuss virtue and integrity as the foundation for individual accountability for practice

- discuss relational nursing ethics and issues of accountability

- describe evolving understandings of accountability and factors affecting accountability in practice

- discuss accountability for others' practice

- describe conflict of interest in practice

- discuss the concept of fitness to practise and how it relates to accountability

- apply the Framework for Ethical Decision Making to a clinical problem related to accountability

The topic of this chapter is the seventh value of the CNA Code of Ethics for Registered Nurses: *Being accountable*. The Code states that "Nurses are accountable for their actions and answerable for their practice" (CNA, 2008, p. 18). That is, they must take responsibility for nursing practice, including, to some extent, the practice of other nurses. This can be a particularly challenging aspect of nursing ethics, as the following scenario will illustrate.

Imagine that you are Maria Estevez, a new graduate who has just started working in neonatal intensive care. You feel very fortunate to get the job because they don't usually hire new grads, but they have been desperately short-staffed and have hired several from your class. Now you have your chance to do the kind of nursing you've always wanted to do. This is your second week on the unit since orientation, and you are very nervous working with these tiny babies. Your orientation was excellent, but you feel overwhelmed most of the time. Tonight you are buddied with Jeanne, an experienced grad who has just gone down to dinner. The unit is extremely busy and all the other nurses still on the unit seem to be responding to urgent patient needs.

Your patient, Stephanie, weighs only 720 g and has a patent ductus arteriosus (abnormal connection between the aorta and the pulmonary artery). She's so fragile-looking that you feel it's a miracle she's alive at all. You are becoming quite attached to her and her parents. You've just given her indomethacin, which is standard care for babies with a patent ductus. Checking her vital signs, you notice that her mean arterial pressure has dropped significantly. Quickly you check her urine output, which is also down. Her perfusion is slow, too, and you recognize the signs of serious cardiovascular problems. You call the medical resident who comes immediately. He's new to the unit, having just rotated in the previous week. He examines Stephanie and agrees with your assessment that her condition is deteriorating. He orders hydrocortisone, 2 mg/kg. You are really worried and believe that the order is urgent and you need to act immediately. You're not all that familiar with the med, but don't think you have time to look it up, and everyone is busy so there is no one to ask. You draw up the hydrocortisone and give it IV, as ordered. Stephanie seems to be looking a little better, and you begin to relax a bit. When Jeanne returns you tell her what happened, feeling sure she will be pleased with your quick action. She looks at you in horror and says, "Oh no! You gave 2 mg/kg of hydrocortisone to a baby on indomethacin? The dose is 0.2 mg/kg, and we don't give it with indomethacin. Didn't you check? It's almost for sure this baby will develop a bowel perforation in the next couple of days. We have to get the neonatologist in here stat, and we're going to have to report this. We've got a problem here!"

This scenario raises many questions that can introduce us to some of the complexities related to accountability. Who should be held accountable for this error? Should it be the medical resident, who gave an incorrect drug order? Should it be Maria, who gave the medication as ordered, but did not check incompatibilities and dosage before drawing it up? Should it be the nurse manager or charge nurse who left a newly hired new graduate on a shift where there was insufficient support for her? Nurses are accountable for their practice, but it is not always clear what their level of responsibility should be when they are working under very difficult circumstances.

Nursing's understanding of accountability has changed as nurses have come to think of themselves as professionals. It has also been altered as nurses have assumed new responsibilities as a result of advanced technology, increasingly complex health care environments and services, and changes in the involvement of patients and families in care. In this chapter we explore aspects of accountability including integrity, responsibility, answerability, advocacy, and moral community, and consider accountability in relation to the evolving nature of nursing practice and health care systems in many settings. We demonstrate that relationship plays a significant role in the enactment of accountability and advocacy. We describe evolving understandings of accountability, factors that affect accountability in the workplace, accountability for the practice of others, and conflict of interest. Exploring accountability in this way helps us show the multiple obligations nurses face in providing safe, compassionate, competent, and ethical care. Finally, we describe some moral implications of accepting accountability in nursing, as presented in two case studies.

THE SEVENTH PRIMARY VALUE: BEING ACCOUNTABLE

You may already have some understanding of the complexity of being accountable in nursing, as it is a feature of everyday practice. **Accountability** is "an obligation or willingness to accept responsibility or to *account* for one's actions" (Merriam-Webster online, emphasis in original) and refers to being answerable to someone for something one has done. **Answerability** means offering reasons and explanations to others for aspects of nursing practice.

In the literature, accountability is often linked with the concept of professional autonomy, because it is assumed that if one is to make independent decisions about practice (autonomy), one must be prepared to accept responsibility for those decisions and subsequent outcomes. Being accountable involves many elements that we have discussed earlier in this book, and you will see much that is familiar in this chapter. That is to be expected, as nurses are accountable for all aspects of ethical practice, including preserving dignity, maintaining privacy and confidentiality, and safeguarding justice. Accountability is grounded in the moral principles of fidelity and respect for the dignity, worth, and self-determination of patients and others with whom nurses work. As accountable professionals, "Nurses are honest and practise with integrity in all of their professional interactions" (CNA, 2008, p. 18). Part of being an accountable nurse means practising within your level of competence and maintaining personal levels of health and well-being in keeping with nursing responsibilities. As members of a moral community, nurses also acknowledge their responsibility to contribute to positive, healthy work environments.

Accountability in nursing happens at two levels. Professional nursing associations are responsible for maintaining overall standards, while individuals are held accountable for their own practice, as defined by those standards. In Chapter 4 we discussed accountability as a characteristic of a self-regulating profession, and described how professional associations monitor and evaluate nurses' competence. We pointed out that the provincial and territorial associations have practice standards that delineate expectations of nurses. Thus the profession as a whole works to ensure that nurses uphold agreed-upon values and practise according to accepted understandings of competence. Nurses who fail to do so can be disciplined, and even denied the right to practise. Aspects of nursing practice are also controlled to some extent by law. Nursing as a profession in Canada is paid for out of the public purse, and there are certain societal expectations that must be met. Nurses will be held accountable under law when a duty of care has been determined and action (or lack of action) results in harm to a patient. The law addresses issues such as battery and assault, consent (or lack of consent), negligence, and breach of standard of care. Each nurse is, therefore, expected to know the law and relevant Acts, and to practise within their boundaries.

Clearly, regulation of nursing practice is of societal concern, and mechanisms are in place to ensure that standards of care are maintained and patients are not subjected to harm. Nonetheless, as we mentioned above, it is important to emphasize that each individual nurse has a moral obligation to provide the best care possible. In the following paragraphs, we will focus on accountability of the individual nurse and how that accountability can be developed and maintained.

INDIVIDUAL ACCOUNTABILITY

Individual nurses are accountable for their own practice, so it seems logical that a discussion of personal accountability in nursing begin with virtue, which we described in Chapter 3 as the moral motivation for beneficent action.

Virtue and Integrity as a Foundation

In nursing, virtue includes the notion of personal integrity. Michael Yeo, a noted Canadian philosopher and ethicist, says that integrity, or wholeness, is the foundation of ethical behaviour, and, as such, keeps us on a path to a moral life (Yeo & Moorehouse, 1996). The word integrity comes from the Latin *integer*, meaning "whole." Each of us lives with many roles, relationships, and commitments, and if we are to be whole, the different aspects of our lives must be guided by a coherent set of principles. A person with integrity demonstrates consistency among values, beliefs, and actions. Nurses are accountable within an ethical framework and are guided by professional values and standards of practice. Nurses who aspire to wholeness also endeavour to achieve consistency and continuity across the various dimensions of their lives. Concepts basic to integrity include 1) moral agency, 2) fidelity to promise, and 3) steadfastness (Yeo & Moorehouse, 1996).

Moral Agency Nurses' integrity is revealed through moral agency. In Chapter 1 we defined moral agency as the ability to act on moral beliefs. The CNA Code of Ethics for Registered Nurses expands that definition by describing moral agency as "the capacity or power of a nurse to direct his or her motives and actions to some ethical end; essentially, doing what is good and right" (CNA, 2008, p. 26). This requires ongoing development. Students and newly graduated nurses often submit to the moral authority of others, doing what they are told without questioning the moral dimensions of their actions. As they grow in experience and confidence they begin to reflect on moral values and principles, and their identities as moral agents are constructed in practice. They learn through reflection to examine their beliefs and actions critically, and begin to make their own moral decisions, thus shaping their own moral code. As their ethical practice evolves they simultaneously develop a growing awareness of themselves as moral agents. Their sense of integrity develops as they assume greater control over and accountability for their moral lives (Yeo & Moorehouse, 1996).

Fidelity to Promise Moral agency is partially bound up with our willingness to promise and to hold ourselves to promises made. Moral agents are expected to be true to their word, to make promises and stick by them. Someone whose word means nothing and who cannot be counted on to keep a promise lacks integrity (Yeo & Moorehouse, 1996). Mila Aroskar, an American nurse ethicist, was one of the earliest to define *fidelity* in nursing practice. She described fidelity as undisputed and primary loyalty and faithfulness to the patient (Aroskar, 1987). That might seem somewhat overstated today, as we become more aware of moral complexity and conflicting obligations in practice, but clearly Aroskar meant to convey that to be a nurse is to make promises and be faithful to those promises. Fidelity is the foundation of a trusting nurse-patient relationship.

Steadfastness To be **steadfast** is to be "firm in belief, determination, or adherence" (Merriam-Webster on-line). Being true to our moral code or promises is sometimes difficult. Sometimes we have to work hard at it. There may be powerful forces constraining what we can and cannot do. Temptations or fears may militate against doing what we believe to be right and good. Sometimes doing what is right carries a price or involves a sacrifice. Steadfastness has to do with being strong in our beliefs and speaking up for what is right, that is, acting as moral agents. People of integrity have an unwillingness to yield their principles and values even when the pressures to do so are great (Yeo & Moorehouse, 1996). However, steadfastness does not mean stubborn adherence to unexamined beliefs. The processes of reflection and thoughtful discourse about the values that guide action are key.

Nursing Accountability as Relational

All nursing involves some kind of relationship, because whether we are carrying out skilled tasks, engaging with patients in discussions about their feelings and experiences, or teaching students, we are interacting with others. Each of us is responsible for our actions in relation to the people we care for, educate, supervise, or work with in partnership. As we have said in earlier chapters, relational ethics lies in commitment to others and a sense of responsibility toward them. Consequently, accountability is largely founded on relational ethics.

We have discussed in earlier chapters that relational ethics is an "action" ethic. John Caputo (1989), a prominent American philosopher, helps us to understand that whenever we act we do so knowing that we do not have all the answers. That is, we are not always certain if we have chosen the right or best action, but we do what seems wisest at the time because something has to be done. Responsibility and accountability are about our actions and how we defend them. Sometimes we are required to act before we are fully prepared, and sometimes our actions are difficult to explain. However, because we have a duty toward the "other," our responsibility cannot be avoided, ignored, or passed on to another colleague. From a relational ethics stance, responsibility is a personal and shared commitment and obligation.

Relational ethics places emphasis on the nurse understanding the other, but at the same time necessitates an understanding of self. For example, nurses in palliative care must pay attention to their own personal assumptions and beliefs about suffering if they are to move toward understanding others' experience. Recognizing their own vulnerabilities and humanity as nurses helps them move beyond their own moral distress to enact moral courage in situations where the other's suffering is unbearable. Moral courage is informed by knowledge, past experiences, and trust in one's own and another's ability to grow. The source of moral commitment is grounded in relationships with others.

ACCOUNTABILITY IN PRACTICE

As a part of accountability, nurses are expected to show how they make a difference in the lives of patients and families. Many nurse scholars have dedicated their efforts to defining the essential nature of nursing practice. It is important to note that when we consider *practice* we do not mean only direct nursing care. Educators practise nursing in the domain of education, while researchers practise nursing in the domain of research. In each domain of nursing we are accountable for what we do.

Evolving Understandings of Accountability

Conceptualizations of nursing accountability have evolved over time to reflect social context and current issues. Factors influencing how nursing has been understood include such things as the changing role of women in society, development of professional nursing standards and a Code of Ethics for Registered Nurses, advanced education for nurses, an emerging interest in patients' rights, and fiscal constraints. Marianne Lamb, a Canadian nurse historian, notes, ". . . between the thirties and sixties, nursing organizations formalized nursing codes of ethics, reflecting a move away from a focus on the character of the nurse to a focus on the nurse's moral obligations and responsibilities as a professional" (Lamb, 2004, p. 29).

Modern nursing is understood as a profession and a practice. Contemporary health care work is at present characterized by:

- multiple relationships among providers and patients who frequently lack any sustained history;
- tensions between goals of the organization and goals of workers, either as individuals or as a group;
- fragmentation of services;
- rapidly changing organizational structures;

- a shift to increased community-based care;

- lack of agreement on what constitutes expert knowledge; and

- diffusion of responsibilities as knowledge is continuously negotiated and redistributed among and between individuals and disciplines.

The growing understanding that nurses work collaboratively, rather than subserviently, in relationship with other health care professionals has led to a shift in perspective on nursing accountability. Nurses are expected to exercise independent professional judgment and moral agency, but boundaries around nursing work are shifting, and it is becoming increasingly difficult to define what it is that separates nursing work from that of many other professionals. Consequently, it is more difficult than ever to state just what it is for which nurses should be held accountable.

Factors Affecting Accountability in Practice

Staffing shortages, increased complexity of care, and reduced resources for health care service often result in little time for nurses to enter into an authentic and engaged relationship with patients, families, and others, which makes it much more difficult to give informed, ethical care. It could be argued that it is not fair or just to hold nurses accountable for knowing what the patient wants and needs and delivering top quality care if structural influences such as limited time and resources make it impossible for them to fulfill those obligations. For example, consider a patient experiencing intense anxiety because he has not received his medication. It may be that the nurse forgot to give the medication because she was too busy. Should she be held accountable for that omission? Is it reasonable to say that it was her fault and that she should be held accountable, despite the fact that the unit was extremely short-staffed, the nurse had five other very ill patients and had just received an emergency admission, and she hadn't been able to take a break for seven or eight hours? It is clear that the nurse made an error in failing to give the medication. What is not clear is whether this is, in fact, an **ethical violation**, that is "actions or failures to act that breach fundamental duties to the persons receiving care or to colleagues and other health care providers" (CNA, 2008, p. 7). An ethical violation only occurs if it is reasonable to hold the nurse accountable for the acts or omissions in question.

Another structural issue that influences understandings of accountability is again related to shortages of staff. The CNA Code of Ethics for Registered Nurses indicates that "Nurses practice within the limits of their competence. When aspects of care are beyond their level of competence, they seek additional information or knowledge, seek help . . . and/or request a different work assignment" (CNA, 2008, p. 18). This seems fairly straightforward in theory, but in practice may be more difficult because often there are no qualified nurses available. Something that we call moral unpreparedness is becoming more common in today's health care environment. **Moral unpreparedness** exists when nurses enter a situation where they lack preparation for giving ethical care to patients and families. An example is Peter's situation. Peter is a newly graduated nurse who is asked to "float" to the intensive care unit (ICU). He tells his supervisor that he does not feel competent to work in ICU, and is told that they can't find anyone else and that they simply need more nurse "bodies." Peter agrees, knowing that he does not have the necessary clinical skills to provide competent ethical care in this environment. This situation is similar to that presented in the introduction to this chapter, and raises similar questions. For instance, in the event that Peter makes an error, who should be accountable? Should it be Peter himself, who has allowed himself to be convinced by his superiors that his going to the ICU is in the best interests of the patient? Should it be those who asked him to go to ICU, reasoning that in a desperate situation even someone inexperienced would be better than no one? The answers to these questions are far from clear. When nurses are placed in situations that compromise their ability to practise to their level of competence, or when their level of competence is unequal to the demands of care, accountability requires that the nurse put forth the best effort possible in the circumstances. Ethical analysis would suggest, as Caputo says, that we "do the best we can" and must be held accountable for our effort, but perhaps not for the final outcome if our efforts are constrained. Legal analysis might see it differently. If a nurse is a licensed professional, the court might hold that he or she is responsible for his or her actions, even under these difficult circumstances.

The CNA Code of Ethics for Registered Nurses states very clearly that when a nurse feels unprepared to meet the requirements of care, she or he is obligated to inform supervisors of the fact and "remain with the person receiving care until another nurse is available" (CNA, 2008, p. 18). In other words, it is not acceptable for a nurse to abandon a patient because she or he feels compromised. Similarly, if a nurse has a values conflict with those receiving care, accountability requires that he or she must continue to provide care until alternative arrangements for care can be made. For example, consider Jaime's concern. As a nurse in a rural hospital, she is expected to work in all areas as the need arises. One day she is assigned to the operating room to assist in a therapeutic abortion. Jaime has been a very strong pro-life advocate in the community, and is horrified to find herself in this position. The patient is a young woman with severe multiple sclerosis (MS) who became pregnant as the result of a rape. Her MS appears to have been exacerbated by the pregnancy. She desperately wants not to be pregnant, as she fears that she will be unable to care for the child and feels her health is in great danger. Three local physicians have agreed that her health was jeopardized by the pregnancy and Dr. Mason has just begun the procedure. Jaime is the only RN on duty in this part of the hospital, and Dr. Mason is expecting her assistance. Jaime is reluctant to take part in this procedure, but the Code indicates that she cannot abandon the patient without any nursing care. Another aspect of accountability rests in the responsibility to recognize the problem and take action. Jaime quickly puts in a call to the Director of Nursing requesting immediate replacement. Soon another nurse arrives from the medical-surgical unit to take Jaime's place, and she hurries to take over the other nurse's duties. In this situation Jaime acts appropriately and it is fortunate that she is able to find a replacement. Another time there might not be a suitable alternative and she might have to compromise her own values in order to ensure that the patient receives the necessary care. This would undoubtedly cause her moral distress. Therefore, Jaime's next course of action should be to try to get a policy in place regarding staffing during such procedures in order that the problem can be avoided in future.

Accountability for the Practice of Others

An interesting and difficult area of nursing accountability has to do with monitoring others' practice. The CNA Code of Ethics for Registered Nurses indicates that "Nurses are attentive to signs that a colleague is unable, for whatever reason, to perform her or his duties. In such a case, nurses will take the necessary steps to protect the safety of persons receiving care" (CNA, 2008, p. 18). It is not always clear what the "necessary steps" might be. As a practice example, consider the situation facing a group of nurses who work on a rehabilitation unit. Their colleague Charlene has just gone through a difficult divorce. The marriage fell apart after the suicide of her teenage son about four years ago. Charlene has been carrying on, but her colleagues have been worried about her. She often seems to be somewhat confused and frequently smells of alcohol. The nurses are concerned that she has a drinking problem that has not been addressed, but they are very sympathetic. She's such a nice person, and she has been through so much. They decide that for the next little while they will take turns covering for her. If she seems to be under the influence of alcohol they will offer to assist her and be sure that she has someone with her when she is giving direct care. They feel that this is the best way to support her at present until she can get her life back on track. They don't want to report her because they think it will just make the problem worse. As one nurse says, "She just needs her friends to help her get through this bad patch. No sense making it worse by having the unit manager on the rampage."

If we consider what the Code says, we would have to question the action of Charlene's colleagues. Although they think they are helping, these are not the necessary steps to ensure that Charlene can perform her duties. A more ethical approach would be to speak to her directly and indicate that it has been noticed that she has been under the influence of alcohol at work. If she refuses to change her behaviour immediately, the supervisor will have to be notified. If the supervisor fails to take action, the professional association should be contacted. Although this would be very difficult, it is essential for patient care and safety, as well as Charlene's own safety, that the problem be dealt with directly. "Necessary steps" are often uncomfortable, but the accountable nurse will not hesitate to do what is required to protect patients. Part of practising as an accountable nurse involves working to create a moral community such that individuals feel safe in reporting such problems, knowing that they will be dealt with fairly and justly.

Accountability and Conflict of Interest

Practice issues in accountability include situations in which the nurse finds her- or himself in a conflict of interest. We discussed this briefly in Chapter 9, where we defined it as making a decision based on what is in one's own best interests, not on the best interests of others who might be affected by the decision. As a practice example, consider Sharon, who works as an enterostomal therapist in home care. Part of her specialty involves wound management. She is constantly being approached by representatives from companies that produce wound management products. Each representative assures her of the superiority of his or her company's product. One day a representative offers to take Sharon as part of a group of ETs to dinner at the best restaurant in the city. He claims it is to thank them for all their hard work throughout the year, but Sharon suspects it is a way of getting the ETs to think more favourably about his products. She declines because she believes this to be a conflict of interest. In effect she feels she is being "bribed" to recommend that company's products.

These kinds of scenarios come up often. It is not uncommon to find industry representatives sponsoring educational sessions, buying pizza or chocolates for nursing units, or giving merchandise such as books, pens, or other such tokens. These kinds of benefits are probably quite benign. However, more elaborate rewards such as dinners and sponsored travel are more problematic. The nurse must remember that the primary purpose of this generosity is to encourage use of the company's products. This is not to suggest that industry representatives are immoral people, but they do have an obligation to try to promote their products, and gifts are one way to do this. Educational sessions about the product are a necessary component of evidence-based practice. However, unrelated educational sessions or other gifts raise the potential for conflict of interest. The concern is that they might cause a nurse to choose a product based on perceived "rewards" rather than effectiveness of the product. The effects of such rewards can be subtle and unrecognized. Nurses need to be acutely sensitive to such possible influences on their decision making and be sure they evaluate the available evidence carefully before choosing a product. To be confident that they have not been influenced, they should resist other rewards. Accountability demands that decisions are made based on available evidence, not personal gain.

MAINTAINING FITNESS TO PRACTISE

We have mentioned repeatedly that each nurse is responsible and accountable for her or his own practice. That means maintaining competence and being sure that one has the necessary skills and knowledge. Note, however, that while competence is necessary for care delivery, it is not sufficient. To provide acceptable care, the nurse must have **fitness to practise**: the physical, mental, and emotional capacities to deal with the often stressful and demanding health care environment. In the CNA Code of Ethics for Registered Nurses, one of the responsibility statements under the value of *being accountable* indicates that "Nurses maintain their fitness to practise. If they are aware that they do not have the necessary physical, mental, or emotional capacity to practise safely and competently, they withdraw from the provision of care after consulting with their employer or, if they are self-employed, arranging that someone else attend to their clients' health care needs. Nurses then take necessary steps to regain their fitness to practise" (CNA, 2008, p. 18).

This suggests, at least at some level, that it is unethical for nurses to work when they have diminished capacity, for whatever reason. This is not to imply that nurses would be unethical if they went to work with the "sniffles," but it does put emphasis on the importance of maintaining wellness.

If a nurse is unable to fulfill the obligations required by the job, undue strain may be put on other colleagues and the system. For example, a morbidly obese nurse working on a busy surgical unit might have difficulty with the level of physical activity required on such a unit. If that were the case, the nurse might be acting unethically if her inability to work to the required capacity put patient care in jeopardy or required colleagues to fill in for her inadequacies, as in the scenario involving Charlene. (In that scenario, Charlene was acting unethically in not addressing her own problems.) Note also that fitness to practise does not just include physical well-being. A nurse must also have psychological stability. If personal worries and stresses impair a nurse's ability to perform to standard, he or she must take steps to remove him- or herself from the situation.

From this perspective, one can see that working as a professional nurse becomes more than just a job; it becomes a way of living. Nurses need to be aware that the choices they make can impact their ability to uphold the value of *being accountable*. They have an obligation to maintain their fitness to practise, which may include leaving a place of employment when they feel they are no longer able to give the best care. This is part of the virtue discussed in earlier chapters. Beliefs and values about those for whom one is providing care also have an impact on the quality of care delivered. Nurses who do not demonstrate the kinds of values necessary for ethical care may be morally obligated to seek another place of employment. For example, a nurse who believes that the frail elderly are not valuable members of society should not seek employment in a long-term care institution.

Maintaining fitness to practise is an institutional responsibility as well as a personal one. Organizations must have mechanisms in place to support employees, and most have an employee wellness program based in the Human Resources department. An **employee wellness program** typically offers a variety of services such as psychological and addictions counselling, as well as safety training and health surveillance. Nurses should know that they have the necessary support to maintain wellness. For example, it is essential that institutions have sufficient casual staff in reserve to ensure that nurses do not feel pressured to come to work when they are ill, especially when they have a contagious illness. Nurses are correct in thinking that institutions are acting unethically if they fail in this regard.

NURSES' MORAL INTEGRITY

Physical, emotional, and psychological well-being are important aspects of accountability and fitness to practise, but we must also take into consideration the issue of moral fitness. Maintaining a sense of moral integrity is important for nurses as its loss can have a profound impact on how they feel about and perform their work.

Erosion of Nurses' Moral Integrity

One sign that moral fitness is being challenged is what we call **moral disengagement**, defined as distancing oneself from the relational aspect of care and focusing instead only on the mechanistic skilled tasks. For example, in an excessively busy environment nurses may find themselves moving into "survival mode" when they know that they are unable to spend the necessary time with patients. They disengage from the patient and avoid meaningful conversations, ignoring the emotional suffering of their patients. Because this is contrary to a relational ethic, those who continue to do this over time may experience moral residue, which the CNA Code of Ethics for Registered Nurses defines as "what nurses experience when they seriously compromise themselves or allow themselves to be compromised" (CNA, 2008, p. 7). They may experience ongoing erosion of their sense of moral integrity, knowing that relationship is foundational to ethical practice. Nurse researchers and philosophers have pointed out that when nurses feel they are unable to act on their values, they experience moral distress. This can contribute to loss of job satisfaction, problems with nurse-patient relationships, and poor quality care (Hamri, 2000; Jameton, 1984; Nathaniel, 2006). Several studies by nurse researchers have examined the profound effect on nurses of loss of moral integrity. Nurses have described a loss to their self-worth, deterioration in personal relationships, feelings of depression, and physical symptoms of stress such as palpitations, diarrhea, and headaches (Wilkinson, 1988). Critical care nurses linked moral distress to feelings of senselessness, anger, frustration, powerlessness, (Rodney, 1988) exploitation, exclusion, and anguish (Holly, 1993). They described their experience using words such as nightmare, headache, miserable, painful, sad, and ineffective (Holly, 1993).

Strengthening the Moral Community

A major concern for nurses is how to maintain moral integrity when their workplace is stressful and they see themselves as powerless to influence change. Moral standards are influenced by group norms and the environment in which nurses practise. When environment or social climate is discussed in terms of morality, it is termed **ethos**, "the distinguishing character, sentiment, moral nature, or guiding beliefs of a person, group, or institution" (Merriam-Webster on-line). The importance of first line nurse managers in establishing a positive ethos cannot be overemphasized. If the nurse manager creates an open, trusting environment nurses will feel more comfortable in expressing their concerns. Nurses must also have a reasonable expectation that action will be taken when they identify their issues. The nurse manager who encourages thoughtful reflection about nursing practice and who models a strong relational ethic will help to strengthen the moral agency of nursing staff.

There is growing recognition of the need to create healthy workplaces that will enable nurses to maintain their moral fitness. Environments in which nurses feel a loss of moral agency are not healthy, and often result in burn-out. A way of strengthening moral agency is working with others in a spirit of cooperation and collaboration for the betterment of patient care. Noted Canadian philosophers George Webster and Françoise Baylis (2000) speak of the importance of **moral community**: a group that works together to enact shared values. Success in creating a moral community depends on the extent to which individuals are willing to bring forward, discuss, and deal with ethical issues in a manner that promotes mutual understanding.

Characteristics of a moral community are well described in the "quality practice environments" framework put forth by the Canadian Nurses Association and the Canadian Federation of Nurses Union (CNA, 2006). This joint position statement was a result of the observation that "The quality of nurses' professional practice environments has a direct impact on job satisfaction, work production, recruitment and retention (and therefore, the nursing shortage), the quality of care, and ultimately, client outcomes" (p. 1). Key elements of the framework include:

- collaboration and communication
- responsibility and accountability
- realistic workload
- leadership
- support for information and knowledge management
- professional development
- workplace culture

In our discussion of relational ethics we identified the importance of *communication and collaboration*. These elements are central to quality practice environments as they are required for effective dialogue about what is going right or wrong in the system. Interdisciplinary dialogue on the moral climate and strategies for increasing respect within the workplace are vital. If open communication is lacking, errors might not be revealed, and without true collaboration, some concerned voices might not be heard. A case example was much in the news several years ago. Nurses in the Health Sciences Centre in Winnipeg had long expressed concerns about one surgeon's practice. Their concerns were essentially ignored, and not brought to light until 12 infants had died and an inquest was performed. A number of recommendations from the inquest pointed in the direction of giving nurses more voice in the institution. As a result, case law around informed consent and protection of whistleblowers was enacted. Had there been a more open and collaborative moral community, such legislation might not have been required.

Responsibility and accountability, the focus of this chapter, are also fundamental to the practice environment. Clearly if some members of the care team fail to take their responsibilities seriously, or are not accountable for their actions, the moral community will suffer. Working in an interdisciplinary setting requires trust, and trust is based on integrity, steadfastness, and fidelity to promise. If I am to work effectively with you, I must be confident that you uphold professional values, hold to your beliefs even in the face of difficulty, and stay true to your word. I must know that if you say you will do something, you will actually do it.

Realistic workload is a foundational value because it allows for continuity of care, enables nurses to develop holistic therapeutic relationships, and creates work-life balance (CNA, 2006). When workloads are too great there is a negative impact on the health of the workforce. For workloads to be reasonable, there must be sufficient nurses to provide safe, compassionate, competent, and ethical care. With recent shortages and changes in care delivery systems, nurses are given very heavy patient care loads on a regular basis, and many nurses are working considerable overtime. Both have negative results. A national survey of Canadian nurses indicated that nurses are absent from work for health-related reasons an average of 14.5 days per year. This rate of absence equates to more than 19,000 full-time nurses not available to provide nursing care; it ". . . contributes to long waits for medical treatment, and care delayed is often care denied. In some circumstances, the shortage produces compromised workplaces, resulting in needless nurse staff injuries and, sometimes, patient deaths" (CNA, 2006, p. 2). Building effective team relationships will make the system more efficient and will help ensure sufficient time for nurses to practise ethically and competently. Nursing leaders, as part of their role accountability, must take a stand and put emphasis on the importance of a healthy and intact nursing workforce. Part of nursing accountability involves helping government and other funding agencies understand the importance of nursing care so that adequate funding is in place.

Effective *leadership* is an essential element for quality practice environments (CNA, 2006). The College of Registered Nurses of British Columbia (CRNBC) has stated that leaders in nursing are not only those who work in management, but also those who act as collaborators, communicators, mentors, role models, visionaries, and advocates for quality care (CRNBC, 2005). Ethical leaders help to establish an ethos where all members of the moral community are encouraged to challenge standards or practices they believe to be unethical. They work to ensure that the mission, values, and beliefs of the organization are translated into practice behaviours.

Nurses work in highly complex organizations with multiple relational networks, where knowledge and morality become tightly linked. Therefore, in quality practice environments there must be *support for information and knowledge management*. This requires time and education. Professional development opportunities must be adequately funded to allow nurses to develop and maintain clinical competence and moral fitness, which translates into strength in moral agency. Institutional support for knowledge development might include activities such as journal clubs and formal educational sessions on ethical issues. The institution could also consider adopting an ethical decision-making model for reflection and action, such as the model used throughout this book. Reflection is vital to growth, as beliefs and values may be shaped by the environment. Recent changes in technology and growing exposure to diverse cultures are examples of factors that can begin to affect beliefs. In such a rapidly changing environment, nurses must be encouraged to contribute to shaping the moral community through interdisciplinary dialogue on issues of moral concern.

Quality practice environments are also characterized by support for nurses' *professional development*. Health care is changing so rapidly that it is a challenge to keep up with the latest developments, no matter what the area of practice. Professional associations demand evidence of continuing competence activities, but these must be supported by the institution. If nurses are to give quality care they require educational and practice opportunities that can help to strengthen their skills. This includes development in reflection and ethical analysis. The CNA framework document points out that nurses who have support and resources for ethical concerns are more likely to endure higher levels of stress and still be satisfied in their positions (CNA, 2006).

Finally, the framework document refers to the importance of *workplace culture* in quality practice environments. In essence, that is what we have been talking about in this discussion on moral community. When members of the health care team trust one another, have open and responsible communication, are accountable for their actions, and are supported with adequate resources and opportunities for ongoing education, the moral community will have greater integrity overall. This is the foundation of accountability, because it is difficult, if not impossible, to maintain moral agency when one is silenced, undervalued, and unsupported. A strong moral community is key to accountability and the delivery of safe, compassionate, competent, and ethical care.

BEING ACCOUNTABLE AS A LIVED VALUE

Our discussion in this chapter has raised some key issues related to the need for accountability in nursing. *Being accountable* is a call to relationship, to responsiveness and sensitivity to others, to excellence in practice, and to upholding the profession's highest standards. By this point in the chapter, you should have a clear idea as to why accountability is a moral imperative in nursing. We will now explore two scenarios common to nursing practice. The first of these is a case involving a nurse who is lacking fitness to practise with a particular patient group; the second relates to working in a small town. Both demonstrate different aspects of accountability, as well as moral dilemmas that can arise when considering aspects of *being accountable*.

Trying It On
10.1 Fitness to Practise and Everyday Ethics

Tara was working in a small hospital in Northern Manitoba. She had moved to this remote area because of the promise of adventure in the recruitment ads and the idea of isolation pay. She thought she would work there for a few years, save her money, and have some fun. It was the end of her first year, and she still hadn't adjusted. In fact, she hated her job, hated the community, and hated herself for making the decision to move to this remote spot.

On days when Tara was scheduled to work she woke up with dread. She always wondered what would come through the hospital doors that day. Her main issue with work was that there was a considerable amount of poverty in the community and a very high incidence of alcoholism.

She felt she just couldn't respect the people who came to hospital. As she said to her friend Wendy on the telephone, "What's the point in what we do? We find them in a field and bring them in, work on them for days, spend incredible amounts of money on drugs and nursing care, and send them back into the same rotten environment. In two weeks they're back again, drunk, smelling to high heaven, filthy, and full of infection. What's the matter with those people? How can they live like that? It's just disgusting."

Tara found that when she met some of the patients for the second or third time she had a difficult time being civil to them. For one thing, she believed that they were so ignorant they wouldn't even notice. She just couldn't waste the energy being polite to people who had so little respect for themselves. She found herself hurrying through her shift so she could get home and forget about work. She didn't bother to go to any of the education sessions the hospital educator put on because most of them happened on her day off, and there was no way she was giving up her precious off-time. She just went to work, did her job, and went home as soon as she could get away. But that was a problem too, because there was nothing to do in the community. She hadn't made any friends, since she didn't want any of those people in her home, and she didn't have any interests to speak of. So her life revolved around her television set. "What a way to live," she thought to herself.

1. Do you see an ethical problem for Tara?

2. What kinds of questions should Tara be asking herself about her care?

3. Does the analysis that follows miss any vital points or questions to consider?

Fitness to Practise and Everyday Ethics

Assessing the Ethics of the Situation: Relationship, Goals, Beliefs, and Values

The scenario described in Trying it On 10-1 reflects a number of issues around Tara's practice and her obligations to provide the best possible care. The first step in understanding the ethics of a situation, whether it reflects concerns with everyday ethics or an ethical dilemma, is to look at the ethical elements. Therefore, the first question to ask is, "What are the relationships, goals, beliefs, and values inherent in the situation?" Using the questions outlined in Chapter 3 as a general guide, one can begin to explore the quality of nurse-patient, or in this case nurse-community, relationships and uncover differences in goals, beliefs, and values.

If we ask questions about the relationships and values in this case, we see that the problem seems to be one of Tara's relationships with this patient population and how she values and acts toward them. This is a problem of everyday ethics. Tara's goal is, presumably, to provide safe, compassionate, competent, and ethical care in her professional capacity as a nurse. However, she believes that many of the patients she is caring for do not have much worth. Her values seem to centre

(Continued)

Fitness to Practise and Everyday Ethics

around a particular understanding of how people ought to conduct their lives. The culture of the community appears to Tara to lead to valuing personal pleasure and alcohol use above self-care. From Tara's perspective, people who abuse alcohol and fail to look after their health are to blame for their own misfortune, and, as such, are not worthy of either her respect or her care. In other words, she is feeling a lack of respect for her patients because they do not share her values and beliefs about lifestyle choices. She finds this very distressing. As a result she is unhappy in what she is doing and is giving less than optimal care. She is impolite and fails to engage with patients in a caring relationship.

If Tara were to consider this situation in view of its ethical components, she would have to acknowledge that she is not demonstrating professional virtues in her dealings with this patient group. In particular, she does not embody caring and compassion in her relationships with them. We see little evidence that she has attempted to learn about the values and beliefs of the community. If there are cultural differences, she has made no effort to understand them. Indeed, she shuns educational sessions and has not tried to learn about the societal, economic, and political factors that might play a role in the kinds of health problems the community is experiencing. She appears to be working exclusively from her own frame of reference, without making any attempt to see things from the perspective of community members. Tara might conclude that her fitness to practise is lacking in this situation.

At this point we have no direct evidence that Tara's work is below minimum standards for safety and competence, but we suggest that it falls short of ethical practice. It seems unlikely that Tara is treating her patients in such a way as to preserve their dignity and sense of integrity. There are values conflicts here, but from the evidence presented we have no way of knowing if they have erupted into full disagreements on care decisions. Nonetheless, with respect to everyday ethics, it seems that Tara is not meeting her professional obligations.

If we look at this scenario from the perspective of bioethical principles, we see that Tara is not meeting the obligation of beneficence. There are no principles in conflict as such, but it is clear that Tara is not fully meeting her obligation to "do good." From the perspective of normative theory, we could look at whether Tara is treating her patients with the kind of respect that Kantian theory would expect. The question that arises is whether Tara understands the issues related to her own accountability and fitness to practise.

Reflecting On and Reviewing Potential Actions: Recognizing Available Choices and How Those Choices are Valued

In order to determine what actions might be possible in this situation, it is first important to understand community expectations of care. Do individuals have any desire to make lifestyle changes? What about the entire community? Perhaps they would like to make changes, but feel powerless to do so. Perhaps there are community beliefs about what is acceptable or even desirable behaviour that would make it difficult for an individual to change his or her lifestyle. Tara would have to consider this issue very carefully and think about what might be appropriate in the community. Sometimes entire communities feel disempowered or alienated, and this is reflected in group behaviours that others from outside the group might have difficulty understanding. That might be part of the problem here. It might also be a general feeling of wanting someone else to take responsibility and look after their needs. To begin to understand why these behaviours are occurring, Tara would need a great deal of sensitivity to the community culture. To develop even a beginning understanding, she would have to be sure that she did not impose her own values and beliefs on others or assume that they see the world in the same way she does. She would have to engage in conversations with members of the community and consider whether their belief system is so different from hers that they could not agree on effective care strategies. She might discover that change for any one individual is very difficult, and might have to reflect on whether she is in a position to influence change at all.

Tara needs to understand that there is a problem before she can reflect on and review potential actions. To be accountable for her practice, she needs to develop an awareness of the ethical dimensions of this situation to see that her fitness to practise is being eroded through her growing dislike of the job and the community and her feelings of low self-worth. Clearly her practice is in need of revision. She must come to an understanding that it is unethical to treat her patients disrespectfully, and do something to rectify the situation. Sometimes such insight comes when someone else points it out, and Tara's colleagues would be right in suggesting to her that she needs an "attitude adjustment."

If Tara feels uncomfortable in her role, she needs to reflect seriously on why this is the case, and what might be done to change it. Actively pursuing information about factors influencing behaviours in the community might be helpful. Attempting to understand the perspectives of the community as a whole, and community members as individuals, is essential. She might consider working with community members to try to come to an understanding of some of the problems the community is facing. Journalling and talking with colleagues might help her to develop the necessary awareness of her own values and beliefs. This might help her to be more supportive and effective in leading change.

Selecting an Ethical Action: Maximizing Good
Tara must select an action, as change is clearly needed. It is her obligation as a nurse to give the best possible care to her patients, and as things currently stand, there is little possibility that she can fulfill this commitment. She needs to consider whether remaining in the community is the best thing for herself and her patients. If she continues in her present mode, and is unable to treat her patients with respect, she is not providing ethical care. She must change her practice or leave the community. This involves weighing the various options. Is there another place she could work where she would have more respect for her patients? Can she change her basic beliefs? She has to consider her own welfare as well as her patients', although patients' needs should take priority. She also needs to consider the possibility that her care could fall below minimum standards, resulting in disciplinary action if someone were to report her, and that she

(Continued)

Fitness to Practise and Everyday Ethics

might do harm to her patients that could result in legal action. Nurses who are unable to deliver safe, compassionate, competent, and ethical care for whatever reason place themselves and their patients in jeopardy.

Engaging in Ethical Action

Tara must be accountable for the quality of her care, which is probably deteriorating due to her disrespect of the patients. She needs the moral courage to do the right thing. It might involve some important changes for her, as she might decide that she has to leave the community. If she were to decide to stay, she would have to change her attitude and behaviours toward her patients. She would need to take into account the fact that, in failing to make change, she would be acting unethically. If

she does decide to stay, she should seek support from her nurse manager in evaluating her ongoing performance.

Reflecting on and Reviewing the Ethical Action

In reflecting on and reviewing the action, Tara would have to look at whether she had made the changes necessary to enable her to give the kind of care patients expect from a professional nurse. She should ask for feedback from her colleagues and nurse manager. Continuing to keep a reflective journal might help her track any changes in her attitude and behaviour. She should also continue to monitor her own feelings of satisfaction in the job, and consider whether she has taken sufficient action to enable her to increase her level of fitness to practise.

Trying It On
10.2 Accountability in a Rural Hospital

In a rural acute care hospital, Emma Foster is a manager on an oncology and medical/surgical unit. Patients on this unit may be receiving intravenous chemotherapy, other blood replacement therapies, high doses of intravenous narcotics, and other adjunct medications. Staffing includes RNs and LPNs. On most days one RN and four LPNs care for 25 patients. The Director of Patient Care has just informed Emma that because of budget issues, staffing changes will soon be announced. Emma informs her staff of this message, and that very week they are informed that starting next

Friday the lone RN on the unit will be the backup for the RN in the Emergency department. LPNs will cover the unit when the RN is helping out in the ER, and will monitor even the sickest oncology patients who are receiving treatment. They will call the RN in Emergency "whenever they think that an RN is required."

Emma and the RNs have immediate concerns about the clinical implications of the new staffing pattern. The LPNs are experienced and capable, but they do not have the educational background necessary to enable them to monitor the very ill patients on chemotherapy and high-dose narcotics. Too many things can go wrong. It is worrying to all the staff that the RN who must ultimately be responsible and accountable for patent care might not even be on the unit to ensure patient safety. Previously, RNs were told that they had to be on the unit at all times, even during their lunch and coffee breaks, so they could be immediately available if there was a problem. A special staff lunch room had been opened so they could stay close by. Now they are being told to leave the unit to cover in Emergency. Neither the physicians nor RNs have been consulted, nor is there any indication that the community has been informed of the proposed change. The Director has clearly stated this change is necessary to meet the budgetary restrictions imposed by their regional board.

1. As an accountable manager, what is Emma's ethical concern?

2. What actions should she take in this situation?

Accountability in a Rural Hospital

Assessing the Ethics of the Situation: Relationship, Goals, Beliefs, and Values

In this case Emma, the RNs, and the LPNs all share the same value: quality patient care. Members of the hospital board would also argue that their interest is quality care. However, they are working with a budget that is inadequate to meet patient care needs. This case highlights how interests of institutional efficiency can conflict with the values of those directly accountable for safe, compassionate, competent, and ethical care. The hospital board has to determine how to run the facility on a restricted budget. Nurses are most concerned about patient safety and are worried that they will not be able to deliver the kind of care they believe is necessary. Thus there appears to be a values conflict. However, the conflict may not be one of values at all, but rather one of lack of resources. The board is not able to produce the money needed for more resources, so must find ways to work within budget, whatever the cost to care standards.

The ethical question forefront in this case is how the hospital board can dictate what staffing patterns are considered safe and ethical. There may be other stakeholders from the larger community who should have input into the business and outcomes of the institution. At this point we have little information about how the LPNs feel about their changing role. Other interested parties whose opinions should be sought include community members using the hospital services, physicians, other health care professionals, the regional board, the director of care, and the facility's liability carrier. The community as a whole might need to be informed of potential liability and professional issues that could ensue.

Reflecting On and Reviewing Potential Actions: Recognizing Available Choices and How Those Choices are Valued

In this situation the nurses are experiencing moral uncertainty as they search for some clarity in how and why these staffing

(Continued)

Accountability in a Rural Hospital

changes are being proposed. Emma has several choices. She can simply accept the decision and emphasize to the staff that the problem is out of their control and they must do the best they can. She can investigate further and determine just how problematic the proposal is to all concerned. If her concerns and the concerns of the nurses are justified, she can then try to get the situation changed. To do this, she must approach the Director with the nurses' concerns related to the staffing change, but she must first gather more information to support her case.

Selecting an Ethical Action: Maximizing Good
Emma first contacts her provincial nursing association and the Oncology Society and finds support for her belief that patients receiving chemotherapy and blood products are at considerable risk and must be monitored frequently. She reviews the professional practice standards and the CNA Code of Ethics for Registered Nurses, and identifies the potential of breaching the value of safe, compassionate, competent, and ethical care. The LPNs are not certified in monitoring chemotherapy infusions and do not have the necessary skills to care for these complex patients. There is also a concern with the possible deterioration in quality of care for the other patients if the RN is off the unit for an extended time. In reviewing professional obligations outlined in the Code, Emma sees that potential breaches of patient safety and justice could jeopardize ethical standards. By defining the issue as one of safety, Emma can argue the nurses' position that the proposed staffing patterns will make it very difficult for nurses to meet their practice standards.

Emma contacts the CNPS to discuss legal ramifications of the proposed staffing patterns. It is determined that a secondary issue of relevance to all of the care providers is the potential liability resulting from unsafe patient care.

Based on this information, Emma feels obligated to take a stand to try to get the proposed staffing practice stopped. One possible solution is to argue to have the acute unit closed until staffing improves.

Engaging in Ethical Action
Once Emma has made her decision, she must find the moral courage to act. She may be fearful for her own job in speaking up. She needs to be aware that taking a stand, especially if she advocates for unit closure, will probably make her unpopular with some of her colleagues and with others in the community, particularly patients who would have to go elsewhere for care. Nurses often feel powerless to make change for such reasons, but they need to make the attempt.

Emma's first action is to meet with the RNs and LPNs. They are all in agreement with her concern. The LPNs are worried about their own liability in being asked to care for patients beyond their scope of practice. She then notifies the Director that she is taking action and organizes a community forum to discuss the issue. She invites local politicians as they can have influence on government funding allocations. At the meeting she discovers that many community members are very concerned and strongly opposed to any staffing changes in the oncology unit, as they or their relatives have been patients on the unit and have recognized the degree of expertise required to care for such seriously ill patients. Some nurses in the community who are not currently working indicate that they would be willing to be on call for emergencies. Emma's next step is to make a proposal to the Director and the hospital board. She proposes that the community nurses be hired on a casual basis to come in on call. She also points out that the neighbouring town has an on-call roster that might be contacted if necessary. She includes in her proposal the concerns about safe, compassionate, competent, and ethical care, and highlights the possibility of liability if care is substandard.

Reflecting on and Reviewing the Ethical Action

In reflecting on her actions, Emma needs to consider whether she has exhausted all avenues and has approached others with due respect. She needs to explore how she has presented her position. Did she help others understand the ethical principles involved in a way that preserved dignity of all involved? Did she make it clear that the primary concern was the patient safety and the quality of patient care? Emma concludes that she has acted accountably in trying to bring this situation to the attention of those who control the funding. Whether or not her actions are successful in changing the practice does not change the fact that she was obligated to act. Her main concern should be whether she has presented her case in a way that is sensitive to the needs and understandings of the community.

CHAPTER SUMMARY

Being accountable is a fundamental value inherent in every situation and action nurses encounter in their practice. Professional associations are responsible for developing practice standards, but individual nurses are held accountable for their own practice. A nurse's accountability is a function of personal integrity, which demands moral agency, fidelity to promise, and steadfastness. Accountability in nursing is essentially relational because all nursing activities occur in the context of relationship. Nurses must relate to others in ways that are respectful and sensitive to their needs. Understandings of nursing accountability are changing because of the complex nature of the health care environment and the expanding scope of nurses' responsibilities. Many factors influence the way in which nurses understand their accountability and are able to act as moral agents. Nurses must balance a duty to care for patients with an equal duty to ensure their own fitness to practise competently. As part of a moral community, nurses acknowledge their responsibility to contribute to positive, healthy work environments for themselves and others. Today's complex working environments can lead to nurses experiencing moral distress. There is potential for accountability to be misunderstood and violated because of power imbalances in professional relationships and the lack of moral preparedness nurses may experience. Nurses must assume a leadership role in advocating for patients through responsible and responsive practices that begin in dialogue and mutual respect for patients as persons. A relational ethic allows us to see accountability as a demonstration of mutual respect, rather than simply a duty. Mutual respect occurs in an atmosphere of interdependence, where nurses strive to build a moral community that supports helping, healing, and caring environments.

Questions for Reflection

1. Think about a situation in your clinical practice where you believe that a nurse you worked with was not accountable in providing patient care. How did you and/or others react? What do you believe impacted the nurse's decision to act in the way he or she did?

2. How has the value of accountability evolved in your practice as a nurse since you began your career? What values guided your decision to accept accountability as a professional? Reflect on a situation in which you did or did not act accountably, and consider the values that governed your choice.

Exercises

1. Read the section in the CNA Code of Ethics for Registered Nurses on the value: Accountability. Suggest how you might revise or update the responsibility statements based on the changing health care system.

2. Examine your institution's policy on accountability as an interdisciplinary team member. How is accountability defined? Does this policy fit with your beliefs and values about the nature of accountability for nurses? Is accountability taken up as relational and shared between team members?

3. Your supervisor asks you to work an extra shift as she is short of staff. In assessing your fitness to practise, what questions would you need to ask yourself to make the decision to determine whether you are fit?

Research Activities

1. Working in small groups, identify relevant Canadian legislation that guides practice related to accountability. Include in your search relevant codes of ethics, practice standards, and provincial labour laws. Each group should work from a different province. Examine similarities and differences.

Key Terms

accountability

answerability

employee wellness program

ethical violation

ethos

fitness to practise

moral community

moral disengagement

moral unpreparedness

steadfast

References

Aroskar, M. (1987). The interface of ethics and politics in nursing. *Nursing Outlook*, 35(6), 268-272.

Canadian Nurses Association. (2008). *Code of ethics for Registered Nurses* (Centennial Ed.). Ottawa: Author.

Canadian Nurses Association. (2006). *Practice environments: Maximizing client, nurse, and system outcomes*. Ottawa: Author.

Caputo, J. (1989). Disseminating originary ethics and the ethics of dissemination. In A. B. Dallery & C. E. Scott (Eds.), *The question of the other: Essays in contemporary philosophy* (pp. 55-62). Albany, New York: State University of New York Press.

College of Registered Nurses of British Columbia. (2005). *Guidelines for quality practice environment for nurses in British Columbia*. Vancouver: Author.

Hamric, A. (2000). Moral distress in everyday ethics. *Nursing Outlook*, 48(5), 199-201.

Holly, C. (1993). The ethical quandaries of acute care nursing practice. *Journal of Professional Nursing*, 9, 110-115.

Jameton, A. (1984). *Nursing practice: The ethical issues*. Englewood Cliffs, NJ: Prentice-Hall.

Lamb, M. (2004). An historical perspective on nursing and nursing ethics. In J. L. Storch, P. Rodney, & R. Starzomski (Eds.), *Toward a moral horizon: Nursing ethics for leadership and practice* (pp. 20-41). Toronto: Pearson.

Merriam-Webster On-Line. Retrieved August 23, 2007 from www.m-w.com/

Nathaniel, A. (2006). Moral reckoning in nursing. *Western Journal of Nursing Research*, 28(4), 419-438.

Rodney, P. (1988). Moral distress in critical care nursing. *Canadian Critical Care Nursing Journal*, 5(2), 9-11.

Webster, G., Baylis, F. (2000). Moral residue. In S.B. Rubin and L. Zoloth (Eds.), *Margin of error: The ethics of mistakes in the practice of medicine* (pp. 217-230). Hagerstown, MD: University Publishing Group.

Wilkinson, JM. (1988). Moral distress in nursing practice: Experience and effect. *Nursing Forum*, 23(1), 16-29.

Yeo, M., & Moorehouse, A. (1996). *Concepts and cases in nursing ethics.* Peterborough, ON: Broadview Press.

Suggested Reading

Altheide, D. (2000). Identity and the definition of the situation in a mass-mediated context. *Symbolic Interaction*, 23, 1-18.

Baumann, A., O'Brien Pallas, L., Armstrong Strassen, M., et al. (2001).Commitment and care: The benefits of healthy work places for nurses, their patients and the system: A policy synthesis. *Canadian Health Research Foundation.* Ottawa: Government of Canada.

Benner, P. (1994). The role of articulation in understanding practice and experience as sources of knowledge in clinical nursing. In J. Tully (Ed.), *Philosophy in an age of pluralism: The philosophy of Charles Taylor in question.* (pp. 136-155), Cambridge, UK: Cambridge University Press.

Bergum, V,. & Dossetor, J. (2005). *Relational ethics: The full meaning of respect.* Hagerstown, MD: University Publishing Group.

Bergum, V. (2004). Relational ethics in nursing. In J. L. Storch, P. Rodney, & R. Starzomski (Eds.), *Toward a moral horizon: Nursing ethics for leadership and practice* (pp. 20-41). Toronto: Pearson.

Bird, F. (1996). *The muted conscience: Moral silence and the practice of ethics in business.* Westport, CN: Quorum.

Bishop, A., & Scudder, J. R. (1990). *The practical, moral, and personal sense of nursing: A phenomenological philosophy of practice.* Albany, NY: State University of New York.

Bishop, A., & Scudder, J. R. (1999). A philosophical interpretation of nursing. *Scholarly Inquiry for Nursing Practice: An International Journal*, 12(4), 17-27.

Canadian Health Services Research Foundation (March, 2006). *What's ailing our nurses: A discussion of the major issues affecting nursing human resources in Canada.* Ottawa: Author.

Falk Rafael, A. (1996). Power and caring: A dialectic in nursing. *Advances In Nursing Science*, 19(1), 3-17.

Flexner, A. (1915). Is social work a profession? In *Proceedings of the National Conference of Charities and Correction* (pp. 576-590). Chicago: Heldman.

Frank, A. (2002). How can they act like that: Clinicians and patients as characters in each other's stories. *Hasting Center Report*, 32, 14-22.

Gadow, S., & Schroeder, C. (1996). An advocacy approach to ethics and community health. In E.T. Anderson and J. McFarlane (Eds.), *Community as partner: Theory and practice in nursing* (2nd ed., pp. 123-127). Philadelphia: Lippincott.

Gotlieb, L., & Gotlieb, B. (1998). Evolutionary principles can guide nursing's future development. *Journal of Advanced Nursing*, 28(5), 1099-1105.

Hartrick, G. (1997). Relational capacity: The foundation for interpersonal nursing practice. *Journal of Advanced Nursing*, 26, 523-528.

Hartrick Doane, G. (2002). In the spirit of creativity: The learning and teaching of ethics in nursing. *Journal of Advanced Nursing*, 39(6), 521-528.

Ladd, J. (1983). The internal morality of medicine: An essential dimension of the patient-physician relationship. In E. Shelp (Ed.), *The clinical encounter: The moral fabric of the patient-physician relationship* (pp. 209-231). Dordrecht, The Netherlands: D. Reidel Publishing Co.

Latimer, J. (2000). *The conduct of care*. Malden, MA: Blackwell Science.

Liaschenko, J. (1998). Response to language, ideology and nursing practice. *Scholarly Inquiry for Nursing Practice: An International Journal*, 12(4), 363-366.

Liaschenko, J., & Fisher, A. (1999). Theorizing the knowledge nurses use in the conduct of their work. *Scholarly Inquiry for Nursing Practice: An International Journal*, 13, 29-41.

Lowe, G. (2006). *Making a measurable difference: Evaluating quality of work life interventions*. Ottawa: Canadian Nurses Association.

May, L. (1996). *The socially responsive self: Social theory and professional ethics*. Chicago: The University of Chicago Press.

McNamee, S., & Gergen, K. (1999). *Relational responsibility: Resources for sustainable dialogue*. Thousand Oaks, CA: Sage.

Moules, N. (2000). Funerals, families, and family nursing: Lessons of love and practice. *Journal of Family Nursing*, 6(1), 3-8.

Pellegrino, E. (1976). Philosophy of Medicine: Problematic and potential. *Journal of Medicine and Philosophy*, 1(5), 5-31.

Rodney, P., & Varcoe, C. (2001). Towards ethical inquiry in the economic evaluation of nursing practice. *Canadian Journal of Nursing Research*, 33(1), 35-57.

Varcoe, C., Doane, G., Pauly, B., Rodney, P., Storch, J., Mahoney, K., Mcpherson, G., Brown, H., & Starzomski, R. (2004). Ethical practice in nursing: Working the in-betweens. *Journal of Advanced Nursing*, 45(3), 316-325.

Walker, M. (1998). *Moral understandings: A feminist study in ethics*. New York: Routledge.

Chapter 11
Ethical Endeavours and Leadership

Chapter Outline

Ethical Endeavours

The Nature of Leadership in Ethics

Ethics Leadership in Direct Care

Ethics Leadership in Administration

Ethics Leadership in Education

Ethics Leadership in Research

Ethics Leadership in Interdisciplinary Practice

Ethics Leadership in International Nursing Practice

Resources for Developing Moral Agency

Resources at the National and International Level

Provincial Ethics Resources

Local Ethics Resources

Chapter Summary

Learning Objectives

After reading this chapter, you should be able to:

- describe some emerging areas where ethical endeavours are important

- discuss the nature of ethics leadership in practice, administration, and education

- discuss the nature of ethics leadership in research and interdisciplinary practice

- discuss ethics leadership in international nursing practice

- identify ways in which nurses can strengthen their own skills in ethics leadership
- identify nursing ethics resources at the international, national, provincial, and local levels

This book has been designed to help you understand the nature of ethics in Canadian nursing practice, and to demonstrate ways in which the CNA Code of Ethics for Registered Nurses (2008) gives guidance for practice. We have selected representative scenarios to illustrate ways in which the values presented in the Code play out in practice. However, this is only a very small sample of the many ethical issues that can arise. Nurses face moral choices in every interaction with patients, families, and colleagues. As we have tried to show, decisions about the way in which we interact as a professional with those receiving our care or with others with whom we work always have moral dimensions. Developing ethical sensitivity and moral courage is an ongoing part of a nurse's professional growth. We can never say "Now I am ethical" and leave it at that. It takes work to practise ethically.

In this chapter we will revisit some areas of social justice and obligations of nursing in the broader social context. We will then discuss some of the different forms that leadership in ethics can take, starting with leadership in direct care. This will be a kind of summary and consolidation of material from earlier chapters. We will consider how leadership in ethics might look as a nurse assumes different roles, and will examine the nature of ethics leadership in interdisciplinary practice. Finally, we will provide you with some resources that can help you as you embark on a lifelong journey toward more ethical practice.

ETHICAL ENDEAVOURS

As you have seen, the CNA Code of Ethics for Registered Nurses is structured around seven fundamental values and their associated explanatory statements. Reading these should give you a good idea about the way in which Canadian nurses understand ethical practice, because the Code was developed by nurses for nurses. The Canadian Nurses Association undertook a number of national consultations in which Canadian nurses were invited to give feedback on various drafts of the 2008 Code. The final version reflects the idea that the values alone are not sufficient to guide nurses in practice, because there are so many complexities and because nurses often have competing obligations. Therefore, the Code was divided into two parts. Part I explains the values and responsibilities. Part II gives a slightly different perspective on ways in which today's nurses might think about their practice. This section is titled *Ethical Endeavours* and is aimed at helping nurses understand their obligations in a broader sphere. The emphasis is on social justice and primary health care.

The nature of health care delivery, and hence nursing practice, is changing rapidly. In the early days of nursing most care was delivered in the home, but as medicine evolved and technology advanced, more and more patients were cared for in institutions. As a result, for a good part of the twentieth century most nurses worked in hospitals, and the emphasis in nursing education was on preparing nurses to deliver care in that context. In fact, nursing education was called nursing training and was primarily hospital-based. Nurses obtained a diploma at the end of their educational program, which was usually three years in length. Relatively few nurses attended university and obtained a bachelor's degree. Those who did were usually expected to work in administration, education, or public health.

In the last three decades, there have been radical changes in nursing education and in care delivery in Canada. Today almost all Canadian undergraduate nursing programs are housed in or affiliated with universities and lead toward a bachelor's degree. Graduate programs in nursing are preparing strong researchers and theoreticians whose understandings are changing the face of nursing practice. Increasingly, nurses are being made aware that their role involves more than the execution of skilled tasks in an acute care environment. A growing emphasis on health promotion, primary care, and social justice is emerging. It is also becoming clear that nurses in the future will have to be leaders in health care reform. The Canadian health care system is not sustainable as presently structured. It is too costly, and there are too many Canadians who do not have adequate access to care.

The *Ethical Endeavours* section of the CNA Code of Ethics for Registered Nurses advises nurses that their moral obligations extend to recognizing "the need for change in systems and societal structures in order to create greater equity for all. Nurses should endeavour as much as possible, individually and collectively, to advocate for and work toward eliminating social inequities" (p. 20). This section of the Code is somewhat visionary, as its statements go beyond "what is" to "what ought to be" in nursing as a profession. It makes clear that nurses must not be satisfied to accept the status quo in health care, but must be active participants in effecting change. Thus, nurses must recognize that part of their role is to work for change at the broader systems level, agitating for revisions to social policy, legislation, and institutional structures. Adding this section to the Code emphasizes the advocacy role for nurses and the need to work to bring about a system that is more focused on prevention, more sensitive to the social determinants of health, more accessible, and more sustainable. This is a daunting task, but nurses of today have the educational preparation and theoretical base to take a leadership role in making the reality of Canadian health care match the vision.

THE NATURE OF LEADERSHIP IN ETHICS

From the discussion above, you may see that ethical practice requires a great deal of commitment. As you develop your own moral sensitivity and moral courage, you may find yourself acting as a leader in ethical practice, whether you are working at the bedside, in administration, as an educator, or as a researcher. Developing your leadership skills in ethics is important if you are to fulfill your obligation to work for change in a system that is currently somewhat flawed.

Ethics Leadership in Direct Care

In Chapter 2 we presented a model of ethical practice (the Ethics Composite Model; see p. 46) and showed that ethical decision making in nursing is influenced by many factors: the nurse's moral motivation (virtue); relationships (relational ethics); professional competence; professional values as presented in the CNA Code of Ethics for Registered Nurses; bioethical principles; normative ethics theories; and contextual features such as institutional, societal, and legal values, as well as the values of other professionals. Societal values are reflected partly in what patients and families expect of nurses, and partly in how the system is structured for care delivery. This includes ways in which nursing care is valued and supported. We showed that the goal of nursing is to act in ways that are beneficent: they serve the best interests of the patient, family, and/or community to whom care is provided.

With all these factors influencing how decisions are made, it is not surprising that at times a nurse might find it difficult to know what to do. The question of how nurses ought to relate to others is seldom at issue. It seems obvious from our understanding of relational ethics that professional nursing interactions must be characterized by a valuing of others' intrinsic worth and respect for them as human beings. Sometimes patients, families, and other care providers can present in ways that make it difficult for us to respond positively, particularly if we feel abused, threatened, or devalued in the exchange. However, we need to be aware that, while we cannot control others' behaviour, we can control our own, and we must strive to keep our responses respectful and professional. Developing this kind of attitude requires ongoing self-reflection. Questions to ask oneself include, "Why did I respond as I did? What were my feelings and beliefs? What values did I portray in my interaction with that person (or those persons)? Whose needs was I attempting to meet in my response, and was this appropriate?"

Ongoing reflection is important, but sometimes questions are about more than relationships. There may be questions of safety, well-being, choice, dignity, confidentiality, justice, or accountability that are hard to answer. Moral uncertainty and moral dilemmas can leave you wondering if you did the right thing. Sometimes the answer is not clear to anyone; sometimes it seems very clear, but values conflict. If you use a systematic approach such as the Framework for Ethical Decision Making we have used throughout the book, you will have a better chance of arriving at a decision that seems right to you.

Ethics leadership in direct care starts with having a clear understanding of the values in the CNA Code of Ethics for Registered Nurses, and trying to live those values. Consider the situation that Mike, an RN working in the emergency department (ED), finds himself facing on an evening shift. Harry, a frequent visitor to the ED, has been admitted yet again suffering from apparent exposure and hypothermia. Harry has many health problems. He lives on the streets and spends his nights in a cardboard box or sleeping on a grate, depending on what he can find. He seldom goes to the local shelter for the homeless as he is unlikely to be admitted. Every day he collects enough cans and bottles from the trash to finance purchase of a bottle of cheap wine, and by evening he is usually too drunk to be accepted by the shelter. Tonight's admission to the ED is assumed to be a result of his being unable to raise enough money to buy wine and consequently suffering from alcohol withdrawal. He was found wandering the street, shivering, incoherent, and shouting at imaginary attackers. This has not been the first time Harry has been admitted in such a state. As soon as he sees Mike, Harry starts hurling abuse, calling him vile names and trying to hit him. Mike has been through this before and realizes that there is no use in attempting to calm Harry; his visual and auditory hallucinations are too frightening to him. Mike calls security to help restrain the patient so they can give him the routine sedative before he hurts himself.

Once Harry is calmer, Mike begins his assessment. He is rather disgusted by the patient, who smells bad and looks worse. Mike wonders if he is in danger of getting lice or fleas, since Harry has clearly not bathed in months. However, Mike pushes aside his feelings of repugnance and talks to the patient gently and respectfully. He tries to make all his movements non-threatening, and explains what he is doing as he proceeds. When he looks at Harry's skin he discovers three large ulcers on the patient's legs, all of which appear to be infected. His temperature is 40.9° C. Mike begins to wonder if his initial assumptions about the patient were incorrect, as it appears that he is septic. Mike notifies the physician and they proceed with further diagnostic tests for sepsis, start the patient on antibiotics immediately, and admit him to a medical unit.

After Harry leaves the ED, Mike starts to think about the care he gave the patient. He realizes that he made a number of assumptions about the patient's condition, and is glad that he took the time to do a proper assessment. Earlier, one of the nurses on duty had said to Mike, "I don't know how you can be so nice to that guy. He's such a piece of trash, and he's dangerous." Mike had replied that he felt it wasn't really his place to judge, as his responsibility was to provide the same level of care for all patients, regardless of circumstances. The other nurse had just shrugged her shoulders and shaken her head in disbelief. Now, however, she approaches Mike and says, "Mike, I really admire the way you looked after Harry tonight. I learned something watching you. We were all thinking that he was just drunk and disorderly, and were ready to just give him the usual sedatives, settle him down and warm him up, then discharge him like we usually do. You looked beyond the assumptions and treated the patient with respect, and probably saved his life. I'm impressed. Next time I'll try to be a bit more careful about judging a patient." Mike feels good about his care. He thinks about how desperate Harry's situation is, and wonders how it came about. He wishes he knew more about Harry's story.

This is an example of one important way a nurse can give ethics leadership at the bedside. Living the values of dignity and respect, and safeguarding the patient's right to good care, are part of ethical nursing. In our society we are often quick to judge others for their lifestyle or choices. We may fail to realize that sometimes people do not really have much choice, that they have been shaped by their environment and circumstances. Even when we are unable to get the patient's history, we need to remember that everyone has a story, and that events and context influence the choices she or he is able to make. Ethical nursing care is fundamentally non-judgmental. Justice demands that we strive to give excellent care to each and every patient.

This is not to suggest that nurses ought to accept abuse from patients, or that they should put themselves in danger. Respecting others starts with respecting yourself, and recognizing that you have rights too. Nurses faced with abusive patients have a right ensure their own safety. In the example above, Mike recognized the danger in the situation, and asked to have the patient restrained. Sometimes it is a difficult decision to take away a patient's choice, but in certain circumstances it must be done. The key to doing this ethically is to reflect on the necessity of restraining action, and whether it was done with respect and the patient's best interests in mind. Acting ethically is not always easy, but persisting in demonstrating respect for patients is a large part of what distinguishes an ethical nurse from one whose values are not so well established.

The nurse who lives the values of the CNA Code of Ethics for Registered Nurses will constantly be on the alert for devaluing of patients and families. Think of the number of times you have heard nurses at coffee or lunch laughing about a patient or complaining about a disruptive family that insists on being in the patient's room. Have you participated in these discussions, or have you had the courage to remind others that talking about patients and families in this way is disrespectful? For example, you might find yourself saying to colleagues at coffee that you are uncomfortable with this kind of conversation, and that if they are going to persist in talking this way you will have to leave. This will not likely make you more popular with your colleagues, but it may make them respect you (and the patients) more.

Being an ethics leader can mean taking a difficult stance with respect to patients' rights. Advocacy is a vital component of ethical care, but too often nurses remain silent when they feel a patient is not receiving the best care, for example, if a patient is being discharged without adequate supports in place. The difficulty often arises when resources for care are scarce, as when beds are badly needed. Decisions have to be made as to whether to discharge a patient who is not quite ready to go home in order to free the bed for another, possibly sicker patient. This can become something of a utilitarian "greater good for greater number" debate, where one person argues that it is better to give everyone some level of care, and another claims that it is better to give excellent care to a smaller number. Sometimes the picture is coloured by hidden prejudices, such as ageism or considerations of relative social worth. As a nurse you need to be attuned to social justice issues and prepared to take a stand when you feel that an individual or group is being disadvantaged. The ethics leader looks closely at the kinds of environments into which patients are being discharged and is prepared to speak up when insufficient supports are available. This has the potential to create conflict. It takes moral courage to take a stand and make physicians and other care providers aware of your discomfort. It also takes considerable skill in communicating in a way that is respectful and non-confrontational but still gets your point across. Making your voice heard is not always easy, but advocacy is an essential part of ethical care.

Being an ethics leader means being vigilant and alert to care that does not meet the value of being "safe, compassionate, competent, and ethical," as discussed in Chapter 4. We have mentioned previously that whistleblowing—or calling attention to another's unsafe, incompetent, or unethical care—is a nurse's obligation. The caregiver who is providing inadequate care should be approached first, but if the problem is not resolved, then further measures must be taken. The supervisor must be notified, and if that does not solve the problem then the professional association must be contacted. We mentioned in earlier chapters that this kind of action can be very difficult, as it can create hostilities with the individual involved, and perhaps with his or her supporters. However, the ethics leader understands that personal discomfort is not an excuse for inaction.

These are just a few examples of how the nurse in direct care can demonstrate leadership in ethics. Modelling best practice is what ethics leadership is about. Interacting with patients, families, and other care providers in a respectful and compassionate way is a first step. Being prepared to advocate for better care and to uncover incompetent care are also important. The nurse who acts as a leader in ethics might feel alone at times, but should be able to find support in her or his first-line supervisor. It is also important to identify others who have similar moral strength and collaborate with them to the extent possible. Making moral choices and then acting on those choices can be difficult, as we have discussed throughout this book, but the ethical nurse will have the assurance of having upheld professional values, which is vital to the integrity of the profession and to excellence in patient care.

Ethics Leadership in Administration

Ethics leadership in nursing administration, like leadership in direct care, is largely relational. The nurse administrator should use the same relational skills and values in caring for staff as in caring for patients and families. All the values in the CNA Code of Ethics for Registered Nurses are applicable to staff as well. Nurses have a right be treated with compassion, to protect their health and well-being, to have choice, and to preserve their dignity. Issues of confidentiality and justice can certainly arise. Ethical practice in administration means attending to these values.

As an example, consider the case of Sharon, an expert nurse working on a surgical unit. She has a great deal of experience caring for patients with ostomies, and even though she is not a qualified enterostomal therapist (ET), she is often consulted by her colleagues on ostomy care issues. On occasion she has covered for the ETs when they needed a day off. Kate is the director in charge of the nursing education department, and as such is the immediate supervisor of the ETs. She is trying to plan for this summer's vacation coverage in her department.

Kate decides that she will ask Sharon if she is interested in a summer secondment to the education department. Sharon is known to be an excellent teacher, and she could easily fill in for the ETs. The two nurses are friends, and Sharon has recently confessed to Kate that she is getting restless and is thinking of trying something new, so Kate suspects that this would be a good move for Sharon. A secondment might meet both their needs. With this in mind, Kate speaks to LouEllen, the director in charge of the medical-surgical units, and explains why she wants to approach Sharon with this proposal.

LouEllen agrees, saying that it sounds like a good idea. Kate's next move is to speak to Sharon to establish if she would be interested, and finds her excited about the prospect of a change, even if it is temporary. She says, "This is just what I need right now. I'm so pleased you thought of me. I feel like I'm stagnant and need a change of pace." Kate tries to contact Heather, the unit manager and Sharon's direct supervisor, but Heather is in meetings all day.

Later that day Kate is working in her office when Heather comes storming in, clearly very angry. She slams the door shut and shouts at Kate, "You are such a scumbag! How dare you try to take one of my best nurses over the summer when you know how short-staffed we are! I can't believe you would do such a thing. I was just lucky that LouEllen mentioned it. Were you planning on telling me, you sneak?" Kate is taken aback by the force of Heather's anger, but she replies quietly, "I can see you are upset, and I'm sorry. I tried to get in touch with you but you weren't available, and I thought it was important to check with LouEllen and Sharon first, in any event. I was planning on speaking to you as soon as possible." Heather is not mollified. Indeed, she seems to become even more upset. She shouts, "You had no right! Understand this: I WILL NOT release Sharon for the summer. She will have to quit my unit before I will let her work for you!" Kate wants to reply that Sharon was thinking of quitting anyway, but feels that it is not up to her to inform Heather of that fact. She had been told in confidence, so merely replies, "I do understand your position. But now you need to consider mine. I needed someone to cover the ET position, Sharon looked like a good choice, and she seemed interested. I hope you will reconsider, but I will not withdraw my offer to Sharon. She has a right to make up her own mind." At that point Heather turns on her heel and slams out of the room.

Kate immediately telephones Sharon and tells her of the situation, saying, "The offer still stands, but Heather is adamant that she will not release you. If you want to reconsider then I will understand perfectly. It's your choice. I'm sorry I put you in such a position, but I do believe you would be perfect for this job. Please let me know as soon as possible what you decide." Sharon replies, "Thanks for giving me the chance. I'll talk to Heather myself and tell her that I will work for you, and if she does not release me I will resign my position, which I was considering anyway. I'm glad you brought this to a head by offering me the summer replacement. This has been one of the problems all along. Heather does not seem to realize that her staff have wants or needs of their own. She needs to understand that it is not about control, but about treating people decently. That's one of the main reasons I was thinking of quitting. I just can't stand being treated like a lower-class citizen because I'm a nurse. Heather is so nice to the patients and families, and even the doctors, but she is just brutal to the nursing staff."

If you think about the values in this scenario, you will see that there are elements of all those mentioned in the CNA Code of Ethics for Registered Nurses. Heather is failing to understand Sharon's need for a change, and is certainly not promoting her health and well-being. She shows no interest in promoting Sharon's right to exercise choice. In denying her the opportunity to take the position without even considering her reasons, Heather is assaulting Sharon's dignity. The issue of justice arises in that Sharon could be offering a scarce resource, her specialized knowledge, to a wider group of people, but Heather has not considered this. Clearly Heather's behaviour lacks accountability. This is an example of what not to do and shows that Heather is not an ethics leader. She needs to ask herself whether her response was designed more to meet her own needs than to those of patients and her staff member. Kate, on the other hand, acts ethically in this situation, treating Sharon, LouEllen, and Heather with respect. She does not react defensively when verbally attacked by Heather, and maintains a professional stance throughout. Kate's first consideration is meeting the needs of ostomy patients while the ETs are on vacation, but she also sees the importance of relational ethics with colleagues. Kate is modelling the behaviours of an ethics leader.

Relationships with staff are one area of concern for administrators. Another consideration is their role in distribution of resources. Sometimes nurses feel abandoned by their managers, believing that they have lost touch with the day-to-day issues that arise in direct care. It is not uncommon to hear nurses complain that their managers pay more attention to the "bottom line" than they do to their staff. Issues arise particularly when there is a perceived conflict between budget and staffing, for example, when the manager will not authorize overtime or decides not to replace nurses who call in sick. Fiscal constraints sometimes make it difficult for managers to practise ethically and they may experience considerable moral distress in having to make choices that they feel compromise the quality of care. There is some debate about whether nurses in administration use a different ethical framework than nurses in practice. One group of Canadian authors (Kellen, Oberle, Girard, & Falkenberg, 2005) has argued that management ethics is driven by a utilitarian argument about the greatest good for the greatest number, whereas the nurse in direct care is more influenced by relational ethics and an ethic of care. Both groups, however, are attempting to act in patients' best interests. The ethics leader in administration will work to make the rationale for decisions more transparent. If nurses understand the reasons for decisions, they may be less troubled by them. It is important that the ethics leader be aware of the difficulties presented by strictly utilitarian arguments and be prepared to present an opposing view. Advocacy is an essential part of ethics leadership in administration. Nurse managers must advocate for the well-being of staff as well as patients. The context in which care is provided is vitally important. Nurses' well-being is essential if they are to provide excellent care. Therefore, the ethics leader in administration is prepared to make strong arguments for decisions that will help to establish a better work environment.

Justice is a key value for ethics leaders in administration, and is often played out in decisions about staffing, as we saw in the case of Sharon just described. There are also issues of fairness in vacation allocation, mediation in staff conflicts, and advocacy with other care providers, notably physicians. In all decisions relational ethics plays an important part, because valuing others as human beings and listening to their concerns is fundamental to understanding their best interests. Sometimes a manager must make unpopular decisions, but they must be based on professional values, not personal preferences. For example, a manager would be unjustified in refusing a vacation request simply because she did not like a particular staff member. Another example would be a situation in which the unit manager is aware of a conflict between a staff nurse and a physician. The physician in this case is acting unprofessionally. She is rude and demanding, and tells others that the nurse is incompetent because he has disagreed with the physician's decision to discharge a patient. This is not the first time this physician has demonstrated such behaviour; in fact, she is generally disliked by the staff as a bully. The manager, wanting to avoid conflict at all costs, speaks to the nurse and suggests that he try being a "bit more diplomatic," without investigating whether he was justified in his objections. This would be unethical conduct on the part of the manager, as she is acting on a personal preference for avoiding conflict rather than addressing the problem. It is her responsibility to examine situations and advocate for staff and patient welfare. Harmony on a nursing unit is important, and nurse-physician relationships are a central part of the context of care. If members of the care team are permitted to behave rudely or exhibit bullying tactics, harmony rapidly evaporates. Nurse managers have a moral obligation to act justly and to work to ensure a smooth-functioning team.

Nurse administrators must also be attuned to issues of social justice. They need to be alert to the many "isms," such as sexism, racism, and ageism, that can adversely affect decision making. They must be prepared to be politically active within institutions, as well as at the government level. In Chapter 9 we talked about the importance of relevant properties in resource distribution, using the example of the need to decide between two programs: one for the elderly and one for new mothers. Here we expand on that idea using Anita's situation to explore other important ethical issues. Anita was the manager of the public health unit that had set up the two programs: the home visiting program for young mothers to assist them in breastfeeding and parenting skills, and the elder care program in which nurses visited the frail elderly to provide ongoing assessment and assist them with a variety of things, including making healthy nutrition choices, mobilizing effectively, and making other lifestyle adjustments. Anita had just received notification that, due to budget cuts, a decision was made to cut the elder care program. She knew her nurses would be devastated, and was very concerned about the potential abandonment of this vulnerable patient group. When she asked for the rationale behind the decision she was told that resources were better invested in the young parents and children, as "they are the future." Anita decided that she would have to act quickly if she were to have an impact on this situation. She quickly began to organize a letter-writing campaign, asking recipients of the elder care program to write about what they had gained from it. She also made several community presentations about the importance of the program and asked people to write to their Member of the Legislative Assembly (MLA) to ask for augmented funding to support this program. She prepared a written proposal outlining the necessity of the program and demonstrating how its continuance would save health care dollars in the long run by keeping people out of hospital. She put up posters in local pharmacies and arranged to be interviewed on local television. Anita's nursing values were the driving force behind this activism, as she felt it was her obligation to ensure that this kind of primary care was available to the elderly.

This is an example of ethics leadership in administration. Anita worked to secure funding for a program to serve a population that has relatively limited power and choice in today's society. Nurses working in direct care can also demonstrate activism, but in reality it is more often the administrators who act in this way, as they have more opportunity to do so. Ethics leadership requires awareness and action. It is time consuming and challenging, but necessary to advance the value of promoting health and well-being for patients and staff.

Again, these examples are only a sample of ethics leadership in administration. In demonstrating ethics leadership, nurse managers must base their actions on the values of the CNA Code of Ethics for Registered Nurses. Dealings with staff and advocating for social justice are just part of the nurse manager's primary obligation, which is to create a context for safe, compassionate, competent, and ethical care.

Ethics Leadership in Education

The values of the CNA Code of Ethics for Registered Nurses must also be demonstrated in nursing education, whether it be with undergraduate or graduate students or practicing nurses. Nurse educators play a pivotal role in how nurses understand and live the values of the Code. Consequently, they have a moral obligation to be ethics leaders and role models for ethical behaviour. You will not be surprised to learn that this begins with relational ethics.

The power imbalance between students and professors or instructors is in many ways similar to the power imbalance between nurses and patients. In both situations the person in power (the educator or nurse) has something the other requires. The educator has opportunities to make life very difficult for students, as does the nurse with patients. This makes students and patients similarly vulnerable. The nurse educator must be acutely aware of this imbalance. Promoting students' health and well-being is part of being a teacher. This does not translate into lowering standards or being reluctant to give deserved low grades. It does, however, translate into demonstrating respect for students and promoting their right to dignity and choice. Treating students rudely, belittling them in front of their peers, refusing to respond to their requests for assistance, or delaying their progress by not attending to their needs, is unethical.

Maintaining confidentiality is also an important element of ethical practice in education. Sometimes students confide personal problems to a professor, just as patients confide in nurses. Both have a right to expect that their personal information will be kept confidential and will not be revealed to others without their permission.

Finally, educators have a responsibility to make decisions with justice considerations in mind. As with nursing administration, ethics leadership in education requires that those decisions be based on professional values, not personal preference. It is not acceptable to give one student preferential treatment simply because that student is more likeable or capable than others. Justice demands that preference be given only to "even things out," as when a student with a learning disability is permitted to write an examination in a separate room and is given extra time to complete the examination. This is an example of the rule of justice that expects us to "treat equals equally and unequals unequally."

Students in the clinical area are also deserving of respect. There is a popular expression that "nurses eat their young," which stems from the observations that nurses in clinical practice are often unsupportive of new learners. Nurses may be overly critical, demeaning, and rude. Students' questions are sometimes perceived as a challenge rather than as a sincere desire for information. From the other point of view, it can be frustrating to work with learners, as they are usually slow and uncertain when experiencing the unfamiliar. When nurses are busy and anxious about their patients they can find it a burden to take the extra time to help a student or explain something that they think should be obvious. This is not an excuse for ill treatment of students, however. The nurse who provides ethics leadership in education will use the CNA Code of Ethics for Registered Nurses to guide interactions with students, doing everything he or she can to protect the students' dignity and self-respect. The nurse will recognize that students are usually apprehensive about making errors. Kindness in interaction does not take longer than rudeness, and it is much more ethical. It also teaches students the value of relational ethics and considering the needs of others.

Similarly, nurse educators who are providing educational support for practicing nurses will find opportunities to be ethics leaders. Modelling ethical behaviour is of great value in creating an ethos that reflects the values in the Code. In Chapter 10 we defined ethos as "the distinguishing character, sentiment, moral nature, or guiding beliefs of a person, group, or institution" (Merriam-Webster, on-line). If the nurse educator acts according to professional values, it is more likely that staff nurses will do so as well. The nurse educator who engages in ethical relationships will have an important influence on staff. Nurses who feel they have been treated with respect will be more likely to demonstrate that same respect in their own exchanges with patients, families, and other staff.

Ethics Leadership in Research

The CNA Code of Ethics for Registered Nurses emphasizes the importance of research as a way of improving quality of care. The Canadian Nurses Association also has an excellent document titled *Ethical Research Guidelines for Registered Nurses* (2002) that gives the basics of ethics in research. It can be ordered for a minimal fee from the CNA on-line bookstore and is a valuable resource for practising nurses.

Referring back to the Code, in Chapter 8 we discussed research ethics and confidentiality. Nurses can demonstrate ethics leadership in research in a number of other ways as well. They can show interest in evidence-based practice, and be alert to possible researchable questions. They can develop research skills and conduct research studies following ethical guidelines. Possibly most importantly, nurses can advocate for patients who are questioning their rights and responsibilities as participants, and assist them in making informed choices.

Truan Ngo's experience will help to illustrate this last point. Truan is an RN working in Hudson Manor, a long term care institution. He enjoys the residents and has developed an excellent relationship with each one. Mrs. Holmes is a 95-year-old woman who has lived in Hudson Manor for a decade. One morning she greets Truan with a concerned look and asks if she may speak to him privately. He agrees, and she tells him that she is very worried. The physiotherapist (PT) who is in charge of her rehabilitation exercises has asked her if she would take part in a study he is conducting. He told her it would really help him if she participated, but that she shouldn't feel obligated to take part. The study will involve a new physiotherapy routine, some blood work, and a number of exercise tests. She really doesn't want to be bothered, as she is finding it hard to keep up her energy for the things she really wants to do, like visit with the other residents and go to Bingo on Mondays. Still, she is afraid to say no. She likes the PT well enough, but has never found him very warm and friendly, and is afraid that if she doesn't take part in the study he will be upset and punish her in small ways. She asks Truan what she should do.

Truan reinforces that she does not have to take part in the study if she doesn't want to, but adds that he will find out more about it and explain it to her if she likes. She agrees, and he decides to call the PT right after lunch when the unit quiets down and the residents are resting. However, when Truan returns from his break in the morning he finds Mrs. Holmes in some distress. She is agitated and upset. Apparently the PT had been in to see her and pressured her into signing the consent form. She wishes she had not signed, but felt she had no choice. Truan is quite concerned and asks Mrs. Holmes if she will authorize him to speak to the PT and straighten things out. He assures her that her care will not be jeopardized if she refuses to be in the study. She agrees and Truan calls the PT. He explains the situation and says, "I know you didn't mean to pressure Mrs. Holmes, but that was her perception. She really does not want to be in the study." The PT responds with concern, saying that he is sorry that she felt that way, and he will withdraw her immediately as a research participant. Truan reports back to Mrs. Holmes, and she is greatly relieved.

This kind of initiative demonstrates ethics leadership in practice and research. Another example of ethics leadership comes from a university setting. Dr. Allen is a nursing professor and an active researcher with several studies on the go. She is currently developing a proposal to try a behavioural intervention with adolescents who have eating disorders. She wants to do the study through schools, and is concerned about how she can recruit participants for her study. She wonders how she can find suitable students, as individuals with eating disorders are usually reluctant to admit that they have a problem. Another concern is how she can conduct her groups without other students finding out about the participants' problem. She decides that the best thing to do would be to go to the schools where she plans to find subjects and tell students about her study. She will set up an anonymous chat line and ask students to help her design her study so that their confidentiality is protected. Dr. Allen's graduate students who are working on the project with her are impressed by her ethical sensitivity and her creative solution to this problem. They agree that she has taught them a lot about ethics leadership.

Finally, consider the situation on the stroke unit in a large urban hospital. This is a very active acute care unit and the nurses are extremely busy. There is the added problem that they have recently had several resignations and are seriously short staffed. Dr. Janine

Bloom is a medical researcher who has just started a drug study on the unit. She has spoken to the unit manager and received permission to do the study, which involves nurses collecting data when patients are admitted into the study protocol. The amount of extra work for the nurses is considerable, and several of them have decided that they will just not do it. Instead of speaking to Dr. Bloom about their concerns, they simply pretend they were not aware the patient was in the study. This is an example of unethical conduct by all involved. The nurse manager who agreed to the study should have been aware of the extra workload and insisted that the study pay for extra assistance on the unit. Dr. Bloom should have talked to the nurses before commencing the study. The staff nurses should inform Dr. Bloom of their concerns. This breakdown in communication and relational ethics has put the study in jeopardy and resulted in unhappy nurses who are experiencing moral distress.

There are many other examples of ethics leadership in research. Those presented above provide some background, but the interested nurse can find many other examples in the CNA document described earlier (CNA, 2002). In essence, the ethics leader in research follows the values of the CNA Code of Ethics for Registered Nurses in interaction with participants, those who decline to participate, other staff involved in the study, and nursing staff.

Ethics Leadership in Interdisciplinary Practice

The Canadian health care system is in a state of rapid change. Care providers are expected to work together more closely than they did in the past, and disciplinary boundaries are becoming blurred. Tasks that were formerly the exclusive domain of one discipline are now frequently done by care providers from other disciplines. For example, until recently legislation in many provinces decreed that giving medications was within the exclusive scope of nursing practice; today, in several Canadian jurisdictions Licensed Practical Nurses (LPNs) are permitted under law to perform this task. Similarly, nurses are now expected to do some of the things that were previously done only by physicians. We can assume that the goal of all health care providers is safe, compassionate, competent, and ethical care. Ethics in interdisciplinary practice is about how we work together as a team to ensure that this goal is realized. You will not be surprised to realize that the basis of this kind of working together is relational ethics.

Two key elements of relational ethics are trust and mutual respect. We are more likely to trust someone whom we respect. Developing respect requires knowing something about the capabilities, understandings, and perspectives of other team members. It also means having the ability to articulate your own disciplinary strengths and knowledge, as well as your personal and professional beliefs. It means having pride and confidence in what you can bring to the health care setting. It has been suggested that nurses are an oppressed group, because the traditional relationship between nursing and medicine has been hierarchical, with physicians directing and shaping nursing practice. That is changing with advances in nursing education. Reverby (1987), a keen observer of nursing and social trends, noted that the motto of nursing in times past was "I see and am silent." A result of hierarchical structures in health care is something that has been called the "doctor-nurse game." This was described in 1968 by Dr. Leonard Stein, who noted that nurses, while pretending to be passive, actually made many recommendations and directed much of the care. The game was that they had to make it look like it was the doctor's idea. Now we understand that good ideas can come from any discipline, and nurses are being taught that they have the right and obligation to offer their informed suggestions as part of serving the best interests of the patient. Nurses are no longer held responsible for supporting the hierarchy for its own sake. With the right to be more equal partners in health care, however, comes the need to be accountable for the form of the communication. Sadly, some nurses have not learned the fine art of effective communication. They believe that stating their position and their concerns is important, but they neglect their obligation to do it in such a way as to ensure that others hear what they have to say. If they are aggressive, rude, or confrontational there is less chance that they will be heard. Part of relational ethics involves being able to work with others in a way that preserves the dignity of all.

Consider, for example, the situation in which Colleen found herself. As a very experienced nurse on an acute care mental health unit, she had a great deal of knowledge about caring for psychiatric patients. One day she had been talking to one of the psychiatrists who was new to the unit. He indicated to Colleen that she should give the patient a particular medication, which Colleen believed was contraindicated because of the patient's other medications. Colleen told the psychiatrist of her concerns but later discovered that he had written the order anyway. She called the pharmacy and inquired about incompatibilities of medications, and her belief was confirmed. She called the psychiatrist and told him what she had found out. He was clearly annoyed, but changed the order. The next day when he came to the unit he pulled Colleen aside and showed her a cartoon. The picture appeared to be a physician talking to a nurse, and the caption read, "Nurse, you showed your *knowledge* in finding my error, but you showed your *wisdom* in not pointing it out." Colleen smiled and said to the psychiatrist, "I hope you weren't offended when I expressed my concerns. I don't like to argue with you as I greatly respect your opinion. However, you need to respect my knowledge and experience also. I hope that we can continue to work together in a collegial way, and that you will see my questioning orders as a good thing. Together we can make sure that the patients get the very best care."

In this way Colleen demonstrated her commitment to best practice, and showed the physician that she was a professional. She made it clear that her desire was to work harmoniously, but that her accountability required her to challenge elements of care that she felt were not up to standard. Her positive and calm response reduced the likelihood that the psychiatrist would become defensive and increased the chance that he would hear and respect her for her position.

This kind of direct approach is greatly preferable to the kind of unprofessional and unethical team behaviours sometimes seen in the health care environment. As an example, consider the nurses who are offended by the behaviour of a medical resident.

Instead of speaking to him directly, they decide as a group that they will "get back at him" and make his life miserable. They know that he will be on call for the next two nights, so they agree to call him as often as possible through the night with the most trivial of questions. They enjoy the feeling of power in knowing they can cause him to get very little sleep. Their reasoning is that he will have to learn to "behave" or suffer the consequences. This kind of approach is anything but ethical. In using subversive tactics such as this the nurses demonstrate a lack of professionalism. They are also putting patients at risk by causing the resident to lose much-needed sleep. Their childish tactics are neither effective nor responsible. Instead, they should attempt to speak to him directly, indicating that they have experienced his behaviour as offensive, and asking him to discuss it with them. This can be difficult, because most of us do not enjoy conflict, but if the nurses want to be considered ethical professionals they must be prepared to change their own behaviour.

Another area of interdisciplinary practice in which nurses often find themselves involves delegation of tasks and supervision. In particular, RNs often work with LPNs and Personal Care Attendants (PCAs). Sometimes the expanding scope of LPN practice makes RNs somewhat defensive, worrying that they will lose elements of their practice to the LPNs. This kind of thinking is not productive, and one might argue that it is unethical. The question should be whether all members of the team are working to their scope of practice, and whether the result is quality care. Nurses who question the evolving role of LPNs are often unaware of changes in the LPN educational program. In times past LPNs had very limited education, but program length and complexity has changed markedly over the years. Teamwork and ethical interdisciplinary practice require that nurses ask themselves if their concerns are rational and related to the best interests of the patient, or if they are more about maintaining traditional hierarchical positions.

Working with members of a team requires that each person in the team be treated with respect. Ethics leadership in interdisciplinary practice means demonstrating supportive, trusting relationships. It requires each person to make a concerted effort to understand and appreciate the various perspectives of team members. It means keeping space open for each member of the team to have an opportunity to contribute to his or her level of expertise. Much of it is simply common sense, and comes down to treating others as you would want to be treated. This is not just a matter of being "nice," but a professional obligation that works to ensure that the team functions effectively in the patients' best interests. Providing ethics leadership in this area is usually a matter of modelling positive behaviours and challenging others who fail to exhibit such behaviours. Again, this may be difficult to do, but nobody says ethical practice is easy!

Ethics Leadership in International Nursing Practice

Nursing exists in every country in the world. Not all countries have their own nursing code of ethics; some are guided instead by the International Council of Nurses (ICN) Code of Ethics for Nurses. The ICN is made up of "129 national nurses' associations

(NNAs), representing millions of nurses worldwide. ICN works directly with these member associations on the issues of importance to the nursing profession" (ICN web site). The ICN Code was first released in 1953, and is revised regularly to make it congruent with current standards and issues in nursing. As mentioned in Chapter 3, the Canadian Nurses Association initially adopted the ICN Code, but in 1979 developed its own Code of Ethics for Nurses. The two Codes reflect similar values, as demonstrated by the opening phrases in the ICN Code. It says,

> Nurses have four fundamental responsibilities: to promote health, to prevent illness, to restore health, and to alleviate suffering. The need for nursing is universal.

> Inherent in nursing is respect for human rights, including cultural rights, the right to life and choice, to dignity, and to be treated with respect. Nursing care is respectful of and unrestricted by considerations of age, colour, creed, culture, disability or illness, gender, sexual orientation, nationality, politics, race, or social status (ICN, 2006, p. 4).

There are four elements in the ICN Code: nurses and people; nurses and practice; nurses and the profession; and nurses and co-workers. Under each element are several explanatory statements. The interested reader can retrieve the entire document from the ICN web site. On first examining the ICN Code you will notice that it is much less detailed than the CNA Code, but reflects many of the same ideas. One of the key aspects of the ICN Code is its emphasis on social justice and the need for nurses to recognize and respond to cultural differences, context, and general understandings of belief systems. The ICN Code reflects that nurses have a responsibility to recognize social injustice related to health, and to work actively to effect change at national and local levels. Canadian nurses are expected to follow the ICN Code as well as their own, but since the values in the ICN Code are subsumed under the CNA Code, this is not a problem. It does, however, emphasize the importance of the social justice considerations we have addressed throughout this book. When working in another country, the Canadian RN is bound by the CNA Code, the ICN Code, and, in countries where there is a separate code of ethics for nurses, by that country's code as well. It is the nurse's responsibility to know the content of all relevant codes of ethics.

The ICN web site has a great deal of useful information for nurses who wish to get a glimpse of some of the issues that arise in other countries. In Canadian nursing we are relatively insulated from issues that are prominent features of everyday life in some of the developing countries: poverty, hunger, religious and political persecution, illiteracy, and many more. Communicable diseases take a far greater toll in developing countries than they do in more developed nations. HIV/AIDS is an enormous problem with many ethical dimensions. For instance, spread of the disease is particularly related to women's rights. There are also concerns with drug testing and availability of access to effective medications. The nurse working in a developing country will find that the moral obligation to attend to social justice issues becomes a central element of practice.

RESOURCES FOR DEVELOPING MORAL AGENCY

Nurses who are interested in ethics and wish to develop their knowledge and awareness can access many resources at international, national, provincial, and local levels.

Resources at the National and International Level

At the national level, there are ethics resources for nurses in particular, and for health care practice in general. The Canadian Nurses Association exists to provide support to Canadian nurses in all areas of practice. A visit to the CNA web site (www.cna-nurses.ca) reveals links under the Nursing Practice tab to pages such as Nursing Ethics, Standards and Best Practices, and Scope of Practice. Under the Nursing Ethics tab one finds documents such as the Code of Ethics for Registered Nurses, Ethical Research Guidelines, Ethics in Practice, and position papers on a variety of topics, including end-of-life issues and nurse recruitment. These have all been developed by Canadian nurses for Canadian nurses, and are useful, practical guides to important practice issues. They can be downloaded or ordered for a minimal fee from the CNA bookstore on-line. Other parts of the web site yield information about current issues that impact nursing worklife and the ability to provide quality care, and as such are linked to understandings of ethical practice. Documents on the web site help the nurse see the work that is being done at the national level to ensure that the first value in the CNA Code of Ethics for Registered Nurses, *safe, compassionate, competent, and ethical care*, is actively supported at the systems and policy level. The *Canadian Nurse* journal, published monthly by the Canadian Nurses Association, often has an ethics in practice column in which case studies are discussed.

Another national ethics resource that is less directly linked to nursing is the Canadian Bioethics Society (CBS) (www.bioethics.ca/index-ang.html). As its name suggests, the focus of this not-for-profit organization is bioethics and bioethical problems in Canadian health care. Its main activities are a national conference/annual meeting that attracts about 400 participants each year, and publication of a newsletter available to members. CBS members come from a variety of disciplines, including medicine, nursing, and philosophy. The conference/annual meeting is an exciting opportunity to hear some of Canada's most prominent ethicists, as well as ethics researchers and students, present on current "hot topics" in health care ethics. It also serves as an excellent learning and networking opportunity for those who wish to become more involved in ethics. Students are particularly encouraged to attend, and there are special sessions and networking opportunities organized exclusively for them.

A few years ago, nurses attending the CBS conference/annual meeting decided that it would be useful to set up a national group of practising nurses, nurse scholars, researchers, and students interested in ethics. Each year at the CBS conference this group meets to discuss current issues. The only requirements for membership are to be a nurse or nursing student and to have an interest in ethics. The group provides a good opportunity to talk with others who might be experiencing similar concerns or have similar questions. Those who wish to find out more about this group can email or telephone the Canadian Nurses Association for current contact information.

Interest in health care ethics is growing, and every year there are numerous conferences with ethics as the primary theme, although some are only marginally related to health care. For example, the Ethics Practitioners Association of Canada (EPAC) was established as a network of individuals involved in organizational ethics, including not-for-profit institutions such as hospitals. It lists events on its web site. Anyone wanting more information on available conferences can easily locate it on the Internet using search terms "Canadian conference ethics."

An emerging area of scholarly interest is research ethics. It is addressed at the national level through several organizations. One that is related specifically to health care research is The National Council on Ethics in Human Research (NCEHR), which was established in 1989 and incorporated in 1993. It is a non-profit organization designed to promote the ethical conduct of research with human subjects/participants. Currently it is supported by the Canadian Institutes of Health Research, Health Canada, the Interagency Panel on Research Ethics, and the College of Physicians and Surgeons of Canada. Most of the work of NCEHR is in the area of ethics education. Members of NCEHR also make site visits to examine processes for ethics review. Although they do not complete an official accreditation, they do offer advice to institutions as to how they might improve their processes. A visit to the NCEHR web site gives access to posted events, documents pertaining to research ethics (such as the Tri-Council Policy Statement we discussed in Chapter 9), and information about latest NCEHR happenings. It is a useful resource for anyone interested in ethical conduct of research.

The Canadian Institutes for Health Research, one of the major federal research funding agencies, also has an informative web site (www.cihr-irsc.gc.ca/e/2891.html) for those interested in research ethics. From the CIHR home page the interested reader can click on the ethics tab and find a number of ethics-related documents, including policies for stem cell research and aboriginal research, funding opportunities, and latest events.

The Interagency Advisory Panel on Research Ethics (PRE) is another federal body. It was established in 2001 by the three major funding agencies: CIHR; the Social Sciences and Humanities Research Council (SSHRC); and the Natural Sciences and Engineering Research Council (NSERC). The Panel was mandated to review and revise the TCPS on an ongoing basis, to ensure that the document continues to be a current and useful resource for researchers and ethics boards. PRE has a number of working committees, and a visit to the web site (www.pre.ethics.gc.ca/english/) reveals various changes to the document that are under discussion.

Yet another national group devoted to questions of research ethics is CAREB, the Canadian Association of Research Ethics Boards. This body is composed of members from Research Ethics Boards across Canada. Of particular interest on the CAREB web site (www.careb-accer.ca/en/links.html) is the "Links" tab, under which you will find a variety of national and international policy statements regarding research ethics issues. Access to the discussion forum is limited to members, but the site does provide some useful information to researchers.

The interested nurse can also find a number of international conferences devoted to clinical and research ethics each year. The American Society of Bioethics and the Humanities is a large organization mostly dedicated to issues in health care. It meets annually in the fall. The Association for Practical and Professional Ethics is a more interdisciplinary group that includes doctors, nurses, journalists, philosophers, those involved in business ethics, and others among its members. Topics at the annual meeting, held each February, are quite diverse and give a perspective that goes beyond bioethics. The International Society of Bioethics is truly international, having membership from around the world. Annual meetings are held in different countries each year. Themes for each meeting are focused mainly on bioethics. For example, the 2007 meeting in Spain addressed topics of freedom and responsibility in research, bioethics committees, decision making at the end of life, and adaptability of bioethics. These are just a few of the organizations that can serve to help you develop your thinking and make contacts with like-minded individuals.

Provincial Ethics Resources

Every provincial or territorial nursing association addresses issues of nursing practice and ethics. Each has a great deal of information available on its web site. The interested nurse can also investigate the possibility of being elected to the directing Board of Council and/or appointed to provincial committees that set practice standards, develop ethics guidelines, and prepare position papers on matters with ethical import. Each association has terms of reference that determine who is eligible for the various positions. Being actively involved in matters that directly affect nursing at the provincial or territorial level can be extremely rewarding and educational. A useful web site called NursingEthics (www.nursingethics.ca) has links to all the provincial and territorial associations as well as the Canadian Nurses Association and a variety of national nursing interest groups. The web site is sponsored by a group called The EthicsWeb bookstore, which has a large collection of ethics books for sale on-line.

Provincial and territorial associations will also offer advice on matters of ethics. Web sites provide some documents, but the nurse with an ethics question may also contact the association directly. In most jurisdictions there is a practice consultant who will answer questions and provide advice about such matters. Another vehicle for disseminating information on practice standards and ethics matters is the provincial newsletter. Most associations have a monthly newsletter in which practice issues are discussed. Some also have a lending library that can be accessed by nurses registered with the association.

The province of Alberta is unique in having the Provincial Health Ethics Network (PHEN) as a resource for health care providers. PHEN is "a non-profit organization which provides resources on addressing ethical issues related to health. PHEN does not advocate for or take positions on particular ethical issues; its role is to facilitate thoughtful, informed, and reasoned ethical decision making from all perspectives" (PHEN, 2007). It was established in 1995 after extensive government lobbying by a group of very committed individuals, one of whom was Dr. Janet Storch, a Canadian nurse whom we mentioned in Chapter 3. Dr. Storch later became the founding Chair. The PHEN web site is useful for anyone interested in health care ethics, whether an Alberta resident or not. It has information on conferences, useful links, news items, public policy consultations, and a variety of other materials. Anyone in Canada may purchase a membership for a small fee, and is then entitled to borrow from the PHEN library, which includes a sizeable number of ethics books. PHEN sponsors an annual ethics conference and will conduct workshops and consultations upon request. To date, none of the other provinces has launched an equivalent organization, but nurses from across Canada can access and become members of PHEN if they choose.

Local Ethics Resources

Most nurses interested in ethics and ethics leadership can find many resources at the local level. These are easily available in the urban environment, but may be less evident in rural settings, particularly in remote areas. The first resource for practice is, of course, your own reflection. You can develop your own moral agency simply by examining your practice using the Framework for Ethical Decision Making that we have presented in this book. Another resource that is usually available is colleagues and supervisors. Discussions on matters of ethics are vitally important in all care settings, particularly in an interdisciplinary environment. Hearing what others have to say on an issue can be enlightening. Just thinking of another way to view a problem can be helpful. Some units have regular debriefings on situations that created moral distress for staff.

Sometimes the nurse will face true ethical dilemmas that cause moral distress and uncertainty. Such problems frequently have to do with disagreements about the level of care, as discussed in Chapter 6. Most often the conflicts are between nurses and physicians, or between care providers and families. Usually this becomes an issue when nurses feel that care is futile and they are contributing to the patient's suffering by prolonging death. Nurses may feel powerless to influence the kind of care that the patient receives. However, many of the larger institutions have a resident ethics consultant who can be called to assist with particular moral problems, or to lead discussions. Ethicists can be an invaluable resource because they can aid in values clarification and help staff work through a problem logically and coherently. They can bring current ethics theory and scholarship to the discussion to help clarify issues.

Another useful resource can be the institutional ethics committee, if available. Most large institutions have a clinical ethics committee that can be accessed by patients, families, nurses, or other care providers. Usually it is the physician who asks for ethics support, but nurses have the right to request an ethics assessment if they feel it is necessary. Ethics committees do not make clinical judgments as such. The final decision is left to the care providers. The role of the committee is to make sure that everyone's voice is heard, to listen to the details of the situation, and to give its opinion about the most ethical resolution. Simply ensuring that everyone has input and then giving a considered opinion can do a great deal toward reducing or eliminating moral distress and subsequent moral residue. Not everyone will agree with the decision, but having an opportunity to make the case and have it understood and evaluated by a neutral body can be very helpful.

Opportunities abound for nurses to develop and strengthen their moral sensitivity and agency. It is essential for every nurse to understand that being and becoming an ethical practitioner is hard work that requires ongoing attention and deliberate strategies. As you consider your own practice and moral development, think about ways that you can build your own understandings. You might also think about how you can support others in their growth. There has never been a time when health care has experienced such rapid change, and nursing practice is changing almost on a moment-to-moment basis across North America and indeed the world. Ethics leaders in nursing will lead the change, creating stronger, better, more effective delivery systems that truly exist to deliver safe, compassionate, competent, and ethical care. To be one of those nurses requires intensive effort, but the support is there for those who seek it.

CHAPTER SUMMARY

Rapid changes in the Canadian health care system mean changing understandings about nurses' moral obligations and accountability. The most recent version of the CNA Code of Ethics for Registered Nurses (2008) reflects some of those changes, particularly the growing emphasis on the need for nurses to attend to issues of social justice and primary care. The section in the Code titled *Ethical endeavours* points out how nurses must broaden their ideas about ethics and ethical practice to include those issues. Moral accountability in nursing must expand to include the broader scope.

What is required for the changing health care system is nurses who are prepared to provide ethics leadership, whether they work in direct care, education, administration, or research. Wherever they practice, their foundational ethic must be relational, as every professional encounter involves some form of relationship. Much of ethics leadership involves modelling ethical behaviour, but sometimes it requires a more active role. Advocacy is a key element of ethics leadership in all areas.

One important area of ethics leadership is interdisciplinary practice. Working to develop strong relationships and opening space for ethical reflection are two ways that nurses can help to ensure that the health care team functions effectively to deliver best quality care. Failing to attend to team functioning is unethical in the sense that a dysfunctional team has a reduced chance of delivering safe, compassionate, competent, and ethical care.

Nursing ethics is of concern wherever there is nursing practice. In international settings nurses need to continue to uphold the values of their own country, while also respecting the values of nursing in the country in which they work. For the most part, nursing values remain consistent across continents, although they might be expressed somewhat differently. What changes are not the values, but the situational context that makes it easier or more difficult to live those values. Ethics leadership in nursing is necessary wherever one works.

To develop qualities of an ethics leader, nurses need constantly to reflect on the nature of their own practice. They can seek thoughtful and experienced colleagues with whom to discuss their concerns. They can use the many resources available at the national, provincial, and local levels. There are myriad resources for nurses on-line, available at the click of a mouse. Conferences and associations provide an excellent way to become connected with others who share concerns about ethical practice. Being an ethics leader is hard work that requires constant attention and reflection. The interested nurse will find much to consider as he or she engages in the pursuit of best practice in ethics—but the goal is definitely worthwhile.

Questions for Reflection

1.   Consider your own practice. What are the key ethical concerns you have encountered? Is there a repetitive theme in these concerns? Which values are reflected in these themes?

2. Have you encountered any ethical problems in education? What, if anything, have you done about them? What does this say about your moral courage?

3. Consider your interactions with colleagues from other disciplines. In these interactions, have you ever been in a position that challenged your ethics? Did you feel you handled the situation skillfully and ethically? Why or why not?

4. In thinking about your own practice, can you identify any social justice issues that have arisen? What, if anything, did you do? Why?

Exercises

1. In small groups, discuss any ethical issues you have identified as arising in a management position. Select one issue and consider strategies for dealing with it. Are you able to agree within your group as to the best approach to take? What values are apparent in the different approaches suggested?

2. On the Internet, find the CNA and ICN web sites. Download one document that you think has relevance for your practice and prepare a brief abstract of the document to share with your group/class.

3. In small groups, select one social justice issue that arises in Canadian nursing practice. Discuss the values that are reflected in that issue and consider responsibilities that nurses might have with regard to this issue. Identify three key points that might be used if you were to discuss this issue with your MLA.

4. Find an article on ethics in nursing in a developing country. To what extent are the issues identified the same as those you experience in Canadian nursing?

Research Activities

1. Meet with the manager on your unit. Ask about the key ethics issues that arise for him/her in managing the unit. Report back to the group/class and develop a list of key ethics issues for managers.

2. Find three articles about nursing ethics in practice. Identify the key values that cause issues for nurses as reflected in the articles.

3. Meet with a colleague from another discipline. Ask whether the values represented in the CNA Code of Ethics for Registered Nurses have relevance for her or his practice, and how. Share your findings with the group/class.

References

Canadian Nurses Association, (2008). *Code of ethics for Registered Nurses* (Centennial Ed.). Ottawa: Author.

Canadian Nurses Association (2002). *Ethical research guidelines for Registered Nurses.* Ottawa: Author

International Council of Nurses (2006). *ICN Code of Ethics for Nurses.* Retrieved from www.icn.ch/ July 26, 2007.

Kellen, J., Oberle, K., Girard, F., & Falkenberg, L. (2004). Exploring ethical perspectives of nurses and nurse managers. *Canadian Journal of Nursing Leadership*, 17, 78–87.

Merriam-Webster On-line. Retrieved August 23, 2007 from www.m-w.com/

Provincial Health Ethics Network. (2007). Retrieved July 26, 2007, from www.phen.ab.ca.

Reverby, S. (1987). *Ordered to care: The dilemma of American nursing*. New York: Cambridge University Press.

Stein, L. I. (1968). The doctor-nurse game. *The American Journal of Nursing*, 68 (1), 101–105.

Suggested Reading

Baylis, F., Downie, J., Hoffmaster, B., & Sherwin, S. (2004). *Health care ethics in Canada* (2nd ed.). Toronto: Harcourt Brace Canada.

Bergum, V., & Dossetor, J. (2005). *Relational ethics: The full meaning of respect*. Hagerstown, MD: University Publishing Group.

Kluge, E.-H. W. (2004). *Readings in biomedical ethics: A Canadian focus*. (3rd ed.) Toronto: Pearson Education Canada.

Murphy, N., & Roberts, D. (2008). Nurse leaders as stewards: At the point of service. *Nursing Ethics*, 15(2), 243-253.

Shirey, M. (2005). Ethical climate in nursing practice: The leader's role. *JONAS Health care law, ethics, and regulation*, 7(2), 59–67.

Storch, J. L., Rodney, P., & Starzomski, R. (2004). *Toward a moral horizon: Nursing ethics for leadership and practice*. Toronto: Pearson Education Canada

Storch, J., & Kenny, N. (2007). Shared moral work of nurses and physicians. *Nursing Ethics*, 14(4), 478–491.

Turkel, M.C., & Ray, M.A. (2004). Creating a caring practice environment through self-renewal. *Nursing Admin Quarterly*, 28(4), 249–254.

Glossary

absolute principle a principle or rule that must not be breached under any circumstances

accessibility one of the principles of the Canada Health Act; requires the health insurance plans of each province or territory to provide reasonable access to insured health care services without extra billing

accountability "an obligation or willingness to accept responsibility or be answerable for one's actions" (Merriam-Webster online)

accreditation a formalized approval process whereby a nursing education program or health care institution is evaluated by external reviewers to see if it meets minimum standards

act utilitarianism requires us to anticipate the outcomes of every act and judge the act on the principle of utility

advance directive or AD a signed document that an individual prepares to be put into effect when he or she loses the capacity to make decisions; it may name others who are authorized to make health care decisions for the individual and/or outline treatment decisions

adverse events "unexpected, undesirable incidents resulting in injury or death directly associated with the process of providing health care or services to a person receiving care" (Hebert, Hoffman, & Davies, 2003, as cited in CNA, 2008, p. 22)

advocacy taking the part of another, speaking for persons who cannot speak for themselves, or intervening to ensure that others' views are heard

ageism "prejudice or discrimination against a particular age-group and especially the elderly" (Merriam-Webster, on-line)

anonymity the state of not being known or identified by name; in research, a situation in which no one, not even the researcher, can link a research subject's identity to his or her data

answerability offering reasons and explanations to others for aspects of nursing practice

applied ethics deals with specific questions about how decisions should be made in particular situations

assent agreement of a patient to receive care; assent requires less understanding than consent and merely denotes agreement with what is proposed

autonomy having both the right and the ability to make meaningful choices for oneself; in health care, the right to choose what one will or will not do or allow to be done with respect to treatment

belief a cherished notion; something we think is true

beneficence acting in the best interests of another; in bioethics, a moral principle that denotes the obligation to do what is best for the patient

bioethics a general term for the kind of principled reasoning used by health care providers in making ethical decisions; a theory of ethics specifically related to health care decision making

biomedical ethics a theory intended to guide medical practitioners in ethical decision making; ethical reasoning for physicians

biomedical model an approach to thinking about the human body and its functioning that focuses on its physiological functioning; an approach to health care that puts emphasis on the physiological determinants of health and disease

bodily privacy freedom from observation or intrusion with respect to one's body and bodily functions; the right to control how much of one's body is exposed to others' sight

boundaries limitations that restrict the extent and nature of nurses' involvements with their patients

capacity   the ability to do or experience something; in ethics it is generally used in the context of discussions about informed consent and refers to the ability to understand what one is told

care encounter   any situation in which a nurse is working in a professional relationship with a patient with the intent to improve the patient's well-being

care theory   ethics theory that places emphasis on having compassion for and caring for others; a type of virtue theory that gives moral weight to caring for others

caring   in nursing, demonstrating that another is valued; using one's professional skills for the benefit of others

Categorical Imperative   in Kantian ethics, a rule that guides conduct and has no exceptions

certification   a formalized approval process involving supervised demonstration of skills to permit a nurse to carry out a particular task; generally involves functions that were formerly under the mandate of another profession (usually medicine) and have been designated to nursing

chart audit   a formalized quality control mechanism whereby someone, usually from nursing administration, reviews charts looking for particular indicators of good practice, such as recording the effectiveness of pain control mechanisms

choice   a decision to select or choose something in preference to something else; in ethics it generally refers to making one's own decisions

clinical competence   demonstrating mastery or command of the psychomotor, relational, problem solving, and organizational skills of professional nursing practice in a particular area of practice

code of ethics   reflects the formalized set of values and acceptable actions agreed upon by members of a profession

coercion   pressuring or forcing someone to do something she or he does not wish to do; limiting choice and freedom

compassion   having a feeling of sympathy or empathy for the pain and suffering experienced by others, often with an attendant desire to assist

competency   a practised ability to perform required nursing actions at a high level of proficiency; "the integrated knowledge, skills and attributes required of a registered nurse to practise safely and ethically in a designated role and setting" (CNA, 2008, p. 23)

competency statements   detailed lists of the skills nurses must have and tasks they must be able to perform in all areas of practice

comprehension   a person's actual understanding of what she or he is being told; in ethics, it is usually discussed in the context of informed consent and denotes full understanding

comprehensiveness   principle in the Canada Health Act that requires provincial or territorial health insurance plans to insure a wide array of hospital, physician, surgical-dental, and other health care services; sufficient services must be insured to provide adequate health care to the population

confidential information   intimate or private knowledge about another that is not revealed to others or available to the public

confidentiality   keeping information private or secret; in health care, the duty of someone (generally a professional) who has received information in trust to protect that information, disclosing it to others only with permission or when rules or laws authorize its disclosure

conflict of interest   occurs when someone makes, or is in a position to make, a decision based on what is in her or his own best interests, not in the best interests of others who might be affected by the decision

consequentialism   an approach to ethics theory that suggests right and wrong are determined by the consequences or outcomes of actions; includes the nature of one's obligation to ensure certain outcomes are achieved

constrained moral agency being powerless to act for what one thinks is good and right; in nursing, the inability to act ethically because of limits placed on the nurse's behaviour by others (including family or other health care professionals), the system, or the law

continuing competence part of the annual registration process in which nurses must indicate to their professional association what they have done to maintain their competence or to learn new skills and knowledge; may be judged by the professional association as adequate or inadequate to permit ongoing licensure

contractarian theories ethics theories suggesting that our duty lies in following rules that all rational people engaged in a social contract would agree were right

culture the beliefs, customs, practices, social behaviours, and material traits shared by a particular group of people

deliberate breach (of confidentiality) occurs when health care professionals deliberately decide to subordinate confidentiality to some other good or value

deontology ethics theory based on the belief that humans have the capacity to think through problems and determine right action based on duty or moral obligation

depersonalization the loss of sense of self as a unique individual

descriptive theory describes phenomena and their linkages as observed; gives an account of something by giving details of its characteristics; is therefore generally an outcome of research

desire fulfillment getting what we most want

determinants of health those factors that contribute to one's health and well-being, including personal characteristics as well as such social, political, environmental, and economic factors as the availability of food, shelter, adequate clothing, clean water, and freedom from persecution

deterrence preventing others from taking action by making them fear the consequences. In the legal system, it is assumed that fear of consequences such as being put in jail will act to prevent persons from committing crimes.

dignity the quality or state of being worthy, honoured, or esteemed; behaviour that accords with self-respect or with regard for due seriousness

discipline teaching people to obey rules and punishing them if they do not do so; in nursing, involves comparison of practice against professional standards and imposing sanctions on nurses who do not meet those standards

dissent to disagree with what is proposed or withhold assent or consent; in ethics, usually discussed in the context of a patient's or family's expressed or implied refusal of treatment

distributive justice concerns how scarce resources can be distributed most fairly; depends on our understandings of what is fair and how we can come to agreement on fairness. Usually used in consideration of how we can get maximum benefit from resources.

duty something we are obliged to do because of certain moral rules or principles; obligation to act in a particular way

dying with dignity being able to maintain a sense of self-worth through the dying process; going through the dying process in a way that is honourable or desirable; in nursing, often connotes dying without unnecessary pain and suffering

Electronic Health Record (EHR) personal health information about an individual collected by health professionals, recorded in a computer and accessible to health care professionals authorized to retrieve the information

embodiment experiencing ethical practice as bodily as well as rational processes; in relational ethics, acting in relationship in such a way that there is recognition that the mind/body split is an artificial one and that healing for both patient and family cannot occur unless scientific knowledge and human compassion are given equal weight

employee wellness program program offered by an employer to employees to assist them to maintain health and wellness; typically offers a variety of services such as psychological and addictions counselling, as well as safety training and health surveillance

empowerment to promote self-efficacy or the ability of another to do what he or she desires or needs to do

engagement connecting with others in an open, trusting, and responsive manner

Epp Report (1986) a policy statement entitled *Achieving Health for All: A Framework for Health Promotion*; recommended fostering public participation, strengthening community health services, and coordinating all sectors of society in health choices

ethical dilemma a situation that requires a moral choice between two mutually exclusive courses of action

ethical violation "actions or failures to act that breach fundamental duties to the persons receiving care or colleagues and other health care providers" (CNA, 2008)

ethics the branch of philosophy that deals with questions of right and wrong, and ought and ought not in our interactions with others

ethos "the distinguishing character, sentiment, moral nature, or guiding beliefs of a person, group, or institution" (Merriam-Webster, on-line)

everyday ethics day-to-day ethical encounters that a nurse has with patients, families, colleagues, and the broader environment; largely concerns the choices a nurse makes in relationships with others

explanatory theory a theory that explains how things might work, what meanings people give to certain events, or how people think about abstract concepts; based primarily on reflection and conjecture

fidelity upholding one's vows and promises; keeping one's word; loyalty to one's promises

fiduciary a relationship of trust and confidence; in health care, a relationship of heath care providers with patients in which they are in a position of trust and are obligated to act in the patient's best interests

fitness to practise the physical, mental, and emotional capacities to deal with the often stressful and demanding health care environment

framework a structure of related concepts that is somewhat more concrete than a model and, consequently, gives more direction for practice

freedom "the absence of necessity, coercion, or constraint in choice or action" (Merriam Webster, on-line); having the right to choose in an environment in which choices are available

golden mean in Aristotelian ethics, choosing the middle ground between excess and deficiency, too much or too little

golden rule in Kantian ethics, the rule that states "do unto others only that which you are prepared to have them do unto you"

health includes physical status, emotional well-being, social relationships, intellectual functioning, and spirituality

health as wellness a state of optimal health or functioning

health care ethics usually taken to mean ethical decision making at the policy and systems level, but often used interchangeably with bioethics

health promotion integrating concepts of health as wellness and fostering activities that move people toward wellness; working to assist others to remain healthy and free of disease/illness

health protection detecting illness early to protect another from its effects or maintain functioning within the constraints of illness

high-level wellness "an integrated method of functioning which is orientated toward maximizing the potential of which the individual is capable, within the environment where he [sic] is functioning" (Dunn, 1977, p. 9)

honesty truth-telling; giving accurate information

human rights those entitlements, freedoms, or privileges to which people are entitled

identifiable data information that would permit identification of an individual; in the health care setting, information about an individual's life or health circumstances, including details about the name or identity of the individual

inadvertent or unintentional breach (of confidentiality) accidental disclosure of information; occurs when care providers do not realize that they are engaging in practices that might result in improper disclosure

independence the ability to do things ourselves, in order for our needs or desires to be fulfilled

individual control a person's right to maintain power or authority over her or his own body and bodily functions, as well as what personal information is given, and with whom and how it is shared

inducement a promise or reward that causes or encourages one to take a certain action; a suggestion or promise that something good will happen if one takes a particular action

informed consent a patient's permission for something (including treatment, research), based on a good understanding of the situation; fully informed consent implies voluntariness, capacity, and comprehension

integrity honesty, sincerity, and uprightness; wholeness

journalling writing about situations and reflecting on what one has written; in nursing, writing and reflecting on practice situations

justice making fair or equitable decisions; sometimes thought about as treating equals equally and unequals unequally

Lalonde Report (1974) a document by the Canadian Minister of Health entitled *A New Perspective on the Health of Canadians*; outlined what was required to attain and maintain the health of Canadians; introduced the "health field concept"

legal rights those entitlements, freedoms, or privileges to which the individual is entitled, as described and protected in law (in this case, privacy laws)

listening to one's own voice a process of knowing personal limits and strengths, trusting judgments, and reflecting on values and philosophy of care

macro level decision making at the level of the broader society or system

maxim a logical principle based on reason; in Kantian ethics, a principle that is reasoned and guides one's actions in all relevant circumstances

Mazankowski Report (2002) A report commissioned by the Alberta government regarding integrity, sustainability, and efficiency of the health care system; suggested spending more public dollars on health promotion and illness prevention and fewer public dollars on illness care

meso level decision making at the institutional level

metaethics the area of philosophy that generates descriptive theory about where our understanding of right or good comes from

micro level decision making about specific individuals or groups

model an abstract representation of reality that can be depicted through pictures, words, or a combination of the two

moral agency the ability to act on one's moral beliefs

moral community a group that works together to enact shared values

moral courage the strength and commitment to act on one's beliefs

moral disengagement in nursing, distancing oneself from the relational aspect of care and focusing instead only on the mechanistic skilled tasks

moral distress a condition of discomfort that occurs when one believes that something should be done but is constrained by institutional or other pressures from acting on that belief

moral relativism   the idea that no single solution to a problem can be considered more right than another

moral residue   the long-standing feelings of guilt, remorse, or inadequacy an individual experiences because of unresolved ethical conflicts or morally distressing situations

moral sensitivity   the ability to recognize the moral dimensions of situations

moral uncertainty   a situation in which one is aware that something is morally amiss, and/or that something should be done, but is uncertain as to what action should be taken

moral unpreparedness   a situation that occurs when nurses enter a situation where they lack preparation for giving ethical care to patients and families

morality   actions that individuals take based on what they believe to be right or good; a doctrine or system of conduct; beliefs about how individuals and groups ought to behave or act in situations

mutuality   a relationship that benefits both and harms neither; sharing within a relationship

non-coercion   allowing or supporting others to choose or make decisions free of force; not forcing others to make particular decisions

non-maleficence   a bioethical principle that denotes the responsibility of the care provider to do no harm; often considered the primary duty of the physician

normative ethics theory   a prescriptive theory that tells us how we ought to think about moral questions based on common agreement or understanding of what is good or right in a particular context

nursing competence   the overall level at which a nurse performs the integrated knowledge, skills, and attributes required to practise safely and ethically in a designated role and setting

Ottawa Charter   (1986) an international consensus statement on how individual and population health could be attained

and maintained; explored the concept of "responsibility for health" and suggested that a balance between medical, behavioural, and socioenvironmental or ecological approaches was needed

paternalism   "a system under which an authority undertakes to supply needs or regulate conduct of those under its control in matters affecting them as individuals as well as in their relations to authority and to each other" (Merriam Webster on-line); in health care, usually connotes providers making decisions that they believe to be in patients' best interests, but they do not seek the patients' consents

peer review   having another nurse at the same level in the organization observe and evaluate one's nursing practice

population health   the health of the entire community; a field of health care that has as its primary mandate the promotion of health and prevention of illness; a philosophical view that the health of people improves only when society tackles all determinants of health

portability   principle in the Canada Health Act ensuring that residents moving from one province or territory to another will continue to be covered for insured services except during a minimum waiting period

power   possession of control, authority, or influence over others

practical wisdom   in health care, knowing the how, when, and why of appropriate interventions, that is, being able to make good practice decisions

practice standards   in nursing, written statements developed by the professional association detailing those things for which nurses are accountable; descriptions of nursing competencies and the minimum level of proficiency nurses must accomplish to be permitted to practice

praxis   reflection in action; practical wisdom enacted

prescriptive theory   ethics theory that tells us how we should think about things or how things ought to be done; usually generated as a result of research and reflection

primary care   accessible and coordinated health services focused on both prevention and cure; basic care at the first level of medical and curative care, focused on promoting health and preventing illness; first level of contact of individuals, families, and communities with the health care system

primary prevention   an action or program designed to help people grow up with or maintain healthy behaviours that will help them resist disease

principle of utility   in Mill's utilitarian ethics, a principle that says that good is to be understood in terms of that which produces "the greatest good for the greatest number"

privacy   freedom from observation or intrusion by others, or from their attention

privacy rights   in health care, denotes a patient's "legislated right to provide or withhold consent with respect to the collection, use, disclosure, or accessibility of personal health information; to access his or her own information and to have personal information recorded as accurately as possible" (CNA, 2001)

proxy   a surrogate or substitute decision maker

public administration   principle of the Canada Health Act that requires health care insurance plans to be administered by the provinces and territories

reflection   conscious effort to think about and evaluate one's own practice and determine what one needs to improve

registration   a formal assessment of credentials and granting of a licence to practise

rehabilitation   in the legal system, teaching criminals how to meet their needs or achieve their desires without resorting to crime

relational autonomy   in ethics, the idea that people who are self-determining seldom make decisions without consultation with or consideration of others; that people make decisions within a complex web of relationships, responsibilities, and social structures

relational competence   ability to engage with others respectfully and authentically

relational ethics   the theory that ethical understandings are formed in, and emerge from, relationships with others

relevant properties   attributes or characteristics that a person must possess to qualify for particular goods or resources

resource allocation   the way in which goods such as dollars, supplies, and staff are assigned to different aspects of health care

restorative justice   a theory of justice that holds that wrongdoers can make amends to society (and to victims) for their crimes by compensating the victims in some way, for example, righting wrongdoing by paying someone back

retributive justice   the theory of justice that believes that proportionate punishment for crime is morally acceptable or desirable

rights theories   ethics theories that tell us that good or right consists in ensuring that human rights are protected

Romanow Report   (2002) report of a federal government commission to look at the health care system and its sustainability, efficiency, and effectiveness; recommended sweeping changes in how the health care system is designed and funded, including changing its focus to primary care

rule utilitarianism   a consequentialist ethics theory that requires us to adopt general rules likely to promote the greatest good for the greatest number

scope of practice   under legislation, activities that only those with the title "Registered Nurse" are permitted to undertake; a less formal definition refers to the spectrum of activities that each nurse undertakes in practice

secondary prevention   a form of health promotion aimed at helping people change unhealthy behaviours; strives for early detection of disease

self-determination   the right and ability to make decisions for oneself; the central idea in autonomy; in health care, the concept of consent and the ability to make decisions about care and treatment

self-efficacy the degree to which a person believes in his or her ability to perform a certain task; a general belief in one's overall ability to do what needs to be done

self-governing or self-regulating having the responsibility under law to ensure accountability for professionals; some professions are designated self-governing under law and have the responsibility of monitoring practice of all members of the profession who are employed in the profession within the jurisdiction of practice

sense of self-worth how we think about and value ourselves

sentient responsive or finely tuned to sense impressions; capable of responding emotionally not just intellectually

social justice "the fair distribution of society's benefits and responsibilities and their consequences" (CNA, 2006, p. 7)

socioenvironmental model a model of health and health promotion that emphasizes connectedness to one's family and community, self-efficacy, self-determination, and capacity to do things that are important and meaningful

steadfast being firm in belief, determination, or adherence

subjective dignity refers to a person's own experiences, values, and beliefs and encompasses his or her idea of what enhances or detracts from a feeling of self-worth

subjects individuals who act with their own desires and intentions

surrogate a person acting as a substitute or proxy

technical competence in nursing, refers to knowledge and skills needed to perform particular (physical) tasks such as changing dressings, starting an intravenous drip, or inserting a nasogastric tube

teleological goal-oriented; related to the study of actions that lead to endpoints or goals

tertiary prevention treatment that prevents a person from becoming more ill or dying from a disease

theoretical competence knowledge of the why and how of possible interventions; scientific and conceptual knowledge necessary for the provision of care

theories of Divine Command ethics theories that say that understanding of good comes from rules delivered by a god or deity and that moral behaviour requires one to follow of the rules

theories of obligation ethics theories that tell us what our duties are based on certain rules, what the rules are, and where they originated

theory a proposition or statement about a set of facts or concepts and their relationships to one another

trust "assured reliance on the character, ability, strength, or truth of someone or something" (Merriam-Webster on-line)

trusting judgments believing that the ethical (and practice) decisions one makes are reliable and valuable

trustworthiness being dependable, that is, someone who can be counted on

undue inducement too much inducement; a promise or reward that persuades someone to do something they would not otherwise do; in research, undue inducement refers to offering persons something they desire, thus persuading them to assume risk

universal dignity the belief that all persons have worth

universality principle of the Canada Health Act stating that every resident of the province or territory is entitled to insured health services

utilitarianism a form of ethics theory that defines "good" in terms of goals or consequences, usually usefulness in promoting happiness and well-being

values core beliefs we hold about what is important to us

values clarification a process used to increase one's awareness about what one values most

values conflicts situations when two or more individuals hold different values calling for actions that cannot both be fulfilled

virtue ethics the school of thought that says good people will make good decisions and explores the characteristics that make people good

virtues moral elements of character

voluntariness making decisions without coercion or pressure; a central feature of informed consent

voluntary euthanasia a patient's decision to end her or his own life or seek assistance from others to do so

vulnerability a risk of being physically or emotionally wounded; in health care a particular vulnerability of persons receiving care may be emotional or physical harm that could rob them of their dignity

vulnerable groups groups in society who are systematically disadvantaged, leading to risk of emotional or physical harm; in health care the harms are related to diminished health and well-being

wellness "a dynamic state of health in which an individual progresses toward a higher level of functioning, achieving an optimum balance between internal and external environments" (Mosby's, 2002, p. 1829)

whistleblowing reporting unethical or unsafe practice of a nursing colleague or other health professional, including such things as errors, incompetence, negligence, or patient abuse

worth a belief about the value of something; in ethics, a belief about the value of human beings or human values

References

Canadian Nurses Association. (2001). *Privacy of personal health information.* Ottawa: Author.

Canadian Nurses Association. (2006). Social justice . . . a means to an end, an end in itself. Ottawa: Author, Retrieved August 2008 from www.cna-aiic.ca.

Canadian Nurses Association. (2008). *Code of ethics for Registered Nurses* (Centennial Ed.). Ottawa: Author.

Dunn, H. (1977). What high-level wellness means. *Health Values,* 1, 9-16.

Hebert, P., Hoffman, C., & Davies, J. (2003). *The Canadian safety dictionary.* Edmonton, AB: Canadian patient Safety Institute.

Merriam-Webster On-line. Retrieved June 23, 2006, from www.merriam-webster.com/ dictionary/ trust

Merriam-Webster On-line. Retrieved July 14, 2007, from www.merriam-webster.com/dictionary/ ageism

Merriam-Webster On-line. Retrieved August 23, 2007, from www.merriam-webster.com/dictionary/ accountability

Merriam-Webster On-line. Retrieved August 23, 2007, from www.merriam-webster.com/dictionary/ ethos

Merriam-Webster On-line. Retrieved August 8, 2008, from www.merriam-webster.com/dictionary/ paternalism

Merriam-Webster On-line. Retrieved August 8, 2008, from www.merriam-webster.com/dictionary/ freedom

Mosby's medical, nursing, and allied health dictionary (6th ed.) (2002). St. Louis, MO: Mosby.

Appendix A

CODE OF Ethics*

FOR REGISTERED NURSES

2008 CENTENNIAL EDITION

CANADIAN NURSES ASSOCIATION
ASSOCIATION DES INFIRMIÈRES ET INFIRMIERS DU CANADA

© Canadian Nurses Association
50 Driveway
Ottawa, ON K2P 1E2

Tel.: 613-237-2133 or 1-800-361-8404
Fax: 613-237-3520
www.cna-aiic.ca

June 2008

ISBN 978-1-55119-182-9

CONTENTS

PREAMBLE

The Canadian Nurses Association's *Code of Ethics for Registered Nurses*[1] is a statement of the ethical[2] **values**[3] of **nurses** and of nurses' commitments to persons with health-care needs and **persons receiving care**. It is intended for nurses in all contexts and domains of nursing practice[4] and at all levels of decision-making. It is developed by nurses for nurses and can assist nurses in practising ethically and working through ethical challenges that arise in their practice with individuals, **families**, communities and public health systems.

The societal context in which nurses work is constantly changing and can be a significant influence on their practice. The quality of the work environment in which nurses practise is also fundamental to their ability to practise ethically. The code of ethics is revised periodically (see Appendix A) to ensure that it is attuned to the needs of nurses by reflecting changes in social values and conditions that affect the public, nurses and other **health-care providers**, and the health-care system (see Appendix B for a list of societal changes envisioned to affect nursing practice in the coming decade). Periodic revisions also promote lively dialogue and create greater awareness of and engagement with ethical issues among nurses in Canada.

PURPOSE OF THE CODE

The *Code of Ethics for Registered Nurses* serves as a foundation for nurses' ethical practice. The specific values and ethical responsibilities expected of registered nurses in Canada are set out in part I. Endeavours that nurses may undertake to address social **inequities** as part of ethical practice are outlined in part II.

---

[1] In this document, the terms *registered nurse* and *nurse* include nurses who are registered or licensed in extended roles, such as nurse practitioners.

[2] In this document, the terms *moral* and *ethical* are used interchangeably based upon consultation with nurse ethicists and philosophers. We acknowledge that not everyone concurs in this usage.

[3] Words or phrases in bold print are found in the glossary. They are shown in bold only on first appearance.

[4] In this document, *nursing practice* refers to all areas of nursing practice, including direct care (which includes community and public health), education, administration, research and policy development.

The code provides guidance for ethical relationships, responsibilities, behaviours and decision-making, and it is to be used in conjunction with the professional standards, laws and regulations that guide practice.

It serves as a means of self-evaluation and self-reflection for ethical nursing practice and provides a basis for feedback and peer review. The code also serves as an ethical basis from which nurses can **advocate** for **quality work environments** that support the delivery of safe, **compassionate**, competent and ethical care.

Nurses recognize the privilege of being part of a self-regulating profession and have a responsibility to merit this privilege. The code informs other health-care professionals as well as members of the public about the ethical commitments of nurses and the responsibilities nurses accept as being part of a self-regulating profession.

FOUNDATION OF THE CODE

Ethical nursing practice involves core ethical responsibilities that nurses are expected to uphold. Nurses are accountable for these ethical responsibilities in their professional relationships with individuals, families, groups, populations, communities and colleagues.

As well, nursing **ethics** is concerned with how broad societal issues affect **health** and **well-being**. This means that nurses endeavour to maintain awareness of aspects of **social justice** that affect health and well-being and to advocate for change. Although these endeavours are not part of nurses' core ethical responsibilities, they are part of ethical practice and serve as a helpful motivational and educational tool for all nurses.

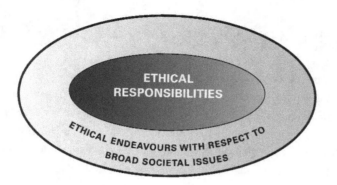

The code is organized in two parts:

PART I: Part I, "Nursing Values and Ethical Responsibilities," describes the core responsibilities central to ethical nursing practice. These ethical responsibilities are articulated through seven primary values and accompanying responsibility statements, which are grounded in nurses' professional relationships with individuals, families, groups, populations and communities as well as with students, colleagues and other health-care professionals. The seven primary values are:

1. Providing safe, compassionate, competent and ethical care

2. Promoting health and well-being

3. Promoting and respecting informed decision-making

4. Preserving dignity

5. Maintaining **privacy** and **confidentiality**

6. Promoting **justice**

7. Being accountable

PART II: Ethical nursing practice involves endeavouring to address broad aspects of social justice that are associated with health and well-being. Part II, "Ethical Endeavours," describes endeavours that nurses can undertake to address social inequities.

USING THE CODE IN NURSING PRACTICE

Values are related and overlapping. It is important to work toward keeping in mind all of the values in the code at all times for all persons in order to uphold the dignity of all. In health-care practice, values may be in conflict. Such value conflicts need to be considered carefully in relation to the practice situation. When such conflicts occur, or when nurses need to think through an ethical situation, many find it helpful to use an ethics model for guidance in ethical reflection, questioning and decision-making (see Appendix C).

Nursing practice involves both legal and ethical dimensions. Still, the law and ethics remain distinct. Ideally, a system of law would be completely compatible with the values in this code. However, there may be situations in which nurses need to **collaborate** with others to change a law or policy that is incompatible with ethical practice. When this occurs, the code can guide and support nurses in advocating for changes to law, policy or practice. The code can be a powerful political instrument for nurses when they are concerned about being able to practise ethically.

Nurses are responsible for the ethics of their practice. Given the complexity of ethical situations, the code can only outline nurses' ethical responsibilities and guide nurses in their reflection and decision-making. It cannot ensure ethical practice. For ethical practice, other elements are necessary, such as a commitment to do good; sensitivity and receptiveness to ethical matters; and a willingness to enter into relationships with persons receiving care and with groups, populations and communities that have health-care needs and problems. Practice environments have a significant influence on nurses' ability to be successful in upholding the ethics of their practice. In addition, nurses' self-reflection and dialogue with other nurses and health-care providers are essential components of ethical nursing practice. The importance of the work environment and of reflective practice is highlighted below.

Quality Work Environments

Nurses as individuals and as members of groups advocate for practice settings that maximize the quality of health outcomes for persons receiving care, the health and well-being of nurses, organizational performance and societal outcomes (Registered Nurses' Association of Ontario [RNAO], 2006). Such practice environments have the organizational structures and resources necessary to ensure safety, support and respect for all persons in the work setting. Other health-care providers, organizations and policy-makers at regional, provincial/territorial, national and international levels strongly influence ethical practice.

Nurses' Self-Reflection and Dialogue

Quality work environments are crucial to ethical practice, but they are not enough. Nurses need to recognize that they are **moral agents** in providing care. This means that they have a responsibility to conduct themselves ethically in what they do and how they interact with persons receiving care. Nurses in all facets of the profession need to reflect on their practice, on the quality of their interactions with others and on the resources they need to maintain their own well-being. In particular, there is a pressing need for nurses to work with others (i.e., other nurses, other health-care professionals and the public) to create the **moral communities** that enable the provision of safe, compassionate, competent and ethical care.

Nursing ethics encompasses the breadth of issues involved in health-care ethics, but its primary focus is the ethics of the everyday. How nurses attend to ethics in carrying out their daily interactions, including how they approach their practice and reflect on their ethical commitment to the people they serve, is the substance of **everyday ethics**.

In their practice, nurses experience situations involving ethics. The values and responsibility statements in the code are intended to assist nurses in working through these experiences within the context of their unique practice situations.

Types of Ethical Experiences and Situations

When nurses can name the type of ethical concern they are experiencing, they are better able to discuss it with colleagues and supervisors, take steps to address it at an early stage, and receive support and guidance in dealing with it. Identifying an ethical concern can often be a defining moment that allows positive outcomes to emerge from difficult experiences. There are a number of terms that can assist nurses in identifying and reflecting on their ethical experiences and discussing them with others:[5]

Ethical problems involve situations where there are conflicts between one or more values and uncertainty about the correct course of action. Ethical problems involve questions about what is right or good to do at individual, interpersonal, organizational and even societal levels.

Ethical (or moral) uncertainty occurs when a nurse feels indecision or a lack of clarity, or is unable to even know what the moral problem is, while at the same time feeling uneasy or uncomfortable.

Ethical dilemmas or questions arise when there are equally compelling reasons for and against two or more possible courses of action, and where choosing one course of action means that something else is relinquished or let go. True dilemmas are infrequent in health care. More often, there are complex ethical problems with multiple courses of actions from which to choose.

Ethical (or moral) distress arises in situations where nurses know or believe they know the right thing to do, but for various reasons (including fear or circumstances beyond their control) do not or cannot take the right action or prevent a particular harm. When values and commitments are compromised in this way, nurses' identity and **integrity** as moral agents are affected and they feel moral distress.

---

[5] These situations are derived from CNA, 2004b; Fenton, 1988; Jameton, 1984; and Webster & Baylis, 2000.

Ethical (or moral) residue is what nurses experience when they seriously compromise themselves or allow themselves to be compromised. The moral residue that nurses carry forward from these kinds of situations can help them reflect on what they would do differently in similar situations in the future.

Ethical (or moral) disengagement can occur if nurses begin to see the disregard of their ethical commitments as normal. A nurse may then become apathetic or disengage to the point of being unkind, non-compassionate or even cruel to other health-care workers and to persons receiving care.

Ethical violations involve actions or failures to act that breach fundamental duties to the persons receiving care or to colleagues and other health-care providers.

Ethical (or moral) courage is exercised when a nurse stands firm on a point of moral principle or a particular decision about something in the face of overwhelming fear or threat to himself or herself.

PART I: NURSING VALUES AND ETHICAL RESPONSIBILITIES

Nurses in all domains of practice bear the ethical responsibilities identified under each of the seven primary nursing values.[6] These responsibilities apply to nurses' interactions with individuals, families, groups, populations, communities and society as well as with students, colleagues and other health-care professionals. The responsibilities are intended to help nurses apply the code. They also serve to articulate nursing values to employers, other health-care professionals and the public. Nurses help their colleagues implement the code, and they ensure that student nurses are acquainted with the code.

A. PROVIDING SAFE, COMPASSIONATE, COMPETENT AND ETHICAL CARE

Nurses provide safe, compassionate, competent and ethical care.

Ethical responsibilities:

1. Nurses have a responsibility to conduct themselves according to the ethical responsibilities outlined in this document and in practice standards in what they do and how they interact with persons receiving care as well as with families, communities, groups, populations and other members of the **health-care team**.

2. Nurses engage in compassionate care through their speech and body language and through their efforts to understand and care about others' health-care needs.

3. Nurses build trustworthy relationships as the foundation of meaningful communication, recognizing that building these relationships involves a conscious effort. Such relationships are critical to understanding people's needs and concerns.

---

[6] The value and responsibility statements in the code are numbered and lettered for ease of use, not to indicate prioritization. The values are related and overlapping.

4. Nurses question and intervene to address unsafe, non-compassionate, unethical or incompetent practice or conditions that interfere with their ability to provide safe, compassionate, competent and ethical care to those to whom they are providing care, and they support those who do the same. See Appendix D.

5. Nurses admit mistakes[7] and take all necessary actions to prevent or minimize harm arising from an **adverse event**. They work with others to reduce the potential for future risks and preventable harms. See Appendix D.

6. When resources are not available to provide ideal care, nurses collaborate with others to adjust priorities and minimize harm. Nurses keep persons receiving care, families and employers informed about potential and actual changes to delivery of care. They inform employers about potential threats to safety.

7. Nurses planning to take job action or practising in environments where job action occurs take steps to safeguard the health and safety of people during the course of the job action. See Appendix D.

8. During a natural or human-made disaster, including a communicable disease outbreak, nurses have a **duty to provide care** using appropriate safety precautions. See Appendix D.

9. Nurses support, use and engage in research and other activities that promote safe, competent, compassionate and ethical care, and they use guidelines for ethical research[8] that are in keeping with nursing values.

10. Nurses work to prevent and minimize all forms of **violence** by anticipating and assessing the risk of violent situations and by collaborating with others to establish preventive measures. When violence cannot be anticipated or prevented, nurses take action to minimize risk to protect others and themselves.

---

[7] Provincial and territorial legislation and nursing practice standards may include further direction regarding requirements for disclosure and reporting.

[8] See *Ethical Research Guidelines for Registered Nurses* (CNA, 2002) and the *Tri-Council Policy Statement: Ethical Conduct for Research Involving Humans* (Canadian Institutes of Health Research, Natural Sciences and Engineering Research Council of Canada, & Social Sciences and Humanities Research Council, 1998).

B. Promoting Health and Well-Being

Nurses work with people to enable them to attain their highest possible level of health and well-being.

Ethical responsibilities:

1. Nurses provide care directed first and foremost toward the health and well-being of the person, family or community in their care.

2. When a community health intervention interferes with the individual rights of persons receiving care, nurses use and advocate for the use of the least restrictive measures possible for those in their care.

3. Nurses collaborate with other health-care providers and other interested parties to maximize health benefits to persons receiving care and those with health-care needs, recognizing and respecting the knowledge, skills and perspectives of all.

C. PROMOTING AND RESPECTING INFORMED DECISION-MAKING

Nurses recognize, respect and promote a person's right to be informed and make decisions.

Ethical responsibilities:

1. Nurses, to the extent possible, provide persons in their care with the information they need to make informed decisions related to their health and well-being. They also work to ensure that health information is given to individuals, families, groups, populations and communities in their care in an open, accurate and transparent manner.

2. Nurses respect the wishes of **capable** persons to decline to receive information about their health condition.

3. Nurses recognize that capable persons may place a different weight on individualism and may choose to defer to family or community values in decision-making.

4. Nurses ensure that nursing care is provided with the person's **informed consent**. Nurses recognize and support a capable person's right to refuse or withdraw **consent** for care or treatment at any time.

5. Nurses are sensitive to the inherent power differentials between care providers and those receiving care. They do not misuse that power to influence decision-making.

6. Nurses advocate for persons in their care if they believe that the health of those persons is being compromised by factors beyond their control, including the decision-making of others.

7. When family members disagree with the decisions made by a person with health-care needs, nurses assist families in gaining an understanding of the person's decisions.

8. Nurses respect the informed decision-making of capable persons, including choice of lifestyles or treatment not conducive to good health.

9. When illness or other factors reduce a person's capacity for making choices, nurses assist or support that person's participation in making choices appropriate to their capability.

10. If a person receiving care is clearly **incapable** of consent, the nurse respects the law on capacity assessment and substitute decision-making in his or her jurisdiction (Canadian Nurses Protective Society [CNPS], 2004).

11. Nurses, along with other health-care professionals and with **substitute decision-makers**, consider and respect the best interests of the person receiving care and any previously known wishes or **advance directives** that apply in the situation (CNPS, 2004).

D. Preserving Dignity

Nurses recognize and respect the intrinsic worth of each person.

Ethical responsibilities:

1. Nurses, in their professional capacity, relate to all persons with respect.

2. Nurses support the person, family, group, population or community receiving care in maintaining their dignity and integrity.

3. In health-care decision-making, in treatment and in care, nurses work with persons receiving care, including families, groups, populations and communities, to take into account their unique values, customs and spiritual beliefs, as well as their social and economic circumstances.

4. Nurses intervene, and report when necessary,[9] when others fail to respect the dignity of a person receiving care, recognizing that to be silent and passive is to condone the behaviour. See Appendix D.

5. Nurses respect the physical privacy of persons by providing care in a discreet manner and by minimizing intrusions.

6. When providing care, nurses utilize practice standards, best practice guidelines and policies concerning restraint usage.

7. Nurses maintain appropriate professional **boundaries** and ensure their relationships are always for the benefit of the persons they serve. They recognize the potential vulnerability of persons and do not exploit their trust and dependency in a way that might compromise the therapeutic relationship. They do not abuse their relationship for personal or financial gain, and do not enter into personal relationships (romantic, sexual or other) with persons in their care.

---

[9] See footnote 7.

8. In all practice settings, nurses work to relieve pain and suffering, including appropriate and effective symptom and pain management, to allow persons to live with dignity.

9. When a person receiving care is terminally ill or dying, nurses foster comfort, alleviate suffering, advocate for adequate relief of discomfort and pain and support a dignified and peaceful death. This includes support for the family during and following the death, and care of the person's body after death.

10. Nurses treat each other, colleagues, students and other health-care workers in a respectful manner, recognizing the power differentials among those in formal leadership positions, staff and students. They work with others to resolve differences in a constructive way. See Appendix D.

E. Maintaining Privacy and Confidentiality

Nurses recognize the importance of privacy and confidentiality and safeguard personal, family and community information obtained in the context of a professional relationship.

Ethical responsibilities:

1. Nurses respect the right of people to have control over the collection, use, access and disclosure of their personal information.

2. When nurses are conversing with persons receiving care, they take reasonable measures to prevent confidential information in the conversation from being overheard.

3. Nurses collect, use and disclose health information on a need-to-know basis with the highest degree of anonymity possible in the circumstances and in accordance with privacy laws.

4. When nurses are required to disclose information for a particular purpose, they disclose only the amount of information necessary for that purpose and inform only those necessary. They attempt to do so in ways that minimize any potential harm to the individual, family or community.

5. When nurses engage in any form of communication, including verbal or electronic, involving a discussion of clinical cases, they ensure that their discussion of persons receiving care is respectful and does not identify those persons unless appropriate.

6. Nurses advocate for persons in their care to receive access to their own health-care records through a timely and affordable process when such access is requested.

7. Nurses respect policies that protect and preserve people's privacy, including security safeguards in information technology.

8. Nurses do not abuse their access to information by accessing health-care records, including their own, a family member's or any other person's, for purposes inconsistent with their professional obligations.

9. Nurses do not use photo or other technology to intrude into the privacy of a person receiving care.

10. Nurses intervene if others inappropriately access or disclose personal or health information of persons receiving care.

F. Promoting Justice

Nurses uphold principles of justice by safeguarding **human rights**, equity and **fairness** and by promoting the public good.

Ethical responsibilities:

1. When providing care, nurses do not discriminate on the basis of a person's race, ethnicity, **culture**, political and spiritual beliefs, social or marital status, gender, sexual orientation, age, health status, place of origin, lifestyle, mental or physical ability or socio-economic status or any other attribute.

2. Nurses refrain from judging, labelling, demeaning, stigmatizing and humiliating behaviours toward persons receiving care, other health-care professionals and each other.

3. Nurses do not engage in any form of lying, punishment or torture or any form of unusual treatment or action that is inhumane or degrading. They refuse to be complicit in such behaviours. They intervene, and they report such behaviours.

4. Nurses make fair decisions about the allocation of resources under their control based on the needs of persons, groups or communities to whom they are providing care. They advocate for fair treatment and for fair distribution of resources for those in their care.

5. Nurses support a climate of trust that sponsors openness, encourages questioning the status quo and supports those who speak out to address concerns in good faith (e.g., **whistle-blowing**).

G. Being Accountable

Nurses are accountable for their actions and answerable for
their practice.

Ethical responsibilities:

1. Nurses, as members of a self-regulating profession, practise
   according to the values and responsibilities in the *Code of Ethics
   for Registered Nurses* and in keeping with the professional standards, laws and regulations supporting ethical practice.

2. Nurses are honest and practise with integrity in all of their professional interactions.

3. Nurses practise within the limits of their competence. When
   aspects of care are beyond their level of competence, they seek
   additional information or knowledge, seek help from their supervisor or a competent practitioner and/or request a different work
   assignment. In the meantime, nurses remain with the person
   receiving care until another nurse is available.

4. Nurses maintain their **fitness to practise**. If they are aware that
   they do not have the necessary physical, mental or emotional
   capacity to practise safely and competently, they withdraw from
   the provision of care after consulting with their employer or, if
   they are self-employed, arranging that someone else attend to
   their clients' health-care needs. Nurses then take the necessary
   steps to regain their fitness to practise.

5. Nurses are attentive to signs that a colleague is unable, for whatever reason, to perform his or her duties. In such a case, nurses
   will take the necessary steps to protect the safety of persons
   receiving care. See Appendix D.

6. Nurses clearly and accurately represent themselves with respect to their name, title and role.

7. If nursing care is requested that is in conflict with the nurse's moral beliefs and values but in keeping with professional practice, the nurse provides safe, compassionate, competent and ethical care until alternative care arrangements are in place to meet the person's needs or desires. If nurses can anticipate a conflict with their conscience, they have an obligation to notify their employers or, if the nurse is self-employed, persons receiving care in advance so that alternative arrangements can be made. See Appendix D.

8. Nurses identify and address conflicts of interest. They disclose actual or potential conflicts of interest that arise in their professional roles and relationships and resolve them in the interest of persons receiving care.

9. Nurses share their knowledge and provide feedback, mentorship and guidance for the professional development of nursing students, novice nurses and other health-care team members. See Appendix D.

PART II: ETHICAL ENDEAVOURS

There are broad aspects of social justice that are associated with health and well-being and that ethical nursing practice addresses. These aspects relate to the need for change in systems and societal structures in order to create greater **equity** for all. Nurses should endeavour as much as possible, individually and collectively, to advocate for and work toward eliminating social inequities by:

i.   Utilizing the principles of **primary health care** for the benefit of the public and persons receiving care.

ii. Recognizing and working to address organizational, social, economic and political factors that influence health and well-being within the context of nurses' role in the delivery of care.

iii. In collaboration with other health-care team members and professional organizations, advocating for changes to unethical health and social policies, legislation and regulations.

iv. Advocating for a full continuum of accessible health-care services to be provided at the right time and in the right place. This continuum includes **health promotion**, disease prevention and diagnostic, restorative, rehabilitative and palliative care services in hospitals, nursing homes, home care and the community.

v.   Recognizing the significance of **social determinants of health** and advocating for policies and programs that address these determinants.

vi. Supporting environmental preservation and restoration and advocating for initiatives that reduce environmentally harmful practices in order to promote health and well-being.

vii. Working with individuals, families, groups, populations and communities to expand the range of health-care choices available, recognizing that some people have limited choices because of social, economic, geographic or other factors that lead to inequities.

viii. Understanding that some groups in society are systemically disadvantaged, which leads to diminished health and well-being. Nurses work to improve the quality of lives of people who are part of disadvantaged and/or **vulnerable groups** and communities, and they take action to overcome barriers to health care.

ix. Advocating for health-care systems that ensure accessibility, universality and comprehensiveness of necessary health-care services.

x. Maintaining awareness of major health concerns such as poverty, inadequate shelter, food insecurity and violence. Nurses work individually and with others for social justice and to advocate for laws, policies and procedures designed to bring about equity.

xi. Maintaining awareness of broader **global health** concerns such as violations of human rights, war, world hunger, gender inequities and environmental pollution. Nurses work individually and with others to bring about social change.

xii. Advocating for the discussion of ethical issues among health-care team members, persons in their care, families and students. Nurses encourage ethical reflection, and they work to develop their own and others' heightened awareness of ethics in practice. See Appendix C.

xiii. Working collaboratively to develop a moral community. As part of the moral community, all nurses acknowledge their responsibility to contribute to positive, healthy work environments.

GLOSSARY

The glossary is intended to provide nurses with a common language for their reflections and discussions about nursing ethics. It may also be instructive, since nurses who read the glossary terms are more likely to investigate these concepts further, especially if they are unfamiliar. The glossary does not necessarily provide formal definitions of terms, but rather it presents information in a manner and language that is meant to be helpful and accessible. Some terms in the glossary are not included in the main body of the code but are in the appendices, others may not appear exactly as noted in the text, and others may not be included in the text but may be useful to nurses in their ethical reflection and practice.

ADVANCE DIRECTIVES: a person's written wishes about how and what decisions should be made if they become incapable of making decisions for themselves. In decisions about life-sustaining treatment, advance directives are meant to assist with decisions about withholding or withdrawing treatment. Also called living wills or personal directives.

ADVERSE EVENTS: unexpected, undesirable incidents resulting in injury or death that are directly associated with the process of providing health care or health services to a person receiving care (Hebert, Hoffman & Davies, 2003).

ADVOCATE: actively supporting a right and good cause; supporting others in speaking for themselves or speaking on behalf of those who cannot speak for themselves

BOUNDARIES: a boundary in the nurse-person relationship is the point at which the relationship changes from professional and therapeutic to unprofessional and personal (College and Association of Registered Nurses of Alberta [CARNA], 2005a).

CAPABLE: being able to understand and appreciate the consequences of various options and make informed decisions about one's own care and treatment.

COLLABORATE: building consensus and working together on common goals, processes and outcomes (RNAO, 2006).

COMPASSIONATE: the ability to convey in speech and body language the hope and intent to relieve the suffering of another. Compassion must coexist with competence. "Compassion is a relational process that involves noticing another person's pain, experiencing an emotional reaction to his or her pain, and acting in some way to help ease or alleviate the pain" (Dutton, Lilius & Kanov, 2007).

COMPETENCY: the integrated knowledge, skills, judgment and attributes required of a registered nurse to practise safely and ethically in a designated role and setting. (Attributes include, but are not limited to, attitudes, values and beliefs.)

CONFIDENTIALITY: the ethical obligation to keep someone's personal and private information secret or private (Fry & Johnstone, 2002).

CONFLICT OF INTEREST: occurs when a nurse's personal or private interests interfere with the interests of a person receiving care or with the nurse's own professional responsibilities (College of Registered Nurses of British Columbia [CRNBC], 2006c).

CONSENT: *See Informed consent.*

CONSCIENTIOUS OBJECTION: a situation in which a nurse requests permission from his or her employer to refrain from providing care because a practice or procedure conflicts with the nurse's moral or religious beliefs (CRNBC, 2007).

CULTURES: the processes that happen between individuals and groups within organizations and society, and that confer meaning and significance; the health-care system has its own culture(s) (Varcoe & Rodney, 2002).

DETERMINANTS OF HEALTH: these include income and social status, social support, education and literacy, employment and working conditions, physical and social environments, biology, genetic endowment, personal health practices and coping skills, healthy child development, health services, gender and culture (Public Health Agency of Canada, 2003).

DIVERSITY: the variation between people in terms of a range of factors such as ethnicity, national origin, race, gender, ability, age, physical characteristics, religion, values, beliefs, sexual orientation, socio-economic class or life experiences (RNAO, 2007a).

DUTY TO PROVIDE CARE: Nurses have a professional duty and a legal obligation to provide persons receiving care with safe, competent, compassionate and ethical care. There may be some circumstances in which it is acceptable for a nurse to withdraw from care provisions or to refuse to provide care (CRNBC, 2007; College of Registered Nurses of Nova Scotia [CRNNS], 2006a). See Appendix D.

EQUITABLE: determining fairness on the basis of people's needs.

EQUITY: in health care, the fulfillment of each individual's needs as well as the individual's opportunity to reach full potential as a human being (Canadian Nurses Association [CNA], 2006).

ETHICS: the moral practices, beliefs and standards of individuals and/or groups (Fry & Johnstone, 2002).

EVERYDAY ETHICS: how nurses pay attention to ethics in carrying out their common daily interactions, including how they approach their practice and reflect on their ethical commitments to persons receiving care and those with health-care needs.

FAIRNESS: equalizing people's opportunities to participate in and enjoy life, given their circumstances (Caplan, Light & Daniels, 1999), and society's equitable distribution of resources (in health care this means an expectation of equitable treatment).

FAMILY/FAMILIES: In matters of caregiving, family is recognized to be those people identified by the person receiving care or in need of care as providing familial support, whether or not there is a biologic relationship. However, in matters of legal decision-making it must be noted that provincial legislation is not uniform across Canada and may include an obligation to recognize family members in priority according to their biologic relationship (CNA, 1994).

FITNESS TO PRACTISE: all the qualities and capabilities of an individual relevant to his or her capacity to practise as a registered nurse, including, but not limited to, freedom from any cognitive, physical, psychological or emotional condition and dependence on alcohol or drugs that impairs his or her ability to practise nursing (CRNBC, 2006a; CRNNS, 2006b).

GLOBAL HEALTH: the optimal well-being of all humans from the individual and the collective perspective. Health is considered a fundamental right and should be equally accessible by all (CNA, 2003).

HEALTH: a state of complete physical, mental (spiritual) and social well-being, not merely the absence of disease (CNA, 2007; World Health Organization [WHO], 2006).

HEALTH-CARE PROVIDERS: all those who are involved in providing care; they may include professionals, personal care attendants, home support workers and others (CNA, 1994).

HEALTH-CARE TEAM: a number of health-care providers from different disciplines (often including both regulated professionals and unregulated workers) working together to provide care for and with individuals, families, groups, populations or communities.

HEALTH PROMOTION: a continuing process of enabling people to increase their control over and improve their health and well-being.

HUMAN RIGHTS: the rights of people as expressed in the *Canadian Charter of Rights and Freedoms* (1982) and the *United Nations Universal Declaration of Human Rights* (1948), and as recorded in the CNA position statement *Registered Nurses and Human Rights* (CNA, 2004a).

INCAPABLE/INCAPACITY: failing to understand the nature of the treatment decisions to be made, as well as the consequences of consenting to treatment or declining treatment.

INEQUITY: an instance of unjust or unfair treatment of each individual's needs; health inequity means a lack of equitable access and opportunity for all people to meet their health needs and potential (CNA, 2006).

INFORMED CONSENT: the process of giving permission or making choices about care. It is based on both a legal doctrine and an ethical principle of respect for an individual's right to sufficient information to make decisions about care, treatment and involvement in research. In the code, the term *informed decision-making* is primarily used to emphasize the choice involved.

INTEGRITY: (1) for persons receiving care, integrity refers to wholeness, and protecting integrity can mean helping them to become whole and complete again; (2) for health-care providers, showing integrity means consistently following accepted moral norms. Implicit in integrity is soundness, trustworthiness and consistency of convictions, actions and emotions (Burkhart & Nathaniel, 2002).

INTERDISCIPLINARY: the integration of concepts across different disciplines. An interdisciplinary team is a team of people with training in different fields: such teams are common in complex environments such as health care (RNAO, 2007b) and may also be referred to as interprofessional teams.

INTERSECTORAL: all sectors of society (government, community and health).

JUSTICE: includes respecting the rights of others, distributing resources fairly, and preserving and promoting the common good (the good of the community).

MORAL AGENT/AGENCY: the capacity or power of a nurse to direct his or her motives and actions to some ethical end; essentially, doing what is good and right.

MORAL CLIMATE: in health care, the implicit and explicit values that drive health-care delivery and shape the workplaces in which care is delivered (Rodney, Hartrick Doane, Storch & Varcoe, 2006).

MORAL COMMUNITY: a workplace where values are made clear and are shared, where these values direct ethical action and where individuals feel safe to be heard (adapted from Rodney & Street, 2004). Coherence between publicly professed values and the lived reality is necessary for there to be a genuine moral community (Webster & Baylis, 2000).

NURSE(S): in this code, refers to registered nurses, including nurses in extended roles such as nurse practitioners.

PERSON/PERSONS RECEIVING CARE: an individual, family, group, community or population that accesses the services of the registered nurse; may also be referred to as client(s) or patient(s).

PRIMARY HEALTH CARE: "Primary health care is essential health care based on practical, scientifically sound and socially acceptable methods and technology made universally accessible to individuals and families in the community through their full participation and at a cost that the community and country can afford to maintain at every stage of their development in the spirit of self-reliance and self-determination. It forms an integral part both of the country's health system, of which it is the central function and main focus, and of the overall social and economic development of the community. It is the first level of contact of individuals, the family and community with the national health system bringing health care as close as possible to where people live and work, and constitutes the first element of a continuing health care process" (WHO, 1978).

PRIVACY: (1) physical privacy is the right or interest in controlling or limiting the access of others to oneself; (2) informational privacy is the right of individuals to determine how, when, with whom and for what purposes any of their personal information will be shared.

PUBLIC GOOD: the good of society or the community, often called the common good.

QUALITY PRACTICE ENVIRONMENTS: practice environments that have the organizational and human support allocations necessary for safe, competent and ethical nursing care (CNA, 2001).

SOCIAL DETERMINANTS OF HEALTH: factors in the social environment, external to the health-care system, that exert a major and potentially modifiable influence on the health of populations (Evans, 1994). See also *Determinants of health.*

SOCIAL JUSTICE: the fair distribution of society's benefits and responsibilities and their consequences. It focuses on the relative position of one social group in relation to others in society as well as on the root causes of disparities and what can be done to eliminate them (CNA, 2006).

SUBSTITUTE DECISION-MAKER: an individual designated by operation of a provincial or territorial statute or in an advance directive of a person in care to make decisions about health care and treatment on the person's behalf (CNA, 1994).

UNREGULATED CARE PROVIDER: paid providers who are neither licensed nor registered by a regulatory body (CRNBC, 2006b).

VALUES: standards or qualities that are esteemed, desired, considered important or have worth or merit (Fry & Johnstone, 2002).

VIOLENCE: includes any abuse of power, manipulation or control of one person over another that could result in mental, emotional, social or physical harm.

VULNERABLE GROUPS: groups disadvantaged by attitudes and systems in society that create inequities.

WELL-BEING: a person's state of being well, content and able to make the most of his or her abilities.

WHISTLE-BLOWING: speaking out about unsafe or questionable practices affecting people receiving care or working conditions. This should be resorted to only after a person has unsuccessfully used all appropriate organizational channels to right a wrong and has a sound moral justification for taking this action (Burkhardt & Nathaniel, 2002).

APPENDICES

APPENDIX A: The History of the Canadian Nurses Association Code of Ethics

1954   CNA adopts the International Council of Nurses' code as its first code of ethics

1980   CNA adopts its own code, entitled *CNA Code of Ethics: An Ethical Basis for Nursing in Canada*

1985   CNA adopts a new code, called *Code of Ethics for Nursing*

1991   *Code of Ethics for Nursing* revised

1997   *Code of Ethics for Registered Nurses* adopted as the updated code of CNA

2002   *Code of Ethics for Registered Nurses* revised

2008   *Code of Ethics for Registered Nurses* revised

The CNA *Code of Ethics for Registered Nurses* is not based on a particular philosophy or ethical theory but arises from different schools of thought, including relational ethics, an ethic of care, principle-based ethics, feminist ethics, virtue ethics and values. It has been developed over time by nurses for nurses, and it therefore continues to have a practical orientation supported by theoretical diversity.

CNA prepares position papers, practice papers on specific ethics issues, booklets and other ethics-related resources, and it maintains an electronic mailing list that provides a forum for dialogue on ethics in nursing. In addition, CNA works with other health professional associations and colleges to develop interprofessional statements (e.g., about no-resuscitation policies) related to issues or concerns of an ethical nature.

APPENDIX B: CONTEXT OF THE CODE

The Canadian Nurses Association's *Code of Ethics for Registered Nurses* is revised periodically to reflect changes that affect the public, nurses, other health-care providers and the health-care system and that create both new challenges and opportunities for nursing practice. Examples[10] of changes currently occurring, as well as those envisioned in the coming decade, can be found below:

Challenges and opportunities affecting the public

- Greater public access to health information from a variety of formal and informal sources

- Increased public use of alternative and complementary therapies

- Increasing health-care expectations by some persons who are receiving care, and increasing disenfranchisement of others who are having difficulty accessing care

- Continued and escalating societal expectations that people will practise self-care

- Increasing societal expectations that families and communities will "look after their own"

- Individual or family isolation in the provision of self-care or care for a family member

- Widening and deepening local, regional and global inequities in health and social resources and in access to health care based upon gender, class and race

---

[15] Reference to these contextual realities are found in the following documents: Government of Canada. (2002). *Building on values: The future of health care in Canada – Final report.* Ottawa: Commission on the Future of Health Care in Canada; Health Canada. (2002). *Our health, our future. Creating quality workplaces for Canadian nurses. Final report of the Canadian nursing advisory committee.* Ottawa: Author; Canadian Health Services Foundation. (2006). *What's ailing our nurses?* Ottawa: Author; Canadian Health Services Research Foundation. (2006). *Staffing for safety.* Ottawa: Author; Villeneuve, M., & MacDonald, J. (2006). *Toward 2020: Visions for nursing.* Ottawa: Canadian Nurses Association; Torgerson, R. (2007). *Not there yet: Improving the working conditions of Canadian nurses.* Ottawa: Canadian Policy Research Networks; UNESCO International Bioethics Committee (IBC). (2007). *Preliminary draft report of the IBC working group on social responsibility and health.* Retrieved on February 22, 2008, from http://unesdoc.unesco.org/images/0015/001505/150522e.pdf

- Demographic shift as baby boomers age and the very old live longer, resulting in increasing numbers of people who require complex health care

- Increasing rates of chronic illness and lack of accessible social supports

- Greater recognition that pain and suffering are underdiagnosed and undertreated

- New and emerging infectious disease

- Increasing rates of infections that originate in hospitals or similar settings (health-care acquired infections) and an increased awareness of other care-related injury and harms

- Threats of natural and human-made disasters, pandemics and bioterrorism

- Continued presence of war, human trafficking and racial tensions

Challenges and opportunities affecting nurses and other health-care providers

- Increasing **diversity** in the populations of people receiving care

- Increasing diversity among health-care professionals and other health-care providers

- A continuing and worsening shortage of nurses and shortage of all health-care professionals and allied health-care providers

- Shortages of clinical support workers with related increasing demands on nurses to do additional non-nursing work so that safe patient care is maintained

- Excessive hours of work and work overload with associated increases in nurse injury, illness and turnover of nursing staff

- Nurse staffing deficiencies that are associated with increased rates of morbidity and mortality among persons receiving care, as demonstrated in research-based findings

- Limited numbers of well-prepared managers to lead the development of healthy work environments and effective nurse retention strategies

- Broader and evolving scopes of practice for nurses and other health-care providers

- Increased numbers of complex **intersectoral** health-care teams that include other health-care professionals and **unregulated workers**

- Increased requirements for well-functioning, innovative health-care teams as a result of the changing roles and scopes of practice of registered nurses and other health-care providers

- Emerging challenges for nurses with regard to potential situations of **conflict of interest** (e.g., relationships with pharmaceutical companies) as roles evolve to broader scopes of practice

- A growing cadre of nurses involved in conducting and participating in research to develop and use evidence-based guidelines and other knowledge for nursing practice and health

Challenges within the socio-political context of the health-care system

- Increasing disparity between resources for urban and rural health-care centres

- Increasing need for health promotion and prevention (primary care), including mental health

- Ongoing tension between individual good and the **public good**

- Ongoing debate within Canadian society over the acceptable amount and mix of public and private interests in the financing and delivery of health care

- Ongoing challenges to preserving an adequately publicly funded, universal and accessible health-care system that equitably serves health-care needs across the continuum of care

- Difficult choices in the allocation of resources, program and services

- Increasing recognition that social inequities drive health-care decision-making and health-care inequities

- A sense that financial gain by health-care agencies and health-care providers in public and private health-care delivery may be influencing health-care decisions (e.g., early discharge of people from hospitals)

- Shorter hospital stays and increased reliance on home and community care and self-care

- Increase in the complexity of care needed in all settings and lack of accessible social supports for people needing care and their families

- Rapid introduction of new technology and pharmaceutical drugs

- Advances in genetics and genomics

- Greater expectations of the public to have access to new technology with the sometimes unfounded expectation that new technology will lead to better health outcomes

- Increasing use of information technology and electronically stored health data in the health-care system

- An accelerating trend toward public-private sector delivery and information systems that increase potential risks to the privacy of persons receiving care

- Rise in the number of policies and legislation related to access to private information

- Increased emphasis on safety and on developing a just culture in health care, in which individuals, organizations and health-care systems share accountability for reducing risks and preventing avoidable harms

- Proliferation of research findings in health care that need to be impartially assessed to determine the quality of evidence

- Ongoing tensions between preserving scientific integrity and maximizing commercial interests in the research and development of health-care technologies and therapies

- Pressing need to understand the relations between human health and environmental health (e.g., global warming) and to act on issues related to the environment on which health depends

APPENDIX C: **ETHICAL MODELS**

An Ethical Model for Reflection: Questions to Consider

The code points to the need for nurses to engage in ethical reflection and discussion. Frameworks or models can help people order their approach to an ethical problem or concern, and they can be a useful tool to guide nurses in their thinking about a particular issue or question.

When it is appropriate, colleagues in nursing and other disciplines, ethics committees, ethicists, professional nurses associations and colleges of registered nurses and other experts should be included in discussions of ethical problems. Legislation, standards of practice, policies and guidelines of nurses' unions and professional associations and colleges may also be useful in ethical reflection and decision-making.

Ethical reflection (which begins with a review of one's own ethics) and judgment are required to determine how a particular value or responsibility applies in a particular nursing context. There is room within the profession for disagreement among nurses about the relative weight of different ethical values and principles. More than one proposed intervention may be ethical and reflective of good ethical practice. Discussion and questioning are extremely helpful in the resolution of ethical problems and issues.

Ethical models also facilitate discussion among team members by opening up a moral space for everyone to participate in the conversation about ethics. There are many models for ethical reflection and for ethical decision-making in the health-care ethics literature, and some of these are noted in this section. The model provided here[11] was selected because it offers a nursing model for considering ethics issues in practice, promotes reflection and is applicable to all types of ethical situations.

---

[11] This model is adapted from *Nursing Ethics in Canadian Practice* by Oberle & Raffin (in press).

Oberle & Raffin Model

1. *Understanding the ethics of the situation: Relationships, goals, beliefs and values*

   In reflecting on what will best fulfil the goal of improving a person's well-being, nurses must first *want* to do good. They clarify their own values as well as the values in the code of ethics that apply to a given situation. They ask some of the following questions:

   - What are my own values in this situation?

   - What are the values of all those involved?

   - What are the goals people hope to achieve?

   - What do others consider to be a good outcome?

   - What is the level of knowledge of the persons receiving care or in need of care?

   - What information do they need?

   - What are the relationships within the family of the person receiving care or in need of care and between the family and health-care providers?

   - What value differences exist among the caregivers and those receiving care or in need of care?

2. *Reflecting on the range of available choices*

   When reflecting on possible choices, nurses ask:

   - What will help individuals and families clarify what they think will do the most good for their situation?

   - What do other health-care providers think is best?

   - What might be the effects of the various choices?

   - What values would society consider appropriate in this situation?

- What economic, political, legal, institutional and cultural factors are at play in the person's health situation?

- What options require further information and discussion?

3. *Maximizing the good*

Nurses try to act in accordance with the capable person's expressed desires. Questions that need to be asked to achieve this end are the following:

- Will what the individual desires conflict with the good of other individuals or of the community?

- Can ways be found to respect the wishes of the person receiving care or in need of care, while keeping the needs of others in mind?

- What might prevent nurses from taking an ethical action?

- Will taking action in this situation require moral courage?

- Will the nurses and other health-care providers be supported in taking action?

4. *Taking ethical action*

Before taking action, nurses reflect on how that action fits with the code of ethics and whether it is what a reasonably prudent and ethical nurse would do in this situation. They assess their ability to act with care and compassion and to meet their professional and institutional expectations.

5. *Reflecting on and reviewing an ethical action*

In reviewing and reflecting on their actions, nurses consider both the process and outcome. They ask if the situation was handled in the best way possible, including both *how* things were done as well as *what* was done. They also consider how everyone involved in the situation was affected, and whether harm was minimized and a good choice was found.

Other Models and Guides for Ethical Reflection and Decision-Making: Resources and Applications

Several other models for ethical reflection and decision-making are in common use. Nurses find that some models are helpful in particular areas of practice (e.g., in acute care practice, long-term care, public health) and that some models are more meaningful to them than others.

Many models include the four principles of biomedical ethics – autonomy, beneficence, nonmaleficence and justice – which some nurses find practical because these models may bridge biomedical and nursing ethics in acute care. Some nurses prefer a model that offers a diagram rather than text: examples of diagram models are the Bergum and the Storch models (CARNA, 2005b). Others prefer an algorithm, such as the one developed by Matthews (2007), and still others prefer a more philosophically based model, such as that offered by Yeo and Moorhouse (1996).

A few key sources are listed below. The first source is likely the most comprehensive, since it analyzes cases using three models.

- CNA's *Everyday Ethics: Putting the Code into Practice* (2nd ed.) (2004b) is a study guide to help nurses use the CNA code of ethics and reflect on ethical practice. It offers three models: "A Guide for Moral Decision-Making" (developed by Chris McDonald), "The Four Topics Method" (by Jonsen, Siegler & Winslade, 1997) and "The Circle Method for Ethical Decision-Making" (by Jan Storch), with examples of their application to practice. Numerous other models are listed and briefly described in the appendix to this study guide.

- CARNA published *Ethical Decision-Making for Registered Nurses in Alberta: Guidelines and Recommendations* in 2005. Included in CARNA's paper is the Bergum model for questioning (in the image of a flower) and a full case analysis using the Bergum model.

- The **Framework for Ethical Decision-Making**, developed by Michael McDonald with additions provided by Patricia Rodney and Rosalie Starzomski, provides detailed questions to consider in ethical decision-making. It is available from www.ethics.ubc.ca/people/mcdonald/decisions.htm

- **Nursing Ethics: Cases and Concepts** (1996) by M. Yeo & A. Moorhouse. These authors provide a way to think through ethical problems using three types of analysis (descriptive, conceptual and normative).

- **Nursing ethics decision-making algorithm** developed by J. Matthews at Brock University (included in the ethics resources on the CNA website).

APPENDIX D:
APPLYING THE CODE IN SELECTED CIRCUMSTANCES

Responding Ethically to Incompetent, Non-compassionate, Unsafe or Unethical Care

Nurses question and intervene to address unsafe, non-compassionate, unethical or incompetent practice or conditions that interfere with their ability to provide safe, compassionate, competent and ethical care to those to whom they are providing care, and they support those who do the same. (Code, A4)

Nurses admit mistakes[12] and take all necessary actions to prevent or minimize harm arising from an adverse event. They work with others to reduce the potential for future risks and preventable harms. (Code, A5)

Nurses intervene, and report when necessary,[13] when others fail to respect the dignity of a person receiving care, recognizing that to be silent and passive is to condone the behaviour. (Code, D4)

Nurses, as members of a self-regulating profession, practise according to the values and responsibilities in the Code of Ethics for Registered Nurses *and in keeping with the professional standards, laws and regulations supporting ethical practice. (Code, G1)*

Nurses are attentive to signs that a colleague is unable, for whatever reason, to perform his or her duties. In such a case, nurses will take the necessary steps to protect the safety of persons receiving care. (Code, G5)

If a nurse encounters a situation where harm is underway or there is a clear risk of imminent harm, he or she should take immediate steps to protect the safety and dignity of the persons receiving care. Some examples

---

[12] See footnote 7.

[13] See footnote 7.

of appropriate immediate steps in cases of actual or imminent harm could include, but are not limited to, speaking up if a potential error in drug calculations is detected, questioning an unclear order, intervening to prevent unsafe restraint practices, protecting patients when a colleague's performance appears to be impaired for any reason (see CRNNS, 2006b) or interfering with a serious breach of confidentiality involving people with sexually transmitted infections. Nurses should be aware of provincial and territorial legislation and nursing practice standards that may include direction regarding disclosure and reporting and provide further clarity on whether there is a clear risk of imminent harm.

When nurses encounter situations where harm is not imminent but there is potential for harm, they work to resolve the problem as directly as possible in ways that are consistent with the good of all parties. As they work through these situations, nurses review relevant statements in the *Code of Ethics for Registered Nurses* and other relevant standards, legislation, ethical guidelines, policies and procedures for reporting incidents or suspected incompetent or unethical care, including any legally reportable offence.

Some additional actions for nurses to consider, if they do not contravene requirements under professional standards or provincial or territorial legislation, include:

- Maintain a high level of confidentiality about the situation and actions at all times.

- Review all information available about the current situation. Separate personal from professional issues. Concentrate on the situation at hand.

- Where appropriate and feasible, seek information directly from the colleague(s) whose behaviour or practice has raised concerns.

- Pay attention to the moral distress nurses are experiencing in trying to find an ethical course of action. Consider the risks of not taking action to persons receiving care, colleagues, self, and the organization, and reflect on the potential harms and breaches in trust that

Canadian Nurses Association

could result if no action is taken. Nurses need to consider as well the consequences that may occur for them and for others in taking various courses of action.

- If possible, speak with an impartial and trusted colleague outside of the situation who can preserve appropriate confidential information and help validate or rule out the conclusions being drawn.

- Seek information from relevant authorities (e.g., supervisor or manager) on expected roles and responsibilities for all of the parties who share responsibility for maintaining safe, competent, compassionate and ethical care.

- Consult, as appropriate, with colleagues, other members of the team, professional nursing associations or colleges or others who are able to assist in addressing and resolving the problem.

- Advise the appropriate parties regarding unresolved concerns and, when feasible, inform the colleague(s) in question of the reasons for your action. Know what immediate help is available to colleague(s) and be ready to help the colleague(s) find these resources.

Nurses who engage in responsible reporting of incompetent, unsafe or unethical care should be supported by their colleagues, professional association and/or professional college.

Ethical Considerations in Addressing Expectations That Are in Conflict with One's Conscience

Nurses are not at liberty to abandon those in need of nursing care. However, nurses may sometimes be opposed to certain procedures and practices in health care and find it difficult to willingly participate in providing care that others have judged to be morally acceptable. The nurse's right to follow his or her conscience in such situations is recognized by CNA in the *Code of Ethics for Registered Nurses* in its provision for **conscientious objection**.

If nursing care is requested that is in conflict with the nurse's moral beliefs and values but in keeping with professional practice, the nurse provides safe, compassionate, competent and ethical care until alternative care arrangements are in place to meet the person's needs or desires. If nurses can anticipate a conflict with their conscience, they have an obligation to notify their employers or, if the nurse is self-employed, persons receiving care in advance so that alternative arrangements can be made. (Code, G7)

Steps in Declaring a Conflict with Conscience (American Nurses Association [ANA], 2006; Registered College of Nurses, Australia [RCNA], 2000)

1. **Before employment**

   Nurses have a moral responsibility to advise their prospective employer if they are conscientiously opposed to certain practices and procedures that are likely to occur in their prospective workplace, particularly if the expression of conflict of conscience "would significantly interfere with the provision of services offered by the employing agency" (RCNA, 2000, p. 1). Similarly, employers should advise prospective employees about services provided by the organization that may be sensitive for some employees.

2. **Anticipating and planning to declare a conflict with conscience**

   Ideally, the nurse would be able to anticipate practices and procedures that would create a conflict with his or her conscience (beliefs and values) in advance. In this case, the nurse should discuss with supervisors, employers or, when the nurse is self-employed, persons receiving care what types of care she or he finds contrary to his or her own beliefs and values (e.g., caring for individuals having an abortion, male circumcision, blood transfusion, organ transplantation) and request that his or her objections be accommodated, unless it is an emergency situation.

Ideally, nurses in positions of formal leadership would ensure that workplaces have a policy in place to deal with matters of conscience so that a nurse can be exempt from participating in procedures he or she considers morally objectionable without being penalized.

3. **Finding oneself caught in providing care that is in conflict with one's conscience**

When a nurse finds herself or himself involved in nursing care that creates a conflict with her or his conscience, he or she should notify the supervisor, employer or, if she or he is self-employed, the persons receiving care. Declaring a conflict with conscience, or "conscientious objection," and requesting accommodation is a serious matter that is not to be taken lightly. In all cases, the nurse remains until another nurse or health-care provider is able to provide appropriate care to meet the person's needs.

Key guidelines with respect to a declaration of a conflict with conscience include the following:

1. The nurse who decides not to take part in providing care on the grounds of moral objection communicates his or her desires in appropriate ways.

2. Whenever possible such refusal is made known in advance and in time for alternative arrangements to be made for persons receiving care.

3. Moral objections by the nurse are motivated by moral concerns and an informed, reflective choice and are not based upon prejudice, fear or convenience.

4. When a moral objection is made, the nurse provides for the safety of the person receiving care until there is assurance that other sources of nursing care are available.

5. Employers and co-workers are responsible for ensuring that nurses and other co-workers who declare a conflict of conscience receive fair treatment and do not experience discrimination (RCNA, 2000, p.2).

6. Nurses need to be aware that declaring a conflict of conscience may not protect them against formal or informal penalty.

Ethical Considerations for Nurses in a Natural or Human-Made Disaster, Communicable Disease Outbreak or Pandemic

Historically and currently, nurses provide care to those in need, even when providing care puts their own health and life at risk (for example, when they work in war-torn areas, places of poverty, in places with poor sanitation, etc.). Nurses also encounter personal risk when providing care for those with known or unknown communicable or infectious disease. However, disasters and communicable disease outbreaks call for extraordinary effort from all health-care personnel, including registered nurses. The code states:

> During a natural or human-made disaster, including a communicable disease outbreak, nurses have a duty to provide care using appropriate safety precautions. (Code, A8)

A duty to provide care refers to a nurse's professional obligation to provide persons receiving care with safe, competent, compassionate and ethical care. However, there may be some circumstances in which it is acceptable for a nurse to withdraw from providing care or to refuse to provide care (CRNBC, 2007; CRNNS, 2006a). Unreasonable burden is a concept raised in relation to the duty to provide care and withdrawing from providing or refusing to provide care. An unreasonable burden may exist when a nurse's ability to provide safe care and meet professional standards of practice is compromised by unreasonable expectations, lack of resources or ongoing threats to personal well-being (CRNBC, 2007).

The following criteria could be useful for nurses to consider when contemplating their obligation to provide care in a disaster or communicable disease outbreak:

- the significance of the risk to the person in care if the nurse does not assist;

- whether the nurse's intervention is directly relevant to preventing harm;

- whether the nurses' care will probably prevent harm; and

- whether the benefit of the nurse's intervention outweighs harms the nurse might incur and does not present more than an acceptable risk to the nurse (ANA, 2006).

When demands on the health-care system are excessive, material resources may be in short supply and nurses and other health-care providers may be at risk. Nurses have a right to receive truthful and complete information so that they can fulfil their duty to provide care. They must also be supported in meeting their own health needs. Nurses' employers have a reciprocal duty to protect and support them as well as to provide necessary and sufficient protective equipment and supplies that will "maximally minimize risk" to nurses and other health-care providers (Human Resource Recommendations, SARS Human Resources Working Group, Ontario Hospital Association, as recorded in Godkin & Markwell, 2003). Nurses will also need to use their professional judgment to select and use the appropriate prevention measures; select, in collaboration with the health-care team, the appropriate agency, manufacturer and government guidelines concerning use and fit of personal protective equipment; and advocate for a change when agency, manufacturer or government guidelines do not meet the infection control requirements regarding appropriate use and fit of personal protective equipment (College of Nurses of Ontario, 2005).

Nurses need to carefully consider their professional role, their duty to provide care and other competing obligations to their own health, to family and to friends. In doing so, they should be clear about steps they might take both in advance of and during an emergency or pandemic situation so that they are prepared for making ethical decisions (Faith, Gibson, Thompson & Upshur, 2005). Value and responsibility statements in the code should support nurses' reflection and actions.

A. **In anticipation of the need for nursing care in a disaster or disease outbreak, nurses:**

- work together with nurses and others in positions of leadership to develop emergency response practice guidelines, using available resources and guidelines from governments, professional associations and regulatory bodies;

- learn about and provide input into the guidelines the region, province or country has established regarding which persons are to receive priority in care (e.g., priority based on greatest need, priority based on probability of a good outcome, and so on);

- learn how support will be provided for those providing care and carrying the physical and moral burden of care;

- request and receive regular updates about appropriate safety measures nurses might take to protect and prevent themselves from becoming victim to a disaster or disease;

- assist in developing a fair way to settle conflicts or disputes regarding work exemptions or exemptions from the prophylaxis or vaccination of staff; and

- help develop ways that appeals or complaints can be handled.

B. **When in the midst of a disaster or disease outbreak, nurses have an ethical obligation to:**

- refer to regulations and guidelines provided by government, regulatory bodies, employers and professional associations;

- help make the fairest decisions possible about the allocation of resources;

- help set priorities in as transparent a manner as possible;

- provide safe, compassionate, competent and ethical care (in disasters, as much as circumstances permit);

- help determine if, when and how nurses may have to decline or withdraw from care; and

- advocate for the least restrictive measures possible when a person's individual rights must be restricted.

Ethical Considerations in Relationships with Nursing Students

Registered nurses in all roles share the responsibility of supporting nursing students in providing safe, competent, compassionate and ethical care. Several statements in the code include specific references to students and their relationships with others in providing nursing care:

> Nurses treat each other, colleagues, students and other health-care workers in a respectful manner, recognizing the power differentials among those in formal leadership positions, staff and students. They work with others to resolve differences in a constructive way. (Code, D10)

> Nurses share their knowledge and provide feedback, mentorship and guidance for the professional development of nursing students, novice nurses and other health-care team members. (Code, G9)

On the basis of these statements in the code, the following guidelines are suggested:

- All teacher-student interactions are to be in keeping with ethical nursing practice.

- All nurses and nursing students treat each other with respect and honesty.

- All nurses endeavour to provide nursing students with appropriate guidance for the development of nursing competence.

- The primary responsibility for the care of the person remains that of the primary nurse to whom the person has been assigned.

- Nursing students ensure that persons receiving care are informed of their student status. The person's right to refuse care or assistance provided by a student is to be treated with respect.

- Nursing students are expected to meet the standards of care for their level of learning. They advise their faculty clinical instructor and their clinical unit nurse supervisors if they do not believe they are able to meet this expectation.

- If nursing students experience difficulties with disrespectful actions from nurse(s) in practice that they are not able to overcome through conversation with the nurse(s) involved, they discuss these incidents with their faculty clinical instructor and, failing helpful outcomes from that discussion within an appropriate period, they enlist the assistance of the appropriate nursing education administrator in their nursing program.

Acting Ethically in Situations That Involve Job Action

Job action by nurses is often directed toward securing conditions of employment that enable safe and ethical care of current and future persons receiving care. However, action directed toward such improvements could hinder persons receiving care in the short term. Nurses advocate for their involvement in workplace planning for the safety of those receiving care before and during job action. Members of the public are also entitled to information about the steps taken to ensure the safety of persons during any job action.

> *Nurses planning to take job action or practising in environments where job action occurs take steps to safeguard the health and safety of people during the course of the job action. (Code, A7)*

- Each nurse is accountable for decisions made about her or his practice at all times in all circumstances, including during a legal or an illegal strike (Nurses Association of New Brunswick [NANB], 2004).

- Individual nurses and groups of nurses safeguard persons receiving care when planning and implementing any job action.

- Individuals and groups of nurses participating in job action, or affected by job action, share the ethical commitment to the safety of persons in their care. Their particular responsibilities may lead them to express this commitment in different but equally appropriate ways.

- Persons whose safety requires ongoing or emergency nursing care are entitled to have those needs satisfied throughout any job action.

- During job action, if nurses have any concern about their ability to maintain practice and ethical standards or their ability to ensure the safety of persons in their care, they are responsible for communicating this concern in accordance with identified lines of accountability so that corrective action can be taken as quickly as possible (NANB, 2004).

REFERENCES

American Nurses Association. (2001). *Code of ethics for nurses with interpretive statements.* Washington, DC: Author.

American Nurses Association. (2006). *Position statement: Risk and responsibility in providing nursing care.* Washington, DC: Author.

Burkhardt, M. A., & Nathaniel, A. K. (2002). *Ethics & issues in contemporary nursing* (2nd ed.). Toronto: Delmar Publishers.

Canadian charter of rights and freedoms, Schedule B, *Constitution Act, 1982.*

Canadian Institutes of Health Research, Natural Sciences and Engineering Research Council of Canada, & Social Sciences and Humanities Research Council of Canada. (1998, with 2000, 2002 and 2005 amendments). *Tri-council policy statement: Ethical conduct for research involving humans.* Ottawa: Public Works and Government Services Canada. Retrieved October 22, 2007, from http://www.pre.ethics.gc.ca/english/policystatement/policystatement.cfm

Canadian Nurses Association. (1994). *Joint statement on advance directives* [Position statement]. Ottawa: Author.

Canadian Nurses Association. (2001). *Quality professional practice environments for registered nurses* [Position statement]. Ottawa: Author.

Canadian Nurses Association. (2002). *Ethical research guidelines for registered nurses* (3rd ed.). Ottawa: Author.

Canadian Nurses Association. (2003). *Global health and equity* [Position statement]. Ottawa: Author.

Canadian Nurses Association. (2004a). *Registered nurses and human rights* [Position statement]. Ottawa: Author.

Canadian Nurses Association. (2004b). *Everyday ethics: Putting the code into practice.* Ottawa: Author.

Canadian Nurses Association. (2006). *Social justice... a means to an end, an end in itself.* Ottawa: Author.

Canadian Nurses Association. (2007). *Framework for the practice of registered nurses in Canada.* Ottawa: Author.

Canadian Nurses Protective Society. (2004). Consent of the incapable adult. *InfoLaw 13*(3), 1-2.

Caplan, R. L., Light, D. W., & Daniels, N. (1999). Benchmarks of fairness: A moral framework for assessing equity. *International Journal of Health Services, 29*(4), 853-869.

College and Association of Registered Nurses of Alberta. (2005a). *Professional boundaries for registered nurses: Guidelines for the nurse-client relationship.* Edmonton: Author.

College and Association of Registered Nurses of Alberta. (2005b). *Ethical decision-making for registered nurses in Alberta: Guidelines and recommendations.* Edmonton: Author.

College of Nurses of Ontario. (2005). *Infection, prevention and control.* Toronto: Author.

College of Registered Nurses of British Columbia. (2006a). *Competencies in the context of entry-level registered nurse practice in British Columbia.* Vancouver: Author.

College of Registered Nurses of British Columbia. (2006b). *Delegating tasks to unregulated care providers.* Vancouver: Author.

College of Registered Nurses of British Columbia. (2006c). *Practice standard: Conflict of interest.* Vancouver: Author.

College of Registered Nurses of British Columbia. (2007). *Practice standard: Duty to provide care.* Vancouver: Author.

College of Registered Nurses of Nova Scotia. (2006a). *Emergency preparedness plan.* Halifax: Author.

College of Registered Nurses of Nova Scotia. (2006b). *Problematic substance use in the workplace: A resource guide for registered nurses.* Halifax: Author.

Dutton, J., Lilius, J., & Kanov, J. (2007). The transformative potential of compassion at work. In S. K. Piderit, R. E. Fry, & D. L. Cooperrider (Eds.), *Handbook of transformative cooperation: New designs and dynamics.* Palo Alto, CA: Stanford University Press.

Evans, R. G. (1994). Introduction. In R. G. Evans, M. L. Barer, & T. R. Marmor (Eds.), *Why are some people healthy and others are not? The determinants of health of populations* (pp. 3-26). New York: Aldine de Gruyter.

Faith, K., Gibson, J., Thompson, A., & Upshur, R. (2005). *Ethics in a pandemic influenza crisis: Framework for decision-making.* Toronto: Clinical Ethics Centre at Sunnybrook & Women's College Health Sciences Centre.

Fenton, M. (1988). Moral distress in clinical practice: Implications for the nurse administrator. *Canadian Journal of Nursing Administration, 1,* 8-11.

Fry, S., & Johnstone, M-J. (2002). *Ethics in nursing practice: A guide to ethical decision-making* (2nd ed.). International Council of Nurses. Oxford: Blackwell.

Godkin, D., & Markwell, H. (2003). *The duty to care of healthcare professionals: Ethical issues and guidelines for policy development.* Toronto: Submission to the SARS Expert Panel Secretariat.

Hebert, P. C., Hoffman, C., & Davies, J. M. (2003). *The Canadian safety dictionary.* Edmonton: Canadian Patient Safety Institute.

International Council of Nurses. (2006). *ICN code of ethics for nurses.* Geneva: Author.

Jameton, A. (1984). *Nursing practice: The ethical issues.* Englewood Cliffs, NJ: Prentice Hall.

Matthews, J. (2007). *Nursing ethics decision-making algorithm.* Available at www.cna-aiic.ca.

Morin, K., Higginson, D., & Goldrich, M. (2006). Physician obligation in disaster preparedness and response. *Cambridge Quarterly Healthcare Ethics, 15,* 417-431. [This paper was prepared for the Council on Ethical and Judicial Affairs of the American Medical Association.]

Neufeldt, V., & Guralnik, D. G. (1988). *Webster's new world dictionary* (3rd ed.). New York: Simon & Schuster.

Nurses Association of New Brunswick. (2004). *Professional accountability during a strike.* Fredericton: Author.

Oberle, K. & Raffin, S. (in press). *Nursing ethics in Canadian practice.* Toronto: Pearson.

Office of the High Commissioner for Human Rights, United Nations. (1948). *The universal declaration of human rights: A magna carta for all humanity.* Geneva: Author.

Public Health Agency of Canada. (2003). *What determines health?* Retrieved October 22, 2007, from http://www.phac-aspc.gc.ca/ph-sp/ phdd/determinants/index.html

Registered College of Nurses, Australia. (2000). *Position statement: Conscientious objection.* Canberra: Author.

Registered Nurses Association of Nova Scotia. (1996). *Violence in the workplace: A resource guide.* Halifax: Author.

Registered Nurses' Association of Ontario. (2006). *Collaborative practice among nursing teams.* Healthy work environments best practice guidelines. Toronto: Author.

Registered Nurses' Association of Ontario. (2007a). *Embracing cultural diversity in health care: Developing cultural competence.* Healthy work environments best practice guidelines. Toronto: Author.

Registered Nurses' Association of Ontario. (2007b). *Professionalism in nursing.* Healthy work environments best practice guidelines. Toronto: Author.

Rodney, P., Hartrick Doane, G., Storch, J., & Varcoe, C. (2006). Toward a safer moral climate. *Canadian Nurse, 102*(8), 24-27.

Rodney, P., & Starzomski, R. (1993). Constraints on moral agency of nurses. *Canadian Nurse, 89*(9), 23-26.

Rodney, P., & Street, A. (2004). The moral climate of nursing practice: Inquiry and action. In J. Storch, P. Rodney, & R. Starzomski (Eds.), *Toward a moral horizon: Nursing ethics for leadership and practice* (pp. 209-231). Toronto: Pearson-Prentice Hall.

Storch, J., Rodney, P., & Starzomski, R. (2004). *Toward a moral horizon: Nursing ethics for leadership and practice.* Toronto: Pearson-Prentice Hall.

Varcoe, C., & Rodney, P. (2002). Constrained agency: The social structure of nurses' work. In B. S. Bolaria & H. Dickenson (Eds.), *Health, illness and health care in Canada* (3rd ed., pp. 102-128). Scarborough, ON: Nelson Thomas Learning.

Webster, G., & Baylis, F. (2000). Moral residue. In S. B. Rubin & L. Zoloth (Eds.), *Margin of error: The ethics of mistakes in the practice of medicine* (pp. 217-232). Hagerstown, MD: University Publishing Group.

World Health Organization. (1978). Declaration of Alma-Ata. International Conference on Primary Health Care, Alma-Ata, USSR, September 6-12, 1978. Retrieved March 19, 2008, from http://www.who.int/hpr/NPH/docs/declaration_almaata.pdf

World Health Organization. (2006). Constitution of the World Health Organization (45th ed. Suppl.). Retrieved October 31, 2007, from http://www.who.int/governance/eb/who_constitution_en.pdf

Yeo, M., & Moorhouse, A. (1996). *Concepts and cases in nursing ethics* (2nd ed.). Peterborough, ON: Broadway Press.

ETHICS RESOURCES

In addition to the resources listed in the references, there is a wide range of ethics resources available from the websites of CNA and the provincial and territorial registered nurses' associations and colleges, as well as from the websites of other national organizations such as the Public Health Agency of Canada, Health Canada, other health profession associations, and ethics or bioethics centres across Canada and internationally.

Nurses should also consult with members of their health-care team, ethics consultants in their agency, ethics committees in their facilities or region, practice consultants at nursing associations and colleges, and others with ethics knowledge and skill in its application to health-care practice.

To visit CNA's ethics resources, go to **www.cna-aiic.ca**.

Appendix B

The ICN Code of Ethics for Nurses*

Copyright © 2006 by ICN - International Council of Nurses,
3, place Jean-Marteau, 1201 Geneva (Switzerland)

ISBN: 92-95040-41-4   Printing: Imprimerie Fornara

THE ICN CODE OF ETHICS FOR NURSES

An international code of ethics for nurses was first adopted by the International Council of Nurses (ICN) in 1953. It has been revised and reaffirmed at various times since, most recently with this review and revision completed in 2005.

PREAMBLE

Nurses have four fundamental responsibilities: to promote health, to prevent illness, to restore health and to alleviate suffering. The need for nursing is universal.

Inherent in nursing is respect for human rights, including cultural rights, the right to life and choice, to dignity and to be treated with respect. Nursing care is respectful of and unrestricted by considerations of age, colour, creed, culture, disability or illness, gender, sexual orientation, nationality, politics, race or social status.

Nurses render health services to the individual, the family and the community and co-ordinate their services with those of related groups.

1

■ THE ICN CODE

The *ICN Code of Ethics for Nurses* has four principal elements that outline the standards of ethical conduct.

ELEMENTS OF THE CODE

1. NURSES AND PEOPLE

The nurse's primary professional responsibility is to people requiring nursing care.

In providing care, the nurse promotes an environment in which the human rights, values, customs and spiritual beliefs of the individual, family and community are respected.

The nurse ensures that the individual receives sufficient information on which to base consent for care and related treatment.

The nurse holds in confidence personal information and uses judgement in sharing this information.

The nurse shares with society the responsibility for initiating and supporting action to meet the health and social needs of the public, in particular those of vulnerable populations.

The nurse also shares responsibility to sustain and protect the natural environment from depletion, pollution, degradation and destruction.

2. NURSES AND PRACTICE

The nurse carries personal responsibility and accountability for nursing practice, and for maintaining competence by continual learning.

The nurse maintains a standard of personal health such that the ability to provide care is not compromised.

The nurse uses judgement regarding individual competence when accepting and delegating responsibility.

The nurse at all times maintains standards of personal conduct which reflect well on the profession and enhance public confidence.

The nurse, in providing care, ensures that use of technology and scientific advances are compatible with the safety, dignity and rights of people.

3. NURSES AND THE PROFESSION

The nurse assumes the major role in determining and implementing acceptable standards of clinical nursing practice, management, research and education.

The nurse is active in developing a core of research-based professional knowledge.

The nurse, acting through the professional organisation, participates in creating and maintaining safe, equitable social and economic working conditions in nursing.

4. NURSES AND CO-WORKERS

The nurse sustains a co-operative relationship with co-workers in nursing and other fields.

The nurse takes appropriate action to safeguard individuals, families and communities when their health is endangered by a co-worker or any other person.

3

Suggestions for use of the *ICN Code of Ethics for Nurses*

The *ICN Code of Ethics for Nurses* is a guide for action based on social values and needs. It will have meaning only as a living document if applied to the realities of nursing and health care in a changing society.

To achieve its purpose the *Code* must be understood, internalised and used by nurses in all aspects of their work. It must be available to students and nurses throughout their study and work lives.

Applying the Elements of the *ICN Code of Ethics for Nurses*

The four elements of the *ICN Code of Ethics for Nurses*: nurses and people, nurses and practice, nurses and the profession, and nurses and co-workers, give a framework for the standards of conduct. The following chart will assist nurses to translate the standards into action. Nurses and nursing students can therefore:

- Study the standards under each element of the *Code*.

- Reflect on what each standard means to you. Think about how you can apply ethics in your nursing domain: practice, education, research or management.

- Discuss the *Code* with co-workers and others.

- Use a specific example from experience to identify ethical dilemmas and standards of conduct as outlined in the *Code*. Identify how you would resolve the dilemmas.

- Work in groups to clarify ethical decision making and reach a consensus on standards of ethical conduct.

- Collaborate with your national nurses' association, co-workers, and others in the continuous application of ethical standards in nursing practice, education, management and research.

Element of the Code # 1: NURSES AND PEOPLE		
Practitioners and Managers	**Educators and Researchers**	**National Nurses' Associations**
Provide care that respects human rights and is sensitive to the values, customs and beliefs of all people.	In curriculum include references to human rights, equity, justice, solidarity as the basis for access to care.	Develop position statements and guidelines that support human rights and ethical standards.
Provide continuing education in ethical issues.	Provide teaching and learning opportunities for ethical issues and decision making.	Lobby for involvement of nurses in ethics review committees.
Provide sufficient information to permit informed consent and the right to choose or refuse treatment.	Provide teaching / learning opportunities related to informed consent.	Provide guidelines, position statements and continuing education related to informed consent.
Use recording and information management systems that ensure confidentiality.	Introduce into curriculum concepts of privacy and confidentiality.	Incorporate issues of confidentiality and privacy into a national code of ethics for nurses.
Develop and monitor environmental safety in the workplace.	Sensitise students to the importance of social action in current concerns.	Advocate for safe and healthy environment.

5

Element of the Code # 2: NURSES AND PRACTICE		
Practitioners and Managers	**Educators and Researchers**	**National Nurses' Associations**
Establish standards of care and a work setting that promotes safety and quality care.	Provide teaching/learning opportunities that foster life long learning and competence for practice.	Provide access to continuing education, through journals, conferences, distance education, etc.
Establish systems for professional appraisal, continuing education and systematic renewal of licensure to practice.	Conduct and disseminate research that shows links between continual learning and competence to practice.	Lobby to ensure continuing education opportunities and quality care standards.
Monitor and promote the personal health of nursing staff in relation to their competence for practice.	Promote the importance of personal health and illustrate its relation to other values.	Promote healthy lifestyles for nursing professionals. Lobby for healthy work places and services for nurses.

6

Element of the Code # 3: NURSES AND THE PROFESSION		
Practitioners and Managers	**Educators and Researchers**	**National Nurses' Associations**
Set standards for nursing practice, research, education and management.	Provide teaching / learning opportunities in setting standards for nursing practice, research, education and management.	Collaborate with others to set standards for nursing education, practice, research and management.
Foster workplace support of the conduct, dissemination and utilisation of research related to nursing and health.	Conduct, disseminate and utilise research to advance the nursing profession.	Develop position statements, guidelines and standards related to nursing research.
Promote participation in national nurses' associations so as to create favourable socio-economic conditions for nurses.	Sensitise learners to the importance of professional nursing associations.	Lobby for fair social and economic working conditions in nursing. Develop position statements and guidelines in workplace issues.

7

Element of the Code #4: NURSES AND CO-WORKERS		
Practitioners and Managers	**Educators and Researchers**	**National Nurses' Associations**
Create awareness of specific and overlapping functions and the potential for interdisciplinary tensions.	Develop understanding of the roles of other workers.	Stimulate co-operation with other related disciplines.
Develop workplace systems that support common professional ethical values and behaviour.	Communicate nursing ethics to other professions.	Develop awareness of ethical issues of other professions.
Develop mechanisms to safeguard the individual, family or community when their care is endangered by health care personnel.	Instil in learners the need to safeguard the individual, family or community when care is endangered by health care personnel.	Provide guidelines, position statements and discussion fora related to safeguarding people when their care is endangered by health care personnel.

8

DISSEMINATION OF THE *ICN CODE OF ETHICS FOR NURSES*

To be effective the *ICN Code of Ethics for Nurses* must be familiar to nurses. We encourage you to help with its dissemination to schools of nursing, practising nurses, the nursing press and other mass media. The Code should also be disseminated to other health professions, the general public, consumer and policy-making groups, human rights organisations and employers of nurses.

GLOSSARY OF TERMS USED IN THE *ICN CODE OF ETHICS FOR NURSES*

Co-worker	Other nurses and other health and non-health related workers and professionals.
Co-operative relationship	A professional relationship based on collegial and reciprocal actions, and behaviour that aim to achieve certain goals.
Family	A social unit composed of members connected through blood, kinship, emotional or legal relationships.
Nurse shares with society	A nurse, as a health professional and a citizen, initiates and supports appropriate action to meet the health and social needs of the public.
Personal health	Mental, physical, social and spiritual wellbeing of the nurse.
Personal information	Information obtained during professional contact that is private to an individual or family, and which, when disclosed, may violate the right to privacy, cause inconvenience, embarrassment, or harm to the individual or family.
Related groups	Other nurses, health care workers or other professionals providing service to an individual, family or community and working toward desired goals.

9

Index

subversive tactics, 289
unethical and unprofessional
   team behaviours, 288
Health Information Act (Alberta), 225
health insurance. *See* health care
   system
Health Professions Act, 84
health promotion
   attitudes, 118–119
   beliefs, 118–119
   current focus, 117
   definitions of, 117, 302
   dying patients, 120
   enhancement of capacity,
      117–118
   identifying and building
      strengths, 117–118
   within illness, 120
   individual teaching, 119
   insufficiency of focus on indi-
      vidual behaviours, 117
   as lived value, 122–123
   and morality, 120–122
   motivation for, 116
   nature of health promotion
      activities, 117
   nurses as leaders in, 117
   and nursing, 116–120
   and resource allocation, 119
   respect and support of indi-
      viduals' rights, 121–122
   and social determinants of
      health, 119–120
   systems issues, 119
Health Promotion Directorate, 112
health protection, 116
Health Sciences Centre, 260
healthy workplaces, 259–260
high-level language, 140
high-level wellness, 109–111, 302
Hippocratic Oath, 194
home care nurses, 92
honesty, 141, 302
Hughes, Bethany, 143, 148
human good, 11
human rights, 165, 303
Hume, David, 9

I

ICN Code of Ethics for Nurses, 31,
   194, 290
identifiable data, 200, 303
inadvertent breach, 200, 303
independence
   and decision making, 138

defined, 137, 303
described, 137–138
and voluntariness, 147
individual accountability
   nursing accountability as
      relational, 252–253
   virtue and integrity as foun-
      dation, 251–252
individual control, 195, 303
individually identifiable data, 200
inducement, 139, 303
information management, 261
informed consent
   and autonomy, 14
   capacity, 139–140, 147–148
   comprehension, 140
   and confidentiality, 195
   decision-making process and,
      151–152
   defined, 138, 303
   honesty, 141
   Kant's view, 7
   power, 141–142
   trust, 141
   voluntariness, 138–139
informed decision making
   choice as lived value,
      150–153
   described, 134
   informed consent, 138–144
   relational autonomy,
      144–145
   understanding choice,
      135–138
institutional ethics committee,
   294–295
institutional policies and rules, 66
institutional values, 47
integrity, 47, 165, 251–252, 303
intentions, 50
Interagency Advisory Panel on
   Research Ethics, 292
interdisciplinary practice, 287–289
   see also health care team
International Conference on Health
   Promotion, 113
International Council of Nurses.
   See ICN Code of Ethics for
   Nurses
international ethics resources,
   291–293
international nursing practice,
   289–290
International Society of Bioethics,
   293

J

Jameton, Andrew, 21, 22
job action, 234
Johnstone, Megan-Jane, 21
joint decision making, 145
journalling, 35, 303
justice
   as bioethical principle,
      222–223
   conflict of interest, 221
   defined, 15, 219, 303
   described, 15
   distributive justice, 229
   ethics leadership in adminis-
      tration, 282–283
   job action, obligations during,
      234
   legal interpretations of justice,
      219–220
   as lived value, 227–234
   in nursing care, 228–231
   Philosopher's Dictionary def-
      inition, 219
   as philosophical idea,
      220–221
   and practice, 49
   promotion of justice, 219
   relevant properties, 229–230
   and research, 225–227
   respect for justice and inclu-
      siveness, 225
   restorative justice, 220
   retributive justice, 220
   social justice, 223–224, 226,
      231–233, 283
   study of issues in systematic
      way, 227
   vulnerable groups, 232
   whistleblowing, 232–233
   in the workplace, 233–234

K

K'Aila, 148
Kant, Immanuel, 5–7, 11, 135, 136,
   151, 167, 220, 221
Kantian ethics
   described, 5–7
   dignity, 167
   justice, 221
   retributism, 220
Keatings, Margaret, 20
knowledge management, 261
Kohlberg, Lawrence, 37
Kramer, Marlene, 47

L

Lalonde, Marc, 112
Lalonde Report, 112, 303
Lamb, Marianne, 19, 253
the law
>   and capacity, 140
>   and confidentiality, 197–201
>   and dignity, 166–167
>   justice, legal interpretations of, 219–220
>   legal requirements, knowledge of, 67
>   and moral agency, 67
>   and nursing competence, 88–89
>   and privacy, 197–201
>   regulation of nursing practice, 250–251
>   tort laws, 67
leadership
>   nature of leadership in ethics. *See* ethics leadership
>   and quality practice environments, 261
>   skills, 95
legal context
>   described, 47
>   influence of social understandings, 150
legal rights, 195, 303
legislation
>   capacity, 140
>   and moral agency, 67
>   Nursing Practice Acts, 84
>   privacy legislation, 194, 198–199
>   scope of practice, 84
liability protection organization, 89
Liaschenko, Joan, 40, 45
Licensed Practical Nurses (LPNs), 84, 87, 287, 289
lifestyle approach, 112–113
limits on freedom of choice, 152
listening to one's own voice, 94–95, 303
local ethics resources, 294–295
long-term relationships, 174
low morale, 93

M

macro level decision making, 119, 303
Maguire, Tom, 146
Manitoba, 84, 106, 198
maxims, 6, 303

Mazankowski, Don, 115
Mazankowski Report, 115, 116, 303
Medical Research Council of Canada, 225
mercy killing, 9
merit, 222
meso level decision making, 119, 303
metaethics, 4, 303
micro level decision making, 119, 303
Mill, John Stuart, 8, 135, 136, 151, 196, 221
minimization of harm, 89–90
misconduct, 67
model, 45, 303
model for nursing ethics. *See* Ethics Composite Model
Model Guide for the Protection of Personal Information, 198
modelling
>   best practice, 280
>   ethical behaviour, 285
Moorhouse, Anne, 15, 20, 200
moral agency
>   constrained moral agency, 65
>   constraints on, and moral distress, 69
>   defined, 22, 303
>   and integrity, 251
>   legislation and, 67
>   local ethics resources, 294–295
>   national and international ethics resources, 291–293
>   nurses as moral agents, 50–51
>   promises and, 252
>   provincial ethics resources, 293–294
>   resources for development of, 291–295
moral community, 259–262, 303
moral courage, 48, 303
moral disengagement, 259, 303
moral distress, 303–304
>   and choice of treatment or options, 66
>   defined, 21
>   feeling constrained as moral agent, 69
>   harm to patient, 90
>   moral uncertainty, 97
>   values conflicts, 97
moral integrity, 258–262
moral philosophy, 4
>   *see also* ethics
moral reasoning, 37–38
moral relativism, 43, 304
moral residue, 22, 259, 304

moral sensitivity, 45, 304
moral uncertainty, 21, 97, 304
moral unpreparedness, 254–256, 304
morality
>   defined, 304
>   described, 2
>   *vs.* ethics, 2
>   and health promotion, 120–122
>   negotiated morality, 45
Morse, Janice, 175
multi-disciplinary environments, 91
Munhall, Patricia, 38
mutual respect, 287
mutuality, 41, 304

N

narrative ethics, 17
National Council on Ethics in Human Research (NCEHR), 292
national ethics resources, 291–293
National Nursing Competencies Project (NNCP), 87
Natural Sciences and Engineering Research Council of Canada, 225, 292
Navajo people, 146
need, 222
need-to-know basis, 200
negligence, 67
negotiated morality, 45
Nelson, Hilde Lindemann, 17, 18
network of relationships, 147
New Brunswick, 106
A New Perspective on the Health of Canadians. *See* Lalonde Report
Newfoundland and Labrador, 106
Nightingale, Florence, 84, 116
Noddings, Nel, 38
non-coercion, 41, 304
non-maleficence, 15, 46, 304
normative ethics theory, 4, 46, 49, 151, 304
Northwest Territories, 106
Nova Scotia, 106
Nunavut, 106
Nurse and Patient (Pearce), 20
nurse-patient relationship
>   *see also* relational ethics
>   as common theme in nursing ethics, 40
>   and dignity, 169–170
>   embodiment, 41, 173
>   respect, 152
nursing administration, and ethics leadership, 280–284

nursing competence
    accreditation, 84
    certification, 88
    chart audit, 88
    competency assessments, 87
    competency statements, 84
    continuing competence, 86–88
    defined, 83, 304
    discipline, 85
    education in basic elements
        of, 85
    and the law, 88–89
    peer review, 88
    practice standards, 83–86
nursing education
    and CNA Code of Ethics, 284
    confidentiality, 284
    ethical fitness, 95–96
    ethics leadership in, 284–285
    nursing competence, basics
        of, 85
    power imbalance, 284
    respect for nursing students,
        285
nursing ethics
    see also ethics
    advances in, 21
    and bioethical principles, 40,
        48–49
    and context, 49–50
    developmental psychologists,
        contributions of, 37–38
    developments in nursing
        ethics theory, 36–40
    Ethics Composite Model. See
        Ethics Composite Model
    ethics in nursing, 34–35
    and ethics theory, 36–43
    evolution of nursing ethics,
        18–22
    evolving nursing ethics theory,
        38–40
    existential advocacy, 22
    and feminist thought, 37, 38
    history of nursing ethics,
        19–22
    as negotiated morality, 45
    and normative theories, 49
    nurse-patient relationship as
        common theme, 40
    practice as moral foundation,
        43–44
    relational ethics. See relational
        ethics
    research, 39
    and virtues, 47–48

Nursing Ethics, 21
nursing practice
    abuse from patients, 279
    and accountability, 253–257
    accountability for others'
        practice, 256
    basic elements of practice, 86
    best practices, 117
    burnout, 176
    business-oriented approach
        to health care reform, 32
    caring practices, 44
    decision making in clinical
        practice, 51
    definitions of, 84
    delegated medical responsi-
        bilities, 84
    and dignity, 169–177
    ethical dimensions of, 3
    fitness to practice, 257–258
    the good in nursing and
        nursing moral identity, 44
    and health promotion,
        116–120
    interdisciplinary practice,
        287–289
    international nursing prac-
        tice, 289–290
    and justice, 228–231
    as moral foundation for nurs-
        ing ethics, 43–44
    moral integrity, 258–262
    personal relationships, guard-
        ing against, 231
    regulation of nursing practice,
        250–251
    scope of practice, 84
    self-evaluation, 32
    self-reflection, 32
    and social justice, 231–233
    treatment of nurses in the
        workplace, 233–234
Nursing Practice: The Ethical Issues
    (Jameton), 21
Nursing Practice Acts, 84
Nursing Profession Act (Alberta), 84
nursing professional organizations, 84
nurturing, 37

O

obese patients, 172
obligation, theories of, 5, 7, 47, 306
OIIQ, 106
Ontario, 84, 85, 106
Ontario College of Nursing, 85

oppression, 18, 40
Ottawa Charter, 113, 117, 304

P

parents, and decision making, 148
paternalism, 14, 121, 151, 304
paternalistic decisions, 136
patients
    abuse from patients, 279
    assent, 142–144
    best interests of the patient,
        68, 147
    consent to disclosure of
        information, 207
    informed consent. See
        informed consent
    obese patients, 172
    power, 141
    safety, 83
    uniqueness of, 171
Pearce, Evelyn, 20
peer review, 88, 304
Pence, Terry, 20
Personal Care Attendants (PCAs),
    289
Personal Health Information Act
    (Manitoba), 198
personal information, 199–200
    see also confidentiality
*Personal Information and Protection of
    Electronic Documents Act* (PIPEDA),
    198–200
Personal Information Protection Act
    (PIPA) (Alberta & BC),
    198–200
Peter, Elizabeth, 18, 40, 45
philosophy
    on autonomy, 195–196
    branches of, 4
    on confidentiality, 195–196
    and dignity, 167–168
    on justice, 220–221
    moral philosophy, 4
    see also ethics
    on privacy, 195–196
philosophy of care, 95
physical environments, 203
political factors, 66
poor work performance, 93
population health, 114, 304
population health model, 114–116
portability, 224, 304
postconventional level of moral rea-
    soning, 37
potential actions, 65–67

A *Theory of Justice* (Rawls), 221
time allocation, 228–229
tort laws, 67
traditions of professional practice, 30–32
Tri-Council Policy Statement (TCPS), 197, 225, 292
trust, 141, 143, 194, 287, 306
trusting judgments, 95, 306
trustworthiness, 47, 306
Tschudin, Verena, 21

U

undue inducement, 139, 306
unintentional breach, 200, 303
United Nations, 166
United Nurses of Alberta, 87
Universal Declaration of Human Rights (UDHR), 166
Universal Declaration on the Human Genome and Human Rights, 165
universal dignity, 165, 306
universality, 224, 306
University of Toronto Joint Centre for Bioethics, 93
utilitarianism
    act utilitarianism, 9
    applying utilitarianism perspective, 10
    and confidentiality, 195–196
    critics of, 9, 10
    defined, 8, 306
    described, 9–10
    dignity, 168
    end justifies the means, 9
    greatest good for the greatest number, 9
    insights offered by, 10
    management ethics and, 282

principle of utility, 9
rule utilitarianism, 9

V

values
    and assessment of ethics of situation, 63–64
    awareness of your own values, 35
    caring, 37
    Christian values, 19
    defined, 2, 306
    developing values, 2
    dominant values, 150
    institutional values, 47
    of nurses, 65
    in nursing, 34–35
    nurturing, 37
    societal values, 277
values clarification, 35, 36t, 306
values conflicts
    defined, 306
    described, 34
    and moral distress, 97
    in support of patient's choice, 151–152
    with those receiving care, 255
Varcoe, C., 18
Veatch, Robert, 21
veil of ignorance, 221
Victorian Order of Nurses, 116
violence, 91–92
virtue-based approach, 48
virtue ethics
    care, 43
    defined, 11, 307
    dignity, 168
virtues
    and accountability, 251–252
    and choice, 151

    and correct moral choices, 11
    defined, 307
    desire to choose well, 63
    excellence in action, 50
    moral courage, 48
    and nursing ethics, 47–48
    understanding of virtue, 47
voluntariness, 138–139, 147, 307
voluntary euthanasia, 176, 307
Vuckovich, Paula, 152
vulnerability, 165, 307
vulnerable groups, 232, 307

W

Wald, Lillian, 116
Walker, Margaret Urban, 45
web sites for Canadian nursing associations, 105–106
Webster, George, 22
well-being
    see also health promotion
    Aristotle's human good, 11
    within illness, 120
wellness
    defined, 109, 307
    high-level wellness, 109
    promotion of, 117
whistleblowing, 91, 232–233, 279, 307
women, and research, 225–227
work-life balance, 261
workplace conflict, 93
workplace culture, 262
workplace justice, 233–234
World Health Organization (WHO), 111, 113
worth, 165, 250, 307

Y

Yeo, Michael, 15, 20, 122, 200, 251
Yukon Association, 106